C000155953

BOOKS
BY THE
SEA
@booksbythesea_lfl

CRITICAL DIALOGUES IN SOUTHEAST ASIAN STUDIES

Charles Keyes, Vicente Rafael, and Laurie J. Sears, Series Editors

CRITICAL DIALOGUES IN SOUTHEAST ASIAN STUDIES

This series offers perspectives in Southeast Asian Studies that stem from reconsideration of the relationships among scholars, texts, archives, field sites, and subject matter. Volumes in the series feature inquiries into historiography, critical ethnography, colonialism and postcolonialism, nationalism and ethnicity, gender and sexuality, science and technology, politics and society, and literature, drama, and film. A common vision of the series is a belief that area studies scholarship sheds light on shifting contexts and contests over forms of knowing and modes of action that inform cultural politics and shape histories of modernity.

Imagined Ancestries of Vietnamese Communism: Ton Duc Thang and the Politics of History and Memory by Christoph Giebel

Beginning to Remember: The Past in the Indonesian Present edited by Mary S. Zurbuchen

Seditious Histories: Contesting Thai and Southeast Asian Pasts by Craig J. Reynolds

Knowing Southeast Asian Subjects edited by Laurie J. Sears

Making Fields of Merit: Buddhist Female Ascetics and Gendered Orders in Thailand by Monica Lindberg Falk

Love, Passion and Patriotism: Sexuality and the Philippine Propaganda Movement, 1882–1892 by Raquel A. G. Reyes

Gathering Leaves and Lifting Words: Intertextuality and Buddhist Monastic Education in Laos and Thailand by Justin Thomas McDaniel

The Ironies of Freedom: Sex, Culture, and Neoliberal Governance in Vietnam by Thu-hương Nguyễn-võ

Submitting to God: Women and Islam in Urban Malaysia by Sylva Frisk

No Concessions: The Life of Yap Thiam Hien, Indonesian Human Rights Lawyer by Daniel S. Lev

NO CONCESSIONS

THE LIFE OF YAP THIAM HIEN, INDONESIAN HUMAN RIGHTS LAWYER

Daniel S. Lev

INTRODUCTION BY *Benedict Anderson*

AND CONTRIBUTIONS BY *Arlene O. Lev*, *Sebastiaan Pompe* AND *Ibrahim Assegaf*, AND *Yap Thiam Hien*

UNIVERSITY OF WASHINGTON PRESS
Seattle & London

This book is published with the assistance of a grant from the Charles and Jane Keyes Endowment for Books on Southeast Asia, established through the generosity of Charles and Jane Keyes.

Printed in the United States of America
Designed by Thomas Eykemans
Composed in Warnock, typeface designed by Robert Slimbach
15 14 13 12 11   5 4 3 2 1

Unless otherwise noted, all illustrations are courtesy of the Yap family.
Chapter 1, "Aceh," is adapted from an essay published in *Indonesia* (October 2006): 97–113.

UNIVERSITY OF WASHINGTON PRESS
P.O. Box 50096, Seattle, WA 98145 U.S.A.
www.washington.edu/uwpress

LIBRARY OF CONGRESS CATALOGING-IN-PUBLICATION DATA
Lev, Daniel S.
No concessions : the life of Yap Thiam Hien, Indonesian human rights lawyer / Daniel S. Lev ; introduction by Benedict Anderson ; and contributions by Arlene O. Lev . . . [et al.].
p. cm. — (Critical dialogues in Southeast Asian studies)
Includes bibliographical references and index.
Summary: "A biography of human rights lawyer Yap Thiam Hien (1913–1989) that focuses on the country's contemporary political turmoil and struggle for human rights, the workings of Indonesia's legal system, and the history of the Chinese community there."—Publisher's description.
ISBN 978-0-295-99114-6 (cloth : alk. paper)
1. Yap, Thiam Hien, 1913–1989.
2. Lawyers—Indonesia—Biography.
3. Chinese—Indonesia—Biography.
4. Human rights—Indonesia.
5. Indonesia—Politics and government—20th century.
I. Lev, Arlene O. (Arlene Offenhender)
II. Title.
III. Series: Critical dialogues in Southeast Asian studies.
KNW110.Y37L48 2011   340.092—dc22   2011017270
[B]

The paper used in this publication is acid-free and meets the minimum requirements of American National Standard for Information Sciences—Permanence of Paper for Printed Library Materials, ANSI Z39.48-1984.∞

CONTENTS

NO CONCESSIONS

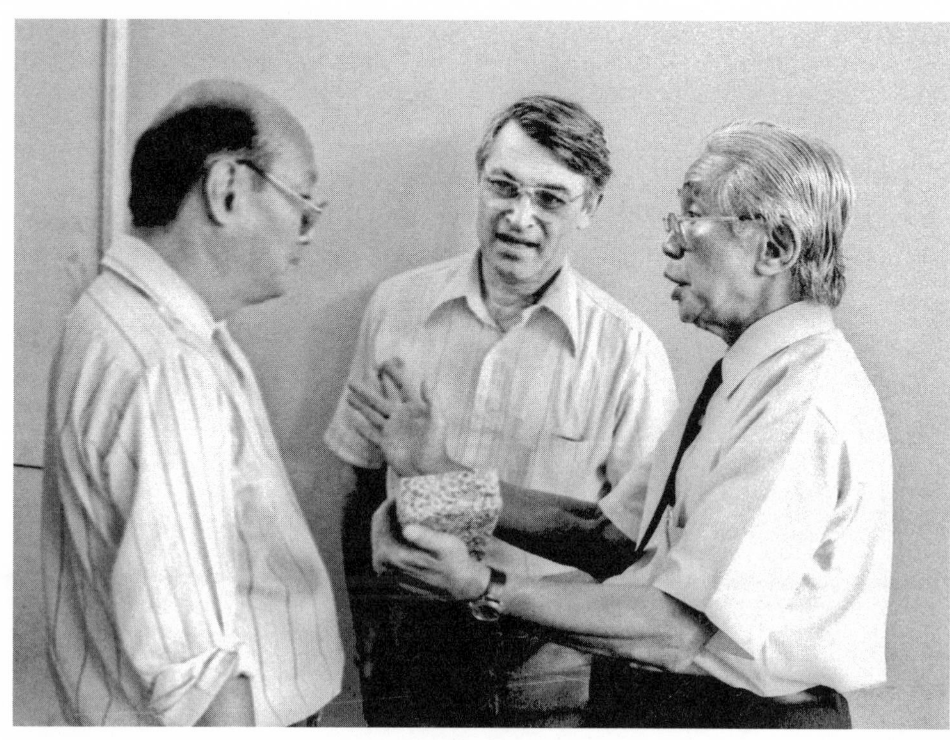

FIG. I.1 *From left*: Ong Hok Am, Daniel Lev, Yap Thiam Hien, 1984.
Courtesy of TEMPO/Nanang Baso

INTRODUCTION

Benedict Anderson

SCHOLARS who write biographies typically write their own introductions, explaining to the anticipated reader why the subject of their work is an unusually interesting and historically important human being. Very often they define the kind of biography they have planned—say, political, literary, or scientific—and discuss the sources they have turned up and the unavoidable lacunae in the "archive." Usually they do not spend much time on themselves, whether out of scholarly modesty and/or because they are already thinking about the next book they will undertake. Alas, Dan Lev came close but did not quite finish this biography of Yap Thiam Hien—on which he had worked for years and which he regarded as the major work of his life. He died on 29 July 2006, leaving no introduction behind. As one of his oldest friends and colleagues, I have here assumed the responsibility of pinch-hitting for him. Perhaps inevitably in such melancholy circumstances, a pinch-hitting introduction must have a peculiar character, part standard fare, part in memoriam. It must set aside Dan's perfect modesty and attempt to explicate the complex of reasons why, and in what spirit, he undertook this last, most difficult, endeavor.

• • •

Scholarly biographies do not fit comfortably into those intellectual boxes that are called the disciplines. Even an inhabitant of the largest box, History, will find herself needing help and inspiration from some combination of Sociology, Anthropology, Political Science, Literary Criticism, Law, Psychology, Economics, and Linguistics. Individual human beings, in their quiddity, are more mysterious than social structures, economic cycles, intellectual currents, legal institutions, and even cultures. Distances of time and place have their own equivocal effects—documents become scarcer, mentalities stranger, languages less legible, and memories more fragmentary and wishful. This is surely the reason why fine scholarly biographies are relatively rare and usually deliberately partial, focused on some aspects of the subject's life that the biographer believes to be of central importance. One could say, furthermore, that the successful biographer feels herself tied emotionally or morally to the subject, even though the affinity can be hostile or sympathetic, or colored by an uneasy mixture of the two.

Biography is also a fairly modern narrative form. Even in England, it does not go much farther back than Boswell's mid-eighteenth-century life of Samuel Johnson. It was born for Asia in the last century and, in the case of Southeast Asia—probably because the region was largely colonized by Europeans until after 1945—only over the last half century. By that time, it had to compete with autobiographies, also a new literary form. It is not easy to remember much about Richard Butwell's pioneering biography of the late Burmese nationalist politician U Nu, but U Nu's own weird "third person" memoir, *Saturday's Son,* is quite unforgettable. Robert Elson's recent political biography of Indonesia's durable dictator is solid and sensible, but seems on a different planet from Suharto's own spooky *Pikiran, Ucapan, dan Tindakan Saya.* Harry Poeze's huge life of Tan Malaka is a monument to years of difficult archival hunting, but it cannot compete with the grand and touching allure of the nomad Sumatran revolutionary's own three-volume *Dari Pendjara ke Pendjara.* In these cases the reader is overwhelmed by the cultural gulf between Burma and the United States, Indonesia and Australia, and the Netherlands and the Netherlands East Indies. A good name for this distance is "balance," but sometimes the reader feels like a visitor at a zoo, watching caged tigers through an iron grille. Even in Rudolf Mrázek's astonishing life of Sutan Sjahrir, Indonesia's first prime minister—a real work of art—Batavia-Jakarta has the scent of Prague and is shadowed by Kafka.

Dan's biography of Yap Thiam Hien is as unique as Mrázek's of Sjahrir, but for completely different reasons. Butwell knew U Nu personally, but he was not long seriously engaged inside Burmese politics; Elson, Poeze, and Mrázek had no personal acquaintance with their subjects and have not participated in the politics of Indonesia. Dan not only knew Yap extremely well, indeed was a close friend, he worked with Yap and continued his legacy after his hero's death. Both men were utterly committed to fundamental reform of Indonesia's legal, political, and moral life. No foreign scholar specialist on Indonesia that I can think of, not even the late Herbert Feith, pledged himself so long, so persistently, and so modestly to this everyday, Indonesian-Sisyphean task. It is significant that Dan started to think about this biography and to amass materials while his friend was still alive. It is quite on the cards that Yap, so reserved in many ways, opened his private thoughts to Dan more than to anyone except his own wife.

Still, many of us have friends we deeply admire and with whom we have long worked, and it does not occur to us to try to write about their lives for contemporaries and for history. Why then did Dan spend years, in an incredibly busy academic and activist career, on this biographical (but not at all hagiographical) project? The answers can only be complex and incomplete. When Dan graduated from Miami University in 1955, he decided to do his graduate work in Cornell University's Department of Government because he was interested in international law. Herbert Briggs, an internationally renowned authority in the field, was still teaching there. But, in a then quite small department, Dan also came under the benign spell of George Kahin, who taught very popular courses on the domestic and international politics of Asia and was also the executive director of Cornell's pioneering Southeast Asia Program. Only three years earlier, Kahin had published his grand *Nationalism and Revolution in Indonesia*, which has become a living classic. Scholarly as it was, the book was also heavily influenced by George's own experience as a student and sometime journalist during the revolution. As a confirmed progressive, he was a passionate sympathizer with the nationalist cause and knew personally most of the Republic's leaders. He sent dispatches from the beleaguered Republic, ran the Dutch colonial blockade, and on his return to the States actively lobbied Congress on Indonesia's behalf. In the process he earned the enmity not just of diehard Dutch colonialists but also of powerful figures in the U.S. State Department.

During the McCarthy era, Kahin was deprived of his passport for some years and slandered as a communist-sympathizer. Not in the least flamboyant, he nonetheless stood out in the quiet little town of Ithaca, New York, and Cornell's quiet little Department of Government. He had shown to his students that not only was it possible (at times) but it was also ethically desirable for a scholar to become involved in progressive politics, not merely in the United States but in other parts of the world. In a time when Government students did research but rarely contemplated "fieldwork," the possibilities of down-in-the-mud engagement was a romantic lure to which Dan, who would have laughed at anyone who called him romantic, was, I believe, subliminally attracted. Best of all, 1955 was the year in which the infant Republic of Indonesia held its first—and until 1999 its only—completely free national election. The two men quickly became very attached. The "Lev" file in the George Kahin archive in Cornell's Olin Library shows only one letter in which Dan addressed his teacher as "Professor Kahin"; after that, it was always "George." We can also read a recommendation letter in which Kahin described Dan as by far the ablest and most mature student under his supervision. For the rest of Kahin's life, Dan was the student closest to his heart.

Dan remained committed to the study of law and legal institutions, but now with a difference. Under Kahin's tactful influence, he was increasingly thinking about law, albeit in an unlawyerly manner. Law was becoming for him a social, economic, and political institution, not a maze of decisions, precedents, and stratagems. Hence, he intended to do his dissertation on the living-dying legal institutions of post-independence Indonesia within a big political-economic-cultural framework. But by the time he was linguistically prepared to go to the field (1959)—he needed a reasonable command of written Dutch, as well as spoken and written Indonesian—the situation in Indonesia had drastically changed. In March 1957 the country was put under martial law; that fall all Dutch enterprises were nationalized and almost all Dutch men and women expelled. In January 1958 civil war broke out, with the CIA blatantly supporting the rebels with arms and strategic supplies. For more than two years the freely elected Constituent Assembly had found it impossible to write and validate a new, permanent constitution. In the summer of 1959, egged on by an increasingly aggressive military, President Soekarno abrogated, completely illegally, the liberal Constitution of 1950 and ordained the reinstatement of the authoritarian 1945 Constitution, which had actually been drawn up in the last days of the Japanese occupation. Constitutional democracy was dead.

But Dan did not arrive in Indonesia alone. He was accompanied by Arlene (née Offenhender), an artist-charmer who won my heart when she laughingly complained of being treated as a "weirdo" in her New York City high school because she was perhaps the only member of her class not undergoing psychoanalysis. But there was also the magisterial Ruth McVey, former Sovietologist, who wrote the only really great book on (early) Indonesian Communism, and ex-Brit John Smail, who went on to become the first person in the United States to be given a permanent appointment as a professor of Southeast Asian history at the University of Wisconsin/Madison. Pioneers all. Wordsworth got it right: "Bliss was it in that dawn to be alive / But to be young was very heaven!"

In any case, the dissertation that Dan eventually defended had very little to do with the law in Indonesia but everything to do with the transition to an authoritarian "populist" system dominated, antagonistically, by the right-wing military and the charismatic, "progressive" Soekarno. Over the years it has also become a classic in Indonesian Studies. I remember that for a long time I felt vaguely resentful about this admirable, soon published thesis. I had the idea that Kahin, in his kindly but effective way, had told Dan that for the moment he should leave his legal studies and write on the momentous and depressing overall changes going on in Indonesian politics. But the Kahin archive shows how profoundly wrong I was. It is mainly full of long, brilliantly formulated letters from Dan on current politics in Indonesia, while very little at all about law is visible. Now I understand why George gently encouraged Dan to change his thesis topic, and why Dan acceded. For Indonesian law, he was probably not yet fully ready.

Although Yap was more than twenty years older than Dan, one could argue that they "matured" together in the constitutional, political, and moral crisis that haunted Indonesia in the late 1950s. One might even go so far as to say that they were political contemporaries. They both experienced the rise of Suharto after the hideous anti-communist massacres of 1965–66 and the long era of corruption, repression, and official lying under his rule. Both were determined to do what they could to fight back on behalf of every kind of underdog. Both were determined believers in human rights. Nonetheless, there were important, productive differences, as this book beautifully shows. Partly, it must have been a matter of character. Dan repeatedly stresses Yap's consuming, only half-bottled-up anger. Yap's religious beliefs and perhaps weak sense of humor made him intolerant of frivolity. Dan was a gifted poker player, with a great sense of irony and humor and an engaging weakness for colorful rogues. I am sure he could get very angry, but I never saw him so; he certainly did not keep grudges, and he was easily forgiving of people, if not of their deeds. Dan was an agnostic, if not an atheist, and was much more open to cultural and moral differences than was Yap. Dan was without star-hunger and had a very exact estimation of his own abilities and potentialities, which he developed to their utmost. On the other hand, after Yap's courageous defense of ex-Foreign Minister Subandrio, a man whom very few people liked or respected, before the Extraordinary Military Tribunal, which the incipient Suharto regime set up late in 1965, Yap was instantly a famous man. His fame only grew with time, so that in 1987 he became the first recipient of the Justice William Brennan Medal for Defending Human Rights.

I suspect, perhaps without real justification, that below the political surface and below the marked differences in the two men's characters, there was something deep that bound Dan to Yap. In this book, the reader will find, quite suddenly and out of the blue, in the middle of a detailed discussion of internal conflicts within Indonesia's "Chinese community," the following: "*There is an analogy, perhaps, with assimilated Ashkenazi Jews in America, who divide in much the same way, some asserting their Jewishness, with or without religion, and finding in Israel a confirming association, while others no longer think it worth distinguishing themselves from other standard white Americans. But Jews in America have an easier time than peranakan Chinese in Indonesia, where the issues and pressures have been constant and public*" (p. 180).

There is a long and often misguided tradition of likening the Chinese immigrants in Southeast Asia and their descendants to the Ashkenazi Jews of Central and Eastern Europe, who migrated across the Atlantic in huge numbers in the late nineteenth and early twentieth centuries. We may well recall the notoriously racist, anti-Chinese tract "The Jews of the Orient," written in the 1910s by King Rama VI (himself 50 percent of Chinese descent) of uncolonized Siam. But if there is any long-haul analogy to be drawn, it is between the situation of Ashkenazi Jews under the autocratic monarchy in imperial Russia and the "Chinese" in the later colonial autoocracies in Southeast Asia, including the Netherlands Indies / Indonesia. Ghettoization, social stigmatization, occupational restrictions, and periodic repression existed in both cases, although the colonial regimes stopped pogroms against the Chinese after the 1760s. But European Jews were never "buffers" in a racially organized social system, with a small group of whites at the top and millions of "natives" below. Furthermore, if one tries to draw a post–World War II analogy between, say, Jews within the world-hegemon, America, and Chinese in newly independent Indonesia, the comparisons that strike one mainly underscore dissimilarities. American Jews are descendants of immigrants in a nation of immigrants (with the exception of the so-called First Americans). They play crucial and public roles in almost all the more respected occupations. They need fear no massacres or expulsions. And Israel, their second, or first, homeland, is, for the time being, the most powerful state in the Middle East, thanks partly to virtually unqualified support from the United States and the European community. In Indonesia, the "immigrant" and his descendants are still largely stigmatized. Their occupational choices have been limited by formal and informal discrimination, and they have no public power in their own right. The number of "Chinese" cabinet ministers since 1945 can be counted on the fingers of two hands. Their second homeland, China, a vast and ancient state, was treated by the West as an international pariah until the middle 1970s, and in the twenty-first century has an independent power and prestige rivaling the United States.

That Dan was aware of these difficulties is evidenced by his temporal restriction of the comparison to that between the Chinese of "Indonesia" (not the Netherlands Indies) and American Jews after the establishment of the state of Israel, and his use of the hesitant "perhaps." Yet his own words seem almost to insist on a filiation. But of what kind? Dan was raised by his Jewish parents in rough-tough, polyethnic, industrial Youngstown, Ohio, a long way from the megacities of the eastern United States. His family did not live in the "Jewish quarter," but in a neighborhood dominated by Polish and Italian Catholic working-class and lower-middle-class families. He did not attend religious schools, was never bar mitzvahed, and knew no Hebrew. His parents were determinedly secular and regarded themselves as heirs of the Bund, Zionism's socialist rival and antagonist in pre–World War II Europe. His father was even a conscientious member of the Bund-derived Working Men's Circle. If that major part of the Chinese community in post-independence Indonesia that had assimilated to local cultures and, with more difficulty, to Indonesianness, which knew no Mandarin and was not much interested in Confucianism, came to be called *peranakan*, was Dan a kind of American *peranakan*? Yes, to be sure; to be even more sure, no.

Social categories are powerful institutions everywhere, so that if you are, for example, taken to be a Jew in the United States, you are forced, willy-nilly, to find ways to deal with the diagnosis: hiding your Jewishness, displaying it, rejecting it, embracing it, redefining it, and so on. Escaping it? Almost impossible. So, what to do with it? I think that Dan's response was affected by the experience of the generation to which he belonged. That generation was the first to "arrive"—after the barely concealed anti-Semitic quotas restricting Jewish entry into the faculties and student bodies of many of the most prestigious universities collapsed and many of continental Europe's most distinguished Jewish intellectuals, fleeing Nazism and fascism, brought about fundamental changes in American higher education. Jews were marrying non-Jews at unprecedented rates. As a huge and increasingly powerful Jewish middle class developed, famous Jews were no longer boxers, basketball champions, and gangsters, but novelists, judges, and politicians. Dan's generation of Jews was very much aware of the progressive roles that Jewish anarchists, socialists, liberals, and communists had played in American domestic politics since the 1880s, but he and his cohorts grew up in an America that had become, after World War II, a ferociously anti-Communist and interventionist world-hegemon. Finally, his was the first generation to grow up with the new state of Israel, and to be faced with the difficult question of what stance to take toward it.

When I first met Dan Lev, in the snow-shrouded Ithaca of January 1958—less than two years after the French-British-Israeli assault on Nasser's Egypt—he already had an outlook which he kept for the rest of his life. I saw him as a progressive in American domestic politics and a thoughtful critic of American foreign policy, especially toward the *ci-devant* Third World and, of course, Israel. He was already distressed by Israel's ethno-religious political basis, and later became ever more concerned about the country's treatment of its Arab citizens, its belligerence toward its neighbors, and its collusion with the United States in interventions in other parts of the world. It cannot have been easy for him, since some of his brothers were vehement financial and political supporters of the new state and its sponsors in Washington. He was also critical of many American Jews who, in his opinion, had abandoned their democratic and progressive traditions in their hunger for prestige, influence, and political power. In later years, after I fell in love with the work of Walter Benjamin, I used to think of Dan as like the figure of the "Righteous Jew," even though I knew he would have laughed at me if I had told him so. What he might have accepted, laughing with me, was "a man for all underdogs."

As we see below in more detail, Yap also grew up in an insignificant town on the northern tip of Sumatra, a long way, in those days, even from Medan, and even more so from the great megacities of Java, where the bulk of Sino-Indonesians lived and worked. The local Chinese population in Kutaradja was quite small and, except for business purposes, kept to itself. Yap's own family had its financial ups and downs and does not seem to have been very "social." It performed the traditional life-cycle ceremonies, but without any pious fervor. The young Yap benefited from an opening of doors higher than those in the United States. By the 1910s, cruel colonial ordinances, which confined residence for Chinese to policed ghettoes and severely hindered free movement around the colony for other purposes, were revoked At the same time, the colonial rulers—worried by the success of China-oriented schools set up by local

Chinese and inspired by the fall of the Manchu dynasty and China's emergence as a nation-state of sorts—decided to open special Western-style schools for Chinese children. From these schools it was possible for small numbers to gain access to what passed for local higher education, separate colleges for law, medicine, architecture, and engineering, and finally liberal arts.

Learning in Western-style schools brought Yap into close contact, for the first time, with Dutch people, as well as different kinds of "natives." Through the former, he eventually became his own sort of Protestant. When he eventually settled on a career, it was as a practicing private lawyer. (In those days, judges and state prosecutors were Dutchmen and natives; and there was no room for a "Chinese" professor in the only small law college that existed.) He matured much more slowly than Dan Lev, and only seriously involved himself in domestic political questions in the 1950s, but these questions were still largely confined to the milieu of the Chinese minority itself. Then, in a startling flash of light, he became famous throughout the nation for his courage and skill in defending the much-reviled Subandrio, on trial before the Extraordinary Military Tribunal. For the rest of his life, he devoted everything he had to (mostly) lost causes within Indonesia's decrepit legal system, his clients coming mainly from non-Chinese groups, and having little else in common than being abused underdogs: Muslims and ex-Communists, peasants and middle-class people. He did not share the fear, the money-hunger, the political opportunism, and the self-enclosure of many in the "Chinese community" and sometimes showed his contempt for them. Nor was he enamored of the "homeland" across the China Sea. Since Indonesia was his country, he felt he had both the right to be ashamed of it and the obligation to ameliorate its fate. You could say, perhaps, that he was a *righteous peranakan.*

What fascinated Dan, and made him wish to write Yap's biography, was the puzzle of how this man had so transformed himself, and at what cost—as well as what conditions had made the transformation uniquely possible. (Paradoxically, how did the young Youngstown Jewish boxer end up writing the best study of Muslim institutions on the other side of the globe and spend years in the struggle for legal and other reforms in Indonesia?). We often understand "human rights" today as a good but abstract principle, enshrined in international charters and a number of constitutions. If one focuses on the identities of those whose "human rights" have been abused or violently terminated, it all seems straightforward. But if one shifts one's angle of vision toward the skilled defenders of such rights, especially in places like Indonesia, then one understands a long struggle to set aside the habits of childhood, the tribalisms of kin and neighborhood, the pull of religious affiliation, the prejudices of class and gender, the provinciality of ethnicity and region, and the animosities of political conflicts. It also means trying to set aside sententious pieties and get down to real work in specific cases, in one's own nation and for one's fellow-citizens.

Employing a contemporary vocabulary and resuscitating an honorable one that has fallen out of fashion, one could say that Dan saw in Yap a man who overcame his various ascriptive "identities" by painfully acquiring "character." Acquiring character can never be a collective endeavor but is always a matter of individual courage and self-mastery. If the reader understands this progression, he or she will then understand the at first surprising shape of Dan's biography. One would expect that a book about an internationally famous trial lawyer, by a scholar steeped in the study of legal institutions, would primarily consist of analyses of the many important court cases in which Yap was involved. But such analyses in fact appear almost tangentially—in the last chapters that Dan managed to complete before his death. Almost all the cases were to be squashed into a single final chapter 14, which his close friends Sebastian Pompe and Ibrahim Assegaf have recreated on the basis of Dan's notes.

The first twelve chapters thus show us in wonderfully nuanced detail how a *mensch* was created, and created himself. Born in 1913, Yap was the great-great-grandson of a tough and enterprising young Hakka, who arrived in the Dutch colony in 1844. The origin of the Hakka is disputed, but it is likely that they were not originally "Han Chinese" but a hill-dwelling "minority" gradually sinified over the centuries. Despite periodic repression by Peking (Beijing), especially under the Ming dynasty, they retained their distinctive style of dress into the nineteenth century and obstinately refused to seclude their women or to subject them to the horrors of foot-binding. Often looked down upon by other "Chinese," they had a deserved reputation for industriousness, "obstinacy," and bluntness of speech. Great-great-grandfather's migration was perfectly timed. Imperial Britain's easy victory in the Opium War of 1840–42 forced Peking to open a number of seaports to international commerce and put an end to the longstanding ban on the emigration of the Ch'ing dynasty's subjects. In 1848, the Hakka mystic Hung Hsiu-chüan began so grand an uprising (known to history as the Tai-p'ing Rebellion) that most of southern China fell into his hands, and he might even have toppled the dynasty if the latter had not hired American mercenaries to train troops in the modern Western manner. Had Yap's ancestor not left in time, he would surely have been swept up into this vast social conflagration, with its countless victims. He entered the Netherlands Indies at a time when the then-dominant Chinese group of settlers were Hokkien, many of them assimilated to local cultures. Hakka and Hokkien were, and are, mutually unintelligible languages, and a "national Mandarin" lay in the distant future. Yap's wealthy, commercially successful grandfather was the last in the lineage to speak Hakka; thereafter the languages were Malay, Hokkien, and, to varying degrees, Dutch. By this time the family had become *peranakan*. But it is not too fanciful to see in Yap's famous obstinacy, bluntness of speech, and workaholic habits the traces of a Hakka origin.

Dan next shows the reader how the young Yap was prevented from becoming a typical member of the small, socially exclusive, and excluded *peranakan* community in the Acehnese provincial town of Kutaradja. First were the consequences of Grandfather's bringing back from a business trip to Saigon, in 1907, a very young Japanese concubine—a mere eleven years since Meiji Japan inflicted a crushing military defeat on a dying regime in Peking. After Grandmother's early death in 1909, this girl, Sato Nakashima, without children of her own, took over the role of beloved grandmother for Yap and his two younger siblings. Till her death, she was the member of the family to whom Yap was most deeply attached. Was there any other "Chinese" boy in the Netherlands Indies who had a Japanese grandmother? Dan suggests that it was the selfless devotion of this woman to her adoptive grandchildren that began the process whereby Yap learned to transcend ghetto complacency and uncritical identification with "we Chinese." Second was Yap's father's successful application, in 1918, to be granted the privileged legal status of a Dutchman. At the age of five, the little boy thus became "Dutch." Though Yap was very bright and studious, one cannot doubt that it was this status above all that allowed him to attend the best primary and secondary schools in the colony, all of them using Dutch as the language of instruction. Few in number, these elite schools brought the youngster into close contact not merely with white Dutch teachers, but with classmates from many parts of the vast archipelago, pure Dutch, Eurasians, Chinese, and upper-class "natives." In these schools, aside from struggling with Latin, he had his first, quite thorough exposure to what was then called "European civilization." Then another fortuity: in his final high-school years, in the royal city of Jogjakarta, the youngster found lodgings with the Eurasian Jopp family, whose warmth and deep Protestant faith made a lasting impression on him.

Up to this point, one can say that Yap's character was largely formed by circumstances over which he had no control. There followed a longer period of the more important self-creation. On graduating from high school in 1933, at the age of twenty, he had to decide what to do next.

The colony then had no university, only a handful of unconnected profession-oriented faculties. His choice of the "Western humanities" stream in high school left him unqualified for medicine or engineering, and though he started to be interested in law, the family's by now very frail finances made entry to the Faculty of Law unaffordable. Furthermore, the colony had been severely hit by the Great Depression. The state was downsizing its bureaucracy and its budget, and in any case *peranakan* were largely barred from entry. Business opportunities were few, so Yap decided to teach in the only schools where there were vacancies, the private missionary schools for Chinese *peranakan* children. (But he did so hoping to save enough to enter the Faculty of Law, which he managed toward the end of the decade.) He discovered that he had a gift for teaching and for combating missionary authoritarianism. The young adult now left the tiny minority of highly educated colonials and entered the larger one of the Chinese *peranakan*, colony-wide in principle.

It was a real but very new minority. In 1920, when Yap was seven, the colonial regime had carried out its first-ever census (followed by a second and last in 1930). For the first time, the state was counting its subjects according to a maze of arbitrary categories, of which the most important were legal status, race, ethnicity, and religion. Published numbers and percentages were now turning all kinds of familiar groups—Catholics and Muslims, Bataks and Javanese, Europeans and "natives," Chinese and Arabs—into something quantified: "minorities" and "majorities." Yap thus was counted, formally, as a member of the tiny (0.5 percent) European minority alongside a 2.5 percent Chinese minority. As in many other countries, the census was creating the first bases for what today we call identity politics.

In Dan's account, the year 1938 was pivotal for Yap's self-creation. It was not only that he had saved enough money to enter the Law Faculty in Batavia, where the mix of his fellow students was very like that in his high schools. In July 1937, the Japanese had launched an enormous invasion of China, carried out massive atrocities in Chiang K'ai-shek's capital of Nanking (Nanjing), and driven the Generalissimo to remote Chungking (Chungqing). As in other parts of colonial Southeast Asia, this merciless aggression caused a wave of outrage among the local Chinese, including even many of the most assimilated: passionate denunciations in the press and large-scale fundraising to send Chiang medical supplies, vehicles, cash, and even some young volunteers for military service. Only too aware of its military vulnerability, and terrified of Japanese retaliation, the colonial regime cracked down on the Chinese press, closing some newspapers and jailing too confrontational journalists. Joining the Help

China movement was Yap's baptism into political activism, a baptism all the more striking in that he had shown not the slightest interest in the native Indonesians' struggle for emancipation now nearing the end of its third decade. "Baptism" may be exactly the right word, for at the end of October 1938, after a long period of reflection and hesitation, he was also baptized a member of the Jopps' Protestant Reformed (Calvinist) Church. (Dan has a superb, intricate discussion of this fundamental decision.) Yap's conversion might seem to be surprising since, in the colony, this church was traditionally a strong, subsidized pillar of the colonial regime (though some impressive dissidents emerged in the interwar years) and, in the Netherlands itself, had a history of repression of Catholics and hostility to any form of socialism. But it was also part of the congeries of cooperating and rival denominations that made Protestantism a global institution, a position out of reach for Chinese Confucianism. After Indonesia's independence was recognized, Yap's political-moral activity was for a long time confined to the Protestant and Chinese minorities, each in its own way a kind of ghetto.

The last big surprise that Dan offers his readers is the story of Yap's decision, at the end of 1945, to take a short-term job as a steward on one of the ships taking home thousands of emaciated and traumatized Dutch survivors of the camps into which they had been incarcerated during the brief but brutal Japanese occupation of Indonesia (March 1942–August 1945). The opportunity arose because of a massive boycott by the "native" crews usually manning these ships, who rallied to the defense of the infant Republic of Indonesia proclaimed on 17 August 1945 against any attempt to restore Dutch colonialism. Dan comes fairly close to implying that Yap was a politically innocent scab. But, as we have seen, Yap had never shown any interest in the independence movement and had sat out the Japanese occupation in the small West Java town of Sukabumi—and he was, after all, still a Dutch citizen and he wanted to complete his law studies in Holland. He stayed in the Netherlands for more than two years as the revolutionary struggle deepened back home. He finished his advanced legal studies, traveled around Western Europe on church-related missions, and above all got himself a real political education. In his middle thirties, he now read widely in Western political theory (including Marxism) and history. Even more important, he had ample opportunity to observe, at first hand, a Western democracy at work, a form of government inescapably tied to national consciousness and the practice of citizenship.

The education came at the right time, since a little over a year after his return to Indonesia, the Dutch gave up the fight and the independent state of

Indonesia was recognized worldwide. At this moment the colonial-era status of *onderdaan* (subject) disappeared in a puff of smoke. Everyone in Indonesia would have to have citizen status, whether Dutch, Indonesian, or Chinese. For most, there was no problem. But for the Indonesian Chinese, a fundamental crisis set in. Dutch citizenship was an option only for a tiny few like Yap. The real choice was between Indonesia, where during the Revolution sporadic but terrible violence had been locally committed against them by gangsterish elements in the revolutionary movement, and China, just mastered by Mao Tse-tung's nationalist, anti-capitalist, revolutionary state. It is an odd lacuna in Dan's account that he does not tell us exactly when or how Yap renounced his Dutchness and took up Indonesian citizenship, but it must have happened before the transfer of sovereignty at the end of 1949. In any case, it was a huge decision, since he could have stayed in Holland and played out his Dutch citizenship for the rest of his life. He could also have opted for Chinese citizenship, but there is no sign of the kind of interest in China that he had had in the 1930s, and to the end of his life he never visited the ancestral country. The important thing is that he *chose* to become an Indonesian, whereas the "native" population had no other even theoretical options and automatically became citizens of their country.

Characteristically, in his brilliant two chapters on the post-independence Soekarno years (1950–66), Dan spends little time on Yap's practice as a by-now highly regarded professional trial lawyer. Nor does he go into much detail about Yap's increasingly important (if typically "opposition") role in Protestant circles. With good reason—for Yap was also plunging himself into the political-legal work of creating what eventually became Baperki (the Consultative Body on Indonesian Citizenship). The original purpose of the organization was to inform and educate the largely apolitical, confused, and sometimes barely literate Chinese population about their options on the citizenship question, and with what positive or negative consequences. It was also intended to be a nonpartisan but comprehensive lobby for the Chinese in top political and bureaucratic circles. Had it remained that way it would have found Yap in his element. But fairly soon the organization came under the control of the wily politician Siauw Giok Tjan, one of the few *peranakan* who had joined the Revolution from the outset and had even on occasion served in the cabinets of that period. Perhaps more aware than Yap of the rising tide of anti-Chinese feeling, especially among entrepreneurial Muslims and the military, Siauw tried quite successfully to turn Baperki into an unacknowledged political party for the Chinese community, and increasingly allied it with President Soekarno and the

Communist Party of Indonesia (PKI). Feeling that these were ominous developments, and also hostile to the PKI, Yap fought against Siauw tooth and nail. But he was always outmaneuvered, sometimes by obviously unethical means. The final parting of the ways came when Baperki felt it had to take a position on Soekarno's increasingly vociferous claim that the liberal Constitution of 1950 had led to nothing but gridlock, while the Constituent Assembly, elected to write a permanent constitution, was, thanks to bitter ideological conflicts, incapable of doing any better. As it became more and more clear that Soekarno intended, quite illegally, to decree a return to the authoritarian Constitution of 1945 (prepared in the last days of the Japanese occupation), Siauw felt he had no choice but to cheer the charismatic president on. Yap was appalled by what he regarded at Siauw's opportunism and betrayal of democracy and the rule of law, which he sensed would lead to later disaster. He proved to be right. When Soekarno's Guided Democracy was destroyed in 1965–66 in an orgy of murder, torture, and imprisonment of people of the Left, Siauw was jailed for years, Baperki was banned, many *peranakan* were killed, Chinese schools were closed, relations with Peking were violently broken, and Indonesian Chinese lost any effective political voice for more than thirty years.

In his mid-fifties, Yap's character was by then fully formed by his upbringing, his experience, his knowledge, and his commitments. One could venture to say, he was ready to become a hero. The trial of the reviled Subandrio, once the second most powerful civilian in Indonesian politics, a Javanese, and of distant aristocratic lineage, gave him his chance to put all his ideals and commitments on the line. In some ways, he was unusually invulnerable. He had few relatives to worry about, and none who was in high position or extremely rich. He was a known anti-communist, even if without fanaticism. He belonged to a religious minority that had never made trouble for any Indonesian government. He was notoriously simple in his habits—and incorruptible. He knew the law which the Suharto regime pretended to respect far better than most judges and prosecutors. In Indonesian society, his age earned him a certain formal respect. He was lucky, too, that the regime, then anxious to appear respectful of legal procedure in foreign eyes, made the huge mistake of allowing the trial proceedings to be broadcast without censorship. Still, he had to have a lot of courage.

What Dan indirectly suggests is that some of this courage had its source in Yap's minority-ness. He was never going to be a cabinet minister, or the leader of a major political party, or the president of a national university. But he was not unique. Kartini became a national heroine only well after her short life was over. As the closeted daughter of a high aristocratic Javanese family, she knew she was going nowhere, except to the silence of an arranged marriage. So, one might venture, she dared to speak about the plight of native women and the need for native emancipation—well before the national movement arrived. Liem Koen Hian, Bandjarmasin *peranakan*, had nowhere to go beyond being a fiery newspaper editor, but he had the courage to form the pro-Indonesian emancipation Partai Tionghoa Indonesia (Indonesian Chinese Party), in opposition to the most powerful groups in the Chinese community and the contempt for the natives widespread in that community, but also against the leaders of the native nationalist movement who closed their parties' doors to Indonesian Chinese. The brilliant colonial era Malang *peranakan* satirist Kwee Thiam Tjing also had "nowhere to go" and died in obscurity, yet he composed the only honest, hilarious, and heart-wrenching account of what it was like to experience the late Dutch colonial period, the Japanese occupation, and the early Revolution. He was also the only person who could record the hideous murder of many of his relatives by gangster "revolutionary" groups and still remain committed to the ideals of Indonesia's freedom. *Peranakan* Soe Hok-gie, who died young, was the only anti-communist who had the courage to denounce the anti-communist massacres of 1965–66. The Arab *peranakan* Munir (perhaps ashamed of the corrupt opportunism of prominent Arab *peranakan* who elbowed their way into cabinet positions to serve Suharto's Machiavellian "opening to Islam") became, after Yap, the most principled defender of the human rights of all Indonesian citizens, till he was murdered by agents of the state intelligence apparatus. The Pasuruan *peranakan* Dede Oetomo, a professional linguist, who knew he was going nowhere in the anti-Chinese world of the dictatorship, became the first Indonesian citizen to declare himself publicly as "gay," and for decades tirelessly worked for the causes of AIDS prevention and the defense of Indonesia's miserable (and sometimes not so miserable) gays and lesbians. Also "going nowhere" was the Tjirebon *peranakan* playwright Riantiarno, who, at the height of Suharto's power, dared to put on plays satirizing the president and his powerful acolytes.

Yet there was one important respect in which Yap differed from these other brave, committed people. They all became famous, to different degrees, when they were still very young—in their twenties or early thirties. If one reads Kartini's letters, Liem Koen Hian's and Kwee Thiam Tjing's iconoclastic journalism, Soe Hok Gie's powerful master's thesis, Munir's daring press releases and legal briefs, Dede Oetomo's missionary magazine *Gaya Nusantara*, and Riantiarno's hilarious and blistering early plays, one feels the fiery force of youthful idealism. (It is true that Kwee's masterpiece was written when he was close to fifty years old, but it was barely noticed in 1947 and was buried until three decades after his death.) Yap, however, had an unnoticed youth and became a hero at an age when Indonesian generals are required to retire and most civilians are thinking about following suit. Yet once achieved, his fame lasted for the rest of his workaholic life. One cannot help but think that here there is another indirect filiation with his ageing, courageous, workaholic biographer.

PRIMARY PLAYERS

FAMILY OF YAP THIAM HIEN

Yap A Sin great-grandfather
Yap Joen Khoy grandfather
Sato Nakashima foster grandmother
Yap Sin Eng father
Hoan Tjing Nio mother
Tan Gien Khing wife
Yap Thiam Bong younger brother
Yap Thiam Lian ("Non") sister
Yap Hong Gie son
Yap Hong Ay daughter

COLLEAGUES, FRIENDS, FOES

Adnan Buyung Nasution Prosecutor; KASI chair; private advocate; founder and leader of the LBH (Legal Aid Institute)
General Ali Moertopo (army) Chair of Opsus; early contributor to LBH
Major General Ali Sadikin (marines) Governor of Jakarta Daerah Khusus Istimewa; patron and board member of LBH
Lt. Colonel Ali Said Presiding judge in Subandrio case; later chief public prosecutor (Jaksa Agung); minister of justice; chief justice of the Supreme Court

Ani Abas-Manopo Medan advocate; Peradin commissioner

Asikin Kusumaatmadja Supreme Court judge

Auwjong Peng Koen (also known as Oyong Peng Koen and P. K Ojong) *Star Weekly* chief editor; Baperki member; *Kompas* newspaper managing editor; director of P. T. Gramedia publishing house; Gramedia Legal Aid Association

Arief Budiman Student leader; reform activist; founding member of LBH

Besar Martokoesoemo First ethnic Indonesian private advocate; secretary general of the Ministry of Justice

Go Gien Tjwan Baperki executive secretary; Antara news agency

Harry Tjan (later Silalahi) Law student; member of the Catholic student group, PMKRI, and LPKB (assimilationist group)

Hugeng Imam Santoso Reform-minded police commandant, 1966–71; member of Pengabdi Hukum

Iskaq Tjokrohadisurjo Law partner of Suardi Tasrif; PNI (Nationalist party); minister of economic affairs; first chair of Peradin

Jamaluddin Datuk Singomangkuto School friend of Yap Thiam Bong in Kuta Raja; AMS Jogja with Yap Thiam Hien; Masyumi Party; Konstituante member; defense co-counsel in Yap's defamation trial and in Oei Tjoe Tat trial; LBH participant/mentor

General E. J. Kanter (army) Military auditor; Kopkamtib (army security agency); Persahi chairman (legal professionals association)

Khoe Woen Sioe Publisher of *Star Weekly;* director *Keng Po* newspaper; president of Sin Ming Hui (peranakan service organization); Baperki deputy chairman

Dr. J.[Johannes] Leimena Medical doctor; Parkindo (Protestant political party) leader; minister in Soekarno's cabinet

Lie Hwee Yoe Senior partner in the Jakarta law firm Yap joined in the early 1950s

Liem Koen Hian Journalist; Surabaya newspaper editor; founded the pre-war PTI; nationalist; served on the occupation-era commission to develop a constitution; founder of the New-PTI

Lukman Wiriadinata Minister of justice in Sjahrir government; PSI; law partner with Hasjim Mahdan and Andi Zainal Abidin; Peradin founding member, vice chair and chairman; LBH advisor

Nani Razak-Muthalib Jakarta advocate and writer on procedural code reform; Peradin commissioner

Oei Tjoe Tat Lie Hwee Yoe law firm partner, with Yap and Tan Po Goan; founding member and president of Sing Ming Hui service organization; founding member of Baperki; minister in Soekarno cabinet; arrested 1966, defended by Yap

Ong Hok Am Later known as Onghokam; historian; member of the pro assimilation group

Oyong Peng Coen See Auwjong Peng Coen

H. J. C. Princen ("Ponke") Member of IPKI party; member of Parliament; chair of Institute for the Defense of Human Rights

Siauw Giok Tjhan Journalist; Surabaya, East Java PTI member; served in revolutionary Yogyakarta; editor of Communist Party newspaper *Harian Rakjat*; member of the Konstituante; member of Parliament; chair of Baperki; arrested in 1966

General T. B. Simatupang (army) Moving force behind Indonesian Council of Churches (Protestant) and the unification of the Chinese churches

Soe Hok Gie KASI student activist, writer

Soemarno P. Wirjanto Surakarta private lawyer and prolific writer; member of Peradin

Sri Widojati Notoprojo First female Supreme Court justice, chair of the Pengabdi Hukum (law professionals' association); chair of Ikahi (judges association), Jakarta branch

Suardi Tasrif Editor of the Masyumi Party-associated newspaper, *Abadi*; law partner of Iskaq Tjokrohadisurjo; Peradin founding member and secretary; editor of Peradin's journal, *Hukum dan Keadilan*; prolific writer

Subagio Defense co-counsel in the Subandrio trial

Subandrio Foreign Minister during Guided Democracy; defended by Yap and Subagio in Mahmillub case

Tan Po Goan Partner, with Yap and Oei Tjoe Tat, in the Lie Hwee Yoe law firm; PSI (Socialist Party); Sin Ming Hui; Baperki; member of Parliament

Thio Thiam Tjong Baperki founder, executive and education committees; ally of Yap against Siauw

Wiratmo Soekito Journalist-intellectual; Pengabdi Hukum member

Wirjono Prodjodikoro Chief justice of the Supreme Court during Guided Democracy period

[Andi or A.] Zainal Abidin Law firm partner of Lukman Wiriadinata; PSI (Socialist Party); founding member of Peradin; co-counsel with Yap in Liem Koe Nio case; defending co-counsel in Yap's defamation case; LBH mentor

ONE

ACEH

ASK just about anyone who knew Yap Thiam Hien and you will soon be told that what accounted for his character is that he was from Aceh. Indonesia's ethnic variety makes for this kind of easy stereotyping: Javanese are soft-spoken, subtle, manipulative, sophisticated masters of compromise; Minangkabau from West Sumatra, businesslike traders; north Sumatran Bataks, tough, vulgar, and self-serving; Acehnese from the northernmost tip of Sumatra, devoutly Islamic, stubborn, independent, and given to violence. Yap Thiam Hien was indeed stubborn, uncompromising, blunt, principled, and outspoken; so it must, of course, be because he was from Aceh. Occasionally, in lighter vein but also with a note of pride, Yap explained himself in the same way.

If only it were so. As tempting as these simple formulae are, they fall apart under even mild questioning. If Aceh explains Yap Thiam Hien, why aren't there more Yap Thiam Hiens, whether ethnically Chinese or ethnically Acehnese, from Aceh? Or for that matter—since Yap's qualities are sometimes attributed to (or blamed on) his Christianity—why aren't there many more Indonesian Christians like him? The questions provoke puzzled silence.

It is not that Aceh is unimportant to explaining Yap Thiam Hien, just not in the simplistic terms of cultural style that most people mean. Actually, he did not have all that much to do with Aceh or the Acehnese, or not enough to have had a profound influence on him. Where he grew up, in Kutaraja (now Banda Aceh, the capital of the province), the majority of the population then were, like him, Chinese. He did not speak Acehnese, or even a Chinese language, but rather Malay and Dutch. His education, from start to finish, was Dutch. And to make matters more complex, the woman who cared for and deeply influenced him after his own mother died was a Japanese immigrant.

Yet, in other ways Aceh explains a great deal about Yap Thiam Hien. That he was born there means, obliquely, that he was not from Java, which dominated the colony and now dominates the independent state. He was always an outsider, in some ways even a stranger, to the intricate networks of family associations and power in the Javanese center. And, of course, Aceh is where he grew up until age thirteen. The earliest formative influences on him—family and education—were obviously from there. These influences make sense, however, only with the help of some light shed by the history into which Yap was born. It is a mistake to try to understand him simply as a Chinese, but it is impossible to understand him without attention to the flow of Chinese immigration, the structure of the ethnic Chinese community, and the colonial state that established the conditions of Chinese existence in the Netherlands-Indies. There is no need here to recapitulate the entire history of the Chinese minority in Indonesia, but a few brief comments will help.[1]

By the middle of the nineteenth century, when Yap Thiam Hien's great-great-grandfather arrived on the island of Bangka, Chinese communities in Indonesia already had a long history that gave them a distinctly Indonesian cast, with its own coloration and fault lines. They were relatively secure but not altogether comfortable in the Netherlands-Indies. Unlike Thailand, where the absorption of Chinese immigrants was eased by ethnic and religious affinity and not obstructed by a European-dominated state, in Indonesia the immigrants were decidedly different in an ethnically Malay society and predominantly (though often superficially) Islamic setting, where colonial authority surrounded them. Unlike in Malaysia, where large numbers of Chinese immigrants—eventually enough to make up about 33 percent of the population—could protect themselves adequately, in Indonesia they constituted only about 3 or 4 percent—maybe more, for a precise and persuasive estimate is hard to come by—and so were always vulnerable. They fit into the colonial economy of the Netherlands-Indies, as elsewhere in Southeast Asia, as a superior source of hard-working talent to fill middlemen roles in which the Dutch were not interested but which, by colonial logic, were best denied to indigenous Indonesians. As a minority, Chinese—since the mid-nineteenth century legally classified as "Foreign Orientals," as were the smaller groups of Arabs, Indians, and Japanese (until early in the twentieth century)—were dependent upon Dutch goodwill. They were never popular with the Dutch, who found them useful but not likeable. They had always to be kept in their place. In 1740 Chinese had been brutally massacred by Dutch and indigenous bands in Batavia (now Jakarta) and elsewhere along the north coast of Java. Few such reminders were necessary.

Although conveniently conceived by the Dutch and most Indonesians as an undifferentiated aggregate, the Chinese, like minorities nearly everywhere, were diverse, with their own elongated class structure and cultural cleavages. They were divided not only by provincial Chinese origins, languages, and customs, but also more deeply by the extent of their adaptation in Indonesia. Like immigrants anywhere, the longer they stayed, the more likely they were to assimilate and acculturate. By the nineteenth century, a distinct stratum had long since emerged of acculturated *peranakan*, "children of the land," or *baba*, as they were usually called in Sumatra and in Malaya across the straits. As Chinese women did not begin to join the men until relatively late, many immigrants married Indonesian women, indicating perhaps that local prejudice needed time, encouragement, and the right conditions to flourish. Some Chinese probably were absorbed into an Indonesian genetic stream. Many others gradually drifted into local cultural streams, adopting local values and norms and relinquishing Chinese roots (though not necessarily identity) and putting down new ones in local history and language. The Indonesian Chinese *peranakan* was as different from Chinese elsewhere as the American Jew was from Jews elsewhere or the French Armenian from Armenians elsewhere.

By contrast, new immigrants, called *totok* (full blood or newcomer) in Indonesian or *singkeh* ("new guest," *xinke*), came fully equipped as always with rich memories of the homeland, mainly Kwantung and Fukien provinces, and their Hokkien, Hakka, and other languages. They remained *totok* beyond the first and second generations as long as these memories and the language lasted. Between *peranakan* and *totok*, the one deracinated but at home and the other with identity intact but essentially foreign, tension was inevitable. Looking down (on) and up (to) at the same time cannot be easy, but it is a discomfort distinct generations of immigrants everywhere have no doubt learned to live with.

The differences between *peranakan* and *totok* were social and economic as well as cultural and became increasingly so in the twentieth century, as new educational and career opportunities arose. The more recent immigrant, limited by language and connections, was more likely to restrict himself (and, later, herself) to whatever money-making opportunities were available. This usually meant opening a shop of some sort, which, with ability and luck, he might develop into something more profitable. Despite the myth of Chinese business acumen, many never made it beyond the cart or small store. By contrast, the *peranakan* equipped with Javanese, say, and Malay and possibly Dutch eventually had a wider range of choices. That person could imagine becoming a doctor, lawyer, clerk, or teacher, as well as a shop owner or businessman. For some, once this happened (from about the 1910s), it became almost a matter of pride not to be good at trading, the mark of the *totok* Chinese.

Like other ethnic groups in the colony, the Chinese were governed indirectly and at minimal cost to the Dutch administration. Basic patterns of indirect rule were established in the seventeenth and eighteenth centuries by the Dutch East India Company, the private ancestor of the colony that was formally created in the early nineteenth century after the conclusion of the Napoleonic wars. The governing principle was that like should rule like, each ethnic community administered by its own leadership: Europeans by the Dutch, Javanese by Javanese, Chinese by Chinese, Arabs by Arabs, and so on. Through the agency of separate ethnic elites, with each of which a mutually advantageous relationship was fashioned, the Dutch governed the whole. Indirect rule over Java, the heartland of the country, was predicated on a political alliance between the Dutch and the Javanese royal houses and the *priyayi* aristocracy. The same pattern basically held elsewhere as Dutch power penetrated the rest of the archipelago.

As Chinese immigrants had no obvious governing class, the Dutch created one for them. *Officieren*—with military ranks of *majoor, kapitein,* and *luitenant,* depending on the importance of the locale and the community—were appointed by the colonial authorities to administer to Chinese needs and Dutch requirements. These Chinese officials were not of the same order of importance as the Javanese bureaucratic aristocracy, or of indigenous elites elsewhere, as the Chinese were considered fundamentally less important in the colonial scheme of things. Conceived as intermediaries between the Dutch and the Chinese, *officieren* were intended to maintain order in their communities, make sure that Dutch orders were carried out, inform the administration about affairs in the Chinese zones, and represent their communities to the colonial government.[2]

Lea Williams has argued that the *officieren* barely deserve consideration as instruments of indirect rule.[3] By the twentieth century, indeed, the institution had begun to collapse, losing the respect of Chinese communities and the economic perquisites and political support once supplied by the colonial administration. When the *officieren* disappeared with the colony, they had long since ceased to exercise any real authority. Still, they meant a good deal until early in the century, a point of some importance here because Yap Thiam Hien belonged to the family of an *officier.* The *officieren* did not have the status of indigenous rulers and were not treated as respectfully, but they received no less by way of advantage. Local aristocracies were compensated for their services to the colony with guarantees of their political positions and social status. The Chinese *officieren* were granted monopolies over the immensely profitable opium trade, for example, and other commercial opportunities. Like ethnic Indonesian elites, they were accorded special privileges of legal status and access to superior Dutch education.

Early in the twentieth century, as new strata of educated Indonesians, including Chinese Indonesians, began to come into their own and to think about change, privileged elites came under attack. Indigenous aristocracies, the Javanese *priyayi* particularly, had no difficulty surviving, because they were essential to the Dutch and no one doubted their authority among the peasant majority. The *officieren* had no such advantages. Before the turn of the century, their dealings in opium had turned especially odious among Dutch reformers, so that this monopoly, among others, was soon taken over by the colonial administration.[4] More than anything else, it was the loss of these financial benefits that destroyed the institution of *officieren.*[5]

Peranakan and *singkeh* alike, affected by the nationalist wave emanating from China, contemptuously lumped the *officieren* together with zoning laws and travel restrictions as humiliations imposed on the Chinese. A Dutch journalist, Henri Borel, distinguished between the officers of Java and those of the outer islands, challenging the former because they were *peranakan* and therefore no longer authentic Chinese, while the latter, to his mind, were more legitimate precisely because they were mainly *singkeh.*[6] While Borel's point reveals some odd thinking about who was Chinese, it also calls attention to the important differences between the Chinese of Java and the other islands. In Java, as Dutch authority and economic control were consolidated, the Chinese population stabilized under the domination of long-resident *peranakan* families well known in Javanese society and Dutch administrative circles. By the middle of the nineteenth century, Chinese immigration to Java had slowed. Outside of Java, where Dutch power began to extend rapidly in the second half of the nineteenth century, new Chinese immigration followed suit as the Dutch sought workers for the plantations of East Sumatra and the tin mines of Bangka and Belitung (Billiton), islands off the eastern coast. At the same time, immigrants were pouring into western Malaya, also to mine tin, and into Singapore.

The resulting demographic changes were less significant for Indonesia than for the British colony to the north, but they were important. In 1860, of the 222,000 Chinese resident in Indonesia, 67.6 percent were in Java, 32.4 percent outside. By 1895 the total had increased to 469,000 of whom 54.6 percent lived in Java and 45.4 percent in outer Indonesia, with 33.9 percent of the total in Sumatra. In 1920, of the 809,000 Chinese in Indonesia only 47.5 percent were in Java, 52.5 percent in the other islands, with 37.6 percent of the total in Sumatra.[7] The numbers of new migrants to outer Indonesia never lent them the influence to match that of ethnic Chinese in Java, from whom they were distinguished in other ways as well. Chinese migrants to outer Indonesia spread out over much larger areas and were economically more diverse—miners, plantation workers, farmers, and fishermen, as well as small shop owners and substantial businessmen.[8] Many were more oriented to the Chinese communities of Penang, Singapore, and the Malayan mainland, where some had recently settled relatives, than to the established *peranakan* groups of Java. Because of the speed and concentration of the new migration, it may be that outer island *singkeh* underwent a slower metamorphosis into *baba* than did those who had preceded them in Java. The outcome was also different, to the extent that the cultural habits they absorbed were as different from those of Java as the local languages were different from Javanese. The process, however, as the Yap family history demonstrates, followed a more or less common pattern.

Yap Thiam Hien's great-great-grandfather joined the exodus from south China in about 1844. In Chinese kinship, the paternal line counts for more than the maternal, so that no one in the Yap family remembers much about the mother's side. As it happens, not much is known either about the great-great-grandfather himself. In the family tree sketched by Thiam Hien's father in the late 1940s, he has no name. But he was a Hakka from the interior of Kwantung province, the district of Moi-yan, subdistrict of Lo-yi. He settled, after the voyage, in Baturusa on Bangka Island. What exactly he did there is unclear, for while thousands of Chinese had come to work as contract laborers in the tin mines, many soon grew pepper instead or fished or took up trades or opened shops. In Baturusa he married a local Indonesian woman, as nameless as he, by whom he shortly had four children, three sons and a daughter. The name of the daughter is also unknown, but the three sons, in order, were Yap A Kang, Yap A Piang, and Yap A Sin (also known as Yap Sin Tjhong). This third son, Yap

A Sin, was Thiam Hien's great-grandfather. Born in Baturusa in 1849, he was evidently a capable and ambitious man, tough and courageous enough to move on in search of better opportunities. It was he who established the family anew in Aceh. Exactly how and when he got there is not clear, but the move greatly improved the family's fortune.

Aceh was not a particularly hospitable or promising place for Chinese, few of whom settled there before the 1870s. By the last third of the century, moreover, political tension in the area finally broke out into a thirty-year war, as the Dutch sought, successfully but not easily, to incorporate Aceh into the Netherlands-Indies. The Dutch presence created more attractive conditions for Chinese. Traders from Penang had been active in Aceh, but few were willing to take up residence until the 1870s, when the Dutch began actively to encourage them with land and opium revenues. In the early 1880s Acehnese attacks on Chinese immigrants encouraged many of them to leave again.[9]

In 1875 the Dutch had little success in recruiting indentured labor from China, but in 1876 had more luck with labor contractors in Penang and Muntok in Bangka. At about the same time, the Dutch administration appointed a Chinese *officier* (a *kapitein*).[10] In about 1874 Yap A Sin married the daughter of *Kapitein* Tjoe Ten Hin of Kutaraja, capital of Aceh. Tjoe Ten Hin was originally from Pontianak, in west Borneo, where the Dutch evidently preferred to recruit their earliest Chinese officers for Aceh from its well-established and relatively autonomous Chinese community. Tjoe Ten Hin's daughter, Tjoe Koei Yin (1857–1915), was born in west Borneo. How she came to know Yap A Sin is not clear, though the meeting could have been arranged by an intermediary in search of a suitable husband for a fairly well-off young woman. If so, Yap A Sin may already have become successful in Baturusa, perhaps as a labor contractor, and would have been known to Dutch officials and to the Tjoe family in Aceh.

Yap A Sin and his new wife apparently lived for a short time in Baturusa, where their first-born son, Yap Joen Khoy, Thiam Hien's grandfather, was born in 1875. Soon thereafter they moved to Kutaraja, where Yap A Sin at length succeeded to the lieutenancy, a position earlier held by Tjoe Ten Hin's son (and Koei Yin's older brother), Tjoe Lim Tzoy. (The latter may have died without a brother to take his place.)

Kutaraja then was small, but it was growing and gathering facilities because of the long Dutch war of conquest. Dutch civil and military administrations were established there, working out of the old Sultan's palace, along with a substantial garrison of troops. There was a new mosque, consecrated in 1881, but also a new church for Christian officials, both Dutch and Indonesian, brought in to administer the war and such peace as there was. There were also Dutch-language schools. By the 1890s Kutaraja already had a tramline and telegraph and limited telephone service, mainly no doubt for military purposes. The population, however, though growing, was still small. In 1896, apart from the military camps, there were 4,799 people in the city, of whom 2,427 were Chinese. There were 1,854 ethnic Indonesians. These were mainly Acehnese but also included Minangkabau from West Sumatra—one of the mature Yap Thiam Hien's close friends, Jamaluddin Datuk Singomangkuto, was a Minangkabau who grew up in Aceh and went to school with Thiam Hien's younger brother. In addition, there were east Sumatrans, Ambonese, Javanese, Menadonese, among others, many of whom worked for the government. Among the rest were 158 Europeans, mainly officials, 22 Arabs, and 338 other "Foreign Orientals," presumably Indians, Arabs, and Japanese.[11] As in other cities in the colony, each ethnic group had its own quarter, a *wijk*, which in the case of the Chinese particularly was something like but not quite a ghetto. The *wijk* was headed by an unpaid but influential *wijkmeester* responsible for registration, travel passes, and other administrative matters affecting the community. The Chinese *wijkmeester* in Kutaraja during Thiam Hien's early years was his grandfather, Yap Joen Khoy.

Through the early 1910s, the family was one of the wealthiest in Kutaraja, though by standards in Java or such major Sumatran commercial centers as Medan and Palembang, the family's lifestyle might be described as "provincial." The population was too small to generate an immense fortune, though inter-island and foreign trade, in copra, for example, helped. Yap A Sin's most substantial income may have come from the opium monopoly or some share of it, depending on his relationship with the *kapitein* (his father-in-law), about whom I have little information. But he also had a coconut plantation, fish ponds, and no doubt other ventures. He and his large house, very imposing as his great-great-grandchildren remember it, were the hub of the family's existence. At this house, the numerous members of the family would gather on Sundays. Thiam Hien, as the eldest son of an eldest son, was privileged to enter Yap A Sin's bedroom, where he witnessed the old man's preparations for smoking opium.

Yap A Sin's business manager was his first son, Yap Joen Khoy (1875–1919), the *wijkmeester* who lived in another substantial house owned by his father on the same short street (fig. 1.1). Thiam Hien spent his first years in this house, where his parents lived, along with many others in the family, in their own comfortable quarters. Joen Khoy and his first son, Sin Eng, were key transi-

FIG. 1.1 Yap Joen Khoy, grandfather of Yap Thiam Hien, Kutaradja, Aceh, n.d.

tional figures in the evolution of the Yap family from *totok* to *baba*. Only forty-four when he died, a year before his father, Joen Khoy never had the chance to assume the lieutenancy to which he was heir, but apparently he was a capable manager of the family enterprises. A stern, handsome man, he belonged to the Chinese community but had connections beyond it. His public clothes were not European but a somber tunic, perhaps not entirely because Dutch officials expected it of him. He had worn a queue, as had his sons, but he cut it off (as did his sons) after the revolution of 1911 in China, and thereafter kept his head nearly bald. Hakka was his first language but he may have used some Cantonese or Hokkien—most of his charges in Kutaraja were Hakkas and Cantonese, with fewer Hokkiens and Hok-Chias, a Hokkien subgroup—but probably not *kuo-yu* (Mandarin; *guo-yu* in *pinyin* romanization). He undoubtedly knew Malay and he used Dutch, which he needed for dealing with officials. What is more important, he insisted that his children and grandchildren learn Dutch well; with his grandchildren, Joen Khoy spoke Dutch. Perhaps under social pressure from the local *totok* community, he forced the grandchildren to attend a standard Chinese-language (Mandarin) school for a time, but they never took to Mandarin or any other Chinese language.

Joen Khoy exercised firm authority over his family and commanded respect—the grandchildren remember him as strict and demanding, befitting a Chinese elder of high standing—but there were tensions, too, at least with

FIG. 1.2 Sato Nakashima ("Omah"), foster grandmother to the Yap children, Hien, Bong, and Non, n.d.

his eldest son, Yap Sin Eng. The root of them had to do with a concubine who played a critical part in the lives of Thiam Hien and his younger brother and sister. Joen Khoy had married Tjoa Soei Hian (1876–1909) from Muntok, who died quite young.[12] A couple of years before his wife died, Joen Khoy went to Saigon and returned with a young Japanese girl, Sato Nakashima (fig. 1.2). Tjoa Soei Hian was not happy about her, naturally. No one would have dared raise an issue with Joen Khoy about it, but Sin Eng evidently resented Nakashima deeply, supposing that she was the cause of the illness that soon killed his mother. In time their relationship changed, a matter to be taken up later.

Yap Sin Eng (1894–1949), Thiam Hien's father, was the first of the line to be identifiably more *peranakan* than *totok* (fig. 1.3). Able to speak Hakka and Hokkien, he was the last to use any Chinese language well, or at all, but he also spoke Malay and Dutch and received a Dutch education, a privilege allowed the children of the *officieren* and other ethnic elites. He dressed by preference in European style, often modishly. He also seems to have been attracted to things European—for instance, he learned to play the violin (as did Thiam Hien later). Eventually Sin Eng took an office job.

Moreover, he took a wife from an unequivocally *baba* family of Hokkien origin, an indication that *singkeh* essences had faded in favor of *peranakan* melding. At age eighteen or nineteen he married Hoan Tjing Nio (1896–1922)

FIG. 1.3 Yap Sin Eng (*left*), father of Yap Thiam Hien, n.d.

from a Muntok family that had become wealthy in retail trade (fig. 1.4). Her parents, lacking a son, adopted one, a common Chinese custom. For the rest, however, her family had acculturated earlier than the Yaps. Tjing Nio's photograph shows a young girl in the typical *baba* dress of Sumatra and Malaysia. At home she and Sin Eng and their children spoke Malay, the only language, apparently, that Tjing Nio knew. It was also the children's first language.

Thiam Hien's generation of the Yap family, then, the fifth in Indonesia, was essentially *peranakan*. One consequence, which they shared with many others, was social marginality, made the more difficult in their case by financial disaster. All three of Sin Eng's children turned out to have remarkable character, filled with fibers of pride, courage, stubbornness, and responsibility. However one tries to figure out the psychological sources of their toughness, the starting place is Kutaraja.

Thiam Hien was born on 25 May 1913; his brother Thiam Bong, on 8 March 1915; and his sister Thiam Lian, on 18 January 1917. Two more children followed, a boy and a girl, one of whom died in less than a year and the other within two years. For a few years the family lived comfortably in their own rooms in Joen

FIG. 1.4 Hoan Tjing Nio, mother of Yap Thiam Hien, n.d.

Khoy's big house, with gardens for the children to play in, secure among a host of parents, grandparents, aunts, uncles, and cousins. What they lacked, as each of them recalls, was intimacy, seldom overdone anyway in many Chinese families, but especially hard to come by amidst a crowd of relatives.

What intimacy there was came at first from their mother, Tjing Nio, and later from Sato Nakashima, their Japanese "Omah" (grandmother, in Dutch). Tjing Nio, only sixteen when she married Sin Eng, was tubercular and never very strong. Five children in as many years probably did not help. At Thiam Hien's birth, she was just seventeen. Only he had much time with her before she died. After a trip to Bangka for the wedding of her adoptive brother, Tjing Nio was ill continually until she died in August 1922. Thiam Hien was then nine, Thiam Bong seven, and Thiam Lian five.

Thiam Hien remembers his mother more clearly than do his brother and sister. He recalls her as loving—worried when the children did not eat, preparing them eggs with thick soy sauce to encourage their appetites—but strict, for fear that their father would be even stricter. As the eldest child, responsible for his younger siblings, Thiam Hien took the most punishment—maybe not very often—from a rattan cane or hard pinches. When he swam in the river, which was forbidden, taking his brother Thiam Bong with him, as he had to, a servant told his mother, who punished him severely enough for him to remember it forever. Thiam Bong recalls his mother as weak and constantly sick. Thiam Lian, the youngest, was with her mother all the time, yet only for a few years; she remembers her least and suffered most from her loss.

As usual in Chinese families then, their father, Sin Eng, was distant. His daughter Lian, nicknamed Non, remembers him affectionately, but Hien and Bong never got along well with him. Sin Eng was strict, though probably no more so than most Chinese fathers of his class and time. He laid down a few hard rules to which there were no exceptions. The family had to eat together, the children had to study hard in school, and gambling, a common pastime, was forbidden. Once he came upon Thiam Hien and some friends playing a card game. Assuming they were betting, he slapped his son, which, despite the injustice of it, evidently drove the point home. Thiam Hien certainly did not drink or gamble or engage in other prosaic vices, even in minor ways, and the reasons precede his conversion to Protestantism in the 1930s.

For the most part Hien, Bong, and Non did not see much of their father and had only a reserved relationship with him. They were cared for by the women of the family, either their mother or grandmothers. There was nothing unusual in this, but after Tjing Nio died the distance between Sin Eng and his sons began to fill up with tension and even dislike, one reason perhaps for the huge fund of anger on which Thiam Hien always drew. It was naturally a time of turmoil for them, not only because their mother had died but also because the family empire, such as it was, evaporated. Sin Eng was still a very young man, only twenty-eight, when his wife died, but he never remarried, though once, when Hien was about thirteen, he came close to doing so, with a woman of mixed European and Chinese parentage. The children hated the idea, partly out of loyalty to their mother but also because they did not want a stepmother. For whatever reasons the marriage was called off at the last moment. Sin Eng had other women friends, and painful and embarrassing rumors got back to Hien and Bong. Kutaraja was a small town and the Chinese community even smaller. They would not have said anything to their father, of course, but they held it against him. Other tensions between Sin Eng and his sons grew indirectly from the dramatic collapse of the family fortunes and status. The children were too young to understand exactly what happened, but the effects of the collapse lasted a lifetime.

The wealth on both sides of the family disappeared in a short period during the 1910s and early 1920s, a bad time for the *officier* class. As a six- or seven-year-old boy, Hien experienced the decline as a puzzling diminution of the gifts of money (*ang pow*) given him by the patriarch Yap A Sin: from the substantial *ringgit* to a *rijksdaalder*, soon a guilder, and finally only half a guilder, each coin smaller than the last. It was a metaphor of the calamity visited on the family as the lieutenancy slipped away and all their property disappeared.

Years later, maybe with a touch of Protestant moralism, Thiam Hien wondered whether the misfortune was not visited on his great-grandfather for the sin of selling opium. More likely, it was because Yap A Sin could no longer sell opium. For the same reason, the *officier* position was no great loss, as the institution itself had already begun to fall apart. Chinese revenue farming—the monopolies over opium, gambling, slaughtering, and so on—was restricted before the end of the century and abolished afterwards.[13] The impact on Chinese *officieren* throughout the colony was evidently immediate, making the positions much less attractive; and the administration was unable thereafter to make them more so. Only if they had already begun to diversify and invest well could the *officier* families recoup the losses from revenue farming. Many went broke. Yap A Sin had taken out loans from banks and companies to support his ventures in the copra trade, among others, a bad investment at the time. His enterprises failed in the economically difficult years following World War I. When the loans were called in, either during the last year of his life or immediately after his death, the family went bankrupt.[14] The houses, including Joen Khoy's (in which Thiam Hien had spent his first years), were sold, along with the coconut plantation, and the family goods were auctioned off.

At the same time, the once-profitable store owned by the Hoan family, on Hien's mother's side, went under, but for different reasons. The store, named Muntok after the home base in Bangka, used to sell heavily to the Dutch officers and soldiers in town. They were not the best customers. Many of them left on transfers without paying off their substantial chits for supplies and liquor. Especially at the end of each year, large bills were run up for Christmas season celebrations. The eternal hope that all would eventually be paid never worked out. It may also be that by the early 1920s, as mopping-up operations following the "pacification" wound down, the military garrison and the Muntok's clientele, reliable or not, shrank. For a while Sin Eng helped out in the store, trying to balance the accounts; he had worked in the Kutaraja branch of the Javaasche

Bank soon after graduating from high school and understood accounts. But it ended badly, and the store and bakery also disappeared by the mid-1920s.

For the children this was a time of instability, beginning with Joen Khoy's death and the disappearance of Yap A Sin's estate. By no means were they destitute, however. Resources were available from the extended families of Yaps and Hoans. But they were suddenly in the unenviable position of being dependent on others, albeit relatives, to which Thiam Bong especially but the others too were sensitive. When Yap A Sin's houses were sold, the family had to move into the big house still owned by Tjing Nio's family. The children were not happy there, for their maternal great-grandmother ruled over the household with a dictatorial hand. They stayed there after their mother died, until Sin Eng, who went to Batavia to find work, returned with a friend to start a supply and catering business serving the military garrison. The children, especially Non, disliked this young man, who they thought had a bad influence on their father. The friend, from Sigli in provincial Aceh, and Sin Eng spent much time together, men about town. It was then that rumors flew about Sin Eng. The business went well for a few years, and Sin Eng rented an apartment in a house owned by the Japanese widow of a Swiss officer in the colonial army, so that he and the children, with Sato Nakashima, were on their own again. Later they rented a substantial house owned by the new *kapitein*. While there, Sin Eng bought a small Austin, which Thiam Hien was once allowed to drive as a reward for good grades, when he returned home during his first year in Java. But the business declined and Sin Eng gave it up. When he returned to Batavia for good, probably in 1927, to work as a clerk in a commercial house, the children and their Omah had to move again to a single room in a house owned by one of Joen Khoy's younger sisters, and then again to an uncle's place. And so it went. In better times, the family had a place of its own, in worse times they were farmed out to relatives.

From Hien's and Bong's point of view, Sin Eng was somehow responsible for their decline, or at least he failed to make up for it. Their resentment—never expressed to him, for his paternal privilege made that impossible—may have been tinged with contempt. In *peranakan* circles, success was even more important than for *totok*, in good part because of a sense that the Dutch were watching and maybe the Indonesian elite, too, not just other Chinese.

Sin Eng seemed to flit from job to job, as his sons saw it. Actually good times were interspersed with bad, but financial stability and security were in the past. For whatever reasons of character, skill, and opportunity, Sin Eng could not replace the family fortune. Like many *peranakan* sons, especially from *officieren* families, he could not, like a *singkeh*, start from the bottom to accumulate capital. Nor apparently did he have contacts with capital to spare in Aceh or in Java. But with a Dutch-language high-school education, he had other possibilities and may have preferred the risk-free security and social status of an office employee. His one business venture, the catering service, eventually failed, and he never tried again. He was also young enough—only twenty years older than Thiam Hien—and in some ways high-living enough not to scrimp merely for the sake of his sons. He might have saved for their educations by taking out insurance policies as some parents did, but lacking foresight or knowledge or concern, or maybe even money, he did not. Thiam Hien and Thiam Bong believed they suffered for it.

They did, though not in fact all that much. No less than most Chinese fathers, especially from educated *baba* strata, Sin Eng saw to it that his sons got good educations. When they wanted to go to Java to finish their studies, he made it possible. It was their sister Non who was hurt most by their father's inadequate income. A sensitive child, she felt most the lack of a mother and the frequent absence of her father. Imaginative, intelligent, and as ambitious as her brothers, she was also a daughter in a culture oriented to sons. Once out of the Dutch-language primary school, she also wanted to go to Java to continue her education. Sin Eng told her that her brothers had prior claim to support from the family's resources, that a woman had less need for education. When first Hien and then Bong left Kutaraja for Java, Non was forced to stay behind with her Omah. She nevertheless found an opportunity to study in a new Catholic school, which in time invited her to join the teaching staff. While still in Kutaraja, she was baptized a Catholic, years before Hien became a Protestant.

After their mother died, the central figure in the lives of Hien, Bong, and Non was their Japanese Omah, Sato Nakashima (1890?–1949). Nothing is as odd in the family's history as this woman. Some basic information about her is missing, unfortunately, because just before the Japanese invasion in early 1942, the family panicked and Thiam Hien destroyed her passport and other papers in an effort to protect her. The children were utterly devoted to her; even in old age, each of them saw her still as a fundamental, formative influence.

When Joen Khoy brought her back with him from Saigon, she was no more than seventeen. Born around 1890 in Nagasaki, Nakashima traveled to Southeast Asia in her teens to live with a relative and find work. According to the only credible explanation of how she got to Kutaraja I have heard—from Thiam Lian—Joen Khoy met her in a Japanese-owned store in Saigon where he bought supplies.[15] When, half joking, he asked the proprietor (her aunt) if he could take the girl, the guardian replied, in effect, why not? Joen Khoy never legally married Nakashima, even after his wife died. Sin Eng apparently resented her, but she was close to Joen Khoy, and the children took her for granted as part of the family.

Outsider though she was, Nakashima made herself a respected member of the Yap family. Intelligent and unwilling to be idle, she had skills—as a seamstress, among other things—and involved herself assiduously in the family's weddings and other rituals. But she was best known as a midwife; she delivered many of the Yap family's babies and did the same for others who asked her help, even when doctors were available. It is possible that she helped to deliver Hien, Bong, and Lian. Sometimes homesick and lonely, in the limited Japanese community in Kutaraja Nakashima found friends with whom she could speak in her own language and play cards. But she moved rather freely in other communities as well, one of few who ignored the real and implicit ghetto lines.

Nakashima returned to Japan twice in the 1910s. On the first trip, a few years before World War I broke out, in Nagasaki she adopted the son of her younger brother. Her family was poor, and her own secure position in Aceh enabled her to help the boy. She brought her nephew to Kutaraja for a time before taking him back to Nagasaki to begin school.[16] None of this would have been thought strange by the Yap family, for the adoption of children, often from relatives, was common in Chinese custom, as it is also in ethnic Indonesian societies. Nakashima's nephew was educated in a naval academy. Sometime in the 1920s, while still a cadet, he contracted cholera and died in Bangkok, according to Thiam Lian. Nakashima never returned to Japan thereafter. After World War II, when Thiam Hien returned from his studies in Holland and offered to take her to Nagasaki, she refused because she knew, she said, that all of her family had been destroyed by the atomic bomb.

When Joen Khoy died, Nakashima was not yet thirty. Whatever his misgivings, Sin Eng, as Joen Khoy's only child, assumed responsibility for her, and she moved in with his family. In turn, when Tjing Nio died, Nakashima assumed responsibility for Hien, Bong, and Lian, since Sin Eng was seldom around. Devoted to the children, she gathered them in at a critical time in their youth. Hien was six or seven when she joined them and barely nine when his mother died. If one can identify any single extraordinary influence on the kinds of adults Hien, Bong, and Lian became, it had to be Nakashima. After Tjing Nio's death, they spent more time, more intimately, with her than with anyone else, and in ways unusual for Chinese families. The children all remember her as very strong psychologically, but, as Bong put it, you could not see her strength, only feel it: "She was wonderful, a remarkable woman. She never raised her voice, never. But what she told us stayed in our minds. She was mother, father, and grandmother at the same time. Our father was not often at home. She was the only person who took care of us."[17]

The family talked in Malay, which Nakashima never completely mastered, but though she spoke with a heavy accent, she was able to make herself understood. At home, wherever home happened to be, she cooked, made clothes—putting up with Thiam Hien's protests over her choice of style—and in many ways established a center of gravity for the family. Nakashima liked to sleep late, and the children made their own breakfasts, but when Hien had an examination at school, she would make him a breakfast of miso soup to calm his nerves. On birthdays she cooked Japanese noodles for long life. Hien had a lifelong taste for Japanese food.

More by example than instruction, apparently, for she was literate but not well educated, she also taught the children values, some of which were bound to challenge those of the Chinese community. When necessary she confronted their teachers, even Dutch teachers—in broken Malay, no less—something Chinese parents, including Sin Eng, out of respect for the authority of teachers, were exceedingly reluctant to do. Nakashima, evidently, was not overly impressed by the privileges of authority, an inclination she may well have passed on to her charges.

She read often to the children, or rather translated and explained what she read in books borrowed from her Japanese friends. She and the three children would lie in bed, Hien always on her right, Lian on her left, and poor Bong always at her feet (and resenting the favor shown Hien), while Nakashima read or told stories about great men and heroes—particularly samurai and their *bushido* code, but also Thomas Edison and the like. From these stories, she drew moral and ethical lessons. They were simple lessons drawn simply: don't be afraid if you are right, because those who are right will win out in the end; be courageous and loyal, like the samurai; and be honest. Nakashima herself, unsophisticated but firmly constructed, exemplified these virtues.

Thiam Hien seems to have been her favorite; Bong was not entirely imagining things. Thiam Hien was the eldest, already a bit independent, and devoted to Nakashima. But for all three, she provided security, affection, intimacy, and a rich source of character. Her values and "Japaneseness" (*kejepangan*), as Thiam Hien once characterized it, also offered a counterpoint to Chinese *baba, totok,* Dutch, and local Indonesian norms and their peculiar interaction in the colonial setting.

For one of the most important advantages in Thiam Hien's life—European legal status—he had to be grateful to Sin Eng. In most colonies, some provision was eventually made to allow local people to assimilate, in some measure, to European status. The application process, always a source both of pride and ignominy, depending on who was judging, was a means of linking elites, of emphasizing European superiority, and of rewarding advantageous behavior. The French *mission civilisatrice* made it necessary, at least ethically, to reward with legal French status—citizenship—any Vietnamese or Algerian, for example, who had a French education, spoke French, behaved French, was to all intents and purposes French.

In the Netherlands-Indies the law was a bit different but the essence was much the same. In the nineteenth century certain ethnic Indonesian aristocrats and high civilian and military officials were subject to the same criminal-law provisions as Dutch nationals. If they (and eventually others) were interested and could demonstrate that they spoke Dutch and lived essentially by Dutch cultural norms, they could request legal equivalence (*gelijkstelling*) with the Dutch. Few ever did so. The same advantage was opened to ethnic Chinese in the early twentieth century, in part, no doubt, as a compromise solution to a widespread Chinese demand to be accorded the same European status as the Japanese at the beginning of the century. Japanese had won the prized European status by Japan's convincing development of military might during the last few decades since the Meiji Restoration. Some politically conscious ethnic Chinese thought they deserved the same, to distinguish them from native Indonesians, rather missing the point that they lacked the convincing weight of an army and navy. By this time in colonial history, however, what with sparks of nationalism, new local organizations, tensions generated by the new Ethical Policy meant to upgrade the Indonesian population, the colonial administration sensed a necessity to make concessions. Consequently, while refusing to consider the gift of Dutch status to Chinese generally, the colonial administration did allow them, like significant ethnic Indonesians, to apply for *gelijkstelling.*

Not many ethnic Chinese actually applied, though proportionately more Chinese than ethnic Indonesians took the step of formal application. Many ethnic Chinese treated the process, and those who undertook it, with contempt. From the cost of the stamps required to register the application or affixed on the return letter that informed registrants of their success, those granted the new status were called "penny and a half Hollanders," or *Belanda toen-phoa* among ethnic Chinese.[18] In the years 1910 through 1920, after which the conversion was no longer allowed, a total of 3,610 applications for *gelijkstelling* were approved, of which 1,711 (47.39 percent) were ethnic Chinese.[19] One of them was Yap Sin Eng, whose conversion, so to speak, also applied to his three children. The transformation was announced officially, in a list of about sixty names, in a statutory instrument (Staatsblad van Nederlandsch-Indië, 1918, no. 49). The immediate impact of the proclamation was that henceforth Jap Sin Eng—Jap is the Dutch spelling—became Sin Eng Jap, and Jap Thiam Hien became Thiam Hien Jap. There is no way of knowing now why exactly Sin Eng took this remarkable step. He might have hoped for some advantage for himself, at least a more weighty status in society or more respect from Dutch officials and others, though there is no evidence in the children's memories that he achieved either one. The family's fortunes were then already in decline, and it is conceivable that Sin Eng sought some kind of symbolic reassurance as his *officieren*-rooted prominence slipped away. None of these possibilities makes a lot of sense, however, for there were few rewards from European legal status to Sin Eng himself. It is more likely that he had the children in mind, precisely because they might well lose the privileges once assured to the *officieren* and their families. Sin Eng himself had a Dutch high school education, which lent him some assurance of both status and employment. If the family lost its position, however, or the *officieren* were no longer needed, Thiam Hien, his brother, and sister might very well lose that critical advantage.

Sin Eng's most generous and lasting gift to Thiam Hien was the opportunity of a good education. Without it, it is hard to imagine the man Yap Thiam Hien.

TWO

JAVA

At puberty Thiam Hien was confident, bright, and ambitious. Family status had made it possible for him to begin his education in the ELS (Europese Lagere School or European Primary School) (fig. 2.1). His command of Dutch was apparently quite good, and he proved to be a quick study. He had done well in the ELS, and thus could move on. The next step was MULO (Meer Uitgebreed Lagere Onderwijs, Extended Primary Education), a middle school from which, if successfully graduated, students might enter high school. This was the route by which the most competent children of the most privileged elite, whether ethnic Indonesian or ethnic Chinese, could acquire superb educations. The odds, of course, were nowhere near as much in their favor as for Dutch children.

Kutaraja had a MULO, though not a Dutch-language high school. Thiam Hien, however, had already developed an itch to go to Java. A Greek-Japanese friend whom he admired had already left for Batavia, and Thiam Hien wanted to follow his example. Like many curious and energetic boys, he wanted the adventure of travel and novelty. In the colony, Batavia was the London and New York. Only Singapore, perhaps, promised more. So Thiam Hien wrote to his father, asking if he could attend MULO in Batavia. Sin Eng agreed.

Sin Eng was then working as a commercial clerk in Batavia but was just about to set up his catering service back in Kutaraja. He may have thought that Thiam Hien and Bong, because their grades showed promise, would enjoy better odds in Java than in Kutaraja. Bong attended MULO in Kutaraja and then

FIG. 2.1 Yap (*seated left rear*), with schoolmates at the ELS primary school, Kutaradja, Aceh, n.d.

followed Thiam Hien to Java. Only Lian, to her misery, was denied the opportunity of attending good government-supported schools, because the boys' education took priority. She stayed in Kutaraja with Omah until the late 1930s.

Java reshaped Thiam Hien's life. In his teens he returned to Kutaraja for visits and spent a year in Medan before high school, but his ties with Aceh loosened and faded. After 1926, when he left for Batavia by boat, he belonged essentially in Java. It was not an unusual story then. Hundreds of educated young men from the outer islands, especially Sumatra, found their way to Java to enter good schools. Like Thiam Hien, they lived with relatives or, while at high school or university, in rented rooms. Few returned home permanently. None of the cities outside of Java, with the possible exception of Medan, offered the educational, social, intellectual, political, or vocational opportunities of Bandung, Semarang, Surabaya, and, above all, Batavia.

Being in Java, however, was not the same as being *of* Java. If few outer islanders returned home, neither did many ever really make Java their home.

Those who learned Javanese had a better chance of doing so, but lack of family connections and cultural patina kept them always apart. This was no less true of outer island *peranakan* than of indigenous outer islanders. Javanese *peranakan* were essentially Javanese—speaking Javanese, linked to one another and often (among the well-off and well-educated) to Javanese elite families and fully at home with the complexities and subtleties of Javanese lore, trade, and political and social gossip. Even when they married into Javanese *peranakan* families, as Thiam Hien eventually did, the outer island ethnic Chinese might never fully appreciate the texture of Java. For those who were interested only in getting along in trade or a profession, it did not matter much. For those who wanted more, as Thiam Hien did, it was difficult to find their way to the center of things. Again, it was not so much that he was from Aceh as that he did not belong to Java. Although he migrated in early adolescence, he remained somehow an outsider all his life, a stranger in a slightly puzzling land. He may not have been interested in being absorbed. Nor were there in his social circles, in and out of school, pressures to assimilate. He never learned Javanese. He was good at languages, but he studied only those of Europe. He was not attracted to Javanese music or art, despite two years in high school in Yogyakarta, a center of Javanese high culture, and several more years teaching in grade schools in Java.

These were well-packed years for Thiam Hien, from 1926 until 1942, when the Japanese invaded. Yet socially and politically he was relatively isolated, not quite oblivious to the serious changes and tensions of the 1920s and 1930s, but not much engaged either. He was only thirteen in 1926, but his social circle was also distinctly limited and hardly given to great interest in the world or even in the colony. By the time he arrived in Batavia, the nationalist movement was in full swing and the colonial administration was busy trying to contain it. Student and intellectual study groups, political parties, and associations were mobilizing and raising issues, including that of independence. Parts of the Communist Party revolted in Banten and West Sumatra in 1926 and 1927, in an incompetent affair easily suppressed by the police. Even Chinese communities, temperamentally reluctant to become politically involved, were not immune to the activity. In 1927, the year Soekarno's Partai Nasionalis Indonesia was established, a Chinese organization, the Chung Hwa Hui (CHH), appeared, led by the conservative pro-Dutch establishment. In 1932 the first ethnic Chinese party was formed, Partai Tionghwa Indonesia (PTI). It never won much support, but its young *peranakan* leaders staked out a position favoring alliance with, or better *in*, the nationalist movement. One of them was Siauw Giok

Tjhan, a journalist from Surabaya, whom Thiam Hien would oppose during the 1950s. Dutch, Indonesian, and Chinese newspapers and journals were filled with critical debates throughout the late 1920s and 1930s, available for anyone with a taste for politics or a touch of curiosity.[1]

Thiam Hien did not, for the most part, take much notice, and it was not just his youth that insulated him. Siauw Giok Tjhan was a year younger but was deeply engaged in politics in the 1930s. So were others on various sides of ethnic Chinese politics. For most Chinese, however, as Go Gien Tjwan has written, politics was *hong-hiam* (Hokkien)—dangerous and unedifying.[2] Neither the right nor the left drew much active support. Both CHH and PTI were tiny clubs. Thiam Hien was mainstream in this respect and distant from the turmoil, if not entirely unaware of it, not well informed or all that interested, and wary of anything that smacked of politics. Only after the Japanese invasion of China in 1937, when he was in law school, did he, like many others, become engaged. In the family, the emphasis was on good grades and a good job, a profession, if possible, and success in the only terms that mattered—financial security and a respectable social standing. Thiam Hien had more in mind, but it had mainly to do with finding himself, to put it tritely. Alone frequently, and a loner always, during the 1930s especially he began to locate himself tentatively in religious and professional vocations.

The five-day trip by boat to Batavia, with a stop in Singapore, was his first venture outwards and he was filled with anticipation. But life in Batavia was not what he expected. He joined his father in the house of his mother's adoptive brother, then a clerk (like Sin Eng) in the Javaasche Bank. The house was in Pinangsia, a district deep in the older part of the city, near the main railway station and major commercial institutions. The thirteen-year-old Thiam Hien had supposed that their situation in the capital would approximate their life in Kutaraja before the family's decline. It did nothing of the sort. Conditions in Pinangsia were not impoverished, but they were simple, for the households of office workers were not luxurious. Thiam Hien and his father shared one room and the same bed. At noon, when everyone, including Thiam Hien, returned home on their bicycles, they had a cold meal "thrown on the table" by a servant. At home in Kutaraja, meals—significant events in Chinese families—had been hot, substantial, and well prepared, all the more so for his father and grandfather. The young boy was now embarrassed and hurt for his father, who worked hard but who by then was perhaps more inured than his proud son to the decline in status these hurried meals implied.

Hurt pride led Thiam Hien to a faux pas that caused his auntie and himself pain. A kind and warm woman, who had given birth just before Thiam Hien arrived, she would allow him to play with the baby on her bed. The bed, he noticed, sometimes had dirty and torn sheets. So did the bed in which he and his father slept. Offended, Thiam Hien wrote a complaining letter to Omah, asking her to send a pillow and sheets. When these arrived, his aunt, angry and embarrassed, chastised her nephew, who felt ashamed and guilt-ridden. It was at this time that he began to understand his father rather more sympathetically. Sin Eng was still young, only thirty-three when Thiam Hien arrived in Batavia, and he was working hard but not successfully. They seldom talked intimately. But Sin Eng was evidently proud of Thiam Hien's schoolwork and placed few restrictions on him, except that they had to eat together. He bought his son presents, including an English Raleigh bicycle. Thiam Hien no longer took the tram but rode his bike to the MULO, located by the Arts Building near Pasar Baru, a modern shopping area across the canal behind the governor-general's palace.

MULO was demanding, like all the European schools, with compulsory courses in Dutch, English, German, French, history, science, and mathematics. As usual, Thiam Hien did well. Before the end of the first year, however, he came down with malaria and had to return to Kutaraja. Because his grades were high, he was excused from taking the examinations and was allowed to complete his first-year courses in Kutaraja. As soon as he recovered, he returned to Batavia for the second and third MULO years, by which time Sin Eng had returned to Kutaraja to establish his short-lived catering business.

Upon graduation from MULO, Thiam Hien did not go on directly to high school. With the critical exception of Dutch, in which he had earned the equivalent of a "C," his grades were good enough for admission, but rather than risk rejection, Sin Eng advised him to repeat the third year of MULO. Embarrassed to do so again in Batavia, Thiam Hien was allowed to go to Medan, the major city of North Sumatra, where he could stay with relatives, Joen Khoy's nephews. Medan was an exciting city, filled with Dutch and English planters—with whom he could practice his English—and a mixed local population of Bataks, coastal Malays, and *totok* and *peranakan* Chinese. Nineteen twenty-nine was a slightly wild year for Thiam Hien. Repeating MULO was easy, and the nearly seventeen-year-old boy spent much time out on the town with his older kin. No prude, Thiam Hien enjoyed dancing and going out, opportunities for which abounded in the large Chinese community. He survived the year, however, and the warnings from his elders about the local high life. In 1930 he was admitted to the first year of the AMS (Algemene Middelbare School, General Secondary School) in Bandung.

AMS needs a word of explanation, though even a long word cannot do justice to the complexity of educational structure in the Netherlands-Indies.[3] Except for ELS, all the schools Thiam Hien attended were new or reorganized after the beginning of the century as the colonial Ethicists tried to accommodate the rising demands of Indonesians for Dutch-language education. Little enough was done to educate villagers or the urban poor, but the expansion of Dutch-language secondary schools provided excellent educational facilities for the small Indonesian elite—and upwardly mobile *peranakan* who disproportionately enjoyed the benefits. High standards of secondary education were assured largely by the admissions policies of Dutch universities, to which the Dutch population of the colony was attentive.[4] Until 1919 secondary education was the province of the HBS (Hogere Burger Scholen, Higher Civil Schools), which provided a five-year pre-university course for entrants from the ELS. In that year the AMS was established as a three-year course, equivalent to the last three years of the HBS, to accommodate Indonesian students who had taken the MULO track as a preparatory link to secondary school. The HBS were always the more prestigious schools, but the AMS were nearly as good. They offered three streams: Western letters (AMS-A), with an emphasis on European languages; natural science and mathematics (AMS-B); and Oriental letters (AMS-C). This last stream, according to J. S. Furnivall, represented an effort to synthesize Eastern and Western cultures.[5] No less than HBS students, however, those in AMS were more interested in "Western" than "Eastern" offerings; few enrolled in AMS-C. At first the AMS-A program was located in Bandung, but in 1931 it was brought together with the B and C streams in the premier AMS in Yogyakarta, directed by the prominent archeologist W. F. Stutterheim.

Secondary school students in the colony, whether in HBS or AMS, were principally Dutch children, automatically elect in the colonial social universe; well-off Eurasians, usually assimilated to the Dutch but lower in status; high-born Indonesians; and well-established or upwardly mobile ethnic Chinese; along with a few Arabs. *Peranakan* Chinese made the most of their opportunities, though their numbers in the schools were exceedingly small. Table 1 shows just how small the educated universe in the colony was during its last twenty years and how large was the Chinese proportion of it. ELS data are included to add some light. Only public schools are included, for they were the most prestigious, though many private schools appeared after the turn of the

TABLE 1 School Attendance by Category

YEAR	EUROPEAN	INDONESIAN	FOREIGN ORIENTAL
	ELS European Primary		
1920	20,357	5387	1416
1925	20,325	4356	1492
1930	19,773	3357	1279
1936	18,295	3659	874
1940	18,076	4034	609
	HBS 5-Year Secondary		
1925	1603	123	156
1930	2203	167	275
1935	2404	460	544
1940	1570	501	480
	AMS 3-Year Secondary		
1919	15	22	5
1925	74	154	28
1930	118	576	178
1935	131	672	202
1940	139	738	185

century. The 1930 population of the colony was about 30 million. In the AMS, Thiam Hien joined the very small ranks of the superior educated. In the "Foreign Oriental" category, ethnic Chinese were the great majority.

Thiam Hien's first year, 1930, was spent in Bandung, where the Western classical program was then located. In 1931 AMS-A and AMS-C, formerly in Solo, were fused with AMS-B in the central Javanese principality of Yogyakarta, where the school occupied a spacious building (still there and still a school) on Jalan Jetis. There Thiam Hien remained until graduation in 1933. The AMS provided him with an excellent education and intellectual confidence. From AMS-Yogya came a generation of well-known nationalist leaders and professionals who went on to universities in Batavia and Holland.

Hien chose to concentrate in Western languages. Although he had done well in math and science, language interested him most, despite his first mediocre MULO grade in Dutch. Dutch and English he had already mastered. In German and French he had a good start from ELS and MULO. At the AMS, he added Latin, in which he proved proficient enough to help other students. In addition, the comprehensive course included history, for which he retained an enduring fascination, and more science. He did well throughout the three-year program, winning half scholarships each year for academic merit. He was not at the top of the class, but always in the first third or half in a rigorous and demanding program. He loved reading and learning, and he developed a taste for intellectual exchange and argument. Like many others with the advantage of European educations in the superb colonial high schools, he also developed more than an edge of intellectual arrogance around his informed and quick mind.

It was also in the AMS that Hien began to become aware of himself culturally and to sense his own marginality. The years 1930–33, as he aged from seventeen to twenty, were uneasy ones in the colony. Indonesian nationalism was intense but suppressed, with occasional outbreaks of turmoil. And the depression, the *malaisetijd*, had set in. For young students on the verge of adulthood, political awakening of some sort was hard to escape. Thiam Hien avoided it as much as anyone could, but he was inevitably affected.

As in ELS and MULO, the ethnic mix and ambience of AMS-Yogya was in contrast to the realities of colonial pluralism. Yet the school was not isolated from the social hinterland, and Hien could not escape his ethnic associations, even if he wanted to. By the early 1930s Indonesian nationalism was widespread among students. Several AMS graduates who later became prominent political leaders in the independent state were in Yogya at the same time as Hien. Among them were Sjafruddin Prawiranegara, from West Java, later a governor of the Bank Indonesia and a leader of the Islamic party, Masyumi; Tandiono Manoe, from Madura, later a socialist (PSI) minister of agrarian affairs; and Jamaluddin Datuk Singomangkuto, from West Sumatra by way of Aceh—where he and Bong had been school friends—who was later also prominent in Masyumi. And there were others. Some Thiam Hien met or knew slightly, but while AMS ties lasted for decades, they meant more later than they did at this time. The one group in which Thiam Hien did not have close friends was the ethnic majority. He had very little to do with Javanese students, perhaps the most culturally self-contained and politically conscious as a group. In part, Indonesian students, precisely because they were politically conscious and, given the invidious cleavages of colonial pluralism, ethnically sensitive, tended to segregate themselves—or, from a different perspective, to exclude all others. In part, too, the advantaged minorities of Europeans, Eurasians, Chinese, and Arabs kept their distance, sensing perhaps a common danger from the "invisible" masses whom the Indonesian students somehow represented.

The distance between ethnic Indonesian and other ethnic students, all of them Dutch-speaking and socially privileged, was essentially political. For Thiam Hien at the time, and in this respect typically Chinese, politics had all the appeal of a dung heap. Most ethnic Chinese, after all, still felt like foreigners—by law they were, at best, Dutch subjects (*onderdanen*)—and had no political toe-hold. Hien's family experience in no way introduced him to politics except to suggest perhaps that it was none of his business. Politically, he was not altogether a blank slate, but the marks on it amounted to little that was intelligible.

Even so, in the AMS there were glimmers of political awakening. The students he knew were politically aware and outspoken, and indirectly that affected him. Fifty years later he still remembered an incident that occurred in a first-year Dutch-language class. Students had been required to present speeches for evaluation, and a boy whom Thiam Hien knew from the MULO in Medan, Mahadi—thirty years later a well-known legal scholar and appellate court chairman in Medan—gave an overtly nationalist speech. The Dutch teacher, a liberal, gently advised Mahadi not to go too far. Thiam Hien was shaken by the talk and the reaction it provoked. It dawned on him that people he knew, for whom he felt some sympathy, actually opposed the colonial regime that he, like most ethnic Chinese, basically supported. It troubled him.

Only years afterwards, in Holland, did he become an Indonesian nationalist. One thread in his own nationalist make-up was a minor sense of guilt for having come to it late and not having associated himself with the Indonesian struggle before the war. A few *peranakan* Chinese had done so. Those who took a stand in the last decades of the colony came to Indonesian nationalism through the *peranakan* awakening, primarily in Java, which ran parallel with the nationalist movement. Thiam Hien later did just the opposite; he came to *peranakan* politics through an inchoate orientation to Indonesian nationalism.

That came two decades later, but during the early 1930s he cleaved to Chinese circles no more than he appreciated nationalist commitments. If his upbringing inclined him to avoid politics and to accept the legitimacy of the colonial regime and its ethnic divisions of labor, it also disinclined him to identify unthinkingly with "Foreign Oriental" Chinese. It may have been partly because he was resistant to submerging himself fully in any group—including, later, the church—but a touch of class arrogance, standoffishness, may also have been involved. He was, after all, the scion, albeit a poor one, of an *officier* family, and had been assimilated to European legal status. Except for his unhappy but brief attendance in the Chinese-language school in Kutaraja, there had been little emphasis on his Chinese heritage. Indeed, his earliest experience with social discrimination came less from Europeans than from *totok* Chinese who laughed at the *Belanda tiga suku* (three-bit Dutchman) and mocked his fall from Chinese cultural grace. Neither could he fully identify with *peranakan* culture, dominated as it seemed to be by the Javanese variant.

In the European schools, from ELS on, he mixed quite naturally with other students, distinguished less by ethnicity than by privilege, even if the privilege rested, as in the case of European children, on ethnic qualification. Then, as later, Thiam Hien seems to have chosen his friends basically without regard to ethnic boundaries and to have felt no urge toward the in-group comforts of a Chinese crowd—though he may at times have been attracted to the special aura of Dutch youngsters.

Thiam Hien's friends in the AMS, as in Aceh, were mainly European or Eurasian, with an admixture of Chinese or, rarely, ethnic Indonesians. The school associations he joined were all polyethnic. Avidly interested in sports, especially soccer, he played on a school-connected team rather than one from a Chinese club. As a result, the local Chinese teams picked on him when they played. Small but combative, then as later, and more inclined to run toward than away from a fight, Thiam Hien responded to fouls with loud invitations to fight. In our discussions, however, he never mentioned anyone taking him up on his invitation.

It may have been then that the young man began consciously to fashion an identity for himself ridged with Europeanness. He rented a room from a Eurasian family, the Jopps, and relaxed with European and Eurasian friends. Accused by other Chinese students of being "Westernized" or putting on "Western" airs (*kebarat-baratan*), he was not pleased, although he may even have taken the slur as an underhanded compliment, for who doubted the superiority of Europe? At any rate, for a *baba* from Aceh, Indonesian- and Dutch-speaking, *gelijkgesteld* to boot (not to mention Sato Nakashima-influenced), it was hard to get a grip on what exactly it meant to be Chinese.

It was not that he ever denied being Chinese, to himself or anyone else, but that he saw himself, culturally and intellectually, as rising above narrow definitions of Chineseness. The charge that he was "Westernized" was no truer of him than of most others with Dutch educations, whether ethnic Chinese or Indonesian, but it may have rung true in his own mind. Throughout his life he ambivalently regarded himself as fundamentally "Western," and yet, somehow, not quite, for he belonged in Indonesia and shared more with other Indonesians—not least, a history—than with Europeans. Moreover, Thiam Hien, like other ethnic Chinese, was not regarded by the Dutch regime, or most Hollanders or other Europeans, as an equal. What exactly did it mean to be a subject rather than a citizen or national? It was, apparently, as others had argued since the legal definition appeared in 1912, a lower order of being. Yet Hien never regarded himself as less worthy than anyone else. The former status of his family and his education prepared him to be confident and proud, and to suffer no fools gladly. Between his own self-regard and the social and political definition of himself as a Chinese there was a large gap, maybe something like the dilemma of the assimilated Jew in nineteenth- and twentieth-century Germany.

Like the assimilated Jew, he was constrained by the contradictions inherent in his identity.[6] Not very clearly or consistently, in Yogya Thiam Hien began to understand his own marginality. If he was "Western" by education, but otherwise not quite, so was he Chinese by birth, but also otherwise not quite. Without the language or customs—for lack of which *totok* Chinese dismissed him and others like him—what else could possibly define him as Chinese but racial origin (a vulnerable, slippery concept) or identification by others? He was Chinese in large part simply because he was nothing else by legal and social definition. There was no room for being Yap Thiam Hien and nothing more. The ethnic rigidities of the colony forced him into an unstable truce with Chinese identity.

That issues of identity troubled him during this period is evident in his initial flirtation with Protestantism in the family with whom he boarded. His brother Thiam Bong, who followed him to Yogya the year after Hien graduated and stayed with the same family, was not similarly tempted and never converted. Thiam Bong was as polyethnically oriented as Thiam Hien, and when he attended the Yogya AMS, he continued to be close friends with Jamaluddin, his ELS chum from Aceh. Jamaluddin had an uncle in Yogya whose Islamic devoutness frightened Thiam Bong, but religion was not much on his mind. He enrolled in the AMS-B science concentration and may have been slightly less inclined than his brother to question his own values. Instead he worried about money, of which there was precious little to support him in Yogya. As later in life, Thiam Hien himself took money problems lightly, but often peered into and tinkered with his own soul.

Thiam Hien was introduced to Protestantism by the Jopp family, with whom he stayed *indekos* (bed and board) during his two years in Yogya. The Jopps were Eurasian, but not of Dutch origin. Hermann Jopp stemmed from German-Indonesian parentage, while Mrs. Jopp was born Nell O'Brien. A Nell O'Brien in Java is about as startling as a Sato Nakashima in Aceh, but Thiam Hien's life was spiced with such surprises. Hermann Jopp, as Yap described him, was a strict but fair man. He worked as a topographer in the *kraton* (palace) geological service. He was not well off but earned enough to support a family of five children, as well as Nell's mother and a nephew or two. Student boarders helped. While Thiam Hien stayed there, they lived in a large house on Jl. Magelang, about two miles north of the *kraton* and not far from the AMS; as the depression deepened they moved to successively smaller homes. Judging from the accounts of both Thiam Hien and Thiam Bong, who were treated like the other children, the Jopp family was extraordinarily solid and loving. Nell Jopp was at the center of it.

Yap Thiam Hien's evolution as a Christian was much too gradual and complex to deal with briefly all in one place, and it will come up again in this and later chapters. Admirers and detractors both assume that Protestantism had always defined Yap's core values and inspired his actions. It is not so simple. The Jopps, particularly Nell, attracted him to the Reformed (Hervormde) Church, the post-Calvin liberal strain in Dutch Protestantism, but he did not actually convert until 1938, and he did not really grasp the religion until the late 1940s, in Holland. "Grasp" connotes the right undertone of intellectual struggle, for Yap never accepted his church altogether on its own terms. He fought with the church as he deepened his own religious and moral convictions. As in much else, he lost the battle. After a conflict of principle in 1965–66, he rarely set foot inside his church again. In time he became a devout Christian, but never an obedient one.

Why people converted to the European religions is no easy question. In the Netherlands-Indies only a fraction did, despite the assiduous work of Catholic and Protestant missionaries. Catholics and Protestants together never rose above 7 or 8 percent of the population. Yet here and there were communities of converts: Protestants in Ambon, northern Sulawesi, Sumba and Sumbawa east of Lombok, the Batak area of North Sumatra, and several places in Java; Catholics in interior Kalimantan and also parts of Java, including Yogyakarta, and Flores and Timor. Proportionately more ethnic Chinese converted than indigenous Indonesians, but most never bothered, keeping more or less comfortably to the Buddhist-Taoist-Confucian admixture of their origins. When ethnic Chinese did convert, the reasons were various. Some were opportunistic. Through the last century, poorer ethnic Chinese sometimes converted to Islam in order to escape restrictions placed on "Foreign Orientals."[7] For the more mobile and ambitious *peranakan,* Christianity, like *gelijkstelling,* offered both liberation of a sort and advantageous cultural links to the Dutch, though few but the wealthiest Chinese ever actually established excellent connections in the European communities.

But it is a mistake to suppose that opportunism was the most compelling reason for conversion. The fact that *peranakan* more often adopted Christianity, and that they were more likely to do so in some areas of the colony than others, indicates that other influences were at work. The famous Dutch Protestant missionary thinker Hendrik Kraemer provided an intriguing discussion of this problem in the 1930s.[8] Kraemer, battling against the doctrinal rigidities and inflexibility of Protestantism in the colony—unlike the culturally adaptable Catholics, remarkably successful in their missionary work despite lack of government support—sought to understand the fit of Protestant ideas with indigenous Indonesian society and culture. This led him to analyze, on occasion brilliantly, the core institutions and values of local societies in order to determine the best entry points for Protestant influence and the needs which the churches must serve. Pretending to no special knowledge of ethnic Chinese, he still provided the best available perspective on what might attract them to Protestantism. Kraemer's point, in essence, was that the most fundamental institution of Chinese culture, the source of its primary values, and the closest analogy to religious commitment, was the corporate family, *hao,* itself. Only when and where—as among the Chinese of Batavia, for example—the extended family had begun to disintegrate (or perhaps even to nucleate) would there be an opening for Protestantism.[9]

The analysis rings true for Thiam Hien, but it cannot help to explain why Thiam Bong, with much the same experience, never felt any need for a religion, let alone conversion. In Aceh the family had had little to do with religions of any sort. Neither Sin Eng nor Sato Nakashima showed any interest at all. Sin Eng's decision to apply for European legal status was an explicit claim to have left Chinese culture behind. Even the family altars were by and large neglected. As a boy Thiam Hien assumed the responsibility no one else wanted for attending the altar of his mother's family. It required no more than lighting joss sticks, but he took the job seriously, partly perhaps because it lent him the kind of minor authority a young boy would appreciate. He himself thought it was an early indication of religious bent. Could it also have reflected an adolescent urge to cement a family coming unstuck? Hien's family, for all its past glory, was then in decline and falling apart. Omah Nakashima, all the children insist, stood in magnificently as mother and father as well as grandmother. But it was no longer much of a family by any standards, let alone Chinese ones, and Thiam Hien left even that behind when he departed for Java. (It is possible that Thiam Bong's additional few years close to relatives there provided him with a different sort of confidence from Thiam Hien's.) Hien's embarrassment for Sin Eng in their Batavia quarters was also a lament for the now raggedly diminished family.

By the time he left for the AMS in Bandung and then Yogya, Thiam Hien, though still financially dependent on Sin Eng, was essentially on his own, distant from the remaining family and increasingly, but never entirely, from older values. On a vacation in Aceh during his first or second year in the AMS, when he was seventeen or eighteen, his maternal grandmother urged him to marry a cousin, a sensible proposal for her generation but already impossible for Thiam Hien. Painfully but firmly, he insisted that he had to finish school and become someone. As self-reliant as he was, he nevertheless regretted the fading family, in which he knew there was strength and support. Perhaps, as Kraemer's analysis would have it, the teenage Thiam Hien was open to the Christianity of the Jopp household as a reassuring substitute.

He was completely taken with the Jopp family, so tight and caring and encouraging and also lovingly intimate—something Chinese families generally, and his certainly, were not. It was a generous family, Nell especially, who made Thiam Hien and later Thiam Bong at home, took an interest in them, and delighted in their successes. In Thiam Bong's last year in Yogya, when Thiam Hien could not send him enough money, the Jopps partially supported him, despite their own straits. As Thiam Hien tried to understand this family, to fathom the inspiration of it, he evidently came up with the wrong causal connection, supposing that the source was Christianity rather than Nell.

The confusion was understandable, for the family was devout and Nell especially wanted to share her commitment with Thiam Hien. On Sundays she invited him to join them in church. Occasionally he agreed, which his younger brother never did, much as he appreciated their solicitude. Thiam Hien went partly out of gratitude to the Jopps, but he also came to enjoy the services, especially the singing, for he liked to sing and eventually learned a few hymns. At the time, he did not learn a great deal more about Christianity, but he was attracted to it. The real magnet, however, was at first the Jopp family and, in another sense, simply Family.

In 1932, before his last year at the AMS, Hien visited Kutaraja, where his father was about to go under as a businessman. Sin Eng told his son that he could not afford to send him to the university. Hien was crushed and angry at his father's lack of foresight in not putting money away or saving through an insurance policy, as an uncle had financed his son's education. Sin Eng had left his job in the Javaasche Bank, failed in business, and now had to find another job as a clerk. For Thiam Hien it was depressing and frustrating. With a superior education, eager to study, and primed to go on, he still could not continue. But there was an alternative.

Thiam Hien graduated from AMS in 1933, not the best of times in the spreading depression unless one had substantial resources, which he did not. Sin Eng was back in Batavia, living in a small rented home, clerking in a large Dutch firm when possible. Thiam Hien returned to Batavia, hoping that something would turn up either to allow him to continue his studies or to earn some money. He was just twenty and, like many well-educated *peranakan* sons, was not oriented to trade but rather to the professions. By this time there were recently established medical, legal, and engineering faculties in Java, and a few local (both ethnic Indonesian and ethnic Chinese) doctors, lawyers, and others from faculties in Holland and the colony. Despite the grumbling opposition of Dutch professionals, the breakthroughs had already taken place, and it was easy, with the right preparation, to imagine achieving professional status.

Thiam Hien wanted such a status, though he did not yet know in which profession, let alone how to pay for the training. He considered applying to the short medical course (STOVIA) for local doctors, but was too late. Given his education, law was a more attractive possibility. In Batavia the Rechtshogeschool, founded in 1924, was a natural magnet for AMS-A graduates. A Dutch-Indonesian friend, the son of a Bandung architect, whom he had helped with Latin in AMS, proposed that Thiam Hien stay with him, at his expense, and they would study law together. Pride made it impossible for him to accept the offer. So he continued to look for a job, in very short supply in the midst of the depression.

After a month, during which he began to feel anxious and degraded for lack of work, an acquaintance suggested that he consider teaching. As it happened, the Dutch Chinese Normal School (HCK) was for the first time accepting applications from AMS graduates. The HCK was recently established to provide teachers for the Dutch Chinese Schools (HCS), which the colonial administration had set up in 1908 in response to Chinese pressures. Indigenous Indonesian teachers for the HIS had their own teachers' schools. Most students went directly from MULO to the HCK five-year program, but high-school graduates required only one year of training. It was wonderfully cheap, only five guilders tuition per month and everything else free of charge. Hien had not considered it before, but teaching was a respectable profession and, during the depression, better paid than many white-collar jobs. So he applied and was accepted. Non and Omah sent tuition money from Kutaraja.

Although he was unaware of it at the time, for the HCK opportunity was a godsend, this move shunted him into the communal pigeonhole of colonial pluralism that he had always avoided. It was as a student in the HCK and a teacher in HCS schools that he began to learn more about Chinese communities.

The HCK was close by in Meester Cornelis (now Jatinegara), on the eastern edge of Batavia. Its teachers were mainly Dutch, but the students were entirely ethnic Chinese, well educated but not wealthy. During the depression, the HCK was an important option for able young men and women who could not afford university educations. Some who made their marks in the independent state—including Yap himself and Oyong Peng Koen, a Catholic from West Sumatra and later a respected publisher and liberal intellectual—got their starts there. It was not a hard year academically, as it consisted mainly of pedagogical methods courses, but it was a strict school, which brought out the rebelliousness in Thiam Hien. Students were in residence, allowed beyond the grounds only briefly during the late afternoon and for a whole day on alternate Sundays, but only if they attended church. For the sake of these Sundays out, Thiam Hien went to church, though more for the girls than the devotions. He chose the Chinese Protestant church—Protestantism (unlike Catholicism) in the colony was also pluralized—because of the Jopps' influence in Yogya. For a while he kept company with a Catholic girl from the HCK with whom he would depart the school on Sundays only to separate at the gate as they went toward their different churches. Occasionally on these off Sundays, he visited his uncle—his mother's adoptive brother and close to his own age—a bright but unambitious man who loved to read and worked in the Kolff bookstore. He helped Thiam Hien with geometry and loaned him books.

Because he was well read and enjoyed talking, Thiam Hien got along well with most of his teachers. One teacher who became a friend was Landsberg, nicknamed Si Botak (the bald one) or Si Macan (tiger), whom most students evidently feared. He called Thiam Hien to the front of the class on his first day and examined his grasp of history. Evidently he liked the answers, and the two would often sit together at meals to talk and exchange jokes.[10] Another friend was Gijsler, the son of a Protestant minister, eventually a minister himself, who taught psychology in the HCK. At the head of the school, however, was a rigidly authoritarian director, as Thiam Hien remembered him, a Catholic who may have extinguished any small likelihood that Hien would drift toward that Christian pole. He dressed the young man down in front of a class for not paying his tuition on time, and warned him against endangering other students with "foreign" ideas, which covered a lot of ground. Students were forbidden to read books that were not in the school library, which was "packed with Catholic materials." Thiam Hien nevertheless smuggled in a book borrowed from his uncle. The book, *Mij Hongert* (I am famished), was in Flemish rather than Dutch. While trying to figure out the language he thought he knew, Thiam Hien was warned by Gijsler to be careful, for the book was on the Catholic Index of banned books. The director's reprimand did not stand well with Thiam Hien. Used to reading and talking in the AMS about whatever he wished, Hien did not hesitate to speak publicly in school meetings. Among other things, he argued that the library ought to have a wider selection. Before he left the school, the director told him bluntly that because he was rebellious he would never be recommended for a teaching job in a government school. He was not, but by this time Thiam Hien was doubtful anyway about working for the government.

After graduating from the HCK, he applied for positions in various independent HCS and promptly left with a friend on a bicycle tour of Java, traveling all the way to Banyuwangi on the Bali straits and back. This friend, his roommate, was Teh Yong Lok, the ablest student in the school, who had entered the HCK directly from MULO four years before Thiam Hien arrived. He was the poor grandson, through a minor wife, of the *majoor* of Cirebon, whose first wife had an only daughter, who turned out to be the mother of the woman Thiam Hien later married. (The odds against such a coincidence seem less impressive given tight kin relations among a relatively small *peranakan* elite.) Teh and Yap rode bikes and train from city to city, staying with HCK pals along the way. In Malang they stayed with Teh's relatives, among whom was the young Go Gien Tjwan, who would be a political opponent of Thiam Hien twenty years later.

On their way back from Banyuwangi, Thiam Hien stopped in Yogya to wait at the Jopp home for word on his job applications. On 30 June 1934, the last possible day of acceptance (the school year began the first of July), he received an invitation to join the staff at a missionary school in Cirebon. Nell Jopp was especially delighted that it was a Christian school. She insisted on buying him a pair of shoes, which he needed but could not afford following the Java tour. Then he rushed to Cirebon, on the northern border area of West and Central Java, to begin teaching on July 1.

He was twenty-one, independent, and pleased to have a good salary from which he could help Bong, now at the AMS in Yogya, and a sudden, heady, rise in status—students and even Dutch school directors called him *mijnheer* and he wore a jacket and tie that he selected from a charity give-away. During the next four years he taught, learned, and became an adult.

He worked in two schools, both private and for Chinese students. The first was the missionary school in Cirebon, the second a HCS *wilde scholen* ("wild school") in Rembang. *Wilde scholen* were schools established by private groups. During the 1920s and 1930s, the government never established enough new schools to meet demands for education from all population groups, so private associations also set up schools tailored to particular political or ideological or charitable purposes. In the Chinese community, the Tiong Hoa Hwee Kuan, a Chinese association founded in 1900, created their own *wilde scholen* that offered instruction in Dutch. Other independent HCS were oriented to Mandarin language instruction. Thiam Hien always taught in Dutch. None of these independent efforts, then as now, had the facilities or prestige of government schools, but they were as well attended. In 1935, a year after Hien began to teach, there were a total of 106 HCSs in the colony, of which sixty-two were public and forty-four private.[11] Overall the private schools for ethnic Chinese were better off than those for ethnic Indonesians, a far smaller proportion of whom were given any education at all,[12] but the colony's educational opportunities were inadequate for either, and in both cases—though here, too, differentially in favor of ethnic Chinese—the poor were served least well. Thiam Hien's teaching experience, for the most part, was with poorer Chinese.

His job at the Cirebon missionary school lasted less than a year, mainly because he could not get along with the headmaster. The school was subsidized by the government, as Protestant church schools generally were. It might have been *gereformeerd,* rather sterner and more puritanical than the *hervormd* variety of Dutch reformed churches, but at the time Thiam Hien did not know the difference. He taught the higher grades, among other subjects, bible studies—mainly bible stories—though he knew little about the religion. As always, he also did lots of sports with the children: swimming, *kasti* (a kind of Dutch baseball), and hikes once or twice a month.

FIG. 2.2 Yap Thiam Hien (*seated on right*) and other teachers and students at the Lasem boardinghouse, Java, 1936.

The headmaster, evidently mistrusting the independent and non-Christian young teacher, got on Hien's nerves. Thiam Hien thought him rigid and sneaky, the sort of man who would come into class in rubber shoes so you did not know he was on his way. On Sundays, when Thiam Hien swam in the ocean, went to the local club, if invited, to play badminton, or rested before correcting student papers and planning lessons, the headmaster thought he ought to be in church. Finally, the headmaster urged Thiam Hien to move to other quarters, some distance away from the school, where it would have cost him forty-five of his sixty-five guilders per month for room and board. He refused, and although he was allowed to stay in Cirebon, he felt ill at ease there.

Consequently, when a friend sent him news of an opening in a Tiong Hoa Hwee Koan school in Rembang, Central Java, he applied and got the job as director. There were two other schools in the vicinity, one a European grade school (ELS) also in Rembang and the other a government HCS (Chinese language) in Lasem, about eleven kilometers away, where Thiam Hien rented a room (fig. 2.2). Both had more resources than Thiam Hien's "wilde" school, with government budgets, enough teachers for every class, and adequate facilities. Their directors were friends of Thiam Hien, including Teh (in Lasem) with whom he had taken the bicycle tour, and they organized sports competitions among the three schools.

For the rest, however, Thiam Hien's school had to make do with limited support. He himself received a reasonable salary of seventy-five guilders per month, from which he supported Thiam Bong in the AMS in Yogya for a year, but on occasion the school board ran low on funds and asked him to accept less, which he had to do. In the entire school of seven classes, with well over two hundred students, there were only four teachers, including Thiam Hien. The students were all from *peranakan* families, some with small shops but mostly rather poor. Better-off families sent their children to the government HCS in Lasem to learn Chinese—then reviving a bit in *peranakan* circles—or further afield to a Dutch-language government HCS. As director of the non-government school, Thiam Hien was responsible for organizing classes and lessons, which he had learned something about from observing the missionaries in Cirebon. For a young man of twenty-two, the responsibility was substantial.

His four years in Cirebon and Rembang, from 1934 to 1938, were important. It was not merely that he broadened his outlook, developed a few skills, and augmented an already adequate supply of self-confidence (or anyway diminished a fund of self-doubts). He also initiated a powerful interest in education that lasted for the next fifty years. And he became familiar with class differences among ethnic Chinese. During the first two decades of his life, Thiam Hien had little enough to do with poor people, whatever their ethnic origins. Because they were everywhere, the poor became all but invisible, a condition noted yet ignored, without essential significance. The Yap family's own financial slippage, serious as it was, led them neither to identify with the poor nor to sympathize with poverty; the memory of wealth and status provided a shield. In the HCK, for the first time Thiam Hien had seen the consequences of being poor, but as a teacher in Cirebon and Rembang he became aware of poverty—not so much among ethnic Indonesians, whose poverty was endemic, but among Chinese, who were not supposed to be impoverished. In Cirebon he had once admonished a boy who fell asleep in class, one who evidently seldom bathed, wore the same clothes every day, and stank. Thiam Hien ordered the child to take a letter home to his father. Another student later courageously told Thiam Hien that the boy was from a very poor family living in a nearby town and had to get up at four in the morning to ride the tram to Cirebon. From this painful Cirebon incident, he learned to be careful, to ask students about conditions at home, and to make an effort to understand. In the Rembang HCS, too, there were pupils whom he saw every day, too poor to pretend they were not.

He became an able teacher, but never intended to stop there. He taught to make a living, as he had gone to the HCK for lack of one, but teaching was not his vocation. At the time, he was uncertain about what his calling was (if he had a calling at all), but he was too ambitious to remain forever in a HCS classroom. So, in 1938, at age twenty-five, he returned to Batavia to find other work and make his way to the university.

THREE

BATAVIA

FAMILY circumstances had begun to change by the time Thiam Hien returned to Batavia in 1938. His brother Bong had graduated from the AMS Yogya in 1936, a bit surly and resentful of Thiam Hien, who could not send him money during his final year. It had been a miserable year for Thiam Bong. No less proud than his brother, he had had to accept the charity of the Jopps and live in utter frugality. No wonder he was inclined to obsess about financial security. In Batavia he found a job first with the trading arm of a bank, which was difficult and demanding work, and then more comfortably in a large import-export firm. From his pay of forty guilders a month Bong set aside twenty, saving enough within two years to bring Non and Omah Nakashima to Batavia. With little money and dependent on relatives, they had long wanted to leave Aceh. When they arrived in 1938, the family rented a house in Mangga Besar, a Chinese district behind the city's principal canal. Non soon found a job selling shoes in a Bata shoe store in Pasar Baru.

As for Sin Eng, after the onset of the economic depression, he no longer worked regularly and began, apparently, to sink into his own humiliated depression. For a time he had a job with a sugar estate, which kept him away from Batavia, but when that gave out there was little else. In general, *peranakan* were harder hit by the depression than *totok*. *Totok* had options. Some returned to China, which was not the homeland of *peranakan*; others engaged in the petty trade that *peranakans*' lack of adequate skills and worries about status made very challenging. Without work or money, Sin Eng lost dignity and stature. As the eldest son, the more self-assured Thiam Hien gradually displaced his father (tacitly, of course) as head of the family.

Two jobs came Thiam Hien's way after he arrived back in Batavia. One was in a "crisis school," a Dutch-language HCS supported by community funds for poor Chinese children. It had been organized by a wealthy benefactor, Dr. Loe Ping Kian. A Catholic priest who had heard about Thiam Hien's teaching experience asked him to take over direction of the school, a position he held just long enough to tangle with Dr. Loe. Loe called the new director on the carpet over some problems at the school but backed off when Hien, not one to take orders or censure easily, insisted on his own authority. His second job, selling telephone subscriptions, provided sufficient income for his needs, so he left the school. Working with a middleman who made contacts for him, he systematically canvassed the Chinese commercial district along the Molenweg (now Jl. Hayam Wuruk). The commission of ten guilders per order earned him about a hundred guilders a month, twenty-five more than his income from the crisis school and enough to cover his expenses for law school. At the time, with everyone in the family working except Nakashima, their funds, though not luxurious, were adequate. When Thiam Hien announced his intention to study law, the family agreed.

In the emergence of Indonesia's small professional class, the Rechtshogeschool (law faculty) played an important part. A product of the educational expansion of the Ethical period, it was founded in 1924 to meet the demand for legal education for those unable to study in Holland. All who could afford it, mainly children from *peranakan* families, or who had support from the colonial administration, mainly children from Javanese *priyayi* families, went to the University of Leiden in Holland, whose prestigious law degrees adorned Indonesia's legal elite for a generation into independence. Everyone else applied to the Rechtshogeschool, which doubled the number of graduate lawyers and diversified them ethnically. Outer islanders, particularly Minangkabau from West Sumatra and Bataks from North Sumatra, flowed in, along with Javanese, Sundanese, *peranakan* Chinese, Arab, and Dutch students. In Batavia, unlike Leiden, from the very beginning Indonesian women were accepted to law studies. Without the Rechtshogeschool, Thiam Hien and many others might never have studied law. By the time Thiam Hein entered, there were already more than two hundred Indonesian (including indigenous Indonesian and ethnic Chinese) graduates from the two law faculties, Leiden and the Rechtshogeschool.

His decision to study law had been brewing for years, not out of a fascination with law or a sense of vocation but because there were few alternatives. Like many educated *peranakan*, he had neither the skills nor the taste for trade. Of the professions that had gradually opened to local entrants, he toyed with the idea of medicine but with no great interest and the wrong educational background. The same was true of pharmacy and engineering, neither of which he considered. Journalism required no university preparation, but mainly attracted the politically aware, which Thiam Hien decidedly was not. In the limited selection that remained, law seemed to offer some options. Then, as now, law drew students who were uncertain about their careers but wanted a degree. Professional advocacy may have occurred to Thiam Hien, but he did not focus on it at the time.

It is worth mentioning here, because it illustrates again the influence of ethnicity in colonial social structure, that once he entered law school his professional choices were all but preordained. In the ethnic division of labor in the Netherlands-Indies, the opportunities available to Dutch and indigenous Indonesian lawyers outnumbered those for ethnic Chinese. In a sense, the lack of options did not matter a great deal because ethnic Chinese enjoyed an advantage in their own substantial commercial base. Ethnic Chinese lawyers were essentially tracked as professional advocates or as house counsel in Chinese firms. Public legal roles—judges, prosecutors, bureaucratic positions—were reserved almost entirely for Dutch or ethnic Indonesian (at first exclusively Javanese) officials. This discrimination, along with the lower pay the few Chinese (and the many more ethnic Indonesian) appointees might expect for the same work as Dutch administrators, served to keep ethnic Chinese confined to the private economy. In the late 1930s there were fewer Chinese than Indonesian lawyers, the latter having entered law courses earlier. But by 1939 there was an equal number of Chinese and Indonesian practicing private advocates—thirty-two.[1] A minority of the Indonesian lawyers had joined the professional advocacy—most had gone directly into the judicial or administrative services; a majority of the Chinese had become advocates. Thiam Hien had no way of knowing it at the time he began his studies, but the odds heavily favored his becoming an advocate.

Originally the colonial administration did not intend to encourage Indonesian lawyers, whatever their ethnic origins, to take up private practice. When an abbreviated law course, the Rechtsschool, was opened in 1912, its first students were lower Javanese *priyayi* who were meant to become judges on the

Landraden (courts for Indonesians). During the late 1910s, several Rechtsschool graduates were sent to Leiden to complete their *meester in de rechten* (Mr., the title graduates would append to their names) degrees, on the assumption that they would return to the courts. With degrees in hand, however, a few courageous souls, in defiance of the government and with impressive odds against success in a Dutch-dominated legal system, opened their own private practices. The first, in 1923, was Besar Martokoesoemo, who began his practice in Tegal.[2] Besar encouraged several others to set out on their own. Almost immediately thereafter, ethnic Chinese lawyers, educated in Leiden at their own expense, followed suit. One of the earliest to do so was Ko Tjay Sing, a Semarang *peranakan*, who joined Besar in the same office. Paradoxically, it was precisely in the private economy, where conflict had already broken out between ethnic Indonesians and ethnic Chinese in Central Java and elsewhere, that the two groups could also collaborate effectively. The difference between Besar Martokoesoemo and Ko Tjay Sing was that the former could have been a judge, while the latter had little choice—if he wanted to use his training, he had to become an advocate.

As important as his legal education was to become, neither in the Rechtshogeschool nor later in Leiden were Thiam Hien's studies quite as pressing as other events in his life. Thiam Hien was never single-minded about a career, nor did he ever conceive of himself purely in professional terms. If anything, his ambitions had less to do with wealth and professional success than with social status, respect, and reputation. He seems to have wanted to make a mark, but did not yet know what kind of mark. He remained uneasy over his own social marginality but was nevertheless outgoing and sociable, fond of arguing and exploring ideas. He began law school in late 1938 or 1939 and finished the equivalent of two years of courses before the Japanese occupation closed down the Rechtshogeschool. Neither in Batavia nor in Leiden was he a superior law student. In the Rechtshogeschool he did well in a course in legal structure and theory, perhaps anticipating later interests, but flunked a course in civil law, though he passed it the second time around after intense study.

In addition to going to classes, he finally became involved politically, or at least occasionally took a political stand. The conquest of Manchuria in 1931 and the invasion of China proper in 1937 had mobilized Chinese in the colony. It is hard to imagine any other issue that could have had such effect on Chinese throughout Southeast Asia. In Indonesia it aroused *totok* and *peranakan* to rare concerted action, though with different nuances, for China provoked differing reactions within the two camps. China was not "home" to *peranakan* in quite the same sense as it was for *totok*.[3] Even so, they began to work together. Many collected money and goods to send to China, a few actually traveled to China to help the war effort—and there discovered that the Kuomintang government preferred money—and just about everyone else argued about what should be done. Thiam Hien for the first time wrote an article or two, for the journal of the Chinese student organization he had joined, evidently taking a very hard line against the Japanese.[4]

But for Thiam Hien, as for most other *peranakan*, including students, there seems to have been little or no carryover from the war to issues of local politics. As always, political affairs were distant, suspect, and perilous, and during the 1930s, though significant conflicts and ideological disputes emerged among some *peranakan* leaders, they were easy to overlook. They were usually of limited local interest and could not compete for attention with the war in China. Only two explicitly political organizations were active among *peranakan*, neither of them very influential. The previously mentioned Chung Hwa Hui (CHH), derisively called the "Packard Club" after the American cars its conservative, pro-Dutch, entrepreneurial establishment leaders favored, was organized in 1927 around its representatives in the colonial deliberative council, the Volksraad. As nearly as anyone can tell, most educated *peranakan* probably agreed, at least passively, with the CHH view that Chinese interests were best served by the Dutch. Thiam Hien was once approached to join the CHH, possibly because Chinese teachers were regarded as usefully influential, but he refused, suspecting the motives of his sponsors and doubting, moreover, that he belonged amidst that kind of money.

Within the limited circles of politically engaged *peranakan*, there was considerable opposition to the CHH. It came in part from the so-called Sin Po group who were pro-China but anti-*peranakan*-establishment and sympathetic to the Indonesian nationalist movement. Unlike the CHH and the Sin Po group, the Partai Tionghwa Indonesia, established in 1932, named itself, significantly, in Indonesian rather than Chinese. Strongest in East Java, particularly Surabaya, the PTI made a strong case for the distinctly local interests and future of *peranakan* Chinese and supported the indigenous Indonesian nationalist movement. Although it defeated the CHH in an early 1930s city council election in Surabaya, it succeeded in mobilizing few activists and was barely known elsewhere.[5] If the party views came to Thiam Hien's attention at all while he was in law school he may well have assumed, like most *peranakan*, that however much indignity the *peranakan* community had suffered from the Dutch, their situation would be worse without them.

Hein did join the Ta Hsioh Hsioh Sing Hui, established in 1926 to foster unity and Chinese nationalism among its members.[6] By 1933 it had become an association exclusively of Chinese university students. The only other student organization it was possible for him to join was the Dutch student corps, which actually had a few *peranakan* members, but they were considered arrogant pretenders. Despite its Chinese name and ostensible purposes, the Ta Hsioh's members typically spoke Dutch, assumed Dutch manners, and often bore Dutch given-names, then much in fashion even among families that had not converted to Christianity.[7] (Hien himself began to sport the English name "John" during this period; and into his seniority he favored it among first-name foreign friends [and some at home as well], but it was the offspring, he insisted, of an off-color joke and not a given name.) He was nowhere near the center of the Ta Hsioh and played no memorable role in it. Leaders of the organization were more likely to be Javanese *peranakan*.

The university revived some of the excitement Thiam Hien had known in the AMS—the fun of reading and studying and mixing and talking with others at a student hangout in Pasar Senin (Monday market), an old Chinese shop area. According to friends who knew him then, he had a reputation for being principled and outspoken. One friend recalls him as a "radical" who took strong, critical, and often contrary positions that he defended tenaciously, which fits the more mature man. It is easy to imagine him delighting in the near serious idea-chatter of student nights. Yet he probably did not fit all that well into the *peranakan* student circles of 1930s Batavia. Older than average in his cohort, he was also much less well off.[8] Peddling telephone lines did not provide enough for any kind of high life. Moreover, he had other concerns, not least religious ones.

From the time he left the AMS, he had drifted, or rather been channeled, back into a Chinese universe, a ghetto no longer demarcated legally by territorial quarters and pass rules but just as effectively by the fundamental premises of colonial social, economic, political, and even legal organization. Through high school his friendships and associations had been mainly Dutch and Indo-European rather than indigenous Indonesian. But once out of the AMS, his choices were tracked ethnically and he was fitted into a Chinese mold manufactured by colonial authority. The HCK was made to order for young men and women like Thiam Hien, with good minds but little money, and the HCSs provided jobs. To sell telephones he naturally plied the Chinese business community. In the Rechtshogeschool it was easiest for him to associate with other *peranakan* students and join the Ta Hsioh.

Easy and natural as it was for him to walk the Chinese corridor, Thiam Hien may not have been altogether comfortable in it. Among educated *peranakan* such ambivalence was not unusual. (The *totok*'s secure sense of identity stood in high contrast.) An emerging *peranakan* left wing dealt with the discomfort of being confined to a Chinese corridor by embracing Indonesian nationalism—in effect, becoming Indonesian politically while remaining Chinese ethnically. Later in Holland, Thiam Hien began to move in this direction, but during the 1930s he was apparently unprepared for it.

Another solution was to adopt a new religious identity. Christianization of ethnic Chinese made less headway during the colonial period than it did after independence. At the end of 1938 there were only 4,045 (0.7 percent) Chinese Protestants in Java and Madura and 1,412 (0.2 percent) more in the outer islands—altogether four out of every thousand. Comparable data for Catholics are unavailable, but their numbers were fewer than Protestants'.[9] Thiam Hien became one of those few ethnic Chinese Protestants in Java. It might seem remarkable that there were any, given the rigidities of missionary Protestantism, but new missionary thinkers had begun to imagine religious responsibilities and obligations in terms of local interests—even nationalism—that transcended European values and colonial claims.[10] But change had occurred on both sides. *Peranakan*, always more inclined to convert than *totok*, had lost enough traditional Chinese values, including the practice of religious rituals and their accepted meanings, to be on the lookout for something to replace them. These were two of the factors working on Thiam Hien.

Chapter 2 dealt with the compelling influence the Jopp family exerted on Thiam Hien. He was entranced by the love and generosity that infused their relationships and that were extended to him and later to Thiam Bong. He was even jealous of the family, of the intimacy that Chinese family structure, at least in his experience, had little room for, and also perhaps of the solidity and vitality that his own family lacked. The Jopps introduced him to the reformed Protestant church (Hervormde Kirk) in Yogya in which they themselves played significant roles. Thiam Hien's belief that that faith explained the wonders of this family may be an indication that he wanted to believe some such thing. Thiam Bong never made that mistake; he knew that Nell Jopp was at the heart of all that goodness and, moreover, that goodness came in various religious packages or even none at all, as nearly as he could tell from Sato Nakashima's example. Thiam Hien evidently wanted something concrete to stand on, something firm to believe in, and a community in which to belong.

Why he chose Protestantism and what it did for him is not all that clear. The simplest answer for his choice, the one he himself offers, is that Protestantism was the Jopps' faith and the one to which he was first introduced. But would he have accepted Catholicism under the same circumstances? Catholic schools attracted some *peranakan* to the faith, including Thiam Hien's sister, Non. One appeal of Catholicism lay in its cultural flexibility. It willingly accommodated local rituals and customs—family altars, for example—which Protestant ministers and missionaries normally sought to extirpate without mercy. The Catholic church was not terribly demanding of its converts, and it did provide the firm organization and leadership that many converts sought. The accommodating spirit of Catholic missionaries probably was not important to Thiam Hien because there were few enough rituals of Chinese tradition that meant much to him. For the rest, he evidently rejected Catholicism in large part because of its hierarchical authoritarianism, exemplified by the overbearing director of the HCK who thought him too rebellious. In his early to mid-twenties, with little religious knowledge of any kind, Thiam Hien had no means of discriminating among diverse Christian dogmas, and he did not acquire the necessary knowledge until he went to Holland in the late 1940s. Before then, and even afterwards, he judged men of faith by their behavior rather than by their beliefs—which may help to explain his later frequent battles with religious leaders.

It is not likely that Thiam Hien opted for Protestantism, as many may have done, simply because it seemed more Dutch and had the tacit blessing of the colonial state. He was too thoughtful for that, and his conversion was too gradual, too serious, and too engaged. From a distance of fifty years it was hard for him, in our discussions, to reconstruct what exactly went on in his mind as he approached Christianity. In an effort to understand better what might have been involved, I talked at length with a young Malaysian, also ethnic Chinese, who had converted a few years earlier at about the same age as Yap was when he joined the church. He shared a few other things with Yap, including an acute mind, an excellent education, and a distant father.

> I have withdrawn somewhat from the church recently. I still attend but am not so spiritually involved now. When I first joined, Protestantism offered extraordinary support for my own individualism. As a young boy, I had a very strong mother, who was basically illiterate. She spoke Chinese and a smattering of English. She was devoted to me. But I barely knew my father, who left when I was very young. As a teenager I was terribly confused.

> I was Chinese but went to English schools and didn't really know who exactly I was. My friends introduced me to the teachings of Protestant ministers. What was extraordinary about this experience, in contrast with Catholicism, was that you really had to stand up and be counted. You had to raise your hand and say you accepted. You had to read the Bible and make a commitment. . . . It was a remarkable emphasis on your own individual choice and being. You did it for yourself, not as part of a group. So, when I was having an identity crisis, quite suddenly Protestantism offered legitimation of my own individual being. Without that, in some ways I never would have made it. I owe a debt to Protestantism for making me aware of my own existence. . . . At a critical time, moreover, I was without a father, and I felt it deeply. Protestantism, with its idea of Christ as God, gave me a sense of the church as father. As a boy I was jealous of other boys whose fathers played with them. I remember once watching a man and a boy playing together, and feeling deeply hurt that I didn't have that. In some ways the church replaced my father, and maybe I was looking for that. [11]

It is not obvious how much of this experience is relevant to the young Thiam Hien, but some of it rings true enough. Whatever other needs it fulfilled, moreover, in some ways at least Protestantism suited his own rigorously rational, principled, and occasionally self-righteous temperament. In later years, both Yap's friends and his critics were inclined to locate his character in Protestant roots, but it may well be at least equally true that the Reformed Church suited an already formed character.

The spirit of Protestantism is one thing, its local tone and organization another. Thiam Hien did not know what he was getting into then, and he would work to change it later, but the Protestant establishment in the colony was problematic. During the 1930s it had begun to be criticized by Dutch religious thinkers, particularly missionaries who kept their ears to the local ground and thus were in a good position to notice the rumblings of contradiction and hypocrisy. Although the colonial regime had always insisted on its neutrality in matters of religion, it favored Protestantism. (Catholic missionary activity was not even permitted before the mid-nineteenth century.)

In exchange for favor, the Protestant churches had loyally reflected the premises of colonial social and political structure. The result was an odd paradox in the small but influential universe of Indonesian Christianity: while the hierarchical Catholic church was locally autonomous, culturally sensitive, and independent of the colonial state, the independent Protestant churches were centralized, slavishly devoted to European primacy, and dependent on subsidies from Batavia. The Catholic priest was wholly within his church and among his flock, but the Protestant minister was also a civil servant. As became more evident later, after Indonesia gained its independence, "protestant" potential was greater in the Catholic than in the Protestant Church, which never relinquished the political quietude that surrounded its colonial privileges. Thiam Hien, whose protestant urges were always legion, consequently could never be fully at home in his own church.

The missionary philosopher Hendrik Kraemer raised these issues most acutely during the late colonial years, to no great effect. His critique more or less defined the program for church reformers of the sort Thiam Hein became. Divorce from the government, he believed, was essential in order to restore the Christian conception of the church:

> As an organization the Protestant Church in the Indies originates from a government decision. It is wholly part of the government in a twofold sense. The appointment and defrayment of its ministers always emanates from the government, and its organization and administration have been modelled upon and fitted into the government system. In other words, the organization of the Protestant Church is purely conceived in centralist-bureaucratic terms, purely from the standpoint of secular officials. . . . Because the Protestant Church has been conceived in centralist-bureaucratic and secular official terms, its basic conception is totally un-Christian and un-Protestant.
>
> . . . A Church based on Christian-inspired thought is, whatever the form and system of its organization, a spiritual brotherhood, and as such one of the visible forms of the one holy catholic Christian Church. The only decisive criterion as to whether it is basically such a brotherhood is only: whether or not this brotherhood is motivated and carried by the clear and conscious will of its members. . . . this is not the case with the Protestant Church in the Indies. . . . [The possibility of experiencing spiritual brotherhood] exists in the Protestant Church in the Indies in spite of its origin, its basic character and the structure of its organization. In spite of its origin, because originally it was not created by the will of its constituent members. In spite of its basic character, because basically it is not a community of people who seek union on the common ground of a certain unity of life and doctrine. It is a government institution for spiritual

> care carrying out this task with the means usually employed by Protestant Churches in general. Without this government, which in principle does not care about life or doctrine in so far as it is outside the Penal Code, the Protestant Church in the Indies will collapse as an institution.[12]

The church did not collapse, but it went through some very difficult times.

Because it was premised on colonial structure, the Protestant church—churches, actually—also faithfully articulated the assumptions of colonial pluralism. More so than the Catholic church, which tended to ignore ethnic boundaries, the Protestant Gereformeerde and Hervormde churches served ethnically exclusive congregations. Members of the churches often preferred it that way. A church could not by itself create a new integrated community that transcended local realities. A few mixed congregations in West Java evidently did not work well.[13] Especially in West Java, the failure to win many converts from Islam and the growing interest of ethnic Chinese in Protestantism, but not in integration with ethnic Indonesian converts, promoted separated congregations. Better education, greater wealth, and more confidence in running their own churches gave local *peranakan* powerful advantages in forming their own congregations. But the churches comfortably went along with these segregated realities and helped to ensconce their implications in the body of the church itself. Not only did each province in Java have its own church and missionary organization, but Chinese congregations, some Chinese- and some Dutch-speaking, worshipped in ethnic isolation.

Finally, underlying the structure of colonial Protestantism was a not too subtle racism, which Kraemer dealt with in another connection. As a missionary, he worried about the failure of evangelical work among Javanese and Sundanese, who remained unenthusiastic about Protestant truths. But he also noted the prejudicial assumptions that fixed the missionaries' posture:

> During this trip I have come to see with greater clarity than ever before that the position of missionaries, which is very difficult anyway owing to their enigmatic status in the church, is rendered even more difficult by the fact that they are allowed to administer the Sacraments to coloured people only, but not to white people. In this country so full of racial antagonisms, this is even worse than the fact is by itself. Anyhow, I cannot think of a single Biblical or authentically Christian reason for this distinction; the reason why this distinction is harmful lies in the fact that it accentuates racial antagonism, as if a theologian of lesser rank in the

> Church were good enough for coloured people, but too low for whites. It is a grave mistake to underline this contrast. Moreover, it hurts the feelings of the missionaries, whose position, as said above, is in any case difficult and ambiguous. [14]

Kraemer's discussion makes it evident that missionaries constituted something of a left wing in colonial Protestantism. Often more attentive to local sensitivities, local politics, and local social problems, they were also more likely to identify with local interests. It was the missionaries, not the ministers, who were inclined to support Indonesian nationalism. They were also more likely to understand sympathetically the concerns and urges of young potential converts, such as Thiam Hien. His interest and conversion were stimulated principally by missionaries of one sort or another, including the Jopp family, and his Protestantism was deepened in the Mission House (*zendingshuis*) in Oegstgeest, just outside of Leiden, where he lived during his studies in Holland.

When Thiam Hien returned to Batavia after leaving the AMS-Yogya, he maintained his contacts with the Hervormde church to which the Jopps had introduced him. While in the HCK he attended a Chinese congregation nearby in Meester Cornelis. It was served by an Ambonese minister who delivered hopelessly dull sermons in a perpetual monotone. (At that time there were not yet any Chinese ministers in West Java. Only one ethnic Chinese minister, Tjoa, was ordained before the war, but he may have been in Central Java.) Thiam Hien, nevertheless, continued to attend, in part because it was the only way to leave the school grounds on Sundays and because he could meet young women at the church—he was twenty-one at the time—but also, no doubt, because he was introduced to missionaries working with youth groups in West Java.

From then on, he occasionally attended outings in a nearby area, Tanjung West, where the missionary organization of West Java ran a rehabilitation center for opium addicts. Missionaries had set up a youth camp in Tanjung West, where young Protestants (ethnic Indonesian and ethnic Chinese) and potential converts gathered for games and talk. It provided just the mix of fun and serious discussion that Thiam Hien enjoyed. There he met two Dutch missionaries who had much influence on him. One was Dominé de Groot, a paster whom the mission had sent to work with the Chinese church in West Java; the other was Dr. van Doorn, precisely the sort of man whom Thiam Hien admired. An economist well placed in the colonial Ministry of Economic Affairs, van Doorn had given up his rewarding position in the government to devote himself to missionary activities. He worked closely with young people, including university students, without regard to their ethnic origins. Thiam Hien was especially attracted by van Doorn's open-mindedness and honesty.

At Tanjung West, while still in the HCK and not yet converted, Thiam Hien helped establish an organization—the Ta Tung (Great East)—for ethnic Chinese high school students in Batavia who had converted. Its members met often in one or other of the few Chinese Protestant churches or in Tanjung West. Only a few years older than the Ta Tung's members, Thiam Hien was proud of his role in creating the organization and he maintained his connection with it while he taught in Cirebon at the mission-supported HCS.

During his year in Cirebon, his involvement with Protestant missionaries continued and deepened. He attended lectures on religion put on by the mission and read widely, largely out of curiosity, about biblical history and the origins of Christianity. The missionaries invited him to meetings of the new Christian Students' Union (Christen Studenten Vereniging, CVS), where he met or became aware of men who later played important political roles. One was Amir Sjarifuddin, an enigmatic politician who later served as prime minister in the revolutionary Republic of Indonesia and was executed on charges that he had supported the Communist rebellion of 1948. Another was Dr. Johannes Leimena, later a leader of the Protestant Parkindo party and a trusted advisor to President Soekarno.

One of the missionaries in Cirebon suggested that Thiam Hien attend the theological academy and become a minister. At the time the church had begun to recruit Chinese schoolteachers to study theology. He laughed off the invitation. Not yet a Christian, he thought the vocation of minister required purer souls than his. Even so, on his return to Batavia in 1938, while in law school but before he was baptized, he taught Sunday school. He did so again later in Holland.

Gradually, then, his contacts with the Protestant mission expanded even as he was being drawn, by force of circumstance, back into the Chinese community. The specific church into which he moved (and remained) was ethnic Chinese, but the Protestant ideas he adopted provided him with an exit to a universalism that transcended simple ethnic identity. Although this offer of an expanded identity was not embraced by all converts, whether ethnic Indonesian or ethnic Chinese, for Thiam Hien it was critically important.

He was baptized in the Tek Wan church in Batavia on 31 October 1938. He was twenty-five, in his first year in the Rechtshogeschool. Dominé de Groot officiated. Van Doorn, whom he would have preferred, was not an ordained minister. There were, again, no Chinese ministers in the whole of West Java, not even in the Tek Wan, the oldest Chinese Protestant church in the capital. Thiam Hien recalled that his baptism did not seem an extraordinary event. There was nothing particularly romantic about it, no stunning revelation, no sense that the spirit had entered him, no sudden recognition of himself as a Christian. If anything, it was anti-climactic. The baptism occurred somewhere in a long process that included both his decision to join the church and his deepening understanding of which aspects of the religion meant the most to him. In subsequent chapters more will have to be said about Thiam Hien's Christianity, but it remains here to sketch the ideas he began with and that continued to influence his own brand of the religion. Precisely because he was persistently rationalist in his religious values, and because he was too independent to submit to a church or to accept its dogma uncritically, it is important to understand the dimensions of his personal religious commitment. He regularly contended with his church, with his state, and with authority of all sorts. Some thought him merely cantankerous, and he harbored enough anger, with assorted roots, to support the charge. But too much reason and thought was involved to dismiss the matter so easily, and few who knew him well did so.

From the start he approached religious dogma critically. He had begun to dip desultorily into the Bible that Nell Jopp had given him but soon began to feel uncomfortable with the Old Testament, whose God he found too harsh, too unforgiving, too quick to wreak destruction. His discomfort later extended to Protestants who took an uncompromising view of God's demands on humanity. Such attitudes made the Hervormde church a more reasonable home for him than the more puritanically inclined Gereformeerde church, though in the 1930s he barely knew the difference between them and, in any case, by that time the differences had begun to soften. His religious inclinations were unequivocally tolerant and open. As sympathetic as he was to missionary perspectives, he increasingly rejected their arrogant treatment of other religions, including Islam. This seems to be his one serious bone of contention with Kraemer, whose ideas in every other way nicely fit Thiam Hien's religious perspective. During the 1960s and thereafter, Thiam Hien worked easily with Muslim and Catholic activists who, more than the members of his own church, shared his sense of public political responsibility. His own occasional attacks of arrogance were always personal, never religious. While Thiam Hien may have sought community in the church, his religious values transcended the organized church and were, if not from the start at least not long thereafter, independent of it. He came to interpret the Christ figure around a core concept of love that was relatively free of dogmatic strictures. In his mature years he understood this idea of love as a motivating force in social action, an example to be followed, but also as a means of self-discipline, a standard by which he must judge himself, a brake on his own failings as a human being.

Thiam Hein was fascinated by and read intensely in theology. Never convinced that he was restricted to or obliged to abide only by Protestant perspectives, his own universalist inclinations in time led him to Lao Tse (Laozi), among others, not out of an urge to return to ethnic roots but in a search for sensible paths to human understanding. Yet, as much as he read in theology, legal theory, and, more spottily, political philosophy, his bent was usually empirical and pragmatic, an inclination that might be too easily interpreted as a Chinese cultural trace in his ideological make-up. Whatever the source, he was inclined to look for exemplary models that turn theory into practice: a van Doorn, who gave up a good job with high status for missionary work, for example. Given his character and background, it is not surprising that Thiam Hein eventually fought with his church. As Kraemer had pointed out, the spirit of Protestantism was in too many ways denied by the history of the Protestant churches in the Netherlands-Indies. Yap's own intellectual independence found a more sympathetic home in modern Protestant thought than in the Protestant church. At age seventy-five, he reflected on his evolution as a Christian:

> It is very difficult to say whether, when I was baptized, I actually felt myself to be a Protestant. If I think about it with hindsight, I felt then [in 1938] that finally I had to make a decision to become a Christian or not. I had to give a firm answer. Because I had been involved in the religion for so long. But can I really say that I was struck by some inspiration? I can't really. There must have been something, but not like those who claim, so arrogantly, that the spirit of Christ entered them. Some people say that at a given moment they became Christian. But for me it is a process [a gradual Christianization]. . . . I must have felt something about God. I believe there is a God, and I must have accepted the idea then. How else could I explain my own life? I came from a very rich family, then became poor, then met good people . . . all this was grace surely. But I read books then about progressive revelation and realized that God does not reveal Himself to us completely all at once. It is too heavy a burden for us. . . . I have to say that I am not a pure [*tulen*] Christian [an obedient Christian]. Why am I no longer so diligent about going to church? For several

> years now I have not gone to church. Actually, my attitude is wrong; it is arrogant, conceited [*angkuh*], I know. But the atmosphere in the church does not match its teachings. This has to do with what is happening in our society now. They [in the church] are afraid, afraid to talk, afraid to take action, afraid to be wrong. Of course, this is in the tradition of pietism. And it has to do with the influence of Dutch policy [in the colony] and of the church itself.[15]

The 1930s, then, were for Thiam Hien a period of intense beginnings: as a teacher, as a Protestant, as a lawyer, but without foreseeable outcome. By early 1942, when the Japanese army invaded, he had finished the equivalent of two years of law school. He was twenty-nine. The Japanese occupation put his life, like that of many others, on hold until the end of 1945.

FOUR

FROM SUKABUMI TO LEIDEN

THE decade of the 1940s was packed, like a Balinese painting, with a thousand commotions. In Indonesia, as elsewhere, World War II divided history. Japanese military forces swept the Dutch defenses aside contemptuously, shattered the myths on which colonial authority depended, and effectively ended the colonial era, though not its substantial residue. After Japan's surrender in August 1945, the Netherlands tried but failed to forestall an unpreventable new period of revolution and independence. No one was unaffected by the events of those years. No one could escape coming to terms, somehow, with realities whose implications were not always obvious. For the Chinese minority, the handwriting on the wall was hardly decipherable. Only a few leaders, themselves divided, bothered to try to read it anyway. Most ethnic Chinese, like most ethnic Indonesians, simply tried to survive. Yap Thiam Hien was among them.

By the late 1930s, predictions of war were common. While few in Indonesia were encouraged by the prospect—some saw in Japanese power a hope for liberation from colonialism—the Chinese had better reasons than most to be apprehensive. Fear lay on the underside of the bitter antagonism that had existed toward the Japanese since 1931. Some ethnic Indonesian nationalists understood the anti-colonial potential of a war in the Pacific, but not even the most pro-nationalist *peranakan* could hope for anything but disaster from Japan. The rape of Nanking did not set hearts and minds at ease.

In Batavia the colonial administration was increasingly conciliatory toward Japanese economic and political demands, but after the Germans occupied the Netherlands in May 1940, there was little enough reason for Tokyo to pay attention. Japan intended to take full control of Indonesia's resources; it hardly mattered what Batavia did, for the colony was isolated and militarily no match for Japanese power. In a peculiar display of priorities, the colonial administration rejected nationalist proposals to arm Indonesians. Instead, during 1941, the government set up Staatswacht units of barely trained, armed, ethnically mixed militia under the command of Dutch officers. Dutchmen, Indo-Europeans, Chinese, and Indonesians joined these green-uniformed squads to mount urban watches against the expected invasion. Volunteers needed to have at least a minimal sense of obligation and loyalty to the colony. With their European legal status, Thiam Hien and Thiam Bong presumably would have been above suspicion. Both joined, received their uniforms and training, and went to different units.

In the meantime the family had become worried about Sato Nakashima. Still a Japanese citizen, she was perfectly aware of the animus against the Japanese and kept quiet. From Aceh, however, came a small stream of Japanese friends, who saw nothing amiss in visiting her. Sin Eng and the others were terrified that the family might become suspect. Sometime in mid-1941, as war loomed, Thiam Hien decided in panic that Omah's documents—her Japanese passport, immigration papers, and other assorted evidence of origin—had to be destroyed. She resisted, wanting to keep her passport at least, but ultimately gave in to Hien's frantic pressure. Unfortunately, getting rid of the papers accomplished little but to wipe out what we can know of her interesting past.

The panic, however, was genuine and justified. On a day in October or November, before the Rechtshogeschool vacation in December, the police came to the house in Mangga Besar and arrested Sato Nakashima in a roundup of Japanese aliens. Thiam Hien was away when it happened, and Sin Eng may have been, too. When Hien learned, probably from his very upset sister, that Omah had been picked up, he rushed off in his Staatswacht uniform to see the Dutch resident about it. The uniform was a conscious political statement. Thiam Hien had two arguments. The first was that the government regulation behind the sweep provided that no one over fifty would be interned and, he insisted, Sato Nakashima was older than fifty. (Maybe so, in which case her papers would have proved it.) Because the Dutch were careful in their treatment of Japanese aliens, abiding strictly by the Geneva Conventions, it was a good case. The second argument was that Thiam Hien was serving the country in the Staatswacht, that this was his grandmother, and that he would assume full responsibility for her. Evidently persuaded, the resident acquiesced and Hien took Nakashima home from detention. But the anxiety raised by the incident did not abate.

Thiam Hien's experience in the Staatswacht was otherwise uneventful, but Thiam Bong's shook him awake politically. When the Japanese invaded in March 1942, his unit of twelve men, commanded by a Dutch lieutenant, was stationed at the prison in Glodok, an old Chinese section of the city. Early one morning, after finishing a two-hour watch on the roof, he came down for breakfast at the command post. The men hadn't eaten for hours, but on the table there was only some bread. As Thiam Bong reached for it, the lieutenant barked that the bread was for the Europeans and he could wait for his rice, if it came. Never slow to perceive a slight, Thiam Bong replied furiously that he and the others had volunteered to defend the lieutenant's country and now they were denied bread that was reserved for whites only. Angrily he decided to desert that morning. Running through some muck outside the prison, he lost his shoes together with the last salary payment he had stowed in one of them.

For Thiam Bong and perhaps Thiam Hien, as for many others, the invasion was itself a political eye-opener. The Japanese were villains but Asian villains, who once more, as in the Russo-Japanese War forty years earlier, laughed off the myth of white invincibility. How easily they brushed the Dutch forces aside! As Thiam Bong put it, "I remember it all very well. Before then all who were white were superior. And afterwards you wondered how it all changed in one minute. That was a bit of a shock—those small Japanese who kicked out the Dutch."[1]

Then the hard times of the occupation began. Despite fears of Japanese retaliation, Chinese suffered no more than ethnic Indonesians, but no less either. *Totok* and *peranakan* activists in the anti-Japanese movement were arrested, as were local Kuomintang leaders, and Chinese political parties, like all others, were banned.[2] For the rest, however, the military administration, concerned primarily with efficient exploitation of resources for the war, maintained the useful status quo. Nothing was done to change the colonial status of ethnic Chinese, who remained politically and legally distinct from the ethnic Indonesian population. Separate organizations were maintained. There were Chinese collaborators as there were ethnic Indonesian collaborators, and separate and equally ineffective Chinese and Indonesian undergrounds. Such cross-ethnic political and social contacts as there were before the war also continued. But, as before, relatively few ethnic Chinese were involved in any such activity. What most knew about were the common hardships of wartime occupation.

The Yap family was no worse off than most, and in some worrisome ways slightly better off. Sato Nakashima, recently an enemy alien, was again the unintentional source of anxiety as she was suddenly transformed into a minor celebrity among the occupation forces. When they discovered her, Japanese officers and men dropped by to pay their respects, bringing gifts of food. These visits were tense and painful for the family, as Nakashima undoubtedly understood, but there was no recourse. To cover their embarrassment, the Yaps divided the food with other households on the street.

At the outset of the occupation the family income quickly dried up. Sin Eng had no work for the duration, and Non, like many other women, gave up her hospital job after the invasion. It was up to Thiam Hien and Thiam Bong to support the family, but neither had a job. The company for which Bong had worked closed shop, as did the Rechtshogeschool. Hien could no longer sell telephone hookups. Paid work was scarce. In desperation, the two men turned to petty trade—*catut*—scratching out a living through small commercial efforts. It was a disastrous failure. If any demonstration were needed to refute the myth that all Chinese had trade in their blood, the brothers were unadulterated evidence. Apparently Hien—according to Bong's accusation and his own admission—was particularly incompetent. Opportunities provided by friends to buy and sell turned to dust. Within months the brothers gave up.

Sato Nakashima's connections were helpful but created more tension. She found work for Bong as a clerk in an occupation agency that shipped goods to Japan. But he hated working for the regime and left after a few months. Learning of a course in sugar technology at the Kian Wan sugar factory in the Malang area in East Java, he applied and was accepted. He departed in late 1943 and remained in Malang for two and a half years.

Thiam Hien's scruples about having anything to do with the Japanese led to a bitter conflict with his father that did not help their edgy relationship. This occurred in 1943, before Thiam Bong left, and at a time when the Yaps had become stonily accustomed to the Japanese personnel who came to chat with Nakashima. Sin Eng caught wind of a friend's project that required contacts with the regime, in exchange for which he would receive a substantial cut. When his father asked him to manage the deal, using Sato Nakashima's connections, Hien reluctantly replied first that he would think about it, but then, the same day, informed Sin Eng that in principle he simply couldn't do it. Sin Eng was furious, accusing his son of ignoring the family's desperate situation.

Nothing more was said on the subject, for Sin Eng was not in the habit of prolonging recriminations, but Thiam Hien knew that his father remained angry. Soon afterwards Hien decided to go to Surabaya, where he had a girlfriend whose family would put him up while he looked for work. He stayed about six months, without much success, and then returned to Jakarta.

Before he and Thiam Bong left, however, they had to see to their sister. Japanese soldiers coming in and out of the house caused special problems for Non. Her brothers worried that she, then in her mid-twenties, might take up with or even marry one of them. So Non, forever the victim of her gender, was pressed into a marriage she did not want. Still set on a career, perhaps as a dental assistant, she had already rejected opportunities to marry. In mid-1943, however, she met Tan Nie Tjong, a law student from a *totok* family in Bandung, who asked Sin Eng for her hand. Thiam Hien and Thiam Bong knew Tan from the *catut* time, and he lived with an uncle whom Hien had known in the HCK. Not very ambitious, according to Bong, Tan was nevertheless a cheerful man who the brothers thought would take care of Non. Although Non was not really interested, Hien persuaded her to marry Tan, for her brothers could not leave until she had someone to look after her. To relieve them of the responsibility, the dutiful daughter and sister finally, reluctantly, agreed. At her wedding Hien met his own future wife, Tan Gien Khing, from Semarang, a relative of Non's new husband.[3]

Shortly afterwards the family scattered again: Thiam Bong to Malang, Thiam Hien to Surabaya and later to Sukabumi in West Java, while Non and Tan established their own household, and Sin Eng, proudly unwilling to live with Non, moved in with a cousin recently arrived from Aceh. Sato Nakashima stayed sometimes with Non, sometimes with Sin Eng, and later, occasionally, with Hien in Sukabumi.

When he returned from Surabaya, Thiam Hien finally took a job for which his legal studies qualified him, with the Weeskamer, a Dutch civil law institution in charge of the estates of widows and orphans. As the need for income waxed, his reluctance to work in the Japanese administration waned, but the Weeskamer was routinely far from the occupation's concerns. Later, however, in Holland he had to justify this choice. For a year Thiam Hien worked in the Jakarta Weeskamer office in charge of enemy citizens—Dutchmen interned during the war—before he was sent to Sukabumi to preside over the estates of friendly aliens—Germans, who had earlier been interned by the colonial administration. It was not a demanding job, basically documentary work, and Sukabumi, with a large Chinese population and a strong Protestant church, was a pleasant enough place to bide time during the occupation. There he remained until the end of the war.

In Malang Thiam Bong tasted more of the occupation than Thiam Hien did in Sukabumi. The sugar factory was garrisoned by a small detachment of Japanese troops. Thiam Bong, the oldest of the twelve students in his dormitory, had an angrily defiant run-in with a drunken noncommissioned officer over numerous late night fire drills, but the soldier was too soggy to do much harm. In 1944 the students were organized into a unit of the Keibotai, the Chinese counterpart of the Indonesian civil defense corps, Keibodan, which the Japanese military administration established as the war began to turn against them. The students were given training but never with real weapons.[4]

After Japan's surrender in mid-August 1945, Thiam Bong remained at the sugar factory. It was a time of great confusion and uncertainty. Soekarno and Hatta had proclaimed Indonesian independence on 17 August, but the Netherlands had no intention of acceding to it. English troops entered Surabaya to accept the surrender and keep the peace, pending the restoration of Dutch authority. On 10 November revolt broke out in Surabaya, a serious battle that sent refugees fleeing south. Many arrived at the sugar plantation. The factory manager wanted to close the area to them, but Bong and his mates insisted on taking them in. Some of the refugees—a mixed group of ethnic Indonesians and ethnic Chinese, mainly women and children—remained under the students' care.

Thiam Bong finally left the plantation in early 1946. A postcard had come from Thiam Hien saying that he intended to depart for China to finish his studies. China! Bong hadn't the slightest idea what to make of this news, but knew that he had to return to Jakarta, either to go with Hien or to take care of his father and grandmother. By the time he arrived, in March, Hien was gone—not to China, which he had written as a code that understandably eluded Bong—but to Holland.

Thiam Hien had not left Sukabumi immediately after the Japanese surrender. But from August onward, conditions there worsened, as refugees and English troops, including Gurkhas and bands of revolutionary youths (*pemuda*), filled the city. Local officials, including judges, left for Jakarta or Bandung or the revolutionary capital in Yogyakarta. Finally, before Christmas of 1945, Thiam Hien closed his Weeskamer office, anomalously (but typically) took inventory, turned in the appropriate forms, and with a friend hopped on a train for Jakarta. It was a harrowing trip. At every stop *pemuda* bands boarded, searched the passengers, confiscated Java Bank currency and left behind only useless occupation notes, and occasionally removed someone from the train. Arriving in Meester Cornelis just before curfew, Thiam Hien luckily found the home of a friend where he could spend the night. The next day he proceeded to Jl. Kelinci, behind Pasar Baru, where Sin Eng and Sato Nakashima had moved in with Non and her husband.

For two weeks he looked for work, until he heard that other young Chinese were finding their way to Europe as hired hands—*corveers*, as they were called, from *corvée*, obligatory labor—on ships repatriating Dutch internees to Holland. In exchange for serving and taking care of the passengers, the *corveers* got free passage, winter clothes, and some money. Several of Thiam Hien's acquaintances had already gone. He asked around, found the recruiting office, applied, and was taken on. It was at this point that he wrote a postcard to Bong (sealed letters were forbidden) that he was going to China, hoping, in vain, that Bong would figure out that he actually meant Holland.

His father tried to talk him out of the idea. Sin Eng could not imagine taking such a risk—without money, experience, or connections. How would he deal with the terrifying cold of Dutch winters or find food, given Holland's post-occupation conditions? Now in his mid-fifties, rather diffident, conservative, and cautious, Sin Eng was not interested in much more than keeping the family together and getting by. He and his son could not have been farther apart. In January 1946 Thiam Hien, at thirty-two, believed he had neither done nor seen enough. Restless and ready for adventure or at least change, he had a few hundred guilders saved up and bits and pieces of information about Holland and how to get along there, gathered from others who had been there. In addition to finishing his law degree, if he could get into the law school at Leiden, he simply wanted to see Europe. In part, it was a lark. The war's end had liberated an ocean of energy. Many young ethnic Indonesians and a few ethnic Chinese poured this energy into the revolution. Many educated Chinese, without any appreciable connection to the revolution and with good reason to fear its consequences for them, went not to Yogya but to the Netherlands.

Thiam Bong, four decades later, expressed it all well. When he returned to Jakarta to find that Thiam Hien had gone to Holland, not China, he was electrified. Internatio, the company he had worked for, had no work for him, and there was little else to do:

> And many young people were going to Holland as *corveers*. Then, all of a sudden I decided to go too. If it were not possible to stay in Holland, then I would come back. It was just to see the world. When father told me that

Hien had gone, I was startled and uneasy. Because my companion was gone. My brother. My feeling was that a new time had been born, and that maybe we could join each other to make a new life. And he was gone. But everybody was uneasy then. It was an unstable time.[5]

Sin Eng, waxing sarcastic about Hien's folly, pleaded with his second son not to follow, but it would have taken much more than that to hold Bong. It was only to see the world, he said, and then he would come back. As it turned out, he never did.

About three months after Thiam Hien, Thiam Bong departed in the same way, on board a refugee ship. He went to Delft to look for work, but found instead an opportunity for free training in textile technology in Enschede in eastern Holland. Not long afterwards, Tan Nie Tjong, Non's husband, decided that he wanted to study in Holland, too. Thiam Hien wrote to advise Non to accompany her husband to Leiden. Within a year or so all three of Sin Eng's children were in the Netherlands.

Thiam Hien had boarded the ship at the Jakarta port of Tanjung Priok, with his savings, a few clothes, a bicycle, and a typewriter. He had had one last petty conflict with Sin Eng, over which he later felt guilty and lacking in filial respect. His father had asked for a nice piece of cloth that Thiam Hien had brought with him from Sukabumi, and Hien refused. But while he was in Holland, Sin Eng sent him cigarettes, and Hien provided his father with a little money from a newspaper commission he obtained before leaving Jakarta.

The commission—to write a series of articles from Holland—was from *Sin Po*, the country's most prominent Chinese newspaper and included, happily, a typewriter. He wrote the articles during 1946, until his time filled up with other activities. They were published in the Indonesian edition of the newspaper under the Mandarin version of his name, Yeh T'ian Hsing (Ye Tian Xing in the new transliteration).[6] As Yap later remembered the articles, they revealed a dawning political and social awareness.

His first insights, basically into the worldwide division of labor, came on board the ship as it sailed across the Indian Ocean, through the Suez Canal, on to the Mediterranean ports, and finally to Holland. He observed (and wrote) that in the Asian and Middle Eastern ports, the workers were always dark and the supervisors usually white, but suddenly, in the European ports, workers and foremen alike were white. At home in Indonesia one took for granted a condition whose significance was suddenly rendered stark by the European contrast. Evidently, by the time he arrived in Holland his eyes were open to the political and social implications of nearly everything in sight, but the revelations had to do mainly with Indonesia. In Holland, Thiam Hien saw for himself that common workers, barbers, street sweepers were all white—something unimaginable in the colony—and many of them, moreover, had their own small but adequate and neat homes.

In many ways, Holland itself was not actually surprising or even novel. Like others who had preceded him over the years to Leiden, Amsterdam, Rotterdam, Utrecht, and Delft, Thiam Hien already knew the country in some respects better than he knew his own. He was not at all disoriented. He spoke Dutch well and by preference and had read Dutch history and literature and seen many photographs of Dutch cities.

Only the mid-winter weather was shocking. On the ship he had been given warm clothes just out of Suez but caught cold and arrived ill. Heading directly for Leiden, he stayed in the room of a friend from Aceh to whom he had written earlier and who had invited Thiam Hien to use his room while he was away on vacation. With no idea how to manage a coal stove, Thiam Hien used a month's ration of fuel in a few days and had to appeal for more. Afraid that he could not take the cold but determined not to run home, he soon struck upon hibernation as the solution. Sleeping late until the warm library at the university opened, he rushed there and stayed near a radiator until closing time at five, ate at a cheap restaurant, and then ran back to bed to begin the cycle again.

This misery did not last. Before long Thiam Hien moved to the Protestant Mission House (*zendingshuis*) in Oegstgeest just outside Leiden (fig. 4.1). Other students had told him about a student hospice there and advised him to talk with E. Looho, a Menadonese Protestant who had come to Leiden in 1939 to study pharmacy. Looho and Thiam Hien became close friends and eventually in-laws, when forty years later Looho's son Stefan married Yap's daughter. The devout Looho had a long association with the *zendingshuis*, where missionaries were trained for overseas work. Near the end of the war, when the Germans were conscripting young men, including Indonesians, to work in the Ruhr, he and two Dutch doctors had avoided a roundup by hiding in the *zendingshuis* cellar. After the German surrender, as there was much space in the huge building, he and others proposed that a hostel be established for students from abroad, many of them arriving from Indonesia. The director of the *zendingshuis* agreed, for these young people fresh from Indonesia, now in revolution, would be helpful in preparing missionaries to work under the new conditions. Many Indonesian students, including Non and her husband, stayed

FIG. 4.1 Yap (*standing left*) and other students on the ice at the Mission House, Oegstgeest, Netherlands, 1947.

there until they found other accommodations. A few, most likely the serious Protestants among them, remained longer. Thiam Hien lived there until he finished his studies and left for other parts of Europe. The *zendingshuis* was a godsend. It cost next to nothing and provided a sympathetic and stimulating intellectual environment.

Thiam Hien's legal studies began as soon as he had justified his wartime employment to a local committee in charge of investigating collaboration. The three-person team, including a priest and a minister, accepted his explanation that working in the Weeskamer was purely a matter of survival. A pre-war concordat between the Leiden law faculty and the Rechtshogeschool guaranteed students of the latter automatic admission to the former. All course work and examinations completed in Jakarta were accorded equivalence in Leiden. Hien had finished the *candidaat* examination in the Rechtshogeschool and had only the final *doctoraal* to do. He was granted scholarship aid in the form of a state study loan of a thousand guilders per year.

FIG. 4.2 Yap's graduation portrait, Faculty of Law, Leiden University, September 1947.

Settling down in law school was difficult after four years away from study, but he graduated in a year and a half, passing the final examination on 26 September 1947 (fig. 4.2). In Leiden, as in the Rechtshogeschool, he was not an outstanding student. His *doctoraalexamen*, awarding the title *meester in de rechten*, was undistinguished, with low passing grades of "3" in civil procedure, criminal procedure, civil code, and *adat* (customary) law. On a 1–10 scale, in which 5 would be unsatisfactory, Hien passed with the equivalent of 6 or 6+.[7] It was not so much that he neglected his studies, but rather that, unlike more accomplished law students, his intellectual and personal priorities were elsewhere, the evidence for which abounds in the other activities he pursued during his years in Holland.

What else he did during those three years in Holland might have exhausted anyone with less stamina and a better sense of direction. Two or maybe three themes dominate his development then: he greatly deepened and refined his religious commitment; he became a nationalist; and in some inchoate way he seems to have decided that he wanted a public role and recognition.

The *zendingshuis*, a Hervormde Church institution now named for the missionary scholar Hendrik Kraemer, became Thiam Hien's home base in Holland and a critical influence on him. In some ways it makes more sense to call this his Oegstgeest rather than his Leiden period. In the huge, solid, four-story brick building, architecturally severe but set pleasantly in a wooded area, Hien was thrown together with young missionaries in training and other Protestant students at a time, in the post-war period, when Dutch Christianity was moving intellectually, and so were the political and social orders of Europe. Thiam Hien was too intellectually curious and receptive to ideas to filter out anything that seemed interesting, but in the Oetgstgeest setting religious issues and perspectives had the advantage.

In the *zendingshuis*, for the first time he was living in an environment that was essentially intellectual, and he thrived in it as nowhere else except, perhaps, the AMS-Yogya fifteen years earlier. Unlike many expatriate students, he was not fixated on making up for lost career time and was eager to talk, argue, and learn beyond his formal studies. It was a time for reading, not necessarily systematically but voraciously, and not only about religion but significantly so. Lectures were offered in the *zendingshuis* on religious, political, and social topics. When time allowed, he took night courses and, in the Volksuniversiteit, summer courses—one, for example, on internal migrations in Europe.

Reading primarily in Dutch and German, he began to explore issues of Marxism and capitalism (in response to the developing cold war), philosophy and politics (*staatslehre*), and social organization and reconstruction. The missionaries soon to leave for Africa or Indonesia or elsewhere were themselves readers and talkers. Some were caught up in the theological and organizational problems of the post-war Protestant churches: issues of the relationship between church and state, church and society, church and church, church and schools, and much else.[8] Thiam Hien got caught up, too. Under the guidance of Dominé Hokerman, an elderly and kind minister who supervised the student hospice in the *zendingshuis*, Thiam Hien read biblical history and exegesis. Karl Barth and other influential German theological writers also figured prominently in his study. From an enthusiastic but shallow initiate at the time of his conversion a few years before, Thiam Hien now began to develop a relatively sophisticated appreciation of Protestant development and thought. Yet, as before, he remained less oriented to theological thinking for its own sake than to theology-based behavior. Theory, abstraction, appealed to him less than how men behaved, what they did—theology in action—and in this, one can imagine Sato Nakashima's influence smiling in the background. Before the war it had been van Doorn, that dedicated religious man who left a rewarding position in the government for the sake of missionary work, who influenced him. In Leiden Thiam Hien read, in Dutch translation, and was completely taken with the sermons of Kaj Munk, the Danish Lutheran minister who had overcome the handicap of physical deformity to become a literary figure and theologian and whom the Germans assassinated for his defense of Jews.

The church in Holland provided Thiam Hien with a home, literally in the *zendingshuis* but also intellectually and ideologically. It came outfitted, moreover, with a network of friends and associates marked less by ethnic than by religious identity. Picking up where he had left off before the war, he taught Sunday school in Holland, serving as a lay minister in an experimental Hervormde children's church, in which children played most of the church roles. He volunteered to work with the mainly Dutch children. Even as he studied law, it is likely that somewhere in the back of his mind was the idea of working permanently in the church.

Yet, as his religious knowledge and commitment deepened, he was never drawn completely into the church or to its tenets. Even the Bible he read critically and a bit skeptically. In some ways, the peculiar mazelike complexity of Dutch religious history suited him well, for with an open mind there was so much to draw on. It is partly for this reason, as well as the fact that he was largely self-taught, that it is so hard to describe precisely Yap's religious commitments. Along with the basically liberal theology of the "modernist" Hervormde Church, inspired since the mid-nineteenth century by a much softened Calvinism, one can ascertain (perhaps) the significant influence on him of Armenian Remonstrants, Anabaptists, and the Mennonite offspring of Anabaptism.[9] Never exclusivist in his religious tastes, Thiam Hien had begun to admire Mennonites and Quakers long before he met with them on human rights issues in the 1970s. In Holland he struck up an acquaintance with an American Mennonite, which was renewed many years later. Still, whatever the mix of his religious ideas, which naturally changed over time, Thiam Hien accepted the Reformed Church as an institutional home until the 1960s.

As he developed religiously in Holland, he also grew politically and ideologically. The revolution at home made it impossible for all but the most oblivious or timid Indonesian students in Holland to avoid taking stands. For Indonesian Chinese, however, the issues were complicated and worrisome. Much was at stake in the revolution, and the signals from Indonesia were confusing. In late 1945 and 1946 ethnic Chinese had come under violent attack here and there. Here and there, too, a few organized to defend themselves, some actively supported the Dutch, a few supported the revolution, but most did nothing, anxiously waiting to see what would happen next. Among ethnic Chinese students in Holland the same patterns held.[10]

Thiam Hien and Thiam Bong emerged as nationalists who, whatever their fears for the Chinese, favored the revolution against Dutch colonialism. On board the refugee ship, Hien's specific observation of the differences in color combinations of foremen and laborers between Indonesia and Europe had generalized into political insight. Bong, in Enschede, argued about the revolution with a teacher, who then invited him to his home to talk further, and when Bong arrived, actually helped him off with his coat. In the Netherlands-Indies people like Bong did not enter the homes of whites. Hien and Bong read the same implications from the fact that Dutch social conditions were so much more egalitarian than those in the colony: that colonialism was neither inevitable nor just and that Indonesian nationalism was a matter of necessity and justice.

Nationalism opened Thiam Hien's mind to politics. He had a mentor of sorts in Tom Sigar, to whom Looho introduced him. Like Looho, Sigar was a Menadonese Protestant who had been in Holland since the 1930s, when his pensioned father had retired there. Unlike Looho, who confined his extracurricular activities to the church, Sigar was politically engaged, though, oddly, only in Holland for he never became active in Indonesia after he returned. A perpetual law student, Sigar was a member of the Dutch socialist Labor Party (Partij van de Arbeid) that opposed Dutch policy in Indonesia. Sigar was younger than Thiam Hien but knew his way around Dutch politics and was aggressively nationalist.

Their first meeting in the *zendingshuis* irritated Thiam Hien, who saw no reason to put up with Sigar's interrogation about his origins and background. But he was nevertheless stimulated by Sigar. Both loved to talk, and they soon became close friends. Their ethnic difference was submerged by their intellectual compatibility and shared religion. The relationship was fruitful almost from the start. For one thing, as Thiam Hien picked up on an organizational interest already manifest before the war, the two of them, along with a few others, established Perki (Indonesian Christian Association), which extended the range of Hien's Christian and nationalist contacts. But it was in other ways that the collaboration most influenced him.

Not for the first time perhaps, but now openly and acutely, Thiam Hien was forced by Sigar to think seriously about the situation of ethnic Chinese in Indonesia. No doubt the questions had occurred to him before, but now they were on the table and painful. Did he know, for example, that most Chinese opposed the revolution? Why were they close to the Dutch, why were they privileged, why were they so well off compared with ethnic Indonesians? Sigar also pointed out that in Holland Chinese students did not contribute much to the struggle for Indonesian independence. A Labor Party publication that Thiam Hien read at the time mentioned the difficulties of ethnic Chinese in Indonesia, but also called attention to their wealth. He could not avoid taking the implied accusations personally:

> On the one hand I resented this raising of ethnic sentiments again. On the other, it also gave rise to a conflict within myself. And this conflict, together with my religious deepening, pushed me to examine things honestly, to see the situation and myself more clearly. After all, I was descended from Chinese. Fine. How come in Aceh my grandparents were so well off? . . . Where I taught in Rembang and elsewhere, how come Chinese owned so much? Why? Now I came to understand all this better. And it provided material for a revolution in one's soul. One could begin to think of these problems not merely from a political point of view but a human one. My interest in human rights and the like really began there.[11]

Beyond these issues, painful as they were, Thiam Hien's association with Sigar drew him into arenas of political and ideological contention where ethnic claims did not count for much. This was a new experience and exhilarating. He made his way enthusiastically, enjoying the arguments and debates and undoubtedly the time he had on stage.

If Yap Thiam Hien was not a stereotypical Christian convert, he was in Holland a fervent nationalist convert. He unfurled a personal style of public discourse—already intimated in his Rechtshogeschool days, according to some who knew him—that suited his temperament but startled his audiences, not to mention his friends: a debating style, actually. Its delivery was blunt, logical, outspoken, argumentative, and often confrontational. Subtlety, diplomatic discretion, and the pulled punch never became prominent in his oratorical repertory. Doubts and ambivalences he pocketed for private reflection. Not long after he had arrived in Holland, he and others from the *zendingshuis* hospice were invited to attend a symposium in Utrecht on the development of overseas territories. There were representatives from Belgium, France, England, and, of course, the Netherlands. Following the presentation of papers, Thiam Hien promptly rose to ask, as this was a conference on overseas territories, where were the representatives of the overseas territories, of the Congo, Senegal, India, and so on. At the same time, he criticized the comments of an Englishman on Vietnam. Another student from Indonesia later warned him that the Dutch government could end his scholarship support or deport him. Nothing of the sort happened, but in any case Thiam Hien felt comfortable with an approach that got attention and satisfied his preference for directness and clarity.

In July 1947 Sigar, Yap, and five or six others were selected by Christian students to join an Indonesian delegation to the World Conference of Christian Youth in Oslo. Thiam Hien decided to go as a gift to himself for finishing his courses at the law school. The Dutch and Indonesian delegates from Holland traveled together amicably by train, but on their arrival in Oslo the news had broken of a Dutch military attack, on 21 July, against the Republic of Indonesia. At Sigar's insistence, the two groups promptly separated, and the Indonesian delegation issued a statement that it would have nothing to do with, and would not even talk to, the Dutch delegation. Thiam Hien went along but felt uneasy and confused, he recalled, by the contrivance of enmity between the Dutch and Indonesian students, who, on the train just a few hours earlier, had been perfectly happy together. He never did become inured to this kind of political maneuver; it was too much like dishonesty. As it happened, a Dutch delegate to the conference, the Protestant minister A. W. Visser t'Hooft, whom Thiam Hien later knew in the World Council of Churches, condemned his government's policies in Indonesia.[12]

But there was more than this to Thiam Hien's political education in Holland. No nationalist, even a neophyte, could avoid an interest in the positions Dutch political parties took on the status of the Republic; curiosity about the parties themselves followed. It was during this time that Thiam Hein discovered the political tack that would remain his preference for the rest of his life.

The Dutch party system, like Dutch society, was then organized along confessional lines.[13] Of the three major ideological/religious allegiances—Catholic, Protestant, and secular—Thiam Hien had no interest in the Catholics, for obvious reasons, and the Protestant parties were unalterably opposed to Indonesian independence. At the time the small Protestant Anti-Revolutionary Party even took the position that God was behind Holland's rule in Indonesia.[14] Many Dutch Protestant missionaries and theologians—among them Visser t'Hooft and Verkuyl, with long experience in Indonesia—opposed Dutch policy, but they had little influence in the political parties. Quite apart from the Indonesian question, the conservative or reactionary social bent of the Protestant parties made them no more appealing. Thiam Hien had little or nothing to do with them and never joined the Protestant Party (Parkindo) in Indonesia either.

The secular Labor Party was most sympathetic to the Republic of Indonesia, and its progressive social and economic programs were attractive to Thiam Hien. Unlike Tom Sigar and a few others, he did not join the party but felt close to it ideologically, on the secular and democratic socialist center-left. Nor did he, in Indonesia after 1950, join the Socialist Party (PSI)—whose sire, Sjahrir, had joined the Partij van de Arbeid—although he shared its outlook more than any other.

With the Dutch Communist Party, which also supported Indonesian independence, Thiam Hien had nothing to do, largely because of his Protestant connections but probably for other reasons as well. A few Indonesian students, including Go Gien Tjwan, were then actively trying to mobilize sympathy for the revolution among the European left, but Hien's path seldom crossed theirs. In 1946, following the Utrecht symposium on overseas territories, he was invited by a student federation to go to Prague and Moscow. The Dutch government, however, denied his request for an exit permit, possibly because of his grating contribution at the symposium, or because it was feared he might be attracted to communism. That was unlikely. He had begun to read in Marxism, which was a topic of conversation and lectures in the *zendingshuis,* and would have had some knowledge of Labor Party literature, but his understanding of the issues was evidently slight. This was brought home to him in an Amsterdam youth hostel, during his last year in Holland, when he was embarrassingly outclassed in argument by a young Dutch man who challenged his anti-capitalist position; he realized that he had much to learn and that grand ideological flourishes were not enough. Like other more or less center-left students, Hien rhetorically plied the middle road between communism and capitalism. Under the influence of the church's attitude, and for other ideological reasons as well, in Holland and later in Indonesia he opposed communism, but not ever rabidly or unthinkingly.

His nationalist activities in Holland may have been a sidetrack from his legal and religious studies, but they had significant if less obvious consequences. By the very fact of his involvement he had decided, maybe subliminally, to return to Indonesia. While most ethnic Chinese returned to Indonesia, many others (like Thiam Bong), then or afterwards, chose to stay in Holland rather than face the uncertainties of independent Indonesia. For members of a small and unpopular minority, it was an obvious choice. Thiam Hien, however, took it for granted that he belonged at home in Indonesia, where he had responsibilities and ambitions to pursue. Although the question of emigrating came up again in later years, if he was tempted, as well he might have been, he never showed it.

FIG. 4.3 The Yap family in Leiden, 1947. *Adults from left*: Yap Thiam Bong, Tan Nie Tjong (husband of Thiam Lian), Yap Thiam Hien, and Yap Thiam Lian (Non).

Thiam Hien's nationalism complicated his sense of ethnic identity without burying it. He belonged to the Chung Hua Hui (same name but unrelated to the CHH in Indonesia) student organization rather than the Perhimpunan Indonesia, the nationalist association organized in the 1920s, and his social circle was still largely Chinese. Non's family was in Leiden, and Hien saw them often and occasionally babysat (fig. 4.3). Thiam Bong was near, as everyone in Holland is. Yet in nationalist as in religious circles, Hien quickly and easily crossed ethnic boundaries. What would happen to the Chinese in independent Indonesia was on many minds, but among nationalists the question was at least partially subordinated to the larger issue of independence itself.

Thiam Hien did not leave Holland immediately after he was awarded his law degree, because the church offered attractive opportunities for training in church work. His own church in West Java had kept tabs on him through Dutch missionaries who had open lines of communication to church and missionary contacts in Holland.[15] His teaching experience and his interest in youth activities during the 1930s called attention to him as a good prospect for youth work in the church. The reports from Holland, possibly from the *zendingshuis*, were good ones. There was no question of his religious seriousness or sense of responsibility. So he was asked, when he returned to Indonesia, to work as a youth leader in the church in West Java. If he agreed, the church would fund additional training for him in Europe. Hien had not yet decided upon a career in law and was already very much involved in church affairs. He accepted.

For the next year he traveled fairly widely in Europe to Christian conferences and training programs, gathering experience and impressions as he went. A mature man of thirty-four with a law degree, confident or at least capable of containing self-doubts, Thiam Hien made intense use of the year, acquainting himself with church issues and approaches to Christian youth.

Following the 1947 Oslo conference, he traveled to Switzerland to spend three months in Savigny, near Geneva, attending a World Council of Churches youth course. It was there, in a forum attended by such prominent missionary figures as Hendrik Kraemer and Kenneth Latourette that he angered an Anglican bishop by asking for the biblical sources of the concept of the Trinity. It was a genuine question, no doubt, but it apparently raised eyebrows and set off some muttering, and he received no answer. He also upset Latourette by pointing out that the historian's discussion of Christianity in Asia provided many facts but no explanations. Latourette replied that he had only intended to present facts. It is a fair guess that Hien, always ambivalent about authority, got a kick out of challenging it. Many years later he returned to Geneva as a board member of both the World Council of Churches and the International Commission of Jurists.

From Savigny Thiam Hien returned to Amsterdam, where he stayed at a kind of YMCA, the Amsterdam Maatschapij voor de Jongeren (Society for Youth). He had written earlier, asking for an opportunity to live there and observe its organization and management, for he considered doing something like it in Jakarta. It was agreed and he spent a month there. England was next. From April through June 1948 he was enrolled at the Selly Oak Colleges in Birmingham for a three-month course in Christian youth work. It was the most valuable experience he had during this period of preparation for church work, partly because England offered a useful contrast with Holland, the one country in Europe he knew well. On the way to Birmingham he stayed for a couple of days in the east end of London at a church-related institution that worked with children from the slums. Those who lodged there paid very little, on the condition that all must share in any work in the house. Confronted with Cockney, Thiam Hien doubted his mastery of English. But he was impressed that children in the school there, unlike those whom he had taught in Indonesia, were spontaneous; they asked questions.

The Selly Oaks Colleges, an English Quaker institution supported by the Cadbury Chocolate Company, brought together a number of different denominations to provide advanced training for Christian service.[16] Thiam Hien found himself in a crowd of older and younger men and women, some with long experience in church work and others just beginning, ministers and laymen. Some were English veterans of the war, others Christian church workers from India, Sri Lanka, and elsewhere around the world. There were young people from various groups and social classes. For Hien it was an opportunity to study and talk about religion again, but now religion in society.

The program combined his twin interests in the church and education. Apart from church organization and management, participants were given instruction in how to teach both religious and secular subjects—the Bible, but also history and science. Thiam Hien's educational concerns were mainly the secular problems of how to encourage learning or how to teach civics in ways that led to new values. From his observations in the classrooms, particularly of the innovative teaching of history, his own particular interest, he was again fascinated by the spontaneity of grade-school students and by the challenging attitudes of teachers, so different from the behavior in Indonesian schools or, for that matter, in the Dutch schools that had influenced them. He left Selly Oaks with ideas that he was eager to try in Indonesia. He still saw himself as an educator, and in some ways always did.

Returning to the Continent, he went off alone to Paris for three weeks of study and sightseeing, then back to Holland and passage to Indonesia. In August of 1948 his European tour ended. It had been an extraordinary time of learning and growth.

FIVE

JAKARTA

YAP THIAM HIEN returned to Jakarta bent on structuring a new stage in life, and life accommodated him with a few surprises of its own.[1] It was not the best of times. The revolution was still on, though the fighting was desultory and far from Jakarta. Thiam Hien was sympathetic to the Republic of Indonesia but had no connection with the events surrounding it. What he knew came from the local press or word of mouth. Jakarta was Dutch territory until the end of December 1949, when the Dutch, having given up and negotiated their withdrawal, formally transferred sovereignty to a short-lived federal state. Like most others, Thiam Hien watched from the sidelines of this history.

In his own history, 1949, his first year back, kept him occupied in a frenzy of change. He flung himself into work—but there were also rites of passage to attend to. In February, only half a year after his return, he married Tan Gien Khing, who had accepted the proposal he sent from Holland (fig. 5.1). But this interesting beginning was followed rapidly by two unhappy endings. In mid-1949 Sin Eng died of a liver ailment, and not long afterwards Sato Nakashima also died. Both deaths were painful, but the pain he felt at each was quite different. Sin Eng left him with a sense of ambivalence, of unresolved guilt for not having shown his father more respect. But Omah Nakashima's connection with Hien, Bong, and Non was untroubled by any emotional burden more complicated than gratitude or less complete than love. When she died Thiam Hien felt orphaned, cut loose from his childhood.

FIG. 5.1 Yap Thiam Hien and Tan Gien Khing, Jakarta, 1949.

Except for his new wife, Thiam Hien was essentially alone, without the immediate family he thought important but seldom, since leaving Aceh, lived with. There were uncles, aunts, cousins, nephews, and nieces here and there, some of them already scattering abroad, but the extended family had never meant a great deal to him. He was responsive when called upon, within limits. Like many other highly educated *peranakan,* he was not moved much by the corporate family of Chinese tradition. In his case, the family that did matter to him had always been too mobile and, since Yap A Sin's collapse, too weak financially to be satisfyingly tight.

I bring this up to interpret a painful conflict between Hien and Bong that may throw some psychological light on Thiam Hien. When Hien returned to Indonesia, Bong and Non were still in Holland. Thiam Bong had finished his textile technology course and was looking for work. As it happened, a friend in Jakarta who had set up an import-export business told Thiam Hien that he wanted Thiam Bong, who had export experience, for a partner. Thiam Hien wrote to Thiam Bong, who agreed. In the meantime, Thiam Bong had met a Dutch woman, Cory, to whom he proposed, and he had second thoughts about returning. It seemed to Thiam Bong that it might be easier for him to live in

Holland than for his wife to live in Indonesia—which was probably true—and he himself had some doubts about surviving in the new conditions of independent Indonesia, where, he had heard, corruption was already becoming common. Thiam Bong was as straitlaced as Thiam Hien and less adventurous. After mulling it over and listening to advice in Holland, he wrote to his friend in Jakarta and to his brother that he had changed his mind and would stay where he was.

Thiam Hien replied to Thiam Bong with an excoriating letter, accusing him of having broken a promise. Bong was outraged and deeply hurt that his older brother would say such things to him. It was months before he stopped hurting, he told me, and nearly forty years later, when he talked about it, the letter obviously still stung. Eventually Hien agreed that Bong had probably done the right thing to stay in Holland, though he may never have apologized for what he had written. But what set off the tantrum? For Thiam Hien, one's word was the essence of character and integrity, a principle so unadulterated and rigorous that, whatever its other sources in his experience, it must have had the force of Sato Nakashima behind it. Yet the letter to Thiam Bong evidently was so unforgiving of his brother's circumstances then and so harsh that neither principle nor self-righteousness seems to account for it adequately. What may explain it better is desperation. Thiam Hien and Thiam Bong were close, more so than either was with their sister. Thiam Bong's decision to remain in Holland left Thiam Hien alone, deprived of an intimate link to the Yap family. If he acknowledged this sad reality to himself, he could not to others, but instead held Thiam Bong responsible for violating a promise. It may be, however, that the promise he really had in mind was an implicit one to maintain the family in Indonesia.

One subtle aspect of Yap Thiam Hien's extraordinary independence as a lay church worker, as a professional advocate, and as a political figure of sorts is his lack of intimate connections outside his immediate family. In the complex of intricate kinship and social networks of Java that became increasingly important in the politics of independent Indonesia, Yap was and remained an outsider, even after his marriage into a Central Javanese *peranakan* family. Always a loner, albeit a sociable one, he concentrated any need for intimacy within his family. That is why his wife was so important and Bong's decision so painful.

Thiam Hien came to depend on Tan Gien Khing far more, I think, than he realized, for he conceived of himself as powerfully independent, while she was generally retiring and usually—not always—very soft spoken. He seemed, and often was, autocratic, quick to make decisions, and firm about sticking to them, while she was inclined to compromise. How she behaved at critical times, however—during a political crisis in 1960, for example, or when Thiam Hien was arrested in January 1968 and then detained for a year in 1974, and when she herself was stabbed in the neck by an intruder in 1981—makes clear that Khing's sweet and pliable softness sheathed reinforcement rods of steel.

Khing was in many ways a typical well-born *peranakan*, culturally more Javanese than anything else, from the old, substantial, solid, and fairly conservative ethnic Chinese community of Semarang, the provincial capital of Central Java. Both sides of her ancestry were thought to be Hokkien. Her mother, Thee Hsia Ling, was from Cirebon. Her father, Tan Siu Lim, was an only son whose own mother dominated the family. Tan Siu Lim spoke a Chinese language (perhaps *kuo-yu*) and had the strong sense of ethnic identity that many *peranakan* acquired in the twentieth century, but he also owned a gamelan (Javanese percussion orchestra) from Solo that was brought out, along with Javanese dancers, on special occasions. Khing's generation, and Khing herself, spoke no Chinese language, only Javanese, Dutch, and Indonesian.

Khing's mother bore seven children who lived (three boys and four girls), and three or four more who did not. Khing was the fifth child, born on 12 January 1919, six years younger than Thiam Hien. All the siblings were well educated in the HBS of Semarang. Her brothers all became successful professionals. The oldest, Tan Tong Ho, became a well-known doctor, an internist, who eventually wound up in Holland. During the Japanese occupation he married an ethnic Indonesian woman, the daughter of a Menadonese man and the younger sister of the famous pre-war nationalist leader Tjipto Mangoenkoesoemo. Her father had at first opposed the marriage but eventually gave in just as *peranakan* fathers were wont to do in the face of generations of precedent. Khing, like her siblings, mixed easily in the Dutch-speaking ethnic mélange of Semarang's educated class. In both her grade school and the HBS, students were from all population groups, and so were her friends.

Like most solid *peranakan* families, the Tans neither converted to Christianity nor, unlike the Yap family, adopted European legal status. In their circle, Chinese "Belanda tiga suku" (three bit Dutchmen) evoked derisive chuckles. Khing's father was a practicing Buddhist and the family maintained an ancestral altar. In a convent elementary school, however, she herself developed a taste for Catholicism, and in the HBS chose the Catholic stream for her required religious studies, though she never formally joined the church. She was baptized a Protestant after her marriage, for Thiam Hien felt strongly that spouses ought to share the same religion. Khing went along, but she always felt more at home with Catholicism, admixed perhaps with Buddhism.

Tan Gien Khing did not finish HBS, for her family fell on hard times during the Great Depression. In 1933, when she was fourteen, her mother died in childbirth, and Khing assumed responsibility for her younger siblings and, in effect, her father. In good times he had been a reasonably successful businessman—tapioca and palm oil factories among other enterprises—but in the bad times of the Depression, like many other *peranakan* entrepreneurs, he gradually lost just about everything. The family moved in with Khing's grandmother. Khing went to a teachers' school and taught for a year before the occupation and then stopped. During the revolution she was in Jakarta, hoping to study again, perhaps dentistry, but never taking the step and regretting it. Instead, at the end of 1945, she took a job in the Ministry of Education.

She and Thiam Hien had met at Non's wedding in 1943 and a few times afterwards, during the occupation, before he left for Leiden. While he was in Europe they corresponded, and when his studies were completed he proposed by letter. They didn't know each other well, but Thiam Hien thought it was time to assume the adult responsibilities of starting a family, and Khing may have felt the same way. She agreed to the proposal, but her father did not, for he had never met Thiam Hien, and she was too much the obedient daughter to act without his approval. Her oldest brother interceded, however; he had known Thiam Hien slightly before the war and vouched for his character and intelligence. For his part, Thiam Hien, in an outbreak of tradition, insisted upon an engagement. Before he returned, Sin Eng announced the forthcoming marriage in a Jakarta newspaper advertisement, ostentatiously using Thiam Hien's new title of *meester*. Thiam Hien and Khing were married on 15 February 1949.[2] In their wedding photograph, Hien, who always took pride in his dress, is wearing a truly ill-fitting suit that he had bought in the children's section of a department store in Oslo, where few adults matched him in size.

Thiam Hien wanted Khing to quit her job at the Ministry, but his income from the church was meager, less than hers, and she insisted on working until he began to practice as a professional advocate in late 1949 or early 1950. He still earned very little at first. They lived in a small house in the Krekot area of central Jakarta and bought their first car on installments. They drove themselves, hiring a driver only many years later after Thiam Hein was released from detention at the end of 1974. In 1957 they bought a larger but still modest home in Grogol, west Jakarta, from the city administration. Though it was inexpensive, they had to borrow from Khing's sister and Non to cover the cost.

They remained in Grogol for the next thirty years. Thiam Hien never did earn a great deal of money, and occasionally there were tensions over his inclination to contribute more to causes than they could afford. Both of them, fortunately, were always genuinely frugal. After he began law practice, Thiam Hien—who thought himself a poor manager and maybe distrusted his own money habits—asked Khing to keep all the household accounts. This she did faithfully, listing every expenditure in a book kept for the purpose. Neither of them was ever house proud or vain enough to spend large amounts on clothes or jewelry. Their social life was limited, more so probably than Khing would have liked, for Thiam Hien was uncomfortable at parties and preferred reading or working late. In the many and diverse parlors of the Jakarta haut monde, the Yaps were at ease nowhere.

If the Yap home remained relatively calm, Khing was the reason. She managed it efficiently and routinely, creating a kind of closed circuit between herself and the two or three servants—a common feature in middle-class urban homes in Indonesia—with whom she always dealt in Javanese. Yet there were perpetual strains in that household that arose inevitably from the different priorities of husband and wife. She was the more conventional, accepting the family as the very center of being, for which, if necessary, she took for granted that her own interests and private wants would be sacrificed. He had a public role, for which he sometimes seemed willing to sacrifice the interests of the family.

Thiam Hien kept Khing informed of his activities—she was his only real intimate—and she took an interest, though she never enjoyed the tensions that increasingly surrounded his work. On the surface an unmistakably goodhearted and empathetic person, Khing was submissive, or maybe resigned, used to the primacy of men. And Thiam Hien was nothing if not dominating. But like many educated *peranakan* and Javanese women, Khing had too much character for endless patience. Early in their marriage, as he engaged in a plethora of activities that kept him away from home, Khing felt neglected or threatened enough to protest. They had an adequate supply of other reasons to argue.

For the most part, however, she provided the measure of reliable solidity, even tranquility, that Thiam Hien could not have done without and still maintain a semblance of sanity. Self-reliant as he usually was, he may not always have understood or wanted to understand this dependence. This judgment is, of course, easier made than shown. But his huge capacity for anger, his impatience, and his easy frustration, all of which quieted with age to a respectable roar, in the early years of their marriage were vented at home in what must have been stunning displays. Khing put up with them, buffering the servants and anyone else in the way, and somehow absorbed the hurricane of wrath until it was spent. As Thiam Hien's public principles were also private ones, and he usually insisted on them as rigorously at home as he did at large, there were bound to be tensions with their two children—their son, Hong Gie, was born in 1953 and their daughter, Hong Ay, in 1957—which Khing also defused or managed as best she could. She did all this, moreover, with the kind of controlled, deliberate, graceful dignity, even in moments of her own quiet but evident anger, that is so highly valued in Java. The chief beneficiary of the smooth routine and interior quietude of the home she created was Thiam Hien.

It was never obviously a "Chinese" home. Khing and Thiam Hien were not collectors of Chinese ceramics or scroll paintings or any of the other ethnic paraphernalia that one often sees in *peranakan* homes (and often too in upper-class ethnic Indonesian homes). There was an occasional vase, more likely than not a gift, and an assortment of Balinese, Javanese, or other regional bric-a-brac, also gifts. There was nothing ostentatious and nothing that presented itself even as revealing an unmistakable Chinese aesthetic sensibility. A partial exception was a makeshift, minimal family altar—Khing's, not Thiam Hien's—barely noticeable as such, consisting of photographs, a small urn, and some joss sticks that no one remembered to light on a table by a wall, giving the impression, often seen in the homes of assimilated minorities anywhere, of a nostalgic afterthought.

The altar represented a bit more than that for Khing, who always took heritage more seriously than her husband and far more than the children, who were as prone as young people anywhere to dismiss old customs whose social significance evaporated along with their enforceability. Even Khing, however, had only a loose grip on the customs, a few of which she might reconstruct uncertainly at opportune times—Hong Ay's and Hong Gie's weddings, for example—but from a dim memory of form and meaning.

Although Thiam Hien, until the mid-1960s, was still very much encapsulated in ethnic Chinese professional, political, and social circles, he had even less connection with any recognizable Chinese tradition. Beyond a few Chinese words, an unremarkable appreciation of Chinese food, and intellectual curiosity about his own origins, culturally he was as marginal a man as one can imagine. In some ways he was typical of the growing group of well-educated, culturally more or less deracinated Indonesians of various ethnic origins who have always been most at home in Jakarta. They form the most visible stratum of what Hildred Geertz once called the Indonesian metropolitan superculture, unquestionably national in language, style, and experience and with only flimsy regional or ethnic identities.[3] Many educated *peranakan* nest most comfortably in this stratum. Thiam Hien certainly did, which helps to explain his tenuous connection with the Chinese community and the relative ease with which in time he left it politically. But so basically did Khing, despite her deeper sense of Chinese belonging and her natural ease in Javanese culture. Not surprisingly, their children, born and raised in the independent state and unburdened by the baggage of colonial experience and memory, were all the more securely part of the cultural mélange of urban Indonesia. Their daughter in time married a Menadonese Protestant, their son a Javanese Muslim, neither of whom has more than traces of local cultural origins.

Nineteen forty-nine was also a year for career decisions. By the end of it Yap Thiam Hien had planted himself in the two vocations, church and law, that defined him ever afterwards. The two callings pulled him into separate worlds made up of different crowds and institutions. By coincidence, during the same time period in the late 1960s, he would be invited to join the boards of both the World Council of Churches and the International Commission of Jurists, as distinct from one another in Geneva as religion and the law profession are in Jakarta, or anywhere else for that matter. Yap somehow entwined them inextricably, never fazed by the oddity of the union he took for granted, or much troubled by the energy each, let alone both, demanded. While Khing sometimes objected to her husband's strenuous schedule, he evidently thrived on it. The more he had to do, he said, the better he felt. Turning away no opportunity for involvement, he seems to have been determined to expend as much as possible of his considerable energy to make a mark of some kind.

Church youth work was not enough; it may have felt confining, and it also did not pay enough. So Thiam Hien finally decided to make his way as a professional advocate. He had entertained the possibility for years, but not always compellingly. If something better had come along, he might have leapt at it, but it is hard to imagine an alternative. Vocational choices were few for ethnic Chinese lawyers in the colony, and they did not multiply in the independent state. In Holland Yap had more or less made up his mind to be a private lawyer, but put it off in favor of working with the church. After a few months in Jakarta, however, he asked his church superiors to allow him to practice as an advocate, explaining that his church pay was insufficient; he would continue his church work voluntarily. It was agreed, and he submitted his particulars to the Department of Justice, then still Dutch administered. On 11 July 1949, he was formally registered as an advocate.[4]

The advocacy was just the right setting for Yap. It provided satisfying professional status along with maximum freedom to extend his activities beyond the church. At about the same time that he registered in the Ministry of Justice, he also joined the Sin Ming Hui (SMH), an organization established in January 1946, a time when Indonesian Chinese were cloaked in confusion and uncertainty. Yap worked with its legal committee, a forerunner of the legal aid movement of the 1970s.

I mentioned in chapter 3 that the ethnic Indonesian component of the professional advocacy was quite young, dating only from 1923, when Besar Martokoesoemo opened an office in Tegal. That first cohort of private practitioners was made up of remarkable men, all Javanese *priyayi* whom the colonial administration had sent to Leiden in the expectation that they would return to staff the courts and higher ranges of the bureaucracy. Most of them did exactly that, joining the Landraden (courts for Indonesians and those assimilated to Indonesian legal status). In time they took over the courts of the independent state; nearly all the Supreme Court (Mahkamah Agung) justices and many of the appellate court judges after 1950 had served on the colonial Landraden. In the colony these were very high-status positions, the sort that well-born Indonesian parents were eager for their sons to achieve. What was extraordinary about the young Javanese lawyers like Besar was their willingness to defy the government and their families to take up private professions.

From the beginning the Indonesian advocacy was on the odd side, constantly out of synchrony with its surroundings.[5] Well educated and self-confident, as they had to be even to think of joining a profession dominated by Dutch lawyers, Indonesian advocates were among the most highly mobilized reformers in the colony—reformers, by and large, but not revolutionaries, except in a quite special sense—and remained so after independence. Soekarno's National Party (PNI), formed in 1927, relied heavily on these new private practitioners and was, indeed, the chief beneficiary of their political commitment and professional skills.[6] The PNI was preeminently the party of a new Indonesian professional class, which provided much of the leadership of the revolution and of the independent state's first, parliamentary, regime. Not all indigenous Indonesian advocates joined the PNI, and some never joined any party at all, but overwhelmingly they supported the nationalist movement. During the revolution a majority of them, but not a large number, were in the revolutionary capital of Yogyakarta. Ethnic Chinese advocates were as ambivalent about the independence movement as were most *peranakan*, but in any case the nationalists among them were excluded from the major parties. There were ethnic Chinese in Yogya, and elsewhere too, who actively supported the revolution, but many who sympathized were uncertain enough about their acceptance or role to remain in Jakarta.

Ideologically, the advocacy tended to the political and economic liberalism that one would expect from a middle-class professional group that depended very little on state support. The kind of state they had in mind for independent Indonesia was not that of Indonesian tradition, nor the colonial version of it, but the modern European *rechtsstaat*, in Indonesian translation, the *negara hukum*. Elsewhere I have described the colonial political order as consisting of two structural models, a "European side" state and an "Indonesian side" state.[7] The former, complete with its own judicial system and rigorous formal codes, incorporated the essential ideas of the *rechtsstaat* (law state). The latter, also equipped by the colonial administration with its own courts and a less-demanding procedural code, was based more on political prerogative than law. Advocates engaged in both, necessarily, but their hearts belonged to the European-side state, where their skills counted most and were rewarded with considerable prestige. While strongly nationalist, few advocates ever became nativist. Already during the colonial period they were loud critics of local *adat* (customary) law and traditional authority. The written codes for Europeans were their métier, and in these complex statutes were encoded the basic premises of the Continental *rechtsstaat*.

As men who had refused to work for the colonial state, advocates were particularly sensitive to tensions between public authority and private right. They were among the earliest intellectuals to question explicitly the assumptions of Javanese (and other Indonesian) political tradition that state and society were fused in a political and moral unity, leaning instead to a perspective that regarded state and society as separate entities.[8] Subjecting the state to controls, keeping guard against it, was a matter of much interest to these advocates. Later, some, but by no means all, who took up positions in the independent state would lose their grip on this idea. But for most advocates, defining and limiting authority by law was the sine qua non of the kind of state they wanted. It was for this reason that Soekarno, under Guided Democracy (1959–65), waved them aside.

Where did ethnic Chinese advocates fit in the Indonesian advocacy as it developed? Among the earliest advocates, ethnic Indonesian and ethnic Chinese were often as friendly as *priyayi* and *peranakan* always had been. The first

Indonesian law office in Semarang was a partnership between Besar Martokoesoemo and Ko Tjay Sing, a very able lawyer and intellectual. Although the men split up during the depression, when work for private lawyers was scarce, they remained life-long friends. There were a few others who worked together. But by and large, indigenous and Chinese advocates went their separate ways, just as the plural structure of the colony would have predicted.

Several reasons account for this tendency. The routes to a legal vocation were different for ethnic Indonesians and ethnic Chinese. Both were enabled by the secondary education that became available at the beginning of the century, but beyond the HBS and AMS young Javanese who went on to law school were most likely to be funded by the government, while young Chinese had to pay their own way. Ethnic Indonesian law graduates who entered private practice were remarkable exceptions, while *peranakan* lawyers, who had little choice in the matter, took to the advocacy as if it were perfectly natural. In a sense it was natural, for commerce needs lawyers, Chinese businesses no less, and they chose ethnic Chinese lawyers, sometimes consciously out of ethnic trust or loyalty. A few Chinese law firms had already begun to prosper before the war as Chinese businesses generated enough work for them. Indigenous Indonesian advocates seldom had anything like this advantage on which to rely.

For another thing, the profession was subtly partitioned around fundamental issues of the independence movement itself. If on some ideological scores—the *negara hukum* above all—nearly all advocates, regardless of ethnicity, fundamentally agreed, nationalism divided them, for the nationalist movement was regarded as quintessentially ethnic Indonesian. During the 1930s even the most sympathetically engaged *peranakan*—the PTI, for example—were denied entry to all nationalist organizations save one. The exception was the small left-of-center Gerindo (Gerakan Rakyat Indonesia, Indonesian Peoples' Movement), which explicitly rejected ethnic exclusions. Perhaps more than journalists, private lawyers are among the most politically aware and sensitive professionals nearly everywhere. In Indonesia, ethnic Chinese lawyers, many of whom supported the independence movement, though often with qualms, for the most part kept their distance from it. During the revolution, when most ethnic Indonesian advocates were engaged in the new republic, only a few ethnic Chinese lawyers were. Tan Po Goan, later one of Yap's senior law partners, served for a time in the cabinet of the republican government; most, however, waited out the revolution in Dutch territory, as did a few ethnic Indonesian private lawyers and many public lawyers. Many ethnic Chinese private lawyers were neither neutral nor lacking in interest, but they had no clear grip on what to do.

The advocacy survived the occupation and revolution but was pared down and a bit misshapen, not least along its ethnic dimensions. After 1945 some of the most prominent ethnic Indonesian advocates joined the revolutionary government and remained in high positions after independence. Besar Martokoesoemo, for example, became secretary-general of the Ministry of Justice; Sartono, speaker of Parliament; Ali Sastroamidjojo, an occasional prime minister and parliamentary leader of the PNI; Iskaq Tjokrohadisurjo, an MP and minister of economic affairs. Many others less prominent followed suit, for the new government was short on educated, competent leadership and personnel; private lawyers, like other professionals, particularly those with party connections, were more or less qualified and usually eager for the opportunity. The advocacy was not emptied out, and a few cabinet ministers—Mohamad Roem, Djody Gondokusumo, Iskaq, among others—returned to practice when their administrations fell, but the profession lost a generation of leadership at a hard time. Their absence also skewed the ethnic balance among private lawyers. Useful data are hard to come by for the first decade following independence, but ethnic Chinese advocates probably predominated nationwide during much of that period.

There were very few professional advocates once the Dutch practitioners departed, as most had done by the time of the transfer of sovereignty at the end of 1949, or shortly thereafter. In 1941, the last year of the colony, there were 194 advocates, down slightly from the peak of 203 in 1939, among whom 122 were Dutch and 72 Indonesian (36 each ethnic Indonesian and ethnic Chinese).[9] Once Dutch advocates were gone and half (at least) of the ethnic Indonesian advocates had taken positions in the government, with only a few new lawyers deciding to enter private practice, in 1950 there were probably at a very rough estimate no more than a hundred or a hundred and fifty practicing advocates throughout Indonesia. Given a population then of about ninety million, this meant at best one advocate per 600,000 people, a meager ratio. (To take up any slack, however, there were also large numbers of ungraduated bush-lawyers, *pokrol bambu*, who had long managed a substantial volume of legal work in and out of court.[10]) About half of the total was in Jakarta, the rest scattered in the major cities of Surabaya, Semarang, Bandung, Medan, Padang, and Makassar.

Yet with independence, the profession was still prestigious and seemed to enjoy a favorable environment. The major reason for this illusion, as it would turn out to be, was that the profession had enough institutional continuity, despite the revolution, to reassure advocates and like-minded others that their universe was secure.

In reality, the occupation and revolution had forced some significant alterations in the legal system, quite apart from political changes that eventually cut deeply into the integrity of the legal process. During the occupation, the Japanese military administration had abolished the European courts, unifying the judicial system around the former courts for Indonesians; and the revolutionary government confirmed the transformation. This left a single line of civil courts, consisting of a first-instance court (*pengadilan negeri*) at the district level, an appellate court (*pengadilan tinggi*) for one or more provinces, and the Supreme Court. In addition, in several areas there remained customary (*adat*) courts, which were gradually abolished over the next decade, and Islamic courts, but private lawyers had never had much to do with these institutions.[11] At the same time, the European codes of civil and criminal procedure gave way to the procedural code for Indonesians, the Herziene Inlandsch (Indonesisch) Reglement (H.I.R., Revised Native [Indonesian] Regulation), as the basic instrument of litigation and lower-level administrative process. Early in the revolution, professional advocates had objected that Indonesian courts should be held to the more demanding standards of the European codes, but for both practical and nationalist reasons they lost out. The formal argument against the European codes was that Indonesian judges and prosecutors had had little experience with them, as in the Landraden only the H.I.R. applied. There is little reason to suppose that well-trained and capable judges could not have adapted quickly and well to the more sophisticated codes. However, the Dutch codes' association with colonial privilege trumped all arguments in their favor. Advocates were not pleased by this development, and perhaps neither were many judges, but they kept the European procedural codes alive in practice as influential sources for rules unavailable in the H.I.R.

Despite these retrogressions, advocates by and large felt reasonably confident, in part because the political leadership was paying symbolic attention to legal procedure—but, more generally, because it appeared committed to creating and maintaining an Indonesian *rechtsstaat*. The Provisional Constitution of 1950, replacing the short-lived federal arrangement sponsored by the Dutch, was a liberal parliamentary charter that provided for a responsible, accountable government and strong courts. This constitution borrowed heavily and impressively from the Universal Declaration of Human Rights. In the parliamentary regime that lasted until 1957, well-known and respected professional lawyers from the PNI, the PSI (Socialists), and the Islamic party Masyumi, as well as several minor parties, including the Catholics (Partai Katolik) and Protestants (Parkindo), were prominent as prime ministers and cabinet members. Independent Indonesia was a *negara hukum* it was assumed—too confidently—and the rule of law guaranteed the legal profession a secure future.

The judicial system, though short on trained personnel and adequate financing, was nevertheless reasonably competent and independent. Major courts were staffed by able judges with experience on the old Landraden. On the Mahkamah Agung were several highly respected judges—among them Wirjono Koesoemo, Wirjono Prodjodikoro, Malikul Adil, Satochid Kartanegara, R. Soekardono, and, above all, the first president of the Court, Kusumaatmadja, who was the only Indonesian judge ever to have risen to the European appellate bench (Raad van Justitie) in the colony. Very jealous of the institutional prerogatives of the judiciary, Kusumaatmadja inspired judges and private lawyers by once facing down President Soekarno on a protocol issue of seating arrangements, threatening to leave unless he were seated next to the president. He died in 1951 and was succeeded by Wirjono Prodjodikoro, a learned judge but, it developed later, politically submissive, which contributed to the disastrous decline of the courts after 1959. During the parliamentary period, judges and advocates got along reasonably well. There were a few hidden tensions between the public officials and the private practitioners, but competent, independent judges had no fear of, and much respect and appreciation for, able professional advocates, colleagues in a single system. This changed for the worse in a few years time, as an older pre-war generation of judges retired and the political regime turned away from the *negara hukum*.

Elsewhere in the judicial system conditions were less edifying but still hopeful. The prosecution had few adequately trained lawyers, but the first chief public prosecutor of independent Indonesia, Soeprapto, was a highly capable and independent man committed to improving the institution and keeping it free of political influence. He lasted until 1959. The national police, too, were led by an able chief, Soekanto, generally trusted by advocates as a man committed to liberal law principles and an accountable police force.

The few professional advocates remained confident in their skills, proud of their independence, and hopeful for the future of legal process. Yet as a group they were oddly inactive, in some ways distant from the serious problems that began almost immediately to infect the legal system. They were barely organized, maintaining no more than the pre-war local *balie* (bar) associations here and there, mainly in major cities. The *balie* groups were little more than local clubs in which advocates occasionally met, largely to introduce newcomers. In the early 1950s prosecutors, police, and judges frenetically organized to extend or defend their territory. Prosecutors demanded the same civil service ranks and pay as judges, which they eventually won, while police sought to wrest control over preliminary investigation from the prosecution.[12] Advocates sympathized with judges in their dispute with prosecutors, but in the main looked on from the sidelines. They did not bother to organize themselves nationally; perhaps because they felt they were too few to be effective or because they already belonged to one of two national associations which included all law professionals (ISHI and PAHI), or because they saw no reason to break with the tradition of local associations for advocates.[13] Moreover, the ethnic Chinese lawyers, probably a majority of the practicing advocacy in the early 1950s, tended to adopt a worried reticence, uncertain of their reception in a legal system that, like the political system, was now suddenly dominated by ethnic Indonesians.

When Yap began practice, there were only a few small law offices in Jakarta, mainly of individual practitioners, including a handful of Dutch advocates soon to leave. Without experience, he could not easily open his own office. Near the end of 1949, he joined Oei Kian Hong (John Karuin), who years later would found one of Jakarta's major law firms.[14] From a wealthy Padang family, Karuin had studied law in Holland before the war and remained there to practice for a time before returning home. Thiam Hien met him in Leiden, where they got along well and Karuin proposed that in future they work together. In 1949 Thiam Hien took him up on the offer. A friend from the church gave them office space in Pintu Kecil, a Chinese commercial area in the old city. It was one room, big enough for two desks. Their practice grew for a short time but then declined, for Karuin, according to Yap a sociable, sympathetic, likeable, but undisciplined man, attracted clients but could not keep them, and Yap was too inexperienced to build their practice by himself. Karuin graciously offered to assure him an income, but Thiam Hien evidently was too proud to accept. The partnership lasted only about a year.

In 1951 or early 1952 Yap joined the law office of Lie Hwee Yoe, where he remained until 1970. He was brought in as a junior partner, without any requirement that he buy in, an indication of trust that he greatly appreciated. His share of the firm's income was always the smallest, never luxurious but adequate to his family's needs. In time, he began to attract clients to the office.

An established firm dating from before the war, the office brought together a remarkable collection of very able lawyers: the senior partner, Lie Hwee Yoe;

his brother-in-law, Lie Kian Kim; Tan Po Goan; and Oei Tjoe Tat. Lie Hwee Yoe, five years older than Yap, was a devout Catholic, a responsible and honest lawyer, and a devoted family man, the only member of the firm who was not politically and socially active. As different as they were in temperament, Yap admired and respected Lie. In 1967, when Yap himself was on trial, charged with defaming a prosecutor and police official, the judge in the case, Soetarno, impugned Lie's integrity. Yap was outraged and protested furiously, half-screaming in open court, according to the press report: Soetarno, surprisingly, withdrew his slur in the next session.[15] Lie Hwee Yoe died in California in 1987.

Lie Kian Kim took his law degree in the Rechtshogeschool and began practice before the war. Yap had met him during the occupation in Sukabumi, where Lie was born, and saw him again when he joined the Sin Ming Hui. It was Lie Kian Kim who, when Yap inquired, invited him to join the law firm. Lie was a founder of the Sin Ming Hui and its chairman from 1948 until 1950, when he died in an automobile accident.

Tan Po Goan, from Cianjur, had been two years ahead of Thiam Hien in the AMS, and he too vouched for him. He had taken his law degree in 1937 from the Rechtshogeschool, practiced in Ujung Pandang (Makassar) and Surabaya, worked for the daily *Sin Po*, and was interned by the Japanese during the occupation. He was active politically. During the revolution he served in Parliament (KNIP), was a member of the third Sjahrir cabinet from late 1946 until mid-1947, was appointed to Parliament in 1950, and elected on the PSI (Socialist) list in 1955. He was also a member of the Sin Ming Hui and the short-lived ethnic Chinese party, the Partai Democrat Tionghoa Indonesia (PDTI) (to be dealt with later).[16] Well known and popular in Jakarta elite circles, an intelligent bon vivant and jokester, Tan Po Goan had friends everywhere and brought many clients to the firm. He preferred criminal litigation, which required courage and a taste for combat. Following his election to Parliament, he seldom showed up at the office, but when he did, according to Yap, it came alive with chatter and political gossip. When the regional PRRI-Permesta rebellion began in early 1958, Tan was abroad with Professor Sumitro Djojohadikusumo, a PSI leader associated with the rebellion, and did not return until after Guided Democracy had disintegrated following the attempted coup of October 1965. He died in Australia in the early 1980s.

Oei Tjoe Tat (b. 1922), the youngest member of the firm, was from Solo, Central Java, and a model of the culturally blended Central Javanese *peranakan* intellectual. He, too, was at the Rechtshogeschool in the late 1930s, a superior student and a member of the Ta Hsioh student organization, but he and Yap were apparently barely aware of one another at the time. Instead of going to Leiden after the war, Oei completed his law degree in 1948 at the Emergency University (Nood Universiteit) established by the Dutch administration in Jakarta. Soon thereafter he joined the Lie Hwee Yoe firm. During the revolution, while in law school, he worked for a Red Cross committee in Jakarta and also for the British-organized War Crimes Committee. Young as he was, Oei was one of the founders of the Sin Ming Hui in 1946 and served as its chairman after Lie Kian Kim's death. He was also active in the PDTI.

Several law firms in Indonesia then housed politically active members, mainly but not solely in Jakarta. The Lee Hwee Yoe firm, well equipped with lawyerly skills, intellectual power, and prominent political players, was one of them. No doubt this activism had much influence on Yap, legitimating and encouraging his own political involvement. He had nowhere near as much political experience as Lie Kian Kiem, Tan Po Goan, or Oei Tjoe Tat, but he learned from them. Following the emergence of Baperki, tension in the office was at times considerable, mainly between Thiam Hien and Tjoe Tat, a study in contrasts between the smooth, adaptable, political insider Oei and the blunt, critical, outsider Yap.

Professionally, as for the most part politically, the Lee Hwee Yoe office was deeply imbedded in the Chinese community. All of its clients, at least in the 1950s, were ethnic Chinese, by and large with commercial concerns. Yap did his share of civil litigation, but soon displayed a preference for criminal defense, a relative rarity among ethnic Chinese advocates. It was not that Chinese lawyers lacked the skill or that commercial law was far more rewarding than criminal law. Quite as important, and increasingly so, minority lawyers were at a disadvantage and risk in a judicial system governed by a none-too-friendly majority. Yap's inclination to criminal practice, however, was not surprising. In Indonesia, private lawyers with a penchant for political and social activism often choose criminal law, which most starkly raises issues of social justice and the contraposition of private rights and public authority. If civil litigation requires knowledge of the civil and commercial codes, negotiating skills, and assiduity in the preparation of documentary exchange in court—which make up much of civil procedure in Indonesian courts—criminal practice demands stamina, analytic imagination, and precise argumentation in confrontation with state power in open court. It also requires some trust in the judicial system, which the Indonesian advocacy enjoyed during the parliamentary years, or dogged determination and courage, which became essential to serious criminal lawyers thereafter. Yap had all the qualities necessary to successfully practice criminal law, save a willingness to bend rules, compromise, and negotiate outcomes that proved helpful to many advocates in criminal procedure later under Guided Democracy and the New Order. A strict orientation to formal law—or what some of his critics saw as rigidity in the extreme—became for Yap a matter of professional skill, ideological commitment, and political strategy.

Yap took his profession seriously and proudly, learning a great deal about practice from Lie Kian Kiem, Lie Hwee Yoe, and another Jakarta advocate with a social conscience and sense of public responsibility, Ting Swan Tiong. But from the start, he seemed to others to be willing to take remarkable risks, or at least to disregard personal interests. Thiam Hien was seldom if ever reckless, but he did insist on taking the letter of the law more seriously than many others who had a realistic appreciation of how legal institutions worked. Oei Tjoe Tat once told me that he began to understand his character when Yap was still living with Khing in the two-room house in Krekot, and Yap risked ever getting a better place by loudly challenging the city housing authority. Yap developed a reputation for putting himself forward in exactly this way, usually at greater risk than the housing authority could threaten, and he may have prided himself on the image of a lone fighter against improbable odds. Maybe, but simple principle figured importantly in his behavior and so did a temper that exploded as easily against unfairness as it did at times against personal slight. When he reacted, with intense focus on the issue he had defined, he seems seldom to have worried about odds and personal consequences. Nor was he easily cowed by authority as novel uncertainties of legal practice began to emerge.

Yap's peculiarly feisty legal style was apparent in several cases he took during the early 1950s, either for the law office or the legal bureau of the Sin Ming Hui. In one of the cases—a conflict over space between two stores that dragged on for twelve years—one store owner, rather than taking the issue to the housing authority, hired a policeman to represent him more efficiently. When Yap brought suit, the policeman tried to scare him off, which nearly led to a fight. It was the first of many clashes with the police. The same policeman picked up Yap's client and took him to the prosecution office, obviously intending to frighten him. (Police-prosecution collusion for extortion later became quite common.) Informed by the client's wife, Yap rushed to the office, where he was just in time to find the policeman and his prisoner getting out of a car. He demanded to see the warrant, which did not exist, and freed his client by threatening to bring a suit. Within a few years saving a client from extrajudicial harm would no longer be quite so easy.

In another case for the Sin Ming Hui bureau, Yap Thiam Hien and Lie Kian Kiem defended a man who sold soy sauce from a bicycle. For some reason, the man had been arrested and detained at a police post in Pasar Baru. This was in 1950, when a few Dutch police officials were still around. The soy sauce hawker had been beaten. Yap reported this breach to the chief investigator, a Dutch detective, who denied that his subordinates would do such a thing but promised to release the man if the allegation were proved. As Yap and Lie were leaving the station, a van drove up carrying prisoners returning from a local clinic, among whom was the unfortunate client—with a bandaged head. The Dutch police official, impressed by this evidence, agreed to release the man.

Another incident reflects both Yap's temperament and the reasonable judicial atmosphere that still prevailed shortly after independence. When Yap delivered his defense (*pleidooi*), he thought the judge had accused him of trying to whitewash a criminal. Insulted, Thiam Hien insisted on an apology. In chambers the judge, laughing, suggested that Yap had misinterpreted the remark and that perhaps he did not understand Indonesian well enough—by implication because he was Chinese—to which the incensed Yap replied that he could use Indonesian as well as the judge. The issue was settled amicably, not unusual then between judges and advocates.

Yap did not limit his aggressions to the police and prosecution, but occasionally he targeted his fellow professional advocates, whose faults he was sometimes quick to judge. A stickler for propriety, from the beginning, he was never able to accept any sort of sloppiness in practice, particularly when it damaged a client's interests. But he also at times went overboard in defending his own clients, to the extent of violating basic rules of professional etiquette. In a civil case in which he represented a poor man against the wealthier client of another Jakarta advocate, Gouw Giok Siong (Sudargo Gautama), Yap accused Gouw, in effect, of lacking a social conscience, a professional faux pas that nearly led to blows and left behind a bad taste on both sides. It was not Yap's last conflict with other advocates.

The incident is indicative of a complex side of Yap that is important to understand in assessing his work and stature. In professional advocacy Yap had found his métier. The law gave him a voice, which he proceeded to use passionately in just about everything he did, not only in court but also in church councils and in politics. But advocacy in itself, much as he enjoyed the law and took pride in his professional status, was never the end point and never enough for him. If he wanted to be known, really known—and he did—it was not simply as a good lawyer but as a reformer with the courage to pursue a vision against all odds. If Yap had a calling, he did not imagine it was in the practice of law but more in the service of significant social and political principles. What these principles were is best made clear in the context in which he fought them out. Basically, in the political field, they had to do with responsible and accountable *rechtsstaat*; in the social (and economic) field, with equality; and in the religious field, with Christian ethics, as he interpreted them. Advocacy was a means of making a living and a means to achieve these principles. If it were nothing more than a living and lacked the larger objective, the legal profession would have been hopelessly inadequate to his grander sense of purpose. This was what distinguished him from many other advocates, and it eventually associated him with the small group of ethnically diverse advocate-reformers who came to life in the New Order after 1965.

Yap's interest in reform and desire for personal significance is what impelled him beyond professional advocacy into public life. Outside the courtroom was the law; beyond the law, the political order; beyond his own church, the Protestant faith; beyond Protestantism, ecumenism; beyond ethnic Chinese identity, Indonesian citizenship; and so on in ever extending reach. During the early 1950s, however, his reach (outside of legal practice) stopped at the boundaries of ethnic Chinese society and the Chinese Protestant church. Within those limits, with which he was never altogether comfortable, he was extraordinarily active. Much of his energy went into church affairs. He held by his promise to the church to work voluntarily after he began to practice law. For a while he practiced law in the morning and served the church in the afternoon. Soon his name was known widely in church circles, for there were not many educated laymen ready to devote as much time to church affairs as Yap Thiam Hien. Indonesian Protestantism and the Chinese churches particularly were in need of leadership, which Yap offered, for the occupation and revolution had imposed sudden and dramatic changes on them from which there was no escape. In the mid-1950s Yap was appointed to the board of the Indonesian Council of Churches (Dewan Gereja Indonesia, DGI), established in May 1950 to promote unity among the numerous Protestant churches scattered in isolated pockets throughout the country. He was also involved in the educational work of his own West Javanese church. There and in the DGI, he made his presence felt through the organizational, moral, social, and political issues he raised, along with the fervent impatience with which he sometimes raised them.

Often he found himself as much at odds with the church and its theological and social tempers as he did with the state and its legal system. During the early 1950s, the Sin Ming Hui appointed him director of an orphanage in the Tanah Abang area of central Jakarta, which was managed by an old and devoted Christian woman. Yap rode his bicycle there in the late afternoon to check on things. Noticing that some of the children seemed malnourished, he thought he had an eminently sensible solution. He knew of a slaughterhouse called Merbabu managed by a socially conscious woman who often helped the Sin Ming Hui. Yap thought that the blood and other normally wasted parts of cows would be nutritious for the children. The manager of the slaughterhouse was willing to donate all this raw protein. Immediately, however, Yap and the orphanage *dominie*, who must have blanched at the idea, fell into a long argument, for the Old Testament, which the *dominie* urged Yap to read carefully, did not condone the consumption of blood and offal. Yap testily reminded the reverend of the existence of a New Testament and suggested that the danger was not in what went into the mouth but what came out of it. He lost. It did not improve his appreciation of the Old Testament, nor of the obstructive irrationalism that seemed to him to obscure the task of the churches.

In his own church there were quite different problems, both of organization and of Chinese Protestants' ability to adapt to a novel and demanding situation in the independent state. If Yap was never fully in tune with his church, he did play an important role in it. His legal skills and penchants helped, for he immediately set to studying the complex organizational layout of the Protestant churches, his own included. This equipped him to lead an effort to unify the churches.

Only gradually, however, could unification proceed, in part because of the traditional reluctance of Protestants to amalgamate. Chinese churches, though only those of Java that had originated from Hervormde Church (East and West Java) and Gereformeerde Church (Central Java) influence, were among the first to come together. More vulnerable than indigenous Christians, Chinese Christians were under more pressure to adapt to the new circumstances of independence. They gave up their churches' Chinese names, for one thing. Evidently the politically more sophisticated church leaders of East Java took the initiative in this connection. Yap's church, originally the Tiong Hoa Kie Tok Kauw Hwee became the Gereja Protestan Indonesia Jawa Barat (GPIB, Indonesian Protestant Church of West Java). General T. B. Simatupang, former commander of the Indonesian armed forces, proposed unification of the three provincial Protestant church affiliations that were largely Chinese. Simatupang, one of the most influential figures in Indonesian Protestantism and a moving force behind the DGI, belonged to the multiethnic but largely Chinese

Kwitang Church in Jakarta, associated with the Central Javanese churches. He and Yap, among others, pressed hard and successfully to bring about unification, which eventuated in a common synod, the "Sinode Am." The synod reflected a relatively rare occasion of agreement and collaboration between these two men, whose complex relationship was normally stormy.

Many of the difficulties Yap confronted in his own church arose less from a Protestant than a Chinese *peranakan* divide. From Yap's point of view, ethnic Chinese were programmed to be culturally too materialistic—a major epithet in his critical vocabulary—and insensitive to the needs of others. On the one hand, those who were wealthy and influential in the church constantly questioned the price of significant innovations that Yap and a few others thought necessary: for example, property acquisitions for the church or its schools or youth services. Every proposal required a struggle. On the other hand, many *peranakan* retained the sense, nurtured in the colonial hothouse, of superiority over and distance from ethnic Indonesians. This was as dangerous and foolish as it was hard to dilute. Most importantly for Yap, it led to violation of Christian norms.

Such a result, one that arose later in the 1950s, was the problematic relationship of the Chinese churches with poorer indigenous brethren in the Sundanese Protestant Church. After 1950, as the Indonesian churches withdrew from the authority of their protectors in Holland, all assets, including church buildings, schools, and related properties were turned over to the local churches themselves. One purpose was to protect the churches from any nationalist backlash against foreign influence, but the churches were now required to manage the properties and to develop their own institutional policies, for little of which Dutch tutelage had prepared them. Yap had ideas for helping the churches cope with their new independence. He successfully urged the schools of GPIB to incorporate into a foundation (whose articles he helped to draft), separate from the Church itself, insulating them from feared potential attacks on the Church. Education, as always, was a crucial issue for Chinese, and Yap's appointment as director of the church education committee was a measure of his stature.

But if Yap had useful technical solutions, he also came equipped with his own sense of Christian ethics, whose implications he addressed at every opportunity. The Church was debating how to handle an offer of property from the West Javanese indigenous church, the Gereja Pasundan. Much smaller than the GPIB, for Dutch missionaries had never succeeded in converting many Sundanese Muslims, the Gereja Pasundan received much less in the division of church assets. In Bandung, there was a small Gereja Pasundan church not far from a larger but still inadequate GPIB church. When the GPIB began to consider expanding its Bandung church and schools, the Sundanese church offered to sell a parcel of its land. Economically, this was a fine opportunity. Yap was opposed, however, and resorted to the parable of Lazarus: the problem of the poor man living next to a rich man. As Christians, he asked, how must you treat your neighbor who is so poor that, in his extremity, he offers to sell you his inheritance? Should you enrich yourselves at his expense? No, Yap insisted, you must, instead, help your poor brother so that he does not have to further impoverish himself. One can imagine the puzzled reaction of the businessmen in his church, but the church council and synod evidently understood and supported Yap. Eventually, in the mid-1960s, after he had already left the chair of the education committee, the Gereja Keristen Indonesia (GKI, Indonesian Christian Church, all-Java successor to the GPIB and other provincial Javanese churches) bought all of the land, but paid enough to allow the Gereja Pasundan church to buy a larger lot for itself. This solution, Yap agreed, was a kind of Christian trade-off based on fellowship.[18]

There were many similar or related problems that Yap took on later, and issues of reform that he would not let go. For all the years that he was active in the church, until the mid-1960s, he could always be found in the middle of a fracas, and in moments of contrition he blamed himself for being too intransigent, too hard. A Dutch minister once told him that he was too arrogant, and Yap took it to heart, but he could not soften his temper, as he admitted, and would not abandon principles that made him what he was.

Yap's intense involvement during the early 1950s in the advocacy, in the Sin Ming Hui, and in the church prepared him for a plunge into politics. The work in these three arenas attuned him to social issues, and those, in independent Indonesia, were also inevitably political issues, and, as he increasingly saw them, issues of human rights.

SIX

HAZARDOUS WATERS

FROM the time of Yap Thiam Hien's return to Jakarta until the mid-1960s, the two passions that most absorbed his energy were the church and *peranakan* politics. His church work lent him enough prominence to represent Protestant interests politically, although only in ethnic Chinese circles. Unlike several others in the Chinese community, including his law partner Tan Po Goan, he did not have the contacts to roam beyond the implicit ghetto lines inscribed by colonial history. But his activity in the church and in the Sin Ming Hui fashioned a habit of involvement and reflected an orientation toward—or more than that, a wish for—public life, as much as possible at the center of things. The political engagement of his colleagues Tan Po Goan and Oei Tjoe Tat may have encouraged him. He set a course of his own, however, without a map and in stormy times.

In this chapter Yap will recede slightly into the background while we explore some dimensions of the arena into which he strode with typical élan and profound unfamiliarity. With hindsight, of course, it is easy to spot the serious dangers for the Chinese minority in the independent state, but at the time little of this was obvious. The complexity of this arena requires some mapping, exploring popular prejudices as well as political realities.

After 1945, and even more so after 1950, once the Dutch withdrew, the minority whom they had despised but also sheltered out of mutual interest now stood quite naked. About 2.5 percent of the population, the Chinese community in all its variety—*totok, peranakan,* rich and poor, Confucian, Taoist, Protestant, Catholic, urban and rural, of Javanese or Sumatran or other origins—was ill prepared to deal with the new situation. It had been peculiarly shaped—or, as some might argue, deformed—by its experience in the Netherlands-Indies. Colonial law had divided the population of the colony into defined racial segments: Europeans, Natives, and Foreign Orientals. Those in the last category, including Arabs, Indians, Japanese (until early in the century), and Chinese, were in effect classified as outsiders, only a special few of whom, like Yap's father, could escape into European legal status. Racial categories became an inherent part of the way the people of the colony thought of themselves, as "prescribed" hardened into "ascribed" status. Where the Chinese were confined to trade as much as possible (partly an intended result of colonial policy), some became wealthy and learned to defend their wealth. Those educated in Chinese schools, whether their own or those provided by the colonial administration, took their group identity for granted. The majority remained socially apart from Indonesians, and some, absorbing the attitudes of the ruling Dutch, were contemptuous of Indonesians, an attitude that did not suddenly change when the relations of political power were turned upside down.

This attitude was part of a colonial heritage that was no easier for ethnic Chinese to shed than it was for Indonesians to see through the haze of myth that surrounded far more complex Chinese realities. The depression, the Japanese occupation, and the revolution had, to varying degrees, punished the entire population—the Dutch colonials, the *totok,* the *peranakan,* the "native" Indonesians—and yet, after the transfer of sovereignty in late 1949, old antagonisms toward presumed Chinese wealth survived. In some ways, once the Dutch began to withdraw, the Chinese became the principal living symbol of a devastating colonial heritage, far overshadowing (and diverting attention from) the less significant minorities of Eurasians, Arabs, Indians, and even the Dutch who had been left temporarily behind in charge of a few agencies and enterprises. For many ethnic Indonesians, the variety of Chinese life somehow disappeared behind the resentful conviction that Chinese were Chinese and therefore rich, exclusive, self-serving, and un-Indonesian.

These old prejudices and fears whispered in the background when in mid-1945 the Japanese set up an investigative commission to prepare for Indonesian independence and to draft a constitution.[1] When it came to matters affecting the minority, considerable hedging was evident among both the Indonesian and the four *peranakan* representatives in this body.

One such issue was the incorporation of a racial qualification into two key articles. The original draft of Article 6 provided that the president must be both Muslim and indigenous Indonesian. The argument that the religious stipulation was unnecessary, as the Islamic majority would elect a Muslim president anyway and that the provision would alienate non-Muslims, led to its removal from the final draft. But the ethnic/racial qualification remained, though exactly the same reasoning should have applied. Yap Tjwan Bing, the one *peranakan* representative present at the session of the preparatory commission that dealt with this issue, evidently raised no objection.[2]

Another article, number 26, raised for the first time the citizenship issue, which would be an intermittent threat to the *peranakan* community for the next fifteen years. Article 26 provided that "citizens" meant indigenous (*asli*) Indonesians and others legalized (*disahkan*) as citizens by statute. Originally, Professor Supomo, very influential in drafting the first constitution, had proposed to make citizens outright of all *peranakan* Chinese, Arabs, Europeans, and others. But a major reason for the final wording was that *peranakan* members of the commission were divided on the issue, as Soekarno pointed out a bit testily. Two favored Indonesian citizenship with a right of repudiation, while two others preferred Chinese citizenship.[3] Nevertheless, a few months after the Proclamation of Independence on 17 August 1945, the first law of citizenship conferred citizenship automatically on Chinese unless they specifically repudiated it.

If the revolutionary government was conciliatory toward Chinese, this was much less true of extra-government initiatives around the country. The signals from revolutionary forces were, therefore, distinctly ambiguous. On the one hand, republican leaders, for reasons both political and ideological, local and international, encouraged the Chinese minority to believe that discrimination would not be countenanced, and the new law of citizenship seemed to confirm their intentions. On the other hand, local populations and roving bands of revolutionary youth (*pemuda*) set off murderous anti-Chinese attacks in Medan, Tanggerang, and elsewhere. Violence was not general, but it did confirm the worst fears of many Chinese. Some responded with the *pao an tui* self-defense corps. That its initial purposes may well have been self-defense did not soften the fact that the *pao an tui* was collaborationist.[4] Some local *peranakan* groups, especially in East Java, actively opposed the *pao an tui*, but the widespread impression was that Chinese supported it and opposed the revolution. In fact, Chinese responses to the revolution varied widely under contrary pressures, enticements, local conditions, and perceptions of the odds. Some foolishly spoke out against it; in 1947 the Chinese Lawyers' Association in Jakarta urgently cabled the United Nations Security Council to oppose recognition of Indonesian independence.[5] A frightened few turned their backs on the Republic and their faces toward either Holland or China. Some, in Dutch-occupied cities, supported the revolution as best they could, contributing money and even smuggling supplies for the fighters. And some fought on the side of the Republic. Most simply looked on apprehensively from the sidelines in Dutch or Republican territory, adjusting their behavior accordingly.[6]

Following the transfer of sovereignty in late 1949 up to 1954–55, violent anti-Chinese incidents were rare. Why was the marked minority allowed such breathing space?

Of the four major parties then—the Nationalists (PNI), the "modernist" Islamic Masyumi, the "traditionalist" Islamic Nahdlatul Ulama, and the Communists (PKI)—the PNI and Masyumi, representing the political center, more or less dominated all parliamentary cabinets during the first six years of the Republic. Neither had an interest in allowing anti-Chinese sentiment to break out into the open. The leaders of both parties, well-educated professionals by and large, were committed to maintaining legal process and the legitimacy of the law-state; the *negara hukum* would have suffered from out-and-out discrimination or public violence of any sort.[7] Financial contributions from ethnic Chinese found their way into party treasuries, particularly that of the PNI, but no doubt of other parties as well. To the extent that the parties lacked their own well-established entrepreneurial sources of support, they relied, when possible, on Chinese funds. The same was true elsewhere in Southeast Asia, wherever ethnic minorities, whether Indians in Burma or Chinese, made up substantial segments of local entrepreneurial middle classes. For a minority, funding a party or two meant both influence and protection.

Although colonial policy and structure had done everything possible to separate Chinese from Indonesians, it had not succeeded completely. As we have seen through the lens of Yap Thiam Hien's life, wealthy and high-status Chinese and Indonesians, Dutch-speaking among themselves, were the first groups to take advantage of privileged colonial education in the ELS, HBS, and AMS schools and in the universities in Batavia and Holland. If the young people sometimes kept their distance from one another for nationalist reasons, they also had a good deal in common and were capable of developing both personal and professional relationships. After independence, those connections would bear political fruit.

The PNI best represented the Javanese social elite, in both its older bureaucratic and newer professional aspects. Some of its leaders had ties to Chinese entrepreneurial circles predating independence. Generally PNI leaders tended not to be overtly prejudiced against Chinese, and some were more than politely sympathetic. Sartono, the PNI speaker of Parliament, for example, had a close personal relationship with Siauw Giok Tjhan, the chair of the *peranakan* organization Baperki, whose leftist commitments did not interfere with their friendship. It is worth pointing out that many politicians in this ideologically defined multi-party system mixed easily with one another across the ideological spectrum. Sartono's brother-in-law, for instance, was a member of the politburo of the Communist Party.

Elsewhere in the party world, relationships with the Chinese minority were less familiar and more tenuous. The PKI alone took a strong ideological stand against ethnic prejudice of any kind.[8] In the Islamic parties, religious issues sometimes promoted anti-Chinese attitudes, but the long-time commercial competition between Islamic and Chinese entrepreneurs may have been a more significant provocation. Yet for a time at least, Masyumi leaders were able to tone down public antagonism, partly out of concern to preserve order and stability, but maybe also because they were not overly bigoted themselves. The same was true of the intellectually influential leadership of the Socialist Party (PSI), as well as of the Protestant Parkindo and the Catholic Party, all of which had ethnic Chinese members. As a general rule, but one requiring caution, the more highly educated the leadership, the more likely it was to be in touch with similarly educated *peranakan* and the less likely to be openly hostile to minority Chinese. At least it would be more likely to want to contain ethnic conflict. Exceptions abounded, however.

Lower down the social-economic-political pyramid, ethnic relationships were more volatile and unpredictable. Some who were in direct competition with Chinese commerce had expected that the revolution would end Chinese "advantage" and became frustrated by the lack of substantial change; they blamed Chinese wealth for continuing exploitation and corruption and Chinese "exclusivity" for arrogantly challenging national solidarity and dignity. Long-suppressed social and economic dissatisfactions had been liberated and mobilized by the revolution. Disadvantaged groups were incorporated into the parties or were represented in other institutions—the army, for a prominent example—or were unrepresented but available for ad hoc mobilization. State leadership could not easily ignore their demands and sensitivities.

What no cabinet could do, even if it wanted to take the risk, was to prevent completely an accumulation of incidents and pressures directed against Chinese business and citizenry. Nothing short of the massive economic, political, and social change that many talked about but no one had the funds and imagination to undertake could have avoided an irate turning on the obvious ethnic Chinese presence. That these incidents were not violent, or very little so, was largely a function of the government's willingness and ability to absorb public pressure and implement policies that satisfied anti-Chinese demands just enough to avoid extreme measures. After the 1955 parliamentary elections, when the political parties began their decline, the leadership's restraining influence over anti-Chinese sentiment dissipated. Most seriously of all, the question of Chinese citizenship was reopened.

The threat to the automatic right to citizenship forced Chinese organizations to face their own internal divisions and weaknesses. Collectively, ethnic Chinese political experience was meager. While the great majority had always shunned politics, the few with political knowledge and will remained divided along the fault lines within the community itself. Before we return to Yap Thiam Hien's plunge into these deep waters, we should look at some distinctions that shaped ethnic Chinese politics, before and in the period following the transfer of sovereignty.

Although outsiders regarded the ethnic Chinese community as an undifferentiated solidarity, in fact cleavages ran deep and naturally produced equally deep political differences. By the time of the revolution, it has been estimated, 70 percent of the ethnic Chinese residents in Indonesia were locally born, since immigration had slowed during the 1930s and then come to a stop. But the proportion of *totok*-minded was higher than 30 percent and carried a good deal of economic weight and the advantage of cultural clarity; some *peranakan* had undergone a process of *totok*-ization as the result of their education during and after the occupation in schools where Chinese was either the medium of instruction or was emphasized.[9] But even among Chinese-speaking *totok*, as among *peranakan*, there were serious differences over their orientations to Communist or Nationalist China after 1949. Among *peranakan*, by and large, the only common political denominator was uncertainty: about their relationship to the revolutionary Republic, to the Dutch, to the independent state; about their status as citizens, their tense relationship with *totok* Chinese, how best to defend themselves, whether to organize and along what lines, and who would provide leadership.

The structure of *peranakan* politics was a microcosm of that of Indonesia generally.[10] As the Javanese heartland dominates Indonesia, so Javanese *peranakan* have dominated ethnic Chinese politics, only more so. It is not merely a matter of numbers—Java contains about 65 percent of the total Indonesian population and 50 percent of the ethnic Chinese population—but of organization, sophistication, experience, and influence.[11] Within Java, provincial differences were no less important, subtle, and complex in *peranakan* than in Indonesian politics. As Chinese absorbed local culture, they took on local political tendencies and habits as well.

West Java may be something of an exception. There, *peranakan* leaders tended to eschew cultural absorption, preferring distance and conservative quietude. Siauw Giok Tjhan has argued that the conservatism of the Chinese elite in West Java was largely an effect of economic history; their ownership of plantation estate land had made Chinese elite and Dutch interests identical. The heavier presence of colonial authority in the region, moreover, made close contact with the Dutch a necessity.[12] Perhaps more consequential for keeping Chinese distant from local culture was the strength of Islam among the Sundanese (in the province's highlands), the Betawi (around Jakarta), and the Bantenese (in the westernmost part of the province).

In Central and East Java, by contrast, established *peranakan* families had long been closely connected with local elites, initially partly through the medium of credit supplied by Chinese opium farmers to Javanese and Dutch officials through the end of the nineteenth century.[13] But the nexus was not merely financial. Business relations often cemented more intimate social connections between notable Chinese and Javanese families. These relationships became reasonably comfortable and routine, helped by the gradual cultural absorption of Chinese and the absence of economic competition between the two groups until early in the twentieth century. Almost by definition, *peranakan* culture is made up substantially of local culture, making *peranakan* vulnerable to the derisive *totok* accusation that they had gone native.[14] Javanese *peranakan* spoke Javanese, listened to Javanese music, partook of Javanese rites and celebrations, mixed with Javanese of like social station and environment, and took to local style, demeanor, and thought—not entirely, but enough to distinguish them from *peranakan* elsewhere. In these circles intermarriage was not unusual.[15]

Of the two Javanese provinces, Central Java has in general been the more socially conservative and politically cautious; East Java, the more socially and economically dynamic and politically freewheeling. The reasons may have to do in part with the influence of the royal principalities of Surakarta and Yogyakarta in Central Java, on the one hand, and the more varied population mix of East Java and the commercial liveliness of its capital city, Surabaya, on the other. In any case, the *peranakan* communities of the two regions followed suit. In Central Java the huge and powerful Oei Tiong Ham firm of Semarang dominated Chinese commerce and firmly negotiated its conflicts with Dutch entrepreneurs. Politically, the Chung Hua Hui and the Sin Po group, the first more or less oriented to the Dutch establishment and the other to Chinese nationalism, were most influential.

In East Java, where President Soekarno was raised and started his political education, Surabaya, Indonesia's second largest city after Jakarta, produced some of the stormiest confrontations between Chinese and Dutch economic interests in the colonial period. Surabayan *peranakan* were also the source of notable challenges to Dutch social prerogatives and of the most radical turns of *peranakan* political thought. The Partai Tionghoa Indonesia (PTI), organized there in 1932, was oriented politically to Indonesian nationalism and even defeated the local Chung Hwa Hui (CHH) in an election to the Volksraad, the colonial era People's Council.[16] Out of East Java came the most experienced and toughest political leadership in the *peranakan* universe—because of its revolutionary credentials, the only group well positioned to make its way in the new state. In the first battle of the revolution, when the people of Surabaya rose up against an English occupying force in November 1945, a Surabayan, Siauw Giok Tjhan, organized a small force of Angkatan Muda Tionghoa (Chinese Youth Front) to join the fight on the side of the Republic.[17] Then, still early in the revolution, a number of *peranakan* leaders from East Java, most prominently Siauw himself, trooped off to Yogyakarta to join the Republic. Siauw, not surprisingly, would become the leader of Baperki, the largest and most effective *peranakan* political organization in post-independence Indonesia. And, not foreordained but also not surprising, Baperki would be heavily influenced by the East Javanese *peranakan* political style.

In Dutch-occupied Jakarta and other major cities, Chinese politics consisted largely of thrashing around in search of a useful organizational format and appropriate leaders. When the Japanese occupation ended, a federation of existing Chinese associations, the Chung Hua Tsung Hui (CHTH), succeeded a similar organization, the Hua Ch'iao Tsung Hui, set up by the Japanese.[18] Pro-republican *peranakan* were active in it, and it was recognized by republican leaders as the principal organization of the minority and a source of financial support.[19] The CHTH brought together *totok* and *peranakan*, but in a spurious unity that soon fell apart over the issue of language. *Totok* leaders insisted on Mandarin, which to many *peranakan* made little sense, literally but also symbolically. By 1948 the CHTH was in mid-collapse as *peranakan* associations pulled out.[20]

One of the most important organizations for the evolution of ethnic Chinese politics was the non-political service organization Sin Ming Hui (SMH, New Light Association), established in Jakarta in 1946 to deal with community problems. It attracted older leaders from pre-war organizations, both CHH and PTI, but also many highly educated younger men in search of significant roles to play. Among them was the able young Oei Tjoe Tat, then politically unattached but knowledgeable and interested, who quickly rose to the top of the organization. Yap Thiam Hien, attached otherwise only to the church, also joined. The Sin Ming Hui somehow contained pro-Dutch, anti-Dutch, pro-Republic, and neutral elements, all in agreement on the obligation to serve Chinese needs.

Harboring much of the *peranakan* leadership that was not in the republican capital of Yogyakarta, the SMH fed into most of the political organizations founded during and after the revolutionary period. The first such organization was the Persatuan Tionghoa (PT, Chinese Union), which emerged from the Jakarta SMH in May 1948. At the same time, the SMH itself broke with the CHTH, organizationally cleaving *totok* from *peranakan*.[21] The PT was chaired by Thio Thiam Tjong, a respected Semarang businessman and former Chung Hwa Hui leader who had been detained in a Japanese camp, where he studied Mandarin, and for a time after 1945 served as an advisor to Dutch Lieutenant Governor-General H. van Mook.[22] Politically he was, therefore, not exactly a wise choice, but at the time many hoped that association with the Dutch might still lend them protection.

In the uncertain period before the transfer of sovereignty, the PT began to stake out defensive positions for the minority. It argued that in any independent state there must be equality for all, regardless of race, religion, or language.[23] It supported the Dutch-sponsored federal structure, assuming federalism would allow the Dutch more influence and the ethnic Chinese more room for maneuver. Finally accepting that the Dutch would have no influence in an independent Indonesia, it embraced the idea that a parliamentary government was in the best interests of the Chinese minority, which might have effective representation in it.

Federalism was thrown out within a year of independence, and the Provisional Constitution of 1950 did establish a parliamentary government and guaranteed Chinese, European,[24] and Arab minorities nine, six, and three parliamentary seats, respectively. With the revolution over and the parliamentary system in place, the question of how ethnic Chinese should act politically became critically important, though there was no clear answer. The PT was organized as exclusively Chinese in membership and concerns, which most Chinese probably thought an obvious course. But joining it appealed little to the majority of *peranakan*, who were still suspicious of political activities of any sort. It appealed even less to the engaged pro-republican center and left. Among them, the PT was regarded as either pro-Dutch or neutral, with its base essentially in the old Chung Hwa Hui.

In February 1950, less than two months after the transfer of sovereignty in late December 1949, Liem Koen Hian, the father of the pre-war PTI, dismissed the PT as politically naive, incompetent to deal with the myriad problems *peranakan* now faced, and lacking the imagination to work effectively with the ethnic Indonesian majority.[25] He established the Persatuan Tenaga Indonesia (Union of Indonesian Forces), known as the New-PTI, explicitly rejecting ethnic definition and encapsulation and identifying with the larger Indonesian universe.[26] In March the PT changed its name, without regrouping in any way, to the Partai Demokrat Tionghoa Indonesia (PDTI, Chinese Democratic Party of Indonesia), reasserting its view that *peranakan* Chinese must organize as Chinese. In effect, the pre-war groupings of Chung Hua Hui and Partai Tionghoa Indonesia had re-emerged in slightly different form, in much the same way as the major national parties established during the revolution picked up from their pre-war pieces.

Neither the New-PTI nor the PDTI drew much support, though the PDTI was probably better known. But it was less in tune with the changing times and came to grief over the issue of whether *peranakan* Chinese should organize exclusive of ethnic Indonesians. (Both parties and other local associations excluded *totok*, allowing only citizens to join.) Some members were outspoken in their opposition, but the PDTI chairman Thio Thiam Tjong and his close associate Khoe Woen Sioe remained unshakeable in the belief that Chinese had no choice but to organize alone.[27]

During the revolution and in the early post-sovereignty period, a small group of *peranakan* leaders, largely from the pre-war left, sought to integrate Chinese into mainstream politics. No longer excluded by most major national parties as they had been in the colony,[28] some joined political parties—mainly the Nationalists (PNI) or Socialists (PSI) or Communists (PKI). Among them, Tan Ling Djie was secretary-general of the PKI from 1949 to 1953; Siauw Giok Tjhan (much influenced ideologically by Tan) was closely connected to the PKI though not a member; Ong Eng Die, just returned from Holland, and the pharmacist Yap Tjwan Bing of the CHTH joined the PNI; and Tan Po Goan (Yap's law firm partner) belonged to the PSI.[29] Eventually a few dissident PT–PDTI leaders, who belonged to national parties, argued that if *peranakan* actively participated in major parties, they could more directly defend their interests. In most major parties—the PNI, PKI, PSI, Parkindo (Protestants), Partai Katolik, and even in the Islamic Nahdlatul Ulama—there were well-known Chinese leaders who were not about to retreat to a ghetto party.

Neither side won the debate, but the argument, though ideologically important, was largely beside the political point. The point, as some understood perfectly well, was that the minority Chinese were wholly dependent on the majority now in control of the state. Ethnic Chinese who joined the major parties never had much influence in them, but an all-Chinese political party also could not have developed substantial influence in the political system. Either way, they could not mobilize enough power to make a difference. It was possible for individuals and groups to buy protection and influence, and the Indonesian leadership was not lacking in good will and a sense of responsibility toward the minority. But the political resources of the Chinese were distinctly limited.

Just how limited they were became clearer after the transfer of sovereignty, when the inadequately organized Chinese minority had to deal with growing discrimination. At one level, Chinese were subjected to pressure from various quarters for financial contributions, often in the form of a protection racket, but also in corrupt exchange for normal government services. It was this that Yap's brother had heard about in Holland when he decided not to return home. There were also occasional street incidents and petty harassments, as ethnic Indonesians expressed their resentment at perceived Chinese wealth and advantage, and some ethnic Chinese proved incapable of recognizing that conditions had changed.

At another and potentially more dangerous level were the escalating public policy attacks in areas of overwhelming importance to *peranakan*—citizenship, education, and the security of Chinese business. The community was badly shaken by political noises about transferring financial and entrepreneurial resources to ethnic Indonesians; these would become loud and clear in 1956 when the politician and businessman, Assaat, demanded economic policies that would explicitly favor ethnic Indonesians over Chinese, citizens or not.[30] The actual policies, as they evolved, did not fundamentally damage Chinese-owned commerce, but there was no way of knowing that they would not.

The problem of education, so important to *peranakan* families, generated quite as much uncertainty and anxiety. The few national universities soon began to impose informal quotas on the admission of Chinese students. Exclusively Chinese schools came under pressure as no longer appropriate in independent Indonesia. In the background was the racial streaming of colonial schools, reinforced during the Japanese occupation when schools in which the language of instruction was Dutch were eliminated and *peranakan* children who had attended them were thrown together with *totok* children in Chinese medium schools.[31] Not altogether out of prejudice, Indonesian educational planners argued for common national education for all children, with emphases on Indonesian language, history, and related nation-building curricula. But many *peranakan*, otherwise willing to give up Chinese language instruction, distrusted the quality of national public schools and may have doubted the wisdom of sending their children to school with Indonesian children. In any case, there were not enough government schools to go around. In Parliament and in the cabinet, rhetorical attacks on Chinese "exclusivity" and on the continued existence of separate Chinese schools escalated.

The question of citizenship was the most fundamental and soul-rattling of all issues, for it went to the very heart of *peranakan* identity and vulnerability. Immediately and painfully, the *peranakan* faced questions of belonging, security, and loyalties.[32] The issue was made all the more complex by colonial law, which had rendered the status of "Foreign Orientals" ambiguously as "subjects," and by the legal claim of China that all Chinese, wherever born, were its citizens.[33] The republican statute of 1946, as we have seen, and the Round Table Conference arrangements of 1949, providing for the transfer of sovereignty, advantageously accorded citizenship automatically to all those born and resident in Indonesia, unless they specifically rejected it. This position did not resolve the claim of Chinese law, which, under the *jus sanguinis* rule, automatically gave Indonesian citizens of Chinese descent dual nationality. Citizenship status became particularly fraught as political pressure, rooted in anti-Chinese animus, demanded that the "passive" system of 1946 and 1949 be transformed into an "active" method requiring formal espousal. By 1953 the possibility of this reversal was much in the air as Parliament considered a draft law on citizenship. Provisions in the draft bill were especially onerous. For example, the applicant for citizenship would have to prove that his or her family had been resident in Indonesia for at least three generations, and the applicant would have only one year after the promulgation of the law to reject Chinese nationality and opt for Indonesian citizenship.

Peranakan anxiety escalated as the government prepared for the Non-Aligned Conference in Bandung in 1955, where China and Indonesia might resolve the question of dual nationality. In late 1954 in Beijing and early 1955 in Jakarta, the two governments negotiated the issues. According to Donald Willmott:

> the Chinese delegation was originally willing to recognize the *status quo* as to the citizenship of Chinese in Indonesia. That is, they would have been willing to draw up a treaty in which China would renounce its claim to all Peranakans who had become Indonesian citizens under the Act of 1946 or the Round Table Agreement. It was the Indonesian side which insisted on a new round of opting, this time according to the active system. This was consistent with the Government's desire to have as citizens only those Chinese who would be willing to make an official and public declaration repudiating their Chinese citizenship.[34]

On 22 April 1955, near the end of the Bandung Conference, a treaty was signed. It applied only to those with dual nationality, not ethnic Chinese who had rejected Indonesian citizenship during the revolutionary years. This meant that all who had been automatically recognized as citizens under the "passive" rules must now specifically declare their intention to remain Indonesian citizens by rejecting Chinese citizenship. Adults were given two years to act, minors one year after they married or reached eighteen years of age. Husbands and wives had to apply independently.[35]

Public reactions to the treaty demonstrated clearly enough that there was no unanimity, not among ethnic Indonesians and not among ethnic Chinese. Nationalists (PNI) and Communists (PKI) supported the new rules, while the Islamic party Masyumi, the Socialists (PSI), Catholics, Protestants, and a few other smaller parties objected on constitutional or moral or related human rights grounds that imposing the "active" choice rule was unfair to ethnic Chinese who had already been recognized as citizens. Jusuf Wibisono of Masyumi called attention to the fact that many Indonesian citizens, ethnic Chinese, might well be lost to Indonesia if they neglected to register—an easy thing to do for lack of public records and private information. He also pointed out that registration of a million or so citizens would be administratively complex, and presciently mentioned the likelihood of corruption in the process.[36]

Reactions within the Chinese community were equally varied and certainly more anxious and confused. As Willmott notes, many regarded the treaty as substantially better than the Parliament's earlier draft law, but still troublesome. Cold war issues intruded as some sympathetic to Communist China supported the treaty, while anti-Communists attacked it. Still others, who were not particularly pro-Communist but felt proud of Chinese achievements, could fall either way. The daily *Keng Po*, according to Willmott, opposed the treaty, arguing that "revoking the Indonesian citizenship of peranakans who failed to repudiate Chinese citizenship would create a serious problem of 'displaced persons.'"[37] "Two weeks later," Willmott wrote, "Mr. Yap Thiam Hin [sic], a leading figure in Chinese Protestants circles and an officer of BAPERKI, gave an even more alarming picture of the possible consequences of the treaty." According to the *Keng Po* report,

> Mr. Yap . . . stated his opinion that the methods proposed in the treaty would have grave social consequences, which could even endanger the stability and security of Indonesia itself. He believed that 80% of the people of Chinese descent, who had already become Indonesian citizens, would now be "uprooted" like displaced persons, because without knowing it they would become foreigners or stateless persons if the treaty were ratified. Their livelihood, judging from the fact that even as citizens it had been interfered with and made difficult, would become even harder, and this might raise criminality, etc. Where would they be sent—those hundreds of thousands of farmers in Tangerang, Bekasi, Bangka, Kalimantan, etc. who, as foreigners or stateless persons would no longer be able to cultivate the soil because of the difficulty of getting land or because their right to rent land would have been snatched away?[38]

Others were softer spoken and more diplomatic in their objections, but the widespread uproar was enough to persuade the parliamentary leadership, led by Prime Minister Ali Sastroamidjojo, to reconsider the treaty, not least because it might be rejected by Parliament. In early June 1955 in Beijing, the Chinese and Indonesian prime ministers exchanged notes that, in effect, amended the treaty. One clarification was that when the twenty-year term of the treaty ended, no one who had opted for citizenship would be required to do so again.[39]Another, oddly, referred to a "certain group" that would be exempted from the "active" rules and would be considered Indonesian citizens without further action. According to Willmott,

> When the text of the notes was released, this provision aroused a storm of comment and speculation as to who would or should be included among those paradoxical persons of dual nationality having only one nationality. Newspapers went to their "informed sources" and "sources near to

> the Cabinet" and found out that before the Prime Minister left for China the Cabinet had discussed this problem, probably at the insistence of the Minister of Health, Lie Kiat Teng, who flatly refused to submit himself to another option procedure. The sources agreed that it had been decided that Chinese-descent Cabinet Ministers, Members of Parliament, and members of the Police and Armed Forces would be released from the obligation of opting again. Beyond this, most sources agreed that all other government employees would also be exempted, while one source went so far as to mention all registered voters of Chinese descent. None of these reports was confirmed by the Government, however, and no further clarification was made.[40]

Those who opposed any requirement of new options promptly argued the case based on these revelations. Siauw Giok Tjhan, representing the *peranakan* organization Baperki, insisted that China left it up to the Indonesian government to determine who should have citizenship, and that Parliament should, in effect, reinstate the validity of the "passive" rules. The PSI soon agreed.[41] Parliament did nothing further on the matter, however, because of the upcoming national elections. But the parliamentary discussions and the apparently responsive changes in the ministerial notes perhaps reveal that constitutional principles and a concern to maintain legal process did count for a good deal among Indonesia's political leadership. The treaty was finally ratified in December 1957, at a time when the parliamentary order, for all intents and purposes, had collapsed. It was not actually implemented until January of 1960.[42]

A tendency to lump aliens and citizens together, denying *peranakan*s a distinction critical to their identity as Indonesians, did not disappear, regardless of the passage of the treaty or its amendments or government promises. If such a distinction was conceded, it came with an asterisk. *Peranakan* citizens commonly were (and still are) referred to as WNI (*Warganegara Indonesia*, Indonesian citizen) or as *warga negara keturunan asing* (citizen of foreign descent) or simply *keturunan* (descent), all of which served to distinguish them from *asli* (original, native) or *bumiputra* or in time *pribumi*, both meaning "native." Chinese themselves used the marker WNI or *keturunan* to indicate a *peranakan*, not always obvious in the case of those who adopted Indonesian names.

Discriminatory pressures on the *peranakan* also were unaffected. They continued for the next several decades, through changes in the law and regulations, creating frequent anxieties, inconveniences, expenses, and uncertainties for citizens who were of Chinese descent. The tensions and schisms in the community, particularly between *totok* and *peranakan*, were no less intractable. One has to wonder how many *peranakan* opted for Chinese citizenship because they could not see a way out of too many dilemmas.[43]

The issues in which Thiam Hien had a special interest were painful and hard. As a former teacher, he had a deep-felt involvement in education and was active on this issue within his church. As a lawyer, it was his concern with the question of citizenship that brought him into Chinese politics beyond that of the Chinese church and eventually into the larger arena of Indonesian politics. Along with several other *peranakan* lawyers in the major cities of Java, he began to publish comments on the conundrums of the law of citizenship.

In 1951, in what may have been his first published article on a legal issue for the *peranakan* journal *Star Weekly*, he addressed the question of passive or active espousal of citizenship. Yap took issue with another lawyer, Gouw Soei Tjiang, over the status of a fictive "Bong A Kew," whose problem was a common one. The question was whether Bong A Kew, born in Indonesia in 1940 of parents who were subjects of China, was an alien or citizen after the transfer of sovereignty. Gouw had argued that he was an alien. Yap replied with a careful analysis of the Round Table Conference agreements, demonstrating that, unless Bong A Kew's parents had specifically rejected Indonesian citizenship in his behalf, he was a citizen with his own right to opt for other legal status. Gouw was persuaded and wrote so in *Star Weekly*.[44] Yap's first article was reprinted in mid-July 1954, when Minister of Justice Djody Gondokusumo and others took the view that "Bong A Kew" was an alien. Enjoying the prominence his article received, Yap continued to write on this subject for various *peranakan* publications.

As we shall see in chapter 7, the birth of the *peranakan* organization Baperki gave him another platform from which to attack, among other targets, the dual nationality treaty drafted after the Bandung Conference in 1955. Yap would be far more outspokenly critical than was the official position of Baperki, which supported the Ali Sastroamidjojo cabinet and was sympathetic to the Chinese government. Characteristically, Yap paid little attention to the prudent politics of the issue. In the requirement that *peranakan* must formally revoke Chinese citizenship or lose their Indonesian citizenship, Yap saw only the potential for tragedy.

SEVEN

AT SEA IN *PERANAKAN* POLITICS

THE title of this chapter has a double meaning, connoting in part a political journey but also Yap's bewilderment along the way. His involvement in Baperki lasted about seven years, from early 1954 through late 1960, a period of intense learning, conflict, and testing of his own character.

In 1957 the family moved from Krekot to the house in ethnically mixed Grogol. In his forties and in energetic good health, Yap poured himself into politics. Khing and his young son, Hong Gie, and daughter, Hong Ay, saw little of him, but on occassion Yap unloaded at home the extraordinary stress of these years in explosions of rage and temper that Khing somehow handled as another item of household administration. His public life took precedence. His passion for punctuality and correctness often imposed unreasonable demands on his wife. They had only one car, which they drove themselves, and the unavoidable conflicts between doctors' appointments for the children and Thiam Hien's law practice or church responsibilities or political meetings were only one source of friction.

In public Yap channeled his reservoir of anger into passionate displays of principle. Although he could be moved by factual and logical argument, he was inclined to operate from general principles, usually unshakeable. This led many who dealt with him to suppose that his character was shaped principally by his religion, or, in a stereotype variation, by his Achenese-ness. But Yap fit none of the molds into which admirers and detractors tried to squeeze him. Had he been less sui generis, it might have been easier to contain him, but no one, either in the church or Baperki, ever really figured him out. Yap was not exactly a loose cannon, but he was a solitary field piece, loaded with personal courage, over which no one else had much control.

With hindsight, it seems obvious that he would drift politically toward opposition in one form or another, partly because the role of critic came easily to him, but also because he had few of the resources necessary for a successful career as a political leader in the *peranakan* community: experience, connections, and the kind of personality commonly recognized as appealing, even necessary, in a leader. When he did enter the world of *peranakan* politics it was obliquely, from the church and the Sin Ming Hui's legal aid committee, where he had made a name for himself as responsible and hard-working, with strong if rigid opinions.

Yap was naturally aware of the immediate post-independence developments among the Chinese political groups, outlined in chapter 6. He read the press avidly and followed political gossip in his law office, but he joined none of the political organizations—not the PT, the PDTI, or the New-PTI, nor even the PSI or the Parkindo (Protestants), the only two national parties for which he had any ideological affinity. He could not submit to party positions with which he disagreed. Nor could he accept the current standards of political morality, which, he insisted, should not differ from personal ethics. About this he argued with Oei Tjoe Tat and Tan Po Goan and a few other PSI lawyers. Politically, Yap was more than a little prim. Ideologically, he was most attracted to the democratic socialist ideas of the PSI, akin to the Dutch Labor Party, but he was put off by the intellectual pretensions of some of its leaders, two or three of whom he had known in the AMS in Yogya. Parkindo was another matter. Small but influential, with a tough and flexible leader in Dr. J. Leimena, it sought supporters in the Protestant community. Yap was approached but refused. This did not sit well with Leimena, who later prevented Yap from getting a seat in Parliament.

If he worried about losing his identity and ethical standards in either party, however, there was probably another reason why Yap shied away from them both. Then and for long after, he was afraid that, as a Chinese, he would not be accepted by the ethnic Indonesians who dominated the PSI and Parkindo, as well as every other major party. In effect, he was ethnically tracked once more, this time, in part, by his own (quite reasonable) imagination. As a result, during the 1950s, he became more consciously "*peranakan* Chinese" than at any other time in his life. When Thio Thiam Tjong announced a meeting in March of 1954, to establish a new *peranakan* organization—not necessarily a party—Yap went.

By late 1953, with ethnic Chinese feeling increasingly under pressure, it was evident that the PDTI did not amount to much. Even Thio Thiam Tjong, its chairman, admitted that a more effective organization was needed.[1] As we have seen, the new draft bill on citizenship requiring an active choice had startled everyone who understood its implications, and other evidence of discrimination was growing. Moreover, as the first parliamentary elections were on the horizon, *peranakan* leaders recognized the need for an organization that could mobilize electoral support for representation committed to ethnic Chinese interests.

By January or February 1954, the PDTI had produced a concept for a Badan Permusjawaratan Warganegara Turunan Tionghoa (Baperwatt, Consultative Association of Citizens of Chinese Descent). Not a party and nonideological, the association would coordinate only those efforts of its members directly affecting the interests of the minority; the only binding commitment was to oppose anti-Chinese policies. By unifying ethnic Chinese, now scattered among a few provincial organizations, Baperwatt could assure the minority at least a minimal electoral presence in the Parliament, soon to be elected by proportional representation.[2] The largest of the local associations, Perwitt, formed in March 1953 in Surabaya, promptly indicated that it would likely give way to Baperwatt.[3]

At 9:35 in the morning on 13 March 1954, in the Sin Ming Hui building on Jl. Gajah Mada, the old complex once owned by the Chinese majoor of Batavia, Thio Thiam Tjong convened the meeting to establish a new *peranakan* organization. Forty-four participants came from around the archipelago, representing existing organizations, major urban communities, and the various enclaves of *peranakan* society (fig. 7.1). Khoe Woen Sioe from *Keng Po* was there, along with Auwjong Peng Koen from *Star Weekly*, who represented Catholic *peranakan*. Yap's partners, Tan Po Goan and Oei Tjoe Tat (the latter was one of the drafters of the articles of the new association), came. Yap was there as one of the Protestant group. They and other lawyers, doctors, journalists, and a few businessmen constituted a kind of center-right coalition, largely out of Sin Ming Hui, with an essentially conservative, defensive understanding of ethnic Chinese interests and possibilities. On the left was Siauw Giok Tjhan (like Tan Po Goan, a member of Parliament) and, among others, his protégé Go Gien Tjwan from the national Antara news agency, whom Yap had once met in Malang on his bicycle trip around Java. Siauw, Go, and a few others had had nothing to do with the Sin Ming Hui.

FIG. 7.1 Baperki branch, Kutaradja, Aceh, n.d.

It was largely Siauw's show, as most participants probably knew—Yap, barely baptized politically, may have been an exception. Mary Somers has pointed out that ethnic Chinese leadership in Indonesia had always served a basically intermediary role with the government; in the colony this indicated the influential, conservative, business class represented in the Chung Hua Hui. After 1950, in a dramatic shift of personnel and ideology, leadership selection now favored those who had supported the revolution and knew their way around the new elite. One of the more fascinating figures in Indonesian politics through 1965, Siauw was the most experienced and capable of the *peranakan* political leaders. In and out of Parliament, he was well connected with and respected by many national political leaders, including Soekarno, then still a constitutional president but very influential and soon to transcend all limits. No one else at the meeting at Jl. Gajah Mada could match Siauw in political skill and insider knowledge. Much of the opposition to him hoped that Khoe Woen Sioe would head the new organization, according to Somers, but when the time came to elect a chairman, only Siauw was nominated.[4]

A quick reading of the sketchy minutes of that founding convention gives the odd impression that much of the day was frittered away on names and words. But these seeming digressions were in fact politically crucial. Those who attended, especially those allied with Siauw, will tell you that Siauw's major contribution was to replace Baperwatt with Baperki.[5] Actually, he contributed a great deal more by way of political counseling, but the name question was critical because it addressed the issue of whether or not ethnic Chinese should organize "exclusively"—that is, on an ethnic principle. Siauw, with well-coordinated support from his home province of East Java and a few select figures from elsewhere, insisted that the term "Tionghoa" (Chinese) be dropped, symbolically registering an intention to create a nonethnic association fully integrated into the mainstream of Indonesian life.

There were intense and lengthy arguments over this issue, made all the more so by Yap, whose political debut demonstrated his capacity for both stubbornness and commitment.[6] According to the minutes, Yap's opinion was "that the words 'Chinese descent' must be retained. We have to recognize the reality that even if we erase the features of Chinese-ness, we will still be treated as aliens. And he [Yap] felt that so long as racial discrimination and sentiments remain, we must keep the Chinese designation." Yap was, in effect, demanding that ethnic Chinese openly and unapologetically confront discrimination. In another display of his preference for an aggressive posture, he asked to add the adjective "berdjoang" (struggle)—thus "struggle organization," probably from the Dutch "strijdorganizatie"—turning Baperwatt into Babperwatt.[7]

Siauw replied that, if the name were not changed, the new organization would be stamped "Chinese," contradicting Article 6 of the draft charter, which stated that all citizens who agreed with the purposes of the organization could join. Holding in mind, he said, that the purpose of the new organization was to eliminate racial discrimination, and that racial sentiments were flaring up, it was not very sensible to react by keeping a Chinese designation. Instead, they must have an organization open to all citizens, regardless of ethnicity, participating without caveats in an Indonesia free of ethnic discrimination.

Yap was supported by the delegations from Semarang and Purbolinggo, the minutes say, and Siauw by Perwitt (Surabaja) and the delegation from Kediri. After a time, Yap's own allies tried to persuade him that the name should not stand in the way of achieving their major purpose, to which Yap testily replied that the attitude of the opposition—his own supporters—was that of "swie poah," abacus calculating. "Names are very important matters. Names impose an understanding of what is being defended. If the content of this organization is characteristically Chinese, why aren't we courageous enough to use the words 'Chinese descent'?" It was vintage Yap. The "swie poah" charge was the same he made against those in his church who calculated money into every decision. But here he applied it to political calculation and compromise.

Yap finally gave in, however. Even as he argued—trying perhaps to deny Siauw the symbolic victory and signal his own intention to be actively involved—he evidently recognized the political wisdom of Siauw's stroke.[8] So Baperki, the Consultative Body on Indonesian Citizenship (Badan Permusjawaratan Kewarganegaraan Indonesia), was born. For the rest, apart from word changes in the charter and rules of order drafted by Oei Tjoe Tat's committee, the organization essentially followed the concept of Baperwatt. It was not to be a party, but a mass organization, whose members could join political parties but were bound by Baperki discipline on the issue of opposing racial discrimination and defending minority interests, particularly, of course, on the citizenship question. Simple as it sounds, it was precisely on these matters of the constitution of the organization and its program that, as far as Yap was concerned, Baperki came to grief.

Siauw was elected chair without opposition. For the four vice-chair positions, thirteen names were put forward. One of them was Yap's, indicating that he had made an impression in the meeting, but not sufficient to be elected. The four with the most votes in order were Oei Tjoe Tat, Khoe Woen Sioe, The Pik Siong, and Thio Thiam Tjong. Yap came in either eighth or ninth.[9] Four others were appointed to the Baperki council, representing West Java, Central Java, Sumatra, and Kalimantan. Siauw chose his close friend and political ally Go Gien Tjwan to be secretary, and Ang Jan Gwan as treasurer.[10] Near the end of the meeting on 13 March, Yap proposed that a collection be taken up immediately for the Baperki treasury. It amounted to the small sum of Rp. 5,700. He himself probably gave more than he could afford—a habit that bothered Khing no end.

Yap poured his energy into Baperki. He was the first editor of the organization's monthly *Berita Baperki* (Baperki News), and he worked assiduously on citizenship issues, giving advice and lectures, persuading ethnic Chinese to become citizens, and speaking out on new developments. In the run-up to the first parliamentary election in August 1955 and the Constituent Assembly election shortly thereafter, he campaigned hard around the country, which meant, first, convincing ethnic Chinese citizens to vote and, second, convincing them to vote Baperki's lotus logo. Yap and Go Gien Tjwan, one a Protestant and the other a communist, frequently campaigned together, demonstrating that ideological differences were subordinate to Baperki's grander purposes and, to Yap, that Baperki was in fact neither ideological nor a political party, even if it was running in the elections.

Yap himself wanted a seat in Parliament, but he did not get it. Baperki's 180,000 votes gave it one seat, which naturally went to Siauw, who used it far more effectively on critical issues than anyone else could have done. Yap hoped for one of the appointive seats set aside by the Constitution of 1950 if the election did not produce nine ethnic Chinese MPs.[11] But the political parties had something to say about this. The one party that might have supported his candidacy, the Protestant Parkindo, which he had refused to join, set his name aside in favor of a financial contributor. Instead, in late 1957, Yap did get a seat in the Konstituante (Constituent Assembly), again not on the Baperki list, which was filled by Siauw and Oei Tjoe Tat, but as a minority appointee. He and four others associated with Baperki whom Siauw was able to get appointed to the Konstituante, including Go Gien Tjwan, constituted a group designated the Fraksi Lima Orang (Five Person Fraction).[12]

The Konstituante added enormously to Yap's work load, though at about this time he left the church educational commission, but he loved it. When the assembly was in session, he traveled by train to Bandung, where it met three days a week. His circle of acquaintances widened substantially, as did his political knowledge and experience. On the station platform in the old city (*kota*) area of Jakarta, he met a Masyumi delegate who turned out to be Thiam Bong's friend from grade school in Aceh and a fellow AMS graduate: Jamaluddin Datuk Singomangkuto, originally from West Sumatra, later became a close friend and colleague in legal aid circles. Yap talked with many others on the train and observed more in plenary sessions and in the committee on human rights and related matters of which he was a member. Anti-communist though he was, he was impressed by PKI organization and principle—how party members stayed in the cheapest hotels in Bandung, studied, prepared well for each session, and in every other way demonstrated their commitment.

Baperki, however, was another matter. Yap's obvious commitment and willingness to work hard paid off in recognition and respect in the organization. In 1955 he was elected fourth vice chair and in 1956 first vice chair, from which position he generated an extraordinary volume of dissonance. By early 1957 he was on the way to becoming the principal voice of opposition to the Siauw leadership. The issues will be explained later, but something needs to be said first about the relationship between Siauw and Yap and, too, about a few peculiarities of Baperki.

In the sideshow of *peranakan* politics, to which few but ethnic Chinese paid much attention, Yap's battles with Siauw constituted another sideshow. Yap never had a chance of winning this war, or even any of the major battles. Politically he was utterly outclassed by Siauw, who took nearly complete control of the organization from the beginning. Comfortable in the minority, defying authority, Yap was bothered by the flight of his allies, particularly Khoe Woen Sioe and Auwyong Peng Koen, but did not mind fighting alone. His courage, however, was no match for Siauw's command of politics and organization.

They were both extraordinary men who, like many others in the *peranakan* minority, in different circumstances might have played prominent roles in Indonesian political life. Oddly, despite appearances, they were much alike and in agreement on a few fundamentals that set them apart from others, even close associates.[13] Siauw, a year younger than Yap, was from a middle-class family in Surabaya, where he graduated from the HBS, worked as a journalist, was active in the PTI, and, firmly planted on the Marxist left, joined the revolution. Politically connected and experienced, he was supple, personable, emotional, and intimate. The better-educated and intellectually avid Yap, religiously devout, a loner, not much given to small talk, tended to uncompromising (and occasionally self-righteous) principle, rigorous logic, and detached, analytical argument. Siauw was capable of public tears in trying moments of anger or gratitude. Yap, whose sense of dignity excluded public displays of emotion—except for an occasional outburst of rage, which somehow contained its own dignity—was nevertheless quick to sympathize and forgive and to rue his own ferocity.

Both men were personally modest. Yap paid more attention to his appearance and liked being neat, but was not particularly vain, while Siauw was usually a picture of informality. Neither was self-serving and both were serious and responsible, qualities they recognized and respected in one another. Yap greatly admired Siauw: his simplicity, his personal honesty, his commitment and sense of purpose, his devotion to his family, which Yap always thought a mark of character. He distrusted Go Gien Tjwan and had doubts about Oei Tjoe Tat and a few others whose inconsistent views and loyalties bothered him. But Siauw he knew to be personally honest. When the two were most at odds politically, Yap did not impugn Siauw's personal integrity, even at home, according to Khing. Yap doubted ideologies and trusted character, which allowed him to respect Siauw as a man while challenging his political views and attachments.

Siauw reciprocated, admiring Yap for his honesty and courage even as he thought him politically a terrific pain in the neck. In his autobiography Siauw describes Yap as "a Christian and prominent among Chinese Christians in Indonesia. He was known as someone who persistently defended his opinions based on the Bible. A hard, stubborn man, firm in his views, but honest and courageous in stating them even if he had to buck a trend. Certainly, his rigidity was often irritating, but his honesty and courage in making his views known even when they went against majority opinion, in discussions meant to find appropriate policies, were very beneficial."[14]

The arguments between Siauw and Yap, then, were in no way personal or petty, but genuinely political and ideological. Both were public men, relatively little influenced by personal ambitions, whose understandings of *peranakan* conditions and possibilities diverged enormously. Siauw and Yap were in many ways typical of educated *peranakan* Chinese in Indonesia. Neither could speak or read a Chinese language. Siauw evidently once tried to learn, but he gave it up as too hard. Yap never even tried once liberated from the Mandarin school to which his father sent him in Kutaradja. Neither, moreover, was naive about *peranakan* limitations, nor given to justifying the privileges many Chinese had gained in the colony and maintained thereafter. Both, indeed, tended to be censorious of bloated wealth, Chinese or other. What each defended was not Chinese commercial advantage, but Chinese minority rights. Yap was both impressed and puzzled by Siauw's defense of Chinese rice-millers when they came under attack by government policy, for the stance indicated Siauw's even-handedness in protecting all Chinese, even if this seemed to contradict his Marxist commitment to deprived classes. Moreover, both men refused to stop short simply with a defense of the Chinese minority. From different starting points—Siauw's, a Marxist critique; Yap's, more eclectically social democratic and idiosyncratically Christian—both assumed that Indonesian economy and society had to change. On the nature of this change they disagreed monumentally, but each had goals that went beyond merely protecting and promoting *peranakan*. Ultimately, Yap would escape the *peranakan* circle to speak to a larger Indonesia. Siauw would not, in part because he was trapped by his leadership of Baperki which confined his imagination and his reputation to Chinese minority interests.[15]

Siauw was at ease in both the Indonesian and the Chinese community, while Yap felt no less socially and culturally marginalized in both settings than did many other highly educated professionals. Siauw was, I think, proud of his Chinese descent, while Yap, who did not regret being Chinese in any way, took it more lightly, often wondering skeptically what it meant, exactly. To Yap, the world of ethnic Chinese politics was a frustrating web of Javanese *peranakan* memories, manners, and obligation; but to Siauw, it was home. He attracted *peranakan* support largely because he seemed to have the inside track to national political leadership, not least to Soekarno himself, but also because, without having to say much about it, he represented ethnic integrity and self-respect and, significantly, pride in China itself. In some ways he combined the old pre-war PTI demand to be Indonesian with the Sin Po group's identification with the Chinese homeland.

Siauw openly supported the Beijing regime, fiercely condemned Taiwan, and hounded Nationalist Chinese supporters in Indonesia. He sent one or more of his children to China for their educations, and when Baperki opened its university in Jakarta imported machinery for its engineering labs from China. Yap refused to have anything to do with Communist China, which he opposed on ideological grounds, or with Taiwan, precisely in order to refute the common accusation that all overseas Chinese, *peranakan* and *totok* alike, paid allegiance only to China. He believed Siauw's attraction to China was mainly ideological and missed the point that emotions may have had more to do with it. Many *totok* businessmen, having no reason to sympathize with communism, seem to have understood this implicitly and were comfortable with Siauw. None evidently regarded him as contemptibly deracinated. Yap, on the other hand, had little if anything to do with *totok*.

With hindsight it is easy enough to say that Baperki was a mistake. At the time it was not so obvious. Siauw's leadership was effective in mobilizing and engaging *peranakan* politically more than ever before. On several important issues, Baperki seemed to wield substantial influence. But in none of its original purposes was the organization successful. It did not unite *peranakan* or end their political disabilities, but in some ways ultimately exacerbated them. It could not even in its own time fully resolve the citizenship question. Nor did it eliminate the *asli-aslian* (native vs. foreign), ethnic Indonesian vs. ethnic Chinese, antithesis, but in some ways helped to consolidate it.

Baperki's promise of unity broke down quickly, because the *peranakan* elites were not in fact united. Older, more cautious leaders resented being shoved aside by the new Siauw group, with its revolutionary credentials. In addition, it proved impossible to ignore the ideological differences that Baperki meant to avoid by focusing on issues of citizenship and discrimination. Siauw himself became the chief focus of conflict, not simply because of his Marxist views, but because his leadership of Baperki could not be separated from these views.[16]

Before the parliamentary elections of 1955, Auwjong Peng Koen, then on the Jakarta Baperki council and a candidate in the Konstituante elections, resigned from the organization amid accusations that Siauw Giok Tjhan was a communist.[17] Khoe Woen Sioe left later. Tan Po Goan withdrew ostensibly because the Baperki leadership had tried to dictate his positions in Parliament. By 1957 others associated with liberal or democratic socialist views, usually seen as belonging to the PSI camp, had withdrawn, too. The effect was to strengthen Siauw's leadership, removing obstacles to a leftward drift. Yap, for one, felt deserted by those who left, especially Auwjong and Khoe Woen Sioe, but he himself had no intention of withdrawing from the organization.

For the rest, at every turn Baperki was caught in contradictions of principle. For one obvious example, Siauw had convinced its founders that Baperki must present itself as a nonethnic mass organization. A few non-Chinese were recruited into its councils, and Siauw was constantly on the lookout for more. But it was only a gesture. Baperki could be no more multiethnic than ethnic antagonisms allowed it to be, which was very little. Overwhelmingly it was, and was understood to be, a Chinese organization. In this case, however, what became of the wish to integrate *peranakan* into mainstream politics? If anything, Baperki had the bewilderingly contrary effect of politically tracking the minority, once more, through an ethnic tunnel—yet not entirely, precisely because it did not or could not unite all *peranakan*. Baperki's political course before 1966 made it easier afterwards for the New Order regime to limit *peranakan* political engagement on any terms.

Finally, as Yap protested more and more loudly, Baperki increasingly behaved as if it were a political party; and having committed itself to oppose all forms of discrimination, it ended up supporting a constitutional prescription of discrimination.

Yap's arguments with Siauw had to do with how best to represent the interests of the ethnic Chinese minority. But the issues were complicated by Baperki's need to adapt to fundamental political change in Indonesia after 1956. Most importantly, the parliamentary order based on the liberal Provisional Constitution of 1950 began to collapse under the weight of regional dissidence, military dissatisfaction, and the popular Soekarno's criticism of national disunity. In late 1956 Vice President Mohammad Hatta, symbolically representing the major islands outside of Java and much respected in liberal political circles, resigned in disagreement with Soekarno. Eschewing the passive role assigned to him by the 1950 Constitution, Soekarno asserted the need for a new political system, one devoid of the political bickering of the country's many political parties and the divisive conflict between Islamic and secular ideologies. In February 1957 he announced his own political *Konsepsi*, which among other things called for including the PKI in the government—which did not happen until much later—and creating a more unified political order. In mid-March the Ali Sastroamidjojo (PNI) government resigned and, to deal with regionalist problems, martial law was proclaimed.

During the next two years, Indonesian politics was caught up in a whirlwind of stunning change. The army, never distant from political conflict since the revolution, now became a central political actor under martial law. Soekarno created a new National Council (to contemplate further political change) and a new "non-party" government, led by Prime Minister Djuanda, in which party representatives were accompanied by non-party appointees and military officers. In November and December of 1957, PNI and PKI labor unions assaulted the major Dutch corporations still resident in the country. The firms were taken over and, in 1958, nationalized and broken up, many of the fragments falling to military control. In February 1958 open rebellion, abetted by the United States, broke out in North and West Sumatra and South Sulawesi and lasted for three years. Islamic rebellions, the Darul Islam, either continued or broke out anew in West Java, Aceh, and South Sulawesi. In mid-1958 all major parties, partly out of anxiety over the increased popular support for the PKI demonstrated in the 1957 regional elections, agreed to postpone the parliamentary elections scheduled for 1959. Only the PKI dissented. With parliamentary legitimacy hence dissipated, army leaders brought pressure to bear for restoration of the strong executive Constitution of 1945. In early 1959 the Constituent Assembly, paralyzed by ideological conflict between Islamic and secular parties, had to deal with this proposal.[18]

Baperki in the meantime was threading its way through a minefield laid by the Assaat movement favoring ethnic Indonesian-owned business over Chinese-owned, and by army martial law authorities dealing with aliens in ways that inevitably, and often intentionally, caught *peranakan* citizens in the net. It was not an easy time and grew tougher as political conflict escalated and the parliamentary system gave way. Siauw adapted quickly to changing conditions over which he had no control, but which he may have believed were headed in the right direction. Yap loudly differed.

Fundamentally their disagreement was ideological, and at every opportunity from mid-1954 on, Yap argued with and tried to contain Siauw's Marxist views. But the ideological divide was nuanced by differences over how best tactically to represent ethnic Chinese interests. While Yap worked from principles that eschewed everyday political possibilities, Siauw approached the problem as a consummate practical politician.

Yap was certainly anti-communist, but never unthinkingly so. His religious education in Oegstgeest and his training for church work thereafter in Holland, Switzerland, and England contained a strong anti-communist bias, but his objections to communism were more political and intellectual than religious and contained no hate-filled rancor. Yap was not much of a cold warrior. If he differed with Siauw on communism, he had no difficulty admiring the man. And, before the 1955 election, he had no difficulty campaigning with Go Gien Tjwan, whom he knew to be a Marxist, in part to demonstrate that men of different political views could work together.

Siauw, for his part, was Marxist, even communist, but with a small "c." The suggestion that he was secretly a member of the PKI is doubtful as well as trivial. Siauw knew PKI leaders well, but also PNI leaders—Soekarno and many others. He also had connections on the political center and center-right just as his opponents—Auwjong, Tan Po Goan, and others—had on the left and center-left. Yap's objection was that Siauw was moving Baperki to the left, by which he meant in part toward the PKI, but also toward what he saw as Soekarno's radical vision of government, soon formulated as Guided Democracy. Although these were distinct issues, they seemed to come together after early 1957, when Soekarno called for the PKI's admission into the government and the PKI drew up behind the president.

The evidence of Siauw's sympathy for the PKI was substantial but easily misinterpreted. As noted earlier, he had been editor of the PKI daily *Harian Rakjat*, from 1951 to 1953. In and out of Parliament he often supported PKI positions. He argued in favor of surplus vote distribution agreements (*stembus accord*) with the PKI in the general elections of 1955 and the regional elections of 1957. He was very close to Tan Ling Djie, former chairman of the PKI. Go Gien Tjwan was his choice for the first Baperki secretary, followed by Buyung Saleh, who did in fact belong to the PKI.[19]

But was Siauw's disposition toward the PKI for ideological or for political reasons? While he sympathized with PKI ideas, it was at least equally important to him that the PKI willingly backed Baperki in opposing all forms of racial discrimination. No other major party offered similar affirmation and support. Moreover, the PKI supported President Soekarno, in whom Siauw placed great trust. When Soekarno called for its inclusion in the government, and it moved from fourth to nearly first in the 1957 regional elections, many, including Siauw, thought that the party's success might herald coming social and economic transformations, essential for the unchallenged safety of the Chinese minority.

It did not matter to Yap whether Siauw's stand on the left was ideologically or politically inspired; Yap's point was that Baperki must remain ideologically *and* politically neutral. This was the original conception of the organization, as Yap thought Article 3 of its charter made clear: a mobilized interest group or lobby, not a party, focused on issues of citizenship and discrimination, not ideology. Throughout his tenure on the executive committee, he argued that any activity beyond citizenship and discrimination violated Baperki's charter. From 1956 onward, Yap unremittingly hammered the point that Baperki's "leftist reputation" not only threatened to split its support, but also incurred unconscionable risks in behalf of ethnic Chinese. The Siauw group replied that Baperki's leadership was reasonably balanced between left and right, true only if one discounted the overbalancing political influence of Siauw himself.

In the circumstances of Indonesian politics after late 1956, it was not easy to avoid choices, and Siauw was much too political, too firmly committed to his own vision, to sit on his hands at a time of change. By late 1956 and early 1957, when Soekarno launched the Konsepsi that anticipated Guided Democracy, Baperki leaders were generally agreed that the parliamentary system had failed to provide adequate protection to ethnic Chinese. The citizenship issue and Assaatism were adequate proof. Yap's approval of the Konsepsi as a corrective to the parliamentary order was tentative. He wanted to see the Konsepsi elaborated and made less vague. Siauw and others on the executive committee enthusiastically supported the president and continued thereafter to do so no matter what turns he took. Yap soon turned his back on Soekarno's vision.

The debate between Siauw and Yap over this issue, which culminated in 1959 and 1960, was long and painful. To make the implications of it clearer, we have to return for a moment to some principles on which they agreed. Sharing a commitment to human rights, including the Universal Declaration on Human Rights, which Baperki celebrated annually through at least 1960, both quite naturally asserted the rights of minorities. They both praised the stipulation of human rights—essentially the Universal Declaration—in the Constitution of 1950. With different emphases, both also embraced egalitarian principles. Neither had any taste for the corruption, inefficiency, economic waste, and self-aggrandizing tendencies of party conflict during the parliamentary period.

But Siauw supported Soekarno, while Yap condemned Soekarno's proposals. In neither case was the position simple. Siauw was convinced that the parliamentary system had to be revised, that its insoluble conflict of ideologies and partisan advantage would lead to national disaster, or in any event to no fundamental reordering of economy and society, and that the evidence for its dangers was obvious in the escalating attacks on ethnic Chinese. Soekarno he knew to be free of prejudice, as were many PNI leaders close to the president, and so was the PKI, which Soekarno argued should be in the government.

Beyond all this, however, Siauw was no less drawn to Soekarno and his vision than were many Javanese. It is essential to recognize this Javanese influence in the trust that Siauw placed in Soekarno. He had known and admired the man since the 1930s and had comfortable access to the presidential palace. But he also shared Soekarno's anger at the colonial deformation of Indonesian history, which Siauw saw as the fundamental cause of Chinese miseries, and he appreciated the president's sense of the need for a radical turn away from it. Believing that Indonesia required revolutionary change to secure the Chinese minority in a political-economic order from which ethnic issues would disappear, Siauw saw in Soekarno the key figure to bring about such a change. Not to support him, from Siauw's point of view, was folly.

Yap's critique of Siauw's position started from the lawyerly assumption that individuals are less promising than sound institutions and legal processes. He, too, admired Soekarno as unprejudiced, but stopped short of wanting to vest more authority in him. Rather, he argued, the most secure hope for Indonesia and the Chinese minority lay in effective law and legal process, which required the Constitution to be taken more seriously than political figures. At informational and training sessions held by Baperki for its cadres and members, while Siauw and Go Gien Tjwan talked about history, colonialism, economics, and social and political organization, Yap introduced the Constitution, legal process, and government institutions.[20] In the crisis years of 1957–58, as political forces realigned and the reliability of legal process began to ebb, he seems to have thought his own position through to a firm outlook, which he expressed clearly in the Konstituante debates of early 1959 over the restoration of the 1945 Constitution (on which issue Siauw and Yap split completely).

In the meantime, as tensions over these issues escalated in Baperki itself after early 1957, Yap began to learn at first hand about political infighting. He was not good at it and did not appreciate the results, but emerged less naive, if also angry and bitter. The issue, which had to do with the critical problem of education, still grated on him thirty years later.

Baperki's influence grew substantially from its attention to education. In 1956 Baperki already had a program of sorts, which expanded quickly in 1957 and 1958 as it took over and ran, under its own aegis, many of the alien primary and secondary schools banned by the martial law authorities.[21] At the same time, Baperki leaders began to address the problem of higher education, because the admission of ethnic Chinese students to the best state universities was severely restricted by quotas. What to do about the matter was a painful question for anyone sensitive to the complex issues. As Yap expressed it:

> We understood perfectly well the fear of Indonesian leaders that only those with enough money to pay for university education, that is Chinese, would have a big advantage . . . compared with indigenous Indonesians, who were poorer. Of course, we understood too the fear [of ethnic Indonesians] that eventually the Chinese, under these circumstances, would be not only financially stronger but also academically and intellectually stronger, if money alone was allowed to determine. All this we could understand: the conditions and the fears. Yet, from the point of view of human rights, equality, and so on, we could not agree [to denying ethnic Chinese children higher education]. The problem was discussed in many circles, including [among] Christians. This is why private universities were set up by various groups. Now came Baperki . . . which wanted to educate Chinese to become good citizens, to understand democracy, the state, and so on. Baperki represented the ideas and wishes of the Chinese group, including Catholics, Protestants, and all the rest. Thus the idea that Baperki itself should establish a university was greeted enthusiastically. All groups wanted to cooperate.[22]

In his report to the Baperki congress in Surabaya in December 1956, Siauw proposed a university to be called the Universitas Bhineka Tunggal Ika (Unity in Diversity, Indonesia's national motto.)[23] A committee was formed of Yap (because of his interest and experience in education), Thio Thiam Tjong, and Kwee Hwa Djin (Oei Tjoe Tat's brother-in-law), which worked gradually through 1957, eventually locating a piece of land in the Grogol area owned by a member of Yap's church. The problem was how to buy it, for Baperki did not have a legally constituted foundation in whose name it could be registered. So the committee decided to purchase the land in the name of Padmo Semasto, a Solo-born lawyer who had been appointed chairman of the Sin Ming Hui, thereby sidestepping Baperki ownership. It seems clear enough that this was not entirely a disinterested move. More likely than not, Yap's belief that Siauw's lean to the left was making Baperki vulnerable to unknown dangers was the reason that he tried to avoid a Baperki imprimatur on the new university. A few years earlier, soon after independence, he had insisted on making the church schools autonomous in order to protect them from any peril directed at the church itself. His fears then were mistaken. In the case of Baperki, as it turned out, they were not.

Education was too important politically for the Siauw group to release control of it or to allow any dissident group to take credit for dealing with it. Before Yap's committee could buy the land agreed on, the national Baperki Section on Education and Culture, chaired by Buyung Saleh, met at Go Gien Tjwan's home on 8 January 1958. There it was decided to establish a Baperki Educational Foundation, to be represented by Go himself, Buyung Saleh, and J. B. Avé.[24] The foundation would assume control over all of Baperki's educational programs, including, it turned out, the establishment of a university.

Two days later, on 10 January 1958, at a national executive committee meeting, Yap was stunned by the fait accompli. Outmaneuvered, his committee's work shoved aside, he felt betrayed, particularly by Go Gien Tjwan, and personally humiliated. Yap assumed that his own slowness in getting the job done was to blame, as in part it may have been. But Go and the others had moved without informing Yap's committee, which Yap thought ungentlemanly, a dirty trick. Yap fought the decision fiercely at the meeting, arguing that Baperki was extending itself beyond the limits imposed by its charter. Nothing was said explicitly about the university, only about existing lower schools, but he undoubtedly had it in mind. He insisted that educational matters should be handed over to other foundations, including those of the churches, or to the Union of Chinese Educators.[25] For if—finally getting to the central issue—Baperki was later accused of being leftist, many would no longer follow it, and then Baperki would become weak. By implication, it followed that the schools would suffer.

Rattled and angry, perhaps embarrassed, Yap had not been prepared for this debate and made a fumbling case.[26] Other members of the executive committee attacked him from all directions, all except Siauw Giok Tjhan, who chaired the meeting in silence almost to the end. Yap, they argued, construed Article 3 of Baperki's charter, which made citizenship the central focus, too narrowly; Baperki alone could do the job of developing educational facilities because people trusted it to get the job done; and despite accusations that it was leftist, Baperki was stronger than ever. Moreover, as Siauw admitted later, expanding its role in education would win Baperki more popular support.[27] Several compromises were proposed to bring Yap around, but he rejected them all. Finally he insisted on a vote, though he had to know that it would go against him. It did, seven to one. Yap thereupon announced that he would have to consider whether to remain on the executive committee or even remain a member of Baperki. It was not the last time he threatened to resign—but he never did.

Baperki leaders succeeded in developing the university by 1960. Funds were raised and land was bought in Grogol near the Sumber Waras hospital, which the Sin Ming Hui had helped to establish. Students and others from the community helped to build the school, to which President Soekarno gave his blessing. Open to both ethnic Indonesian and ethnic Chinese students, within a few years it emerged as a creditable institution. It was not named Bhineka Tunggal Ika University, after all, but at first was called simply Baperki University and, then, picking up on the title of a Soekarno speech, Universitas Res Publica (Ureca). Yap thought Res Publica a wonderful name, but he never got over the blow to his pride, nor over his anxiety about connecting the school with Baperki. In this he proved right, for after the coup of 1965, Ureca was attacked and burned, largely by other ethnic Chinese, and was taken over by the government and renamed Trisakti University. The effort begun by his own committee continued independently but less effectively, eventually with financial help from the GKI–West Java church and the Sin Ming Hui. It opened in 1962 as Tarumanagara University, then nowhere near Ureca's standard. It is still a rival of Trisakti, though students probably no longer know why.

Following the blow-up over the education issue, which Yap kept simmering, his relations with the Siauw group went steadily downhill. There was no lack of issues to fuel the conflict. The pace of political change after early 1958 was extraordinary, and Baperki's efforts to keep up generated contentious internal debates. Most of those who differed with Siauw gradually became silent, until Yap stood nearly alone in outspoken opposition.

In February 1958 the PRRI/Permesta rebellion had broken out, with support from the United States and Taiwan. The army reacted quickly, recapturing centers in Sumatra and Sulawesi, though the rebellion dragged on until 1961. Washington began to repair its relations with Jakarta in April, but they remained brittle thereafter, while Siauw stepped up his attacks on the Kuomintang. At the same time, the political system, led by Soekarno since March 1957, was still very much interim and uncertain, for the "non-party" Djuanda cabinet and the new National Council sat alongside a still-functioning Parliament and Constituent Assembly, which continued to work on a new constitution.

But the political party system was in turmoil. Masyumi and the PSI were badly hurt by the involvement of several prominent party leaders in the rebellion. The PNI, always eager to remain close to the president—who founded it in 1927, but now stood above all parties—was divided over his intentions. Soekarno indicated his displeasure with the party's conservatism and encouraged a splinter, Partindo (Partai Indonesia), to which Baperki loaned a few of its members. Oei Tjoe Tat, among others, became enthusiastically active in the party, which may have relieved him from the tension of his own ideologically centrist position in Baperki. Of the major parties only the PKI remained both whole and on the move, gaining popular support and also political advantage from the rebellion, the turn against the United States, and the turn to the left by Soekarno, whom Communist Party leaders praised lavishly and encouraged. But the PKI, too, had to deal with its powerful nemesis, the army, whose leadership under General Nasution was strongly anti-communist and fully able to take its own initiatives under martial law. Increasingly, during the next six years, Indonesian politics was largely defined structurally by the standoff between the army and the PKI, with most other groups drawn to one or the other.

Soekarno was at center stage from 1957 on. His public speeches set a tone of dramatic change, of eliminating "free fight liberalism" and other imported Western ideas, of restoring Indonesian traditions—*gotong-royong* (mutual assistance) and *musyawarah-mufakat* (discussion and consensus)—of return to revolutionary unity and purpose and the "spirit of the Proclamation of 1945," of movement, and of transformation. But no one knew exactly what to expect. Soekarno himself was uncertain. At a time of military coups elsewhere in South and Southeast Asia and the Middle East, the army accumulated leverage and exerted pressure simply by denying its intention to mount one. Soekarno, with no organization of his own, had to mobilize popular support around his own figure, while playing the political field by ear and coming up with ideas around which, somehow, to develop a new political order. Guided Democracy, which he began to press in 1958, had no certain content at first other than that it would be Indonesian rather than foreign, unifying rather than divisive, and oriented to revolutionary purpose.

Peranakan understood the meanings of this rapidly changing situation no more than anyone else. What was obvious was that their situation had not greatly improved since early 1957 and in some ways was growing more threatened. Assaat's association with the regional rebellion in Sumatra had discredited him personally, but Assaatism was still in the air. The association of indigenous Indonesian businessmen, KENSI (Kongres Ekonomi Nasional Seluruh Indonesia, All Indonesia National Economic Congress), continued to issue anti-Chinese diatribes. Late in 1958 Siauw actually tried to work out an accommodation with KENSI, but to no avail. Citizenship issues remained, with worrisome consequences for ethnic Chinese, citizens and aliens alike. The citizenship agreement with China would not be ratified until early 1960, but even then was subject to troublesome interpretations. Moreover, the army, now an active political force, made few bones about its anti-Chinese sentiments, though local army commanders were already working out their own accommodations with Chinese businessmen. The army was responsible for alien school closures in 1957 and 1958, and in 1959 encouraged and helped to implement Government Regulation 10, which placed shattering, disruptive restrictions on alien traders—essentially Chinese without Indonesian citizenship—in rural areas. As a result, more than a hundred thousand Chinese boarded Chinese ships for China in 1959 and 1960.

The strain of these difficult times showed in Baperki, partly as organizational problems and partly in escalating tensions over policy, particularly between Siauw and Yap. Baperki suffered no less than other electoral organizations, except for the PKI, from the emergence of Guided Democracy. The difficulty was not in popular support, which had increased in the 1957 regional elections, but in the declining importance of popular support once the likelihood of future elections faded.[28] Dues payments declined, the activities of local branches slowed, and, as in other national organizations, the more important Jakarta politics became, the more Baperki's head outweighed its body.[29]

In late June 1958, at Baperki's fifth national congress in Solo, the Siauw group and Yap clashed throughout. As first vice chairman, Yap presided over the opening of the congress, because Siauw was in Parliament for a discussion of citizenship matters. In response to Siauw's annual report, in which he criticized well-off businessmen and professionals for their lack of support, Yap accused Siauw of divisiveness and of failing to understand why Baperki did not attract those whose skills it needed. The ensuing discussion highlighted their ideological and political differences. Siauw replied acutely that common folk had to learn how to act without leadership from the economically strong and educated, who were not about to provide it:

> [Yap Thiam Hien has misunderstood me. I made the point that] in developing their activities the branches shouldn't rely only on the strong social-economic and educated groups. It is clear that these two groups generally do not feel the same pressure as the group of small traders and hawkers or labor, and so do not feel compelled in the same way to struggle

> along with BAPERKI, whose members come largely from the weaker groups. No doctors are complaining who have lost their livings because of racial discrimination. Yap Thiam Hien says that we should not be political ostriches, but we see quite realistically that the social-economically strong and educated prefer the way of least resistance in seeking to improve their lots. The conditions of our society are not yet free of colonial characteristics. It is still possible to bribe, buy, or rent people to avoid losses due to racial discrimination. In the face of this reality, if BAPERKI is only willing to move when the economically strong and educated are ready to join, then we can organize and carry on our struggle only when conditions are too difficult to improve.[30]

Siauw's argument could not persuade Yap, who was convinced that Baperki should include businessmen and professionals. Those former supporters had been driven away by Baperki's association with the left, not by class reluctance to oppose the status quo. Yap believed that ideological neutrality and a narrower program would unite the membership. Siauw could not accept so severe a limitation or agree to abjure politics—committed politics—which to his mind necessarily implied class struggle.

Yap's initial critique addressed other issues raised in Siauw's report, laying down a number of principles:

> We have to be democratic in carrying out our program; we must take steps in all matters where there is injustice and defend justice, even when those who face injustice are our opponents. If a religion experiences unjust treatment, we must defend it; also if there is a ban against the PKI, we must act to oppose it. Now, just recently the ban against publishing the newspaper *Keng Po*, for reasons unknown, suggests that this military measure was based on racial discrimination.[31]

Addressing only the *Keng Po* issue, Siauw replied that Baperki should not risk being drawn into a sticky situation.[32]

A day later the tension between Yap and Siauw blew up into an emotional scene. At issue was a proposed election law in which, at Soekarno's insistence, the number of parties would be reduced. (No one knew before September that the 1959 parliamentary election would be postponed.) Since Baperki, as a self-defined non-party, could not run, Siauw wanted the national congress to give the executive committee discretionary authority to decide whether to enter into electoral agreements with political parties. Immediately, a noisy debate broke out. Some branches wanted no such agreements, others wanted them only with small parties, and still others supported Siauw. Those opposed, particularly Yap, suspected that Siauw wanted to throw Baperki's support to the PKI.[33] Siauw at length bitterly denounced the suspicions and proposed that the meeting be resumed the next day, when the issue could be resolved calmly.[34] The next day, after Siauw explained the problem more clearly and announced a solution all could accept, he and Yap both made conciliatory statements that did not quite apologize but excused one another.[35]

At this congress Yap was elected again to the executive committee, but with the second smallest vote, 130 by a weighted system, just one more than his ally, the circumspect Thio Thiam Tjong.[36] He was placed in charge of contact with businessmen, and later, in August, was appointed to the legal commission of the organization. He seems not to have done much in connection with the first position, but was reasonably active in the second, which dealt with legal issues of citizenship and related matters. His time was limited, however, for he was in Bandung for Konstituante sessions three days a week, was still active in church affairs, occasionally gave speeches and advice on citizenship questions, and was practicing law. He also spent a good deal of time worrying about what would happen next in Baperki.

What came next was his most serious battle with Siauw, over Guided Democracy and, not long after, the 1945 Constitution. In this prolonged struggle, the two men played out their roles as if directed by a tragic playwright. Judging from the evidence of Baperki conference minutes, both understood the situation, and each may have appreciated the unhappy path the other felt he had to take. Even though in late 1958 Soekarno's vision of Guided Democracy remained vague, Siauw was convinced that Baperki had no choice but to support him early and completely. It was an optimistic bet that Soekarno would be able to consolidate the forces on the left for the sake of fundamental change. Yap was convinced this choice would lead to ideological errors and political dangers, and demanded, once again, that Baperki limit itself to the issue of citizenship.

Siauw fought off Yap's challenges but did not attack Yap personally—though others did—while Yap often reiterated his respect for Siauw's opposition to racial discrimination. Both had satisfaction of a sort. Siauw won in the short term, but Yap proved right in the long, though there was little enough joy in the fact. If any doubt remained about Yap's courage, his behavior during the months after December 1958 had to dispel it. But few outside of Baperki circles were aware of his actions, for ethnic Chinese politics hardly counted for much on the national scene. On the inside, however, Yap's single voice caused considerable turmoil and consternation, though partly at least because Siauw countenanced the dissension. Crushing Yap at that point might well have alienated others who had the same doubts.

The issue broke at the plenary meeting of the executive committee in Jakarta in mid-December 1958. Of the twenty-one national and provincial Baperki leaders who attended, most supported Siauw. He nevertheless came prepared, in an eleven-page report, to make the strongest possible case for Guided Democracy. He wanted, if possible, to avoid dissension on the issue, for unanimity behind Soekano would enhance Baperki's standing. Were it not for Yap he might have had it.

In his report Siauw promptly asserted that Baperki had already endorsed Guided Democracy, and he then went on to paint a promising picture of what it meant. He told the executive committee that on 5 December, the president and cabinet had met in an "Open Talk," which had, according to Minister of Information Sudibio, produced an understanding that Guided Democracy was based on the Pancasila. (The Pancasila consists of five principles enunciated by Soekarno in 1945 as the state philosophy: belief in the one Almighty God, humanitarianism, nationalism, sovereignty of the people, and social justice.) Thus, said Siauw, Guided Democracy, as a means of implementing the Pancasila, was better than the parliamentary system: it was more suited to conditions in Indonesia, which guaranteed that the government would rule with the consent of the people. It assured democracy of a more perfect sort.

Moreover, said Siauw, Sudibio emphasized (as did Siauw) that Guided Democracy would bring about the equality of political rights stipulated in Articles 1, 23, 35, and 131 of the 1950 Provisional Constitution; economic rights, as in Articles 37 and 38; and social rights, as in Articles 36, 39, 41, and 42.

> Even if it was not mentioned concretely, still it is certain that Guided Democracy naturally covers the effectuation of art. 28 . . . which assures every Indonesian citizen . . . of the right to work . . . and . . . also art. 30 . . . which assures every citizen of the right to education. In short, guided democracy is democracy meant to implement human rights, so that it can be presented precisely as a means of implementing in practice the daily life of the Pancasila as state principle.[37]

"With this understanding," Siauw went on, "BAPERKI supports the idea of guided democracy, because guided democracy will facilitate the implementation of article 3 of BAPERKI's constitution, which means facilitating national development, guaranteeing to every citizen a life free of fear of being unattended and free of fear of poverty." Siauw continued giving assurances, citing authorities, putting the best face on what Guided Democracy would do for all citizens, including ethnic Chinese. Baperki, he said, must do everything possible to mobilize support for Guided Democracy.

Very little in Siauw's report did not distress Yap, who had come to the meeting prepared, as usual, to urge Baperki back to what he conceived of as its proper course. Siauw's tone was irritating. He had begun to adopt the kind of political rhetoric, filled with ritual phrases—the just and prosperous society, the ideals of the 1945 Proclamation of Independence, among a hundred others to come—often borrowed directly from Soekarno's speeches, that marked public discourse under Guided Democracy. Yap hated it as thought-throttling sloganeering. His two copies of Siauw's report and the minutes of the discussions that followed are red-penciled with huge, angry, exclamation points; question marks; marginal comments of doubt, challenge, disagreement; accusations of subjectivity; and worse. Others at the December meeting had doubts, but Yap made them plain, generating enough heat to come through even in the mimeographed minutes. During the three days of the conference only one session, on the morning of 14 December when Yap was absent for some reason, proceeded more or less quietly.

Yap pursued Siauw relentlessly. When discussion of the report opened, he immediately challenged Siauw's statement that Baperki endorsed the idea of Guided Democracy, demanding to know when this decision was made. Uncertain issues, he insisted, must be discussed, and Guided Democracy's content and effects were unquestionably uncertain. Everything that Siauw had said about Guided Democracy sounded grand, but he had no way of demonstrating any of it. Yap himself had long since begun to think about the political system and now put up a defense of parliamentary democracy. As a member of the Konstituante committee charged with drafting the new constitution, he had come to appreciate much in the 1950 Constitution, especially its specific inclusion of human rights, but also the parliamentary system itself. This, he thought, provided more guarantees and better assurances of some kind of democracy than Guided Democracy did. It was not parliamentary democracy that was wrong, he argued, but those engaged in it thus far, and it was they who had to be changed. Finally, Yap returned to his established position that Baperki was violating its original purpose. No longer did he have much faith that the organization would confine its struggle to citizenship, but still he urged it to do so. Reacting against Siauw's call to mobilize public opinion behind Guided Democracy, Yap asked rhetorically whether it would not be more principled to keep a distance from matters outside its ken.[38]

Siauw conceded that Baperki had never made a decision to support Guided Democracy, "but it can be concluded from various other decisions that BAPERKI as a mass organization could do no other than to support the idea of guided democracy."[39] First, he explained, Baperki ran in the elections of 1955 for fear that the parliamentary seats constitutionally set aside for citizens of Chinese descent would be filled by the kind of party horse-trading (cow-trading in Indonesian idiom) that would be eliminated under Guided Democracy. Second, Baperki promoted the Pancasila in its campaigns out of the belief that it would lead to the best resolution of the citizenship problem, and Guided Democracy was intended to guarantee the Pancasila. Third, Baperki sought to settle the citizenship question by eliminating racial discrimination, and Guided Democracy was a means of achieving equality of political, economic, social, and cultural rights.[40]

Yap did not buy any of it. He proposed that the chairman's report be considered Siauw's own personal position, not that of Baperki. So heated were the arguments that the respected elder Thio Thiam Tjong stepped in to cool tempers with a compromise of sorts.[41] It did not help much. Soon another debate broke out over the executive committee's control of provincial branches, which Yap wanted to prevent from taking their own public stands on significant issues of policy.[42] He most likely had the East Javanese branch in mind. Chaired by Siauw Giok Bie, Giok Tjhan's brother, Baperki–East Java was in the habit of publicly anticipating the Siauw group's objectives.[43] Yap made little headway here, too. Having the support of a majority of Baperki's leaders, Siauw was determined to move ahead on every issue. In one vote at the December meeting, perhaps on the question of supporting Guided Democracy, Yap lost sixteen to one.[44]

Yap was frustrated and angry after the December meeting. He continued to see Guided Democracy as vague and potentially dangerous. Moreover, his sense of political ethics had been violated. Siauw's declaration of Baperki's support for Guided Democracy struck Yap as dirty politics, a fait accompli like that of February 1958 when educational policy was worked out behind closed doors and in violation of democratic procedure. The same was true of the East Java branch's intentional manipulation, publicizing its own approval of Guided

Democracy before the plenary executive committee had completed its deliberations.

During February 1959 Yap engaged in a tense correspondence with the executive committee, via its first secretary, Buyung Saleh, demanding to know when it had ever made a decision, at a formal meeting with himself present, to support Guided Democracy. Siauw had eluded this question in December, but Buyung Saleh came up with the argument that Yap, like others, had agreed to Soekarno's Konsepsi in February 1957 and that this implied approval of whatever the president proposed thereafter, including Guided Democracy.[45] Incensed at this spurious argument, Yap could only answer that "because of the attitudes, character, and atmosphere that have developed I feel there is no longer a place for me in the central executive committee [*pengurus harian pusat*, the small, permanent executive in charge of daily affairs], which from the start I trusted as honest men of whom one could be proud, even though we did not always share the same opinions."[46] He stopped attending the executive committee meetings.

In the meantime Baperki leaders were racing to keep up with political developments. Until early 1959 conflict over Soekarno's proposals had brought matters to a standstill. The primary issue had to do with Soekarno's plan, backed by the army under General A. H. Nasution, to introduce a corporatist concept—functional groups of various sorts, including the military—into representative institutions. This would reduce the influence of the political parties, and the parties were naturally disinclined to go along. Yet they could not do the one thing that might have given them an edge of political initiative: complete a new constitution in the Constituent Assembly. Although much of the text had been agreed upon, closure was made impossible by ideological conflict between Islamic parties, which sought an Islamically defined instrument, and all others, which were unalterably opposed to anything of the sort. Neither side had the two-thirds majority necessary for approval.

In January and February of 1959 the solution to the stalemate appeared in the form of a proposal to preempt the efforts of the Konstituante by restoring the Constitution of 1945, which provided for a very strong executive and representation of regions and undefined "groups," and made no mention of Islam. For army leaders, the 1945 Constitution was particularly compelling, not only because it symbolized the revolutionary period in which the army had been born and played so significant a part, but also because it created the opening for their expanded political participation. In 1957, at a National Council meeting, General Nasution had suggested reinstating the 1945 Constitution, and now, in early 1959, he urged it again on the Djuanda cabinet. Soekarno went along. When the proposal broke into the open at the end of January, the PNI and several other parties eager to stay close to Soekarno supported it. The government decided to take the idea directly to the Constituent Assembly.[47]

In Baperki Siauw, already committed to Soekarno and Guided Democracy, had little choice now but to approve the 1945 Constitution proposal as well. But it was an especially problematic choice for ethnic Chinese, because this Constitution contains two distinctly discriminatory provisions: Article 6, which stipulated that the president must be a native Indonesian, and Article 26, which stated that citizens are native-born Indonesians and others naturalized according to law.[48]

On 26 February KENSI issued another in a stream of anti-Chinese missives, this time referring happily to Article 6 of the 1945 Constitution. On 27 February, the Baperki management committee, absent Yap, met to respond to the KENSI challenge. Its statement to the press afterwards began with an emphatic endorsement of the 1945 Constitution and especially of Soekarno. The spirit of the 1945 Proclamation, the statement declared, was revolutionary and democratic. Article 6 was only the result of a strategy meant to avoid the appointment of a Japanese as president in 1945.[49] However, Article 27, which provides that all citizens shall have the same status in law and in government, reflects the true intention of the 1945 Constitution. The statement continued with a reminder that returning to the Constitution of 1945 meant returning to the spirit of 1945, which would correct all deviations, including that of nativism, and "we have full faith in President Soekarno as the highest executive authority, who it is not possible would continue the policy of the nativism game."

When he read the statement, Yap reacted strongly in a letter addressed to the executive committee and the management committee. He said that replying to KENSI was one thing, which he approved, but supporting the 1945 Constitution was another. As a vice chairman of the management committee, he said, he had never been invited formally to attend a meeting to discuss this issue.[50] And he accused "a certain group in BAPERKI" of trying to force its views on others and presenting those who will not give in with faits accomplis. Yap sent copies of the letter to *Pos Indonesia* (successor to *Keng Po*), *Sin Po*, the PSI-oriented *Pedoman*, and *Republik*. Baperki's secretariat replied with a blistering rebuttal that was published in *Republik* on 4 March immediately below Yap's letter.[51]

Yap's split from the rest of Baperki's leadership was almost complete as the correspondence tirades continued through March and April. On 3 April Yap wrote to the executive committee again, summarizing a few issues thus far. First, he said, the executive committee had never in formal session discussed and taken a decision to approve Guided Democracy. Second, the reasoning of the committee that, because in February 1957 it had approved the basic objectives of the president's Konsepsi, therefore it automatically agreed to Guided Democracy, meant that anything else proclaimed in the framework of the Konsepsi also had to be accepted automatically, without discussion or decision. "Now I begin to understand," he continued, "that the view of the Central Management Committee, which has already approved the 1945 Constitution with its discriminatory provisions (see Articles 6 and 26), must be regarded in the same light and consequences." Under these circumstances, he could no longer share responsibility for the policies of the committee and would continue to absent himself from its meetings. He would retain his mandate from the Baperki congress, however, until the next congress, when he would exercise his rights to report fully on all deviations from Baperki's principles and goals to the full executive committee and the congress itself, which he did, dramatically, in December 1960.[52] The committee replied that it would no longer explain anything to him by letter, as he always misinterpreted their letters, and accused him of violating his responsibilities as a member of the committee.[53]

EIGHT

THE BAPERKI WARS

A LESS determined or less principled man, or a more sensible one, might have fled the ordeals Yap faced one after another in 1959 and 1960. But he seemed to thrive on them. It was an astonishing period for the energy he expended on lost causes. Only in his church did he and other ecumenists enjoy some success in creating a unified synod for the three provincial Chinese reformed churches of Java. But for the rest, Yap rushed from one disastrous front to another. In Baperki he refused to relinquish his largely solitary and entirely hopeless battle to restore the organization to its original purpose, as he understood it. In the Konstituante in mid-1959, he delivered a memorable speech against adopting the 1945 Constitution, to no effect except to enrage other Baperki leaders. A year later he engaged in the most significant debate yet, in *Star Weekly*'s pages, over the integration-assimilation issue, where he opposed the dominant positions on both sides. In December 1960 he gained some unwanted respite, absenting himself from Baperki meetings after his open confrontation with Siauw at the Semarang national congress.

The struggle over the issue of supporting the 1945 Constitution began in Baperki but then shifted from that obscure *peranakan* stage to the national arena of the Constituent Assembly, where the dilemma became plain. On the merits, because of the obviously discriminatory Articles 6 and 26, the 1945 Constitution had to be unacceptable to *peranakan* citizens. But the Siauw group had attached Baperki to Soekarno's star, which complicated its position. On 25 April 1959, Baperki members of the Konstituante, including Siauw and

Yap, met at Oei Tjoe Tat's home to discuss the situation. On the question of what to do about the 1945 Constitution in the debates, Siauw told the group that Baperki had not yet determined its position. He agreed with the general disapproval of Articles 6 and 26, but stated that the problem now was how to make the best of the situation.[1]

This apparently meant swallowing hard and supporting the 1945 Constitution. Siauw himself was torn. In his speech to the Konstituante on 11 May, his misgivings were obvious. Despite the 1945 Constitution's shortcomings, said Siauw, Baperki nevertheless saw no reason to reject the government's proposal to restore it in full, without amendment. But Siauw treated Article 6 at length, as he had to for the sake of Baperki's membership, insisting that it had to be viewed in its historical context and that the spirit of the Constitution was not racist. He hoped that the new People's Consultative Assembly, the highest organ of state under the 1945 Constitution, would eventually improve the document and eliminate all references to *asli* (native).[2] Siauw and the three other official Baperki delegates would, therefore, support the government.

Five other delegates who were Baperki members, the so-called "Faction of Five" which included Go Gien Tjwan and Yap, split four to one, with Yap going off on his own to give one of the most compelling addresses in the debates. Go half-jokingly reported that the "Faction of Five minus one" supported the government proposal to restore the 1945 Constitution. When his statement appeared in the press the next day (13 May), Khing was furious at Go for spotlighting her husband. At a time that was so politically tense and uncertain, danger seemed pervasive and Khing was nervous. Yap appeared to be alone and vulnerable and taking chances. Within Baperki, the reaction to his stand was hostile, and there were angry demands that he be thrown out, but no other repercussions.[3] Outside of Baperki and a few curious Konstituante circles, however, no one paid much attention to him.

Yap had labored over his speech, which turned out to be an exercise in both political courage and realistic, prescient political analysis. His losing battle with Siauw freed him to speak beyond Baperki, and for the first time he addressed issues and an audience unconstrained by minority ethnic or religious interests. Yap's arguments with Siauw over Guided Democracy had revived his longtime interest in constitutional law and deepened his newer worries about abuse of power. The political drift of Guided Democracy confirmed all of his suspicions. Not least, the legal system had begun to erode, setting off alarms in Yap's mind. In early 1959 Chief Public Prosecutor Soeprapto had been dismissed for political reasons connected with the trial of a Dutch national. The army under martial law had taken to closing down newspapers at will. Restrictions on public activity became frequent. Soekarno himself was openly contemptuous of lawyers and their slavish devotion to "Western" notions of state organization and process. While others saw hope in the kind of change that Soekarno promised, Yap saw evidence of decay and few optimistic signs of regeneration. Others in Baperki took up Soekarno's calls to revolution, movement, and the spirit of this and that, while Yap thought more cautiously and conservatively about institutions, guarantees, controls over power, human rights.

Yap was among the very few in the Konstituante debates who refused to treat the 1945 Constitution question as a matter of partisan or ideological interest. This alone sets his speech apart, not so much because it was courageous as because it ignored the political givens of those times. Many who knew Yap in connection with Baperki believed that he opposed the 1945 Constitution because of Articles 6 and 26 alone, which would place him squarely in the *peranakan* camp, albeit opposed to Baperki's political choices. It was not so. Near the middle of his speech, he did address the minority problem directly, speaking to his opponents in Baperki as well as to the Konstituante generally:

> Article 27 (1) speaks of the equality of rights of all citizens in law and government. But article 6 (1) provides that the President be a native Indonesian. In my opinion article 6 (1) contradicts the equality of rights of all citizens in article 27 (1).
>
> Considering the provisions of article 26 (1) which classifies Indonesian citizens as "native Indonesians" and "others," I have to doubt that article 6 (1) does not establish racial discrimination. In a democratic state there ought to be equal opportunity, really equal, for all citizens, in all matters, including the highest position in the state.
>
> Thus to avoid suspicions abroad or at home that the Indonesian Constitution has an odor about it of "Blut und Boden" or "Apartheidstheorie," unlike another honorable member of the Constituent Assembly [either Siauw or Go] who rather preferred to convince and comfort himself with various excuses that the above provisions are not racially discriminatory . . . I on the other hand am inclined to a solution, more sympathetic and responsible to the group of Indonesian citizens for whom I was appointed a representative in this Constituent Assembly . . . that is, that the provisions in article 6 (1) and article 26 (1) be brought into line with the Spirit of the Proclamation of 1945.[4]

But these comments on Articles 6 and 26 took up less than one of eight folio pages. The speech began on a quite different note:

> What are the motives and objectives of the Government in its proposal "to return to the Constitution of 1945?"
>
> If I do not misunderstand, the motives of the Government are: to stop irregularities in political, military, and social-economic fields, to end corruption, to unify all the people . . . to overcome all the difficulties of people and state.
>
> These are glorious motives and objectives, which deserve the highest respect from everyone who loves the Indonesian homeland and who possesses a sense of responsibility to land and nation. . . .
>
> Having agreed with the motives and objectives of the Government's proposal it remains only to consider and discuss its means, that is, the Constitution of 1945 and Guided Democracy. . . .
>
> The history of constitutional states is the history of the struggle of people against tyranny, despotism, and absolutism; the struggle for fundamental human rights and freedoms against absolute power. The constitution is a manifestation of the victory of justice over arbitrariness, victory of "Recht" over "Macht." Therefore a constitution is intended to establish and guarantee in its body fundamental human rights and freedoms, to formulate and limit Government authority, and to control the exercise of that authority. . . .
>
> The history of the struggle for Independence of the Indonesian people is also a struggle for the supremacy of "Law" over "Power," of justice over arbitrariness. Therefore, the Indonesian Constitution must share the same character and purpose as other constitutions.
>
> What good were the sacrifices of the Indonesian people for the sake of Independence, if Indonesians can still be detained at will, without knowing what they are guilty of, without trial, and then released just like that without the right to sue for revision and damages, just as in the colony?
>
> What good are the sacrifices of the Indonesian people in the struggle for Independence, if, as in the colonial period, Indonesians [still] do not have the right and freedom to think, to write, to organize, to hold meetings, to join political parties, to act in opposition, to strike, and so on. . . .
>
> What good are the sacrifices of the Indonesian people for the sake of Independence if in Indonesian society and state there is a division of

citizens into several classes and there is racial discrimination, as in the colonial period?

What good, finally, Mister Chairman, is all the suffering and misery of the Indonesian people in defeating the colonialist, if the Indonesian people fall back into the grip of other oppressors, even of their own nation?

In order to avoid making senseless all the sacrifices, suffering, and misery of the Indonesian people, now and in future, the Indonesian people require a Constitution like the one analyzed above.

Just about everyone in the Konstituante debates understood perfectly well that they were merely symbolic, giving an aura of legitimacy to the transfer of power from the parties to Soekarno and marking an end to ideological conflict by resolving the standoff between political Islam and its opponents. What went on in the Asia-Africa Building in Bandung, where the assembly met, had relatively little to do with constitutional principles. The major parties—except for the Nahdlatul Ulama, whose leaders were caught in a tug-of-war between the government and their party constituency—had already decided how they would vote on the issue and had announced their positions. So had Baperki. Yap, however, insisted on taking the Constitution itself seriously, eschewing immediate political questions in favor of larger issues of state organization and its consequences for the Indonesian citizenry. His analysis was remarkable for the accuracy of its predictions.

Following his opening remarks, Yap went on to say that he did not expect a perfect constitution, but one with fewer imperfections was better than one with more. He built his detailed analysis of the institutional problems inherent in the 1945 Constitution around the question: "To what extent are the fundamental rights and freedoms of human beings and citizens guaranteed in the Constitution of 1945?" This crucial matter, he argued, was addressed in only five articles (27 through 31) of the 1945 Constitution, compared with twenty-eight articles in the 1950 Constitution. And even the 1950 Constitution was inadequate in this respect. Anticipating the reform agenda taken up years later by the new association of advocates, Peradin, Yap argued that the 1945 Constitution was seriously flawed because it did not include habeas corpus, judicial review, the imposition of criminal penalties for human rights violations, or the right of religious conversion. It was in this context that he discussed, among other issues, Articles 6 and 26.

He went on to raise the critical matter of the authority vested by the 1945 Constitution in the president. The highest body of state is meant to be the

People's Deliberative Assembly (MPR), consisting of Parliament and such additional regional delegations and "other groups as are determined by law." Yet the president, in Article 5, is given legislative powers. He could, therefore, issue laws and regulations determining the make-up of these "groups as are determined by law," and, Yap implied, usurp or at least diminish the independence and authority of the legislature. This, indeed, presidents did before and after 1965.

Moreover, Yap argued, since the president had authority under Law 1 of 1950 to appoint members of the Supreme Court, he indirectly holds judicial powers as well. What fundamental rights and freedoms, Yap asked rhetorically, do the people have to balance these powers of the President in the 1945 Constitution?

Turning next to Guided Democracy, Yap noted that, although the government regarded it as democracy,

> democracy is no longer democracy without the freedoms to think, talk, write, organize, join parties, and meet. Excesses in exercising these freedoms cannot at all justify the elimination of such freedoms. Anything good can be abused or used for ends that are not good, but it is surely wrong for us to throw out the good, simply because we have abused it or used it for things that are not good. A right or freedom bears an obligation, the obligation to heed the same right of others, or otherwise be punished. This punishment is the one restriction that may be imposed against the exercise of the freedoms to think, talk, write, and so on.

Yap passionately argued that once these fundamental freedoms were restricted, others could be too, including religion, education, and work. Referring then directly to the government's determination to "simplify" the party system, he noted that "from restriction, or in the Government's terms, 'simplification,' to elimination is only a short distance." This too was an accurate prediction.

He brought these issues into a sharp focus on the notion, averred by Soekarno, that the essence of Guided Democracy was deliberation (*permusyawaratan*) and consensus, not debate and challenge which ends in a contest of power and a vote.

> Deliberation, in my view, presupposes that at least two equal sides are speaking. But if only one side in the discussion has authority to determine

> at any time when the other side is [speaking properly] and when he is debating and [being oppositional], then from the start this deliberation is like that between a sergeant major and an underclass common man under martial law.

Yap insisted that in his references to the presidency he did not mean President Soekarno personally, or the person of any future president, but the concept and function of the presidency occupied at any time by any Indonesian person. Before summarizing, he concluded on this note:

> Mr. Chairman, in my first speech in a session of this Constituent Assembly I once read a quote, in English then, to the effect that if humans were angels, no government would be needed. And I added: nor would a constitution be needed. But humans are not angels. Indeed, humans often do evil things that are not desired, and do not do the good things that are desired. We are aware that all power carries with it the potential for abusing that power, and as power grows so does the abuse of power. For this reason, those in authority [or power] must have their authority limited in order to protect them from themselves and to protect others from them.

Mincing few words, Yap recapitulated his discussion:

1. As the legal basis of a stable system of government the document of the 1945 Constitution is a "masterpiece."
2. As the legal basis of a democratic law-state [*negara hukum, rechtsstaat,* rule of law] the 1945 Constitution does not fulfill the minimum conditions.
3. The propositions of Guided Democracy are not convincing [on the point that] they are identical with the essentials of democracy.
4. With the 1945 Constitution as a foundation and Guided Democracy as the instrument, it is possible that the Government can transport the Indonesian people to a just and prosperous society, but also possibly to suffering and misery. Only God knows.

Citing his position as a member of the Konstituante as his mandate from the people, and the second letter of Peter 1:4 as a mandate from God, Yap voted to reject the government's proposal that the 1945 Constitution be accepted without amendment, but did accept it as no more than valuable material to be used in drafting a permanent constitution according to the normal procedures of the Constituent Assembly.[5] He was one of only two or three members, out of 533, who openly broke with his faction on the issue and made his "no" vote public.

His speech was inspired by moral outrage, informed by liberal political values, and filled with coolly skeptical and pessimistic political foresight. In it, Yap broke with Baperki in more than one sense. While rejecting the 1945 Constitution and Guided Democracy, he also began to break out of the suffocating confinement of ethnic identity. He spoke less as a *peranakan* Chinese with formal Indonesian citizenship than as an Indonesian citizen who happened to be a *peranakan*. In this there is some irony, but also a reflection of the complexity of the *peranakan* condition. It was the Javanese insiders, Siauw, Go, and others, who, starting from the PTI insistence that ethnic Chinese be treated as Indonesian, ended up organizing as a minority and acquiescing to a structure of authority that promised them more than it could deliver. The outsider Yap, who fought against turning Baperki into anything more than a narrowly defined interest group, acted like a fully empowered citizen, doing what Yap believed every citizen must, criticizing and opposing authority on issues of principle.

The government's proposal failed because the Islamic parties finally drew together to deny it a two-thirds majority.[6] By this time it hardly mattered, for the new regime did not include or need parliamentary institutions. After the final Konstituante vote, in early June General Nasution imposed a ban on all political activities and proceeded to generate pressure on Soekarno, then abroad, to decree the restoration of the 1945 Constitution. This Soekarno did on 5 July 1959. The Constituent Assembly was adjourned forever. In 1960 the Parliament, elected five years earlier, was dismissed and reconstituted, with a large number of new appointees selected by Soekarno, as the Gotong-Royong Parliament (DPR-GR, Dewan Perwakilan Rakyat-Gotong Royong). It was all very much as Yap had predicted.

From then on, until October 1965, the politics of Guided Democracy whirled, increasingly frenetically, around Soekarno, the army, and the PKI as the essential power centers. Soekarno tipped toward the PKI, largely as a means of countering the army, while remaining parties and groups looked to one camp or the other as the hope of the future. It was a time of shrill political conflict and tension. As the economy declined, much of it fled underground as an inflationary spiral sped upwards. Corruption grew to alarming levels as the central and regional bureaucracies that had almost been subjugated by the parties during the parliamentary years were restored to places of prominence and extractive competence commensurate with their colonial origins. In 1960 Yap and many other like-thinking lawyers were shocked by Soekarno's cavalier dismissal of the separation-of-powers principle and his appointment of Wirjono Projodikoro, the chairman of the Supreme Court, to the executive cabinet.[7] But Soekarno's symbolic declaration of independence from "Western" constitutional models, along with the populist rhetoric and patrimonial organization of Guided Democracy, legitimated much worse than what was in practice. As Yap forecast, human rights counted for less and less.

By mid-1959 Siauw was in complete control of the Baperki organization. For the next three or four years, his close support of Soekarno seemed to make good sense politically. Baperki was actively involved, effective in running its schools and making headway in establishing an education faculty and then a university, and its voice was at least heard in the government on issues affecting ethnic Chinese. There were misgivings here and there in the organization, and Siauw himself may have had more than most.

Yap was unpopular in Baperki following his Konstituante vote. Even those who admired him thought him reckless, while most believed he was politically simple-minded, naive, and obstructionist. Between January and August 1959, although the secretariat routinely invited him to executive committee meetings, he attended only one. His sympathizers there—among them, Thio Thiam Tjong and Mrs. Lauw In Nio, also a Protestant—grew silent and at length quietly withdrew from the organization.

Yap, by contrast, grew noisier. Estranged as he was and boycotted by most other Baperki leaders, he got bits and pieces of information about the organization's activities from his law partner, Oei Tjoe Tat. The two argued often and occasionally bitterly, for Oei, though hardly on the far left, nevertheless supported Siauw. When Oei told him that an extraordinary congress would be held at the end of August 1959, Yap wrote to the executive committee to propose another item for the agenda: to wit, his charge that the executive committee had perverted the principles, objectives, and struggle of Baperki.[8] A few days later, on 7 August, he wrote again in connection with Presidential Regulation 2/1959, which forbade civil servants from belonging to political parties. Because Baperki had engaged in trying to affect state forms and policies, he argued, it fell under the definition of a political party according to the new regulation. It followed that the chairman of Baperki, as a member of the High Advisory Council (Dewan Pertimbangan Agung), thus a civil servant, should resign from his position and membership in the organization, a party. The executive committee replied that his first accusation could be entered in the agenda, but that on the second matter, if Yap had read the regulation more carefully he would not have written as he did.[9]

Had Yap attended the sessions of the congress held from 28–30 August, he might well have made an enraged scene. These meetings had been called basically to review developments after the restoration of the 1945 Constitution and to consider organizational changes, including Siauw's efforts to attract non-ethnic Chinese members. There were several indirect attacks against Yap, with Siauw, for example, referring to "those afraid of their own shadows" who had objected to Baperki's establishing a university in its own name.[10] Oei Tjoe Tat, in his report on the Constituent Assembly, however, offered a veiled defense of Yap, pointing out that nothing bound all Baperki delegates to a single position and no pressure was imposed.[11]

But Yap was not present, for he did not stay at the conference beyond the evening of 27 August, when the plenary executive committee met. There he insisted that his letter of 3 August be read and that his accusations against the executive committee be placed on the congress agenda. His demand sent the session into a tailspin, with the Jakarta delegate urging that something be done to stop Yap from continually interrupting the discussion. Buyung Saleh suggested that, as the martial law authority's ban on discussion of the Constituent Assembly deliberations was still in effect, Yap should postpone his proposal until the next regular congress. Yap replied that if it were not discussed, he would leave the session. He did not intend to discuss constitutional issues, but rather wanted to prevent Baperki from getting involved in problems of state principles. The Jakarta delegate protested again that Yap had already talked several times, and no one else had had a chance to speak. Finally Siauw asked Buyung Saleh to read Yap's letter. The minutes do not report whatever discussion followed, but it must have been tense, as Oei Tjoe Tat, always eager to avoid open conflict, asked for a recess. When the discussion resumed, the executive committee agreed that Yap's accusations should be taken up at the next congress, setting the stage for Yap's dramatic address in Semarang in December 1960. Yap left the meeting. Immediately afterwards Tan Foe Khiong proposed that Yap's behavior be discussed, accusing him of neglecting his responsibilities as a member of the executive committee. Siauw replied that such a discussion would not be fair, for Yap was not present, so this too should be postponed until the next regular congress.[12] This was the last Baperki meeting Yap disrupted before the Semarang congress.

Although Yap had begun to reach beyond ethnic boundaries in the Konstituante, he nevertheless remained essentially bound by them. As he put it years later, in the early 1960s he was still "very ethnic." *Peranakan* issues were the ones he felt least reluctant to address. Address them he did in the integration-assimilation controversy that broke out in 1960, staking out a position quite independent of all others.

The differences between integrators and assimilators had long been latent in *peranakan* history, as they are perhaps in that of all adapting minorities. At extremes, the question was whether the minority should maintain itself as a recognizable group or whether it should disappear. Seldom, however, was the question put that way. Ethnic Chinese in Indonesia had made choices at any number of points along the continuum between those extremes, without necessarily generalizing their choices into principle. But in 1960 the question suddenly turned political and ideological. As it did so, all the contradictions and paradoxes of *peranakan* existence became painfully manifest.

The debate broke out in public at a time of extraordinary tensions. Setting the stage was the 1959 ban on alien (read: citizens of China) retail trading in rural areas, which had an appalling effect on the entire minority community, citizens of Indonesia and aliens alike.[13] A complex affair, involving economic nationalist and anti-Chinese motives in the Assaatist mode, it began with a policy announcement of the Minister of Trade in May, while Soekarno was abroad. Soekarno apparently did not favor the ban, but neither could he rescind it in the face of considerable public support. In November he reluctantly issued Presidential Regulation No. 10 (PP10, Peraturan Presiden 10), which clarified and softened the policy, but not enough to make a difference. As a result, in 1960 over a hundred thousand Chinese left Indonesia for China on Chinese ships, amid much name-calling between Beijing and Jakarta.

Quite apart from the human misery and economic disruption caused by the ban, which occurred at a time of growing economic tension generally, it cast a pall over the whole minority community. Little physical violence occurred, for the animus behind the policy was not local but national. But violence was implicit, and the vulnerability of all ethnic Chinese became plain as anti-Chinese sentiment broke out openly. Distinctions between alien and citizen Chinese, never very convincing to many, were simply lost; and the departure of many for China confirmed the common myth that, when push came to shove, all Chinese preferred China to Indonesia.[14]

In this severe crisis Baperki's influence counted for little, despite Siauw's connections with Soekarno. Although Soekarno had spoken out in mid-1959 against anti-Chinese discrimination, he could not—or did not—take the risk of trying to bury the issue. At most, he was able to ameliorate its effects slightly in the final form of PP10. Baperki was paralyzed. At a meeting of its executive committee in Batu, East Java, in mid-April 1960, with Yap still absenting himself, Gouw Jam Hok proposed issuing a statement on PP10. Siauw declined to do so, confirming Yap's prediction that Baperki's political drift would inevitably weaken its ability to defend the Chinese minority. "[Gouw] must hold in mind," said Siauw, "that in the present situation we must avoid arousing the suspicions of other groups, in this case the majority group. Many suspicions have now arisen against Baperki, so that [I] don't agree to issuing a written statement concerning PP10, because it will cause suspicions without advantage."[15] Yap's outrage is indelible, in red, on the margins of his copy of the minutes.

The PP10 crisis demonstrated that Baperki's clout was limited, but also, to Baperki's *peranakan* opponents, that its political perspective was dead wrong. By 1959 and 1960 the Indonesian political universe was increasingly polarized between the PKI and the army. Soekarno leaned to the left partly out of preference for its promise of dynamic change but as much, perhaps, out of the political logic that he needed to balance the army's strength. The army leadership actively contested with the PKI and other groups for influence, establishing its own political fronts or assisting others in the right-wing camp. At just about every turn, organizations on the left were countered by organizations on the right that were created, directed, and supported by the army—labor unions, youth groups, women's organizations, student groups, and so on. From the start, the assimilation cause had army support so it was inevitable that the army would be interested in creating an ethnic Chinese organization to counter the presumably integrationist, left-wing Baperki. When, in 1963, it finally produced such an organization, the Institute for the Promotion of National Unity (LPKB, Lembaga Pembinaan Kesatuan Bangsa), its chair was a naval legal officer, K. Sindhunata (Ong Tjong Hai).[16]

The assimilation movement went public in early 1960, in the middle of the PP10 crisis and a smattering of advice from all sides about how to deal with the minority's problems. One government minister, speaking at a Baperki seminar no less, urged *peranakan* to give up "exclusive" activities and gradually assimilate culturally, economically, and even biologically. Another, in a meeting with *peranakan* youths, advised adopting "Indonesian" names. Siauw Giok Tjhan replied on 13 March, Baperki's anniversary, that such assimilation was undemocratic, opposed to human rights, and, in any case, impossible.

On 24 March, ten well-known *peranakan*—including Auwjong Peng Koen, Injo Beng Goat, and Ong Hok Ham—issued a statement entitled "Towards Genuine Assimilation" that set off several months' worth of polemics and many more of intricate infighting with Baperki for government support.[17] Calling attention to the ministers' remarks and Siauw's refutation, as well as to a speech by Soekarno in December in which he had urged more intermarriages among the country's many ethnic groups, and to the long history of biological mixing in Indonesia, the signatories declared that: (1) they fully supported the views of President Soekarno; (2) the minority problem could only be resolved via the route of free and active voluntary assimilation in all fields; and (3) they could not approve of measures and statements that artificially deterred the process of assimilation, but neither could they agree with measures that forced such assimilation.[18]

So began a public struggle that never really ended but took a few startling turns over the next three decades. Battle lines were drawn between integrators and assimilators, with outriders here and there on both sides prepared to launch variations on the themes. Strident rhetoric was filled with name-calling and politically loaded accusations, for in part the issue was greatly exacerbated, as Yap had insisted for years that it would be, by Baperki's politicization of it. The ten prominent supporters of assimilation were all opposed to Baperki, which they saw as communist and pro-China and not so much "integrators" as separatists devoted to maintaining a status quo that was colonially inspired. Ironically, there was enough truth in this accusation to sting. Baperki leaders, for their part, regarded the assimilation movement as a Catholic or PSI conspiracy, or both, led by liberals who—as the word war turned nastier—had been absent from the revolution, a heavy missile in the armory of Guided Democracy supporters.[19]

The pages of *Star Weekly* especially, but also Baperki's daily *Republik* and other *peranakan* journals, pursued the debate during the first half of 1960. Invective and innuendo aside, the analyses and discussions were serious, painful, and full of paradox. The terms "right" and "left" became even fuzzier than usual. For while assimilators tended to come from the political center, the idea of assimilation can be seen as much to the left of (or at least more far reaching than) the integration idea. Left-leaning Baperki took a conservative position with respect to the protection of the minority's right to maintain itself, while the centrist, liberal assimilationist group, claiming the pre-war PTI among its ancestors, tended to the quite radical argument that members of the minority were right to choose to disappear into the majority, as long as no coercion was involved. Sensible cases could be made for either view, but the implications of both were easily spun to extremes that no one intended. With equal absurdity, integrationists were accused of supporting segregation; assimilationists, of approving forced interethnic marriages.

The differences among these equally well-assimilated *peranakan* were at once starker and more subtle and variegated than they themselves could easily make clear. In part the differences were political, distributed from left to right of center on a continuum of Indonesian ideological choices spread between the PKI and the PSI, though, in fact, many integrationists were closer to the political center than to the political left. In larger part, however, the differences had an uncomfortable affinity with choices of personal identity. There is an analogy, perhaps, with assimilated Ashkenazi Jews in America, who divide in much the same way, some asserting their Jewishness, with or without the religion, and finding in Israel a confirming association, while others no longer think it worth distinguishing themselves from other standard white Americans. But Jews in America have had an easier time than *peranakan* Chinese in Indonesia, where the issues and pressures have been constant and public.

As the conflict among these *peranakan* was substantially over identity, so it was substantively condensed to a question of names: to keep Chinese names or adopt "Indonesian" ones. (I enclose "Indonesian" in quotation marks to make the point that in ethnically diverse Indonesia, Chinese names are, in one sense at least, no less Indonesian than Batak, Javanese, Sundanese, or Menadonese names.) Integrationists contemptuously repudiated any proposal that *peranakan* should give up their names. Siauw and Yap, fleetingly in agreement, waxed livid on this question. Assimilationists varied hugely from enthusiasts who adopted "Indonesian" names without compunction to more measured actors who adjusted their names symbolically or kept their own names. Auwjong Peng Koen became P. K. Ojong (later, following the language reform of the early 1970s, Oyong). Ong Hok Ham became Onghokham. Lauw Chuan Tho, a Protestant signatory of the assimilation statement who eventually converted to Islam, became Lauwchuantho and then Junus Jahya. For integrators, all this was nonsense and worse, a denial of origins and enraging cowardice, or opportunism, or self-delusion.[20]

Although on the issue of integration versus assimilation Yap and Siauw were on the same side, they were not together. For Yap, this was a watershed period, into which, while ethnic issues still dominated his imagination, other matters were intruding. For all intents and purposes, he had broken with Baperki, though he was still waiting in mid-1960 for one last chance to turn Siauw away and Baperki back. The PP10 crisis troubled him deeply, not simply because it was anti-Chinese but because it was inhumane. By 1960, too, the consequences of Guided Democracy had become all too clear. Under martial law the army was everywhere and dictated its own law, while the civil legal system had begun to rot, as prosecutors and police became increasingly extortionate and judges increasingly shaded their eyes. Yap, as a devout lawyer, hated the corruption of the law even more than the slogan-filled and hypocritical public discourse of Guided Democracy. Yet, despite his speech to the Constituent Assembly, he felt on safer ground focusing on ethnic issues.

Yap leapt into the integration-assimilation debate with a series of three articles—actually longish letters to the editor—for *Star Weekly*, in April and May 1960. In them, he managed to attack every other side of the argument, without producing a practicable solution of his own. These articles, by crystallizing and sharpening the issues, became an essential centerpiece of the polemic drama. He worked hard on them, leaving dozens of drafts in his files. The intense debate itself and Yap's contributions to it set off more, and more acrimonious, correspondence than *Star Weekly* had ever received.

The first short article was entitled "Two Therapies (Part I) to Cure the Sickness of Racial Discrimination."[21] The title gives away its integrationist position, locating the problem as one of racial discrimination whose source is the majority, rather than one, as assimilationists were wont to argue, for which the minority itself had to assume substantial responsibility. Yap's target in the first piece, however, was Siauw. Siauw himself had sharply challenged the assimilationist position in a letter to *Star Weekly* on 2 April, accusing its proponents of having caused great anxiety among *peranakan* about forced name changes, intermarriage, and religious conversion. Quoting his own earlier speech to Baperki, and obliquely charging assimilationists with sins of which they were not culpable, Siauw said that forcing people to change their names or religions or to intermarry was a violation of human rights and would not, in any case, soon solve the problem of racial discrimination. Only the establishment of a just and prosperous society, which Soekarno said would end the exploitation of man by man, could achieve this end.

Yap's first article confronted this argument. The original draft was more vitriolic than the one published. In a long introductory paragraph he had excoriated "Nazi-fascists" and their treatment of Indonesian citizens of Chinese descent. In the published version this paragraph and all references to "Nazi-fascists" were excised by Oyong, who explained to Yap that the article was too long but who undoubtedly had other worries (for both Yap and *Star Weekly*) in mind. Instead, the article opens by saying that, although on the subject of assimilation there is more than one point of view among Indonesians of Chinese descent, only one would be discussed here. Yap then proceeded to lay this view out in the following way: racial discrimination is merely a symptom of a more fundamental illness, which is that Indonesian society remains feudal, colonial, and capitalist; the only appropriate cure for that illness is a radical operation to remove the heart, lungs, and liver and replace them with new ones, or, in political terms, raze the feudal-colonial-capitalist structure of society and erect a new society; what kind of society? a communist society, with the Soviet Union and China as models. This view, wrote Yap, is that of those who control Baperki under Siauw's leadership. (Yap seldom resorted to the circumlocutions of Indonesian public political discourse, as in referring to "a certain figure.") "This kind of cure we will call the Communist therapy or Siauw Giok Tjhan's therapy."

Wielding nationalist tenets, Yap then attacked Siauw's premise that the only way to cure racism is to perform radical transplantation. Replacing the present political system, he wrote, is unnecessary, for the minority's safety and equal treatment would be assured if only Indonesia were faithful to its own principles of Bhinneka Tunggal Ika (Unity in Diversity, the Indonesian national motto) and the Pancasila, Democracy, and Human Rights.

According to Siauw's therapy, Yap continued, the disappearance of racial discrimination must depend on whether, and when, the communists were successful in transforming Indonesian society. An evaluation of Siauw's therapy is thus necessarily an evaluation of whether, and when, the communist group would succeed in controlling Indonesian state and society. This is difficult to predict, wrote Yap, but given that 72 million of Indonesia's 80 million people were Muslims, another 2 million were Christians, and one million were Hindus and Buddhists, all noncommunist—a simplistic generalization on Yap's part—it is obvious that it would take more than a little time for communism to win out. Is there anything positive in Siauw's therapy? Of course, Yap said, for it seeks to end not the minority but the minority problem. Nevertheless, the proposed therapy must be rejected because it embraces totalitarianism, but also because it is unrealistic.

Taking umbrage, Siauw replied in *Star Weekly*, 23 April, accusing Yap of McCarthyism, and then reciting Soekarno's prescriptions to which, by implication, Yap stood vulnerably opposed.

Yap's second article addressed itself to the assimilationist proposal of the ten *tokoh* (prominent persons), which he evidently regarded as more dangerous than Siauw's view because it seemed more obvious.[22] To the claim that the "minority problem could only be settled by voluntary, active, and free assimilation in all fields," Yap replied that this was one but certainly not the only way. Other means included enforced laws against ethnic and racial discrimination;

public education on the meanings of nationality, human rights, and democratic principles, on the evil of discrimination, and on the fact that national unity and loyalty were not endangered by the existence of minorities; and public policy that created good relations among ethnic and racial groups.

Yap next confronted the social naiveté of assimilationists, as he had the revolutionary optimism of Siauw, with a skeptical analysis of reality. "Say, for the sake of argument, that the proposition of those ten persons is correct, still it must be seriously doubted whether in the situation and atmosphere that exist *now* the desired assimilation could be carried out. Why?" Because, first, assimilation is a "two way process." If the minority wants to assimilate to the majority, but the majority rejects it, then there will be no assimilation. Second, discriminatory regulations and practices had established a minority, and, in response, minority consciousness had deepened. His point could well have emerged from some self-observation; at no time had he himself felt more "Chinese," and it was in reaction to external, not internal, impetus.

Yap also had an objection of principle that is critically important to his political and social outlook. "Our objection to this theory [of assimilation] is that, in essence, it wishes for a leveling [*nivellering*] of the culture of ethnic and racial groups by eliminating their special characteristics. In a situation that embraces a wrongly oriented nationalism, this view contains the danger of extremism that will force 'uniformization,' like that practiced by Hitler's Germany and totalitarian states."

The publication of this second letter opened the dam of the debate, as a flood of letters reached *Star Weekly*, some supporting Yap's arguments, others attacking him in favor of the assimilationist view, and still others, both ethnic Chinese and ethnic Indonesian, offering their own strikingly blunt observations on the problem.[23] Oyong, although making no bones about his assimilationist preferences, kept the pages of his journal open to all sides.

Yap's third and longest piece, in which he offered his own therapy, appeared on 17 May. He wrote it after reading as extensively as he could in the literature on race relations available in Jakarta's bookstores. In some ways the essay represents him at his intellectual best: detached, analytical, rigorous, even-handed, and unremittingly critical. But it ends on a note—his solution—of amazing inanity.

He focused again on the assimilationist argument. Drawing on the works of Louis Wirth, Arnold Rose, and Claude Lévi-Strauss and on the Declaration of Human Rights and other sources, Yap's analysis portrayed minorities as the creation of dominant majorities—defined not by their size but by their power—and, he argued, not only is the creature thereby harmed, but also its creator. "One cannot long discriminate against a people without generating in oneself a sense of guilt and at the same time creating in oneself a conception of oneself as being God."[24] As the dominant group excludes and discriminates, the minority becomes isolated, consolidates, and eventually reacts in acts of "protest or opposition in various forms and means which sometimes are no longer obviously protest and opposition, for example, flight, name changing, racial passing." Thus from its very inception a minority problem consists of an interaction between two groups, each shaped by distinctive experience and psychology. It follows, that the problem cannot be resolved by examining only one side and demanding a correction of that side alone—as the assimilationists do.

Who transformed the resident ethnic Chinese into a minority? he asks.

> At first the colonialists as the dominant group separated out the 'NederlandseOnderdanenVreemdeOsterlingenChinezen' [Netherlands Subjects Foreign Oriental Chinese, three distinct terms that Yap runs together here in bitter mockery] from other Netherlands Subjects, isolated [*meng-exclusifkan*] them from agriculture, civil service, within the schools, and in 'social traffic,' and discriminated against them with the travel pass and residential restriction system . . . and other regulations. Indeed, during that period the Indonesian people were also made a minority. Now the colonial period has passed, and Indonesia is independent and sovereign. We hoped and wished that with this Independence and Sovereignty too all minority status would be abolished. But almost all the discriminatory colonial regulations still remain. Indeed, Assaatism and Kensiism arose, which paradoxically caused the Ali-Baba system.[25] The travel pass system was revived under the name STKI [Surat Tanda Kewarganegaraan Indonesia, Indonesian Citizenship Identification Card], proof of citizenship. Discrimination in the fields of education, economy, and civil service remain. . . . The dominant group has changed, but its status and psychological complex remain the same. . . . And the Chinese minority also remains.

Reviewing the experience of minorities around the world—Jews in Europe, blacks in the United States, among others—Yap noted that physical or cultural differences were the bases on which groups of citizens had been turned into 'minorities.' The ten *tokoh,* he argued, assume that erasing those critical differences would be the sine qua non for erasing discrimination. But are they right in supposing this was the only way to do it? No. Switzerland, Hawaii, the Soviet Union, and China demonstrate that national unity and coexistence were possible without the brutal leveling of Hitler's Brave New World. Yap was wrong about the Soviet Union and China, of course, but fifty years ago this assumption, which Siauw made much of, was common.

Yap was challenged by assimilationists for comparing *peranakan* to European Jews and American blacks. Indeed, the analogies were imprecise and undeveloped. African Americans had never had the economic power and influence of Indonesian Chinese. Although Jews and *peranakan* do offer interesting comparisons, nothing in modern Indonesian experience suggested quite the same kind of hatred or murderous intentions against *peranakan* as Jews had experienced.[26] Yap insisted on casting *peranakan* Chinese as more downtrodden than they were.

But the essential thrust of Yap's analysis was not with these, perhaps vulnerable, comparisons, but with the minority condition itself, discrimination and the social realities that sustain it. "The form, means, gradation, quantum, quality and motive of discrimination are not the problem and do not reduce the fact of discrimination," he quoted Arnold Rose.[27] Yap used Rose's point against assimilationist logic: Understanding its origins and measuring its severity cannot make racial discrimination any less racial discrimination, he chided. Prejudice cannot be justified, no matter how small its scope, no matter who is to blame. We are not freed, from the obligation to condemn and to fight it. Cultural self-obliteration is surrender, not solution, and finding a solution to our minority problem can be accomplished only by taking into consideration existing social and political realities, not by wishful thinking. We must ask, do existing conditions make the proposed solution, assimilation, more or less possible?

Replying to the arguments of Lauwchuantho, the sharpest and most persistent of his critics, Yap conceded that, under optimum circumstances, assimilation is possible, perhaps desirable, as a multidirectional process of give and take (thereby distinguishing himself from the many other integrationists for whom assimilation was anathema).[28] Yap then proceeded to muzzle his concession and attack Lauwchuantho's logic.

> Concerning the Chinese minority the ten *tokoh* have no doubts about their therapy: the minority should best dissolve itself into the "dominant group" in order to "escape" from minority status and for the sake of facili-

> tating the process of development. The "dominant group" becomes the "recipient" host.
>
> But what about the other [Indonesian] ethnic groups? Which of them must be regarded as the recipient? What is the criterion for becoming a "culture recipient"? The number of members of the ethnic group? Or the "good," "less good," or "bad" quality of one culture compared with others? In this case, who is competent to be the judge?

Yap proceeded to a reasoned defense of cultural pluralism and then to a reasoned critique of assimilationism. He must have been aware of the oddness of his position, for on the minority issue he stood closer to Siauw than to Oyong and others with whom he was in fundamental agreement on all but the minority issue. It may be for this reason that his language softens into a persuasive mode.

> While we greatly value and respect the intention and objective (a homogeneous nation) of the ten *tokoh* . . . still, and precisely for the sake of similar ideals, we cannot avoid pointing out the deficiencies and weaknesses of their therapy. . . . Once you have accepted the *principle* of eliminating physical differences or those of mores and customs, why not also accept the elimination of differences of opinion, ideology, religion? Do not differences in these areas contain the greater potential and possibility for conflict, antagonism, or discrimination, obstructing the process of developing a unified and homogeneous nation?
>
> The ten *tokoh* and their friends certainly do not interpret "homogeneous" to mean uniform, though it is doubtful whether they are yet fully aware of the consequences of their views. Who does not want to bear responsibility for the drift of the ideas and words of Lauwchuantho, you or I?
>
> And there is no intention at all here to frighten people, but rather to make you aware, to convince you [Lauwchuantho] and your friends, of the danger of the principle of leveling, which is only gradationally different from uniformization. Lauwchuantho and his allies, who with myself stand against totalitarianism, should be careful not to propose anything that will lead to what is not intended for lack of attention and forethought about problems with more than one facet. . . .
>
> Assimilation of a minority into a "dominant group" cannot possibly be achieved if only the minority wishes it, while this objective is rejected by

> the "dominant group." And if we do not hesitate to point out that at present there is a part of the "dominant group" that rejects assimilation of the Chinese minority, it is because the facts speak loud and clear. Up to the present, Indonesian citizens of Chinese descent still experience "restriction of employment opportunities, lack of access to facilities that are meant to serve the population in general, the presence of bias and antagonism among law enforcement officials and many other manifestations of prejudice" [quoting the UNESCO publication by Arnold Rose]. Can such "discrimination and exclusion" be regarded as signs of the acceptance of the proposal of Lauw Tjoan Tho [*sic*] et al.? . . .
>
> We do not oppose assimilation *an sich*. We are only trying to explain that assimilation, as a means of resolving the minority problem, is not now appropriate. For discrimination has damaged the relations between groups, and bad interrelationships do not provide the right soil and climate for the cultivation and sprouting of assimilation.[29]

There were flaws in Yap's sociology, and he had not acknowledged the contributions of the *peranakan* minority to its own predicament. On this point, Lauwchuantho, no less combative than Yap, took the offensive:

> Every initiative to find the best "way-out" for all of us deserves praise. So does the effort of Mr. Yap who has proposed his therapy and, free of doubt, like a judge who has been given the right to render judgment, has articulated his sense of the matter and laid down his decision with the pronouncement that it is the majority who are responsible for everything that has happened, while the *peranakan* Chinese minority never did anything.
>
> This attitude of "injured innocence" [*vermoorde onschuld*], which at first feels very comfortable for the minority involved, is of doubtful moral advantage for us all, all the more so seen from an ethical point of view and that of religions that instruct us to examine from time to time our own shortcomings.[30]

This was in some ways a just criticism of Yap and other integrationists, but it also missed his point. Yap was not unaware of *peranakan* attitudes and habits that generated friction with ethnic Indonesians. He did not focus on them in part, no doubt, because he, like others, found it hard to take a genuinely detached, even-handed view of the matter. Temperamentally, he needed to locate responsibility and blame, and I suspect, he felt more comfortable, as Lauwchuantho charged, belonging to the injured party. But assigning blame was not his central concern; it was understanding, confronting and finding a solution to the problem of existing discrimination.

What was Yap's own therapy, to which all his analysis was prologue? Following a clear-headed, reasoned argument contra Siauw and the assimilationists, Yap's conclusion took an astonishing leap into an abyss of confusion. Yap knew a blind alley when he saw it, and I suspect that writing these articles convinced him that there was little hope for resolving the *peranakan* dilemma satisfactorily. Having rejected Siauw's simple structural and the assimilationists' even simpler analysis, at the end of his third article Yap asserted that "the problem is man himself." The remedy?

1. Not "brainwashing" but "heart-cleansing."
2. Not a change in the structure of society but a change from the materialistic and homocentric to a Christocentric view of man.
3. Not the elimination of physical and cultural differences, but the elimination of prejudice, egoism, and hypocrisy.
4. That there no longer be a "dominant group" but instead a "ministering elite" [*dienende elite*].
5. Not the retooling of man, but the rebirth of man in Jesus Christ.[31]

What exactly was in Yap's mind when he wrote this, and to whom was it directed? Did he mean that it was Chinese who had to turn to Christ, or ethnic Indonesians, or all Indonesians?[32] Did he really believe any of this prescription made sense, or did he, failing all else, fall back on the one source of hope that was constant—his religion? He never said. Yet for all its startling naiveté, was Yap's therapy much more naïve than Siauw's revolution or the assimilationists' voluntary absorption?

The public debate petered out in mid-1960, partly because *Star Weekly* itself closed down. Oyong buried it rather than submit to government demands to toe ideological lines. The debate had been reduced to a struggle for position between Baperki and the assimilationists operating under the aegis of the army.[33] It revived noisily after the coup of 1965 when Baperki was eliminated and the assimilationists, who had a hand in crushing it, suddenly had the field to themselves. It was then that the name-changing issue reignited, and Yap again dove into the center of the dispute, the last time he took up a cause specifically connected with *peranakan* problems. Again, he was alone, condemning the adoption of "Indonesian" names with all the passion and foresight he had displayed in 1960. The episode will be taken up in chapter 9, but it is worth pointing out that his argument, in 1967 as in 1960, proved quite correct.

Even during the therapies debate, Yap was waiting for the open confrontation with Siauw that had been much on his mind since mid-1959. The opportunity came in December 1960, at the Baperki congress in Semarang. Since August of 1959 he had attended no executive committee meetings and was not in touch with other members except, most likely, for his one or two allies and Oei Tjoe Tat, whom he saw at the law office. But Oei was on the other side, deeply involved in Partindo, the new party inspired by Soekarno, and not all that forthcoming. The two men did not get along well: Yap doubted Oei's political ethics and honesty, while Oei thought Yap politically naive and irrelevant.

Oei Tjoe Tat was both wrong and right. Yap, still a vice chair, had become irrelevant to Baperki in the sense that his influence had all but evaporated. As Siauw took the organization to the left and behind Soekarno, its liberals departed in a steady stream. They had their outlets in *Star Weekly* and the Surabaya journal *Liberty*, but had no organization to contend with Baperki. Of the original centrist founders of Baperki, only Yap and Thio Thiam Thong and perhaps one or two others remained active, but they were swamped by Siauw's supporters. Yap was no longer politically naive. Six active years in Baperki, along with his intense involvement in church affairs, had equipped him with enough knowledge and experience to become politically pessimistic and perhaps a bit cynical, without, however, losing his commitment to principle.

Strict principle and outrage drove him to the Baperki congress in Semarang in late December 1960. Convinced that Siauw had subverted Baperki's original purpose and endangered the minority on behalf of an abhorrent ideology, Yap was utterly bent on making his case publicly. In April 1959 he had refused to attend any more executive committee meetings until his protest was put on the agenda. Now it would be on the national congress agenda. He knew well enough that there was no chance of swaying the membership; neither Siauw's championship of the 1945 Constitution nor his refusal to condemn the alien traders' policy (PP10) evidently shook his support. It was believed that Baperki was as close to the center of things as any *peranakan* organization could hope to be only because Siauw had Soekarno's ear. And it was all right to be pro-China, even proud of China, given Soekarno's interest in a left-leaning international alliance against the neo-imperialist West. Anomalously, a few middle-class professionals took to wearing Mao jackets.

Yap understood all this and found it idiotic and dangerous. No one would have blamed him for withdrawing from a hopeless battle. Friends in and out of Baperki advised him to abandon the struggle, and, especially, not to speak at the congress. The word was out that Siauw's backers would retaliate viciously if Yap attacked him publicly. The East Javanese delegation evidently had prepared some petty harassment for him. Oei Tjoe Tat knew about the plans, and thought them vulgar and untoward, but said nothing to Yap. Rumor was that much more than vitriol could descend on Yap. Khing was frightened and did not want him to go.

Everything about the Semarang congress was tense and bothersome, and Yap suspected the motives of the Siauw group at every turn. The invitation from Secretary Buyung Saleh, in mid-November, announced that the executive committee plenary session would be held on 24 December and the congress would begin on December 25. Yap was incensed, supposing that Siauw and his cohorts either meant to exclude Christians or in any case to ignore Christian sensibilities. In a flurry of testy, irate correspondence Yap, Buyung Saleh, and Siauw himself flung charges, counter-charges, suspicions, and denials at one another.[34] The dates stood, but Yap was assured a time slot on the agenda for the day after Christmas, for "his problem," as the secretariat put it.

But Yap had spent too much time thinking about Baperki, Siauw, and the Chinese minority not to have his say. For months he prepared. His files are filled with drafts of the speech he intended to deliver, written in longhand in small tablets, on folio paper, and on the backs of old documents and official forms. Despite last minute hesitation, Yap declared he would go, and Khing gave up trying to dissuade him. He thought, as he explained to Khing in an effort to allay her anxieties, that the Siauw group was not interested in hurting him, for they already knew his position, but in getting rid of fence-sitters. Did he think he could rally the fence-sitters? Maybe, but there was more to it than that. He called the speech his "protest speech" (*protesrede*), but also his "J'accuse" speech, suggesting that he wanted to hold Siauw accountable for what had happened to Baperki and, by extension, what might happen to the *peranakan* community. But "J'accuse" suggests something else: that Yap had come to accept that his role in Baperki was as a conscience, and like a heroic Zola, he was prepared to go it alone without expectations.

Yap left for Semarang the day after Christmas. Even his departure was soaked in tension and anxiety. A week or two earlier he had asked Oei Tjoe Tat to tell the Baperki secretariat that he would travel by train, but, changing his mind, he later wrote to the secretariat himself to request a plane ticket.[35]

As it turned out, he went by train after all. At 3 a.m. on 26 December, he and Khing were startled out of sleep by a car honking its horn and gunning its motor. When Yap went out to check, the driver said he had come to take Yap to the train station at Gambir. Khing was frightened, thinking Yap would be kidnapped. (Actually, Yap may have ordered the car from the secretariat and forgotten to tell Khing, but in any case he, too, suspected something might be up for the car to come so early.) Yap telephoned Oei Kim Seng, a Baperki member whom he trusted, to ask if he knew what was going on. Oei did not, but advised Yap not to go to Semarang at all. Yap ignored the advice, but gave in to Khing's plea not to go in the car that was waiting out front. She drove him herself to the station in their old Austin.

He was among the last to arrive in Semarang. Some were waiting there to warn him not to take a hard stand at the congress. The word was out—possibly from, among others, Oei Tjoe Tat, who witnessed Yap working on his speech in the office—that Yap meant to cause trouble, and no one who was aware of his long battle with Siauw or his speech in the Konstituante doubted that he had the gall to do so. The secretariat had not arranged for anyone to meet him, but Thio Thiam Tjong badgered Oei Tjoe Tat into coming with him to pick Yap up at the station. Yap chose not to stay in the hotel with other congress participants, however, but with his sister, Non, and her husband, who lived in Semarang.

Yap's speech that night at the Chinese Chamber of Commerce hall, where the congress was held, was yet another study in plain courage or foolhardiness—or both, depending on one's perspective. Everyone knew that he meant to challenge Siauw at a time when Baperki, like every other organization, wanted to maintain solidarity, necessary for weathering the perilous times of Guided Democracy. As a vice chair, Yap had the right to speak to the whole congress. For that session Siauw stepped down from the chair, turning it over to a designate, so that he could reply to Yap. By all accounts, the hall was extraordinarily tense.

As always, Yap constructed the speech like a brief in court, each argument built tightly from detailed evidence.[36] There was little new in it, for he had made most of the arguments before in the executive committee, but this was the first time he spread out the map fully and in public. Starting with a review of the original limited objectives of Baperki—a mass organization without ideological commitments, concerned solely with citizenship and the promotion of human rights—he demonstrated how, from year to year, its character and purpose had been turned upside down and subverted until it was transformed into a political organization with an ideological stake. Yap had carefully reread all the minutes of the executive committee plenary sessions in order to gather his evidence of how decisions were preempted by the Siauw group, how regional branches were used to force through positions, how internal debates were squelched, and how the original charter and rules of order were violated, then altered to justify the violations.[37] He began by accusing Siauw of self-contradiction.

> Along with Thio Thiam Tjong and several other members, I take the view that confronting our membership and the organization with faits accomplis is very hard to call parliamentary and democratic. If one claims to carry on a struggle for democratic principles and human rights, as can be heard in every speech and read in nearly every sentence of the Chairman, then one must begin first by practicing those principles oneself in the life of the organization. If not, then it will be easy to assume that what are called democracy and human rights are really democracy and human rights intended only for certain persons.

The second part of his indictment, dealing directly with the issue of the 1945 Constitution, was blistering and irrefutable. There could be no doubt about the discriminatory content of Articles 6 and 26, he began.

> Despite our internal and principled agreement [that Articles 6 and 26 of the 1945 Constitution condoned racial discrimination], yet in his Konstituante speech of 12 May 1959 the Chairman at great length defended tenaciously the view that these articles were NOT racially discriminatory. Even though both the charter and rules of order of Baperki obligate us to oppose all legal provisions that are racist. What name must we give to these actions of the Chairman that were fully supported by the friends of the Chairman in the Konstituante and in Baperki? What name is usually given by the public to those actions which consciously dismiss one's responsibility and loyalty to the undertakings and bases of an organization? If I am not mistaken, the public names such acts treason or apostasy (*murtad*). So the provisions in the Constitution that contained the term "native" (*asli*) were affirmed and defended to the end, and yet still [Siauw] requested the Presidential Cabinet to issue a firm instruction: to eliminate the terms *native Indonesian citizen* and *not native*. (Emphasis added.)

But what had caused this abandonment of principle? Here Yap took up his third accusation, that the violation of Baperki's original mission had to be understood as a subordination of this mission to a grander ideological commitment. In chapter 7, I wrote that Yap may have overestimated Siauw's attachment to Party interests and underestimated the influence ethnic loyalties had on him. Yap may not have understood the pull of ethnic identification because he was himself more ideologically than ethnically attuned. In any event, he presented the unsympathetic congress audience with a full analysis of the communist purposes and style of Siauw and Go Gien Tjwan, citing their speeches and comments on the class struggle, the bourgeoisie, the economic system, the wonders of communist states. He paid special attention to the problem of the People's Republic of China:

> In the minutes of the executive committee *pleno* in Batu in 1960 . . . are very interesting comments. The Chairman said . . . that "we must remember that in the present situation we must avoid arousing suspicions among other groups, in this case the majority group. Now much suspicion has arisen about Baperki, so [the Chairman] did not agree to issue a written statement concerning P.P. 10, because there is nothing to gain from encouraging suspicion. . . ." Concerning P.P. 10 Mrs. Tjoa Hien Hoey said that "in this problem many people are accusing Baperki of being pro PRC." Every observer who is free of preconceptions must admit that in this matter of the prohibition of foreign small traders in the villages, the Chairman and his colleagues have acted "more PRC than the PRC," so that of course the Government and society doubt whether Baperki is a Chinese political organization of the PRC or of Indonesia. The attitudes of national and local leaders of Baperki in this connection have fueled the suspicions of the majority—in this case with good reason . . . concerning the loyalties to Indonesia of Indonesian citizens of Chinese descent.

Yap went on to accuse Siauw of toadying to Soekarno, a tactic that he found personally distasteful and politically outrageous.

> The reports and speeches of the Chairman—especially about Manipol/USDEK, the just and prosperous society, Pancasila, and so on— . . . very liberally quote the pronouncements of President Soekarno.[38] Evidently everything is fully accepted by the Chairman, including the state philosophy based on belief in the One God.[39] His acceptance of and support for

every concept of President Soekarno gives one cause to think, [especially] when one reads the chairman's discussion of Manipol/USDEK, in the 'Minutes of the [Nineteen] Sixty National Congress of Baperki.' On page 54 [of the minutes] . . . he says that Baperki is not a [political] party and differs from political parties, which emphasize the form and name of a political matter, while for Baperki it is content that counts. Thus Baperki can accept liberal democracy or guided democracy, a federal or a unitary state, a socialist or . . . (unfortunately here the contrast is not mentioned, but logically it can be filled in, for example, with a colonial/imperialist society or a Communist one...because for the Chairman the name is unimportant), as long as the content accords with the ideals and struggle [of Baperki]. So it follows, Manipol/USDEK, Socialism based on the Pancasila with its principle of Belief in the One God can be accepted (because these are only names, no?), [and there is no need to] question first what is the content, the meaning, the objective, and so on.

. . . I am convinced that among those present here not a few of you respect our Chairman, as I myself do. There is also a group that even praises him endlessly and regards him as "our King who can do no wrong." . . . His private life is beyond reproach. Yet, Baperki is not a private bailiwick. . . but an association, an organization. . . . [And] as it is an association we have the right to examine it, to scrutinize the course along which our Baperki is being taken by our Chairman and his allies.

After this mild mockery of Siauw's logic and his supporters' devotion, Yap appealed to the congress not to forget Baperki's origins and originators, their objectives and sacrifices, for that was the way of opportunists, the "abacus minded." Reminding his audience that many of those founders had left the organization—among them Khoe Woen Sioe, Auwjong Peng Koen, Kwee Hwat Djien, Tan Kian Lok, and Gouw Soey Tjiang—he asked them to consider the causes of those departures. There may have been many reasons, he said, but the most fundamental was the actions of the chairman and his allies, "whom I accuse." Yap went on to demonstrate in his own case, how the tenor of Baperki had changed.

Several friends, also members of Baperki, urged me not to come to this Congress, or at least to be very careful in pronouncing my accusations and indictment. [Recalling past incidents in Baperki], I too became terrified. All the more so as I thought of how some persons, in a totalitarian-fascist way, had tried to play off the President and myself, falsifying my "Therapy'" articles in *Star Weekly* on assimilation, falsely accusing me of being anti-Baperki and anti-Manipol/USDEK and so on. . . . All this was known to the Central Executive Committee, which still, as far as I know, has not yet disavowed either the public or secret writings, and therefore I assume these writings have the blessing of the Executive Committee. So I am a bit frightened to face the Chairman and his allies. But as someone who tries to be a devoted follower of Christ, I am reminded of God's message that we must fear God who can crush us body and soul more than we fear those who can only destroy our bodies.

He concluded both with an appeal to idealism and on a pessimistic note:

Let us ask ourselves why in actuality we established Baperki, why we exhausted ourselves, sacrificed our time and thought and money, often also sacrificed harmony in our households [was this an apology of sorts to Khing?] humor and health? Here I set aside those who jumped into Baperki for the sake of money, power, prestige or position, whether in Baperki or in government, or out of other materialistic and egoistic purposes. . . . But I want to limit myself to [worthy] members of Baperki. What drove them to struggle without tiring, without thinking of personal advantage, their health, or their own safety? I think it was nothing other than feelings of humanitarianism and justice, two senses that originate in a single source with many names, but which I and my fellow believers call God. . . . Mr. Chairman [of the session], honored Congress, given the power and influence of the Chairman, I don't have much hope that my voice will surpass "the voices that scream from the battlefield." But I believe that among you there are still some who can distinguish between truth and untruth, between the just and unjust. For this reason too I needed to come before you with my charges and indictment and to ask for a decision. . . . I believe, Mr. Chairman and honored Congress, whatever your decision, that only History and Society will be the final court to try . . . the leaders of Baperki and myself. And also the decisions of you who make up this seventh Congress of Baperki. I pray that Justice alone will be the motive and inspiration for those who support the true ideals of Baperki, guiding your considerations and decisions.

Yap's prayers had no chance in that hall. Of those who certainly agreed with him, and many others who probably did, not one said a word. The room was filled with Siauw's supporters, including new faces, many of them ethnic Indonesians, whom Yap supposed had been imported, possibly from the PKI, to pack the session. Siauw himself, though he had left the chair in order to be able to reply to Yap's expected attack, declined after all to respond. It was not the time to answer Yap's charges, he said. But a more appropriate time never came. Given the complexity of the man and his respect for Yap, his thoughts may well have included one that recognized the worrisome truths in his adversary's words.

Others replied instead, and viciously. During and after Yap's speech, the audience hooted and stomped their disapproval. By this time in the evolution of Guided Democracy, parties and associations met to proclaim unity and acclaim leaders, not to countenance dissent. Buyung Saleh rose to speak after Yap, not to take up his arguments but to fling invective. It was the standard invective called up then against the critics and doubters of Guided Democracy. Not only Yap himself, but Khing, too, was flayed by Buyung Saleh, though no one I have asked, not even Yap, was willing to admit remembering what was said about Khing. Yap, said Buyung Saleh, was a lackey of the West, too westernized to understand Indonesian ideals and purposes. He had been absent from the revolution. He opposed Soekarno, Guided Democracy, Manipol/USDEK. Buyung Saleh was cheered as he slashed away at Yap's reputation. Yap was booed.

Yap did not stay at the rostrum after Buyung Saleh's speech. He knew, long before he finished his own speech, that he had lost utterly. He walked out through the crowd, listening to the catcalls, and got into his brother-in-law's waiting car. Years later, in a conversation with Yap and me, Oei Tjoe Tat remembered how impressed he was by Yap's courage at the Semarang congress.[40] As Yap left the hall, defeated but with his head held defiantly high, Oei said he thought, "how extraordinary this man is." Everyone at the meeting was screaming at Yap and pounding their tables. "Including you?" Yap asked. "Yes, including me," Oei replied with a small laugh, "because at the time I was politically opposed to you." Yap smiled, but in a way that indicated he still had a hard time understanding that kind of political morality.

Yap had nothing more to do with Baperki after Semarang. He refused to resign his membership, however, insisting that the Executive Committee take the initiative in forcing him out. This Siauw and the others refused to do. So technically he remained in the organization until the end.

Ethnic Chinese problems did not recede under Guided Democracy but rather, if anything, proliferated. Entrepreneurs were hurt by the economy's decline, the citizenship issue remained unresolved, even after the treaty with China appeared to solve it, for government regulations implementing the agreement posed new difficulties. The attack on alien traders in rural areas (PP10) generated enormous tensions. Thousands of aliens and even a few *peranakan* citizens felt driven to board ships for China, and some wealthier ones, despairing of their future in Indonesia, left for Europe and North America—a quiet spurt in the steady stream of emigration. The more chaotic the economy became, the more anti-Chinese sentiment spread, until in May 1963 a violent pogrom of sorts was set off in West Java, probably by an army faction. Baperki itself began to feel a severe financial pinch, as dues declined along with the enthusiasm of its members, partly perhaps because the likelihood of national elections had dimmed. The same was also true of the major parties, with the exception of the PKI. As in the parties, in Baperki too, following the model of Guided Democracy, attention came to be focused more and more on the organization's leadership. Siauw, though himself democratically inclined, nevertheless became Baperki's Soekarno.

The end came shortly after the coup of 30 September–1 October 1965, when Baperki, like the PKI but less brutally, was destroyed. Siauw and Go Gien Tjwan were detained, along with many others, including Oei Tjoe Tat. With the help of Adam Malik, his friend and superior in the Antara News Service and later vice president, Go was released soon after his arrest. Before he left for Holland, he came to see Yap in Grogol. It was a visit that implied an apology of sorts, or at least a recognition, as he admitted in an interview, that Yap had been right. Yap asked Go to promise that he would do nothing abroad to hurt the cause of *peranakan* Chinese at home. Go promised. They did not see each other for another twenty years, when Yap visited Go in Amsterdam.

Siauw was detained without trial for eleven years. During that time Yap was concerned for Siauw's family, whom Khing visited from time to time to help in whatever way she could. Siauw was released in 1977 to get medical attention for his eyes in Holland, where he remained until his death in November 1981. In 1980, when Yap received an honorary degree at the Vrije Universiteit in Amsterdam, he agreed to give a talk in Rijswijk, just outside The Hague, to the Indonesian Chinese community. Siauw came. In the course of his address on the *peranakan* situation in Indonesia, Yap pointed out that Baperki's history had hurt citizens of Chinese descent. Siauw rose in defense. Some say that Yap was too hard on Siauw, that he was too self-righteous, and that Siauw, stung by

Yap's comments and their exchange, left the meeting. According to an account by Siauw's son, the two men chatted amicably but formally afterwards.

From early 1961 through the end of 1965, Yap paid careful attention to *peranakan* affairs, but from the sidelines, angrily, pessimistically, and no doubt often bitterly. In his files are clippings on the various arguments between Baperki integrators and the assimilators, on issues of discrimination against Chinese and on the May 1963 anti-Chinese riots in West Java, against which Baperki was powerless to do anything except thank Soekarno for condemning them. For the rest, Yap attended to his law practice, which picked up during those years, not in spite of but because of the economic shambles of Guided Democracy. There were bankruptcy cases and debt collections and the like. He continued to advise *peranakan* clients and others on citizenship problems and difficulties arising from national and local discriminatory policies. And through it all, he watched Baperki and the *peranakan* community head for the disaster he knew was coming.

NINE

OUT OF THE ETHNIC CAGE

"IF in his heart of hearts a Chinese *peranakan* wants to join his fate with that of Indonesians in this land of Indonesia, then he too must be considered a true Indonesian." So said Liem Koen Hian in 1934.[1] In his packed decade of the 1950s, Yap had first engaged, not altogether comfortably, as a Chinese. The 1960s liberated him to become at ease as an Indonesian. For *peranakan* men and women of his generation it was not an easy thing to do, and few bothered to try. This was not, after all, entirely a matter of choice. To be Indonesian in one's own mind could not dictate acceptance as Indonesian by ethnic Indonesians, as Yap had pointed out to the assimilators. Many who joined Baperki did so precisely because there seemed to be no other choice but to fall back on a Chinese identity that did not fit well the template of *peranakan* existence. A later generation of *peranakan*, which came into its own after 1965, produced more figures who had no compunction and little hesitation about participating in Indonesian politics, albeit in a skewed way dictated by New Order rules. Yap was in awe of their ease; he had had to struggle toward air from the submerged state of ethnic confinement.

Exiting Baperki with principles intact helped. But so did the principles themselves, which he now had time to think about more deeply. Yap's speech before the Constituent Assembly indicated clearly enough that he had more in mind than minority issues. He already knew then that *peranakan* Chinese, like all other citizens, would be affected by the shape of the political system. Freed from the constant flow of ethnic signals generated by Baperki, this idea that *peranakan* citizens had interests in common with all citizens grew increasingly important to him, as did the notion of citizenship itself. Being Indonesian meant being concerned with all Indonesians and, moreover, having the right to act on issues of concern to all Indonesians. *Peranakan* Chinese disabilities could not be treated in isolation, for they were, he came to understand more fully, only part of a larger problem that had to be addressed first.

It was not that he wanted to deny his Chinese origins; he never did and had contempt for those among the assimilators who he thought might be motivated to do so. Nor did *peranakan* issues lose their significance for him. During the early 1960s, after the Semarang congress, he continued to help *peranakan* clients (and nonclients) with difficulties arising from discriminatory laws and policies. He clipped newspaper articles on issues affecting Chinese. The 10 May 1963 riots against Chinese in West Java, evidently organized by an army faction, dismayed and angered him. So did the continuing debate between Baperki and the official assimilation group. And after the 1965 coup, when suddenly the assimilators had the advantage, Yap again attacked them in utterly uncompromising terms.

But there was a difference in the way he understood *peranakan* issues before and after he left Baperki. If he previously viewed *peranakan* problems as *sui generis*, afterwards they became part of a much larger continuum of human rights issues incurred by state and social structures. He remained *peranakan* Chinese by ascription but was increasingly unwilling to accept the usual consequences of the accident of having been born Chinese. A person was a citizen or not, and for the public man citizenship overrode all other attributes. This argument he had long maintained. Now, more than ever, he was inclined to act on it. To be inclined, however, was not the same as being fully prepared. Yap's sense of principle and personal courage, considerable as they were, nevertheless required a modicum of encouragement to be completely engaged. He was perfectly capable of the solitary act of protest, a fierce defense in court, a speech in the Konstituante, or a dogged pursuit of an idea elsewhere. When Soekarno appointed Supreme Court chairman Wirjono Prodjodikoro to the cabinet, Yap wrote an article critical of this nullification of the separation of powers for the Protestant daily *Sinar Harapan*. *Sinar Harapan* refused to publish it, deeply disappointing him for its lack of courage. He also talked about the appointment with the then minister of information, whom he knew from schooldays, trying to persuade him that the appointment was a serious mistake. Later he wrote in protest against the arrest and detention without trial of several prominent Masyumi and PSI leaders, among them Sutan Sjahrir,

Subadio Sastrosatomo, Mochtar Lubis, Mohammad Natsir, Mohamad Roem, and H. J. C. Princen, whom he came to know particularly well after the coup.[2]

No less than others, Yap needed an arena in which to act. Baperki had offered him that. So did the Konstituante. So did the church, where he remained very active. Out of Baperki and unalterably opposed to the new assimilationist association, he was effectively denied an organizational forum for speaking out on Chinese issues, but neither did he have one for dealing with wider Indonesian issues. Neither his church nor the new General Synod of Chinese Reform Churches in Java was much inclined to public engagement.

Along with an arena, he needed associates, colleagues, some sort of community. One obvious home for him was the legal profession, which he, like most other advocates, took for granted as a very loosely articulated club without a clubroom. Post-Baperki, Yap had more time for chatting with other advocates in and out of court. In his own law office, only he and Lie Hwee Yoe were around and practicing. Tan Po Goan had been abroad since 1958, unwilling to return—partly on advice from the law office—for fear that he would be arrested, along with a few other PSI leaders, for complicity in the regional PRRI rebellion. Oei Tjoe Tat, fully engaged in Partindo, had little or no time for practicing law. But Yap's own increased attention to professional matters put him in touch with other lawyers, most of whom had plenty of time on their hands to talk politics and complain about the decline of law and the miseries of litigation.

Yap was guarded in his relationships with his ethnic Indonesian colleagues during the early 1960s, out of fear that they would never accept him. Yet it was far more his problem than theirs. Senior advocates of that generation, almost all of them dead now, were an extraordinary group. Usually high-born, well educated in the HBS or AMS and in the law faculties of Leiden or Batavia, well-read and intellectually inclined, many of them traveled politically in PSI circles, or were in any case quite comfortable there. Few were seriously infected by ethnic prejudice, or to the extent that they were, professional standards and commitments had more influence on them. Yap began to mix more with these men in the years after 1960, but not until the mid-1960s did he take his place comfortably as a member of the select in-group of senior advocates. Only then did their behavior convince him that it did not matter to them that he was Chinese.

The legal profession—once a small association, Peradin (Persatuan Advokat Indonesia, Indonesian Advocates' Bond), was formed—became Yap's substitute for Baperki, both symbolically and practically. In time, indeed, it replaced even the church (not his religion but the church) as the repository of his cache of significance. Not only did he devote himself to the profession with as much energy as he had earlier given to Baperki, but he also found there the closest friends of his mature life. Peradin helped to liberate him from the suffocating asthma of ethnicity, providing him with a forum for engaging with Indonesia. In 1963 Yap was fifty years old and about to leap into the waters of a different sea, no less stormy than those in which Baperki had made its way, but more satisfying to his sense of life purpose.

Yap was always most comfortable as an underdog, and in the professional advocacy he found a whole underdog institution. Guided Democracy had made a mess of the legal system, destroying its autonomy, subjugating it to political authority, and reorienting its institutions, on the one hand, to the beacon of executive will that shone from the Presidential Palace, and on the other, to the joys of corruption. No legal role, however, suffered as much as that of professional advocate. Nor, consequently, were any public or private lawyers anywhere near so committed to political and legal reform as were professional advocates. A brief sketch of the convulsions visited upon the legal system during those years will clarify a few of the issues.

During the parliamentary years, the legal system, was in reasonably good shape. The liberal Constitution of 1950 was predicated on assumptions of the *negara hukum* (*rechtsstaat*), or rule of law, which parliamentary political leadership took quite seriously as the ideological underpinning of the state. There were problems and tensions in the legal system—lack of graduated lawyers, conflicts over status between judges and prosecutors, inadequate salaries and working conditions—but its autonomy was respected and its procedures honored.

Private lawyers—advocates and notaries—were no less respected than public lawyers. Yet latent tensions existed between them that became manifest as the legal system was wrung out under Guided Democracy. These tensions had to do, largely, with the different characters and orientations of public and private lawyers. In the independent state, as in the colony, most graduated lawyers had entered public service as judges, prosecutors, or administrators, for bureaucratic office provided both security and high status. More so in Java than elsewhere, these advantages of government employment were a magnet to all but the most independent-minded souls. The latter, by and large, became private lawyers. Ethnic Chinese, who had much less leverage on public employment but had more in the private economy, flocked to the notariat and advocacy. So did Batak and Minangkabau law graduates, whose home economies in West and North Sumatra had developed strong commercial bents.

The differences between public and private lawyers were relatively unimportant in the parliamentary years, in part because colonial legal habits remained influential throughout the legal system but also because *negara hukum* ideology distributed legitimacy to all the legal professions, and the legitimacy of the private sector extended to private professions. These conditions changed dramatically under Guided Democracy as the state bureaucracy was greatly strengthened and public ideology subordinated the private sector and private roles to state purposes. Soekarno, formulating an ideology that would break the psychological hold of European domination in the same way that the revolution had broken direct colonial control, emphasized national cultural resources in the shaping of an Indonesian identity: *Kepribadian Indonesia*. The one European influence on which lawyers particularly depended was the idea of the law state itself and its accompanying ideological baggage of republican organization. Slapping lawyers with Liebknecht's argument, "You cannot make a revolution with lawyers," Soekarno also hacked away at the liberal addiction to such principles as the separation of powers (*trias politika*) and judicial autonomy. The president was unmoved when Yap and other professional advocates wrote public critiques of his appointment of a willing Wirjono Prodjodikoro to the cabinet. In 1964 Soekarno went further with two new laws on judicial organization to subject the courts to political authority in matters of "national interest."[3]

Public lawyers themselves were ambivalent about the transformation of their roles under Guided Democracy. On the one hand, older judges and prosecutors especially objected to the politicization of the legal system and resented their loss of autonomy and pride, with judges being particularly incensed, for their professional authority, status, and self-respect suffered from the loss of judicial independence rooted in *negara hukum* ideology. The prosecutorial corps, on the other hand, adjusted more easily, expanding their political services as required. Their adaptability won them substantial rewards in the currencies of power, influence, status, and money. In 1960 the prosecution was allowed to withdraw from the Ministry of Justice and establish its own, independent, ministry. The police, competitive with the prosecution for position in criminal procedure, did the same. But judges, with whom prosecutors had long competed for equalization of status and salaries, remained under the administrative jurisdiction of the Ministry of Justice.

In addition, the prosecution profited enormously from its control over preliminary investigations, which gave prosecutors broad opportunities for extortion. The corruption of criminal procedure during this period was appalling, setting a pattern that endured through the change of regime in the late 1960s. Perhaps the most common practice was simply to arrest, on legitimate or trumped-up charges, someone who was wealthy enough to pay ransom for release. Or a civil debt might be transformed into a criminal action for fraud, in exchange for a substantial fee passing from the creditor to the prosecutor willing to sell these services. Less potentially profitable criminal matters were left to new prosecutors or those unwilling to play the game. Their entrepreneurial opportunities provided prosecutors with leverage over the police and especially judges, who, with little institutional pride left, were more and more easily suborned by offers of a cut for accommodating decisions. Corruption in the judicial system was no worse than in the bureaucracy generally, at a time when low salaries depressed the entire civil service, but to any who took the law seriously, it was by far more cynical and disturbing.

In the entire judicial order, however, no one suffered more than professional advocates. They were squeezed out of the system. Even if judges were made miserable by their loss of stature compared with prosecutors, they were still civil servants, *pegawai negeri*, which bore the high status that had always belonged to the Javanese *priyayi* elite and counted for a good deal in the strong bureaucratic state restored by Guided Democracy. Official status in general counted for more and more, while private sector roles declined precipitously. In the judicial system, judges, prosecutors, and police, whatever the tensions among themselves, shared in the brotherhood of officialdom. From this collegiality, advocates were excluded, to the disadvantage of their clients and themselves. Even notaries fared better, for they seldom had to deal directly with the courts. Notaries, essential to private law in the Continental civil law tradition, remained quietly and often profitably in their offices, turning out the documentary work for which demand remained more or less constant.

But advocates were barristers, quintessential litigants, who had no choice but to be in court, where they had always been accepted as legitimate and prestigious participants in the system of judicial roles. Now, increasingly, they were pushed aside by intimately collaborating judges and prosecutors. The fact that prosecutors sat next to judges on the judicial bench took on new symbolic meaning for advocates, even as it sometimes confused accused persons about who exactly was in charge. Robed in black like judges and prosecutors, but below and away from the high bench in the courtroom, advocates were as private as their clients and truly at the mercy of the court. As if to call attention to the distance between public and private roles, prosecutors replaced their robes with military-style uniforms. Judges awkwardly followed suit, though at the first opportunity, after the coup of 1965, they cast off the uniforms and donned robes again. By 1964, advocates alone wore togas, often tattered at that.

But attire in court was the least of their problems. At the height of Guided Democracy, a new institution was established—the Panca Tunggal, "five as one"—which constituted a coordinating session of local administrators (*pamong praja*), army commanders, police, prosecution, and judges. Its purpose was to deal with local security problems, but it also cemented the fellowship of officials. Not only did the Panca Tunggal violate the advocates' sense of procedural propriety, it also firmly established them as outsiders—and, in the eyes of some judges and prosecutors, as intruders upon the legitimate authority and prerogatives of state officials. In court, increasingly, advocates were treated abusively or frequently simply ignored. Tensions between judges and advocates grew steadily from the early years of Guided Democracy, in some ways more so than between prosecutors and advocates. Professional lawyers had always regarded themselves as supporters of strong courts and allies of the judges who now often spurned them. From prosecutors, natural opponents at best, powerful enemies at worst, advocates came to expect very little anyway.

The professional lives of advocates changed quickly once Guided Democracy set in unequivocally in 1959. During the parliamentary years, advocates had been a small but confident group, known for their legal skills and personal independence, sometimes resented but also respected by public lawyers. Several prominent advocates had given up their profession to serve in the government: Sartono was Speaker of Parliament; Besar Martokoesoemo, secretary-general of the Ministry of Justice; Iskaq Tjokrohadisurjo, a minister of Economic Affairs; Ali Sastroamidjojo, a prime minister. Others were politically influential. The professional absence of these men weakened the advocacy but seemed to bode well for it. Advocates optimistically waited for the rest of the legal system to catch up with their skills. Less optimistic judges, prosecutors, police, and bureaucrats of every ministry organized frantically for defensive or offensive purposes. Advocates, used to working alone, watched with interest but saw no reason to get involved.

By 1959–60, advocates had lost everything but their sense of independence and political values, neither of which had much currency. Soekarno had contemptuously dismissed their political and legal commitments as irrelevant to Indonesia's destiny, and they were isolated in the judicial system. Some made reasonable livings, but others lost clients and income to more effective fixers, and all lost any sense of professional satisfaction. Cut off from judges and other public lawyers, and unhappy with the drift of Guided Democracy, increasingly they talked only with one another. For advocates who had once been politically active but had lost their influence or their parties, the advocacy became the sole outlet for their energies. Masyumi and the PSI, the political parties to which many advocates had belonged, were banned permanently in mid-1960 on grounds of their putative support for the PRRI/Permesta regional rebellion in 1958. Lukman Wiriadinata and his two office partners, Hasjim Mahdan and Andi Zainal Abidin, had belonged to the PSI. Jamaluddin Datuk Singomangkuto was a Masyumi leader, and Suardi Tasrif, the editor of Masyumi's daily *Abadi*. When *Abadi* was banned, Tasrif took a law degree at the University of Indonesia and opened a practice, sharing an office with Iskaq Tjokrohadisurjo. Mainly centrist liberals, their prominence in the advocacy helps to explain both its activism and its political orientation before and after the coup of 1965. But other advocates who were nonparty, among them for example Soemarno P. Wirjanto from Solo, Ani Abas Manopo from Medan, and Yap himself, were of much the same stripe.

During the early Guided Democracy years, faced with a precipitous decline on all fronts, advocates began to organize. The first to do so were the small group of Semarang practitioners, most of them ethnic Chinese, who revived a local Balie van Advocaten, little more than a professional club on the old model. Jakarta, Bandung, Surabaya, and Medan soon followed suit. These five cities contained the great majority of professional advocates, then totaling perhaps 150 or so nationwide, of whom more than half were in Jakarta. At the same time talk began of a national association.

On the initiative of Jakarta advocates, a national body finally took shape, to little notice, in March 1963, at a National Law Seminar sponsored by the Indonesian Lawyers Association (Persahi, Perhimpunan Ahli Hukum Indonesia).[4] The handful of advocates attending the conference met in a University of Indonesia cafeteria, where they agreed to establish the Persatuan Advokat Indonesia (PAI, Indonesian Advocates Bond), toasting their decision with orange crush. Only fourteen advocates from around the country were there,[5] Yap among them. They reached into their own pockets for the treasury and came up with Rp. 14,500—no great sum. In August 1964, in Solo, the organization held its first congress, which replaced the abbreviation PAI with Peradin. To succeed the first interim chairman, the former PSI minister of justice Lukman Wiriadinata, the congress chose the former PNI minister of economic affairs,

FIG. 9.1 Members of Peradin enter a celebration arm in arm, 1968. Suardi Tasrif is second from left; Yap Thiam Hien, second from right.

Iskaq Tjokrohadisurjo, partly in the hope that he might wield some influence on behalf of the profession with his old friend Soekarno. Some worried at the time that the government might actually abolish the advocacy.

Yap did not play a significant part in the early Peradin. Years later, in fact, he barely remembered that he was a founding member. It did not register because, during the early 1960s, he still felt himself to be an outsider, as both Christian and *peranakan* Chinese, among ethnic Indonesians. Again, however, it was he, not they, who held back. Yet he belonged in that odd circle of sophisticated and accomplished figures, and in time he drew close to several of them, especially Lukman Wiriadinata, Hasjim Mahdan, A. Z. Abidin, Suardi Tasrif, Soemarno P. Wirjanto, and Ani Abas Manopo (fig. 9.1).[6]

Like most advocates, these men were all outsiders in one sense or another, if for no other reason than that they remained advocates in a legal system that no longer appreciated them. All in that generation were Dutch-educated and Dutch-speaking, more or less culturally marginalized, ideologically committed to republican principles and, of course, to legal process. None had any taste for Guided Democracy, nor for Soekarno's patrimonial-populist movement poli-

FIG. 9.2 Yap addressing the fifth national Peradin Congress, 1977. The Peradin emblem, with "Fiat Justitia Ruat Coelum," is prominently displayed.

tics, nor for his search for operative principles from local tradition. They saw the rhetoric as inadequate to a modern state in a society as complex as Indonesia's. Most held on to symbols and standards that rubbed directly against the grain of Guided Democracy's nativist appeals. Peradin's emblem provides a perfect example. One of Minister of Justice Sahardjo's proudest achievements was to establish a new national symbol of justice, replacing the blind goddess and scales inherited from the Netherlands-Indies with a banyan tree inscribed with the Javanese word *Pengayoman* (succor), referring to the king's, now the government's, patrimonially conceived responsibility to care for subjects. Peradin's emblem, designed with quite as much pride by Suardi Tasrif, stubbornly stuck to the scales, now appearing under crossed swords and surrounded by the adage *Fiat Justitia Ruat Coelum*—"let justice be done, though the heavens may fall" (fig. 9.2). It was a declaration of independence that frankly admitted the profession's European origins. Similarly, the first Peradin congress rejected the Indonesian term *pengacara* (literally, "procedurer") in favor of *advokat*, which bore more symbolic weight for them: even a lawyer who had not graduated could be a *pengacara,* but the status of *advokat* required a degree and proper registration in the Ministry of Justice.[7]

In a similar but weightier vein, Jamaluddin, Tasrif, and others produced a code of ethics that was strangely dreamy in its insistence on professional norms that made little sense in the institutional conditions of Guided Democracy or thereafter. It too was an act of defiant independence, an impractical and nonpracticable claim to legal propriety at a time when few people placed much trust in law. But at the time few people paid much attention to the advocacy either. Defiant as it was, the profession was also stagnant and depressed. Until the end of Guided Democracy, Peradin never had more than 150–200 members.[8] The advocacy grew older by the year for lack of new recruits. Law graduates applied to the judiciary for status and to the prosecution for money and influence. The advocacy showed little promise except to those few lawyers who lost government jobs.

For Yap, however, the advocacy offered a very promising place to roost. Not only was the profession small and filled with lawyers whose backgrounds were in many respects like his own, but it was an institution that stood for right and justice in the midst of unmistakable political and social injustice, corruption, and lawlessness. And it offered fellowship of the sort he had found neither in Baperki nor in the church, both riven by ideological and political conflicts. Peradin members agreed from the start not to allow political party differences among them to affect the advocacy's purposes, though, in fact, the ideological spread among them was quite small. During the late Guided Democracy years, the founding members of Peradin and a few others in Jakarta met often, usually once a week, ate together at a restaurant—steak, if they could find it—and complained about the politics of Guided Democracy, talking about the need for legal reform and working out their ideas for a political system. Not surprisingly, they were all in agreement.

Gradually the circle enclosed Yap. Sometime in 1964, when Minister of Justice Astrawinata, a former Bandung judge who appreciated advocates, asked Peradin for its views on a draft law concerning legal representation the ministry was considering, the group invited Yap to develop a concept for one section of it. Nothing came of the law, but Yap's deeper involvement in Peradin began then and grew more and more intense. It was actions not words that persuaded him that other advocates accepted him without ethnic or religious qualm. It was important to him that he had been asked to work on Peradin's advice to the Ministry of Justice. Two events made an even more significant difference to him. One involved his own arrest and trial in 1968, discussed in chapter 11. Another was the Liem Koe Nio case in Surabaya, which began in December 1964 and lasted through August 1965. The Liem trial was not very unusual during the Guided Democracy period, nor do many people remember it as extraordinary. Yap's defense of Soekarno's first deputy prime minister/foreign minister, Subandrio, in 1966 and several other political cases he represented thereafter are the ones that called public attention to him. But for Yap himself it was the Liem case that evoked his most enthusiastic memories. It was a threshold, a transition to the kind of human rights and political litigation that would later mean so much to him. More than that, at a very difficult, even perilous, time, this case set the pattern for many of his later political defenses. More than twenty years later, he still talked about that trial with flair and enthusiasm, as if enjoying every moment of it again even as he pointed out the misery and corruption it represented.

In the Liem Koe Nio case, only the law was simple and straightforward. Everything else was mired in political and economic corruption. It is a perfect case for revealing the institutional pathologies of Guided Democracy that continued with slight variations thereafter. The case provided Yap with a hefty fee, but his affection for it rested on the extraordinary opportunity it offered him to make official corruption and incompetence plain.

Liem Koe Nio, a forty-year old *totok*, illiterate in both Chinese and Indonesian languages, was East Java's most successful and influential businessman, with bases in Surabaya and Jakarta.[9] He had made a fortune in textiles, structural steel and reinforcement bars, and a variety of other commodities that he bought, often from state companies, stockpiled, and sold at substantial profits. His operations, like many others of the sort, depended on close connections with local and national officials, many of whom he no doubt paid handsomely for their help. In Surabaya he was evidently linked to several top regional officials, including the powerful Governor Samadikoen. Liem himself was connected with the Kuomintang (KMT), but his younger brother, who ran the business in Jakarta, was a communist.

In 1964 Liem began to run into trouble for a number of related reasons. He lost valuable influence when Governor Samadikoen and his staff left office, immediately rendering Liem vulnerable to challenges by other local entrepreneurs who resented his power and operations. Evidently Liem was a channel for pay-off funds, which he collected from other businessmen, some of whom may have questioned whether he himself contributed to the accumulated funds. Weakening or destroying him was undoubtedly tempting to other businessmen who hoped to improve their own positions. But with less protection, Liem also became fair game politically for those who either opposed the Kuomintang or who sought public support by attacking rich entrepreneurs. The former included the PKI and Baperki, while the PNI and associated groups belonged to the latter.

Quite apart from these groups, another interested party was the local prosecution, which had to gain substantially by showing itself to be aggressively protecting the public against corruption, while helping itself to any goods seized in a criminal action. During the late years of Guided Democracy, the public prosecution's reputation for predatory greed was so bad that efforts were made to impose some limits. These efforts had relatively little effect, for by then the corruption was fully institutionalized, widely distributed, and grounded in a sense of official entitlement at a time of bureaucratic power and low official salaries.

At the same time, as it happens, the law of criminal procedure had changed favorably for prosecutors. As the economy declined, political conflict intensified, and Indonesia became internationally embroiled in a border war against Malaysia, the government eased legal controls over criminal process. The criminal code (KUHP) and code of criminal procedure (H.I.R.) then in force were legacies of the colonial period. Although their enforcement was lax, depending on the willingness and experience of police, prosecution, and courts, still they provided a range of guarantees to which appeal might be made. But in October 1963, a Presidential Decree, Nr. 11/1963, was promulgated to facilitate the suppression of subversive activities.[10] In the tradition of sedition acts, the decree made the work of civil and military prosecutors easier. Powers of detention for a year, the elimination of certain procedural restrictions, and the imposition of heavy punishments—including the death penalty—all facilitated prosecution. The act was not utterly devoid of guarantees (imported by way of reference to the conventional codes), but these were vitiated by the powers granted to prosecutors already infamous for their rapacity and lack of accountability. Not surprisingly, the advantages of relying on the Anti-Subversion Decree encouraged prosecutors to use it as much as possible against any criminally accused person who stood a chance under conventional criminal procedure.

Liem Koe Nio was arrested at the end of December 1964 on charges of economic subversion. At the same time, the prosecution sealed seven of his warehouses in Surabaya and Jakarta and seized a well-appointed villa on the elite street Jalan Darma in Surabaya, as well as ten vehicles, one of them a new Chevrolet Impala.[11] The prosecutor, Susanto Bangunegoro, announced that he would try the case as subversion, that he was working closely with other "revolutionary instruments," and that he had firmly rejected all attempts to buy Liem out.[12] Soon, however, a prosecutor had moved into the villa and Susanto himself, as Yap later protested, was driving the Impala. Such convenient use of impounded evidence—including goods with no evidentiary value—had become quite common among prosecutors, who also graciously lent cars, houses, and other luxury items to assorted influential figures.

By early January the daily *Trompet Masjarakat* began running an unremitting campaign against Liem, the "steel king," "money king," and "billionaire."[13] On 25 February 1965, moreover, the day the trial began, the newspaper also prominently reported a statement of the minister/chairman of the Supreme Court Wirjono Prodjodikoro to the effect that judges must integrate themselves with the people, side with revolutionary forces, and listen to society rather than read Western-derived textbooks.[14] But *Trompet Masjarakat* was not the only source of pressure on the judges. Every day of the trial, spread out intermittently over the next six months, crowds of demonstrators from the PNI, PKI, and other organizations surrounded the courthouse. Delegations visited the judge's chambers to deliver petitions that Liem be sentenced to death.[15] Judge Djoko Sugianto, who years later rose to the Supreme Court, was not unsympathetic to the defense, but he and the two other judges on the panel were hemmed in on all sides. Few if any judges had the courage and fortitude necessary to face the uncertain consequences of deciding this kind of case on its merits. Liem's fate in court was preordained.

Initially, his defense attorneys were from Surabaya: the senior advocate, Sudarno, and his son, Ernanto. Five others later joined the team. In mid-March, however, all seven withdrew from the case, despite the promise of substantial fees, following numerous anonymous telephone threats.[16] No other local attorneys would represent Liem, who was refused an offer of court-appointed counsel. At length, Liem's brother in Jakarta came upon A. Zainal Abidin and Yap Thiam Hien, who agreed to consider the case.

From an aristocratic Buginese (South Sulawesi) family that had long been exiled to Kalimantan, Abidin was about Yap's age and shared the same educational history. As a young boy he had been sent to school, ELS and HBS, in Surabaya. His knowledge of the city and of Javanese was helpful in the Liem case. He and Yap had first met casually in the Rechtshogeschool. In those years, according to Abidin, Yap had a reputation for being "less Chinese in character than Indonesian and international."[17] During the 1950s and especially the early 1960s, when Yap had too many clients, he sent those he could not represent to Abidin. The law school connection was important, but Yap also trusted Abidin's personal integrity and legal skills. Peradin brought them closer together, along with Lukman, Hasjim Mahdan, and Suardi Tasrif. Rather alike in some ways, the two men prided themselves on being professional, principled, and hard to frighten. By turns calm or raging, they complemented one another well in the Surabaya *pengadilan negeri*. For Abidin, as for Yap, it was a memorable case, the sort one talks about forever. But for Yap their collaboration was also charged with a more subtle nuance, which was that ethnicity had nothing to do with it. It meant more to Yap that he was working with the ethnic Indonesian Abidin than it did to Abidin that he was working with the ethnic Chinese Yap.

As it happened, ethnic bells sounded on their first trip together to Surabaya, at the end of March. Abidin was put up in the city's prime hotel, the old Oranje with a new Indonesian name, but Yap was installed in a small *losmen*, a cheap inn, near the bank of the Brantas River. Yap asked why he and Abidin had been separated. Liem's younger brother explained that because of the anti-KMT agitation against Liem, he worried for Yap's safety, and so hid him away in the inconspicuous *losmen*. They had no such worry about Abidin, because he had been in the PSI, which opposed the KMT, but also, obviously, because he was ethnic Indonesian. Yap protested the separation, partly because he and Abidin had to confer about the case, but also quite clearly because he felt the indignity of it. He was moved into the Oranje.

They talked with Sudarno, Liem's first counsel, who told them about the anonymous telephone calls and admitted he was afraid to take the case. That same night, when Abidin answered the telephone, a caller asked threateningly whether he was brave enough to defend the KMT. Yes, if we want to and think it necessary, replied Abidin. He told Yap about the call, asking his views. Like two young cocks exulting in their own toughness, the two fifty-year-olds agreed that they would not be frightened away from the case. (Years later, during the 1980s, Yap and Abidin independently described these events so similarly that I do not doubt their accuracy.) The next day Abidin, who knew Surabaya well and spoke Javanese, got them to court to meet with Judge Djoko Sugianto. They were shocked to find the courtyard swarming with demonstrators and the courtroom filled by, among others, police and law students, there to observe trial procedure. Outside, PKI and PNI banners were waving. Inside the courtroom, prosecutor Susanto himself had had a PNI flag hung. Abidin and Yap, celebrating the courage of Makasarese and Acehnese, decided they would represent Liem.

In the circumstances, Judge Djoko insisted on providing protection for the defense. Yap wanted to reject the offer, for lots of police would simply call attention to them and cause tension. Nevertheless, a military police (CPM) detail accompanied Abidin and Yap to and from court. The Javanese-speaking Abidin quietly provided some additional security by asking pedicab drivers in front of the hotel to report any suspicious happenings to him.

From the time the new defense team took over, Yap made Susanto's life miserable. He had few illusions about anything in the trial. Although Liem was illiterate, he was intelligent and had an astonishing memory; his aides would read him newspaper articles, which he would memorize verbatim. There was little doubt that Liem had freely used money under the table to make a great deal of money everywhere else, but then so had all other entrepreneurs. The trial, however, was fundamentally corrupt, not only for the political pressure involved, but also for the prosecution's hypocritical abuse.

Yap's strategy in this case, as in others later, was to focus as much on official wrongdoing as on the relevant legal issues. Given the extraordinary power of the prosecution and police, and the growing tension between advocates and judges, few advocates were willing to take such risks. Even Abidin tended to caution in this respect. Yap took a rather different view of the matter, one informed partly by outrage at official misbehavior and partly by the sense that a proper defense in criminal trial required forcing public lawyers to obey the law. It did not always help his clients, however, and in time he himself suffered for it.

At the outset Yap insisted that the PNI banners must be removed from the courtroom. Susanto resisted, but Judge Djoko understood and quietly had the flags taken away. Next, after Abidin and Yap had studied the list of seized property, Yap protested that Susanto was using, had even driven to court in, Liem's red Impala. He requested that the car be turned over to the court and that the prosecution be enjoined from using it. Susanto again protested.

The relationship between Susanto and Yap, having started so unpleasantly, got much worse. Before Abidin and Yap arrived, Susanto had intensely examined Liem and others on the stand to good effect. The defense now turned the tables, putting the prosecution on the defensive by insisting that the court, prosecution, and Liem's counsel must examine all the warehouses to make sure that their contents matched the lists compiled by the prosecution. After all, the state, to which the goods would revert if Liem were convicted, had an interest in the matter. The contents might be eaten by mice, said Yap in court, drawing a knowing laugh from the audience. Judge Djoko allowed his request, and Liem's Surabaya warehouses were opened. They were bulging with textiles, building materials, automobile parts, and much else that Liem had bought up and hoarded, waiting for higher prices. It quickly became clear, however, as Yap suspected, that the goods did not match the lists. Djoko ordered a count, which showed that there was more on the lists than in the warehouses. Everyone knew perfectly well that the prosecution had helped itself to these items. Yap respected Djoko for trying to get at the truth.

The judge even agreed to examine Liem's warehouse in Jakarta, where all hell broke loose, partly because the politically more variegated Jakarta press had greater leeway to report on the case. The Jakarta warehouse was huge, big enough for a truck to drive into. Evidently one had done so, removing about three-quarters of the contents, according to Yap. On seeing this, Susanto promptly fled the scene. It turned out that he had opened the warehouse in order to take porcelain tile to give to a deputy chief prosecutor who wanted to construct a small public zoo in his own yard, where he happened to keep a pair of tigers. The deputy chief prosecutor, Soenarto, a Catholic and an army brigadier, had been appointed, ostensibly to reduce corruption, during the reign of Jaksa Agung Gunawan, who was responsible for some of the prosecution's worst abuses. Known as the Macan (Tiger), not just because he owned one or two of the animals, Soenarto was brutally tough, having severely beaten and broken the ribs of another prosecuting official for carrying on with an army officer's wife. It says something about Yap, and the times, that he respected the Tiger for his honesty: Soenarto had taken the tile not for himself but for the zoo, and after being arrested for a short time as a Soekarno loyalist in the aftermath of the coup of 1965, he went on to make an honest living as a truck driver.

Yap and Abidin had reported to the police that a prosecutor, perhaps Susanto, was living in a house seized from Liem's brother. The Tiger summoned them, yelled at Abidin for sitting improperly, then at Yap for saying that both he and Abidin were responsible for the police report, when only Abidin had signed it, and then accused them both of trying to play the police off against the prosecution. They managed to persuade him that they had no such intention and were merely following proper procedure. Practicing law under Guided Democracy was full of traps.

Back in Surabaya, Yap made the most of the revelations, accusing Susanto of playing Santa Claus with property seized from Liem and then making off with evidence. Susanto went wild, and the audience screamed at Yap. Through April, May, and June, the trial sessions became increasingly tense, as Yap and Abidin attacked both the prosecution and its case. *Trompet Masjarakat* stepped up its campaign, putting on its front pages speeches by Soekarno and Minister Sudibjo (secretary-general of the National Front) calling on judges to support the revolution.[18] The newspaper barely touched on defense arguments, though here and there Yap's forays against Susanto seem to have provoked some journalistic interest. When Yap infuriated the prosecutor by suggesting that perhaps Susanto himself should take the witness stand and be questioned, *Trompet Masjarakat* did report it, but underplayed it, emphasizing Susanto's protest and Judge Djoko's admonition of Yap.[19]

Abidin and Yap worried Susanto enough for him to fill his *rekwisitoor*, the summation of charges and demand for sentence, with appeals to Soekarno's speeches, the ongoing revolution, and the rest of the standard repertory of political slogans of the late Guided Democracy period.[20] Stung by Yap's revelations of prosecutorial abuse, of which Judge Djoko indicated his disapproval, Susanto at several turns singled out Yap for sneering attacks. The prosecution's legal case, however, rested basically on Article 1(1)d of the Anti-Subversion Law (Presidential Decree 11/1963), which condemned as subversion, inter alia, any obstruction "of industry, production, distribution, trade, cooperatives, or transport managed by the Government, or based on Government decision, or which bears extensive influence over the People's standard of living," and the president's Economic Declaration of the same year, which sought unsuccessfully to halt the hopeless economic decline. Susanto asked for a sentence of death.

Yap's defense was uncomplicated.[21] He pointed out numerous instances of vagueness in the prosecutor's indictment, but the core of his argument concerned the application of the Anti-Subversion Law. As *Trompet Masjarakat* reported Yap's statement, he insisted that the essence of a subversion charge was political but that the prosecution had failed to show any political motive at all. Without a copy of the defense plea, it is hard to ascertain where Yap meant to take this argument. One possibility is that he was trying to obfuscate the relevant article by burdening it with an implicit requirement of political motive. Another, however, which is more likely, is that he was making a more general point that the very nature of subversion demanded a political impetus, which the prosecutor had made no effort at all to demonstrate. Finally, Yap had a less subtle and more damaging argument, ignored both by the prosecutor and *Trompet Masjarakat*, which was simply that many of the charges were ex post facto. Much of the activity for which Liem Koe Nio was indicted occurred before Presidential Decree 11/1963 and the Economic Declaration were promulgated; his actions were not illegal at the time.[22] Yap asked for dismissal of the charges. When he finished reading the *pleidooi*, the audience in and out of the courtroom screamed its disapproval and became threatening. Judge Djoko, a large man, shielded Yap and Abidin, taking them to his office for protection. Two days later Susanto replied with a ringing appeal to Revolutionary Law—*Hukum Revolusi*, Soekarno's catchword, Soekarno's speeches, especially the Political Manifesto of 1959, and the unsurprising announcement that he was sticking to his demand for the death penalty. Yap's response, equally unsurprising, reiterated his appeal for acquittal.

Legal issues, again, had little to do with the disposition of the case. Susanto, Djoko, Yap, and Abidin went through the theatrical motions, but only Yap and Abidin could act them out genuinely as if law mattered, for they had no choice. Predictably, on 31 July, Judge Djoko announced the judicial panel's decision—death.[23] All of Liem's property was to be turned over to the state, and he had to pay court costs. The crowd shouted its approval of the decision, praising Judge Djoko Sugianto and Prosecutor Susanto Bangunegoro. Liem appealed and lost all the way up to the Mahkamah Agung, which rendered a decision after the coup of 1965. On a final jarring note of legal impropriety, Soerjadi, the chair of the Supreme Court who heard the case, was also chair of the *pengadilan tinggi* (appellate court) in Surabaya when Liem's case came up.

As a better end to a bad case, however, Liem was never executed. Unlike the New Order period post-1965, when the death penalty became real and common, without trial more often than with, Guided Democracy's bark was worse than its bite. No one was ever executed under Presidential Decree 11/1963 until after Guided Democracy had disappeared. Liem's lawyers requested presidential amnesty, which Yap thought was granted some twenty years later. Liem's brother in Jakarta, who paid Yap's and Abidin's fees, was also ruined, but apparently fled to Singapore, where he opened a successful emporium as an outlet for goods from China.

In itself, the Liem case was not unusual in the annals of Guided Democracy's jurisprudence. But Yap had turned the case into something extraordinary by raising issues that were almost never aired in a courtroom. A couple of years later he did the same thing in another trial, the P. T. Quick case, with electrifying effect. The Liem case, however, was his first venture into that peculiar genre of criminal trials underlain either by political purpose or official abuse of power, which provide courageous or visionary advocates access to public influence. Yap's name appeared prominently in the press whenever the trial was reported, and no longer in connection with *peranakan* politics. But for Yap himself, the case provided a model for his own brand of reform advocacy thereafter. It opened the curtain on a stage, an Indonesian stage, where he could stand at the center, making an argument to an infinitely larger audience than Baperki ever offered. It was for this reason that the Liem case meant so much to him, and why it could still elate him decades later. It was his debut as a serious reform advocate with ideas about how to use a judicial trial as a weapon.

The case was a debut, but not the beginning. The beginning probably had come most clearly with the onset of Guided Democracy, which led Yap to think more deeply both about the political foundations of justice and about his own political vocation—by which I mean to convey a slightly religious edge. Having taken the parliamentary *rechtsstaat* for granted, like many others, the rise of Soekarno and Guided Democracy forced Yap to think seriously about politics, not as a partisan matter (partisanship he regarded as a necessary but repugnant fact of life) but as the foundation of state, society, and justice. During the early Guided Democracy period he read a great deal (largely in Dutch and English) about political systems and change. What he thought then was well reflected in his Konstituante speech, in which he broke with Siauw and for all practical purposes with Baperki.

From then on, ethnic issues did not disappear for Yap, but were submerged in a larger concern for human rights that extended to a much wider universe. Only once thereafter did he engage publicly on a *peranakan* question, the name-changing debate of 1967, which he also cast, more clearly than before, in the general terms of human rights rather than the narrower frame of Chinese minority issues.

From 1961 through late 1965, Yap prepared himself for the extraordinary trials—in all senses—of the New Order regime that followed upon the catastrophic demise of Guided Democracy. It was a genuine time of transition, during which his focus on *peranakan* affairs shifted to the grander front of political and legal reform in Indonesia, symbolically represented by his stride from Baperki to Peradin. Liem Koe Nio's case honed the tools he liked best.

TEN

INTO NEW ORDER INDONESIA

On the morning of 1 October 1965, two months after he and Abidin had finished their defense of Liem Koe Nio in Surabaya, Yap drove as usual to his office on Jl. Gajah Mada. He noticed that it was unusually quiet for Jakarta, but thought little of it. Only after he arrived at the office did he learn of the violent events of the previous night. The attempted coup that had occurred changed Indonesia's life, and with it Yap's.

Much about the coup, including basic issues of origins and causes, remains murky.[1] Even the term "coup" is ambiguous, for there were actually two attempts to unseat the government: a first that failed, and a second, the army's, that crept up behind it and succeeded utterly. Only the essentials for understanding what happened, and how Yap responded, will be taken up here.

Given the spiraling tension during the early 1960s, a dramatic denouement was inevitable. If a turning point in the Guided Democracy period can be located, it was probably November 1963, when First Minister Djuanda, a moderating influence, died. To succeed him, President (and Prime Minister) Soekarno chose Foreign Minister Subandrio as first deputy prime minister. A medical doctor by training who had been a diplomat since 1947 and foreign minister since 1957, Subandrio had a reputation for arrogance and opportunism. Attached to no party and without other visible means of political support, he was utterly dependent upon Soekarno, who entrusted him with huge responsibilities: first as deputy prime minister, then as foreign minister, chief of the Central Intelligence Bureau (BPI), head of the Government Institutional Retooling Commission (Kotrar), and much else.

As the economy slid into inflationary chaos, foreign affairs claimed center stage but hardly dampened the heat of domestic political turmoil. The confrontation with Malaysia produced a war along the Indonesia-Malaysia border in Kalimantan that led nowhere. Soekarno pronounced new alliances on the international left, invited the United States to "go to hell with its aid," and at the end of 1964 withdrew Indonesia from the United Nations.

Foreign adventure, however, fed back into the frenzied activity of political conflict at home, where the PKI seemed to grow more influential by the day. Indonesian politics during the last two years of Guided Democracy was complex, intense, brutal, and uncontained by institutional rules.[2] Politics was all sandlot with no arena or umpires except for Soekarno himself. Formal institutions had collapsed into corruption, abuse, and inefficacy. As if to spread responsibility, Soekarno expanded the cabinet enormously, culminating in the "Cabinet of a Hundred Ministers" (seventy-seven actually) of September 1964. Oei Tjoe Tat was appointed to the cabinet at that time.[3] The press, controlled, cautious, and generally bound by party lines, was a poor source of information. Bloated rumor circuits took up the slack, contributing substantially to public enervation.

Soekarno, as the pivot of the political system, had relatively little control over it. Nor did anyone else. All was contention, with the PKI as the most aggressive party, the army as the one force with enough raw power to contain the communists, and other parties and interests distributed uncomfortably around these two poles. The PKI alone seemed to know what it was doing. Sticking closely to Soekarno, who appreciated its dynamism and support, the party became increasingly confident in its initiatives. The most important of these was land reform, promulgated as law in 1960 but consistently blocked by landed interests associated especially with the Nahdlatul Ulama and a wing of the PNI built around the *pamong praja* regional administration. In 1964 the communist Indonesian Peasants' Front (BTI, Barisan Tani Indonesia) began to force the issue by means of "unilateral actions" against recalcitrant landowners and government forest reserves. In Central and East Java, Bali, and North Sumatra, tension spread as Communist, Nahdlatul Ulama, and PNI interests attacked each other. The terrible violence that followed the coup in late 1965 was adumbrated a year earlier particularly in those areas. In December 1964 Soekarno had called party leaders together to negotiate an end to conflict, but to no effect, partly because the PKI Central Committee could no longer fully control the provincial BTI.

At the same time, however, the PKI parried all efforts to limit its growing power and effectively undercut its most determined opposition on nearly all fronts. One key to its success was Soekarno, who saw in the party not only the most progressive force in the country but also the best organized counterweight to political Islam and to the more worrisome threat, the army. The army alone, despite political dissension and dissatisfaction within the officer corps and the jealous resentment of the air force and navy, was quite capable of denying the PKI and fending off Soekarno as well. Both had footholds in the army officer corps, and more so in the air force and navy, but the army leadership was sufficiently unified politically to hold its own. In early 1965 army leaders rejected a PKI effort to extend Soekarno's Nasakom concept—the amalgamation of Nationalist, Islamic, and Communist orientations—to the armed forces. Soon afterwards, a proposal to create a "fifth force" (alongside the army, navy, air force, and police) of civilian irregulars equipped with weapons from China was firmly rejected by General Yani, the army commander.[4] Still, army commanders continued to feel pressure both from PKI criticism of "bureaucratic capitalists" and from suspicions among the president's staff of army intentions. In April or May 1965 rumors began to circulate of a coup-minded Generals' Council (Dewan Jenderal). These rumors gained credence from the revelation of a secret memo from British Ambassador Gilchrist mentioning "our local army friends." In his trial in October 1966 Subandrio insisted that he had not taken the rumor of a Generals' Council seriously, nor had he supposed that the Gilchrist letter referred to an army conspiracy. He was probably telling the truth. Many others, however, were either encouraged or worried by the prospect of military action to stop the PKI.

By mid-1965, then, Jakarta's political temperature was distinctly overheated, with rumors flying about all sorts of possibilities, reasonable and fantastic. Then, on 4 August, Soekarno fell ill, vomiting in the presence of army officers and others attending the palace for a meeting. For years rumors had cropped up regularly about Soekarno's failing health, but now there was evidence. Whatever illness upset the president, it turned out not to be serious, as evidenced by the fact that he would survive another five years under the depressing conditions of what amounted to house arrest. But at the time, doctors were called in, including a team from China, leading to additional rumors that the PKI had inside information about the president's precarious health. On

17 August 1965, Soekarno delivered his last Independence Day address before the roof caved in on both Guided Democracy and himself.

On the night of 30 September, small contingents of troops kidnapped six army generals, including army commandant Achmad Yani, but botched the attempt to capture Armed Forces Chief of Staff A. H. Nasution, mortally wounding his young daughter. Three of the officers were killed on the spot and the others, including Nasution's aide, a young lieutenant, were put to death at a place called Lobang Buaya (Crocodile Hole) located at Halim Perdanakusuma air force field, near Jakarta, which served as the base for the coup effort. The next morning Lt. Colonel Untung, commander of a battalion of the Cakrabirawa palace guard, announced on the radio that the September Thirtieth Movement had overthrown the Generals' Council, preventing a coup, and had extended its protection over President Soekarno. Troops from the Central and East Java divisions in Jakarta for Army Day on 5 October were deployed around the huge field in front of the presidential palace, commanding the radio station and the offices of the Ministry of Defense. Soekarno himself was whisked off to Halim air base. Later on 1 October, Untung announced the names of forty-five members of a revolutionary council committed to the president's policies that would assume governmental authority. Few if any of those on the list, an odd grab-bag drawn from across the political spectrum, evidently had any inkling of a "revolutionary council."[5]

By any standard it was an incompetent coup and was promptly crushed by Major-General Suharto, commander of the Army Strategic Reserve (Kostrad), located in the Jakarta area. By 2 October he had succeeded in persuading the dissident troops to leave Independence Field by the palace, had taken over the radio station, brought Jakarta under control, and then taken command of Halim, while Soekarno moved to the presidential palace in Bogor. These moves, however, were only the beginning of what became a well-orchestrated reaction.

Who exactly had planned and initiated the coup was unclear. There was little public discussion of the matter, however, for the Jakarta press was promptly closed down and, when allowed to publish again within a few days, all newspapers on the left had been banned. Despite the fact that the 30 September Movement was apparently led by military officers, General Suharto suggested that the PKI was behind it, and the anti-communist press immediately took up the cry. There was little evidence for this charge, and not much more has come to light in the years since. The peripheral involvement of members of the Communist Youth (Pemuda Rakyat) and women's (Gerwani) organizations was seen as sufficient grounds for the accusation. Blaming the PKI suited many interests. Army headquarters issued lurid reports—apparently false—that the slain generals had been tortured and mutilated by Gerwani members. Suddenly the party, riding high so recently, faced fierce retribution by the groups it had hammered during the previous several years. Islamic groups, Catholics, Protestants, student organizations, intellectuals, and much of the army officer corps moved together in a natural but fleeting alliance whose one common concern was to eliminate the suddenly hapless PKI.

Within a week supporters of these groups began to pour into the streets. PKI headquarters in Jakarta were burned on 8 October. Later, so was Baperki's Res Publica University. Communist leaders in Jakarta were arrested by army units. Within two weeks, army shock troops (RPKAD), who had been deployed to Central Java to help round up officers who had supported the coup, also helped by upsetting local political balances and lending a hand to a terrifying massacre of communists, mainly by Islamic youth groups backed and abetted by troops.[6] The killings spread to East Java, Bali, and North Sumatra, all areas where conflicts over land had been especially vicious. Violence occurred too in Aceh, West Kalimantan, and elsewhere, though less prominently. Calculating how many died is nearly impossible because of the lack of hard evidence; the figure of 500,000 commonly referred to is simply midway between low and high estimates. The worst of the killing orgy was over by early 1966, but it continued here and there long afterwards, with the political and moral consequences extending far into the future. Despite the misunderstanding abroad, relatively few ethnic Chinese were slaughtered, except in West Kalimantan in 1967. It was not an anti-Chinese pogrom, and none of the rhetoric that justified the killings had to do with Chinese. Economic, religious, and social factors supported the terror, which also provided the opportunity to settle personal scores, but it was legitimized entirely in anti-communist terms. The sin of the PKI was not to have prepared its members for the possibility of such violence. By the time the terror stopped, there were hundreds of thousands dead and hundreds of thousands more crowded into concentration camps and prisons around the country.

The obliteration of the PKI was complete. Its leadership was gone. D. N. Aidit, chairman of the party, was shot upon capture by troops in Central Java. Others were presumably killed outright when they were caught, still others were later brought to trial and sentenced to death, and a few lucky enough to have been abroad stayed there. The party, the third largest communist organization in the world, was vaporized in a matter of months.

Without the communists, the political structure of Guided Democracy collapsed. Its other prop, the army, now stood essentially alone, hardly winded by the mayhem of late 1965 and surrounded by a crowd momentarily grateful to it for having rid them of the communist threat. Soekarno was too able a politician not to have realized that his game was likely over. He put up a fitful struggle to maintain his grip but had little to work with once the PKI lever was gone. His substantial pockets of support—in the PNI, Partindo, here and there in the military and police—were seriously weakened in part by their own fawning attachment to him. They were no match for the previously suppressed groups, whose energy now exploded furiously not only against the PKI but against the Guided Democracy regime itself, and even against Soekarno. The politics of the post-coup period was more complex and intricate than its easy violence, but nearly as inexorable. Soekarno spoke out against the killings and asserted his political prerogatives, while Subandrio tried to mobilize PNI students against newly organized opposition groups that not only demanded the formal abolition of the PKI but showed little respect for Soekarno's authority. By mid-March 1966, however, Soekarno was forced to sign over the authority for restoring order to General Suharto. From then on the New Order regime, as it called itself, had only to mop up politically. A year later Suharto became acting president and Soekarno was confined to his home, where he died in 1970. The unpopular Subandrio was not only publicly vilified by students and others but was arrested a month after Soekarno's surrender on 11 March and brought to trial in October. Yap defended him.

Like many others, Yap was startled and frightened when he learned about the coup on the night of 30 September. He thought, terrified, that the communists had taken over. He could not make sense of Lt. Colonel Untung's revolutionary council list, which included the names of Siauw Giok Tjan, who might have belonged if the coup were on the left, but also Leimena, then second deputy prime minister and chairman of the Protestant Parkindo, and others who certainly were not on the left. By day two, however, Suharto had begun to take control of Jakarta. Yap was relieved and, as the anti-PKI reaction set in, began to be hopeful that the communist problem would be done with. He was convinced that the PKI was behind the coup. Only later, did he begin to doubt.

Even while he still believed the PKI to be responsible for the coup, however, the dark side of the anti-communist reaction affected him early, deeply, and in part personally. After the burning of the PKI building, Baperki's Res Publica University (Ureca), which years earlier had caused him such pain, was also burned, an affair managed largely by *peranakan* members of the Catholic student association (Persatuan Mahasiswa Katolik Republik Indonesia, PMKRI). Among them were the law students Harry Tjan and brothers Liem Bian Kie and Liem Bian Koen, who played important parts in the reaction and later became prominent figures in New Order politics. Soekarno condemned the burning of Ureca as racist, but, according to Tjan, it did not occur because the university was Chinese, but rather because it was a stronghold of the communist student organization Consentrasi Gerakan Mahasiswa Indonesia (CGMI, Concentration of Indonesian Student Movements), which had just held a conference there.[7] Yap saw the conflagration driving home from the office. He pulled over and watched—weeping, by his own account—as students, many of whom had helped to build the university, were chased and beaten.

Yap's emotions must have been more mixed as he witnessed the devastating end to Baperki, whose fate, as he had predicted was now linked to that of the PKI. What may not have been so obvious to him was that Baperki's destruction would be left to ethnic Chinese themselves. As Siauw had tethered the *peranakan* community to Soekarno, new leaders on the right now arose to accommodate the post-coup power structure. Those who burned Ureca also hounded known Baperki figures, along with CGMI members living in the vicinity of the university, quite close to Yap's home in Grogol. Violence was evidently tempered by family and friendship connections, but only unreliably.

Yap's own family was caught up in the terror. One of Khing's nephews belonged to the CGMI and had to leave the country immediately. But her brother, marked for having been to China and bragging endlessly about it, was reluctant to go. At a chance meeting, Liem Bian Kie told Yap that his brother-in-law had best get out. Yap, who did not get along well with Khing's brother, relayed the warning and persuaded him to leave for Europe. October 1965 was an anxious, frenzied time for the family.

Soon after, rumors and then hard news of the massacres in Central and East Java began to filter back to Jakarta. There, as elsewhere, the most common reaction to the killings was on the lines of "if the PKI had come to power, they would have done the same to us." Only Soekarno and perhaps a few others publicly condemned the violence, but their opinions were read politically, not morally. The surviving press, including Oyong Peng Koen's much-respected liberal *Kompas*, was too delighted with the demise of the PKI to express qualms over the holocaust that followed. (The same was true of much of the American press, which observed Indonesian events then as a cold war victory.) The brutal slaughter of so many during late 1965 still has not been confronted openly in Indonesia. Only in fiction has the terror been touched on, albeit cautiously.

Yap, too, was publicly quiet, but he did openly express horror at the violence in the one available forum where the issue could not easily be avoided, the church. Despite his own anti-communist convictions and relief that the PKI had been crushed, as early as October 1965 he sharply distinguished political from moral issues and came down hard against the killings. Eliminating the PKI was one thing; terror, revenge, and murder were another. It was at this time that the tension between him and T. B. Simatupang began to blossom into a long-running battle in the General Synod of the Reformed (ethnic Chinese) Churches of Java, between the Protestant Church of Indonesia (GKI, Gereja Kristen Indonesia) and the Indonesian Council of Churches (DGI, Dewan Gereja Indonesia), in both of which Simatupang was a dominant figure.

During the Guided Democracy period, the DGI had been quiet on public issues, to Yap's dissatisfaction. In part it was a matter, as always, of minority Protestants looking to the government for protection. In addition, Dr. Leimena, whose authority in Protestant affairs was enormous, was very close to Soekarno, as his second deputy prime minister and intimate political advisor, and not much inclined to allow criticism of Guided Democracy.[8] Troubled and frustrated by the reluctance of the churches to take a public stand, Yap was eager after the coup for the DGI to speak out clearly on issues where Christian ethics were relevant, and as usual he generated tensions by loudly voicing his own views.

In mid-October 1965 the council met to discuss the post-coup situation. The debates lasted for months. News had started to drift in from local ministers, missionaries, and others about the killings and the involvement of Protestants in them. From Medan, for example, came information that Gerakan Mahasiswa Kristen Indonesia (GMKI, Indonesian Christian Student Movement) students had been given a quota of one truckload per night of communists to slaughter. Fierce arguments broke out in the meeting over the appropriate posture of the churches. Some insisted that Protestants must take part in destroying the communist enemy. With Yap at their forefront, saner views of Christian responsibility won out, and, in this case, Simatupang agreed that limits must be imposed. GMKI students, already involved in the action fronts organized after the coup, were allowed to remain active but were forbidden to participate in the violence.

It was the one debate whose outcome satisfied Yap in some measure, but it was not enough to stem his growing alienation from the Protestant establishment and the church. Increasingly, as in Baperki, he felt himself isolated and out of tune with the mainstream.

By 1965 Yap's religious and political views had fused into a conception of responsibility that was consistent and equally demanding religiously and politically. What often confused his various associates was the fusion itself, which was undeniably idiosyncratic, irritating the theologians whom he debated and befuddling the political allies who thought him too quick to take risks. Several principles underlay Yap's outlook in his early fifties, none of them obvious to someone looking for an easy summation of the man. Those who saw him as a fanatic Protestant, or a tough Acehnese, or a rigid legalist missed the point of his own thoughtful integration of values. Yap's God was real but a mystery, who, like Lao Tze's Tao—his own analogy—surpassed human powers of comprehension. No one, not theologians, not Simatupang, not Leimena, could pretend to uncontested authority to interpret God's word. His own, and anyone else's interpretation, deserved respect: a fundamentally democratic and quite Calvinist view with significant political implications.

As I pointed out earlier, Yap had, rather un-Calvinistically, chosen the New Testament over the Old and saw his God as both loving and progressive. The love extended, without distinctions, to all of humanity, for God had sacrificed his son for all.[9] Add to this the notion of witness, particularly important for Yap both as religious and political principle, and the implication is that one must respond to every transgression against any human being. No political or social or personal interest could possibly intervene to stop that response, inspired as it was by love for a loving God. Any intruding interest had to be hypocritical and self-serving.

A progressive God who embraced all of humanity had to favor justice and equality, which could only be achieved, even if imperfectly in an imperfect world, through the honest adherence to just laws equally applied to all citizens. Why laws? Not because laws are important to lawyers—for higher principles count more—but because any other means of rule implies greater inequality in the distribution of power. Responsibility to just legal principle, then, makes sense of God's progressive love. In effect, Yap read his legal training and political attitudes into his religion, but also infused his politics with religious inspiration.

What seems to be missing in all this is defense of the ethnic Chinese minority that had consumed so much of his energy during the 1950s and early 1960s. The Baperki fiasco had released him from an involvement forced on him from the start, for lack of other opportunity and for lack of confidence to move politically beyond the *peranakan* community. But more than that, Yap had become convinced that he was obliged to move beyond a single concern. His religious views revealed the contradiction in defending the rights of only one group, but so did political analysis, already evident in his Konstituante speech of 1959, that demonstrated that the human rights of any one group depended on their universal applicability.

Yap's reaction to the brutality that followed the coup and his insistence that the DGI condemn it are perfectly understandable, then, but so was his angry frustration with the unwillingness of the DGI or his own church to go further to make their disapproval public. From late 1965 on, many rank-and-file Protestant ministers and Catholic priests extended help to those who were persecuted and in prison, winning large numbers of converts as a result. Yap approved of this and wanted even more of a commitment from the Protestant leadership. Simatupang and Yap debated this issue at length. Once, years after the coup, in a meeting with GMKI students at a DGI or GKI rest house, the discussion became heated. Simatupang offered the standard argument in defense of imprisoning communists: that, had the PKI won, Yap himself would have been slaughtered. Yap replied that this was speculation, that he had never seen any of the rumored PKI blacklists. What he knew was that PKI members, not others, had been killed or imprisoned. At one point, when Simatupang justified the violence, Yap insisted that in his (Simatupang's) heart he did not mean what he was saying, that it was wrong and created a bad impression. A student rose to say that Yap was right. Simatupang broke into tears, and Yap immediately regretted his words, for Simatupang was caught in a hopeless contradiction between political credo and religious value.

In the years that followed Yap and Simatupang fought constantly, not only about the human rights of PKI members but about the dominance and behavior of the army, the meanings of Indonesian nationalism, and the appropriate role of the churches, not to mention the management of Universitas Keristen Indonesia (UKI). Yap was not unsympathetic to the man, but saw in Simatupang's demeanor a peril intrinsic to Indonesian political culture:

> No one had the courage to oppose him, because of his authority, his stature as a former general, his profound intelligence, and also his personal discipline, exactly like Siauw Giok Tjan. . . . Like Giok Tjan too, he is too much on a mountain, [one] who will not descend, like Moses. He does not mix with common people, who are afraid to approach him, again like Moses. (May 1985)

Yap's own occasional arrogance, which he himself recognized, was less personal or political than intellectual. He was a fairly consistently egalitarian, both by personal inclination and political orientation. But his objections to

Simatupang (and Siauw) struck more deeply in a critique that extended to the churches, the attitudes of Christians, and some qualities he thought peculiar to Indonesian politics. Some time in the early 1970s, Yap went to Simatupang with a map indicating the extent to which forestry concessions in Kalimantan had been divided up among army officers. He asked Simatupang to use his influence in the army to do something about it. Simatupang said nothing.

> I know he thought it wrong, but he refused to deal with things openly. This is what I regret. He doesn't want to discuss such issues. For me, Christians cannot be quiet when there is a wrong. Christians should not be arrogant, or pretend to be better, or pretend that their religion is better, that we are smarter or deeper. I said this to Sim and he replied yes, but people cannot be changed. I disagree.

Years later his views extended into a more general critique of Christian history and attitudes, as his political experience fed his religious discomforts, but all the seeds were already well planted in 1965.

> In the Netherlands I talked about Sim with Professor Verkuyl [a prominent *Gereformeerde* missionary, influential in Indonesian Protestant circles, with whom Yap had become close, and who defended Simatupang as a church leader.] I asked how the church could treat corruption and the like so lightly. It lacked the courage to witness. And when there is criticism from abroad, the church—Simatupang—says don't interfere and don't support foreign criticism. The Bible teaches us to be brave, to talk with anyone. Why not the Indonesian church? I think we are too arrogant. What the Western church has taught us is too Christian-centric, too ghettoist. In the world there are not only Christians, but Buddhists, Muslims, and so on. Now [in 1985] Muslims are under attack [by the government]. It is dangerous if we join in the attack [which many Christians thought a good idea]. That is political, but what about humanitarian concerns?

In 1965–66 Yap pressed these views in his own church, the Gereja Keristen Indonesia, insisting that it must speak out courageously against the killings and other violence visited upon communists. It is not likely that many agreed with him. Ethnic Chinese Christians, the double minority, had no stomach for what must have seemed the extraordinary risk he asked of them, to put themselves forward for what? To defend communists, who, some no doubt believed, had it coming? To expose themselves against the majority mainstream? Very little in the history of *peranakan* or of Christianity in Indonesia made sense of such behavior. As Siauw had made more sense to most members of Baperki, so Simatupang made more sense to most Protestants.

The failure of the church to act morally, to see the public responsibility that seemed so obvious to Yap, did not surprise him. For years he had faulted the church membership for their caution, their unwillingness to support poorer churches, their lack of courage to criticize Guided Democracy, their constant accommodativeness. In 1963, following anti-Chinese riots, the GKI had gone along with advising Chinese to adopt Indonesian names, which infuriated Yap. His aggressive style did not help his case. Even those who agreed with him thought him a source of too much tension and conflict. His wish for the church to lead was overwhelmed by the church's inclination to follow.

The church's failure to condemn the post-coup brutality was the last straw. Yap was discouraged, frustrated, depressed, and disgusted. So he left his church. He did not make a big issue of it but gradually, in 1966, simply stopped going. Thereafter, when a family presence of any kind was required, Khing, never all that comfortable in Protestant circles, went in his stead. Yap remained active in the DGI and spoke out on religious issues, but his congregation did without him.

Leaving the church was not as dramatic as his break with Baperki at the Semarang conference in December 1960, but it had a similar effect of liberating him to speak out and act independently, without institutional fetters. If anything, his religious commitments deepened as those to his church lapsed. By 1966, however, Yap's commitments were undergoing another kind of change. His frustration with the church was matched by a growing optimism about the law, which began to absorb more and more of his time. Law was for Yap a religion of sorts. When he left his church, he was already engaged with Peradin, where, among like-minded activist reformers, he found far more satisfaction. Peradin became the congregation he had always wanted.

For all that he hated the violence of its origins, the New Order that succeeded Guided Democracy seemed as promising to Yap as to many others. Gradually naive optimism eroded into realistic pessimism, but, for the first few years, reformists were encouraged.

For one thing, lots of new faces were milling around. Not many thought about it at the time, but the changing of the guard was also a change of generations. Guided Democracy was the swan song of the nationalist leadership who began their careers in the 1920s and 1930s. They were swept away by senior army officers who came of age in the revolution, aided by civilians, many just born during the Japanese occupation or revolution. New faces often came equipped with new ideas and styles.

The change that first struck Yap was among young *peranakan* activists, more of whom now strode confidently into the political arena as if they belonged there. As Baperki supporters scattered, the representation of the *peranakan* universe shifted quickly from left to right toward young, prominently Catholic figures closely connected with army political intelligence leaders and generally associated with the assimilationist group. At the same time, however, young *peranakan* intellectual critics emerged, among them Soe Hok Djin, who adopted the name Arief Budiman, and his younger brother, Soe Hok Gie, both very active in the new politics. Yap was much impressed by the Soe brothers; to Arief, he once quietly mentioned how good it was to see young ethnic Chinese engaged politically. Ethnicity apart, the streets and meeting rooms were filled with young activists in the students' action front (KAMI) and the intellectuals' action front (KASI) who were saying much the same thing that Yap, and many of his senior colleagues in Peradin, had been saying for years. Yap, as yet hardly well known beyond *peranakan*, Protestant, and senior advocate circles, saw hope for progress all around him.

The advocacy itself was suddenly revived from the torpor induced by Guided Democracy. In the early New Order period the symbols of constitutionalism and legal process, submerged by the Soekarno government, quickly reemerged to become a principal source of ammunition against Guided Democracy. Intellectuals, university students, advocates, and even some judges allied to take their revenge on the Old Order that had waved them aside. Newspapers were filled with revelations and criticisms of the Soekarno years—corruption, interference in the courts, abuse of power. Younger judges and students hounded Wirjono Prodjodikoro, chairman of the Supreme Court, until he resigned. Judges tossed out their khaki uniforms and donned robes again. Prosecutors came under fierce attack, not least from judges, who began to insist that they step down from their seats on the judge's bench.

In May 1966 the University of Indonesia and KAMI and KASI put on a seminar—"The Rise of the Spirit of '66: Exploring a New Ground Plan" (Tracee Baru)—in which the enthusiastic participants poured optimistic hope into discussions of ideology, domestic politics, foreign policy, the young generation, the economy, and culture.[10] The make-up of the panels was itself indicative of a new era: well-known scholars, intellectuals, journalists, student leaders, and economists. Several *peranakan* figures were there, among them Oyong Peng

Koen from *Kompas*. Professional advocates were in a particularly enthusiastic frame of mind during early 1966. Never having climbed on the Guided Democracy bandwagon, and having suffered for it, their credentials were unimpeachable. Peradin's members quite suddenly were sharing a bit of the limelight as critics of the Old Order and proponents of reform in the New. Several around the country began to write prolifically for the press on legal reform. Prominent among them were Suardi Tasrif and Yap, whose articles for the next six or seven years appeared frequently in the press, mainly in *Kompas*. Possibly under the influence of the university symposium, in mid-May Yap wrote a long piece for *Kompas* in the form of an open letter to Soesanto Bangoennagoro, the prosecutor in the Liem Koe Nio case, a letter dripping with irony, demands for rectification in the name of the rule of law, and an "invitation to a dialogue," to which Soesanto did not respond.[11]

With hindsight it is easy to see how wrongheaded the optimism was. But until the early 1970s, when the consolidation of army control and purpose became incontrovertible, there were just enough mixed signals to provide reformers with constant, though dwindling, hope. General Suharto's gradual approach to removing Soekarno from office—Suharto became acting president in 1967, president in 1968—his rhetorical emphasis on constitutionalism and legal process, the apparent willingness of army leaders to work through appropriate political institutions, and, perhaps above all, the improving economy seemed to promise fundamental change just over the horizon. Change came, but not quite the sort reformers dreamed about.

Counter-evidence—of the variety *plus ça change, plus c'est la même chose*—was equally ample in the army's political initiatives, the organization of a Special (Political) Operations (Opsus, Operasi Khusus) group under General Ali Moertopo, and the military's interference in every significant political event. In 1966, however, the civilian-military alliance against Guided Democracy still held, and the army's political intentions were not altogether clear.

Immediately after 11 March 1966, when Soekarno transferred authority to Suharto, the process of pulling down the Old Order began in earnest. The PKI was formally banned. So was Baperki. On 18 March fifteen cabinet ministers were detained "for their own safety," it was at first announced.[12] Subandrio, the biggest political fish of all save Soekarno himself, was arrested in early April. From then on, despite a great deal of tension and uncertainty, Suharto was fundamentally in control.

Baperki's leaders, identified with the PKI, were picked up, too. Oei Tjoe Tat, still Yap's law partner, was arrested with the other ministers on 18 April.

He was tried eleven years later. Yap insisted on defending him. Siauw Giok Tjhan was detained but never tried before his release thirteen years later. Go Gien Tjwan was arrested but soon released with the help of Adam Malik, his longtime friend and boss at the news agency *Antara*, who replaced Subandrio as foreign minister and later became Suharto's vice president.

If anyone had the right to gloat over Baperki's vaporization, it was surely Yap, who had predicted something like it. He remained angry at Siauw and Go Gien Tjwan and the others who, he believed, had violated all the original purposes of Baperki and endangered the *peranakan* community. But he did not crow. Others did, including Oyong, who editorially approved the arrests of Siauw and other Baperki leaders. Yap thought the arrests morally and legally wrong. He felt badly for Siauw, whom he respected, and over the next few years Khing regularly dropped by to see Siauw's wife and children and to offer help.

Go Gien Tjwan, whom Yap especially resented and distrusted, came to Grogol to see Yap before leaving for Holland after his release. In an interview years later Go said that in the end Yap's critique of Guided Democracy and of Baperki's support of Soekarno turned out to be right. As they said goodbye, Yap made Go promise not to say or do anything abroad that might hurt *peranakan* at home.[13]

By this time, in mid-1966, Yap was less engaged with *peranakan* issues than with Peradin efforts to influence the reconstitution of an effective legal regime. There were only a couple of hundred members of Peradin then, half of them in Jakarta, but many of these were active, and the organization had begun to attract attention, some of it unwanted.

In early 1966 the trials began of prominent civilian and military figures accused of supporting the coup. These trials, which dragged on for years, served various purposes. Not only did they help to de-legitimate the Soekarno regime, they also kept the coup before the public as a reminder of the debt owed the new regime for saving the country from communism, and they demonstrated, particularly to Europeans and Americans who would be asked for financial assistance, the New Order's commitment to legality and proper order. Fundamentally, however, despite the appearance of judicial process, the trials were a sham, their outcome predetermined and inexorable. No one was acquitted, either in the military tribunals extraordinary (Mahmillub), which tried military figures and civilians accused of complicity in the coup, or in the civil courts that later heard lesser cases of subversion. Of the sixteen men tried in the Mahmillub by the end of 1966 in Jakarta, Yogyakarta, and Medan, thirteen were sentenced to death and three to life imprisonment.[14]

On the surface, the trials looked real. Every effort was made to put on a good legal show, complete with defense attorneys. The military auditor's office asked Peradin to provide legal assistance to the accused. At first, none of Peradin's leaders, including Yap, was willing. Some said they would not defend communists, but in the main they were afraid, as Yap was. Nineteen sixty-six was a highly uncertain time, as KAMI, KASI, and various Islamic and other groups, pro- and anti- New Order, milled about angrily. For the next year or two, the army provided numerous civilian officials with bodyguards. Defending communists, military insurgents, and despised political leaders of the old regime was a worrisome project both professionally and personally. Yap and one or two others, perhaps, began to doubt that Peradin should hold back, raising the issue of professional responsibility to provide *pro deo* assistance in capital cases. What finally brought the senior lawyers around was, evidently, a matter of machismo. In the first major trial the auditor's staff struck a deal with Trees Sunito Heyligers, a Dutch-born lawyer married to a detained official, to defend the communist leader Njono before a Mahmillub in exchange for her husband's freedom to accompany her to Holland. Yap himself argued that if a woman, a foreigner moreover, appeared in court, surely Peradin advocates could not refuse. Conditions were anxiously stipulated, to which the auditor agreed. Unlike Mrs. Sunito, who appeared alone, Peradin advocates would always serve as a team of at least two. Moreover, they would be appointed officially by the court rather than volunteer. And adequate protection would be supplied.

The splashiest of the trials, eagerly awaited by everyone, was that of Subandrio, a man easy to detest for his arrogance, opportunism, and oily ambition. Subandrio became the principal target of those who hated Guided Democracy, because Soekarno was politically out of bounds. Since early in the year, when he had openly invited Nationalist (PNI) students to meet violence with violence and terror with terror against opponents of the Soekarno regime, anonymous pamphlets and street slogans had accused Subandrio of a hundred evils and branded him a Durno, the devious and cynical royal adviser in the traditional Javanese puppet theater version of the Mahabarata epic. No evidence connected Subandrio to the coup, but he was a powerful symbol of the old regime, in some ways a stand-in for Soekarno, and a useful political scrap to throw to the street crowds.

Every ambitious military lawyer wanted to sit as judge in Subandrio's Mahmillub trial, which promised a brilliant career thereafter.[15] The position went to Lt. Colonel Ali Said, a 1960 graduate of the Military Law Academy, who had tried Njono (PKI Politburo member), and who went on to become chief public prosecutor, minister of justice, and finally chairman of the Supreme Court. No one, on the other hand, wanted to defend Subandrio, who agreed to have the tribunal appoint his defense.[16] Peradin merely reiterated its position that it would provide defense counsel only if appointed by the tribunal. Just a few days before the trial began, Major Soewarno from the auditor's office was still frantically racing around in search of a lawyer. He found Subagio Djojopranoto, a Jakarta advocate and PNI member, who was a possibility. Probably on the advice of other Peradin leaders, Soewarno called on Yap and convinced him that if he agreed, so would Subagio. Yap finally acquiesced.

The Subandrio trial made Yap a national figure. A reasonable American analogy to the Subandrio case is the Scopes "monkey" trial, where Clarence Darrow defended his client's right to teach Darwin's theory of evolution. It is not so much that both lawyers faced very long odds and lost, but that they, like other great lawyers, had the social and intellectual vision, as well as a superb command of the law, to transmit a powerful message despite defeat. Both men made prosecutors sweat and judges squirm, transforming one-sided routines into dramas staged around powerful social critiques and political statements. It takes greatness to do that. Darrow had institutional advantages that Yap lacked, making Yap's performance all the more remarkable.

It would have been easy for Yap to offer a pro-forma defense, as most defense counsel did in the Mahmillub and civil court trials. All expected to lose anyway, and few, if any, had their hearts in the defense. Yap, however, was not really capable of pro-forma work in court, certainly not in a criminal trial. As a civil lawyer, he was competent, professional, and hard working, but not particularly imaginative. Commercial cases did not excite him. Criminal trials, which in Indonesian procedure make heavier demands on counsel than civil litigation, were a different story. Yap loved criminal defense, which gave full play to his competitiveness, distrust of authority, quickness of mind, and capacity for forensic eloquence. Cross-examination, for which Indonesian procedure allows much less leeway than in common-law procedure, particularly excited him. An avid reader of American mystery stories, Perry Mason among others, he liked the mold of the defense lawyer in American courts.

Yap's style in court was almost always a study in thoughtful strategy and severe logic. Sometimes nervous before trial—and he was genuinely anxious in the Subandrio case—once in the courtroom he became cool and focused, rather like an experienced athlete when the match begins. It was his stage, and his knowledge of the law and sense of vocation made him comfortable there as nowhere else. A routine defense was as much out of the question then as a routine move is to a chess master with a brilliant combination at hand. No better proof exists than Yap's performance in the Liem Koe Nio case, in which the dangers and risks were greater than in the Subandrio trial. After Yap read his formal defense (*pleidooi*) in the Subandrio trial, Umar Seno-Adji, a former prosecutor, legal scholar, and later minister of justice, evidently impressed by Yap's show, asked him whether he was serious. Taken aback, Yap replied "of course," and years after was still amazed enough by the question to recall it.

The symbolic weight of the Subandrio trial was evident in the decision to schedule it precisely on the anniversary of the coup.[17] Public interest that had begun to flag in the other Mahmillub cases picked up immediately when Subandrio was brought to trial. The press, even the respected *Kompas*, with the widest circulation in the country, made no pretense of objectivity but vilified the defendant day after day. Ali Said, the judge, publicly referred to Subandrio as Durno. General Suharto, when he formally handed over the case materials to Ali Said, said that justice, not revenge, was the crux, but also reminded everyone of his feelings when he saw the bodies of the murdered generals.[18] A Mahmillub spokesman said that this trial was the biggest of them all because "Dr. Subandrio is the chief figure, the architect of the old order, the intimate friend of Gestapu."[19] The trial was guaranteed massive attendance, as anyone with influence scrambled for a place in the National Planning Board (Bappenas) building, where the Mahmillub sat. Five thousand requests poured in for four hundred seats.[20] One hundred and fifty local and foreign correspondents registered.

Before the trial began, Yap and Subagio had lunch with Ali Said and the other judges on the panel—one from each of the armed forces, including the police—and the military auditor, Lt. Colonel Achmad Durmawel. Yap asked how much leeway in cross-examination they would have, to which Ali Said promised the defense complete freedom to question witnesses directly.[21] Yap also urged, in view of the importance of the trial, that it should be broadcast in full over the radio and that journalists should in no way be restricted. Other trials had either been reported on the radio or had their opening statements broadcast. Subandrio's trial was indeed broadcast in full—television was added later—with thousands glued to their radios throughout. The government and the Mahmillub officials must have seen some advantage in this, but it was Yap to whom the broadcasts drew attention. Far more than the daily press, where Yap's performance was submerged, the radio transmitted his case everywhere.

The trial opened at 8 p.m. on 1 October 1966, a Saturday evening. Khing, who no doubt wished that Thiam Hien had refused the case, insisted on accompanying him. Unaware that the defense would have their own parking privileges, he had to park far from Taman Suropati, where huge crowds had gathered. For a couple of days Jakarta had witnessed noisy demonstrations marking the anniversary of the coup. Trucks filled with students had gone through the city's major streets, at one point wrecking a store that sold Chinese books. Stores had closed in the Chinese commercial districts of Glodok, Pintu Kecil, and Pancoran.[22] The Subandrio trial rode a peak of tension. Khing and Hien walked through the crowds anonymously but anxiously. His anonymity disappeared after the first session.

In every respect but one—the Mahmillub's power to render decision—the case against Subandrio was weak.[23] The substantive charges were divided between the pre- and post-coup periods. In the first, the indictment was basically that during the period 1964–65, Subandrio had abetted communists and certain military officers in preparing or facilitating rebellion against the government.[24] The evidence adduced by Durmawel was circumstantial at best: that in May 1965 Subandrio, as head of the Central Intelligence Bureau, did not investigate rumors about a Generals' Council although he did, at that time, disseminate information about the Gilchrist letter, referring to "our local army friends," which tended to confirm these rumors; that in July 1965, after PRC and Indonesian doctors had examined the ailing Soekarno, he called Aidit home from a trip abroad in the USSR and the PRC; that in September 1965 he ignored reports about increased PKI activity, rumors that the PKI would undertake a coup, and reports about military exercises involving PKI members at Halim airbase; that in late September he went to Sumatra, where he delivered inflammatory speeches urging the people to crush bureaucratic capitalists, economic dynasties, and the like; that on 1 October, still in Sumatra, he was informed of the coup but decided nevertheless to continue his tour rather than return to Jakarta; that he must have known that these actions would damage the government's economic, security, and foreign policies.[25]

Part two of the indictment essentially charged Subandrio with obstructing General Suharto's efforts to restore order after the coup, attempting to reestablish the forces behind the coup, and seeking to vitiate the significance of the 30 September Movement as a counter-revolutionary act.[26] These charges were proven by Subandrio's failure to act or investigate reports about PKI activities before and after the coup, his accusation in October 1965 that the press was paid by the CIA, his comparison (in a November briefing) of the excesses of the communist revolt at Madiun in 1948 with those following the 30 September coup, his attempt to rally Nationalist students in February 1966, and, finally (but irrelevant to the charges), his decision at the end of 1965 to transfer $500,000 from the Indonesian Embassy account in Switzerland to an account controlled by the Central Intelligence Bureau. Unlike the first group of charges, subject to the criminal code and Presidential Decree 5/1959, the provisions relevant to the second group were drawn from the Anti-Subversion Decree of 1963 and other acts dating from 1963 through September 1966, which were referenced in order to establish the authority of the court and its procedures as well as Subandrio's guilt.[27]

Subagio and Yap had barely any time to prepare, either alone or together. Three days separated their appointment from the first session of the trial. As required by law, they saw Subandrio to ask whether he agreed to their service, which he did, and whether he agreed with the charges, which he did not. Yap had not liked Subandrio as a public official and liked him as a client even less; Subandrio was suspicious, devious, and unforthcoming, Yap thought. Afterwards, the two advocates rushed to examine the voluminous materials in the case, which they had to read in place as there were only three copies. Without time to coordinate, they agreed to divide up the defense arguments: Subagio to address the political issues, Yap the legal questions. As the case developed, however, just the reverse happened, with Yap making the strongest political case for Subandrio. With little knowledge of military law, Yap asked the tribunal staff for a full set of the relevant statutes, which he studied along with the interrogations of Subandrio and prosecution witnesses.

In the very first session that Saturday night, after Durmawel read the indictment, Yap stunned the court with a complex of demurrers that they did not expect and could not really deal with.[28] The strategy, which he had worked out in just a few days, comprised an assault on the jurisdiction of the court and, failing that, a defense of Subandrio's actions that rested on their appropriateness under Guided Democracy. Both arguments were distinguished in part by their originality, but largely by the thoroughness and consistency with which Yap developed them. The speed with which he was able to put together his case was partly the legacy, I think, of the similar analysis he had done a year earlier in the Liem Koe Nio trial.

Yap's demurrers, which addressed issues of competency and legality, wove a tight net of legal reasoning. Instead of merely questioning the jurisdiction of the Mahmillub to try civilians, as advocates in a few other cases had done, Yap raised the issue to a new level by casting it in the light of constitutional legitimacy and legal propriety. Presidential Decree 16/1963 that established the Mahmillub, he argued, was in conflict with Article 21 of the 1945 Constitution, which provided that judicial organization and authority must be determined by statute, that is, a parliamentary rather than an executive act. It was also in conflict with three other major statutes on similar grounds.[29] So, therefore, was Presidential Decision 370/1965 that designated the Mahmillub as the jurisdiction to hear the coup cases. Moreover, in the decree which established the Mahmillub, there is no provision allowing the president to delegate authority to designate the accused, but here President Sukarno had delegated this authority to General Suharto, who was thus acting extra-judicially. This Mahmillub was out of compliance with its own establishing decree as well as with existing laws and the Constitution.

In addition, as Yap discovered in the code of military criminal procedure, an officer must be tried by higher-ranking officers. Subandrio in office had been given the titular rank of air marshall (*laksamana udara*), but Ali Said, the officiating judge, was only a lieutenant colonel. These arguments were only the beginning of a cascade of demurrers that had occurred to Yap's fecund legal mind. They were not inventions or mere cavils, nor were they rooted simply in his considerable knowledge of legal structure and ability to read statutes. Rather, what made them impressive was their foundation in concepts of legal integrity and constitutional governance that Yap himself took seriously, at a time, given the experience of Guided Democracy, when many others, including lawyers, doubted their relevance. His next demurrers brought this point home, for they stemmed from constitutional provisions that Yap insisted on treating as if they meant something. Article 27(1) of the 1945 Constitution provides that all citizens are equal before the law and obliged to uphold the law. All citizens, including the accused, have the right to be tried in a legally constituted court, which Yap had demonstrated the Mahmillub was not. As the Mahmillub heard cases in the final instance, without appeal, it therefore violated principles of existing statutes (5/1950, 19/1964, 13/1965), which provided for the right to appeal and established the Mahkamah Agung as the apex of the judicial system. Being tried by the Mahmillub deprived Subandrio of his human right to be tried according to law.

Yap had not yet run out of objections. Next he pointed out that Presidential Decision 370 and the Order of General Suharto, which laid the basis for bringing Subandrio and others to trial, were both promulgated in December 1965 and were therefore ex post facto to the acts of which the defendant was accused. This meant that these acts were not illegal when they were committed. The two presidential decrees, one of them the Anti-Subversion Act, also changed rules and procedures prescribed in the criminal code (most egregiously by increasing penalties), but they themselves were not legislative products (i.e., laws). The case, therefore, violated the principle that no one may be accused, tried, or punished except on the basis of a preexisting law. Yap then reminded the court of the provision in Law 19/1964 that anyone falsely arrested, detained, indicted, or tried had the right to seek compensatory damages. On another substantive issue, he attacked the inadequate distinctions made in the indictment between the several charges.

Yap's demurrers were a tour de force. In the audience, there in the Bappenas building and in front of radios, informed listeners (as some have told me) were riveted by Yap's cascading arguments.

The judges and auditor must have paled as Yap laid out his points one on top of the other. Ali Said later asked him how he had come up with so many arguments in such a short time. The problem was not volume, however, but that they were unanswerable. Ali Said called a recess of twenty minutes for the auditor to consider his reply to the demurrer of defense counsel. After the allotted time, the auditor requested another half hour, and then more. Every lawyer in the audience—the minister of justice, chief public prosecutor, legal scholars, advocates—understood the difficulty. There were whispers and chuckles.

An hour or more later, the tribunal reconvened to hear Durmawel's reply and then adjourned.[30] The next morning, Ali Said read the interlocutory decision, accepting Durmawel's arguments and rejecting all the demurrers. Of the decision's six pages, one and a half dealt with Subagio's arguments, the remainder with Yap's. If Yap's objections were free of cavil, the court's reasoning was not.[31] On the issue of the Mahmillub's constitutional legitimacy, Ali Said argued that constitutionality was adequately proven by the fact that the tribunal had not been dismissed by the New Order administration, an administration incontestably devoted to the 1945 Constitution. If Law 19/1964 on the judiciary provided that the organization of all courts must be laid down by statute, the reality was that no such laws had yet been promulgated—an argument which hardly met Yap's objection. If Presidential Decision 16/1963 did not provide for delegation of presidential authority, neither did it forbid it. On the matter of Subandrio's civil status, from which followed a right to trial by a civil court, Ali Said simply fell back on Presidential Decision 16/1963 and surrounded it with a jumble of words, in Indonesian and Dutch, without a sensible conclusion. As for the ex-post-facto problem, the interlocutory decision set forth the definition from Black's Law Dictionary, which actually supports Yap's interpretation, but then rejected Yap's argument. To Yap's point that the indictment confused the charges, Ali Said replied that they seemed clear to him.

On the issue of Subandrio's titular military rank being higher than that of the judges, Ali Said said nothing at all in the interlocutory decision, though he dealt with it inadequately, following Durmawel's reasoning, in the final decision.[32]

At this point, the very beginning of the trial, it must have been perfectly clear to everyone, even the most naive, that Subandrio did not have a chance. For all that the leadership of the New Order asserted they were following a new tack in which legal process counted, the Mahmillub gave ample indication that little had changed. Yap himself and many others could not have missed the point that the Mahmillub trials were only a more orderly version of the legal travesties of Guided Democracy. Yap was not surprised. But his anticipation of the outcome did not affect his defense. It did not because he was addressing imperative issues and an audience beyond the Mahmillub. Several of his arguments in the Subandrio trial would become standard fare for reforming advocates in ensuing years.

Yap's impressive performance throughout the trial won him the regard and sympathy that was denied his client. Subandrio did himself little good, for his answers to Durmawel's questions tended to be longwinded and meandering, giving the impression that he was trying to weasel out of each predicament. His defense oration was better, but its efficacy necessarily depended upon the unlikely willingness of the court and audience to accept the assumptions that governed the politics of Guided Democracy. Much of Yap's strategy, in contrast, had to do precisely with making these assumptions quite clear and using them to explain Subandrio's behavior, without justifying it. So effective was he that for many years some who had heard him could immediately recall his defense and its implications.

Yap's objectives in the trial were twofold: to soften or discredit the testimony of hostile witnesses and to undercut the prosecutor's reasoning. He could not achieve either without adequate freedom to cross-examine. Ali Said stuck to his promise to allow counsel complete leeway, for which Yap and Subagio praised and thanked the court profusely. In some ways the Mahmillub was more generous procedurally than the civil courts, where hostile judges imposed severe limitations on advocacy. Yap used the opportunity to good effect in skilled cross-examination of witnesses, some of whom had a distinct self-interest in supporting the prosecution's case. One witness from the Foreign Ministry testified, in answer to a question from Durmawel, that Subandrio's transfer of $500,000 to the Central Intelligence Bureau account was illegal. As he was leaving the stand, Yap called him back and asked him which law had been violated. He did not know. Yap accused him of talking through his hat, and Ali Said upbraided the official. Yap publicly embarrassed Suwito Kusumowidagdo (Subandrio's deputy in the Foreign Ministry, who went out of his way to support the accusation that Subandrio was close to the PKI), in part by demonstrating both his bias and his ingratitude, but mainly by showing that the witness himself had never at the time criticized Subandrio. No witness who supported the prosecution case, which was contrived to begin with, was left untouched by Yap, who repeatedly extracted testimony that either vitiated or diluted the prosecution's charges.

In the cross-examination of Subandrio himself, Yap fashioned his defense around a subtle and powerful political critique. Subandrio insisted all along that he was nowhere near as influential as Durmawel made him out to be, that he was Soekarno's deputy and no more and that, if he was in touch with the PKI, so was he with all other significant parties, including the PNI and NU, as was the president. Yap brought out the same points from his client and other witnesses, but went further to reconstruct the atmosphere of Guided Democracy, when few had dared contest the will of the regime. Again and again, Yap forced his audience to reflect on the problem of political responsibility under the old regime and, by implication, the new.

On the second day of the trial, following Durmawel's questioning, Yap directed Subandrio to answer his questions briefly and to the point, establishing that Subandrio was only one of many influential members of the Cabinet of a Hundred Ministers, and he then raised the issue of the Gilchrist letter, which, according to Durmawel, Subandrio had used to imply the existence of a Generals' Council:

Y: So [in the various bodies that you headed or were involved in] it was not as if you could dictate everything?

S: No, I couldn't.

Y: Were there disagreements in the meetings?

S: Yes.

Y: Often?

S: Often.

Y: In the meeting of the President with the military commanders: now I will focus on the matter of "our local army friends." [The offending phrase in the Gilchrist letter.] When the Gilchrist document was discussed, were there protests from the Commanders present there concerning the phrase . . . "our local army friends?"

S: No.

Y: There were not. No one said to the President that it did not mean the army?

S: No one.

Y: Afterwards, do you know whether there were protests about the phrase to the President or to you?

S: No.

Yap then established that the military intelligence bodies, more experienced than the Central Intelligence Bureau, also did not investigate the Gilchrist letter, as far as Subandrio knew. Then:

Y: One more question . . . about the period from the last quarter of 1964 through October 1965 for which you are being charged. What was the view of the people in general about the policies of the Government, as far as you knew?

S: Well, the society at that time was in a situation . . .

Y: What I want from you . . . is concrete, to the point. What was the general assessment of Government policies during that period, good or bad in general?

S: Good.

Y: Good.

S: Good.

Y: Was there support or not?

S: There was support.

Y: Did you yourself or through the President ever receive criticisms from the people concerning your policies as First Deputy Prime Minister . . . ?

S: No.

Y: From other offices?

S: No.

Y: From other Ministries?

S: No.

Y: In that case, can we conclude that the People and other Ministries, as well as the other [military] Forces, more or less approved your policies?

S: Yes.

Similarly, on relations with the PKI, Yap, fully engaged in a duel with Durmawel, showed that Subandrio was hardly alone in cooperating with the communists at a time when Soekarno urged it.

Y: . . . I take you back to the reception for the anniversary of the PKI in [May] 1965. At this reception were you the only one to speak?
S: No.
Y: Who else gave speeches, as you remember it?
S: From the Presidium [of the Cabinet] the Third Deputy Prime Minister [Chairul Saleh] and I. . . . And then the PNI, a representative of the PNI, then a representative of the NU, and other parties, all the parties . . . spoke.
Y: Among all of those parties was there one who detracted from the greatness of the PKI or did not wish long life to the PKI?
S: They all praised it.
Y: All praised, wished it long life?
S: Yes, Yes.
Y: Not one criticized the PKI, said that it shouldn't have a long life?
S: None.
Y: So all of them in fact publicly approved NASAKOM?
S: Yes.
Y: . . . Clearly this is not the case now, and of course in fact there was no real desire to praise the PKI then. So, can we call [the praise by the other parties] a political tactic?
S: Yes.
Y: Is this method of "the ends justify the means" really usual for political parties, both abroad and here?
S: True.[33]

Yap was not merely demonstrating that Subandrio was no more to blame than anyone else for what happened under Guided Democracy, but rather that the practices of Guided Democracy were rotten and that nearly everyone participated in the rottenness. His own political and ethical views obviously infused the critique that he constructed, brick by brick, throughout the trial. Much of what he led Subandrio to admit, Yap had anticipated in the Baperki debates and in his 1959 speech to the Constituent Assembly rejecting the 1945 Constitution. Thus, on the matter of constitutional practice during the Soekarno period, Yap asked Subandrio who determined the course of state policy. According to the 1945 Constitution, this was the function of the People's Consultative Assembly (MPR, with an S added to indicate that it was still provisional). Subandrio answered that state policy was established by the government under the leadership of Soekarno.

Y: Is that so? Is this in accord with the Constitution?

S: Yes, afterwards it was approved by the MPRS.

Y: . . . So it was not the MPRS that determined state policy and then sent it to the Government for implementation?

S: No.

Y: No?

S: No.

Y: Oh, it was just the reverse . . .

. . . .

Y: I return to the DPR [Parliament]. Did the DPR also have representatives of the nine political parties?

S: Yes.

Y: And from the functional groups and the like?

S: Yes.

Y: Were many Presidential Regulations, Presidential Decrees, discussed in the DPR, as far as you know?

S: Yes.

Y: Was it ever pointed out that this was in conflict with the Constitution?

S: No.

Y: Never. Was all this simply accepted, just like that?

S: After discussion.

Y: After discussion, it was approved.

S: Yes, approved.

Y: So, even though now it has been pointed out that all that was in conflict with the Constitution.

S: Now it is pointed out.[34]

Yap was as relentless in this line of questioning as he was in blocking and turning every attempt by Durmawel to paint Subandrio into a solitary corner of culpability. Time and again he returned to the point that those who might have criticized Subandrio—and by implication Soekarno and the government generally—did not, and in their failure shared responsibility.

In the fourth session, during the evening of 3 October, Yap, following Subagio, questioned Subandrio about foreign policy issues, particularly Indonesia's friendship with the People's Republic of China:

Y: Did you carry out our Government's policy then in your own interest or in the interest of State and Nation.
S: In the interest of State and Nation.
Y: Was your implementation of Government Policy opposed or approved by the MPRS?
S: Approved.
Y: By the DPR?
S: Approved.
Y: By political organizations and mass organizations in our country?
S: There was no opposition.
Y: It wasn't opposed?
S: No . . .
Y: Was there one political organization or mass organization that opposed the foreign policy, you and our Government?
S: No.
Y: . . . In your opinion the members of the MPRS were ducks [parrots] or persons of Character . . . who were capable of thinking for themselves?
S: They could think for themselves.
Y: Not ducks?
S: No.
Y: . . . So we can say that they weren't just following but agreed to it all?
S: Yes.[35]

But as everyone knew, in fact they were just following, and it was this that Yap wanted to press home. Again, during the evening of 8 October, after Durmawel had combed Subandrio's speeches of 1964 and 1965 for implicating evidence, Yap asked Subandrio whether President Soekarno had ever reprimanded him or expressed anger at any of his speeches.

S: No.
Y: . . . Ever by the MPRS?
S: No.
Y: Ever by the DPR?
S: No.

Y: Was there ever a protest against you by one of the [military] forces in this connection?

S: No.

In our discussion of the case long afterwards, Yap said that if he had wanted to be cruel, he would have asked whether Subandrio had heard protests or criticism from any judges, prosecutors, or military law officers—but he refrained. Yet, so effective was he in this litany of questions, that some at least in the audience remember him as having asked precisely those questions. A prominent human rights figure, the late H. J. C (Ponke) Princen, who became Yap's close associate but who did not know him until the Subandrio case, began to weep, sob really, as he told me of the effect Yap's line of questioning had on him. Dramatically he recounted how Yap had asked Subandrio whether army officers had spoken out, the members of the court, the auditor, the audience—none of which Yap had done at all. But the implication was inescapable to an audience that knew well the level of complicity in the miseries of Guided Democracy.

In his long summation on 17 October, Yap addressed imperative political issues as much as legal ones. By this time, the anxiety he had felt before the trial had disappeared. He had managed his defense capably and effectively. His *pleidooi*, which he and his law office secretary typed, was confident, direct, and far-reaching, speaking not only to the case at hand but to its significance for the Indonesian political system. Having thanked the court for its consideration, Yap at the outset raised the issue of the rule of law, to which he and other advocates, he said, were ready to contribute. But about the "Rule of Law of Our Revolution," to which Ali Said had referred in his interlocutory decision on the demurrers, Yap had serious reservations. He must have seen in the formulation the same wish for discretionary authority that Soekarno had sought when he first spoke of revolutionary law. "Is not our society and nation in revolution very much in need of basic legal regulations inspired by norms rooted in values that transcend the tides of revolution, as a protector and guarantor of rights to live in accord with the dignity of humanity, the creation of God?"

As in the Liem Koe Nio case, Yap distinguished himself in the Subandrio trial by refusing to ignore the environment in which it took place and by simply telling the truth. In his *pleidooi* he promptly regretted that Subandrio had already been convicted by public opinion, that there had been an intense and systematic attempt to prejudice the case, and that this stood in conflict with the principles of a democratic rule of law.[36] Such campaigns, said Yap, were typical of what was now called the "Old Order."

He also had a few warnings to deliver about the New Order. Between old and new orders, he pointed out, 1 October 1965 was accepted as an artificial dividing point without attention to the historical and social continuities. The "New Order" was not a new creation out of nothing, he insisted. It was a prescient comment, and its implication that the New Order and Guided Democracy had much in common became a more widespread insight a few years later. In addition, said Yap, driving the point home, to see those supporting Guided Democracy as all devils and those supporting the New Order as all angels not only obscured the situation, but also implicitly, unconsciously, constituted an admission of oneself as the child of a devil. Finally, Yap confirmed that the aim of the New Order was to restore justice, truth, and honesty and to implement the 1945 Constitution, "as the slogans say."

Having delivered this brief but compelling political sermon, Yap summed up his defense of Subandrio. He reiterated the legal issues raised in his demurrers, but then went on to a political defense that constituted a plea for a more tolerant understanding of modern Indonesian history. Taking up Durmawel's misunderstanding of dialectics, which had been offered as proof of Subandrio's own Marxist inclinations, Yap pointed out that every period of explosive change in Indonesia had been marked by cooperation and opposition. This, too, was a dialectical process, one most recently evident in the conflict between the PKI and the army. In short, Yap tried to persuade the court to understand Subandrio's actions in the context of normal politics in a complex state with a violent history.

Analyzing the evidence, Yap gave a more credible explanation of Subandrio's record than did Subandrio himself, who had rather less perspective on it. The difference, in some measure, was that Subandrio tried to justify, while Yap explained, concluding that Subandrio had no means for or purpose in weakening the state or governmental authority. Nor did he have a special relationship to the PKI. In the matter that actually was of most interest to the Mahmillub judges, Subandrio's alleged attempt to damage the army, Yap's analysis of the evidence demonstrated the shallowness of the auditor's case.

Yap had bigger fish to fry than Subandrio in his summation, however, and near the end of his speech he returned to these points. First, he confronted the death sentence demanded by the prosecution. Here Yap borrowed from the arguments he had developed earlier in the Liem Koe Nio case. Only God, he insisted, not other human beings, could justifiably take a life. The death penalty is an atavism in a modern criminal law system, one that marked a society that placed no value on a human being. Yap approved the Dutch philosopher

J. Huizinga's view that the quality of a culture rested not in its technology or aesthetics but in its capacity for sympathy and forgiveness.[37] For Yap, redemption was a value far superior to revenge.

Second, appealing to modern social science, Yap insisted that each of us is shaped by his environment; Subandrio was a timely product of Indonesian history and society. Unless one recognized the influence of culture, society, and history, in effect, one could not expose and defeat evil. This idea lay behind his argument that Subandrio was only one among most in shaping the miseries of Guided Democracy.

> Indonesian society itself gave the opportunity and means to this "second in command" to manage and arrange the "res publica," our common affairs, according to predetermined policies, that is according to what have been formally called "the outlines of state policy."
>
> Mr. Chairman, Indonesian society, we together, Civil as well as Military, private as well as public, left and right, all of us agreed consciously or not, purposefully or not, we all approved the actions of the Accused in his various functions, which now in different states of emotion we criticize and condemn. At the least, together we allowed the Accused to act for us and in our name, as he did, from 1959 through April 1966.
>
> I know, Mr. Chairman, that our Criminal Law does not recognize "ethical or moral responsibility" but only "criminal responsibility." Even so, Mr. Chairman, a modern judiciary acting in the name of "Justice based on the One Almighty God" and which has the function of providing "Succor" . . . has a new responsibility, that is to review and consider [all the charges comprehensively in relationship to the individual and to the social, political, economic, and cultural settings] in accord with—to borrow the honorable auditor's lovely words—"not an arena of revenge, but an arena of truth and justice based on philosophy, law, and sociology which must balance one another." In any understanding of these words it is awkward to hear the honorable auditor say "There are no mitigating circumstances, except that the accused has never been sentenced."[38]

Yap ended his defense oration with the biblical story of Christ and the adulterous woman about to be stoned to death. "Let you who is without sin cast the first stone," Yap in effect abjured the court.[39]

If nothing else, that parting shot got to the Mahmillub, provoking an outburst in the otherwise predictable decision read by Ali Said on 25 October. The

Court, he said, regretted Yap's unfortunate comparison of the Mahmillub trial with that of a wife who had committed adultery. Could he not have found a story from the Holy Book more suitable to the problem faced by the Mahmillub, whose heavy, even holy, burden had been entrusted to it by every layer of the Indonesian people except those who supported the G30 S/PKI? "Should the Court take it from this story that we should leave because we too participated in and are responsible for the sins of the Accused, that we participated in the 30 September Movement/PKI?"[40]

It was not an adequate answer to Yap's point, but rather narrowed down the sin to the single, discrete event of the coup, which Yap had insisted was only part of a much bigger problem. In emphasizing the persistence of political culture, Yap proved to be right, as the New Order soon established another version of Guided Democracy, without Soekarno, the PKI, and economic chaos.

For the rest, the Mahmillub decision simply rejected all defense arguments, with no more serious consideration (or more convincing reasoning) than it had counsel's demurrers. Ali Said did address Yap's argument—and that of Subagio as well—on the death penalty, for the court's decision made necessary a justification of it. His reasoning may have been closer to the view the country favored than Yap's, but, more importantly, was undoubtedly a more accurate reflection of New Order thinking than anything Yap had to say on the subject. Taking a swipe at Yap's reference to European and American philosophers and social scientists, Ali Said noted that the court felt it unnecessary to cite the views of Western philosophers, but rather cleaved to the world view of the Indonesian people, simple but filled with piety to God Almighty. Agreeing with Yap that human life was in the hands of God, he proceeded to argue nevertheless that God intended that on earth there should be justice, truth, discipline, and order. As executors of God's will, humanity seeks to maintain balances within society. When the balances are threatened, action must be taken to restore them and to eliminate conflicts that violate the sense of justice. This requires firm steps, "for the sake of justice and legal certainty."[41] For Muslims interested in the religious side of the question, Ali Said recommended the Surah Al Baqarah, paragraph 178, in the Qur'an, which, as it happens, was not easily applied to Subandrio.[42]

The sentence, of course, was death, though it was never carried out. Subandrio promptly requested presidential grace, and in 1970 his sentence was commuted to life imprisonment. Yap never got to know him well, although halfway through the trial Subandrio evidently began to trust his counsel. Despite the effort on his behalf, he never bothered to thank Yap, and years later when Yap ran into him while visiting another client in prison—Latief,

I think—Subandrio had either forgotten him or for other reasons did not acknowledge him.

This reaction did not bother Yap. For him, Subandrio was less important than his trial. As in the Liem Koe Nio case, but more so as conditions were more opportune, Yap meant to use the trial as a forum for raising issues of principle that had become, to him and many other senior advocates, key planks in a platform of reform. In this effort he both won and lost. There is no question but that his arguments, stated so bluntly but also elegantly and genuinely, hit home. For years afterwards, people remembered them and respected him for making them.

Yet the Subandrio trial did more for Yap, as for Ali Said, than for the principles Yap was pressing. It made the two men famous, but for the rest, it was a tragic failure. Not only for the Mahmillub personnel, but also for the politically active public, KAMI, KASI, and the press, the Subandrio trial, like all of the 1966 trials, was a political event that was allowed to obscure far more serious institutional issues. Despite pious avowals that the Mahmillub sought justice, not revenge, revenge was indeed a primary objective. The press, including *Kompas*, *Sinar Harapan*, and every other major Jakarta daily, attacked Subandrio relentlessly. Ignoring its implications for Indonesian political evolution, they applauded the Mahmillub for shorter-sighted reasons. Mochtar Lubis, one of Indonesia's most famous journalists, who had himself been detained under Guided Democracy and would be again under the New Order, wrote about the Subandrio trial as if hammering Subandrio, and through him Soekarno, was all that counted.[43] The press did not ignore Yap entirely, but by and large ignored the huge issues he raised. The demurrers and *pleidooi* of Yap and Subagio in the Subandrio trial received little more attention in the Jakarta papers than his and Abidin's defense in the Liem Koe Nio case had in the Surabaya press before the coup.

Yap was not the only one who understood that the Mahmillub trials set a depressing precedent for New Order justice, but he was one of very few who made the political and moral implications plain and public, in the Subandrio trial itself. No less than the Baperki debates and his speech to the Konstituante in 1959, his defense of Subandrio is filled with significant warnings about the political system, now of New Order Indonesia.

For the first time, Yap became the chief draw to the Lee Hwee Yoe law office, and for the next decade or so he had no difficulty in finding clients. The same people who delighted in Subandrio's fall were also impressed by the straight-talking Yap. Even the army auditor's office and the Mahmillub staff came to

FIG. 10.1 Yap Thiam Hien greets then Attorney General Ali Said, 1977. Ali Said was the presiding judge in the 1968 Subandrio trial.

respect him for his tough defense. When Yap was arrested early in 1968, both Durmawel and Ali Said spoke out in his support (fig. 10.1). His law practice benefited because his name automatically popped up when anyone asked for a good lawyer. He did not become wealthy, though many other advocates did as the economy flourished, but he and Khing were reasonably comfortable. Khing would have been pleased had Thiam Hien simply stuck to his law practice after the Subandrio trial. By then, however, Yap was as fully engaged publicly as he had been in the 1950s.

ELEVEN

EARLY NEW ORDER BATTLEFIELDS

FAR from withdrawing into a comfortable law practice after the Subandrio trial, Yap did precisely the opposite, leaping into—better yet, doing his bit to generate—crisis upon crisis. If anything is clear from the pattern of his activities from then on, it is that he saw himself as a public man, a responsible citizen, entitled and obliged to engage. Others began to see him as something akin to a mounted gaucho charging into troubled crowds with bolos twirling, scattering people in all directions. Yap could not be trusted to play anyone else's game, as the Subandrio case had shown decisively, and it made him dangerous. Yap felt increasingly comfortable with the calling of reformer, and only in Peradin, filled with reformers, did he feel at home.

For Yap, one meaning of the Subandrio case, like the Liem Koe Nio case earlier, was that he could, in fact, speak out frankly without suffering unduly for doing so. He did not land in jail or get beaten up. A few anonymous telephone threats were manageable. Speaking truth, he found, actually won him respect and a receptive audience. The Subandrio case made him a hero of sorts. He received letters, some signed, some not, full of praise, and friends expressed their admiration for his courage. Yap was too sensitive to the dangers of pride and egotism to let the adulation go to his head, but it nevertheless had an effect, making it all the more likely that he would continue to act as his principles dictated.

While Yap left the Subandrio trial with a sense of personal elation, Khing was filled with relief that it was over. Their children were growing into their teens in noisy times, and Khing wanted for them and herself as well the quietude and security that Yap seemed incapable of enjoying. It was bad enough in the early 1950s, when he was constantly off at a dozen meetings. Now the situation was worse, for he was not only away from home but too prominent, and loudly contentious, for comfort. Khing grew more and more anxious after 1966.

Even before the Subandrio trial, Yap had devoted himself, apart from his law practice, to issues of legal reform and human rights. Like several other Peradin advocates, he began in 1966 to write on issues of criminal procedure and the courts. He also wrote two long essays for *Kompas* on political detainees, arguing that those arrested during the Guided Democracy years should be released immediately, but making a more general case against the practice of detention without trial. He was one of very few to take up this issue, at a time when the army was still rounding up thousands of communists and others vaguely on the left for internment. Many agreed with the detentions, and many who did not thought it wise to keep quiet. It is hard to find firmer public statements on the question than Yap's.

During 1966 he wrote nothing about ethnic problems. He remained concerned, of course, as anti-Sinitic tremors accelerated during the year, but his perspective had drastically shifted. His dominant line of thought now grew out of his Konstituante speech of 1959, and his organizational home was no longer Baperki but Peradin. When anti-Chinese shrieks rose to a crescendo, however, he stepped back into that arena just long enough to create a terrific furor for the last time over specifically *peranakan* questions.

The October coup had exactly the same effect on *peranakan* politics as on Indonesian politics generally, erasing the left and leaving a clear field to a slightly startled but delighted right.[1] Yap had been correct in warning that Baperki would suffer for being identified with the PKI, but wrong in supposing that the peranakan community would suffer by association with it. Precisely because ethnic Chinese citizens were politically divided, as they had always been, an alternative leadership was in the wings waiting for Baperki to fail. *Peranakan* suffered, it is true, but less because of the Baperki disaster than because they were likely to suffer in any serious crisis.

The new leadership group among the *peranakan* was substantially Catholic, closely associated with the military, and actively engaged in the post-coup action against the PKI and the old regime. Its organization was the Institute for the Promotion of National Unity (LPKB), led by the naval officer K. Sindhunatha. The LPKB organized the demands to abolish Baperki beginning in mid-

October 1965, worked with the government in taking over Baperki schools, including Ureca, and set about winning over *peranakan* support. On the surface, it was not all that difficult. As in every other threatening crisis, ethnic Chinese gravitated to whoever offered help. After the coup there were few choices. Many who had supported Baperki hurriedly reoriented to the LPKB, whose members held Baperki responsible for having misled them.[2] Yet the LPKB never matched Baperki for enthusiastic popular support. If anything, Baperki's experience ultimately confirmed the intuition that politics of any kind was dangerous for *peranakan*. At any rate, the New Order regime, unlike Guided Democracy, was not much interested in popular mobilization.

As far as their clientele was concerned, the critical difference between Baperki and the LPKB, both of which depended on an intimate association with the regime in power, lay in their contradictory solutions to the "*peranakan* problem." In contrast to Baperki's emphasis on *peranakans*' right to participate without altering their identity, the LPKB from the start insisted that ethnic Chinese must finally surrender their distinction as Chinese and assimilate into the ethnic majority. After the coup, the assimilation side of this long, never-resolved debate had a huge advantage.

The pressure felt by *peranakan* in late 1965 and 1966 originated in the growing tension between Indonesia and China, as allegations, never substantiated, that Beijing had encouraged the coup and sent arms escalated into demonstrations against Chinese consular offices and into occasional violence.[3] Eventually formal relations between the two countries were broken, not to be restored until 1990. The long resentment against Chinese in Indonesia exploded into the usual accusations of Chinese exclusivity, cultural separatism, money grubbing, exploitation, and nationalism. Distinctions between Chinese aliens and ethnic Chinese citizens were quickly lost to the less discriminating perception that Chinese were Chinese. The violence that ethnic Chinese had escaped in the immediate aftermath of the coup now descended on them in outbreaks around the country. In Aceh, Medan, Ujung Pandang, Surabaya, and Jakarta, from late 1965 through 1967, there were anti-Chinese incidents, some violent, quite enough to remind the minority of their permanent vulnerability.

Warnings and appeals against racism by younger KAMI and KASI leaders and by General Suharto and others had little effect. What did have an effect was the shattered economy; continuing inflation, brought under control only after 1966–67; and the visibility of ethnic Chinese as a commercial stronghold, as well as the tension with China. Assaatism broke out again as KENSI, the Indonesian entrepreneurial association, revived its demands to move control of the economy into ethnic Indonesian hands. The new regime, still mopping up Soekarnoist influences while trying to establish its credentials with sources of assistance in Europe, Japan, and the United States, seemed to waffle on the problem of ethnic Chinese citizens. Suharto's assurances that the government would brook no anti-Chinese actions were rendered otiose by anti-Chinese actions taken by the chief pillar of the government, the army.

In late August 1966 army leaders gathered formally at the Staff and Command School in Bandung to establish the dimensions of the army's new post-coup role. This was a critically important meeting, in which civilian economists and others contributed to developing the New Order's programs, but its sole decision on the ethnic Chinese problem was petty and vindictive. It was to drop the terms Tiongkok (China) and Tionghoa (Chinese) when referring to the Peoples Republic of China, in favor of Tjina—Cina, in the new spelling. Obviously an intentional slap, it was comparable to an official ruling to call Italians "wops," or Jews "kikes," and while on the surface it applied to China, it was immediately and commonly applied to Indonesian Chinese as well, as was no doubt the intention. According to Charles Coppel, this decision by the army seminar may have been a concession made to undercut the more severe anti-Chinese measures some officers wanted and the civilian economists opposed.[4] Perhaps, but its meaning for *peranakan* was painful and threatening. Ethnic Chinese themselves adjusted to Cina, using it commonly along with everyone else, including *peranakan*-owned newspapers. In itself this was a defense mechanism, but adequate only after enough time had passed to take the edge off the epithet. Yap and Khing, who also habitually used the term Cina, admitted to still finding it insulting and hurtful. But not to use it would only make matters worse.

Yet, New Order policies toward ethnic Chinese were more favorable than the imposed epithet Cina implied, which warrants a more complex analysis. While criticism of Chinese remained constant and not a single *peranakan* was appointed to a cabinet-level position, ethnic Chinese commerce was allowed a free pass. In fact, almost immediately the relationship between ethnic Chinese entrepreneurs and the regime—and many army officers, including General and then President Suharto—blossomed into a fruitful intimacy that eventually produced astonishing wealth for those engaged. Apart from the oil boom of the 1970s, much of Indonesia's economic growth after the late 1960s was the result of the encouragement given to ethnic Chinese finance and investment, often to the detriment of ethnic Indonesian entrepreneurs. As always, there was less political danger in ethnic Chinese economic power than in ethnic Indonesian economic power, so long as *peranakan* or *totok* businessmen could be confined to the economic sector and kept dependent for protection on the political elite. Intentionally or not, the political-economic relationships worked out after the coup, hardly unprecedented in Indonesian history, operated in exactly this way. Social resentment of *peranakan* economic influence and occasional anti-Chinese violence, often set off by the connection between political power and entrepreneurial talent, served to maintain the symbiosis.

Although this problem had long been evident, no one addressed it adequately in public until the early 1970s, when students and intellectuals fiercely raised the issue of ethnic Chinese *cukong* (financial backers) and their politically influential front men. Little came of the protest then or afterwards. During the late 1960s, the debates over the Chinese problem generally (but not entirely) skirted the complex issues of economic structure, focusing instead on the apparently easier questions of the minority's failure to adapt to the majority. Vitriol was more common than reason, and solutions were more superficial and vindictive than real.

In this atmosphere the old integration-assimilation debate burst forth again. The LPBK made several sensible proposals to lower ethnic barriers, but most of these were essentially symbolic. In December 1966 the cabinet agreed to eliminate the old colonial classification of population groups, dating from the mid-nineteenth century, into European, Native, and Foreign Oriental categories.[5] But the issue that received the most attention, name-changing, was the one whose symbolic significance was most likely to cause ethnic Chinese pain without effectuating deeper change.

From mid-1966 on, as anti-Chinese signals proliferated, LPKB activists revived the invitation to *peranakan* to adopt "Indonesian" names.[6] On the first of June, most of the citizens of Chinese extraction in Sukabumi, West Java—more than 6,000 people—publicly agreed to change their names in a mass ceremony marking the birth of the Pancasila. They did so under pressure from both the LPKB and local government officials.[7] As existing regulations made name-changing harder than the officials knew, in December, on the LBPK's urging, the cabinet simplified the procedures. Coppel points out that the new regulation, by contrast with the law of 1961 that it temporarily replaced, applied only to citizens, not aliens, only to ethnic Chinese, not Arabs, Indians, or Europeans, and was in effect only until 1 March 1968, when the 1961 rules would revive.[8]

Immediately afterwards, the two Christian dailies, the Catholic *Kompas* and the Protestant *Sinar Harapan*, along with several other Jakarta newspapers, were filled with articles and signed columns urging that ethnic Chinese adopt "Indonesian" names, explaining the procedures, and promising that this measure would help the assimilation process. "Indonesian" names would not only distinguish the Chinese who adopted them from alien Chinese, but would lend credibility to their commitment to Indonesia, all the more so as the move was voluntary. *Peranakan* citizens had their doubts. Some refused to change their names, including a few who urged others to do so. A number of people went along, some enthusiastically, some in the hope it might make a difference, others rather cynically for whatever advantage it offered. Many ethnic Indonesian commentators also had doubts. Some were sympathetic to the problem *peranakans* faced, others angrily accused ethnic Chinese of changing their names only cynically, and still others admonished them that they must do more than simply adopt Indonesian-sounding names. Damned if they did or didn't, *peranakans* nevertheless heard few public voices that said they shouldn't.

Until Yap wrote. How ironic his position was then. It seemed as if his was the last Baperki voice to be heard, as one or two critics charged.[9] But Yap's argument was his own, as it always had been, only now it was even more clearly rooted in human rights principles than in an ethnic commitment. He was incensed by the pressure on ethnic Chinese to change their names, and even more by the failure, particularly of religious leaders, to consider the ethical implications of what they were doing. Gereja Keristen Indonesia leaders had discussed the issue and come out in favor of name-changing, much to Yap's chagrin. This stance influenced his decision to stop attending church. In the rush to adopt new names, despite the contention that it was voluntary, he saw, as he had in 1960, little but coercion and hypocrisy and irresponsible burdening of many who had inadequate resources to deal with the financial costs and bureaucratic exploitation involved.

His three-part article on the subject, which appeared in the January 25, 26, and 27, 1967, issues of *Sinar Harapan*, was addressed directly to ethnic Chinese Protestant leaders.[10] He wrote as a member of the West Java GKI and one who opposed "the decision and attitude of some ministers, theologians, and church officials" in support of changing Chinese names. In part it was a recap of his 1960 "Therapy" articles for *Star Weekly*. Yap's first installment exuded anger, sarcasm, and regret as he reviewed the recent writings of Protestant figures on the name-changing issue. For each of the *peranakan* correspondents with an "Indonesian" name, he added the original Chinese name in parentheses, until he came to Pek Hien Liang, who had not yet changed his name and whom Yap evidently disliked, and there he added snidely "(original name as yet unknown)." He chastised each of the writers for demanding that Chinese give up their identity, along with their names, without analyzing the root causes of ethnic conflict in Indonesia, without considering the ethical issues involved, and without trying to bring religious principles to bear on the human pain caused.[11]

In the second and third parts of the essay, Yap turned to his own analysis of the Chinese problem, in which, more clearly than in the "Therapy" debate, the subtle mix of his religious, ethical, and political commitments became evident. The Chinese problem, he wrote at the outset, was a human problem, a problem of relations between human beings living together, a problem of individuals and groups from the Chinese minority and indigenous majority. "Yet we have and recognize principles to manage our social and national life: that is, Pancasila Democracy, Human Rights, and the Rule of Law. And above all these: The Rule of the Will of God!!!!" None of the writers he mentioned, said Yap, tried to analyze the Chinese problem from the point of view of these principles.

Human problems, he wrote, require all the power of science to understand and resolve, but for Christians this alone is inadequate, for the root of all human problems lies in the relationship of people with God. Since the Reformation, the responsibility shared by religious leaders and laymen together—a swipe particularly at the former—has been to ask "What is the will of God in dealing with this problem?" A true relationship with God is one that submits to and obeys God's will. "To obey God means to love one's fellow humans, including friends and enemies, one's own or foreign people [*bangsa*]."

> To love fellow humans also means to protest and oppose all wrongdoings, injustice, all oppression, all torture visited upon mankind, according to the means willed by God. And to search for and approach those unfortunate people, including our enemies and foreigners, in order to comfort them with the word of God. NOT to distance ourselves from them or to close our hearts to the screams of their misery. Wherever and however this command to love takes us, to hatred and enmity by our own people, to jail or exile, He who commanded us to love is greater than obedience to the demands of nation or group, greater than the urge or pressure of instincts to save and calm our lives. We must not forget that for us Christians to suffer in the Name of God—that is, for our fellow men—is something that pleases God (1 Peter 2:20).

Much to the discomfort of judges and prosecutors, let alone Protestant ministers, Yap often fell into the language of sermons when dealing with moral issues. There may be a touch of self-righteousness in that paragraph, but no hypocrisy, which angered his opponents but limited their response.

Opponents could respond politically but not ethically or religiously—no one tried publicly. Yap went on to make plain his objections to name-changing. First of all, it was necessary, he wrote, to examine the political conditions under which name-changing became a problem. What the Jakarta GKI meeting had admitted privately and Yap made public was that anti-Sinicism had become rampant since the coup. The Chinese minority, as always, was a scapegoat for all the political and social frustrations that needed an outlet. In these conditions *pribumi* Indonesians sympathetic to citizens of Chinese descent revived the name-changing idea. (In fact, however, it was not only *pribumi* but also *peranakan* leaders who pressed the issue.) Their intentions, he said, were good: to differentiate Chinese citizens from Indonesian citizens of Chinese descent. The same sympathetic purpose led them to urge Indonesian Chinese to condemn the Peoples' Republic of China, to wear "indigenous" Indonesian clothes, and to use distinctly Indonesian store signs and the like. The cabinet decision to facilitate name-changing could be understood in the same light.

But, in the anti-Chinese social atmosphere, Yap asked, what actually were the motives of Chinese who changed their names? His troubling answer was that the motivation was essentially egocentric. It had to do with self-preservation and the defense of property, the search for personal security and economic safety. Here Yap simply threw off the cover from a sticky reality that most wanted to ignore.

> In danger a chameleon can change its color, but humans cannot. But clever people are not put off. They can avoid danger by changing their clothes, changing their alliances, changing their loyalties. They can also change their Chinese names. And they can distance themselves as far as possible from dangerous surroundings—that is, [among] other Chinese—or they can condemn and torture Chinese. In this way people think that they can reach safety. . . . There are also some Christians who believe they can assuage and quiet their consciences or delude others with such slogans as "for developing national unity" or "for carrying out the Christian calling."

But such rationalizations, Yap insisted, make the selfish motives behind them obvious. It was not merely the feelings of fear and desire for self-preservation behind name-changing that bothered Yap, but, also, the way that people were being pressured and frightened into this self-serving, dishonest behavior. Would it help? Not at all, according to Yap, and in this he proved to be depressingly right.

> But changing names will not satisfy racism. Nor will it promote good feelings or respect among upright pribumi who think rationally. For the development of national unity name changing has no meaning or advantage at all. It is very naive to suppose that changing names represents a positive step toward national unity. And . . . assimilation/integration of the Chinese minority into the *pribumi* majority is not a sine qua non for national unity, which depends upon other factors that are many and complex. So what good is name changing? It is useful only to those who seek an egotistical personal end: to secure a position, to guarantee entrance to a school/university, to guarantee the future. Idealists who change their Chinese names may protest these hard words, but even idealism can be misled by the wish for security. . . .
>
> In itself, to change one's name is a personal right and freedom. . . . But like [other] rights and freedoms name changing can be abused. For example, if in a crisis situation name changing is intended to or has the effect of drawing a dividing line between "the patriotic and unpatriotic" or "those who fulfill the Christian calling and those who do not," this is to "thump one's own chest" (self-righteousness). And if the intention and effect of changing one's Chinese name is to distance oneself from [other] Chinese because they are treated as enemies . . . such acts are an abuse of apostolic and pastoral responsibilities. They are also not in character for one who loves his nation and state, and who [seeks?] in Indonesian societies a collective life and personal and group relations that are peaceful, just, and free, in the image of God's Peace, Justice, and Freedom. Such a person will struggle for an Indonesian state and society in which there is the least screaming and weeping because of hunger or oppression, so that human dignity and Human Rights are recognized and respected, not only for every Indonesian but also for every foreigner who seeks protection from the Indonesian Government. He will struggle so that the name of the Indonesian nation and state will be . . . respected by all nations, and so that the Indonesian nation and state will not be scarred because

> of racialism, fascism, or the rape of human rights and international rights. . . . Anyone who loves the nation and state of Indonesia will also be courageous in pointing out the wrongdoings of the nation and its state and, too, point out the ways and means of correcting the faults. All this calls for the replacement of egoism by altruism, the replacement of the survival instinct with a readiness to emphasize public interests and safety. But it does not call for the replacement of names.[12]

Yap ended his appeal with a quotation from Matthew 5:4, 7, 9, 10: "Blessed are those who mourn . . . blessed are the merciful . . . blessed are the peacemakers. . . . Blessed are those who are persecuted for righteousness." Any readers who took their religious commitments seriously had to be tempted to follow his call to witness. Others must have been discomfited at least by the accusation of hypocrisy implicit in the argument.

If religious value, even a touch of naiveté, prompted Yap's epistle to *Sinar Harapan,* a dose of political realism, even cynicism, drove him to shoot a quite different missile in the direction of *Kompas,* published on 26 January, the day his articles began to run in *Sinar Harapan.* This piece offered advice to those busy seeking appropriate names to replace their Chinese names, especially the poor. First, he wrote, the Cabinet Presidium's decision provided an opportunity to change one's name but did not require it. Second, he explained the documents necessary to secure a change. Third, he listed thirteen documents—birth and marriage certificates, identity cards, utility bills, driver's license, etc.—on which the name would have to be changed. Finally, he itemized eleven payments that would be required, never saying, though anyone with experience understood, that such charges might well mount up to considerably more as a result of bureaucratic extortion. The charges, he suggested, would be at least Rp. 1000. "This of course does not include the exhaustion of one's body and one's heart." Yap concluded with the hope that those who urged people to change their names would not stop there, but would help the poor, especially with the financial charges. He directed this request specifically to Christians and their churches that should not, he insisted, limit their assistance only to members of the church.[13]

Yap's articles set off a stormy debate, indicating that the name-changing issue was not as simple or settled, either among ethnic Chinese or ethnic Indonesians, as assimilationists hoped. He touched so many raw nerves and evidently worried proponents of the policy that they might lose momentum.[14] Replies to Yap, mostly angry but a few ambivalent, flew out in *Sinar Harapan* and *Kompas*. In an interview defending the cabinet decision on name-changing as wise and radical, Harry Tjan—who only later added the Batak clan name Silalahi to his own—suggested that Yap, whom he did not name, feared being thought an opportunist, opposed assimilation and social homogeneity, and in his heart longed for his ancestral land.[15] Michael Tanok, a Protestant, furiously attacked Yap by name and criticized *Sinar* for running the articles, which, he said, were insulting and, hinting darkly, perhaps communist-inspired. He pointed out that Yap's position was exactly that of the late Baperki.[16] Sufwandi Mangkudilaga accused Yap of wanting to return to "the glorious past 'met Kapitein der Chineezen.'"[17] The charges against Yap's sarcasm, at least, were reasonable—Sufwandi pointed out that Yap was hardly demonstrating Christian forgiveness—but little in the attacks on Yap was. He might have been accused of naiveté, of an overdose of idealism, of demanding too much of people, but to raise such issues required confronting directly his substantive analysis and arguments based on religious principle. No one did. Knowingly or not, the invective against Yap missed the point of his argument completely. Yap was not interested in reviving the colonial past, nor did he long for China. His criticism of name-changing—that it was in fact coercive, that it was anti-Chinese, that it encouraged people to act selfishly, and that it avoided deeper causes of ethnic conflict—was rooted in values that demanded a longer view of Indonesian politics and society than many others were capable of adopting.

Yap had a discomforting influence on the debate, but not much on the outcome.[18] Many ethnic Chinese did adopt "Indonesian" names. Exactly how many is unclear. One report indicated that as of August 1967, 50 percent of ethnic Chinese in Jakarta had changed their names and suggested optimistically that by the deadline in March 1968 all would have done so.[19] Nothing of the sort happened. There were many holdouts who refused to give in to pressure or simply did not bother. Some of those who did change their names did so, no doubt, for precisely the opportunistic reasons Yap suggested, others because of social or political pressure, still others in the hope of removing one barrier to integration.

Was Yap right that name-changing would have little effect for the good and perhaps much for the bad? Was his case against assimilationism reasonable? On balance, judging from a brief review of the evidence, his argument, shorn of its theological foliage, was basically correct. The assimilationists never claimed that name-changing alone was more than a token, but they did not follow with anything more substantial. Government measures were potentially significant yet essentially symbolic, such as the rescission of the colonial classification of the population by race and the promise of a civil registration for the entire population, not just Europeans, Chinese, and Christians. For the rest, however, neither economic nor social policy showed any serious interest in resolving tensions that would never disappear without fundamental economic change. If anything, the economic dimensions of the "Chinese problem" simply grew, and so did the hostility that served to keep *peranakan* dependent on government protection.

Perhaps some who changed their names escaped overt discrimination, but so did others who retained their Chinese names, including Yap. As he predicted, ethnic Indonesians predisposed to bigotry did not become less so as names changed, and many believed the effort a ruse. An "Indonesian" name might disguise a *peranakan*, but passing as a *pribumi* was not all that easy, and word usually got around. Twenty-five years later, many ethnic Chinese with "Indonesian" names regretted having adopted them, partly because the change made no difference, but also because it had incurred a sense of indignity to no unquestionably useful end. In the 1990s the *peranakan* condition was much as it was in the 1960s.

Had any of the charges against Yap in the name-changing debate been true—that is, that he was bound by his own Chinese identity—he would have stopped there, eschewing engagement in any issue irrelevant to the Chinese problem. That he did not, but instead poured his huge store of energy into legal and political reform, makes clear that his commitments had much less, if anything, to do with ethnic identity than with the responsibilities, as he understood them, of citizenship. Other serious reformers understood this implicitly. It was what attracted them to Yap.

For anyone interested in reform, the possibilities of the late 1960s were fairly rich. At the very center of reform issues was the remaking of the political system or, to put it more grandly, the redefinition of the state. For Yap, as for other professional advocates and for many others, the legal system was the key arena of change. How legal institutions worked represented the relationship between state and society, ideologically and practically. As the political battle lines of the New Order took form, beginning in 1966, legal process became a principal issue of contention, one that generated extraordinary tension, precisely because the stakes were so high for both public authorities and their critics.

Nearly everyone agreed that the corruption of public institutions under Guided Democracy had to be reversed. General Suharto, almost from the start, promised that the New Order would be bound by the constitution and the rule of law. Reformers tried to hold the government to its commitment, but it soon became clear that serious reform threatened the New Order regime in ways that it would not countenance. No less than Guided Democracy, the New Order presumed a strong state, one backed by a politically involved army that would not allow any weakening of control over state institutions. This premise directly challenged reform interests in restoring more responsible, accountable, and accessible legal institutions.

The early New Order period was filled with the efforts by reformers to press their demands, and counterefforts by the government to shunt them aside. Reformers active in KAMI, KASI, and Peradin demanded the revival of parliamentary institutions, the eradication of corruption, and the strengthening of responsive legal institutions. The Tracee Baru seminar of 1966 devoted as much time to the *negara hukum* as to economic policy. A new and critical literature on human rights and civil rights began to blossom during the same period, as legal scholars and practitioners revealed the corruption and abuse of authority under Guided Democracy and outlined the dimensions of change. Professional advocates from Peradin for the first time became prominent contributors to the debates over reform. Suardi Tasrif, Soemarno P. Wirjanto, Yap, and a few others wrote extensively for the press on constitutional and legal issues. Yap focused on human rights, particularly the problem of detentions after the coup, criminal process, and the role of courts and judges.

It was also a time for new organizations. Political parties, floundering after the experience of Guided Democracy and hemmed in by the army, held little attraction for New Order activists. KAMI and KASI were themselves party-substitutes of a sort. KASI, the intellectuals' action front, drew upon a variety of professionals, many of them lawyers. Yap did not join KASI but was close to many of its members. Instead, he became active in two other organizations that were more specifically oriented to his reform tastes.

The first was the Institute for the Defense of Human Rights (Lembaga Pembela Hak-Hak Azasi Manusia), established in 1966 or 1967. Its first chairperson was Mrs. Hidajat, well known in Islamic circles and the wife of a general; but the driving force behind it was its vice chairman (later chair), H. J. C. Princen, one of the more intriguing figures in Indonesian reform politics. Netherlands-born Princen arrived in Indonesia in 1946 as a young draftee in the Dutch army, which he left to cross over to the Indonesian side. Romantic, adventurous, politically engaged—he was a member of the minor party Ikatan Pendukung Kemerdekaan Indonesia (IPKI, League of the Supporters of Indonesian Independence) and served as a member of Parliament until it was prorogued in 1960—and courageously outspoken on liberal political principles, Princen spent the last two years of Guided Democracy as a political detainee. Different as they were, Yap and Princen became quite close. Princen was impressed by Yap's writings on political detention and criminal process. Yap appreciated Princen's courage and commitment to principle and probably admired and enjoyed his quirkiness and unpredictability, so unlike Yap's own outward character.

The Human Rights Institute was essentially Princen, with Yap and perhaps one or two others available for support. It provided Princen and Yap with a forum and a dais from which to write letters of protest, to support efforts in the MPRS to adopt a human rights charter, and to disseminate information on human rights violations. In 1968 Princen made headlines with startling revelations of the massacres that had taken place in Purwodadi, Central Java, and the continuing brutality in the prison camp there.[20] Regional army officers promptly attacked him as a communist, which was nonsense, as other officers who knew him pointed out. Gradually during the next several years, however, the institute became inactive, until Princen revived it in the late 1980s.

The other organization that engaged Yap's enthusiastic attention was the Pengabdi Hukum (Servants of the Law), an interesting but short-lived attempt at reform from within the legal system itself. Formed in October 1967, it originated in the concern of a few judges, prosecutors, and police officials, as well as professional advocates, to recover from the devastation of the judicial system under Guided Democracy. It was common knowledge that the entire legal system was corrupt, especially the prosecution, whose reputation for extortion and abuse of authority was rank, but also the courts and police.[21]

Treating the pathology, however, was exceedingly difficult because of the complex political and bureaucratic interests at play. The regime's need to control the civilian security apparatus required concessions especially to the prosecution and police. The prosecutors, judges, and police officials—tied together in a corrupt system that was mutually beneficial but also mutually competitive—needed to protect their economic interests. For example, the prosecution and police had long battled for control over preliminary investigation, which offered opportunities for extortion but also a sense of procedural significance. Equally difficult were conflicts between prosecutors, judges, and the police on the one hand and the Ministry of Justice, on the other, for positional advantages, here attached to economic benefits, there to bureaucratic status. The Ministry of Justice, having lost control over the prosecution in 1961 and been left with only the judges, was eager to extend its reach again. A subtler problem lay in the status concerns of all the players. They were all officials, civil servants; even though competitive for privilege within the bureaucracy, they allied against any attempt to subject them to non-state influence—for example, by the professional advocacy.

Few of these concerns, however, had anything to do with serving the public interest in reasonably fair, efficient, and inexpensive justice. Beginning in 1966, popular protests against judicial corruption, court backlogs, and much else evoked government promises of reform. Ad hoc solutions were worked out for the backlog problem, and judicial officials were encouraged to cooperate in the interests of justice, but little if anything was accomplished by way of effective institutional reform. New legal officials were appointed who seemed to offer hope of change. Umar Seno Adji, a former deputy chief public prosecutor and legal scholar who had gained a reputation for principle during the Guided Democracy years, became minister of justice. Young judges and KAMI students forced the chairman of the Mahkamah Agung, Wirjono Prodjodikoro, to resign. His successor, Surjadi, whose selection Soekarno had influenced, lasted only a year before he too was forced out, to be replaced by Judge Subekti, a liberal who actually did have some effect before his retirement in the early 1970s. After a struggle, the chief of the National Police, a supporter of Soekarno, was replaced by Hugeng Imam Santoso, a very popular man, committed to reform. The new chief prosecutor, significantly, was General Sugih Arto, who had no legal training; every one thereafter, until rather late in the tenure of President Suharto, was a military officer.

None of these appointments, including those of Hugeng and Subekti who did try, achieved much in the way of reform, for genuine reform depended on the commitment of the regime. The New Order leadership gave far less priority to serious institutional reform, which would have caused a storm of bureaucratic conflict, than to political security and consolidation of the state apparatus. Standing above the judicial system was the Command for the Restoration of Security and Order (Kopkamtib), led at first by General Suharto himself and little constrained by legal process. In matters of political concern the civil apparatus toed the line, in exchange for which, as under Guided Democracy, its various parts were allowed considerable discretionary authority. Consequently, corruption and other abuses remained endemic in the judicial system.

Judicial officials themselves, those who had survived Guided Democracy with integrity intact, took their own initiatives. Among them were two young judges, Asikin Kusumaatmadja from the Mahkamah Agung and Sri Widojati

Notoprodjo, a young appellate judge and a leader of the Jakarta branch of the Indonesian Judges Association (Ikahi). Widojati, who later became the first woman appointed to the Supreme Court, was instrumental in bringing down Wirjono Prodjodikoro and leading the opposition to his successor. Incorruptible and sensitive to the decline of the courts, she was a prime mover in the effort to restore some semblance of autonomy to the judicial system and to clean it up. In late 1966 and 1967, when the reaction against Guided Democracy was still strong and reform was in the air, she and several other politically active judges, prosecutors, police officials, and advocates (including Yap) began to meet periodically to discuss legal conditions. In October 1967 they created the Pengabdi Hukum as an intralegal system conference consisting of all professional legal associations. Widojati was its first chair. Yap, as Peradin's delegate, served as one of the vice chairs.[22]

Yap saw great hope in the Pengabdi Hukum, whose ambitions matched his own hopes for an Indonesian *rechtsstaat*. Reforming judges and advocates saw the organization not only as a means of cleansing the legal system and making it responsive to popular demands, but also as a vanguard of legal ideology in "the struggle for the realization of the principles of constitutionalism and a *negara hukum*."[23] For public lawyers, Pengabdi Hukum was a means of asserting their institutional independence and taking responsibility for their degradation under Guided Democracy. In some ways it was nothing less than an effort to build legitimacy for the legal system itself.

While it lasted, Pengabdi Hukum worked more or less effectively, responding to problems in criminal process particularly by bringing responsible officials together for discussions. Tensions and conflicts between prosecutors, police, and judges were ironed out directly, without public confrontations. Rights issues were taken up at the urging of Princen and Yap. In fact, the issue of citizens' rights against malfeasant officials became a dominant concern of the organization, which began to evolve as a kind of ombudsman. No other institution existed to serve this purpose until the Legal Aid Institute of Jakarta was established in 1970.

Ironically, it was Yap, for whom the Pengabdi Hukum was so important, who put its premises to the test and helped destroy it. This was one unintentional consequence of the famous Yap affair of 1968.

The affair started in 1967, with Yap's defense of a client, Tjan Hong Liang, the owner of a company called P. T. [Ltd.] Quick. This case, in every respect but one—Yap's representation—was typical of the corruption of the judicial system. In some ways it was a replay of the Liem Koe Nio case, but in different conditions that gave Yap rather more leverage. A few details of this complex case will serve as a prelude to its extraordinary consequences.

To begin with, it was actually a civil case, the result of a commercial dispute between Tjan Hong Liang and a well-connected businesswoman, Lies Gunarsih (Lao Giok Sie). Sometime in 1966 the two arranged to import Isuzu cars, the license for which Lies had acquired through another corporation. Later, they disagreed on the division of the profits. Impatient and evidently feeling that Tjan was tricking her, Lies sought help from a few close friends in the government, among them Simandjuntak, a prosecutor at the appellate level, and Mardjaman, a police inspector-general. The three had met in the early 1960s in Ujung Pandang, where Simandjuntak and Mardjaman had been stationed and Lies had lived and worked, among other things at smuggling coffee, which required well-positioned acquaintances. (She was once caught, but only fined and never brought to court.) In Jakarta, where Lies lived well in the suburb of Kebayoran, their friendship continued.

At the time of Lies's dispute with Tjan, Simandjuntak brought pressure to bear on him, not in connection with the commercial debt but rather with a shadow issue, P. T. Quick's failure to repair a Chevrolet Bel-Air that Lies had brought to Tjan and had paid for, she claimed, in advance. Tjan was summoned again and again to the prosecution offices, without any stipulation of the charges against him, and was kept there for hours, interrogated, and threatened with detention. P. T. Quick's books were seized and kept by the prosecution. Intimidated, Tjan finally signed an agreement, written up by a prosecutor, acknowledging a debt of Rp. 6,000,000 to Lies. When execution of the agreement was delayed, however, Lies, now relying for leverage on Mardjaman and a tax official, forced Tjan to write six fore-dated checks for Rp. 500,000 each. By this time, Tjan had sought legal help from the Lie Hwee Yoe firm, where Yap took the matter in hand. Three of the checks had been cashed, but the other three were backed by insufficient funds. Lies gave these checks to Mardjaman, who pursued Tjan, urging him to make good on them, to apologize, and to dismiss the Lie Hwee Yoe law firm. On Yap's advice, Tjan refused to sign but kept the concession document that had been dictated by Mardjaman. The document was evidence of blackmail.

In the meantime, the Lie Hwee Yoe office had asked the Siliwangi Bank not to honor the checks, on the grounds that they had been extracted by coercion. By this time the checks were held by Simandjuntak, who sent another prosecutor to the bank to cash them, which he had no right to do even by the rules of criminal investigation. The bank refused to cash the checks, but nevertheless retained them. Thereupon the prosecution charged Tjan with passing rubber checks, or empty checks (*cek kosong*) as they are known in Indonesia.

The pretrial maneuvering in this case was standard operating procedure. It represented one variation in a repertory elaborated by prosecutors and/or police, often with the collusion of judges. The preferred target was an ethnic Chinese businessman, usually willing to pay under pressure for lack of any other recourse, but others able to pay were also targeted. Prosecutors and police generally warned their victims against hiring lawyers, on threat of more severe treatment. However, if called upon, attorneys faced several difficulties in such cases. Once engaged, counsel had to decide whether the client's interests demanded a defense or a quick compromise in order to avoid prison or a heavier ransom or the failure of a business. If the client agreed to a defense, the odds were against winning because of the prosecutions' influence over judges, but also because it was hard to find sufficient evidence of extortion.

Given Yap's reputation, Tjan must have been either extremely angry or extremely frightened to engage him as counsel, and he evidently had second thoughts during and after the trial. For Yap, on the other hand, the case was attractive precisely because the proof of extortion was abundant, and Tjan was willing to reveal everything in open court. In December 1967 the case came up in the Jakarta district court, just up the street from the Lie Hwee Yoe firm. The trial was well attended, by the press, too, partly because Yap himself was a draw. Before long the courtroom filled to overflowing, as Yap startled the court and everyone else by accusing Simandjuntak and Marjaman of extortion. Thereafter reports of the case appeared in the press every day. Widojati showed up to observe the trial on behalf of Pengabdi Hukum.[24] It did not help. For whatever reason, the trial judge made things very difficult for the defense, ruling against Yap procedurally; rejecting his witnesses; refusing to allow him to show the relationship among Lies, Mardjaman, and Simandjuntak; and confining the issue to the bad checks alone. Tjan was convicted.

This was only the beginning of the Yap affair. What followed makes sense only if Simandjuntak and Mardjaman were either arrogantly vindictive or (along with their colleagues) worried enough about their enterprise to want to teach Yap a lesson. Yap himself thought they were moved by revenge, but more may have been involved. In any case, on New Year's Eve, a police contingent set up watch on Yap's home, and the next morning, 1 January 1968, which was an Islamic holiday that year—Lebaran, the end of the fasting month—he was arrested and taken to jail. Startled and utterly unprepared, Yap told Khing to go to the Pengabdi Hukum.

The charges were that Yap was a member of Baperki, hence—irony of ironies—a communist and maybe a supporter of the 30 September Movement. His captor was army Lt. Colonel Djohan Arifin, who was in charge, for the Grogol area, of special operations against communists and those involved in the coup. Arifin was polite to Yap on the way to jail, emphasizing that he was just doing his duty. They ended up in a small police post in Grogol, where political prisoners were held, under military command, along with common criminals. Yap remained in jail for six days. It was a new and troubling experience. Word had gotten out, probably from the jail staff, that Yap had been arrested, and when he arrived at the jail more than twenty political prisoners stood and shouted a welcome, which Yap found upsetting because he did not understand whether the greeting was meant to be kind or threatening. A few of the prisoners expected that someone like Yap might help them.

Yap was summoned to Arifin's room only on the third day. He was fearful, having heard from other prisoners that they were beaten. One of his two cellmates—both ethnic Chinese, one a Baperki member—was held only because he was the younger brother of a wanted man. Beaten to extract information about his brother, he returned to the cell hurt and shaking so badly that he could barely put on his pants. (Impulsively, and typically, Yap complained to the prison authorities about this.) Usually, Yap learned, two men stood behind the prisoner, one on either side, beating him on a signal from the interrogator. So when he was finally called, Yap glanced back anxiously but found that he and Djohan Arifin were alone. He was not mistreated.

Nor was he actually interrogated about Baperki or anything else related to the allegations. Arifin insisted to the press that Yap's arrest had nothing to do with the P. T. Quick case, which few believed to be true.[25] Yet apparently he had nothing to ask Yap about the charges, either because he knew they were trumped up or because, as it turned out, there was no time. Instead the two men merely talked, until Yap felt at ease or at least out of danger. Arifin was a hard man, slightly unbalanced it seemed to Yap. While convening prisoners in the yard, rumor had it, he once drew his pistol and shot a chicken who happened to be scratching there; and he had no compunction about once ordering one of his own men to be slapped in front of police families and others gathered in the area. But Arifin was cordial with Yap. What they talked about mainly was the problem of political prisoners. In their first talk, Arifin announced that he hated communists and thought that they and their families should be killed. Yap replied that you can't do that in a *negara hukum*, or even in war, let alone peace. It was not right, and Arifin, as a Muslim, surely could not believe it. The interrogator, unimpressed, dismissed the argument as irrelevant to his job, which was to crush those behind the coup. Yap pointed out that some of the detainees in Grogol, picked up on the street or at home or at work, had been held three weeks without charges. What had they done wrong? Well, it was only three weeks, said Arifin.

Gaining confidence, apparently, Yap complained to the commander of the police post about conditions in the jail. The men were allowed to walk only along the short aisle in front of their cells, which were dirty, for they had no soap or brooms. The next day the cells were opened and the men delightedly roamed the yard. They were given soap and cleaned their cells. On the fourth or fifth day, while Khing was visiting, the Pengabdi Hukum leadership—Widojati, Martono, Subagio, Wiratmo, and Abdul Kadir Besar—showed up. When they asked about his condition, Yap cautiously emphasized that he himself had been treated well, hoping they would understand that others were not, but they missed the point and did not pursue the matter further. Arifin, who was anxious about the Pengabdi Hukum visit, was delighted with Yap's reply, regarding him as a fast friend thereafter, even embracing him when they ran into one another in the jail.

During those few days, Yap came to know both the political prisoners and the generally better-treated criminals. Among the latter was a group of bandits, all originally from Ujung Pandang in South Sulawesi, led by a well-known armed robber named Taufik (or Taufic). The bandits were funny and had all the prisoners laughing at stories about their escapades. (A few of the group sold all the clothes from two other prisoners from Tanggerang [charged with stealing and killing an ox or two for the holiday] who came dressed up for Lebaran.) A romantic and impulsive side of Yap that was usually suppressed occasionally broke through the surface with people quite different from himself. It had shown up earlier in his respect for the prosecution official, the Tiger, whom he knew from the Liem Koe Nio case, and in his friendship with Princen. It also attracted him to Taufic, whom he may also have viewed as a fellow critic of state authority. Taufic asked Yap to represent him and his band when they were brought to trial. Yap did so six months later.[26]

Outside, meanwhile, Yap's arrest blew up in the faces of Simandjuntak and Mardjaman. Such abuses of authority had become so common since the onset of Guided Democracy that officials and the public took them for granted, the one as a normal prerogative, the other as an inescapable fact of life. Yap's case was an exception to the rule before and after.

His arrest set off a hurricane of activity by Khing and by Yap's Peradin colleagues, Pengabdi Hukum, and the press. Khing, who never hardened to such crises, was beset by contradictory advice. Lie Hwee Yoe, Yap's senior law partner, told her that he had a client who knew an army officer, but Khing, perfectly aware that Yap disapproved of working that way, held him off. Haryono Tjitrosubeno and Soekardjo from Peradin told her not to do anything and that they would take over the matter, but she was unwilling to sit still. Then as later, Khing followed her own instincts, more attuned to reality than Yap, resorting to whatever channels of influence she could muster. She contacted Pengabdi Hukum, talking with Abdul Kadir Besar and Widojati, who returned from Central Java to deal with the problem. She also called on General Suharto's *peranakan* doctor, Tan, who had once quietly visited Yap to express his support, perhaps in connection with the name-changing issue. Tan evidently could not be of much help, and Khing upbraided him, asking why when he visited Yap he encouraged him to take public risks. She could not do much more.

Neither could Pengabdi Hukum, which was paralyzed by its members' cross purposes. When push came to shove, both the prosecutor and the police members retreated to defensive positions. Whatever the commitments of Sugih Arto and even Hugeng Imam Santoso to reform, they were reluctant to risk the disenchantment of their corps. Police General Sujud, Hugeng's deputy, discussed the matter with me in an interview at the time. He admitted to the corruption and abuse, but claimed that it was mainly at lower levels.[27]

> In the past, under Guided Democracy, the tendency was to demand that police perform all kinds of other, political, functions. [Former police commandant] Soekamto opposed this and was consequently fired. . . . Now there is an effort to re-establish properly defined functions of all institutions. [In the Yap case] the police were unfairly put upon by others. In the Pengabdi Hukum other members unfairly attacked the police for Yap's arrest. But nothing was said when Chinese were beaten up and killed in Glodok by RPKAD [army commandos] troops at about the same time. [Sujud heard that] only Princen from the Human Rights Institute raised the issue of the Glodok affair, but no one else in Pengabdi Hukum wanted to discuss it. After all, the rule of law means establishing rules for everyone, for every violation of law is a serious challenge to the rule of law. But while everyone criticized the police in the Yap case, no one wanted to take up the more serious situation of [the army] at Glodok.[28]

Even some judges in Pengabdi Hukum, identifying as government officials, were resentful of the public sympathy for the private attorney Yap, and were lukewarm about defending him. Thus, only on 5 January did Pengabdi Hukum issue a statement condemning Yap's arrest as a violation of law and rejecting the accusation that he was a communist.[29] The organization did little more. During the first week of January, its executive committee met with Suharto, but mainly to introduce the organization. The Yap affair was mentioned, but essentially in passing.[30] Adnan Buyung Nasution, in his memorial essay on Yap, asserts that the affair killed Pengabdi Hukum by highlighting its internal conflicts.[31] Yet it was doomed from the start. The tensions set off by Yap's arrest were inherent in the legal system itself and were played out fully in his subsequent trial.[32] Pengabdi Hukum's demise resulted from the utter failure of the legal system to accomplish the reforms the organization had meant to inspire. Ironically, when Pengabdi Hukum faded out of existence in 1969 or 1970, its last chairman was Haryono Tjitrosubeno from Peradin.

It was primarily the press that brought about Yap's release from jail by mobilizing public anger against abuses of public authority and rattling the government's windows. Newspapers immediately reported Yap's arrest, along with the reactions of New Order reform activists; among the first was Buyung Nasution, a former prosecution official and KASI leader who became one of Indonesia's most prominent advocate-reformers and Yap's close ally. Within a day or two *Kompas* and *Sinar Harapan* especially, but also many other Jakarta dailies and even regional newspapers, were filled with reports of Yap's detention, which appeared in the foreign press as well. The Jakarta press, by and large except for government-supported papers, pointed out the injustice of the allegations, calling attention to Yap's anti-communism and his conflicts with Siauw Giok Tjhan in Baperki, which were better reported in 1968 than when they had occurred years earlier. Copies of his December 1960 speech at the Baperki meeting in Semarang circulated.[33] Yet attention focused less on this issue than on Yap's willingness to do battle with corrupt officials. KASI, KAMI, the Human Rights Institute, Peradin, and several student organizations all issued statements protesting the arrest and praising Yap.[34]

Even the substantial number of people who had fought fiercely with Yap on various issues rushed to defend him. Both Sindhunata, chair of the LPKB, and the young Soe Hok Gie, who had served on the Jakarta military command's research group on Baperki, spoke out against the charges. Arief Budiman, who had argued with Yap about name-changing, wrote two essays in praise of him as a man of ethical principle in pursuit of the New Order's own slogan of "Truth and Justice."[35] These were all *peranakan* figures, but the support for Yap crossed ethnic lines. Most strikingly, both because they were his antagonists in the Subandrio trial and because army officers generally supported the official case against Yap, Ali Said and Ahmad Durmawel spoke out in his behalf. Ali Said was rather cautious, but Durmawel not at all so in dismissing the Baperki accusation as nonsense and defending Yap as an able and dedicated lawyer.[36] Durmawel said he was shocked by Yap's arrest and insisted that the whole process should be reviewed seriously.

The public uproar interrupted a cabinet session on 5 January, when Jaksa Agung Sugih Arto reported the matter during a discussion of security problems and an impending visit by Philippine president Ferdinand Marcos. Foreign Minister Adam Malik told Yap later that he first heard about his detention then. Hugeng Imam Santoso, chief of the national police, told the cabinet he knew nothing about the affair, that lower police officials must have been responsible, but that Yap had to be released, for otherwise KASI and KAMI students would create havoc.[37] According to a press report, Suharto ordered Sugih Arto "to pay attention to the sharp reactions of the public about the detention of Yap Thiam Hien S.H. and as quickly as possible deal with the negative impressions of the problem."[38]

So on 6 January, Djohan Arifin, who had never lost a detainee, seemed to Yap amazed and worried as he informed his prisoner that a letter had come ordering his release. Later a car from Adam Malik's office arrived to pick him up. In it was the lawyer Padmo Sumasto, chairman of the Sin Ming Hui and a friend of Malik, who knew Yap well.[39] They drove to Adam Malik's house, where Yap chatted with the foreign minister and then was taken home to Grogol. What struck Yap most about the whole adventure was its arbitrariness: arrest, detention, and release were all at someone's whim. Oddly, others from Arifin's jail were released soon after Yap. Several came to thank him, for had he not been there, they still would be. Although legal process had nothing to do with it, many believed the affair had a promising effect, and, with reservations, so did Yap, for it exposed widespread abuse of authority, called attention to corruption, and showed that something could be done about it. Even before Yap's release, a Jakarta lawyer, Jetty Rizali Noor, called the affair a blessing in disguise for the cause of law.[40] Others, including Simatupang, agreed, while Arief Budiman, connecting the issue with the ideals raised by the 10 January student demonstrations against the New Order regime, thought the Yap affair a serious test case for the New Order.[41]

The real test, however, was yet to come, for Mardjaman and Simandjuntak brought a civil case against Yap for slander and set off a criminal prosecution for defamation. The criminal trial, which took precedence, was heard in July and August 1968.[42] It was a remarkable case, replete with powerful tensions and subtle nuances. Nearly everyone directly involved—Yap, his defense counsel, the prosecutor, the judge, Mardjaman, and Simandjuntak—had tacit interests in the case that went beyond the issues before the court. So did many who were not directly involved: the judicial corps, the prosecution, the police, the bureaucracy, the professional advocacy, and crowds of activists angry at corruption and abuse of power. The courtroom was packed to overflowing nearly every day of the trial, which the Jakarta press covered in detail. Yap himself was usually in attendance, which made judges and prosecutors uncomfortable, but popular interest in the case reflected awareness, obvious in press reports, that more was involved than a show.

The trial had a significant impact on Yap even before it began. When he was charged, three Peradin colleagues—Zainal Abidin (his co-counsel in the Liem Koe Nio case), Hasjim Mahdan, and Jamaluddin Datuk Singomangkuto—promptly stepped forward to act as his defense counsel. All were ethnic Indonesians, and they volunteered their services. For Yap it was a revelation, irresistible proof that, among his fellow advocates at least, it did not matter that he was Chinese. Their action was deeply important to him, lifting a painful burden of doubt about his acceptance. There may be no connection, but at about this time, in early 1968, a new press photograph of Yap appeared, showing him smiling and at ease, almost jaunty.[43]

The trial itself was a fascinating travesty, filled with nuance, in which the charge of slander obscured a fierce struggle over critical issues. At stake were some of the same institutional interests that ultimately condemned Pengabdi Hukum and that also bore tacit but profound political implications. On the second day of the trial Yap explained to Judge Soetarno Soedja that he had made his accusations in the Quick case "in the interests of the defense and in the public interest."[44] Yap and his attorneys had two immediate objectives: first, to prove the allegations against Mardjaman and Simandjuntak, and second, to confirm the right of advocates, with immunity, to marshal all relevant evidence for the defense.[45] While long extant in Dutch-Indonesian law and jurisprudence, this professional capacity in legal process had been whittled down de facto during Guided Democracy, when the courts and prosecution allied, as colleagues in public authority, to squeeze private lawyers out to the periphery of the judicial system. Advocates wanted to reenter the system, which implied, however, that there be not only a measure of control over public lawyers, prosecutors and judges particularly, but also a recognition of the legitimacy of private interests against public authority.

Public authority, for its part, took the obverse view. The prosecution was desperate to convict Yap, partly to teach him a lesson and through him the entire professional advocacy, but theirs was an effort in which the whole bureaucracy had an intense interest. In effect, the Yap case was a contest between official prerogative and private rights. This confrontation, not slander, was the prime connection with the P. T. Quick case where Yap had seriously challenged extortionate officials. At a time before the army-dominated New Order was fully consolidated, when the relationship between state power and social organization was still at issue in the streets, in the press, and in government councils, Yap's trial awkwardly brought that question into the courts.

Most of those who followed the trial knew, more or less acutely, what was at stake in Yap's challenge and the riposte to it. Prosecutors and police especially had the reputation and authority of their corps to protect. Prosecutors, much criticized for past (and ongoing) abuse, were particularly tender and defensive. But for judges, too, and the bureaucracy generally, Mardjaman and Simandjuntak were not merely corrupt officials who got caught. They represented official status and its privileges, which, for some, significantly included the right to extract additional income, but this was hardly the sole dimension of the problem. Officials tended to identify with Mardjaman and Simandjuntak, not in the first place as corruptors, but as officials, *pegawai negeri* (civil servants), representatives of the state, who were under attack by mere private parties. It was a kind of lèse-majesté, threatening not only the bureaucracy but the state itself conceived around its bureaucracy. For this reason, only government or army-connected newspapers bothered to emphasize police reports that Yap had "confessed" that he had never resigned from Baperki.[46] It may also explain, in part, why Djohan Arifin publicly supported the charge against Yap, though evidently he did not take it seriously enough to interrogate him.

How seriously the prosecution took the matter is evident in the choice of a senior prosecutor, Dali Mutiara, attached to the personal staff of the *Jaksa Agung*, to handle the case—for a charge of slander in a district court? The judge was R. Soetarno Soedja, for whom Yap's case turned out to be the last. On the first day of the trial, the largest courtroom in the Jakarta *pengadilan negeri* was packed with judges and prosecutors, along with members of Pengabdi Hukum and Peradin and Human Rights activists.[47] The press, there in force, divided predictably in its presentation of the case: private newspapers favored Yap, in part by reporting the sessions without comment, while government-related journals defended the officials.[48]

Yap did not expect a fair trial and took its odd turns in stride. A week before the trial began, the Kejaksaan Agung withdrew the permission it had just granted earlier that day, 25 June, for Yap to leave the country to attend a LawAsia conference in Kuala Lumpur at the beginning of July and a World Council of Churches meeting in Sweden in the middle of the month.[49] The prosecution's reason was that Yap's trial was scheduled to begin on 2 July but, even after the trial ended, for a time he was prevented from leaving the country, making other motives obvious. In a pre-trial press conference, Yap, foreseeing difficulties, briefed reporters on judicial process and expressed the hope that the "rules of the game" would be obeyed.[50] They were not.

This was the case in part because important rules had fallen into disuse over time, or had been turned on their heads to the disadvantage of accused persons and their counsel, who had lost the leverage necessary to keep such rules intact. One example: prosecutors, either because it was easier or because they lacked or wanted to avoid precise charges, often failed to specify the charges in summonses; or, another, judges would overlook improprieties in the summons to court. Both happened to Yap, who refused to heed the first, angering the prosecution, and protested the second, upsetting the judge. The judicial summons to trial came only one day, instead of the three required by law, before the hearings began. When Judge Soetarno Soedja asked Yap whether he objected to starting the trial despite the error, Yap replied yes, requesting more time to study the case materials. Soetarno Soedja overruled him and opened the trial anyway.[51]

Yap was a stickler for legal rules, which led both friends and critics to label him legalistic; but written law, after all, was the only advantage advocates had if they were committed (as some were not) to legal process. To be ideologically consistent in their assertion of the *negara hukum*, advocates had to insist that legal rules must be obeyed, not least by officers of the law. Yap's trial quickly became theater, as Judge Soetarno Soedja protested at one point, but only because Yap, Zainal Abidin, Hasjim Mahdan, and Jamaluddin acted as if written rules were to be taken seriously. In *that* there was drama, as bench and prosecution, for whom law often enough was a legitimating cover for other assumptions, were thrown continually on the defensive. A large audience, many of whom noisily approved Yap's assault, made the stage uncomfortably bright.

Much of the trial was a replay of the P. T. Quick case, with many of the same witnesses, including Mardjaman, Simandjuntak, and Lies Gunarsih, who were grilled to consternation by defense counsel and by Yap himself, who, accused of slander, was allowed by law to prove his allegations. As in the first trial, here too the defense suffered from the judge's hostility. Judge Soetarno Soedja seemed to make an effort to be even handed, now and again chiding prosecutor Dali Mutiara for his interruptions, but these reprimands hardly compared with his treatment of the defense. Such behavior was not unusual in criminal trials, then or later.[52]

Soetarno Soedja's demeanor reflected both judicial submission to the influential prosecution and the usual sensitivity, evident in his decision, to the prestige of the state officials Yap had assailed. Moreover, Yap's own demeanor in court, always legally correct and professionally courteous but never informally submissive or ingratiating, most likely irritated the judge (fig. 11.1). This, too, was not unusual. Relatively few judges, since the retirement of prewar-trained staff, had the legal confidence to deal with acute advocates, especially seniors with the kind of command of law and procedure Yap possessed. Unlike many professional advocates, who adjusted flexibly to changing conditions of practice and won cases accordingly, Yap made no concessions, and his clients occasionally suffered for it.[53] Yap suffered, too, in his own relationship with judges and prosecutors, but the issues he raised made this likely anyway.

Soetarno Soedja again and again prevented Yap and his lawyers from developing obvious lines of proof to demonstrate the intimate relationship of Lies, Mardjaman, and Simandjuntak and their intention to blackmail Tjan Hong Liang, the accused in the first trial and a witness in the second. When Yap raised the possibility of a sexual connection between Mardjaman and Lies, the indignant judge refused to allow him to pursue the point. He angrily denied Yap the opportunity to compare the testimony of a witness in the first and second trials.[54] He blocked other relevant openings, making it difficult for Yap to prove his point, as he argued in his own defense statement. Along with his frequent flare-ups at Yap, Soetarno Soedja also made clear his view of professional advocates, at one point referring to them as *tukang pukul*, hatchet men or hired guns.[55] At another point, he referred insultingly to Lie Hwee Yoe, Yap's senior law partner, which provoked Yap's one burst of fury in court and the next day generated Soetarno Soedja's one apology.

The worst performance, however, belonged not to Soetarno Soedja but Dali Mutiara, who pursued an insidiously obvious tactic against Yap. With a weak legal case but strong political motive, Dali tried to put Yap on public display as

FIG. 11.1 Court in session, *pengadilan negeri*, Jakarta, 1971. Yap is seated facing the judges' bench. Courtesy of TEMPO/Beng Bratanata

a Chinese, probably disloyal at that. As nearly as one can judge, the tactic did not work, for Yap's reputation made him relatively invulnerable to racist lunges, but Dali thought it worth the effort. On the second day of the trial, Yap, in an exchange with Soetarno Soedja, mentioned the abuse, inefficiency, and neglect that infused both civil and criminal legal institutions, arguing that the judiciary was the proper place for revealing the corruption. The overflow audience, split between private citizens and officials, broke out into cries of "Hidup Yap" (long live Yap) or "Yap gila" (Yap's crazy), as Soetarno Soedja banged his gavel.[56] At this, his first opportunity, Dali asked whether Yap was really defending his client or engaging in cheap agitation in his own interest, "like a tricky ploy from Mount Tay San [Tai Shan]."[57] To defend the Rule of Law, said Dali, moving on to less subtle approaches, requires expertise and a patriotic character. In this connection, he asked, where was the accused, Yap, on 17 August 1945, when independence was proclaimed, and on 21 July 1947 and 19 December 1948, when the Dutch attacked the revolutionary republic. Yap and his counsel immediately protested the irrelevance of such questions, which Soetarno Soedja disallowed, but Dali had already displayed his armory.[58]

Thereafter, Soetarno Soedja proved less willing to stop Dali's line of attack. In the next session Dali promptly returned to the issue of Yap's patriotism, asking whether he was a republican or a foreigner, and whether he was loyal to the Indonesian state and nation. This demanded an answer, he said, because the accused had defamed state officials on grounds of defending the public interest. Dali then claimed that he had Dutch documents indicating that in 1950 Yap was a foreigner—that is, a Foreign Oriental—and had even worked against the Republic in the Sin Ming Hui. Yap replied that there was no need to doubt that he was Indonesian, for how else could he have practiced as an advocate for twenty years. But he went on to point out that some foreigners had in fact defended Indonesian national interests, while some citizens had not.[59] For the rest, Yap delayed responding to Dali's innuendo until he delivered his own defense statement.

Dali did not let up, raising questions about Yap's citizenship, his membership in Baperki, and his loyalty to Indonesia.[60] A prosecution witness, one Thamsir Rachman, claimed to have met Yap in a Baperki connection after the 10 May 1963 anti-Chinese riots, which was unlikely as Yap had by then severed his ties to the organization; but the bench would not allow Yap to cross-examine.[61]

Dali's summation focused less on legal than more potentially damaging issues. The brunt of it was in part a defense of Simandjuntak and Mardjaman, and in part an extended ad hominem assault on Yap, whom he accused, as a Baperki figure, of wanting to make a political comeback and trying to make political hay of such ideas as the rule of law and human rights. Addressing the question of public interest raised by Yap, Dali argued that defaming state officials could hardly be said to be in the public interest, but instead was done in the interest of a client and Yap's own fee. He hedged his bets a bit, however, revealing his concern for the reputation of the prosecutorial corps, as Yap's counsel later pointed out. Dali argued that, even if the allegations against Mardjaman and Simandjuntak were proven, they were only the acts of individuals. "But by blowing up the matter even though unproven, the accused purposefully 'assailed' State institutions and the official corps of the government in their entirety in order to obtain political advantages for himself; that is, he tried to portray the acts of the witness . . . Simandjuntak as identical with the acts of the entire corps of prosecutors, and similarly the acts of . . . Mardjaman as identical with all Police Generals or Military [ABRI] generals."[62] Alerting the army officer corps to its interests was a considered stroke.

Dali concluded with an adage attributed to Gajah Mada, the famous prime minister of the fourteenth-century empire of Majapahit, who said to his admiral, Lembu Nala, about to lead an armada to Bali: "Only one thing need I say to you, if there is a flame, put out that flame while it is still small, before it burns down the house." The term Dali used for "flame" was *pelita*, a poor choice, for it also means an oil lamp. Later Yap's counsel would make much of this double meaning.

The *pleidooi* of the defense team called attention to Yap's trial as a test case, not only for the right of advocates to defend their clients but also for the quality of New Order politics, indicated by the widespread public attention drawn to the case in and even outside the country. The Indonesian people, they said, were now eager for truth and justice, sick of corruption and the lip service of those who called themselves leaders. Quoting Jaksa Agung Sugih Arto himself on the need to clean up the prosecution and eliminate tolerance for official corruption, the defense team pointed out that Dali Mutiara's *requisitoir* nevertheless read like a defense of Mardjaman and Simandjuntak and Lies Gunarsih, who were not the accused in this case.[63]

Following a long discussion of Yap's history in Baperki, his arrest earlier in the year, and his principles, the defense team turned passionately to Dali's Gajah Mada story. Yap and his counsel, in separate summations, addressed the ambiguous moral of Dali's story as they took up the issue of public interest. Implicitly they asked, "whose house is in danger of burning down? The prime minister's, the king's, the emissary's, the Balinese people's?" Here, Yap's defense attorneys argued, was the key to the prosecutor's view of this trial and the role of everyone in it. Dali saw himself as Gajah Mada, Soetarno Soedja as the admiral Lembu Nala, and Yap as the leader of the revolt in Bali, whose *pelita* had to be extinguished.

> Certainly, Mr. Chairman, such a picture is not appropriate, a joke that is not funny. What tickles our fancy is the choice of the example of a *pelita* . . . [A]ccording to the "common sense" in our possession, people use a *pelita* as a means of illumination . . . and not as a means of burning down houses. In reality, if the accused, Yap, is pictured as a *pelita* in the usual sense, the example is altogether appropriate, for he is regarded by society as an illuminator, a torch bearer who guides seekers after peace through dark passages to find Law. But if he is regarded as a rebel from Bali, who

must be crushed by Lembu Nala on the order of Gajah Mada only because he has the courage to speak out before the Court in defense of the public interest and that of his client, then such a view is very excessive."[64]

Yap, as he addressed the legal issues of slander and the rights of counsel, planted his defense in a more general consideration of the role of courts and law in the Indonesian state. He bluntly accused Soetarno Soedja of being predisposed against him, favoring the officials and their witnesses, and he demonstrated article by article in the procedural code (H.I.R.) how the court had failed in its responsibility to stand as umpire above the adversaries. He lectured the court on the meanings of a fair trial and the presumption of innocence, detailing the practices of arrest, detention, and seizure of property before any evidence had been collected, and in court he pointed to Soetarno Soedja's insults, innuendo, and mocking of Yap's case. Turning, near the end of his *pleidooi,* to Dali's ethnic attack, Yap defended the contribution to Indonesia of nonindigenous citizens. Love of one's country, like love of truth and justice, was not something inherited from one's parents, and therefore had nothing to do with foreign or indigenous origins.

> Someone of foreign descent, therefore, can have a sense of love and loyalty to his chosen nation, possibly also greater than that of someone who obtained Indonesian nationality by the mere chance of having been born of "indigenous" parents.
>
> Speaking of proof of Indonesian citizenship, Mr. Chairman, I have full proof that I was born in Indonesia of parents who also were born in Indonesia and, consequently, I possess legal proof of my Indonesian nationality. Can the honorable public prosecutor say the same and prove incontrovertibly that he is actually of Indonesian nationality, and not of Malaysian nationality, for example?
>
> Finally, who has more love and is more loyal to Indonesian state and nation, Mr. Chairman: someone who respects and obeys the Constitution and laws or someone who violates his oath of allegiance to the Constitution and laws and who treads upon them in his own interest or in the interest of the corps or his close friends?

Like his counsel, Yap also leapt upon Dali Mutiara's Gajah Mada parable. The moral, said Yap, of these "pearly words"—*kata mutiara,* a pun on Dali's last name, which means pearl—addressed via the court to society and specifically to all *pelita* in Indonesia, is a warning, a veiled threat:

> Oh, all you arrogant *pelita* . . . dare you shine a bright light in the darkness created by ignorance of law and justice of the people who have been my property for decades? You don't quake at my power, [which is] like a thousand headed dragon, and you dare to point your fingers at the arbitrariness which is the quality of my absolute power? You dare to try to attack the fortress of my power, my right seized from the powerless people? Oh! The moment of your death has arrived; I will extinguish you and cast all of you into the darkest darkness.

This threat, said Yap, is the scream of one who is himself threatened with destruction by the fire of Truth and Justice.[65] In all this passion, born of anger and principle, there was also sound political analysis on the one hand and optimism on the other. The optimism, the implication that Truth and Justice would soon win out, was excessive.

Given his own analysis and Soetarno Soedja's demeanor, Yap could not have been surprised by his conviction. Like Dali, Soetarno Soedja interpreted the legal issues involved to fit his determination to sentence Yap, but the core of his reasoning was elsewhere. Defending his own impartiality and rejecting the political issues raised by Yap and his defense team, the judge, quoting an American Bar Association president's concern that the pendulum had swung too far in the United States toward favoring the accused, warned that in Indonesia the same problem should not be allowed to develop—as misplaced an admonition as one can imagine. His emphasis was on the possibility of abuse of guarantees by accused persons. Constitutional and procedural safeguards, he insisted, might cause police, prosecution, and courts to act with too much restraint, even when convinced that a crime had been committed. Balance, he said—as if it existed at all in the current criminal process—had to be maintained between the rights of the accused and the interests of society. "Therefore, it is necessary to create an atmosphere in which legal officials can carry out their responsibilities unaffected by influences or pressures from outside."[66] In other words, officials should be left alone. At every turn, Soetarno Soedja gave Mardjaman and Simandjuntak the benefit of the doubt and accused Yap of trying to make a laughingstock of the prosecution: "the consequence and influence of this will tend to be negative. The consequences will be no more trust, or the disappearance of trust, on the part of society not only for the apparatus of the prosecution and the apparatus of the police, but for the whole State apparatus."[67]

The sentence, laid down on 14 October 1968, was a year in prison. Yap promptly appealed. The appellate court of Jakarta, apparently caught between its sense of responsibility to the judicial corps and its responsibility to the law, worked out an awkward compromise. Admitting that advocates may bring all evidence to bear in defense of their clients, but considering that Yap had gone too far, the appellate panel reduced his sentence to fourteen days, suspended, as long as he committed no punishable offense during a probationary period of six months.[68] It was a typical face-saving decision, in which the appellate court kept the sensitivities of the judicial and prosecutorial corps in mind. Only in the Mahkamah Agung, to which Yap naturally appealed, was the issue sensibly resolved. Then still headed by Professor Subekti, a quiet liberal sympathetic to the criticism of legal process since Guided Democracy, the Supreme Court finally acquitted Yap in a 3 January 1973 decision that was a landmark in the modern history both of the court and the professional advocacy.[69] Advocates celebrated the decision, but it did not count for much, because the fundamental issues raised by Yap in the first-instance court were never resolved. If anything, their situation worsened, as prosecutors, judges, and police remained hostile and resentful of the intrusion upon officialdom that advocates represented.

Still, Yap survived the trial well, which cannot be said of most of his antagonists. Immediately after the trial, Soetarno Soedja—whether because of his performance in the case, as everyone thought, or because he was due for a transfer, as the Supreme Court claimed—was ordered to a court in Kalimantan. He refused and left the judicial service. Simandjuntak and Mardjaman fared worse.[70] Dali Mutiara's reputation was not helped by the trial. It was too common to call it a paradox, but Yap, twice condemned to prison, in 1968 and again in 1987, never served either sentence, yet spent two periods in detention, the week in 1968 and almost a year in 1974, for which he was neither indicted nor tried.

TWELVE

REFORM FRONTIERS

NINETEEN-SIXTY-EIGHT was a stunning year for Yap, filled with baptisms of fire and personal confirmations. Surrounded by controversy and official animosity, enjoying public adulation and international recognition, he had become a symbol of the reform movement, such as it was. In Indonesia, especially Java, where personal status is a powerful stimulant usually taken for granted, few observers of Yap, even antagonists, thought that he acted from personal ambition. If anything, he was generally regarded in head-wagging awe as purely a man of principle, some thought to the point of nuttiness. "Quixotic" often turned up in conversations about Yap, sometimes with a slight edge of opprobrium, sometimes with gleeful appreciation. Ethnic Chinese were ambivalent about him, either taking pride in his courageous citizenship or worrying that his noise would affect the *peranakan* community. Ethnic Indonesians, particularly in reform circles, began to forget that he was ethnic Chinese, or they ignored the fact as irrelevant.

However one views this puzzle—what mix of personal ambition and principle motivated Yap—it has no simple answer. At age fifty-five in 1968, Yap himself probably could not have answered the question with certainty. He did have a strong need for recognition and had his share of status anxieties, which showed up in flashes of anger or sarcasm at anyone who talked down to him. But he dealt with these common afflictions in ways incomprehensible to any for whom status attached to official rank, position, or wealth. Many ethnic Javanese who knew him well saw in Yap the personification of the rarely obeyed cultural prescription of dispassionate, non-self-serving (*sepi ing pamrih*) devotion to duty and principle.

After Yap's release from jail in January 1968, the journalist-intellectual Wiratmo Soekito warned him not to let it all go to his head, not to take himself more seriously than the principles involved. According to Wiratmo's wife, Sri Widojati (then already a Supreme Court justice), Yap replied, "Of course." Yap needed no reminder about the dangers of egocentrism, he had condemned it often enough in his writings on the assimilation issue, to monitor his own tendencies in that regard. Before and after his ordeals in jail and court, Yap spoke and wrote publicly about his personal experience only when it was relevant to the principles that he insisted were paramount, and even then the first-person pronoun was almost entirely absent, not only in published pieces but also in preliminary drafts.

If for Yap 1968 was intoxicating, for Khing it was filled with anxiety, terror, and foreboding. Their arguments, the tension between them, were not altogether secret. The young Soe Hok Gie, an updated version of Yap, learned about the situation from a friend who was dating the daughter of Yap's law partner Lie Hwee Yoe. He reflected on the tension in his diary.

> From Bambang I just learned that there is a conflict between Yap Thiam Hien and his wife. Yap wants to maintain justice without considering the obstructions, while his wife, like other mothers and wives who always want security, doesn't agree. I am reminded of the difficult situation for idealists (like me???) who perhaps have to fight on two fronts—against their own circle and against outside enemies. They live in eternal loneliness. Maybe I have to learn to love loneliness.[1]

These words are both true and one-sided, lacking much appreciation of Khing's situation, like that of many other women whose bargaining positions were hardly commensurate with their responsibilities. Constantly anxious for Yap, worried about their children, concerned about household funds, Khing had her own kind of courage, in some ways rather more impressive than Yap's. He enjoyed the public conflict, the risk, and the limelight; she capably managed the shambles that he occasionally left behind. As early as 1968, perhaps, but particularly in the early 1970s, Khing began to think about leaving Indonesia, moving to calm and untroubled Holland, as many other *peranakan* had done in waves of crisis since 1950, but Yap consistently refused and Khing went along, not altogether quietly, but loyally.

She wrote anxious letters to Thiam Bong and his wife in Holland about Yap's doings and dangers, with hints that maybe he should leave the country. Her letters and reports in the Dutch press about the murderous tensions in Indonesia and about Yap too—his case was widely reported—convinced Thiam Bong that he ought to do something about Thiam Hien. Bong had written to Hien, urging him to leave for Europe, but Hein's answer was always the same: what could he possibly do in Holland? In Indonesia he had a purpose. Bong decided to visit Jakarta for the first time since the revolution. He went alone, sometime in late 1969 or early 1970, to offer his older brother moral support, basically, for there was little more he could do. He stayed with Thiam Hien and Khing in Grogol for about a month. Little came of the visit, other than Bong's own surprise at the changes in Indonesia. He found things not so bad after all, and he returned home somewhat reassured that his brother would be all right. Khing never felt that way.

Yap was aware of Khing's anxiety and misgivings, yet he took them rather lightly, partly at least because to do more would have burdened his own sense of mission and involvement. He had to assume that her fears were exaggerated, that she did not understand matters. As the burdens became heavier, particularly after his arrest in early 1974, Khing began to dream of leaving, even on her own if Thiam Hien would not go. When she disclosed this in her letters to Thiam Bong, he sympathized but reminded her that she belonged with her husband. The advice was hardly necessary.

Before, during, and after his trial Yap kept busy, as much or more with reform advocacy as with the income-producing kind. His articles on judicial reform, human rights, and reform of criminal procedure were featured prominently in *Kompas* and drew favorable responses from the public in letters to the editor. Less publicly he wrote letters of protest to officials on behalf of unjustly detained or mistreated prisoners who had asked his help. He was in demand by prospective clients, particularly in criminal actions, for Yap's reputation as an advocate had spread widely since the Subandrio trial. Accused persons whose cases seemed hopeless sought him out. Yap could pick and choose, and did not hesitate to set conditions. The cases he chose were likely to be reported; even his routine trials drew audiences.

He was quick to accept cases, paying or not, that involved abuses of authority or legal process, or engaged his interest in other ways. Difficult cases were his forte. One such was that of Carmel Budiardjo, an English national married to an Indonesian man. Both were detained without trial after the coup, like many others, because of their alleged associations with communists. Carmel's family in London sought her release with the help of an English solicitor and, in late 1968, contacted Yap for information about Carmel's detention.[2] Little happened for a couple of years. While the British government was unwilling officially to request her release, assuming she was subject to Indonesian law, the British ambassador did at some point raise the matter privately with Foreign Minister Adam Malik, who apparently advised Kopkamtib (an army-based security apparatus) that holding her might cause difficulties.

The problem was to find a way around Indonesian legal jurisdiction over Carmel, who had renounced her British citizenship in 1954. Yap researched the matter and discovered that the Budiardjos, wed in Europe, had failed to register their marriage in Jakarta and hence in Indonesia were not legally married. He so informed the British ambassador, suggesting that, if his government rescinded its earlier declaration that Carmel had relinquished her citizenship, she would be English again. This formula or one like it was adopted, and Carmel was released on 1 November 1971, on condition that she not complain about her treatment and that she leave the country immediately, as she did the same day.[3]

Yap's own vistas opened wide in 1968, with invitations to join the World Council of Churches (WCC) and the International Commission of Jurists (ICJ). Suddenly he was an international player in the two arenas, religion and law, that meant most to him. He was eager both for the roles and the experience. In neither organization did he actually assume a position until early 1969, when he was allowed finally to leave Indonesia. Then, for the first time since 1948, he returned to Europe, and thereafter until the mid-1980s traveled fairly often to Geneva, with occasional short side trips to Holland, and more widely around the rest of the world on official missions.

In Holland, along with his Dutch contacts, he could visit Thiam Bong and his family and attend to his son, Hong Gie, who spent much of the 1970s in the Netherlands. As a teenager Hong Gie had been in some difficulty, which Thiam Hien and Khing resolved by sending him to the Netherlands to finish high school and find a vocation. For years father and son, both strong willed, did not get along. Slowly, during Yap's visits, they began to repair the tension between them.

For nearly fifteen years in both the WCC and ICJ, Yap traveled to Africa, Korea, Hong Kong, Vietnam, and India, whose poverty made a lasting impression on him, as well as to Europe and elsewhere. The experience abroad was rewarding, lending him perspective as well as comparative information that fed back into his work in Indonesia. It confirmed his own vocation as reformer, made him even more confident in his own views, and supplied him with trustworthy contacts and channels of support outside of Indonesia. Increasingly, he no longer thought of Indonesia as a special case, but one of many, some better and some worse, in which economic misery, abuse of power, corruption, greed, and political unaccountability were common features. While European political models and cultural styles remained influential in his thinking, he became more aware of problems there too.

The qualities for which Yap had become known at home he brought with him to the WCC and ICJ: blunt outspokenness, a lawyerly passion for detail, willingness to ask questions, and a quick eye for misbehavior.[4] His work in the ICJ was routine, for the most part, and included reviews of human rights violations here and there, from which he learned about other legal systems and their abuses. Among his ICJ colleagues there was little occasion for conflict. In the WCC, however, Yap seems to have been an occasional cause of tension, which he remembered with pride. The WCC may have engaged his attention more than the ICJ, partly because he felt more confident in his command of Protestant values than of the complex variations and murkier evidence of the legal universe. Moreover, the WCC had a wider mission than the ICJ, one that afforded more leeway for Yap's interests than the relatively straightforward work of the ICJ.

Yap served two consecutive, seven-year terms in the WCC, the first as a member of the World Church Service Commission, which dealt with local church requests for assistance, and the second on the International Affairs Commission. At first his own church nominated him via the Indonesian Council of Churches, but his second term was at the request of the WCC commissioners themselves. On the World Church Service Commission, where he sat as one of four vice chairs, Yap evidently made his mark early as someone from the Third World who would not stand for condescension. Sometime in 1969, for example, the representative of a French church showed the commission a film on Vietnam. Afterwards the German chair of the commission admonished the members to evaluate the film critically, for it might be propaganda. Yap, typically, took umbrage, asking the chair whether he thought the members incapable of making their own judgments. His remarks evidently raised eyebrows, some approvingly, some not.

At a general meeting of all the commissions in Geneva, perhaps in 1974, the discussion had to do with church administration. Criticism arose of the imbalance between administrative and program expenditures in Third World churches. Too much was spent for personnel and church costs, not enough for programs. Yap thought it a serious critique and supported it, but for the sake of consistency insisted that the WCC explain to the session how it disposed of its income. He demanded, moreover, that a report be delivered at the current session. When the stenciled report was compiled, with considerable difficulty, it appeared that Third World church expenditures, encumbered with travel and similar expenses, were not very much more than those of the WCC, where salary items were higher.

Another more serious matter sheds light on Yap's thinking. Here Yap questioned the judgment of Visser t'Hooft, a former secretary-general of the WCC and a man of great prestige and influence in Protestant circles. The issue involved the appointment of a new financial administrator to direct the organization's special fund; the appointment was to be made by the WCC financial advisory board, of which Visser t'Hooft was a member, and Yap was one of those responsible for interviewing candidates for the advertised position. While this process was still under way, Visser t'Hooft and a Swiss bank director informed the members that they had found, and by implication favored, another candidate, an emeritus minister from the United States well known in the WCC, appropriately experienced, and in all respects well suited to the position. Yap was angered by this attempt to short-circuit his own committee work and bluntly accused Visser t'Hooft and others of subverting established procedures. In a meeting meant to secure approval of the American candidate, Yap refused to go along, startling the other members. The session broke up, and t'Hooft's candidate was not approved. It emerged that the American's qualifications were not all they should have been, but it was mainly on the procedural question that Yap stood fast. Later, in his hotel, an English minister and others on the staff pointed out to him that never before had anyone questioned Visser t'Hooft's authority, let alone made him stand down. It was one of the things Yap did best, as he knew well, for it was the essential point of the story as he related it to me.

In this affair, as in others, Yap's baggage of experience from Indonesia made a difference. His reaction to Visser t'Hooft's end-run was much like his reaction to Siauw's coup in Baperki's higher education effort. Both events involved personal sensitivity to being undercut, but also a principle of procedural consistency that Yap believed produced better odds of integrity. In another instance, opposition arose in the WCC to funding a small banking effort to assist needy churches. Yap angrily objected to his own well-off commission's doubts about helping another commission's useful service. The project was funded. His argument was phrased in exactly the same terms as his plea to his church, during the 1950s, to assist "our brethren" in poorer Indonesian churches.

In the WCC as at home, Yap had misgivings about organizational interests and the self-serving tendencies of elites, which he believed had to be held accountable constantly, but he trusted the basic decency of ordinary members, as he did of ordinary citizens. He was impressed in the WCC by the willingness of rich American and European churches to help poor churches elsewhere, even beyond the ideological divide of the Iron Curtain, which he took to be an expression of faith that deepened his own. He was encouraged by American churches that either opposed the war in Vietnam or gave assistance to Vietnamese, communist or not. Yap distrusted American purposes in Vietnam, suspecting that colonial or "Western" interests were involved or, in any case, a failure to recognize the Vietnamese struggle for freedom. The ability of some churches to ignore the issue of communism, to give aid to the "enemy" in effect, reinforced his own sense of Christian purpose.[5]

This sense of mission led to serious tension between Yap and Simatupang at the WCC assembly in Nairobi in late 1975. Simatupang headed the Indonesian delegation to the conference, held every seven years. Yap's term on the World Church Service Commission had ended, but in early 1975 he received a special invitation to attend the conference, possibly because he had just been released from prison at the end of 1974. In view of his fresh experience, he was asked (or perhaps himself requested) to sit with the human rights commission at the assembly. Yap touched off a controversy in the well-attended commission discussions by protesting that the lion's share of speaking time went to well-known figures and rather less to participants from new states, where most human rights violations occurred. Moreover, he pointed out, those whose language was not English should be allowed more, not less, time to express their views. The session was chaired by an African American woman who sympathized with Yap's point and who asked permission to allot more time for speakers from Third World countries. Yap himself spoke, in fluent English, demanding attention to and assistance for Indonesian political prisoners detained since the 1965 coup. His refusal to exempt his own country from criticism anticipated the conflict that followed within the Indonesian delegation.

While the assembly was in session, news broke of the Indonesian army's invasion, on 8 December 1975, of East Timor, the small colony that Portugal had released over a year earlier. While East Timorese political groups debated issues of independence, Indonesian troops invaded, brutally occupied, and soon annexed the territory, setting off a resistance movement that lasted until after Suharto's fall.[6] The Indonesian delegation at Nairobi, out of the country for weeks, was unprepared when an Australian minister, John Brown, asked for information about the invasion and proposed a resolution condemning it. Immediately the Indonesian and Australian delegations confronted one another, coming close to a fight. Simatupang defended the invasion, insisting that it was an Indonesian affair, in which no one else had a right to interfere. Yap, chagrined, challenged Simatupang. Tension was high. At a recess, the secretary-general of the Indonesian Council of Churches, Nababan, said that he would smash the Australian if he spoke again. Yap confronted Nababan, reminding him that he was a Christian and warning him that if he did anything of the sort, he, Yap, would condemn him publicly. Nababan apparently quieted down, but the delegation was split, with Yap in the minority. By insisting in that setting that the invasion should be judged, first of all, according to moral, not nationalist, standards, Yap had raised an exceedingly sensitive issue that did not sit well with Simatupang.

In Jakarta during the late 1960s Yap had been fully engaged and creative, by turns optimistic and pessimistic but at a peak of energetic work, in and out of court. He was in demand as an advocate and as a spokesman for change. His circle of associates and friends had widened enormously since the early 1960s. Close to other Peradin seniors, he was now well known to younger admiring advocates, KAMI and KASI activists, intellectuals, and journalists.

Soe Hok Gie, judging from his diary, felt free to drop by Yap's home; and his older brother, Arief Budiman, was in touch. Through the Pengabdi Hukum organization Yap knew Wiratmo Soekito and such judicial reformers as Widojati and Asikin Kusumaatmadja, both on the Mahkamah Agung. He and Ponke Princen, so different in character, became fast associates in the League for the Defense of Human Rights. Another close relationship dating from this turbulent period was with the also turbulent Adnan Buyung Nasution, from the office of the chief public prosecutor, a KASI leader who confronted Suharto over army corruption and resigned in protest from the prosecution to become one of Indonesia's most prominent professional advocates and the founder of the Legal Aid Institute. He sought Yap out after the Subandrio trial; and twenty years later, in Brussels, was at Yap's deathbed. Many others from Jakarta and the provinces linked up with Yap during this period, all in one way or another committed to change.

What were the odds in favor of change? The period from 1966 through 1970 was full of equivocal signals on reform, optimism and pessimism mixing inexorably in favor of the latter as the Suharto circle consolidated its control over the New Order regime. As the army leadership became increasingly heavy-handed, there still were officers who sympathized with reformers. General Nasution and his staff helped critics of the regime. Other allies included Marine Major General Ali Sadikan, who became governor of the Jakarta metropolitan district.

The discrete, decrepit, corrupt universe of the legal system was surrounded by hostile reformers, and on the inside, too, a few promising figures held powerful positions. Minister of Justice Seno Adji, though his reputation as a liberal reformer faded fast, at first seemed to be an asset. General Sugiharto, brought in as chief public prosecutor to put that charnel house in order, said the right things about cleaning up the system and now and then acted as if he meant it. Hugeng Imam Santoso was well known as a police commandant with integrity, and in the Mahkamah Agung the new chairman, the mild-mannered Soebekti, was capable, honest, and altogether sympathetic to legal reform. Politically none of them counted enough to make a difference, with the partial exception of Hugeng, who was out by 1971, but their presence encouraged the civilian opposition. So did the early rhetoric of the Suharto leadership, which promised a restoration of the *negara hukum* and the *trias politika* and an end to corruption.

Among the most prominent activist reform groups was the professional advocacy, which, small as it was, was extremely vocal, not only in condemning the Old Order of Guided Democracy but in confidently outlining necessary reforms in the New Order. More than any other single group, advocates, represented by Peradin, had a long list of precise demands at hand and a phalanx of articulate spokesmen in and out of Jakarta to press them (fig. 12.1). Among the best-known spokesmen were Suardi Tasrif, Yap, and Nani Razak from Jakarta and Soemarno P. Wirjanto from Solo. Tasrif, Yap, and Soemarno wrote frequently on a wide variety of legal and basically political-legal issues for the national (i.e., Jakarta) press, *Kompas* and *Sinar Harapan* especially but also *Indonesia Raya* and *Nusantara*. Tasrif's journalistic experience, contacts, and discipline made him a particularly consistent contributor.[7] Yap was only slightly less prolific, with much to say that Oyong Peng Koen at *Kompas* was always ready to publish. Yap wrote well, and much that he wrote, for conferences and similar forums, was actually meant to be spoken. He enjoyed writing and his files contained lots of notes, clippings, and unfinished pieces. Neither before nor after, however, did he write quite so much as he did during the late 1960s, when it still seemed that worthwhile change was a real possibility.

Yap's writings then represented a fairly common consensus among senior advocates in Peradin on issues of both law and politics, which to their minds

FIG. 12.1 Peradin directors, November 24, 1983. *Front row, left to right*: Suardi Tasrif, Lukman Wiriadinata, Yap Thiam Hien, Amartiwi Saleh, and Todung Mulia Lubis (LBH).

were joined in the institutional structure of the Indonesian state. Their narrow focus was on institutional reform: cleaning up the prosecution and police and redefining their responsibilities, strengthening the courts, restoring judicial respect for the advocacy, and reorganizing the professional advocacy itself—all subsumed in the creation of new procedural codes. The broader concern implicit in these demands was the need for institutional control over political authority and for redefinition of the relationship between state and society; it was this that drew other reform groups to the lawyers. As Soemarno put it, the issue was between the rule of law and the rule of (political) discretion. The debates across this divide were particularly frequent from 1966 through the early 1970s, but they never actually ended.

The entire legal system and all aspects of the law—constitutional, civil, commercial, criminal, administrative—were at issue, but criminal procedure above all displayed dramatically the reality of state-society relations. If the press treated the massive detentions following the coup ambivalently or circumspectly—though newspapers did publish protests by Yap, among a few others—the rampant abuse of criminal process was spared not at all. From early 1966 onward the press was filled with complaints and protests against police and prosecutorial corruption, malfeasance, brutality, arbitrary arrests, extortion, long detentions without trial, coerced confessions, prison conditions, and maltreatment of accused persons amounting to torture.

Yap, whose métier was criminal procedure, spoke out lucidly and persuasively on these issues, not only in court but also in public lectures and in the press. His writings during these years reflect his two meshed sides. As a critic he was blunt but measured, down-to-earth, analytical, documenting every point with substantial evidence. But as a reform thinker he often soared, tossing aside received wisdom and legal tradition in ways that seemed politically dreamy but made quite good sense as an agenda for change.

For all that he was sometimes accused of being too "legalistic," exactly the reverse was true. Yap was less inclined than others, even Tasrif, to approach reform issues from a narrowly legal or professional perspective. He could not separate law from politics. The logic of his position started from a human rights premise, that the decent and fair treatment of all people required a political system devoted to that end. Good will alone, however, was unlikely to generate such a system. To Yap's mind, power and authority, concentrated especially in the state, were the principal sources of danger to society, which he conceived not in the first place as an abstract collectivity but as individuals who could be hurt and suffer. Only two means existed to control such power, he believed. One was consistent and open legal process, limiting the inclination of authorities to act in their own selfish interest. But because legal process is often inadequate—a leash in the hands of the officials it is meant to restrain—a second and more important control is needed—popular political participation and the concomitant courage of citizens to act politically.

Yap's religious and political convictions met and meshed in his focus on human suffering as the essential measure of public policy, requiring no sophisticated analysis but simply a recognition of pain. To ignore pain, like injustice of any kind, was outrageous and sinful. Hence Yap's refusal to let go of the political detentions issue following the coup. The tens of thousands whom the army rounded up and confined to prison camps in late 1965 and 1966, often subject to inhumane conditions and treatment, received attention from abroad—Amnesty International, the United Nations Development Program, and the ICJ—but less so at home. The detentions were a delicate political issue, about which even those who thought the government's actions wrong—many did not—were seldom willing to risk speaking out. Princen's League for the

Defense of Human Rights, consisting of Princen himself and a few others including Yap, protested the issue.[8] KAMI was the only major political organization to condemn the massive detentions. Yap, always on the lookout for optimistic signs, was encouraged:

> It is very significant that precisely the Indonesian Students Action Front, a social element that [firmly opposed the totalitarian PKI and Old Order] also asks for public concern and attention to this problem of G 30 S/PKI detainees via the press, TV panel discussions, and so on. KAMI's attitude, filled with a sense of responsibility concerning this national and international problem, truly warms the heart. It gives faith and hope for national state leadership in the hands of these *spes patriae* in future.[9]

Pursuing the issue unrelentingly, Yap took the opportunity to point out that, along with the 80,000 or (considerably) more political detainees, there were an additional 25,000 prisoners awaiting trial. Apart from the financial burden to state and families, he argued, other considerations dictated deep concern: the danger that innocent detainees in jail would turn into criminals or that they would seek revenge. As such detentions are inhumane, they also have a dehumanizing effect on the jailers. It was a point Yap returned to often, making it a powerful critique of officialdom:

> But the matter least often considered is that the "detention game" [or "wait for a decision" game] gradually generates in the soul of the officials involved an attitude towards fellow human beings that is inhumane. This attitude is quite obvious in the formalism, bureaucratism, and lack of courage to assume responsibility involved in allowing detainees to be robbed of their freedom for months, even years. Such negativism is not limited to the officials concerned alone, but rather spreads to their wives and children. . . . Just imagine how widespread and influential this negative social force will become if allowed to grow for years without correction.[10]

Detention without trial was not an isolated problem, of course, but was linked to a hundred others in an ascending spiral of institutional and political pathology. Piecemeal solutions, Yap understood, were impossible. An opportunity to engage higher on the spiral evidently appeared in 1966, when the government, in response to public criticism of the prosecution and police, promised to consider a new code of criminal procedure. Replacing the colonial code of criminal procedure (H.I.R.) was not a new idea. In 1964 the Ministry of Justice had produced a draft that introduced significant changes—e.g., allowing accused persons professional counsel after their arrest. The prospect of a new code set off tremors in the souls of senior advocates eager to have a say in reorganizing criminal process and with it the whole of the judicial system. Peradin turned to Yap to draft a concept of the code on behalf of the professional advocacy. Yap was surprised but pleased by the confidence they placed in him. Although his concept was not actually presented to a Peradin congress until July of 1969, he may have finished a rough draft as early as 1966.[11] In any event, the ideas in this document are the same as those in his newspaper articles from 1966 through 1968. Like other senior advocates who had suffered the procedural miseries and professional distress of Guided Democracy's legal system, Yap had begun to think that effective reform required not piecemeal change but an utter transformation of the legal system, one based on altogether different institutional assumptions. The revolution in criminal procedure that he and a few other advocates fantasized about was a fundamental shift away from a civil law inquisitorial to a common law accusatorial process, particularly the American form. Civil law procedure, they recognized, weighted the scales too heavily in favor of the state, while common law practice, which Yap and others knew partly from standard texts but also from Ellery Queen and Erle Stanley Gardner, offered advocates efficacy and prestige and their clients better odds. Yap and Tasrif went furthest in urging the American model, but others were intrigued.[12]

Yap consistently concentrated on protection of the individual against the state. As early as March 1966, he wrote a long article for *Kompas* focusing on arrest and detention and the rights of accused persons.[13] The government draft code of criminal procedure, he made clear, was inadequate. Yap lucidly explained existing procedural law, the H.I.R., analyzing its shortcomings and those of the government draft and proposed improvements. His basic points were that the authority of prosecutors and police was not clearly delimited and was therefore subject to abuse, that in neither the H.I.R. nor the government draft did judges have adequate control over arrest and detention, and that accused persons had few rights or recourse.

In mid-1968, when he was most likely at work on his own draft code, Yap published a two-part article—"Proposals for Change in the 'Law of Criminal Procedure'"—in which his startling suggestions amounted to a transformation. The essay began with the comparison of two extradition cases then in the news, one the arrest in Jakarta of Bob Liem Tjie Sian, wanted for murder in Hong Kong, and the other the arrest in London of the suspected assassin of Martin Luther King. Yap's emphasis was on the arrests, in which Liem was detained with few protections, while James Earl Ray had counsel and legal recourse. Using the contrast to introduce the "Anglo-Saxon" system, Yap proceeded to argue the case for accusatorial process, *habeas corpus*, bail, and further guarantees of individual rights.[14] Another article followed immediately, this one on timely justice as a human right, in which he compared the speed with which Robert Kennedy's killer, Sirhan Sirhan, was brought to trial with the exceedingly long waits of accused persons in Indonesia.[15] Again he explained the protective instruments available in America that Indonesian criminal procedure lacked.

Reminding his readers of the International Year of Human Rights, 1968, Yap concluded this piece with an appeal to legal officials, members of Parliament, the government, law faculties, and the public at large to "examine our legal system and to pay concerned attention to the 'Law in Action' in our country, so that we can amass enough facts and data to create a legal system that genuinely respects and extends equal protection to human dignity, without distinction of any form in matters of race, descent, religion, national origin, culture, politics, social or economic standing. . . . What we need is not additional authority and power, but additional skill, efficiency, and sense of responsibility. But above all we need to increase our concern and love for fellow human beings."

All these ideas and more came together in Yap's own sketch of the procedural code, which went to Peradin members and the Ministry of Justice, perhaps to a parliamentary committee, but not much farther.[16] It is an interesting document, partly for Yap's assessment of the politics of change and the impediments to it. The genesis of the revision he saw as the result of pressure from "social forces" on an otherwise reluctant government that, he implied, would prevent change if it were strong enough. This was exactly right, though at the time Yap may have assumed that the "social forces" had a chance to compel new law and the "democratic" political system that went with it. The difficulty he saw in achieving the kind of change he wanted—predicated on the existence of free and responsible individuals determined to keep official leadership in check—was a cultural predisposition to bow to authority (*mendoro*) inherited from a feudal and colonial past.[17]

In Yap's draft, police and prosecutorial functions were carefully defined, with the prosecution limited to court work alone, while police were given full responsibility for arrest, detention, and preliminary investigation.[18] The courts were to be fully independent, by implication, no longer the administrative responsibility of the Ministry of Justice. The role of defense lawyer in the judicial process was to be equal to that of prosecutor and judge. Advocates were to have the right to be present at preliminary investigations from the time of arrest. *Habeas corpus*, unknown in civil law process, was incorporated and developed in detail. So was bail. Restrictions were imposed on arrest, detention, and investigation. Courtroom procedure rendered prosecutor and advocate equal in all respects. On the last page of his draft Yap offered a sketch of the new courtroom layout required by accusatory procedure. Most importantly, prosecutors were no longer on the bench but now sat below the bench across the room, on the same level as with advocates.[19]

Nothing came of Yap's draft, and little more of the wishes of the advocacy generally. In the 1970 law on judicial organization and the 1981 code of criminal procedure the few concessions were backed by none of the elements of control over legal process that might have made them real.

By 1968–69, as earlier hopes faded, Yap realized perfectly well that his draft code and the political dreams behind it had little chance. Not only was the Suharto regime efficiently consolidating its authority, but also existing political parties were quite weak and under pressure from the army, while the reform alliance of KAMI students, KASI intellectuals, and liberal political activists of various sorts, never all that solid, had begun to disintegrate. In early 1969, in response to talk of getting rid of KAMI, Yap defended it, arguing that an activist student organization was needed for the sake of balance in the political structure.[20] KAMI soon disappeared.

For all their efforts, reformers had accomplished relatively little since 1966. The pattern was clear enough in the MPRS, until 1969 the institutional arena for debates about the regime, where the military, parties, and assorted new groups were all represented. It was easy, given a victorious consensus, to dismantle Guided Democracy, abolish the PKI, remove Soekarno from the presidency, and overturn various MPRS policy statements from the earlier period. Reconstructing the political system was another matter. Everyone, including Suharto, agreed that the *negara hukum* would be restored, that the *trias politika* would be revived, and that the judiciary would again be independent. In fact, not only was the 1945 Constitution left intact, so were the repressive legal instruments that Guided Democracy had added to the colonial repertory, and none of the protections for citizens demanded by reformers were enacted into law.

In 1968, when the MPRS made Suharto president and approved the responsibilities of his cabinet, it failed to erect any significant institutional or legal impediment to the exercise of governmental authority. By this time reform interests in the MPRS constituted a minority opposition, to whom it was made clear that Suharto's government had no interest in accepting unnecessary limitations. Especially depressing for Yap and others, the human rights charter failed, a result partly of Islamic objections to a right of religious conversion, but also of the absence of regime support.[21] Moreover, MPRS Committee II, responsible for reviewing the legislation of Guided Democracy, sent on to Parliament recommendations whose import was unmistakable. Most telling, Presidential Decree 11/1963, the Anti-Subversion Decree that so outraged Yap and many other professional advocates, far from being rescinded, was re-promulgated as a law.[22] It was not an oversight; every regulation of use to the new regime was retained.[23] The only concession to reformers was the rescission of the laws of 1964 and 1965 on judicial organization that made the courts subject to presidential interference, but while this step seemed to promise much and set the stage for a major battle over institutional change, it turned out to mean very little.

It became obvious by 1968–69 that the army leadership intended the New Order regime to be its own. Political stability and policy direction were assured by the army's subordination of the bureaucracy (in which appropriately ranked officers were strategically placed) and by the security apparatus, which was fully controlled by the army and stood apart from the conventional state legal machinery but directed it at will. The combination was politically formidable.

The consequences of the army-bureaucracy alliance were clear in Yap's trial, in which prosecutors, police, and judges unreservedly asserted their prerogatives as civil servants against private interests. The corruption and abuse of power that had been rampant under Soekarno did not disappear under Suharto, but rather flourished, not only in the judicial system but also in the bureaucracy generally. Neither the few reforming officials, Soebekti and Hugeng among them, nor the anti-corruption committees, appointed from time to time, ever exercised any noticeable influence.

In these circumstances, Yap and his fellow reformers did not entirely give up hope for dramatic change, but they realized that it would require a longer struggle. By lowering his sights Yap was able to preserve a modicum of optimism, to which he may have been slightly more inclined than others. He was not unrealistic but he needed hope. Like a few others, especially older advocates for whom judicial reform was imperative, Yap was quick to welcome any meager evidence of change, though always with a demand for more. Lawyers were pleased by the so-called Cibogo agreements among judicial officials meant to speed up trials, reduce huge case backlogs, and render judicial process less corrupt and perilous. In 1968 Chief Justice Soebekti began to submit to the president reports on the legal situation, in which he openly admitted myriad serious problems in and out of the courts.[24] In January 1969 Yap praised the Jakarta *pengadilan negeri* and prosecution for publishing statistics on their work. Their action was, he wrote, a sign of new "openness" by conservative institutions, and it did not matter whether it was the result of public pressure, or concern to please superiors, or a new self-awareness. Openness and public disclosure, he insisted, were essential to democracy, and he promptly demonstrated their importance by asking pointed questions: what was the breakdown of charges in summary trials, what goods were seized, what kinds of fines were levied, what were the indictments against the 14,289 persons detained by the prosecution in Jakarta, could they contact legal counsel, were they fed well?[25] They were genuine questions, but they were also indictments, which the government did not answer.

Yap's slightly optimistic comments on the legal system in 1969 were sparked in part by somewhat hopeful signs in the first major constitutional battle to shape up in the New Order period.[26] It was not over a new code of criminal procedure—that battle was postponed for more than a decade—but rather over a new law on judicial organization (Law 14/1970) in which advocates, judges, and the government all had a substantial stake. Since the new law was meant to replace the law of 1964 that allowed direct presidential intervention in judicial process, it was momentous for the issue of judicial independence. But it also was symbolically relevant more broadly, and once the judicial independence issue was broached, the floodgates opened on other complex institutional and political questions.[27] Much that Yap wrote from 1968 through 1970 was, in one way or another, connected with the debates over the new law on judicial organization.

Oddly, these debates brought advocates and judges together in an awkward alliance that lasted only as long as it took to pass the law. For quite different reasons, both sought two fundamental goals: to extract the courts from the administrative jurisdiction of the Ministry of Justice, placing them fully under the control of the Mahkamah Agung (Supreme Court), and to grant the latter powers of judicial review. If the courts were completely independent of executive power and the Supreme Court had powers of judicial review, the judicial corps hoped to regain the sense of authority and significance that had been lost under Guided Democracy. Soebekti, Asikin Kusumaatmadja, and Sri Widojati on the Mahkamah Agung, and a few other judges scattered throughout the appellate and first instance courts, appreciated the grander constitutional implications of institutional autonomy and judicial review, but for most judges the first consideration was a rise in status.

For advocates the issues were far more complex and layered, involving constitutional, professional, and reform purposes that only those few senior judges shared. In a mandated judicial review and a judiciary freed from the Ministry of Justice, they saw hope for limiting executive power, but also for rendering judges more genuinely independent of bureaucratic interests. Indonesian judges have always considered themselves *pegawai negeri*, civil servants, which implies, formally independent or not, a primary obligation to the state and its leadership. Their identity, institutionally and psychologically, is within the state bureaucracy; this establishes a deep divide between judges, as public lawyers, and professional advocates, as private lawyers. Formal independence, advocates hoped, would not only stiffen judicial spines against executive prerogative but would distance judges from bureaucratic colleagues in the prosecution and police, and, by reconstituting the judicial system on new premises, allow advocates back into the judicial fellowship as equals.

The government, whose spokesman was Minister of Justice Umar Seno Adji, had no intention of allowing any such erosion of its authority. When the public debate over Law 14/1970 began, in the National Law Seminar at the end of December 1968, Justice Asikin Kusumaatmadja laid out the arguments for judicial independence, judicial review, and other reforms, while Seno Adji fended them off in a defense of traditional Continental civil law theory.[28] Seno Adji's stake was in preserving the integrity of the Ministry of Justice, which had lost control of the prosecution in 1960 and would have been all but emptied out by the exodus of the courts.[29] But it was also in defending the New Order regime from the desire of advocates, some judges, and liberal reformers to impose controls over political authority.

Beyond these issues, however, was an ideological divide of lasting significance. Both sides in the struggle over Law 14/1970 insisted that they were devoted to the *negara hukum*, but they meant quite different things by it. From the start, the Suharto regime had promised restoration of the separation of powers, judicial independence, and constitutionalism, but by the letter and without compromising the government's political freedom of action. Constitutionalism was only to be restored "as far as possible," not at the sacrifice of political stability or the effective authority of the regime. The regime's interpretation of the *negara hukum* left no doubt about state primacy. Amalgamating old Javanese political lore with colonial political traditions, the New Order government, like that of Guided Democracy before it, assumed responsibility for the ordering of society and, it followed, retained a lion's share of political privilege and prerogative, which it had adequate power to defend.

On the other side of the debate was an Indonesian variant of political and social liberalism. In its proponents' view, the *negara hukum* distinguished society from state and was emphatically oriented to containing state power by subjecting both it and society to legal process. Support for this view came more or less consistently from disparate social groups—professionals, university students, intellectuals, business circles not blessed with regime connections, religious and ethnic minorities for whom protective rights were imperative—all those, in short, who for reasons of interest or ideology sought to redefine state-society relations.[30] No single group had as much reason to support this view as professional lawyers. Peradin's commitment was unequivocal, and no one articulated it more devoutly than Yap. All the arguments for this view of the *negara hukum* are evident in his writings from 1966 on. Like others, he had doubts that Indonesian culture would allow it to be realized, but he saw no reasonable compromise on the only form of state—which he understood as a law-oriented democracy—that promised respect for human rights. It was not culture, however, but power that dictated the contents of Law 14/1970, allowing the Mahkamah Agung no review powers and leaving the courts administratively within the Ministry of Justice. The law's few concessions to legal reform interests—the right of accused persons to counsel after arrest, for example—while important in principle, remained unfulfilled by the ancillary legislation they required. The public prosecution had every interest in withholding any such advantage to the defense, and no other official instance saw good reason to grant it.

Advocates, including Yap, were disappointed, but by this time only the most naive could have been surprised. Whether out of professional interest or ideological commitment, many saw little choice but to persist in what they now accepted would be a protracted struggle. Senior advocates in command of Peradin continued their own reform initiatives. Peradin was transforming in the early New Order period, though nowhere near so impressively as the private legal profession at large. Government encouragement of economic growth and foreign and domestic private investment generated an immediate demand for legal advice and counsel. For the first time since the early Guided Democracy years, new lawyers opened offices, shooting off in professional directions that were unfamiliar to the senior advocates. As the profession was poorly organized and regulated, not all of these new lawyers bothered to register as advocates with the Ministry of Justice. Nor did all, or even most, join Peradin. Enough of them did, however, to multiply the original twelve founders by ten times, to 122, by July 1969.[31]

The influence of these advocates was disproportionate to their absurdly small number. They were, after all, highly educated professionals who, moreover, possessed unquestionable credentials as critics of Guided Democracy. In addition, many of the reform issues of the early New Order were peculiarly their issues: the *negara hukum*, constitutionalism, official abuse of power, human rights, judicial reform, prosecutorial reform, police reform, and more. From 1966 onward, Peradin was much in the news as a critic of Guided Democracy, as a provider of counsel in the Mahmillub trials, and as a prime source of legal criticism and reform proposals. Yap and Hasjim Mahdan represented Peradin in the Pengabdi Hukum. Tasrif took the organization into the regional LawAsia, and efforts were made to establish other international connections.

At its second congress in December 1966, Peradin installed a new board of senior advocates, with the Jakarta lawyer Soekardjo as chair and Lukman Wiriadinata as vice chair.[32] Tasrif joined the board in 1968 as secretary, injecting a large dose of enthusiasm, drive, and imagination. More than anyone else it was he who accomplished much of Peradin's early program and designed Peradin's new emblem, portraying the blind goddess of justice holding scales and surrounded by *Fiat Justitia Ruat Coelum*. New articles and an ethical code were drafted. Seeking influence, Peradin tried to inject its members into Parliament, the MPRS, and the Institute for the Development of National Law. It had no success: a few advocates did sit in those institutions, but not as representatives of Peradin. Nor, for technical reasons, was Peradin accepted into the regime organization Golkar, which some but not all members wanted to join. The board, Tasrif pressing, also sought government recognition of Peradin as the sole professional organization of advocates in the country. In this too it was unsuccessful; neither the Ministry of Justice nor any other instance in the official legal system was willing to allow the hypercritical organization such cachet.[33]

At its third congress in August 1969, Peradin elected a new board filled with committed reformers: Lukman as chair, Zainal Abidin as vice chair, Tasrif as secretary, Soekardjo as treasurer, and, as commissioners, Nani Razak-Muthalib, Amartiwi Saleh, Ani Abbas-Manoppo, Moh. Dalyono, and Yap.[34] This congress took an even more activist stance toward both professional upgrading and legal reform. It undertook to improve its own ethical code, establish refresher courses for advocates, and train new advocates, as well as collaborate with law faculties in an effort to improve advocates' command of "development law," particularly with respect to such issues as foreign investment, taxation, and banking. The board was also urged to establish relations with law organizations abroad in order to widen the knowledge of its members. The congress prepared a draft code of criminal procedure, having listened to extensive discussions by Yap and Nani Razak on the subject.[35] It also agreed to establish a journal, which the experienced and efficient Tasrif promptly brought out by the end of the year; the journal, called *Hukum dan Keadilan* (Law and Justice), lasted until 1981, which was as long as Tasrif was willing to run it.

Finally, and significantly, Peradin's membership passed two distinct resolutions, agreeing to explore legal aid in and out of the courts. Under the first of these, an ad hoc committee was formed to draft a law on legal aid to urge on the government and Parliament. Little ever came of it. The second resolution, however, which called on the board to initiate a pilot project in legal aid for the indigent, was much more successful. It marked an important break with tradition, which since colonial times provided only for *pro deo* (*pro bono*) counsel appointed by the courts in serious crimes. The idea for a legal aid program sponsored by the advocacy itself came not from the seniors but from Adnan Buyung Nasution, new to the profession and not yet even a member of Peradin. Ebullient, energetic, ambitious, outspoken, and mercurial, Buyung had been a ranking prosecutor, a protégé of the independent and able chief public prosecutor, Soeprapto, who had been ousted from office in 1959. As the chair of KASI (University Graduates' Action Front) in Jakarta, Buyung had courageously, maybe foolishly, confronted Suharto on the issue of corruption among army officers. Rather than accept a transfer to distant Medan, he resigned and set up a private law office, which quickly developed into a profitable concern with both local and foreign clients. An activist by nature, Buyung saw in legal aid, which he had surveyed on trips to Australia and the United States, a potential force for reform altogether independent of government resources and control. He needed a legitimate sponsor for the effort. Yap, whom Buyung had met after the Subandrio trial, encouraged him to bring a proposal to Peradin.

When Buyung's proposal came before the 1969 congress, it was by no means greeted with unanimous approval. It reached far beyond any narrow understanding of legal aid, to social education and training grounds for law students and young lawyers.[36] If Peradin's leaders, Yap especially, were enthusiastically oriented to an aggressive reform effort, many of its members were concerned primarily with professional issues, not least their incomes, at a time that had begun to look promising after years of drought. Some advocates feared that

FIG. 12.2 Adnan Buyung Nasution of the Legal Aid Institution (LBH) is seated (*second from left*) on the dais with Yap Thiam Hien (*left*) and Suardi Tasrif (*third from left*), at the sixth national Peradin Congress, Bandung, West Java, 1981. Courtesy of TEMPO

an active legal aid program would draw paying clients away from their offices. Lukman, Tasrif, Yap, and others fought hard on the issue and succeeded in winning approval for a "pilot program." Buyung, who joined Peradin, was put in charge of the effort and promptly recruited the enthusiastic Yap as a member of its board (fig. 12.2).

In 1971 the Legal Aid Institution (of Jakarta) (Lembaga Bantuan Hukum, LBH) opened the doors of a small office not far from the *pengadilan negeri* and Yap's own office.[37] Buyung's drive and imagination produced and sustained a remarkable institution whose ken extended far beyond legal aid for the poor to an activist program of legal reform so ambitious that few on the outside took it seriously. Had the government realized how effective the LBH would become, it might well have stopped the effort in its tracks or preempted it with a government program, which did emerge a few years later but too late to compete with the popularity of Buyung's organization. The LBH's staff initially consisted of about eight young lawyers, carefully interviewed by Arief Budiman and Yap, among others, and selected because of their commitment, intelligence, and skill. With a subsidy from the administration of Greater Jakarta, then led by the sympathetic governor Ali Sadikin, the new organization did indeed provide legal aid to the poor of Jakarta and nearby areas. But it did so in surprising ways, which included something like a class action suit against Ali Sadikin himself, on behalf of local farmers whose land had been condemned. The conflict was negotiated, with Sadikin conceding slightly increased payment for the land. It was nevertheless an eye-catching start for the LBH, which became very good at attracting attention.

In a short time, LBH evolved into a major source of legal criticism, enacting programs in legal education for key groups, and threatening publicity against abusive prosecutors and police. It also became a preferred source of legal defense in political cases, with Yap himself frequently serving on defense teams. Supported by an excellent press in Jakarta, the LBH was soon a major irritation for the government. The first major reform NGO in the country, its success, not least in surviving, made it a model for other NGOs that took form over the next two decades. For a few years angry army officers in the Javanese provinces enjoined it from expanding, but by the late 1970s it was allowed to establish branches elsewhere in the country.

Although the LBH staff was young, senior jurists consistently helped out. At the start a retired judge from Surabaya was recruited to advise in litigation. In later years Yap's friend Jamaluddin had an office there, and Zainal Abidin and others often showed up for seminars and discussions. Journalists and political sympathizers hung out in its offices. The LBH's active curatorial board brought together tough professionals and reformers, including over time such figures as the famous journalist Mochtar Lubis and Ponke Princen from the League for the Defense of Human Rights. Despite his early confrontation with the organization, Governor Ali Sadikin continued to subsidize it and years later, in retirement, joined its board.

Yap loved the LBH, on whose curatorial board he served until his death. It was exactly the kind of activist, courageous, consistent reform organization that appealed to his own sense of social responsibility. He and Buyung were as different as night from day, but also close. Although they argued fiercely at times, which was easy for both men, Buyung always addressed Yap respectfully as Pak (father), as did nearly everyone else. Yap provided a moderating, calming influence on Buyung and a steadying influence on the staff. Always a stickler for punctuality, consistency, and careful preparation, Yap constantly insisted that the younger lawyers, and Buyung himself, play by those rules. But he also encouraged and supported them. Never short of internal conflicts over issues of policy, the LBH required just the sort of even-handed intervention

Yap offered. Both of Buyung's young successors in the 1980s, T. Mulya Lubis and Abdul Hakim G. Nusantara, whom Yap helped to select and adopted as protégés, relied on him as troubleshooter and advisor.

By the time the LBH took shape, whatever reform optimism remained from the late 1960s had fizzled out. A different game had begun, in which critics of the New Order were as often as not on the sidelines. As if to prepare for the new situation, Yap left the Lie Hwee Yoe law firm with which he had been associated for almost twenty years and began practicing on his own.

Lie's firm had only three partners in the late 1960s, one of whom, Oei Tjoe Tat, was in prison. Tan Po Goan, in Thailand and Singapore since the outbreak of the PRRI rebellion in 1958, returned after the coup and asked to be reinstated. Yap voted yes, but Lie and Oei were opposed, presumably fearing that Tan's presence might hurt the firm. Yap thought this terribly unfair, for Tan had helped to build it. Tan opened his own office, but he eventually emigrated to Australia, where he died. Yap faced other problems in the firm. Following the Subandrio trial his name brought in more cases than ever before, but some resentment developed around his extra-office practice and notoriety. Lie Hwee Yoe had no objection, but his wife, who used to grumble about Yap's work in the Konstituante, now complained to acquaintances about his absences in Europe and his other outside engagements. Khing heard and deeply resented these criticisms. Another irritation involved a junior lawyer in the firm, a cousin of Lie Hwee Yoe, whom Yap thought dishonest and who, moreover, refused Yap's request to take notes at his trial. Given his relationship to Hwee Yoe, Yap did not want to make an issue of the young lawyer's behavior.

Above all, however, Yap himself had begun to feel restless because of his many other activities, his WCC and ICJ responsibilities in Europe, and the spread of his commitments to legal and political reform. Yap wanted room to do what he chose, to come and go independently, free of responsibilities to partners and concern about the firm. He and Khing mulled over the possibility of opening his own office. Finally, early in 1970 he asked a cousin of his, a smart young man who ran the Speed Building, not far from the Lie Hwee Yoe office on Jl. Gajah Mada and just around the corner from the *pengadilan negeri*, whether there might be some spare space. His cousin offered him a corner office in the back of the building, two floors up, with a small anteroom and an inner office adequate to Yap's needs. He moved in on 1 May 1970, but did not have to pay rent until September, and then not much. Finally independent, free to go to the office or not—though he was always a compulsive office-goer—and free to do whatever his vocation and conscience dictated, Yap liked his office in the Speed Building. He stayed there until just a couple of years before his death, when his small amount of work could no longer justify even that meager space.

Symbolically the move signified an important change of direction for Yap, or an ending and a new beginning. In the years 1966 through 1970, his public life had been transformed: from obscure lawyer to nationally known lion of the courts, from slightly apprehensive ethnic Chinese to confident Indonesian citizen, from provincial professional to international traveler in the service of the WCC and ICJ. His circle of political associates had grown enormously, his friends and intimates, too. Peradin had become the comfortable public home Baperki never was. By the start of the 1970s, Yap seems to have set his future agenda, essentially more of the same but better grounded in a realistic appreciation of odds and possibilities. If his priorities seemed to be human rights, improved criminal procedure, judicial reform, and political change, in that order, he in fact understood perfectly well that these issues were inextricably enmeshed with one another and could not be pursued one at a time. Focusing on legal process, he had to believe it was possible to win concessions here and there, but any success required constant demands, pressure, public education, and, along with this, cultural change. Yap seldom turned down a chance to speak on human rights and criminal procedure. His newspaper articles and speeches drummed constantly on the need to ask the police for arrest-warrants, to report abuse, to insist on one's rights.

In June 1969 he talked with Soe Hok Gie about an idea for establishing a new journal.[38] Yap thought the journal should teach readers about the law, especially criminal law, with articles about violations of human rights and reportage on court cases concerning poor people without adequate counsel. (Buyung's LBH proposal may have been on his mind as well.) And Yap wanted letters, signed letters with addresses, from readers who had tried official channels and found them wanting. He had some funds for the journal and wanted Hok Gie to find young people for the editorial staff. He thought he could persuade Hasjim Mahdan, who had newspaper experience, to help out.

Nothing came of the idea, which he also talked about with others, but it indicated a few dimensions of Yap's vision, one shared with other professional advocates and many young activists. Yap's democratic dream amounted not merely to institutional reform but to a kind of cultural revolution which would create a society utterly uncowed by authority, insistent on doing everything legally and properly, and willing to challenge any official who corrupted or abused legal process. To achieve such a society, he thought, people had to be instructed in how to use the law, how to understand and defend their rights. His own behavior he saw as an example for others to follow, which may help to explain why, even in small matters, he insisted on taking startling stands of principle. It was not a realistic dream, but in such matters "realists" did little or nothing. Yap was one of a small flock that did enough that was unrealistic to make a significant difference.

THIRTEEN

LAW AS POLITICS

A SIDETRIP TO DETENTION

THE essential patterns of New Order politics, conflict, and debate were established during the years from 1967 through early 1974.[1] Once it was clear that the army leadership had no intention of sharing authority with, or even paying much attention to, its political allies of the immediate post-coup period, the students, intellectuals, and Islamic groups that had hoped for a different political order were now compelled to rethink their positions. Although the officer corps was not completely united, it was incomparably more solid than the emerging opposition and had most of the advantages in any conflicts of interest or policy ideas.

The debates over Law 14/1970, on judicial organization, which seemed to many an arcane struggle among lawyers, epitomized the critical issues, demarcated political fissures, and highlighted the problems of reform. By rejecting judicial autonomy and judicial review, the New Order regime made it quite clear that it would not submit to institutional controls, and that the limits of its authority would be defined by the reach of its power. While insisting that it took constitutionalism seriously, the government also made clear that it would be a limited constitutionalism, given the priority of economic development and its precondition of political stability. Suharto stated flatly that the 1945 Constitution was not subject to amendment of any kind, as if saying that political change was out of the question.

The political structure that evolved rapidly after 1966 left in its wake much dismay among hopeful reformers. In only two or three years the optimism of the immediate post-coup period faded into the serious doubts of the late 1960s and early 1970s, and then grew into the disappointment, anger, and opposition that blew up in late 1971 and again, even more explosively, in early 1974. Yap's own case was emblematic of the transformation. Although his quick release from detention in 1966 had encouraged hope for change, the aura surrounding his trial and conviction in 1968 suggested that nothing in fact had changed, and, if anything, that conditions had grown worse. Reformers were stymied at just about every turn. After 1967 it became increasingly clear not only that army leaders would not step aside, but that they had no intention of sharing any power with the students, Islamic groups, and intellectuals who had helped to bring down Soekarno. Suharto as president, receptive and rather open at first, grew distant from and antagonistic to any but his own intelligence and military advisors.

Reformers might have imagined a new regime in which they and their demands for more democratic institutions, a *negara hukum*, and more egalitarian development programs would play a central part, but army leaders had a different plan in mind. While civilian reform groups reacted against the whole of Guided Democracy, army leaders assumed part of it as their own heritage. General Nasution's "Middle Way of the Army" translated into the Dwifungsi (Dual Function) of the armed forces (ABRI[2]): security on the one hand, political and social engagement on the other. The officer corps had never had much respect for the civilian leadership, which seemed to them self-serving, corrupt, indecisive, and ineffective. It was now the military's turn to run the country.

President Suharto and his advisors committed themselves to two related lines of public policy: economic growth and political stability. *Pembangunan* (development) became the New Order's watchword. International and domestic investment was encouraged, partly through the agency of the Inter-Governmental Group on Indonesia established after the coup by Indonesia's primary international creditors. The promise of investment, however, depended on stability, control over labor costs, and the assurance of protection for investors. In large measure, the structure of the regime was focused on this need for security and control. It left little room for accountability, which would have required some means of institutional or popular control over the regime itself.

Given the purposes of the New Order government and the outlook of army officers, effective institutional oversight of any sort was hard to conceive. If anything, Suharto and his staff were determined to achieve just the opposite by centralizing their control over the bureaucracy, making parts of it more efficient and installing active or retired army officers in key positions in all ministries, partly as patronage but also to impose uniform lines of command. The same was true of the regional bureaucracy, the *pamong praja*, and even of the villages, where hundreds of retired NCOs found jobs as *lurah*, village heads. As in the Guided Democracy years, the bureaucracy was compensated for its loyalty by enjoying relative freedom from outside supervision or challenge. This was an unstated key issue in Yap's case. In the judicial system judges, prosecutors, and police all understood what was required of them; only a few challenged the arrangement, and they—like Hugeng Imam Santoso, chief of police—were soon silenced or removed from office.

The same was true of Parliament (DPR) and the People's Consultative Assembly (MPR), which met every five years in order, basically, to approve government policy and to elect (in fact, re-elect) the president. Here the issues and the process were more complex, involving as they did the problem of political parties. Long hostile to the parties, army leaders may have preferred simply to abolish them but they could not do so. The promise of "constitutionality" and "democracy," symbolically important for local and international reasons, dictated a more delicate operation of emasculation.

Anticipating elections, in which army leaders at first had no great confidence, the corporatively conceived Golkar ("functional groups") was reorganized as a regime party, which would not actually be called a party, to serve as little more than an electoral vehicle. At the same time, the Special Operations group (Operasi Khusus, Opsus) run by General Ali Moertopo, a consummate operator who enjoyed Suharto's support, undertook to deal with the still-active political parties. The most important of them left more or less intact by Guided Democracy were the PNI, Parmusi (Partai Muslimin Indonesia, successor to the banned Masyumi), and the Nahdlatul Ulama (NU). The government intervened directly in the PNI and Parmusi, either dictating or manipulating their choice of leaders, rendering them capable of little more than occasional obstreperousness while remaining dependent on the regime. The NU, with a long history of willingness to negotiate its presence in any government, required no such direct pressure.[3]

In the elections of 1971 Golkar exceeded expectations, receiving over 62 percent of the vote, while the PNI was reduced to under 7 percent, Parmusi to 5 percent, and the NU remained relatively strong with more than 18 percent. Whatever doubts there might have been about Golkar's chances, the regime party in fact enjoyed all the advantages. The army supported it, as did the bureaucracy, once a bastion of the PNI whose control of the *pamong praja* had meant direct influence in village Indonesia. Now, however, the Ministry of the Interior, to which the whole of the *pamong praja* was responsible, was led by General Amir Machmud, who mobilized the same support for Golkar. Given the government's interest in maximizing its vote, widespread electoral abuse was hardly surprising.[4]

Following the elections, Parliament belonged to the New Order government no less than it had to Soekarno under Guided Democracy. Along with the substantial Golkar majority, one hundred appointive seats reserved for military representatives made the DPR's orientation unequivocally clear. For the next twenty-five years, the body initiated no legislation at all. Critics could approach Parliament and sometimes found sympathetic ears, but no hands, among its committees. With minimal influence over policy, the DPR was taken for granted. The same was true of the MPR, half of whose membership was drawn from the DPR; the rest were appointed from functional groups and the provinces.

Having won the elections, the government set about reformatting the party system. Contending that villages should be spared the dysfunctions of ideological conflict and that the rural population in fact formed a "floating mass," the government denied parties access to villages except during brief election campaigns, which meant that villagers were themselves denied access to party influence. Golkar was exempted from this restriction, for it was not officially a party, but in any case it retained contact with the villagers through the *pamong praja*. Then, in 1973, picking up on the process of party "simplification" left undone during the Guided Democracy years, when the number of active parties was reduced to eight, the government legislated the fusion of the remaining seven parties into two.[5] The Partai Persatuan Pembangunan (PPP, United Development Party) consisted of the former Islamic parties, including the NU and Parmusi; the Partai Demokrat Indonesia (PDI) was made up of the PNI, Protestants, Catholics, and IPKI. At best, both could cause ripples and each had future potential, but for more than twenty-five years neither had much impact on the political balance in the New Order.

By the early 1970s, not only had Soekarnoist support been dispersed, subjugated, or cowed, but also nearly all other political potential outside the army and bureaucracy had been marginalized, denied useful organizational channels. What remained was a highly centralized political system built on a military platform made explicit in the idea of Dwifungsi. Natural child of General Nasution's "Middle Way of the Army," Dwifungsi now flourished in ways General Nasution might not have imagined. (Shoved aside as chair of the MPR during the late 1960s when he showed signs of disapproval of Suharto's policies, the retired Nasution developed into a disgruntled critic of the Dwifungsi.) As the army had no pressing external defense requirements once Soekarno's war with Malaysia was resolved, the security half of Dwifungsi focused on domestic issues, which meant repression. In the Command for the Restoration of Security and Order (Kopkamtib), the regime had an army-based political security apparatus that paralleled and, at will, either dominated or superseded the civilian legal system, itself dependably responsive to political authority.

The New Order government had quickly become a powerhouse, from which all who were not directly useful or relevant were excluded, some gently and some not. Inside, rivalries, policy differences, and contests of status and advantage imposed the only limits on its power. Almost inevitably that power spiraled upwards to Jalan Cendana, the street where President Suharto lived and usually worked, except on state occasions and during formal meetings. The civilian activists who regretted Suharto's increasing reluctance to listen to them may have overlooked his natural home in the army and his long political experience. Neither naive nor politically incompetent nor shallow, as many thought him during the early years of the New Order, Suharto possessed considerable political skills. Like Soekarno before him, but with the substantial advantage of directly controlling usable power, the president quickly occupied the determining position within the political system. From this pinnacle, surrounded by civilian economists and military staff, Suharto was able to fashion the political decisions meant to assure stability and to choose among the policy alternatives for achieving economic "development." From there, too, he distributed compensation and perquisites to his supporters, never failing to reserve a substantial share for himself and the first family.

Until 1974, however, New Order politics retained some porousness that left room for ambivalence and uncertainty about the future and encouraged public debate and conflict. The daily press was relatively outspoken and critical, and policy issues were debated. University students were organized and engaged. There remained some question about whether it made sense to work for change from within or from without the regime. The government blandished rewards of status, cars, and commercial opportunities on those willing to join it in one capacity or another. Some KAMI and KASI members accepted offers of positions in the government or joined Golkar. Others who were tempted by the opportunity to make a difference joined and then later recanted.

Many of the activists who also wanted to make a difference were unconvinced by the promises of the New Order. Those most inclined initially to see a new age in the New Order, and most attentive to its development, had good reason to be disappointed, angry, and skeptical. The MPRS debates of 1967 and 1968, when it became clear that the army had no intention of giving way to civilian leadership, brought many KAMI and KASI activists up short. So did Ali Moertopo's Opsus operations, which recruited some of the activists but left others with a bad taste in their mouths. Students who had poured into the streets in 1965 and 1966 were not about to remain quietly on their campuses. Discussion groups in the universities, not least the University of Indonesia, insistently took up the economic, political, and social issues that spanned Guided Democracy and the early New Order. Their inclination was to be critical, the more so as no one in the government, except perhaps a few of their own professors now serving as economic advisors, seemed interested in their views.

Among those worried about the New Order's direction were Peradin lawyers whose disappointments were at once narrowly professional and broadly political. Only too aware of the chasm between public and private lawyers, senior advocates were not very surprised at the events surrounding Yap's case in 1968, but it was a miserable sign. The failure of deep reform in Law 14/1970 was far more serious, for it demonstrated the government's fundamental reluctance to give up any advantageous power and also revealed the reformers' lack of enough influence to compel change. Nor did their momentary alliance with judges alter the advocates' relationship with the courts, which remained hostile to private lawyers on all other grounds.

Yap shared these sentiments and experienced the same slide from optimism through concern to pessimism, but his outlook was mixed with touches of brightness. Having left the Lie law firm in 1970, and content with his new office in the Speed Building, his solitary practice gave him freedom to leave the country for meetings of the International Council of Jurists and the World Council of Churches and to pick and choose his cases as he wished without worrying about partners. He was active with the Legal Aid Institute (LBH), the Indonesian Council of Churches, and Peradin. His professional earnings had risen, for he was in demand as one of the best-known and most popular attorneys around; he appeared often in the press, was a member of Peradin's board, and was fully engaged with the growing profession's seniors. By 1970 his anxieties over his Chinese identity were behind him, a liberation that he found as edifying as his sudden rise to international recognition. Chinese issues rose again in the form of the problem of the *cukong* (Chinese financial backers of high-ranking army officers, including the president himself), but no one gathered Yap into that net, and he did not feel touched by it. Chinese questions

FIG. 13.1 Yap reading, n.d.
Courtesy of TEMPO

had become more complex since the coup, what with the rise of a new generation of *peranakan* engaged politically on both the right and the left. While Ali Moertopo's advisors included a strong Catholic contingent around Liem Bian Kie and Harry Tjan, the regime's critics included the courageous and respected Arief Budiman, the late Soe Hok Gie's older brother, and others.

If anything, Yap extended himself more and more actively into what he knew had to be a long-term struggle over law, constitutionalism, and human rights (fig. 13.1). He continued to work with Princen in the Institute for the Defense of Human Rights, into which he quietly injected his own limited funds when needed. And he was on call to give advice to the young LBH attorneys, whom he and Arief Budiman had examined and helped to recruit.

Yap wanted to set an example of how an informed citizen should behave in the face of official malfeasance, abuse, or corruption, much as he meant to set an example for professional advocates. Some who had to deal with his criticism, such as prosecutors, police officials, assorted figures in the bureaucracy, the Indonesian Council of Churches, and elsewhere, read it as arrogance. Khing often thought that in some ways his efforts went too far by way of self-denial or self-sacrifice or self-endangerment. For one thing, at a time when advocates or the new consulting lawyers who specialized in commercial law were demanding huge retainer fees of hundreds, even thousands, of dollars—often, in fact, in U.S. dollars—Yap and Lukman Wiriadinata stuck to old rules that limited their retainers to what rapidly became laughably minuscule amounts: in the vicinity of Rp. 50,000, for example, around US$50 in the early 1970s, and much less later. Even symbolically, as a model for others, this made little sense, but both men evidently felt ethically safer living according to standards established long ago in the colony and retained because so few lawyers paid them any attention. No one else who had a choice was impressed enough to follow their lead.

Once the battle over Law 14/1970 ended, leaving many unhappy senior advocates in its wake, Yap was convinced that they had to prepare for a long-term struggle challenging official abuse, educating the population about rights and legal process, and persuading the government that reform was essential. Idealistically more than naively, he had to believe that it was possible to appeal to justice, fairness, and rationality. In court he insisted on proper procedures, etiquette, and correctness, at a time when many other advocates had little compunction about marching into judges' chambers, using influence and money when they could, and winning the cases that Yap would probably have lost. A few advocate-reformers adjusted to the realities of the judicial system and used them to trap abusive or corrupt prosecutors. But Yap was incapable of this kind of strategy, which ultimately did little to change the institutional pathology. What he was capable of was rigorous insistence on the law and its procedures, which made him fearsome in court but which alienated judges, prosecutors, police officials, and others.

The cases he was inclined to accept left him little choice. His approach to issues of abuse of power and official malfeasance was aggressive, bulldog-like, and often imaginative. Along with other advocates, he learned to use the press to his advantage, which was easy for him because he made good copy in Jakarta newspapers. Press reports of trials were likely to headline Yap in defense, a courtesy seldom extended to other advocates. After his own trial in 1968, Yap took the case of one Andreas Akijuwen accused of falsifying cables ordering Garuda Indonesian Airways tickets. Prosecutor Thamsir Rachman had initially detained Andreas for thirty days and then, without obtaining court permission, for an additional thirty days. Instead of limiting himself to a defense, Yap promptly brought a civil action against Thamsir Rachman and the chief public prosecutor, Major General Sugih Arto, claiming a million rupiah in damages for their violation of Andreas's legal rights.[6] The action went nowhere, as Yap no doubt expected, but it had the effect, at least, of forcing the prosecution to deal with the issues in court and of making them public. Few advocates were willing to risk the animosity of prosecutors and judges in this way.

Defenders of the New Order insisted that reform would come, that critics needed to be patient and sympathetic, that the officer corps would become more sophisticated and less paranoid, and that the government would deal with corruption and institutional reform but needed time to establish stable economic growth. Critics replied that, if anything, corruption was increasing as military officers greedily joined in the take, that efforts to control the prosecution and police had not been serious, that economic policies were doing little to alleviate poverty, and that the regime remained too repressive. The same arguments were repeated endlessly over the next thirty years.

Much of the early, though limited, openness of the regime that had made some observers a bit optimistic arose from its own lack of political solidity, mainly within the army, which still harbored officers unattached to and unimpressed by Suharto. Contention existed between professional military officers and those who played special roles around the presidency: between, for example, some of the staff of Kopkamtib and Ali Moertopo's freewheeling Opsus (special operations) group and Suharto's personal assistants. Both sides had their own contacts among students and other reformers. Similarly, there were differences within the cabinet, between civilian members—including the influential economic planners, academic economists who kept in touch with their students—and the military officers and cabinet ministers bent on political careers who distanced themselves from "expert" outsiders.

These cleavages provided little leeway for reformers, and none of their demands for change received much attention. The political system had in fact become an updated and top-heavier version of Guided Democracy, with the PKI and Soekarno replaced by a powerful and politically efficient army. After the massacres of late 1965, scores of thousands of political prisoners were held in camps in Java and elsewhere, including the newly established prison-island of Buru. Only a few had any hope of a trial and of those none, given the precedents, had hope of acquittal. Nor was the legal process in any other way fundamentally improved.

What had become of the courts, prosecution, and police under Guided Democracy remained the same in the New Order, but in spades. Once it became clear that the regime did not intend to allow legal institutions any independence, corruption burgeoned and became the system's symbolic center of gravity. Promising to deal with the problem, the government set up a commission to do so, but nothing came of it. If anything, corruption spread ever wider. Economic growth seemed to spur a determined avidity among officials or anyone else blessed with regime connections.[7]

Critics saw in the flourishing corruption a blatantly unjust enrichment in utter disregard of the massive poverty of the country. Army officers established relationships with ethnic Chinese financial backers to whom they offered both connections and protection in exchange for substantial returns. The president himself established close ties with, among others, Liem Sioe Liong, a *totok* businessman whom Suharto had known since his days as commandant of the Diponegoro division in Central Java in the 1950s, and who soon became one of the richest men in the world through the favor of government-protected monopolies. Government-driven economic growth soon generated an increasingly wealthy elite, both military and civilian, with a powerful interest in maintaining the regime.

Frustration among the reformers graduated into outrage over many inextricably related issues. The fairer economic distribution that some had hoped for was reversed as the expanding economy, while relieving poverty at least for a time, dramatically enriched a small group willing to serve the purposes of the regime. The interests involved militated against any major political or bureaucratic reform that might have imposed limits on the New Order elite, which had the most to lose from any genuine reform. From the early 1970s on, in just about equal measure, the government pressed both an expanding economy and a concerted political and ideological effort to consolidate its authority.

Those who cast their lot with reform had to conclude not only that change would take much longer than they had hoped, but also that it would have to be pursued against the interests of the most powerful regime independent Indonesia had yet known. Although a more or less sympathetic audience for reform existed, reliable activists consisted basically (and most significantly) of a steady flow of engaged university students, some former KAMI and KASI members, independent intellectuals, journalists, and professionals, especially a limited number of professional advocates. With political inclinations ranging from left to center, these reformers often lacked agreement on much more than the need for change.

The Legal Aid Institute quickly established itself as a prime source of reform energy, initially in Jakarta but with outwardly rippling effects. Buyung Nasution's own endless supply of energy and courage, along with his mercurial impetuousness, drove the institute along at remarkable speed. Its ten or so young lawyers did not always satisfy Yap's standards, but Buyung, Yap himself, and one or two other senior lawyers helped to shape them. Buyung's law firm, established after he left the prosecution in 1967, was increasingly successful in its commercial practice with foreign and domestic investors, allowing him to spend as much time as he wished at the LBH. Running on Buyung's high-powered fuel, in no time the LBH filled the front pages of Jakarta's papers.

Buyung's vision of the LBH, which Yap also embraced, was not limited to helping indigent clients, though this was its basic function and kept its lawyers busy with hundreds of clients who began to crowd its office.[8] Had legal aid alone been its mission, it might have settled back into busy but relatively quiet and unremarkable routine. But Buyung turned the LBH into a noisy center of reform activity embracing a huge range of social-legal and political-legal actions. On the one hand, he himself, once a prosecutor, used the telephone to threaten abusive prosecutors with publicity and fed sympathetic newspapers a steady flow of information, complaints, and news on the legal front. On the other hand, the LBH sponsored seminars for young lawyers, journalists, and others to inform them about the law, social-legal problems, and the need for reform. Senior advocates, among others, spoke before these educational conferences. Yap was an active participant, explaining criminal procedure and its failings, exhorting participants to use their legal rights—to demand arrest warrants, for example—and not to allow the police or other officials to get away with violating them.

From the outset the LBH generated enough static to attract the attention of General Ali Moertopo, who personally came to its offices in late November 1971 to donate five motor scooters on behalf of Golkar, an organization to which Buyung no longer belonged.[9] Ali Moertopo may well have seen in Buyung a potentially useful figure who was worth cultivating. As a member of the LBH board, Yap attended the donation ceremony, which he regarded a bit skeptically, commenting on how many in the room maneuvered around Ali Moertopo.[10] Yap had affection for Buyung, making allowances for his occasional recklessness and egocentrism. He was pleased by Buyung's speech, which paid close attention to the problems of the poor and the need for political-legal reform.

More than anything else, what inclined Yap toward pessimism was a conflict that arose at the end of 1971. President Suharto's wife, Hartinah—known as Ibu (Mother) Tien—undertook to develop a large and expensive theme park, "Indonesia in Miniature," on the outskirts of Jakarta, meant to represent Indonesian diversity.[11] Under the aegis of the Suharto family's Our Hope Foundation (Yayasan Harapan Kita), the project required substantial land acquisition and capital. The president himself blessed the idea.

Once it became public, Project Mini almost immediately provoked severe criticism from intellectuals, university students, and others still committed to the reform hopes of the fading KAMI and KASI. It was a foolish waste of scarce resources, they insisted, a luxury and a silly priority in the face of Indonesian poverty. Rumors, many of them well founded, had it that the land acquisition deals for Project Mini involved huge profits, many of them accruing to Ibu Tien and her financial backers. Critics, prominent among them Arief Budiman, Ponke Princen, Buyung, and young faculty members and students at universities in Jakarta and elsewhere in the country, announced formation of the "Thrift Movement" (Gerakan Penghematan)—a movement, not an organization, and one uneasily including those inclined to spontaneity and others who preferred structure and planning.

The Thrift Movement generated headlines, street demonstrations, and conflict among its participants and also within the government, Kopkamtib, and the army. Public opinion was divided on the issue. The tensions grew in complexity as various interests played their particular cards and alliances shifted. In mid-December local thugs suddenly showed up to attack demonstrators in front of the office of the Yayasan Harapan Kita, sending several to the hospital.[12] This kind of proxy violence became a common pattern in the following years.

Government officials who sympathized with reform efforts were caught in the crossfire as reformers attacked a program that the officials felt obliged politically to support. The governor of Jakarta, Ali Sadikin, for instance—who was as much appreciated by reformers for his toughness, imagination, and goodwill as for his funding of the LBH, his support of the new weekly *Tempo* edited by the young poet and intellectual Goenawan Muhamad, and his establishment of the Jakarta arts center, the Taman Ismail Marzuki—was torn on the Mini issue. If he wanted to remain governor, as most reformers wished him to, he had little choice but to accede to the request of Suharto's wife (and, indirectly, of Suharto himself) for land and possibly for discretionary funds. Yap called the governor on the issue, embarrassing him and starting a minor feud between the two men.

Oddly, given the many sides to the Mini issue, a few observers held Yap particularly responsible for its progress. Although he naturally sympathized with the Thrift Movement, he was not very active in it. In an interview he gave to *Sinar Harapan* on Project Mini, he told the reporter how embarrassed and upset he felt for not having been courageous enough to state his position earlier. In this interview he raised the key questions of principle involved in

Project Mini that others either did not recognize or were reluctant to address openly. What right, asked Yap, does the president's wife have to talk with the governors at all? She is a private person, taking advantage of her husband's position; this, he charged, was a throwback to Guided Democracy. And under such pressure, he said, the governors cannot help but suppose that their response will affect their futures. Yap made clear that, despite this, ethically the governors should reject the pressure, which must have made men like Ali Sadikin uncomfortable.[13] Yap would enrage Ali Sadikin even more at the end of the year by demanding fifteen minutes of his time to discuss corruption in the capital administration.

One member of the University of Indonesia law faculty argued that Yap's interview helped to set off the demonstrations in the second half of December, for "his was the most to the point statement . . . and provided the demonstrators with sounder intellectual grounds on which to act."[14] Others involved referred to Yap's position with admiration. Whatever its effect on the Mini affair, however, in security circles the interview evidently called attention to Yap, whose apparent influence on students and perhaps other critics could make him a serious problem for the government. He confirmed the point in early 1974.

Project Mini came to a startling conclusion not long after it began. On 5 January 1972, in a speech at the opening of a hospital, President Suharto unleashed a thunderbolt, setting off repercussions of political anxiety and depression. Referring to Soekarno's transfer of authority to him for restoration of order on 11 March 1966 (Supersemar[15]), Suharto angrily warned that, if necessary, he would use force against critics of the Mini project. To many on both sides of the issue this reaction seemed altogether out of proportion. Even cabinet ministers were astonished. Until then there still seemed to be some good will, at least, between Suharto and his post-coup allies. Now rumors flew everywhere. Some thought Ali Moertopo had misinformed the president about the street demonstrations. Others, including civilian cabinet members, believed Suharto was genuinely incensed by the attacks on his wife, or may have thought it time to let everybody know who was in charge. Whatever the case, the speech was stunning. It had the effect not only of focusing attention on Suharto himself, but of emphasizing his reliance on the army and making clear to outsiders how little they actually knew about what went on inside the center of power, especially at Cendana.

Arief Budiman, Ponke Princen, and several others distressed by Suharto's speech met to draft a striking statement under the title "Januari Kelabu"

(Ashen January), protesting the threat and, in effect, commemorating the end of old hopes.[16] Soon afterwards, Arief and a dozen others were arrested as they sat outside a hotel where Mrs. Suharto was giving a briefing on Project Mini, from which the protesters had been barred. The LBH, called by Arief, protested to no effect. Princen and several others were also detained. Arief was released after several weeks and left later in the year to study for his PhD at Harvard University.

Project Mini went forward without further obstructions, but it left behind a changed political atmosphere. Between the New Order regime and its critics, whatever trust and confidence remained on either side was dissipated, and the gulf was filled with anger, suspicion, and force. One acute observer, formerly in the administration, described his feelings, as I recorded in my notes at the time:

> Frustrated and angry, he thought of writing a letter of protest to the newspapers against the president's speech but knew this would be the end for him and didn't. He too senses that Ali Moertopo may have been behind much of the trouble, but more so than others takes the wider view that . . . influential army officers are taking the Guided Democracy route. They are nothing but PNI people in new guise. . . . He sees here the same kind of cultural nationalism, narrow-minded ethno-centrism, inability to accept criticism, corruption, and political and cultural self-centeredness. For him the president's speech simply blasted open the door to all the evils in the regime, and he is full of profound misgivings about the future."[17]

Yap had similar misgivings, but his expectations had been more modest in the first place. Working from first principles, in politics as in law, he saw relatively little that was encouraging and too many bad signs. On the political detainee (*tahanan politik, tapol*) issue, not only had the army rounded up thousands, but there was too little public discussion of it, which he found outrageous. In the political sphere, the concentration of power was overwhelming, and much as he admired their will, he found the critics unorganized and no match at all for the military force behind the regime. Corruption grew, if anything, more flagrant, and anyone who had an opportunity seemed to be getting in on it.

The touch of optimism that Yap had felt during the early discussions of the judicial powers act evaporated when Law 14/1970 was promulgated. What had replaced optimism was not utter discouragement but an almost stoic acceptance that change required commitment over the long term. The outcome of the Project Mini debate deflated others into anxious inaction, but Yap, though not happy, saw hope (as he had in KAMI) in the Thrift Movement and the willingness of young people to put up a fight. He was sincere when he said, during the *Sinar Harapan* interview, that he was embarrassed for not having spoken out earlier. Thereafter, he continued to take cases that provided an opportunity to challenge abusive prosecutors and policemen, but he devoted more time to the LBH and to speaking and writing about the need for legal reform. In his mind, legal and political reform were two sides of the same coin. Yap's political effort thus consisted of little more than reasoned criticism and informing people of their rights, which constituted the accusatorial grounds for which he spent 1974 in detention.

The context was Malari (*Malapetaka Limabelas Januari*, the 15 January [1974] disaster), foreshadowed by the Project Mini brouhaha but far more complex, and with more maneuvering, more violence, and more far-reaching results. This disaster was a key turning point in New Order politics.[18]

The issues and influences involved in Malari were much the same as in 1971–72, but were heightened and even more critical: on the inside, there were tensions between the army's professional field officers and the political staff around the president, similar to the competition between Kopkamtib's director General Soemitro and Opsus's General Ali Moertopo; on the outside was the increasing anger among intellectuals and students over the growing presence of foreign, particularly Japanese, economic influence, over the poverty existing amid ever more ostentatious wealth, expanding corruption, and the closed-door influence on President Suharto of his chosen assistants. In addition, in 1973 the political temperature rose as Islamic groups mobilized against a new marriage bill, and anti-Chinese riots broke out in Bandung, for which the West Javanese Siliwangi division had to assume some responsibility. Moreover, in October news arrived from Thailand of the student uprising that had brought down the military regime there. Inevitably, this last item meant a good deal to students in Indonesia and something quite different to the officer corps.

In October 1973, following the election of a new chair for the University of Indonesia Student Council, Hariman Siregar, a politically astute medical student, protests began to pour out of the campus about corruption, abuse of power, economic problems, and the misuse of law and legal process. An active and relatively free press kept the issues alive. By the end of 1973, the government was on the defensive against an onslaught of criticism, at a time when it was preparing for the state visit on 14 January 1974 of Japan's prime minister,

Kakuei Tanaka. Student activists, Ali Moertopo, General Soemitro, and others were no doubt preparing for the same visit.

Exactly what happened and at whose instigation, from about 10 to 17 January, is subject to differing interpretations. Before Tanaka's arrival, students from several university campuses in Jakarta had been demonstrating for two or three days when new participants—pedicab drivers, residents of poor districts, and truckloads of unknown out-of-towners—suddenly appeared on the scene, to turn what started as a student protest into a riot of destruction. There was some consensus that Ali Moertopo was behind the riots, using the opportunity to undercut General Soemitro, who had taken a soft line with the students, and to provide the excuse for a crackdown on regime critics. If this is true, as seems likely, it was a brilliant maneuver, and what followed was disastrous for the reform movement, such as it was.

The results were a virtual coup. President Suharto's only concession was to promise to do something about his personal staff, which meant little more than eliminating their titles. On the other hand, General Soemitro was dismissed, and other military critics of the regime and its policies were sent abroad or otherwise removed from influence. Critical newspapers were permanently shut down. And hundreds of students, including many student leaders, Hariman Siregar among them, and other activists who had participated in the demonstrations, were rounded up. Among others who were regarded in some way as inciters or abettors were Buyung, Princen, and Yap.

Yap had been much involved in the protest activity, speaking to students and writing in the press. As tension on the campuses rose in January, the Christian University of Indonesia (UKI, Universitas Keristen Indonesia) was not exempt. Yap taught at the law school there and may actually have been ad interim dean at the time. UKI was also the site of considerable tension between Simatupang, as chair of the board, and a constantly critical Yap. Simatupang, who was not exceedingly popular among students, called on Yap to speak to the students and calm them down. Yap agreed, but what he said was probably not quite what Simatupang, who wanted no trouble with the government, had in mind. Yap told the students that as a Christian he understood that they might want to demonstrate, and he would join them in a just cause, but not if they were violent. He expressed these views not only to the students from UKI and other institutions, but also in his newspaper articles and interviews, where he insisted that applicable law did not forbid demonstrations; it was the students' right to protest, but they should avoid violence and not pick fights with the police. Violence did break out, however—rocks were thrown and Japanese flags burned, and more—but Yap did not participate. At the time, a Protestant minister accused him of doing so, but it was not true.[19]

When students were arrested, Yap and Princen, the bulk of the Human Rights Institute, rushed to police stations to do what they could. Buyung and the LBH were similarly active. Even had they done nothing at all, they might still have been detained, for, probably since the Mini issue, Kopkamtib and Bakin (the intelligence coordinating body) had marked each of them as potentially dangerous to public order.[20]

Yap had anticipated these events.[21] Princen and others began to be picked up on 15 January, and Yap promptly packed his own bag with essentials to keep in the car. On 21 January, 1974, while he and Khing were eating dinner, soldiers came with an arrest order signed by a military police general. Yap asked for a duplicate and in Dutch told Khing to get it photocopied. She rushed to a neighbor, who made several copies, one of which Khing hid in the car, for she knew that all copies would have to be surrendered to the authorities.[22] Having finished his dinner, which the soldiers politely allowed, Yap was taken to the military detention center (RTM) at Jl. Budi Utomo.

Yap did not know who exactly had ordered his arrest. One of those involved in the decision was General E. J. Kanter, then a military auditor seconded to the Kopkamtib.[23] Although they later became friendly, in 1974 Yap and Kanter, also a devout Protestant, had never met. In a private interview at Yap's home in mid-1986 Kanter explained what had happened. The following is from my notes:[24]

> On 15 January, when the demonstrations were in full swing, he had two meetings. One was in Kopkamtib, the other in Persahi [the national organization of public and private lawyers, of which Kanter had become chair a few years earlier]. The Kopkamtib meeting went very quickly. These were army people, after all, and they knew there was danger in the streets, and you couldn't wait long to act. Lives could be lost. . . . There was a long list of people who should be arrested. [This list obviously existed, then, before the 15th.]
>
> Several hundred people were picked up, among them Yap and Buyung. He [Kanter] specifically agreed with the arrest of . . . Yap and Buyung. Along with all the other officers in the Kopkamtib he agreed that these were dangerous men, capable of inciting people, particularly intellectuals. So he had no compunction at all about arresting Yap and taking him off the streets. . . . Now, the second meeting, with the Persahi executive

> board, was later, at one in the afternoon of the 15th. This meeting went on for hours, because of course they were all lawyers, a civilian organization, and everything had to be discussed, which they did at great length. [My impression from Kanter is that his primary objective was to persuade the other members of the Persahi board to endorse the decision Kopkamtib had already taken: that the situation was serious and many people had to be put away. He wanted a measure of legitimacy for what would happen, approval or no.] Many members of the board were there, but he could remember only Haryono Tjitrosubeno and Albert Hasibuan.[25] After a long discussion, the executive board went along, agreeing that what was happening in the streets was subversion [!].[26]
>
> At the time, he did not mention the Kopkamtib list, and certainly did not mention Yap and Buyung. But they did agree to define the action on the streets as subversion, and he said emphatically that he has a signed document to that effect. He never made the document public but has it.[27]
>
> When I asked again why Yap was thought to be dangerous, Kanter approached the problem from two directions: one the ideas Yap promoted and the other Yap's character. Human rights, said Kanter, were an imported idea unsuitable to Indonesian values and conditions, a common view in the officer corps, but his effort to argue the point was formulaic and murky. On Yap himself, however, he was direct. Yap had courage, was tough and principled, outspoken, and hard, and so lots of people looked up to him. As a Christian, Kanter said, he knew that Yap's perseverance came from Christian principles and values, and that this made him especially dangerous. And so, again, he had no compunction about putting him away. Other officers felt similarly, and were uncomfortable with Yap, because his principles and toughness made him dangerous, and he needed to be controlled.

So Yap was detained for nearly a year, until the day before Christmas of 1974. The detention was hard (though he didn't speak of it as miserable) but less threatening than his week's incarceration in 1966, an experience that was probably useful to him in 1974. Forbidden at first to have any reading material other than the Bible, he asked for copies of the Bible in German, English, and French, so that he could improve his languages. Later he was allowed other books, one of which was the Holocaust survivor Viktor Frankl's *Man's Search for Meaning*, on the psychology of survival in Germany's concentration camps, whose ideas he recommended to others at the RTM.[28]

For the first forty days, during which he was allowed no visitors or food from outside, he was interrogated every morning, mainly by a Lt. Colonel Kartono.[29] Aside from a threat or two—"we can be kind or we can be tough"—nothing untoward occurred. But his interrogators had little to ask, and Yap, given any opening at all, was inclined to turn questions into debates or lectures. The questioning was a fishing expedition that had little or nothing to do with Malari. His interrogators raised the issue of his membership in Baperki, insinuating a connection with the PKI and the coup, but that did not go far, in part because Yap evidently used the issue to ask why detainees charged with involvement in the coup were treated so badly.

The rest of the interrogations concerned the reasons for his detention. When Yap took the initiative to ask why he had been arrested, his questioners initially refused to tell him, but gradually it emerged that he had been detained because of his newspaper articles, his assistance to those arrested, and his advice to them on how to deal with the police. He had abetted the demonstrators. Yap turned the questions back: why weren't the demonstrators arrested at the time of their protest rather than a day or two afterwards, one by one. They were not arrested in the act. The police had misinterpreted the law.

Yap insisted on engaging his interrogators, arguing about this with Buyung (in a different RTM block), who refused to answer any questions at all, let alone debate with his interrogators. Furious, Buyung took a hard stand of principle, but Yap's principle was different: that one should try to bring the interrogators around to understand the evil in which they were complicit. Moreover, as he tried to convince Buyung, there was no point in fighting a hopelessly uneven battle; rather, one had to make the best of the situation. So Yap debated his examiners, partly perhaps as entertainment but also because he believed in rational discourse. "I did this quite consciously," he said, "for I didn't want to follow [the interrogators'] game plan. I wanted to show them that they had misused or abused this or that law."[30]

As General Kanter indicated, there was no plan to indict Yap; he was to be detained, not taken to court. Consequently, he could take the lead, forcing his questioners to engage with him, as they had no obvious objective and little else to do. And, of course, he chose the ground with which he was most familiar, the law, in which his advantage lay in knowledge and expertise but also in a powerful ideological commitment. Everybody in the interrogation room—Kartono, a prosecutor, and a police official—must have known that the sessions were both pro forma and sham. Confronted with Yap's discourse on law, his interrogators understood perfectly well that law did not determine the situation. But Yap's game was different; he too knew that law was irrelevant, but it could be used morally and ideologically as an argument that his questioners could not simply dismiss.

The argument concerned, for example, the law applicable to demonstrations, a subject that Yap was well equipped to debate, because before and during the protests leading up to 15 January he had studied all the relevant laws and regulations. And on legal grounds the government, as Yap showed his examiners, had no cause to forbid the demonstrations or to arrest its participants.

Yap's interrogators joked that every day they received lectures from him. At first, a *proces verbaal* was given him of each session, which he would correct. But after a time, the interrogators tired of their daily discussions and Yap's lectures and the verbal questioning came to a halt; instead they would say good morning and give Yap a sheet or two of written questions to which he was simply to write his replies.

For the rest, Yap made reasonably good use of his time in detention. He evidently understood well how important it was to keep himself occupied. He organized prayer sessions, complete with sermons, for Protestants, but others, Catholics and Muslims, occasionally came. He gave lectures about law, not only to his interrogators but also to anyone else among the prisoners interested enough to listen. And he met and talked with companion Malari detainees, particularly student leaders—Hariman Siregar, Marsillam Simandjuntak, Dorodjatun Kuntjorojakti, and Sjahrir, among others.[31] He became familiar with a large segment of the Jakarta reform crowd, filled with knowledgeable and capable young thinkers, and they with him.

There were only a hundred or so Malari detainees in the detention center, however. Most of the others in the mixed population there were G30S (coup) detainees, whose condition preoccupied Yap a good deal. The two groups were treated differently, much to the advantage of the Malari prisoners. For one thing, the food budget for the G30S group was less than that for the Malari group, but, in addition, Malari detainees were allowed to receive food delivered by their families. Yap once protested this situation to a military inspector who replied that it was not his province and he could do nothing about it. On another occasion, when a temporary commandant was in charge, Yap got news from the Council of Churches that it had sent 10,000 vitamin pills and 100 kilograms of sugar to the RTM. Unable to locate the delivery, Yap went to the commandant, who claimed that he had given the pills to the polyclinic. Yap checked, but they were not there. He angrily confronted the temporary commandant, who stood fast. Assuming that he had probably sold the pills and the sugar, Yap raised the issue with the regular commandant upon his return, but nothing was done about it.

It was not unusual for corrupt officers to take an entrepreneurial view of the detention camps spread around the country. Ponke Princen revealed as much in 1968 in his exposé of the brutal conditions of the camp in Purwodadi, Central Java, for which a number of officers resented him deeply. G30S detainees, after all, lacked resources and were fair game. Not only could their food be sold but so could anything else contributed by friends from outside. The prisoners themselves could be put to work outside the camps, essentially as slave labor, for the benefit of commanding officers, and evidently women were occasionally put to profitable use as prostitutes. In our discussion, Yap, who had persuaded Dutch contacts to send tools to the prison island of Buru, wondered whether they were used there to make money for some officers.[32]

Yap adapted to life in the RTM and made the most of it. He exercised, read, talked with other Malari and G30S detainees, and argued as much as he could with the administrators, not taking extraordinary chances but not submitting quietly either. Khing sent good food, and he could see her at visiting times, when they talked about the children, home, when he would get out, and what she should do. Yap ordered her not to beg for his release and, above all, not to thank anybody in the government for helping him. No one was owed gratitude for an injustice. Nor should Khing go out of her way to get Yap released. Buyung took the same position with his wife, Ria.

Khing by and large ignored Yap's rules. Nineteen seventy-four was in many ways a much harder year for her than for him, but alone she proved tougher than either he or she thought, and resilient, persistent, maybe surprising herself. There were difficult problems—the children, money—and she was determined, despite Yap's strictures, to do whatever she could to get him out. Her experience during his arrest in 1966 was useful, not least as a precedent for doing as she thought best, his views on the matter notwithstanding.

The first concern, as always, was for the children. As in 1966, when Yap defended Subandrio, and later too, the possibility that someone might take revenge on their children terrified Khing. Their son was now at school in Europe, and Khing tried to enroll their daughter, Hong Ay, in the international school in Singapore, but it did not work out then. Financially, they were not prepared for this kind of emergency, for their savings were relatively meager. Soon after Yap's arrest, Oyong Peng Koen, the publisher, sent an envelope of money, which Khing put away for use only if necessary. Others, too, came to help with funds. When Yap was released, all the money was returned. A nephew of Khing's suggested that she sell one of their two cars and rent out the other, which he would manage. She then invested most of their savings in a new car, a relatively inexpensive Toyota, for the family's use. Unfortunately, an ethnic Chinese friend informed her that, according to Chinese custom, if none of their children married, they should not use the car for family purposes. Whether or not this made sense, Thiam Hien was also against her using a new car while he was in detention. So she put the Toyota into the car-rental pool managed by her nephew, and it provided a monthly income that was more than adequate to the family's needs.

The more harrowing problem was to gain Yap's release. Khing was in touch with the Peradin leadership—Hasjim Mahdan, who had come to see her immediately after the arrest, and Tasrif and Lukman. They offered advice but told her they could offer little more, for if they did anything overt Peradin might suffer. She should, therefore, act on her own. Tasrif gave her the name of a general to contact—Kanter—who as it happened she had once met. Kanter's son, Chris, and Hong Gie were friends from school, and Khing had taken Hong Gie to the Kanter home to say goodbye before he left for the Netherlands.

Although using connections is common practice in Indonesia, and often necessary, Khing hated the idea of asking for help. She and Ria Nasution, Buyung's wife, talked about it. Khing urged Ria to come with her to see Kanter, but Ria demurred because Buyung had forbidden it. Khing replied that she wasn't asking Yap's permission any more and that she would go alone but report back to Ria. Her brother, a notary, took her to Kanter's house at 6:30 a.m., a time when he would be at home, but she felt unable to go in and left. With a mixture of fear and embarrassment, she returned the following morning, when Kanter received her.

To Khing's everlasting gratitude, Kanter and his wife proved sympathetic and helpful. The Protestant connection undoubtedly helped, as Kanter's later comments to me indicate. Knowing that nothing would happen to Yap, Kanter could give Khing his personal assurance that her husband would not be beaten or mistreated. He told her that he had placed Yap at the RTM, which was close enough for her to visit him, though she would not be able to do so until the interrogation was over. She asked whether she could come again, if necessary, and he said of course.

Kanter's help was essential, for Khing had no other powerful contacts and did not know her way around officialdom at all. Even his assistance, however, was not always effective. When Khing decided to take Hong Ay to Singapore, in March 1974, the immigration office refused to allow them an exit permit and took Khing's passport, indicating that she needed a letter from Kopkamtib. That afternoon she and her brother reported the matter to Kanter, who wrote a letter for her signed by himself and the new head of the Kopkamtib, Admiral Soedomo. When she gave the letter to the director of immigration, West Jakarta office, however he informed her that Bakin, the intelligence coordinating body, had forbidden her to leave. This may have been a ploy in search of a bribe, all the more so with an ethnic Chinese involved. Having no idea what Bakin was, Khing at first assumed that it was a person—Pak (Father) Bakin—but insisted on seeing him or it. The immigration official bridled and refused to return her letter. Remembering an old school friend of Yap's in the Central Immigration Office, Z. H. Pulungan, she got in touch with him. He called the West Jakarta office, insisting that there was no point in holding her passport as she had nothing to do with Malari. Khing got her passport back. Bakin evidently had nothing to do with the issue.

But there was no word on when Yap would be released. Khing stayed in touch with Kanter, asking constantly for news, until finally in October he told her it was time to meet with Admiral Soedomo—also a Protestant, as it happens—who had replaced the out-maneuvered General Soemitro as head of the Kopkamtib. Kanter apparently felt that others in the Kopkamtib had softened enough on Yap that a bit of pressure would help. After all, if Yap was dangerously principled and popular, he was also a solitary Chinese, and nowhere near as worrisome as a Buyung or the student leaders who could and might mobilize people on the streets. Kanter himself apparently argued the case for releasing Yap. In any event, he instructed Khing to write a letter to Soedomo, in her own words, asking when her husband would be released. Warning her not to tell Soedomo or anyone else that he had told her what to do, Kanter explained where to find Soedomo's office and how to approach him.

At 7 a.m. on 28 October, which she did not realize was a celebratory day—Youth Pledge Day, commemorating the national oath of 1928 to one country, one people, one language—Khing went to the Ministry of Defense. She walked to and fro looking for Soedomo's office, while pretending she knew her way around, until a young naval adjutant asked where she was going. She replied that she intended to see Pak Domo, as if she knew him. Eventually finding the office, she registered but wrote nothing in the book about the purpose of her visit. She waited until 9:15 a.m., when she was told that Soedomo had to leave for the Palace and that she should come back the following day. Khing refused, insisting that she would wait until he returned. An adjutant consulted Soedomo, who invited her in to the office. Bedecked in white and covered with medals, Soedomo informed Khing that Pak Yap would indeed be released. It was clear to them, he said, that Yap had no dangerous intentions. But he warned her that when she saw Thiam Hien, she should be wary of reporters.

> I asked whether Hien would be released before Christmas. Soedomo looked at me, as if I were too forward or pushy, but I knew he is a Christian and would understand. I suggested that perhaps I should see the *jaksa agung* [chief public prosecutor] myself. No, no, he said, he would do it himself. I thought, oh my, to depend on this one person, Soedomo himself. But he told me clearly not to contact the *jaksa agung*. Later I began to realize why this was necessary, so that I wouldn't be manipulated. If so, he would have to get involved again, holding off various others. I was so happy. Then I went to Hasjim's [Mahdan] home and told him that it had to be kept secret, and then to Simatupang to tell him.[33]

The release still took nearly another two months. As the decision had evidently been made, it is not clear why Yap was not simply let out of jail, though it may have been a concession to those, either among the Kopkamtib officers or in the prosecution, who wanted to hold him as long as possible.[34] Or it might have been a bureaucratic omission. Soedomo had agreed that Yap would be out by Christmas. Nervous and angry, on 21 or 22 December, Khing telephoned the office of Jaksa Agung Ali Said, who was now formally in charge of the Malari detainees. A deputy, Sobari, dismissively (and insultingly) refused to arrange an appointment with Ali Said. Instead he told her that none of the papers for her husband's release had been signed yet, and that she should get in touch on December 26. Then he hung up.

By this time Khing was less frightened of officialdom than angry and in no mood for compromise. Yap had to be released before Christmas. Furious, she called Kanter about her conversation with Sobari. On 23 December, Kanter brought the matter up with Soedomo, reminding him of his promise.[35] Soedomo said he would talk with the police and then Ali Said. The next day, December 24, Khing went to see Soedomo, who told her that Yap would be taken home that day.

> I promised you, he said, and, then, Merry Christmas. And I thought he cannot lie, he is an important person, we have to trust him. That evening [Christmas eve] I called Kanter again—how tired he must have been of all my calls—and it is evening, can he be brought home? Kanter said yes, if

> not tonight, maybe tomorrow. Certainly, he said. And so, stupidly, I went [with her brother and others] to the Hotel Borobudur to eat a Christmas Eve dinner.

And when she got home, Yap was there. At the RTM earlier he had given up hope that he would actually be released and, with others, watched a movie on television. Suddenly he was called out, and two prosecutors with a release order asked whether he wanted to leave that evening. Of course, he replied; if the order is for today, it must be today. They typed the order and took him home, where their servant, Suppiah, greeted him happily.

After celebrating Christmas with the family, on his own volition Yap returned the next day to the RTM. He had promised to return as part of a Church Council effort to help G30S prisoners who had not seen their families in years. Of five detainees, presumably all Christians, the DGI found the families of only three, of which one, a wife, refused to go, but the other two did. Yap and the son of Soekarno's old loyal minister, Leimena, led a service for the families. One of the detainees, a former police officer, who for some reason disliked Yap, begged his forgiveness and thanked him for bringing the man's son to see him.

Not more than an hour after returning home, Yap and Khing had a serious argument. He told her that he intended to represent the student leader, Sjahrir, who was thinking of suing the government over his arrest. Khing promptly blew up. All the pain of that year poured out, how hard it was for her while he was detained. If he took that case, Khing told him, she would leave. But, as she said to me in recalling the outburst, where would she go? In the face of her anger, Yap was quiet. In the end, the issue was moot, for no case was brought.

There were other cases, however. Within a week, Yap was back in his office. He had been released as much as six months before most other Malari detainees. Buyung remained at the RTM. Princen was still held at another facility. Several of the student leaders, a few of whom would be tried, were also held. Later, on their release, some decided that the time had come to withdraw from activism, not to fight a hopeless battle against the New Order government but to take care of their families and get on with their careers. Others remained politically active in various ways, but without much éclat. A year or year and a half in detention was sobering. Yap, Buyung, and Princen went back to acting much as they had before Malari. And Khing went back to containing herself.

EPILOGUE

A STEADY COURSE

Arlene O. Lev

DAN Lev's manuscript ends with the first weeks of 1975. He had planned to write another chapter, so chapter 13 is an accidental conclusion. However, it is a sufficient one. By 1975 Yap Thiam Hien had traveled through all the stations necessary to reach his destined professional and moral home. He had moved through wider and wider arenas, from the implicit Chinese ghetto in Kutaraja to elite schools in Java and university in Europe, to the Reformed Protestant Church and its educational organizations, to the battlefields of *peranakan* politics, to the practice of law and the collegial world of Peradin, to Indonesian activist politics, and to international religious and legal organizations. In each he had acquired and then refined conceptual and practical skills, and by 1975 he had what he needed for the roles he was to play for the rest of his life.

Perhaps even more propitious, he had gradually been freed from the wariness that is the demanding twin of minority identification; his ethnic Indonesian colleagues and friends seemed to take no notice of his *peranakan* identity, and he too could ignore it, at least most of the time. It is odd to say about a man whose adversarial anger continues legendary, but Yap now felt more at ease. He no longer thought of himself simply in terms of his *peranakan* origins. Study and travel in Europe had confirmed his view of himself as Indonesian. Reform Protestantism had early broadened his self-identification; he was a Protestant as well as a *peranakan*, a member of a worldwide community. But broader still, he came to believe, in the religious language he was comfortable with, that all people, irrespective of the accidents of religion, nation, "culture," or station, are children of God and created in his image. Now his community was without boundaries. "Identities" became at best partial truths.

Partial they may be, but to deny them is both traitorous and futile. He angrily condemned the *peranakan* assimilationists, and when the Suharto government pressured the Chinese to change their names to "Indonesian" names, he accused those who complied of self-serving cowardice. In his great 1959 Konstituante speech, he defended the right of Indonesian Chinese to participate as equal citizens; but at greater length, he argued for civil and political rights for all Indonesians and for their protection from unfettered authority through "the supremacy of Law over Power." Finally, he placed the effort to achieve those rights within "the struggle for fundamental human rights and freedom."[1] Before he cast his vote against accepting the 1945 Constitution, Yap cited his mandates to vote his conscience as coming from the second letter of Peter 1:4 and from the people. Principles born of sectarian religious commitment had met and married the idea of fundamental human rights. Throughout his career, alongside defending statutory and constitutional rights in court and in published articles, Yap argued for universally binding human rights and was impatient with popular arguments that culture, Indonesian or Asian values, or political realities nullified these rights.

After 1974, during the remaining fifteen years of his life, Yap continued on the course he had by then set, with no diminution of energy or anger against injustice. He was more and more identified as a fighter for human rights, especially abroad where an international human rights movement was gaining momentum. He traveled widely, responding to the many invitations from legal, religious, and human rights organizations. At home, he was seen as part of a developing movement advocating political reform and democracy—a movement that without objection accepted the human rights premise. As before, he wrote, published, and practiced law. His cases often were political, frequently in defense of statutory and human rights, and dependably caught the newspapers' and the public's attention. The Lembaga Bantuan Hukum continued to engage him; he was fully involved in "giving advice and encouragement, helping to resolve issues and to set new agenda, trouble shooting, and defending political cases in cooperation with LBH attorneys."[2]

In 1981, seven years after Malari, the hopes of Yap and the other reform-minded advocates of Peradin and LBH for a Law State were once again raised by the passage of a new Code of Criminal Procedure (KUHAP), which redefined "the balance in relationships between state agencies and private citizens."[3] KUHAP incorporated some of the procedural changes Yap had recommended in the mid-1960s: prosecutors lost and police gained responsibility for preliminary investigation, "to the chagrin of the prosecutors and the delight of the police";[4] the judge's pre-trial role was enhanced; and the accused gained new rights to immediate legal representation. However, "even the subdued satisfaction legal reformers drew from these statutory developments did not last . . . for they were accompanied by none of the political and institutional changes that might have made sense of them."[5]

The New Order government continued for the next seventeen years to subordinate, distort, and ignore the legal system, but, even more than government actions, corruption and incompetence crippled the administration of justice. The government, however, could not ignore the persistent opposition of the small group of human rights advocates and the activist lawyers in Peradin and LBH, and it took a number of threatening steps against them.[6] But a generation of lawyers had come into its own, one that embraced Yap's argument that the legal system could be a battleground in the struggle for political change. And this generation would be practicing law and advocating reforms longer than Suharto's reign would last. Yap, however, would not see the hoped-for political change. Dan Lev wrote about his sudden death in 1989:

> Just a month short of his seventy-sixth birthday, on Sunday, April 23 [1989], Yap Thiam Hien died at the start of the INGI conference in Belgium. The cause, apparently, was an aortic aneurysm. Until the end, as one would expect of him, he was working among colleagues concerned with issues of justice in Indonesia. The news that he was gone quickly spread grief and a numbing sense of loss. Pak Yap himself evidently had expected it soon and mentioned the premonition to friends. Over the last few years he had begun to complain lightly that his body had slowed and his concentration slipped, but he could not stop working. After the death last year of his close friend Lukman Wiriadinata, he wrote a will and began to take leave from those who did not want to hear of it.[7]

In 1992 the Yap Thiam Hien Award for achievement on behalf of human rights was established in his memory by the NGO Yayasan Pusat Studi Hak

Asasi (Human Rights Study Center Foundation); the honor has been conferred fifteen times since then.

The political change that Yap, Buyung, Ponke Prinzen, the young lawyers of the LBH, the senior lawyers of Peradin, and the other NGO activists had envisioned, argued for, and gone to prison for came in 1998. The New Order government fell, and a stream of legislation intended to erase its authoritarian legacy followed. In 1999 the Parliament began to pass a series of amendments to the 1945 Constitution that Yap had so bitterly opposed. The amendments dilute presidential dominance, strengthen the legislature, remove army representation from the legislature, and grant powers of judicial review to a new Constitutional Court, all measures that address weaknesses Yap had challenged.[8] In particular, Amendment 28 (A through J) is fundamentally a Bill of Rights and incorporates, in its entirety, the Universal Declaration of Human Rights that Yap so intensely admired. As one of the early acts of the new government, Parliament passed a law creating the National Human Rights Commission (Komnas HAM). The commission has continued to bring human rights abuses to the public's attention and is respected and effective. However, it has no executive powers, only the power to investigate and recommend, and execution is, of course, reined in by political realities.[9] In 2009 the commission courageously called for an investigation into the human rights abuses committed during the 1965 massacres and throughout the New Order period, still emotionally and politically charged issues.

In 2004 the courts were moved from the administrative purview of the Ministry of Justice to that of the Supreme Court. Yap had, in part, blamed the courts' indifference to defendants' rights on judges' identification with the interests of the executive; judges knew themselves to be, above all, *pegawai negeri*. After the restructuring, they became part of a separate branch of government and were insulated from direct executive control, if not from subtler political pressures. However, they were not insulated from the temptations of corruption with its equally corrosive effect on defendants' rights. And, as everywhere, judicial incompetence had not been, could not be, legislated away.

New NGOs began to monitor the legal system almost as soon as Suharto fell. Like the LBH legal aid lawyers, they were the citizens Yap had hoped for: "uncowed by authority, insistent on doing everything legally and properly, and willing to challenge any official who corrupted or abused legal process."[10] The young lawyers of the PSHK (Center for Indonesian Law and Policy Studies), LeIP (Institute for the Study of and Advocacy for an Independent Judiciary), and MaPPI (Indonesian Judicial Watch Society) criticize shortcomings, reveal abuses, bring class-action cases against the government, and recommend and lobby for concrete changes to laws, procedure, and court administration. Like Yap, they insist that legal system probity is a prerequisite of a just society.

Pak Yap's often disappointed optimism would have been energized by the New Order's collapse. After a lifetime in opposition, he probably would have been gratified by the new official support for changes he championed. He certainly would have condemned its limitations and demanded more and better. And, as always, he would have challenged power fearlessly.

Yap during court recess during the Sawito Kartowibowo case, 1977.
Courtesy of TEMPO

POSTSCRIPT

NEW ORDER LANDMARK CASES

Sebastiaan Pompe and Ibrahim Assegaf

DAN Lev planned a final chapter in which he would discuss important cases handled by Yap Thiam Hien in the years following 1974. He listed cases for inclusion, the files for many of which we found in the basement of Lev's Seattle home. The case files rarely include the briefs in which Yap set out his arguments and there is not a single court decision. (Lev himself had noted how incomplete the defense files were.) Yap rarely wrote his arguments in full, since it was not required by law at the time: "From the early days I would hardly ever write down my full defense argument. The prosecutor must write up his indictment, but the defense lawyer does not need to do so. So in developing our defense, we can simply follow the indictment point by point, present our case orally, without writing it down, and I often did it that way."[1]

Yap tended to develop his argument as part of the usual jousting in court rather than to prepare it beforehand: "I like the court sessions, how to question, cross examine, how to make objections, sustain, overrule, etc."[2] He found developing and writing briefs an arduous process and he went through many drafts: "I may be too perfectionist. That is why I spend too much time when I have to write something. When I write a brief, I tear up page after page. Even after the first concept is completed, ah, this word is bad and so on. Change again, change again. But then, when I hand it in [to the typist], I am satisfied.

But when it comes back, I ask, ah, why did I say it this way, why did I argue it along these lines? [laughs]"[3]

New Order conditions may have made it hard to approach things differently. Defense lawyers were generally given very little time to prepare for cases, as Dan recounts in chapter 10 on the Subandrio trial. As defendants were denied access to counsel until the last minute, their lawyers were forced to make up the defense on the fly.[4] Additionally, the increasingly ramshackle court process under the New Order, in which pretty much everything could be challenged, forced an improvisational litigation style. Yap explained:

> There is so much misuse or abuse of evidence. Sometimes the same pamphlet [or evidentiary instrument] is used for different cases. Or the same gun. I understand this, for I know that even though the labels state that something happened on such and such a date . . . it turns out that the person who did the seizing actually was absent, the commanding officer was not there, and so on. So you start to question [during the trial], and it turns out that the seizure documents do not have the signature of the accused, only of the platoon commander and this and that. So I argued that these cannot be accepted in evidence, and in fact some of the judges accept that argument.[5]

The case files tended to be most solid on demurrers and summations. Usually demurrers must be presented at the beginning of trial proceedings and summations at the end. Hence lawyers could prepare in advance for these parts of the criminal process, even in the constrained New Order settings. Yap pointed out that in the political trials of the 1960s and 1970s, he could use the same demurrers for different cases and so they became somewhat routine. Even so, the demurrers and summations are often missing, and, if present, they are never complete. Thus, the famous summation in the Asep Suryaman case, which we will discuss later, is clearly the final paragraph of a fuller text that has been lost. We tracked down the published text through a newspaper article in Lev's files (see Appendix). Yap recounted that in one case he taped his summation because he had submitted to the court only a summary of the major points, which he said was usual procedure.

As for the substance of the cases, we generally ran into a mass of little handwritten notes on the backs of envelopes or torn calendars, with parts of the text crossed out and additions inserted. These little scraps are vivid: the deep imprint of the pen and the heavy slant of handwriting suggest pressure and emotion. They evoke the "question, cross-examination, how to make objections, sustain, overrule," which Yap said he liked. It has not been possible to patch these notes together into the cogent argument that Yap presented in court. We cannot even be certain that these little notes were used during the trials. They may merely be ideas that Yap considered but discarded. Finally, we do not have court transcripts (which are not used in Indonesian courts), and in most cases the final verdict is missing.[6]

Next to the case files, we relied heavily on Lev's interview notes as a source of information. His notes are a unique historical document, a nearly unbroken record of Indonesian legal and institutional development, going back to the late 1950s.[7] They record how Indonesia's professional and political elites and civil society actors viewed developments and shaped them. The notes are the product of phenomenal discipline and intellectual focus, written by a uniquely knowledgeable, insightful, and well-informed observer. They testify to an extraordinary commitment.

Lev's interviews with Yap Thiam Hien started in November 1971, initially in the form of written notes and moving to tape transcripts in the 1980s. These were wide-ranging discussions on why Yap felt certain cases were important, on how he handled them, and on the trials' contexts (such as interaction with the judges, mistakes, rumors of government pressure, threats, the media circus, etc.). The notes are not comprehensive in a legal sense, for, indeed, the law was not what mattered most to Lev or Yap as it became increasingly irrelevant in the New Order.

Heavy on facts and context and light on legal technicality, what shines through the interviews is a good deal of humor and outrage, often closely entwined. Notably in the later tape transcripts, Dan throws in exclamations, expressions, gestures, bringing life to these documents even after many years: "Angry." "Yap feels very angry." "Laughing it off." "Something funny for we both laugh." "Wah, dia tidak senang. Much laughter." [8]

There are accounts of the two men in Jakarta or in the Lev home in Seattle: Yap, vocal, emotional, gesticulating, jumping out of his chair to make a point, and Dan asking, debating, exploring, making a joke here and there. The notes show a great friendship between two persons who in some ways were very similar, with energy and intelligence and capable of humor and fury in equal measure.[9]

Many of the cases on Dan's list are in the interview notes. Some are covered in considerable detail. Others are discussed in a more contextual way, such as the Latief case or the cases involving the suppression of religious rights in the

1970s and 1980s. The interviews also bring up cases that are not well known, such as the Pertamina cases. Dan was clearly thinking of including them, and we have done so.

Dan Lev would have been able to give the reader a sense of why these cases are important, drawing on his deep friendship with and knowledge of Yap and his equally profound understanding of institutional development in Indonesia in that critical period. In a real sense and unlike us, he lived through it. We cannot follow this route. Neither of us knew Yap Thiam Hien in person, nor do we pretend to match Dan's intimate knowledge of events. We still hope that our account brings out the things that Yap and Lev shared: their political principles and interests, their focus on basic rights, their appreciation of the 1950s and what these years meant for modern Indonesia, their deepening concern about political developments, and their enduring love for the country.

Nearly all cases discussed in this chapter are criminal cases that were actually litigated in court. As Dan has pointed out, Yap Thiam Hien was first and foremost a litigator and seemed less at ease in civil law. There are two exceptions: the Heru Gunawan case was a sting operation that arose in the context of a separate civil case Yap was litigating. It led to the criminal indictment of the judge for corruption, in which Yap had no role. Strictly speaking, therefore, the Heru Gunawan case is not a court case but a set of events that Yap set in motion.[10] Also, the first Pertamina case was a civil case settled out of court.

THE COUP CASES: BASIC HUMAN RIGHTS, DUE PROCESS

After the Subandrio trial (see chapter 10), which made Yap a public figure, he took up three more cases related to the 1965 coup—those of Asep Suryaman (1975), Oei Tjoe Tat (1978), and Colonel Latief (1978). All three came to trial a decade or more after 1965.

The dual sources on which we relied are quite different for the three cases. On Latief, the case file is very slim, largely because Yap came to the case when it was already well under way. Conversely, the files on Asep Suryaman and Oei Tjoe Tat are quite comprehensive. The interview notes on Asep Suryaman, however, are few and wide apart (and Yap's accounts show lapses of memory). On Oei Tjoe Tat, the notes are extensive, as Dan interviewed both Yap and Oei. In the Latief case, Yap's account is impressionistic, focusing on three aspects of the case: the brutality of Latief's arrest, Latief's subsequent courage, and how the courts handled the trial. The essence of Yap's approach was the way in which state authorities openly violated the whole gamut of basic rights and basic rules of Indonesian legal procedure. What interested him was what the state actually did, not what Latief may have done or may have known.

Our treatment of the cases reflects this variety. The Asep Suryaman and Oei Tjoe Tat cases are discussed in some technical detail. Our discussion aims to bring out Yap's "detailed, careful, analytical method."[11] Latief's account is presented here as an excerpted summary of the interview notes.

On the surface, the three cases seem quite different. For one thing, Suryaman was a communist, Oei a nationalist, and Latief a military officer. Suryaman was not a public figure prior to his arrest, but he attracted more and more attention after being detained. Oei, on the other hand, was a cabinet minister in the Soekarno administration right up to the day of his arrest in March 1966. Latief evolved from an unknown mid-level officer into one of the most intriguing and best-known characters for that critical period.

Yet when one considers how the state treated the three men, it is the similarities that stand out. All three were accused of subversion, overthrowing the legal government through violent means. They all categorically denied doing anything unlawful or intending to overthrow the government. In no case could the prosecution bring compelling evidence. In all cases, basic human rights and due process (as defined in Indonesian law at the time) were violated in the most blatant manner, as the state authorities themselves admitted. In none of the cases were warrants issued, nor did any court order detention; access to counsel (and family) was denied, and the accused were deprived of food and reading materials. All three men were subjected to treatment that qualified as physical or mental torture by Indonesian and international legal standards. There can be no debate that the ultimate court conviction in all three cases lacked proper statutory basis.

The backdrop to the cases was somewhat different from that of the dramatic Subandrio trial ten years earlier. The passage of time had reduced the sharp political tensions of that era. The political kangaroo courts (Mahmillub) had been disbanded. The cases in the 1970s were conducted before the regular courts (Colonel Latief's before a regular military court). While this change by no means guaranteed a fair trial, it did somewhat dilute the one-sidedness of the Mahmillub. The political pressure was still there, but it was not as frantic or heavy-handed as it was in the 1960s. If judges were so disposed, they had some leeway. The outcome of the cases was never in doubt, but rather than the crude contrasts of the 1960s trials, those of the 1970s were marked by shades of gray, degrees of injustice.

The Asep Suryaman Case (1975)

> The tapols are treated like the dregs of society, deprived of the most elementary rights enjoyed by all other citizens, like mere objects that can be moved from one place to another. . . . They have no power and no voice, no right to complain or protest against their interminable imprisonment, against torture, insult, hunger or disease. They have no power and no voice in the face of this abuse against their dignity and person. (Yap Thiam Hien, defense speech)

The Asep Suryaman case became famous because of Yap's glorious summation (see the Appendix).[12] Suryaman was accused of subversion, or the attempted overthrow of the legitimate government. There was no evidence of his involvement in the 30 September Movement, as the prosecutor himself acknowledged. The sole basis of his indictment was his membership in the Communist Party, which, as Yap pointed out repeatedly, was a perfectly legal party until October 1965. The statutory bases of the subversion charges were questionable. These consisted in part of regulations that had been invalidated by the government and in part on regulations that were applied retroactively in violation of basic legal precepts and Indonesian law. Condemned to death, Asep Suryaman remained on death row until he was released in 1999, at the age of seventy-two. In that period he was told at least twice by the authorities that he would be executed, and at one point in 1990, he was moved out of his cell for execution. Yet Yap's summation speech had drawn international attention to the case. Suryaman had been placed on watch lists of international human rights agencies. Both times the execution was called off because of external pressure. In that sense, even though Yap lost the case in court, he may have delivered in the end.

Yap's defense consisted of three elements: (1) to challenge the constitutionality of the case by establishing that the statutory basis of the indictment was flawed (simply put, as the law stood in 1965, his client had not done anything illegal); (2) to demonstrate that the basic rights of the suspect had been violated under Indonesian law, and according to principles of international law, in the method of arrest and the prolonged detention; and (3) to establish that Suryaman's treatment in detention violated basic principles of Indonesian and international law on the humane treatment and basic rights of prisoners. Finally, Yap brought these elements together in a famous summation, demonstrating how they constituted a comprehensive abrogation of the most fundamental precepts of the legal order. Asep Suryaman stood for many others whose rights were being similarly violated by a state that increasingly abused the legal process. Is this what our Republic set out to be? Yap asked.

FLAWED STATUTORY BASIS AND THE ISSUE OF CONSTITUTIONALITY

Yap recounted in his interviews that he had done a lot of work on the subversion regulations upon which all his cases were built. He knew the subject and had written an article on it (though it was never submitted for publication). This knowledge served him well in this case and in cases that followed. His argument was that there was no valid statutory basis for the indictment.

The indictment was based on a 1963 Presidential Decision (Penetapan Presiden nr. 11/1963), which was amended in 1969 (Law nr. 5/1969). Yap pointed out that, since the 1969 statute was enacted after the occurrence of events for which Asep Suryaman was indicted, the case directly violated the fundamental principle (acknowledged in Indonesian criminal law) that one can be held criminally liable only on the basis of a preceding law. Also, the 1963 Presidential Decision relied on a Decree of the MPR (People's Deliberative Assembly) that had been repealed. (Yap: "Consequently, the Presidential Decision lacks basis in law, as well as in morality or in philosophy.")

Yap adroitly quoted Indonesian state authorities in support of his arguments. Had not a senior Department of Justice official himself in a recent publication raised the conflict between the 1963 Decision and the 1969 Law, and argued that the 1963 Decree must be deemed "suspended"? Had not the prosecutor himself said that the pre-1965 Political Manifesto (Manipol), the ideological basis of the 1963 Presidential Decision, was designed by the top PKI official "and must be the work of the devil"? How could he then base his indictment on a decision based on that satanic ideology?

> Considering all the above, the issue is so self-evident that the defense really does not understand why this defunct Presidential Decision nr. 11/1963 is still used. It is a theater piece, as funny as Chekhov's One Man. We must give credit to the Prosecutor for having entertained us with this massive distortion of logic. (Yap Thiam Hien, demurrer)

He challenged the authorities in a subtle game that exposed the political inconsistencies of the regime and the intellectual dishonesty of its officials. In upholding the integrity of the law, he also challenged a professional culture that increasingly attached greater importance to persons and power than to law and institutions.

FLAWED INDICTMENT AND THE ISSUE OF DUE PROCESS AND BASIC HUMAN RIGHTS

Yap then challenged the legality of the arrest and subsequent detention as violating basic human rights and due process. Asep Suryaman had been arrested twice: the first time in March 1966, when he was detained until November of that year; and then he was rearrested in October 1971 and detained until brought to trial in 1975. In none of the arrests or subsequent detentions did the prosecution honor elementary principles of Indonesian criminal law on warrants or court-approved detention orders. There was no warrant or court order. Yap's argument that the prosecution had blatantly violated criminal procedure was uncontested: the prosecutor acknowledged that there had been no warrants or court orders for Suryaman's arrest and detention. Yet the court did not dismiss the case on this ground, as it should have. The failure of the court to serve as effective guardian of the rule of law and basic rights infuriated Yap.

TREATMENT OF PRISONERS: BASIC HUMAN RIGHTS AND CIVIL RIGHTS

The next step for Yap was to consider the way his client had been treated while in detention. He brought up two issues in this regard.

The first was basic human rights. Yap stated before the court that Suryaman was not permitted to meet his lawyer or his family, that he had had no access to newspapers or books (other than religious materials), did not get sufficient food or medical attention, and, last but not least, had been tortured. These were all major issues and caused considerable discomfort all around.

Yap's other angle on basic human and civil rights attracted even more attention. For here he did not raise the individual mistreatment of a human being, but rather focused on how this abuse percolated through to the prisoner's broader environment and legal status. It is in this context that Yap launched the concept of "civil death," in which he referred to a condition in which citizens are deprived of their ability to act as legal persons, a condition that affected everyone implicated in the 30 September Movement even after their release from detention.

Civil death was an innovative concept. Yap argued that the political prisoners, who had been arrested and were being detained without any legal title, for unknown duration, were being deprived of their most basic right to be recognized as human beings. Instead, they were regarded and treated as chattel, devoid of any legal right either active or passive, to be disposed of in completely arbitrary ways. Even after being released, they could not exercise even basic rights like other citizens. Broad sectors of employment were closed to them, including education, journalism, the law, local administration, and the electricity and telecommunications industries. They could not purchase real property. Yap raised the simple issue of moving house. This required approval from the Kepala Rukun Tetangga (neighborhood administrator), the Kepala Rukun Warga (ward administrator), the Lurah (sub-district administrator), the local head of police, the local military boss, and the district head. Ex-detainees also needed a letter testifying to their good conduct from the local district head.

And this civil death extended to their families.

SUMMATION: THE EROSION OF THE RULE OF LAW

Yap's stirring summation is the culmination of the Asep Suryaman case.[13] Its vocabulary is not dry legal jargon and it does not aim to make a legal argument. Instead, Yap uses words that arouse emotions: "compassion," "concern," "anxiety," "outrage." The summation was a way to break free from obscurantist technical legal argument and the closed world of court insiders and reach out to society at large. It aimed to tell society that the case of Asep Suryaman involved basic principles that touched each and all. Suryaman was a citizen of the Republic, whose basic rights as guaranteed under Indonesian law were being systematically violated. (A translation of this speech is included in full in the Appendix.)

FRAYED AFTERMATH

During the Asep Suryaman case, any rapport that might have existed between Yap and the prosecution frayed. Yap had a way of heaping disapprobation on the head of the prosecutor, who found this hard to swallow. In many of the cases that followed, Yap would often find himself in personal tiffs with prosecutors. Rather than attempt to paper over the cracks, Yap seemed to relish the spats, saying things that made them worse. In the Suryaman case he all but described the prosecutor as a pedantic and incompetent ass:

> In the hearing of 16 July 1975, the Honorable Prosecutor called for the Defense to respect the session, because the Public Prosecutor they were facing was a representative of the State, whilst the Defense only defended a private citizen. Let me first establish that the defendant Asep Suryaman is [to be considered] entirely innocent before a final court decision

establishes his guilt. Therefore, the Public Prosecutor must uphold proper standards [of conduct] with an Indonesian citizen whose guilt is not established.

But if we follow the logic that the Prosecutor represents the state, is not the state representative also a public servant who must honor the rights of citizens? The conduct of the Prosecutor, who refused to assist us in finding documents in support of our case, who failed to give us a single copy of his indictment, is clearly far, very far, removed from the idea of a public servant.[14]

Yap's personalized approach made both the law enforcement agencies and the defendants queasy about either facing or using him as a lawyer. The courts and the prosecution would put pressure on suspects not to hire Yap.[15]

The Oei Tjoe Tat Case (1976)

> Of course I am defending Oei Tjoe Tat, but above all I must defend truth, justice and the law. (Yap Thiam Hien, quoted by Oei Tjoe Tat)[16]

Oei Tjoe Tat, a senior politician and cabinet minister, was the complete opposite of the relatively unknown Asep Suryaman. In both of their trials, the prosecution had a hard time identifying where they had violated the law. Oei's prominent position with the previous regime and his unwavering loyalty to Soekarno made it almost impossible to bring charges of subversion against him, for whom would he be subverting, if not himself? His principal fault seems to have been getting on the wrong side of Suharto.[17]

Oei Tjoe Tat was arrested in March 1966. After an initial period of house arrest "for his own safety,"[18] he was detained for nearly eleven years before being brought to trial in 1976.[19] During this detention, Oei was interrogated and put under pressure to sign a statement to the effect that during cabinet meetings prior to 1965 Soekarno had discussed an impending coup. This would show Soekarno had stage-managed or was complicit in the 30 September Movement. Oei refused.

> [The prosecutor] would always lay his pistol on the table and use much psychological pressure. For example, he would show photos of Oei['s] wife and children, and ask whether he knew them, did he want to see them

again, they were having much difficulty and so on. All he had to do to see them again was to sign the *proces-verbaal* that was already drawn up.[20]

At one point there was a clear implication that he would be secretly shot unless he complied.

> I think in the 1970s Oei was told that he should pack his bags. This was known to mean that one would be taken out never to return. That is, shot secretly. When [detainees were] ordered to pack, it was commonly understood in the detention center that this meant death. He was of course frightened [but was] then told that to avoid this he needed only to sign the statement which implicated Soekarno.[21]

Oei recalled his mind racing with great clarity, as he realized that, even if he were to sign, nothing would guarantee his safety. And if not, well at least he would die with some sense of dignity, and doesn't one die at one point in time anyway? So he refused. His interrogator was livid and told him to pack up. Oei did so and went to the front office to wait for what seemed the inevitable. He ran into the camp commander, called Sutomo. When Sutomo asked what was going on, Oei told him. Sutomo said "What nonsense, nothing will happen, just go back to your room." As it turned out, the commander was a decent fellow and a friendship sprang up between the two men. Even so, Oei would not give in.

It was clear that the Attorney General's Office (AGO) was struggling to bring a case. There were rumors that Oei would be released in 1973, but conditions changed with the Malari riots in January 1974, following which the AGO announced that Oei Tjoe Tat would be charged after all. The charge, inevitably, was subversion. The case progressed at a snail's pace. In July 1974 the AGO issued a statement that the case was under preparation and in September announced that the case would be postponed indefinitely because it had proved impossible to complete the file. It is reported that the court refused to hear the case in 1974 on grounds that there was absolutely no case to answer. Still, the AGO persisted, the principal reason being, it is said, that Suharto himself expressly instructed it to do so. So Oei Tjoe Tat, status unclear, languished in prison until finally after two more years the AGO mustered all its energy (and fantasy, no doubt) and brought the case. Surely, as the International Commission of Jurists commented on the case, "any testimony first produced 8 years after his arrest must be virtually valueless."[22]

The AGO was in a difficult position. The president wanted a conviction, but even by the much-diluted New Order legal standards, there was little to go on. All senior prosecutors begged off and the AGO carted in an inexperienced junior prosecutor from Bogor to head the prosecution. The poor fellow was very reluctant. He did not ask any pressing questions, indeed hardly asked any direct questions at all. The presiding judge was manifestly well disposed to Oei.[23] And so the case seemed to stumble to a positive end after all, in which Oei would be condemned to an eleven-year prison term, identical to the period of his detention, which would allow him to walk out of court a free man. On decision day, the court was crowded with the press and TV cameras ready to record the event. But things turned out differently.

Yap Thiam Hien became involved as counsel to Oei Tjoe Tat almost despite Oei, who was worried about the way Yap made "an issue of principle out of every molehill" and lost cases as a result.[24] Yap's involvement was in part decided by economics. Yap was willing to argue the case for free, as were his two associates, Albert Hasibuan and Jamaluddin. No one else of Yap's prominence would agree to this arrangement and Oei, whose family had survived for more than a decade by selling off their jewelry, had no money. There were, of course, the fixed trial costs, such as paper, typewriter, postage, copies, court fees, etc. Yap had developed a method to cover these. It amounted to holding up colleagues and friends. He would confront them, point out the great importance of the case, and then ask for a contribution. He would then add that unless they paid up, he would no longer talk to them. Oei would later recount this with a mixture of distaste and admiration. Yet, if lacking in subtlety, Yap's tactics were also effective. The funds for the trial costs were there in no time.[25]

Oei Tjoe Tat was charged on the basis of the Anti-Subversion Law: "Subversion of lawful authority, spreading of hatred, and causing large-scale conflict and unrest in the community etc." The initial part of the case was taken up by the demurrers. Much as in the Asep Suryaman case, Yap sought to have the case thrown out because of basic flaws—violation of the basic rights of the defendant and the principles of due process, including the failure to present proper court orders approving detention.[26] Furthermore, indicating the time constraints in Indonesian criminal procedure (allowing for only a thirty-day detention of a suspect, which needed to be approved by a court of law), he challenged the legality of holding the defendant for more than a decade, without court approval. He also referred to the basic principle of speedy justice laid down in the Indonesian basic law on the judiciary (Article 8 Law nr. 14/1970), as well as in Article 11 of the Universal Declaration of Human Rights and Article 14 of the International Covenant of Human Rights, which he quoted at length.

As with Asep Suryaman, Yap challenged the validity of the anti-subversion regulations, notably the way in which the prosecution applied them retroactively. Referring to Article 1(1) of the Indonesian Criminal Code, he argued that this principle had been upheld even by the colonial government and courts, so how could it be disregarded by this nation now that the nation was free and independent? He then proceeded to show that this was an internationally recognized principle, referring to Article 11(2) of the Universal Declaration of Human Rights.

Yap had to contend with government manipulation in the case. Witnesses were put under pressure: Yap found that a defense witness had been withdrawn overnight ("due to high blood pressure") after being subjected to the attentions of the military police. Technical flaws were ignored: when Yap challenged a witness's statement because the man was a Buddhist but the oath had been taken according to Islam, the argument was dismissed. Clearly pressure was also being exerted outside the court: initial press reports exposed the fact that the prosecution was fumbling and that Yap was running the indictment through the grinder. But after a couple of days, the press was instructed to uphold the basic principles of Pancasila, and it suddenly became either compliant or silent. On the written documents, less open to manipulation, Yap was on more solid ground. He disclosed how evidence had been tampered with and brought out the fact that one key witness never knew he had signed an affidavit advanced by the prosecution. Yap also knew that the initial interrogation report concluded that Oei Tjoe Tat had to be released, but the document had gone missing from the file.

The principal challenge for the prosecution was to establish that someone who had been a loyal senior minister in the previous administration had also plotted its overthrow. Grasping at straws, the AGO had come up with the following logic. Oei Tjoe Tat, besides being a minister, also was a senior member of the Partindo party. On October 3, 1965, Suharto gave an address in which he strongly condemned the 30 September Movement. Shortly thereafter (between October 1 and 4, according to the indictment), Partindo issued a statement saying that the G30S was an internal matter of the armed forces (which also was the position of the Communist Party). "This constitutes legal evidence of a subversive act," argued the AGO, who further claimed that the Partindo statement had received wide publicity that had caused major unrest in Central and East Java and led to the killing of many Partindo members. So here were the core elements of the subversion law: overthrowing legal authority and causing unrest.

Yap challenged all the building blocks of the argument in detailed and methodical fashion (Lev notes):

Partindo statement. Yap showed that while the Partindo meeting leading up to the October statement had been conducted at Oei's house, Oei had not attended. He did, however, leave express instructions that if Partindo were to issue a statement, it should reflect full loyalty to President Soekarno and support him in resolving the current situation. Oei had disagreed with the statement that was issued and requested that it be amended. This amendment was in fact issued on 8 November.[27]

Subversion. Yap asked rhetorically, How could Oei be a subversive? Who constituted the legal government in the critical period of 1–4 November 1965? Surely the prosecution could not seriously contend that a radio speech by Suharto constituted executive authority? Surely authority still rested with President Soekarno? In view of all this, how could Oei have been subversive? After all, was he not a minister? Just to underscore the issue of loyalty, Yap submitted in evidence a letter which Oei had written to President Soekarno and Vice Prime Minister Leimena during that precise period, in which he pledged his complete loyalty to them. Yap also pointed out that in November 1965, Oei was appointed by Soekarno to a range of sensitive positions, hardly conduct one would expect from a president who suspected his minister's loyalty.[28]

Social unrest. The case of the prosecution depended entirely on the general public being informed of the Partindo statement, which then caused unrest. Yap first established that the press had gone to ground by November 1965 and had not published either the earlier Partindo statement or Oei's subsequent amendment. The assertion of the prosecutor that the statement had received wide publicity was simply wrong. On the unrest, Yap challenged the prosecution by asking whether it could present witnesses or produce other evidence showing that Partindo members were killed because of the Partindo statement. The prosecution could not do so.

One by one Yap ticked off, as factually incorrect or just plain lies, the assertions of the prosecution. When the prosecution argued that Oei Tjoe Tat had been in Surabaya in September 1965 to foment unrest, Yap demonstrated that his client had not been to Surabaya once that year. When the prosecution argued that Oei had been secretly informed on 25 September 1965 that some generals were planning a coup (and hence his failure to prevent that attempt showed complicity), Yap simply pointed out: "Look at his passport. He was out of the country at the time and only returned on 28 September 1965." When the prosecution argued that Oei Tjoe Tat had given a financial hand-out to demonstrators who torched the U.S. Information Office building in 1965, Yap showed that, in fact, the incident had happened in 1964, that it was official policy to support the action, that the disbursement was valid, and that all these actions had been supported by the Armed Forces at the time. No subversion.

Yap was upset by the way the AGO had created a case out of thin air, and had lied and dissimulated. Obviously, the injustice of what had happened to Oei Tjoe Tat was personally troubling to him. But Yap was no less alarmed by the way in which the entire case had been concocted by the authorities to secure a desirable political outcome, with fabricated evidence that violated elementary principles of due process and human rights as recognized even in Indonesian law. Like the Asep Suryaman trial, this case was not just about an individual, it was also about the rule of law. And in the Oei Tjoe Tat case, the fabrication of false evidence and twisted logic was perhaps even more obvious. Yap would not let it pass. He dealt with each and every fabrication advanced by the AGO and expounded the principles in Indonesian and international law. He also went on to speak at length about what actually constituted facts, legally relevant facts, causal effects, how these were to be established, and what were suppositions or fabrications.

Yap's file notes here are very detailed, as, like a surgeon, he dissects issues, facts, and logic with precision and sets down the basic rules involved in criminal prosecutions:

> The acts set forth in the indictment:
> Did they actually happen?
> Are they rumors, historical constructs, fiction?
> Are they legally relevant?
> Is there a relationship between the acts and the results of which the suspect is accused?
> Is there a connection between the defendant and the "facts and circumstances"?

> Can the "facts and circumstances" be proven? Did they have the effect the prosecution asserts?
>
> How does the prosecutor propose to prove his asserted "facts and conditions"? With witness statements, or just because he says it?
>
> (Yap Thiam Hien, handwritten notes in his case file, 1978)

And so, with the prosecution a shambles and everyone pretty well shaken up, the case was coming to a close. Everyone expected Oei Tjoe Tat to be set free, and the press had turned up in force. But then the judge unexpectedly deferred the decision. Oei himself claimed that the judge, who had made up his mind to release him, received a last-minute instruction apparently originating from Suharto that this would not do.[29] Some shabby negotiating went on behind the scenes, with the president's men insisting on a sixteen-year sentence and the judiciary holding out for an immediate release. In the end they settled on thirteen years, which was two years and nine months more than Oei had served.[30] The judge found Oei guilty of one thing only, namely, that while Oei had not issued the Partindo statement, he had not protested against it in sufficiently strong language. The argument was patently absurd, as the judge surely knew. It also clearly failed the statutory burden of evidence as no causal connection with the 1965 violence (the unrest argument) had been established. Clearly, the sentence was completely disproportionate to the alleged crime. Underscoring this fact, the actual author of the 1965 Partindo statement was sentenced to a shorter jail-term than Oei Tjoe Tat, who had protested against it.

The verdict came as a shock to Oei, but he did not follow Yap's recommendation to appeal, applying instead for remission, which to general surprise he received. Yap commented that Oei was quite rational about such matters, perhaps implying that he himself might be less so.[31] There was pressure from abroad, and indeed senior state officials sympathized with Oei Tjoe Tat and made an effort to secure his early release.[32] But the greatest effort was expended by Oei's wife, a remarkable woman, and by Yap Thiam Hien, who made the most of his contacts with key officials such as General Kanter and Admiral Soedomo.[33] When Oei's daughter married shortly after his release, senior state officials turned up in force, including the speaker of Parliament and the chief justice and mixed happily with Oei's former guards and wardens who also attended. It is hard not to view their presence as silent acknowledgement of past wrongs and a vindication.

The Case of Colonel Latief (1978)

Colonel Latief, then commander of the First Brigade of the Jakarta Metropolitan Command, was accused of complicity in the 30 September Movement. He was arrested two days after the key events took place and was detained without trial for thirteen years. His case finally came up before the High Military Court in 1978. The court imposed life imprisonment. The prosecution appealed to the Supreme Court, which took five years to deny the appeal (1982).

Colonel Latief was little known in 1965, but when he was released in March 1999, by which time he was eighty-two years old, he was not only one of the last but also one of the most famous of the remaining 1965 political prisoners.[34] His fame in part rested on a widespread conviction that he had inside information about the 30 September Movement, notably on Suharto's role in it. It was believed (including by himself) that Latief had been locked up less for what he did than for what he knew, and people wondered how it was that he had been permitted to survive.

The brutality of Latief's arrest, and his notable courage, added to his aura. Yap was deeply disturbed by the arrest and admired Latief's courage. He would return to these issues several times in the interviews.

> This was a sad case, he was still hobbling when he came to court, even though he had been ten years in detention by then. His story is terrifying. When his house was ransacked and he was seized, he was dragged out of his house and his legs were shot. Both his knees were shot. He was thrown in a cell and for several months his legs were not taken care of. Over time they became infected. An operation was suggested but he wanted none. Let him have a limp, let him die, he refused an operation. He told me his wounds were so bad that they were crawling with maggots.[35]

Latief was extraordinarily tough, both physically and mentally, as events would show. The authorities fully intended to have him die from his wounds, but he refused to do so. "He screamed, asking for medicine. . . . And there were those who looked at him and said, 'kamu belum mati?!' [you're still not dead?!]. But he said, [it was] such a miracle, for I lived."[36]

Latief refused to ask for forgiveness because he felt he had done nothing wrong. Most importantly, he refused to keep his mouth shut.[37] It was his unrelenting testimony during the trial that brought him to the attention of the public and made him one of the most intriguing personalities of the 30 September Movement.[38]

> [Yap speaking:] Oh, he was a real military man. He refused to apologize, he admitted everything. . . . He did not deny his actions. Yes, [Latief said,] I sent a platoon to here and to there. But it was my duty. I was ordered to send a platoon, so I did.[39]

Yap was intrigued by Latief's account of the role of Suharto in the immediate run-up to the coup.

> "But on Suharto," [Yap] said, "I have begun to have doubts." Why didn't he do anything? Latief went to see him twice to report that something was going on. Two days before, at night, and on the morning of 30 September Latief saw him at the Gatot Subroto Hospital. He wondered why Suharto did not take any steps because the whole episode could have been prevented still.[40]

Dan Lev commented: "So [Latief] threw it all into the open. Whether true or not [I don't know]."[41] Yap wondered about Suharto's role, and it troubled him, but he would not go too far down this road, recognizing its speculative character. On the same tape, Lev comments that "[Yap] is unwilling, apparently, to go so far as to suggest that Suharto set it up, but it appears quite clear that he feels that what is known about the coup is incomplete, that something very strange was going on here."[42]

Latief's arrest, which in its cruelty violated basic human rights and fundamental principles of Indonesian law, his prolonged detention without trial, and, in the background, the questions about Suharto's role, would affect the way Yap looked at the New Order regime as a whole.

Latief himself had requested that Yap defend him, but Yap was then serving as the lead lawyer in the famous Sawito case. As a result, he missed most of the Latief testimonies.[43] The limited sources at our disposal, including a very slim case file, must be in part attributed to the abbreviated role Yap played in the trial.

Lev had a copy of Latief's book, filled with pencil markings and notes. The book consists in large part of the pleadings in court. Part of it might in fact be Yap's work, even though he is mentioned nowhere in the book: Chapter 2 is legal-technical and mostly refers to "the accused" when talking about Latief, whereas in the rest of the book Latief refers to himself simply as "I." The book includes a four-page, detailed account of Jesus's trial before the Council of the Elders, complete with biblical references (John 18:20–23) and Christian religious literature.[44] The account seems rather out of tune for Latief, who was Muslim and is shown at Muslim prayers in the book.[45] The book contains objections on grounds of violations of due process: disregard for Latief's physical condition, failure to provide him with adequate equipment to prepare his defense (paper, writing materials), the extremely short time given to prepare for the case, and basic mistakes in court procedure (for instance, disregarding the sequence for hearing witnesses required by law).[46] It is all very familiar and comes right out of the Asep Suryaman and Oei Tjoe Tat cases. Then there is a part, equally familiar from the previous cases, that challenges the statutory basis for the case, 1963 Presidential Decision (Penetapan Presiden nr. 11/1963), as amended in 1969 (Law nr. 5/1969).[47] There also are six pages dealing with the poor food in prison, detailed down to the minimum daily intake of calories, which are quintessentially Yap and resemble his angry complaints in the Sawito case.[48] In the absence of supporting sources, we cannot confirm that chapter 2 is in fact Yap's work. But clearly there is a very close correspondence in the line of argument and the issues mentioned with those brought up in Yap's other cases dealing with the 1965 coup.

One interesting angle comes up during the discussions between Yap Thiam Hien and Dan Lev on this case, which we will quote here at some length.[49]

> Lev: So what happened at the trial?
> Yap: Yea, well, those judges. . . . [Yap falls silent for a bit, and ponders the issue.] The funny thing was, and it still surprises me thinking about it, during breaks in the hearings or at lunch, we the advocates and the prosecutor (auditor) would be routinely invited to join the judges for drinks or something to eat. It was me and the other advocates from Peradin with the military judges. It became a routine affair, drinks, snacks, always we were invited. And we would talk. Not about the case, but about other matters. I am not sure the judges did the same with the others, but with me, the judges talked a lot. They knew, especially after my demurrer in the Subandrio case, that they had to get their stuff in order.
>
> I would challenge them, and I think this is why they liked me. I never beat around the bush, I challenged them directly, how can you do this or that, I pointed out the illegality of the Subandrio trial since he was sentenced to death by a court that was unlawful (because the judge-officers

were of inferior rank to the defendant). Oh, it embarrassed them all right. But they liked it all the same. People know I am honest, maybe, and I have no political ambitions. Sure, I am hardheaded, not supple, cannot be bent. . . .

Two years later, Yap and Dan were again discussing Latief.[50]

Lev: So why were you chosen to defend him?"
Yap: Latief himself asked for me. . . . The judge at the Military Court of Appeal was actually very good. He operated very independently. The prosecutor at one point wanted to stop Latief from presenting testimony, when Latief actually went into describing the role of Suharto and the brutality of his own arrest. But the judge denied his objection, and ordered Latief to continue and spill it all out. He was really nice. . . .

Yap: Now the prosecutor [laughs], he wanted the death penalty. I knew he was a Protestant. I argued against it. And then the prosecutor in his rebuttal (which was oral) quoted the Bible, Romans 13: "Whoever rebels against government authority rebels against God." A very Lutheran idea, and the prosecutor was a Lutheran.

So in my response, all of which was oral, I said that the prosecutor was right in quoting the Bible, but the specific passage cannot be read out of context. In Revelations 13, it is written that there are governments which are rotten, that emerge out of the sea with many heads and so on, that it is a monster that can be destroyed by the Almighty. So do not blindly assume all government is good.

Afterwards, as had become our habit by now, the judge invited me over for lunch, and the prosecutor was there also. And the judge said, with a smile, "Ach so, Pak Yap, you don't just know the law, but also the Bible." The prosecutor sat there in silence. . . .

Yap: The decision was a life sentence. And for the last time, we had our lunch together, the judge, the prosecutor and I. The prosecutor was angry. He raised his voice with the judge, he swore at him. The judge stayed composed. He said: You have to understand, we are talking about a situation of many years back. Had Latief been arrested in 1965 and tried within several months thereafter, he likely would have received the death penalty, like all the others. But much time has passed since then; we are in different times.

> And look at how this man has suffered. You yourself saw in court, and heard his testimony. He could not be tried because of his wounds. Should we not consider his suffering in our decision? So the prosecutor cooled down; he said, "Sorry, but I will still have to appeal because my function is to secure the death penalty."

The prosecutor did appeal but was turned down by the Supreme Court, which took a horrifying five years to make up its mind.[51] Several years later, Yap ran into Latief in prison, when he was visiting clients in another case. Latief said he was thinking of applying for an amnesty.[52] The decision was very slow in coming, and Yap thought that it was all engineered and a lost cause anyway because Suharto would never let Latief go free since he knew things that might damage the president.[53]

And so it happened. Latief recounted in his book how it seemed to him that Suharto was determined to keep him in jail, more so than all the others. When in 1988 Latief qualified for an early release at the determination of the minister of justice, he found that the law had been changed just a few months earlier to make release dependent on the president. Every year between 1988 and 1999, Latief applied for an early release for which by law he qualified. In 1995 Subandrio and the other senior generals detained after 1965 were released. Yet Latief remained in prison, even though his application had been filed in conjunction with the others. When the press started asking questions, the minister of justice claimed disingenuously that he had not actually seen Latief's application. In 1998, after Suharto's fall, Latief submitted his application three times. Each time, the Department of Justice requested that he resubmit, without addressing it in substance. At long last, Latief was released in 1999.

Dan observed that the Latief case was a dismal example of the shabby and manipulative use of the law by the New Order government. When Yap talked about the ostensibly technical ins and outs of the Latief case, in reality he was making a more general point regarding the "extraordinary cynicism and corruption of what is happening now. In Jakarta, in the courts. This conversation . . . went on, and Yap mentioned that the key figure here is Latief."[54]

BASIC POLITICAL RIGHTS: FREEDOM OF EXPRESSION AND ASSOCIATION, RELIGIOUS FREEDOM

If the conversations between Dan Lev and Yap Thiam Hien on the 1960s and 1970s focused on the cases that emerged out of the 30 September Movement and the coup, by the late 1970s and the 1980s their discussions dealt mostly with cases that involved political rights, generally those with a religious tinge.

The first case handled by Yap that fitted this new category was the 1976 Sawito case, involving a mid-level civil servant who claimed that he had received heavenly instruction to mobilize forces against the government. While Sawito was driven by a mixture of Javanese mysticism and Islam, he also tapped into a rich vein of economic and political discontent with the New Order.

Following the Sawito case, Yap in the 1980s handled a series of cases that, while rooted in similar economic and political discontent, had a much clearer Islamic profile. These include the Tanjung Priok case, the Basuki Rahmat case, the A. M. Fatwa case, and the Sanusi case. Dan and Yap would sometimes refer to these as the "Islamic cases."

The Islamic cases of the 1980s were triggered by a 1984 riot in the Jakarta port district of Tanjung Priok. It was put down with great brutality by the Indonesian armed forces, resulting in many deaths, as many as four hundred, by some accounts. The riot had Islamic and anti-Chinese overtones, and in fact it was put in motion when military personnel entered a local mosque without taking off their boots. But the root of the unrest lay in the simmering economic, social, and political discontent in a poor part of town. After the riot, the government indicted thirty people on grounds of subversion.

The Tanjung Priok riot had a broad impact on Indonesian politics. In the early 1980s an informal opposition group called Petisi 50 (Petition 50) emerged, made up of "retired military officers, bureaucrats, and pre-New Order party officials shunted aside by Suharto."[55] Even though the group was little motivated by religious dynamics, some of its members were quite close to Muslim activists. After the Tanjung Priok riot, the Petisi 50 put out a White Paper that blamed the authorities for creating the social, economic, and moral causes behind the riot, as well as for slaughtering the rioters. The government responded by indicting the White Paper's author, A. M. Fatwa, for subversion. Sanusi, a former member of Parliament and a cabinet minister, was accused of complicity in the bombing of a local bank.

It is generally accepted that the real target in the Fatwa and Sanusi cases was the Petisi 50 group. Dan Lev attended some hearings of the Sanusi case, where he ran into Ali Sadikin, the respected former governor of Jakarta (and member of the Petisi 50 group). Ali Sadikin said that he was there because Sanusi was a friend, but also, and principally, to show solidarity with the Petisi 50 as a whole, which he thought was the actual quarry of the trial. Underscoring the religious tincture of the case, Dan recounted that the courtroom was filled to the brim with young people from the Islamic mass organization Muhammadiyah.[56]

From the mystic Sawito to the overtly Islamic cases of the 1980s, the mix of religion with social and economic discontent was a mobilizing political force. Yet for Yap these cases involved the more general issues of properly secured legal rights and fundamental principles, which is why he took them on (often pro bono).

> I recently defended someone, in the case of the bombing of BCA [a local bank]. He already admitted it, and some people asked: "Why are you still willing to defend him?" Well, this involves the broader interest, after all. We want to be sure that a person who has admitted his deed is given his full rights in court. First, how was he treated to obtain a confession? Was he beaten, given electric shocks, or did he confess voluntarily? Second, in accordance with the Indonesian Code of Criminal Procedure, was he informed by the investigating officers that he had the right to have a lawyer present during the examination? These rights are what we fight for, and these rights are not only the rights of the accused, but are also the rights of other citizens. It is this general, broader interest which we lawyers fight for.[57]

After bridging political divisions in the 1960s, in these cases Yap Thiam Hien transcended the religious classifications that traditionally shaped the Indonesian social and political universe. In the 1980s cases Yap had to work closely with defendants for whom Islam (often in combination with anti-Chinese sentiments) was a core element in their thinking. The fact that he managed to bridge that ethnic and religious divide and came to be accepted by the Islamic defendants made him seem a man who transcended all categories: "He fit no mold that would have made him obvious."[58]

In the Tanjung Priok case, for instance, the defendants at first insisted that only *muballigh*s would be on the defense team, for was the case not about understanding the Qur'an?[59] Yap could not be their lawyer, they argued, for as a Chinese and non-Muslim, he represented everything they fought against, and some of their group had died in the battle. Yet the Legal Aid Organization (Lembaga Bantuan Hukum), which managed their defense, convinced them to bring in Yap and in the end they grudgingly agreed.[60]

When Yap stepped up, however, through his open contact with the defendants and his vigorous defense in court, they began to see him in a different light. By the time the trial ended, they had developed great respect for him. From the interviews, one gets a strong sense that this was in no way a matter of artifice or design on the part of Yap, but quite simply reflects the integrity that he himself had a hard time explaining.

> Lev: In your defense of them, did you notice that their attitude [*sikap*] toward you changed?
> Yap: I saw that they did not see me as a Chinese [*golongan tionghoa*] etc. They saw me in terms of my performance as advocate, as jurist. For myself, well how? [*bagaimana*], I didn't know . . . I had no feeling of being inferior or such [*perasaan minder*] toward them because they are original Indonesians [*pribumi* or *asli*] . . . I am used to getting along [*saya biasa bergaul*] . . . maybe I am democratic or egalitarian. . . . I often am like that [*saya sering begitu*].[61]

The other cases show a similar dynamic. Sanusi made a point of stating in his defense speech that Yap Thiam Hien was not really Chinese, he was *pribumi*—an original Indonesian. Rahmat Basuki before presenting his defense speech apologized to Yap for what he was about to say about the Chinese, and said that it did not apply to him. He went on apologizing and clarifying, even in court; Rahmat's friends also came up to reassure Yap.[62]

To Yap, what mattered was that basic rights should be respected and upheld. It was not that he agreed with the substance of the defendants' message in these various cases, but he would fight to the end for their right to express it: "And I said to them, 'Go ahead. You have a right to your opinion and I will defend your right to your opinion. Even if I do not agree.'"[63]

We struggled a lot with this section, as the case files either are missing or dramatically incomplete, and the interviews consist of scattered references. Because it is clearly so important, we diverged from our original approach and tried to trace the records of the Legal Aid Organization in Indonesia and talked to some of the Indonesian lawyers who were on the defense team with Yap. It all generated very little. Regrettably, we had to draw heavily on work done by others, and we limited ourselves to the Sawito case.[64]

The Sawito Case (1976)

Before 1976, Sawito Kartowibowo was an unknown former employee of the Department of Agriculture. He was elevated to popular hero status when he was charged on multiple counts of subversive activities for having composed several controversial documents detailing the failings of the Suharto regime. The documents would have been insignificant had they not included the signatures of many well-known people, most notably the founding father and former vice president, Mohammad Hatta, religious leaders, and high-ranking military men.[65]

The socioeconomic and political backdrops of the trial were perhaps equally significant. Religious and to some extent military groups increasingly criticized social inequality, large-scale corruption (in particular at the collapsing state-owned oil company Pertamina), and the conspicuous spread of multinational firms. Dissatisfaction with the Suharto regime itself was implicit. To top it all, Indonesia was preparing for general elections in 1977.

In September 1976 the authorities announced that some prominent figures had been deceived into signing a number of documents evidencing moves to replace the president unconstitutionally. Among the key documents, "Towards Salvation" was signed by former Vice President Hatta, Cardinal Darmoyuwono (Catholic primate of Indonesia), T. B. Simatupang (former Armed Forces chief of staff and one of the chairmen of the Indonesian Council of Churches), and Hamka (Haji Abdulmalik Karim Amrullah, a prominent Islamic scholar and head of the Indonesian Council of Islamic Scholars). According to the authorities, the document contained "very negative evaluations of the present day situation [and] called on those who love their country and people . . . to contribute toward a 'General Restoration' in accordance with their capabilities." The bulk of it criticized the moral degradation perceived to have blighted the New Order leadership.[66]

Another document, unsigned, proposed that Suharto choose a successor (it named Hatta specifically) who would govern pending an election. A document, titled "Letter of Transfer," transferred the president's mandate from Suharto to Hatta and was modeled on the Supersemar document that had transferred the mandate from Soekarno to Suharto. During the course of the trial, two other documents surfaced: "Letter of Authority," closely resembling the "Letter of Transfer," and "Welcoming a Just Government in Indonesia," which was signed by Hatta and Sawito, among others. The official announcement also contained statements from the signatories that Sawito was the instigator of the affair and had tricked them into signing the documents.[67]

Following the disclosure of these documents, sweeping "anti-subversion" measures were taken against many people affiliated with Sawito. In October 1976 it was announced that Sawito was to be put on trial. He was charged, under the 1963 Presidential Decree, with engaging in conduct that undermined the authority of the lawful government and spread enmity, discord, and disorder among the people, including the composition and distribution of false news. He was also charged with plotting to overthrow the government and intentionally slandering the president.

In July Yap offered to defend Sawito free of charge. However, according to Sawito, the prosecution repeatedly implored him to appoint "anyone but Yap," asserting that Yap's involvement would incur the wrath of the presiding judge, who was an old Yap adversary. But he nevertheless went ahead and appointed Yap, who was joined by four other lawyers from Peradin and LBH Jakarta, one of whom was Abdul Rahman Saleh.

Yap and the other lawyers did not have direct access to Sawito until the trial actually began. Having had no chance to study the charges, the defense at the first sitting was granted a three-week suspension. Nevertheless, the skills of the defense lawyers compensated for their lack of preparation time. Apparently, Sawito's oratorical skills and the legal acumen of Yap and his colleagues proved to be a lethal combination for the prosecution.

The main thrust of the defense was to argue that Sawito's trial was a political show, designed not only to get rid of Sawito but, more importantly, to teach the people that they must obey the regime.[68] In his summation, Yap declared that it was "the Indonesian people who were on trial for their freedom."[69] This was a political case, Yap argued, and so Sawito's right to a fair trial would inevitably be trampled on. The judges would not, indeed could not, be impartial. Yap based his argument, as in other cases, on the flawed structure of the judiciary: Judges are part of the civil service (Korpri) (here Yap made specific reference to the presiding judges) and are therefore under the minister for Home Affairs. They are also administered by the Ministry of Justice. Consequently, judges' salaries, promotions, or demotions and court assignments are determined by ministers who are appointed servants of the executive.

In political cases such as Sawito's, Yap submitted, not only did the judiciary trample on the presumption of innocence, but the prosecution too became a tool of those in power to attack anyone threatening the status quo. He went on to demand that the chairman of the panel of judges respond in open court to the following questions:

> Do you have any personal interest in this case, either directly or indirectly?
>
> After reading the government's allegations and studying the dossiers against Sawito for the past 2 months, have you [already] decided for yourself as to the defendant's guilt?
>
> Even though you are part of the corps of judges and therefore cannot escape the executive's influence, do you accept that you and the other presiding judges have to protect all the defendant's human rights and free yourself from any influence from the executive or other party and that you will decide this case solely on the basis of facts revealed before this court in line with the noble profession of a judge and in the interest of justice?
>
> Are you willing to swear that you will abide by the judges' oath and code of ethics and the 1945 Constitution and to all laws and regulations and that you will implement all rules of procedure as best you can?[70]

Although there are no accounts to confirm whether or not the judges responded to Yap's demand that they take the oath during the hearings, probably they did not. As Yap predicted, the judges failed to preside impartially.

This bias was evident in the judges' heavy-handed and, in Yap's words, "inept and sloppy" management of the proceedings. The prosecution's concealment of evidence and withholding of key witnesses were mostly endorsed by the judges. In a letter to the presiding judges, Yap protested their decisions, citing the perception that they sided with the prosecution.[71] In addition, a key witness was not produced by the prosecution, who claimed that he was held by the military. Only after almost two months was his testimony finally heard.[72] Furthermore, the judges overruled as irrelevant most questions the defense addressed to the witnesses. In some instances, the judges even forbade the witness to answer the defense's line of questioning.[73]

Nonetheless, the defense lawyers managed to squeeze from the witnesses some key testimony, poking holes in the prosecution's case. Three witnesses testified that they had helped draft the "Letter of Authority" and other similar documents. One witness accepted responsibility for "Welcoming a Just Government in Indonesia." A second witness acknowledged that the initiative for "Towards Salvation" came from someone other than Sawito. Witnesses also testified that they had been coerced by interrogators into producing statements against Sawito. No witness supported the prosecution's allegation that Sawito coerced the signatories.[74]

The prosecution, nevertheless, concluded that Sawito had been proven guilty of all charges and demanded a twenty-year prison sentence. On July 1978, almost two years after the proceedings started, the presiding judges sentenced Sawito to eight years in jail. In late 1982 Sawito appealed to the High Court, which upheld the conviction but reduced his sentence to seven years. A further appeal (*kasasi*) to the Supreme Court was lodged, then another one (*peninjauan kembali*), both in February 1983, but both were rejected. Yap remained as Sawito's unpaid counsel throughout these proceedings.

COMMERCIAL FRAUD AND CORRUPTION CASES

Yap Thiam Hien may have ventured into civil cases but these were not his natural habitat, as Lev's notes point out. The law of contracts, torts, property rights, and the (often) negotiated civil process never quite suited him. He did not take to cases in which right and wrong were not clearly set out. His expertise, spiced with a tinge of paranoia perhaps, was in justice and injustice, for which the more compound world of civil disputes was a poor fit. Dan wrote in his notes that Yap tended to criminalize the civil process: he reconceived the civil dispute as a kind of prosecution in which he again could engage in a battle between good and evil. This explains why his relations with opposing lawyers in civil cases were often frayed, for he would look upon them much as he looked at prosecutors and accord them comparable treatment.[75]

It is cause for little surprise, then, that when Yap and Dan in their discussions, went beyond the political cases, Yap would focus on cases involving injustice, often straddling the civil and the criminal. What set these cases apart from ordinary civil disputes was that they were marked by power imbalances: some wretched fellow put through the grinder by a big company or swindled by the state.

> I have this habit. I do not accept all cases, unlike other advocates, who accept whatever clients come in. I don't. I always say to them first, give me time to look into the matter. . . . I do not want to just give it a shot. So if I take a case I have really studied it, and only then do I take it. So why did I take this case with the Italian? Because of the injustice. A strong party against a weak party. The Italian was in this second position, weaker.

> And the government did not want to meet its obligations because it felt strong.[76]

We have grouped these cases under the rubric of "commercial fraud and corruption," for they seem to have these issues in common.

It would be a mistake to view commercial fraud and corruption cases as being any more sedate than the more political cases on which Yap built his reputation. In some ways they cut even closer to the bone of the regime. We should remember that in the political cases, the government in a way needed Yap. Within obvious limits, his participation perversely helped legitimize a stage-managed process, as Dan commented in his notes.[77] In fact, the more outspoken and confrontational Yap's reaction, the more it conveyed an image of an open and legitimate legal process.[78] Yet the state retained control through it all, and indeed often continued to enjoy considerable public support no matter what it did, notably in the criminal cases that emerged from the 1965 coup.

The commercial fraud and corruption cases were different. These cases exposed institutional dysfunction, often involving members of the political elite or senior officials. They exposed the entwining of government interests with those of big business and revealed the murky edifice of off-budget payments and backroom deals that marked the New Order. Hence they tended to create great discomfort for senior state officials. The threat that sensitive documents might be produced as trial evidence, indeed even the mere prospect of publicity, sometimes caused the government to react more vehemently than in criminal cases.

Consequently, Yap Thiam Hien ran a bigger risk in some of these apparently sedate commercial fraud and corruption cases than in high-profile political litigation. This certainly is what Yap himself believed. It was not during the political cases but during the commercial fraud and corruption cases that he and his family were physically threatened.

The Heru Gunawan Case (1981)

> "I told her: get the name on tape. So back she goes, yes Pak Heru Gunawan, no Pak Heru Gunawan, on and on. And so his name was all over the tape."
>
> Yap Thiam Hien

Heru Gunawan was a judge in the most important district court of the land, the Central Jakarta District Court. He was caught in a sting operation, the first and only successful sting against a judge in the first half-century of the Republic's existence. Yap Thiam Hien was the principal engineer of the operation.[79]

The case was one of institutional fraud that reached up to the highest levels. Although it started out as a simple civil default case, Yap gave it a criminal twist. What happened to the civil case and the unsung heroine of the story, which appropriately perhaps involved a Ms. Maria chasing a diamond, is a bit of a mystery.[80] What people remember, and indeed what became legend over the years and well into the Reformasi period, is how Yap and Maria got a judge recorded on tape asking for money, had him pocket a check, which was predestined to bounce, and then nailed him.

One of the regrettable reasons why this story is so well known in Indonesia is that in the pre-Reformasi environment of rampant institutional corruption, it is unique. The Heru Gunawan case continues to be held out as an ideal to which many aspire, even today. The case makes decades of ineffectiveness and failure in addressing deepening judicial corruption ever more gloomily apparent. This long-term failure makes the one moment of success all the more formidable. The facts are convoluted and can be presented here in simplified form, mostly as Yap recounted them to Dan Lev.

Yap's client, Ms. Maria, was a broker in diamonds. On behalf of the owner, she arranged for the sale through a middleman. The purchaser claimed he paid for the diamonds, but the middleman denied having received payment. Ms. Maria was left holding the bag. There was no evidence or paper trail, because that is the way of the diamond trade. And so Ms. Maria filed a case against the broker in the Central Jakarta District Court, which is where Yap enters the story (amended in places for the flow of argument).

> Then, lo and behold, Ms. Maria is called before the presiding judge, called Heru Gunawan. He asks her whether she has a lawyer. She said she didn't have one. Well you don't need one, said Judge Heru, just give me Rp. 50 million and I will handle this case. That's a bit hefty, said Ms. Maria (a trader if ever there was one). After some haggling she got the fee down to 30 million, payable in installments. In the process, Ms. Maria got a tape recorder that fitted into her handbag and began to record the conversations. So then one good day she turns up at my office and I'm blown right out of my socks.

The first thing was to perfect the evidence and I got Ms. Maria to go back with the tape recorder and make certain his name was on tape and the transaction specified. Also, I changed the payments to be principally in cheques (1 million in cash and 9 million in cheques), which could be blocked. The second thing I did was to get the Opstib (the anti-corruption squad) involved. So when everything is set up, back Ms. Maria goes, yes Pak (Mr.) Heru Gunawan, no Pak Heru Gunawan throughout the conversation, it's all on tape. The judge takes the payment and puts it in his briefcase. Ms. Maria leaves his office where the Obstip squad is waiting. It's in his briefcase says Maria, they go in to seize the case and arrest Heru Gunawan.[81]

Yap said he had little trouble getting the anti-corruption squad involved. The squad knew the courts were messed up but previously never could get a handle on them. So this was a unique opportunity. Judge Heru Gunawan was indicted. During the interrogations Heru "sang like a bird" (Yap's words) and the scandal started to spread.

Yap recounted how Heru Gunawan exposed a system in the Central Jakarta District Court in which cases were put out to bid among the judges by court chairman Soemadijono and his clerk. They would assess cases on their approximate market value when they came in, and then in weekly meetings "auctioned them off"[82] to the judges who were willing to pay. (Some judges refused to participate in the racket.) So Judge Heru Goenawan got the diamond case by promising money to the district court chief. This corruption funnel went all the way up to the Supreme Court and the chief justice. It was a system by which judges at all levels were under pressure to generate funds, with the superior judges pressuring the junior judges, and in the end the parties to the disputes. Naturally, judges would take their cut at all levels.

Judge Heru Gunawan was sentenced to seven months in prison. The hearing was held at noon when the court was empty so the case would not attract attention. Soemadijono was dismissed.[83] Four other judges were dismissed, including Staa, the chairman of the Jakarta Court of Appeals who had covered for them and passed the funds up to the Supreme Court.[84] But no charges were filed against any of these higher-ups at the insistence of Chief Justice Ali Said who had just replaced Seno Adji. According to Yap, Ali Said remarked: "Ah those poor judges, they have suffered enough. After all, they have been dismissed, their children are teased at school, why pursue this further?"[85] For its part, the anti-corruption squad investigations clearly showed that the chief justice was part of the racket, but it did not dare investigate him because he was part of the powerful political elite. And so the case fizzled out.

Asked by Lev whether the judges felt burdened or embarrassed by what happened, Yap noted with wonder that these judges were not in fact embarrassed at all. Soemadijono, Staa, and the others now serve as advocates, no doubt making good use of their court connections, and they are members of Ikadin (the Indonesian Bar Association). There is a provision in the Ikadin code that its members must never have been sentenced for a crime, and in fact they never were.[86]

Could they not have been brought to trial, Lev wondered? The whole point, replied Yap, is that no matter the crime you have committed, no prosecutor will bring a case if your rapport with the Supreme Court is good. The judges were not indicted, not because there might be evidentiary problems (such that no one could have a good shot at proving the charge) but because they were protected. "Thus we saw in the case of Heru Gunawan, he was the only one tried, and he was of Chinese descent! Chinese descent. And he was the only one sacrificed. Corruption is not a game."[87]

In a perverse way the Heru Gunawan case had the opposite effect from the one it aimed to achieve. A sense of impunity took hold of the higher echelons of the judiciary, for if this highly visible scandal could not touch them, what could? Rather than shore up the flagging standards of the institution, perversely the Heru Gunawan case accelerated the rot. The inability of the anti-corruption squad to secure indictments against the senior judges and roll back the networks and practices helped drive a nail in the coffin of judicial independence and authority. Lev and Yap then discussed what the case signified.

> Lev: Is there still hope for the courts?
> Yap: No hope whatsoever. How can we respect the judges? We talk about respecting the symbols of—Justice, Judiciary—but with these people, how is it possible we respect them?
> Lev: I asked General Kanter about corruption. He had an interesting response. He said that of course we know that corruption is widespread, in the courts, in the government, but it is not yet considered so serious as to destabilize the government.
> Yap: [laughs] Yes, difficult, difficult.[88]

The Pertamina Cases (1983 and 1984)

> Ah, pissed off, how pissed off I was. Cases such as these in which the law is being ignored and justice is trodden upon. I hate them, I was absolutely furious, furious. But what can one do, Pertamina was very powerful.
>
> Yap Thiam Hien, on the Pertamina oil theft case

The Pertamina cases are prime examples of the way in which political and economic interests had become entwined under the New Order, and how the regime had become reliant on corruption. These were cases about institutionalized corruption and the casual arbitrariness and brutality that sustained it. Yap was involved in a number of Pertamina cases and often discussed the following two closely connected ones as being of major import.

PERTAMINA COMPANY HOUSING CASE

The first Pertamina case never came to court but is an important backdrop to the Pertamina oil theft case that followed. In 1983 a senior Pertamina official, who had retired, came to Yap Thiam Hien with the following account. The official (and a number of his colleagues) lived in company housing, which was nicely located in central Jakarta. According to an internal Pertamina regulation, after residing a number of years in a company house the occupant would have the right to buy it. The official came to see Yap because he and his colleagues had received summonses from the Housing Department of the Jakarta City Government instructing them to leave their homes. The officials wanted to assert their rights under the Pertamina regulation and refuse to move.

Yap managed to dig up an internal Pertamina document that listed state agencies getting routine payments from Pertamina. The Jakarta Housing Department was on that list. Yap discovered that what was really going on was that Pertamina wanted the retired employees to vacate their houses, and it tried to get around its own internal regulation by enlisting the Jakarta City Government for the job. It was for services such as these that Pertamina had paid the city government all along. The case was significant because it demonstrated how institutional corruption served to pervert the law and the legal process.

One of the remarkable aspects of the list was that it revealed where the Pertamina funds were going on a routine basis, and this included the courts and the law enforcement agencies. In fact, there was a fixed line item for the courts. So the list documented the off-budget financial connections between state agencies and state-owned enterprises and how legal process could be manipulated.[89]

Yap informed the city government that if the case were pursued he would publish the Pertamina list of off-budget payments. The government (and Pertamina) were well aware that publication of the list would be damaging. The mere threat killed the first Pertamina case. It evaporated; the Jakarta City Government was never heard from again, and the retired employees were permitted to keep their houses.

THE SECOND PERTAMINA CASE: OIL THEFT

The second Pertamina case involved the prosecution of the Greek master and Polish first mate of a tanker (carrying oil from Singapore to Jakarta) for alleged theft of the oil. The tanker had been chartered by Pertamina in 1984. When the ship arrived in Jakarta independent inspectors verified the cargo manifest. In fact, the load had been inspected on a number of occasions and each time had been found to be correct. Nevertheless, shortly after the Jakarta inspection the Greek master and the Polish first mate were accused of having stolen oil en route. They were detained.

Of the ship's twenty-seven crewmen, four were Indonesian. It was the four Indonesians who told Pertamina that the oil had been stolen. According to their testimony, on the way from Singapore late at night near the island of Bangka, the ship had transferred oil to another tanker. The Indonesians said they did not help transfer the oil, but they saw it happen. They said they each received US$50 to keep mum. But they felt a surge of nationalist pride, as they put it, and decided to report the event.

The twenty-three foreign crewmen were not heard by the prosecutor and after three days were instructed to leave the country. The alarmed Greek consul arranged for them to issue a notarized statement before they left. The statement denied that there had been any irregularities at all while the ship was underway and corroborated the inspector's report. There were strong suspicions that, in reality, it had been Pertamina officials themselves who had stolen the oil after the tanker arrived in port. By blaming the foreign crew, who had no idea what they had gotten themselves into, and pressuring the Indonesian crew to bring false testimony, the officials were aiming to cover up their theft and make themselves appear patriotic.

Yap argued there was not enough evidence to bring a case under Indonesian law. The only documentary evidence was from the inspector, an independent agent recruited by Pertamina, and it attested to the oil having arrived in good order, a fact corroborated by various other statements. The case rested not on evidence but on a conspiracy among Pertamina officials, the prosecution, and the court.

The commercial fraud, in which courts, prosecution, high-level company officials all conspired to blame innocents, angered Yap. In interviews with Dan, he kept coming back to the fact that this was the first visit of the Greek master and Polish first mate to Indonesia; with no knowledge of the country, they had been purposely sacrificed. Also, the first mate had been diagnosed with cancer, and this was his last trip before going into treatment. Keeping him in jail for a prolonged period of time, and thus preventing treatment, might turn out to be a death sentence.

Yap's anger showed in court, and relations with his colleagues soon became acrimonious; his arguments were cut short by the prosecution and the court at every attempt.

Yap requested that the notarized statement of the foreign crew be accepted as evidence. The court rejected this because it had not been made under oath (which in fact under Indonesian law notaries are not empowered to administer).

Yap asked for a deferment to bring the foreign crew back and get their testimony. The court rejected this.

Yap asked for testimony by expert witnesses and the inspectors, who, he pointed out, had been hired by Pertamina itself. The court rejected this.

Yap asked the prosecutor to testify. He wanted him to explain why he did not interrogate the twenty-three foreign crewmen and instead instructed them to go home. 'Could you please state in court, under oath, why you did this?' Yap asked. If the prosecutor had agreed, his reply would have shown that he had failed in his duty to hear all witnesses. But the prosecutor refused. The court upheld this refusal.

Yap brought a witness who testified that Pertamina itself had siphoned off the petrol when the tanker was being unloaded in Jakarta. After his initial testimony, the court recalled the witness but he didn't turn up. When he finally was tracked down and did come, he was a changed man. From being assertive and talkative, he had turned into a shaking wreck who could not say a word. He had been beaten up by military figures.

The prosecution brought two witnesses. The first was the traffic controller for the Tanjung Priok port. He said he had gone to the ship master and told him he knew petrol had been stolen en route, and he would report this to Pertamina unless he was paid. He said that, indeed, he was then paid. The second witness said he witnessed this transaction. But in cross-examination, Yap established that the second witness had been too far away to see the alleged meeting clearly, if at all. The traffic controller by his own admission was a blackmailer and a totally unreliable character. The master and first mate denied it all. Despite the absence of corroborating evidence, the court upheld the testimony of the prosecution witnesses and rejected the defense of the master and first mate.

The four Indonesian crewmen had been coached by the prosecutor. But their statements were conflicting. One said that he had signed on with the ship on such and such a date, and it turned out he was still in Sumatra at the time. The whole case was a construct, with Pertamina painting itself as a victim and filing the complaint to cover up the oil theft by its senior officials.

Yap recounted: "The court was hostile throughout the case and clearly was in cahoots with Pertamina." He wondered how the court could ignore the statement of the inspectors who were independent although appointed by Pertamina itself. Who could be more objective? Instead the court relied on the testimony of the four Indonesian crew and the harbormaster, who had admitted that he was a blackmailer. The two foreigners, newcomers with no knowledge of the country, had been chosen to take the fall for a crime that had been in the works for a long time.

Yap was put under great pressure in these cases. He recounted how he was getting threatening phone calls. His dog was poisoned (he had it autopsied to make certain). The death deeply affected his family; his wife loved the dog and began to feel increasingly insecure. Someone shot at his house. There was a bullet hole in the window precisely at the height of Yap's head. Yap was not so much frightened as feeling he should report the attack to the court, so that if anything happened to him the court and authorities would know there might be a connection to the case. The attack was reported in the newspapers and the police came to investigate. Yap had no idea why they came, because he had not reported the incidents. The police found nothing and said that the hole in the window had been made by a stone. But Yap was convinced it was a rifle shot.

"A truly remarkable, modest, intelligent, and humane man."[90] This quote of 21 August 1971 originates from Dan Lev's first note on meeting Yap.[91] In August 1971 they sat down for a serious talk for the first time, without distractions.

The mutual interest and admiration was immediate. Dan's notes rarely were as explicit as they were about Yap: "As a public man he set a superb example, certainly for his courage, but also for his ability to remain outraged by injustice of any kind."[92] "What a great soul this man has!"[93] Dan met Yap again the following October and November, visiting his office for the first time and starting to ask questions about Yap's background.[94] From those initial meetings sprouted an extraordinary friendship—and eventually this book.

APPENDIX

DEFENSE SUMMATION IN ASEP SURYAMAN TRIAL

AUGUST 13, 1975

Yap Thiam Hien

Mr. Chairman and respected members of the Court,

The experiences of the accused, Asep Suryaman, are not unique; what has happened to other tapols is similar and in many cases worse.

Shortly, we Indonesians will be celebrating the thirtieth anniversary of our country's independence. At that time, all Indonesians, moved by a variety of emotions, will celebrate their liberation from colonialism and its many forms of subjugation. At that time, the government and people of Indonesia throughout the country and throughout the world wherever our embassies happen to be will celebrate this anniversary. In mosques, temples and churches, they will give thanks to the gracious Lord for the blessing of independence. But at the same time, countless tens of thousands of fellow Indonesians are still languishing in countless prisons and detentions camps where they have been held since their arrest in October 1965 or after.

The tapols too will celebrate Independence Day; they will do this spontaneously, without the encouragement of their prison chiefs or camp commanders. They will organize their modest celebrations without in any way condemning the Government or the State apparatus responsible for their imprisonment. At these celebrations, they will read the Independence Proclamation as well as verses from the Koran and the Bible. They will do it solemnly, movingly, saying a prayer that they may be blessed with God's truth and justice, with His mercy and His love, praying that the country will be run wisely and will be taken forward to a just, peaceful, quiet and prosperous life. And they will pray too for the safety and protection of their loved ones from whom they have been separated for so many years—their loved ones left without protection or care. For in so many cases, whole families have been split up and the members scattered so far from each other that they do not know where their closest relatives are or whether they are alive or dead, free or in prison.

The tapols are treated like the dregs of society, deprived of the most elementary rights enjoyed by all other citizens, like mere objects that can be moved from one place to another, put out "on loan" to another authority or interrogation, to give evidence or to meet the personal needs of some official; and they are not even told why they are put "on loan" or where they are being taken. They have no power and no voice, no right to complain or protest against their interminable imprisonment, against torture, insult, hunger or disease. They have no power and no voice in the face of this abuse against their dignity and person.

Many of them have become automatons, going to sleep, getting up and taking their meals like persons without any spirit, for they are not permitted to read newspapers, magazines, or books except religious literature, nor are they allowed to write their loved ones.

They live a sterile life, devoid of all hope and full of anxieties for their loved ones because often they do not know where they are and have no contact with them. Such a life leads them to break down under the strain. Some have become insane, others have committed suicide, some have tried to rebel against their predicament with horrifying consequences.

"We are like leaves on a tree, just waiting to fall to earth and become one with it," said one tapol, "Help us to get our freedom back, to rejoin our unprotected families. Help us at the very least to be brought to trial so that this uncertainty which destroys the spirit can end. Whatever is required, we are ready to sign so long as we can be released. Please, Mr. Yap, now that you are free, do not forget those of us who are still in captivity."

Mr. Chairman, how can we forget our fellow Indonesians who, together with their families, have been plunged in this terrible depth of suffering? How can our government, our people, our religious and party leaders, go on living happily and contentedly with their families, how can they tolerate this suffering of fellow citizens that has gone on for nearly ten years, for one third of the period our people have been living in independence?

This suffering whose only end is the grave, this intolerable situation goes completely against all the sacrifices made during the struggle of independence. It is a flagrant violation of Pancasila, to which we have pledged ourselves. It is totally against the objectives of development and the values and laws of the state, and is contrary to those principles and rules which Indonesia acknowledged and endorsed when it rejoined the United Nations, the principles and rules stipulated in the Universal Declaration of Human Rights and the Standard Minimum Rules for Treatment of Prisoners. This injustice, this inhumanity, cannot be allowed to continue; it is like a cancer destroying the very fabric of our lives and our efforts at construction.

To be honest, we must admit that the Government has tried to do quite a lot to alleviate the situation. We should wholeheartedly respect and welcome these efforts, while not overlooking the very real problems and obstacles that obstruct them. But it must be admitted that these efforts are nothing more than a tiny drop in this vast ocean of hardship and suffering. And the efforts toward improvement are proceeding so slowly that there is every reason to fear that many tapols who might have been released will no longer be in a position to enjoy their freedom.

The utterly arbitrary treatment of the tapols is not merely a violation of man-made laws; it is first and foremost a gross infringement of the commandments of God who bids us to love one another, who exhorts us to be merciful towards one another.

It is an internationally accepted practice to pardon and release prisoners on a country's national day. May the merciful God soften the hearts of our state leadership and people on this thirtieth anniversary of our Independence, moving them to end this situation, which is undignified both in human terms as well as for the state. May they grant freedom and restore to normal life all those tapols who are clearly not guilty and against whom there is no evidence for a charge in court, and speedily bring to trial all those against whom there is sufficient proof of guilt. This would earn the blessing of God and we could then enter our thirty-first year of independence with a sense of relief, with heads held high, looking boldly forward to a life of peace, tranquillity, freedom and happiness.

Mr. Chairman and respected members of the court, my own deep beliefs convince me that human integrity, respect, and dignity, freedom and basic human rights are values that far exceed even the noblest things in human and social life. And the source of these values is the Creator of Life, who is also the source of all law and justice, the source of freedom and basic human rights.

[Yap Thiam Hien concluded his address by reciting Psalm 72.]

GLOSSARY

ABRI. Angkatan Bersenjata Republik Indonesia; Armed Forces of the Republic of Indonesia

adat. Custom, customary

AMS. Algemene Middelbare School; General Secondary School

Angkatan Muda Tionghoa. Chinese Youth Front (Revolutionary period)

ang pow. Gifts of money

asing. Foreign

asli. Native

ASPRI. President's Personal Assistance staff

baba. Acculturated Chinese (used in Sumatra and Malaysia)

Bakin. Badan Koordinasi Intelijens Negara; State Intelligence Coordinating Body (New Order)

balie. Bar (lawyer's association)

Baperki. Badan Permusjawaratan Kewarganegaraan Indonesia; Consultative Body on Indonesian Citizenship

Baperwatt. Badan Permusjawaratan Warganegara Turunan Tionghua; Consultative Assembly of Citizens of Chinese Descent

Bappenas. Badan Perencanaan Pembangunan Nasional; National Development Planning Board

BPI. Badan Pusat Intellijen; Central Intelligence Bureau (Guided Democracy)

BTI. Barisan Tani Indonesia; Indonesian Peasants' Front

bumi putera. Native; literally, son of the earth

catut. Petty trade (often illegal)

CGMI. Consentrasi Gerakan Mahasiswa Indonesia; Concentration of Indonesian Student Movements

CHH. Chung Hwa Hui; Chinese Association (in Indonesia)

Chung Hua Hui. Chinese Association (in Holland)

CHTH. Chung Hua Tsung Hui; Federation of Chinese Associations (revolutionary period)

corvée. Obligatory labor

CSV. Christen Studenten Vereniging; Christian Students' Union

cukong. Ethnic Chinese financial backers

Darul Islam. House of Islam (movement to establish an Islamic state)

DGI. Dewan Gereja Indonesia; Indonesian Council of Churches

DPA. Dewan Pertimbangan Agung; High Advisory Council

DPR. Dewan Perwakilan Rakjat; People's Representative Council (Parliament)

Dwifungsi. Dual function (of the armed forces)

ELS. Europese Lagere School; European Primary School

G30S, Gestapu. Gerakan September Tiga Puluh; September 30 Movement

gamelan. Javanese percussion orchestra

gelijkstelling. Legal equivalence

Gerindo. Gerakan Rakyat Indonesia; Indonesian Peoples Movement

GKI. Gereja Keristen Indonesia; Protestant Church of Indonesia

GMKI. Gerakan Mahasiswa Kristen Indonesia; Indonesian Christian (Protestant) Student Movement

Golkar. Golongan Karya; functional groups

gotong-royong. Mutual help

GPIB. Gereja Protestan Indonesia Java Barat; Indonesian Protestant Church of West Java

HBS. Hogere Burger Scholen ; Higher Civil Schools (five-year secondary schools)

HCK. Hollandse Chinees Kweekschool; Dutch language Normal School for Chinese (teachers college)

HCS. Hollandse Chinees School; government (primary) schools for Chinese

H.I.R. Herziene Inlandsch (Indonesisch) Reglement; Revised Native (Indonesian) Regulation(s) (code of criminal procedure)

HIS. Hollands-Inlandse School; Dutch Native School (primary school for ethnic Indonesians)

hong-hiam. (Hokkien). Dangerous, unedifying

ICJ. International Commission of Jurists

IGGI. Intergovernmental Group on Indonesia

Ikadin. Ikatan Advokat Indonesia; Indonesian Advocates Association

Ikahi. Ikatan Hakim Indonesia; Indonesian Judges' Association

indekos. Bed and board

IPKI. Ikatan Pendukung Kemerdekaan Indonesia; League of the Supporters of

Indonesian Independence (political party allied with the army)

ISHI. Ikatan Sarjana Hukum Indonesia; Indonesian Law Graduates Bond

jaksa. Prosecutor

jaksa agung. Chief public prosecutor, attorney general

kabupaten. Regency, district

KAMI. Kesatuan Aksi Mahasiswa Indonesia; Indonesian Students' Action Front

KASI. Kesatuan Aksi Sarjana Indonesia ; Indonesian (University) Graduates' Action Front

Keibodan. Indonesian civil defense corps (Japanese occupation)

Keibotai. Chinese civil defense corps

KENSI. Kongres Ekonomi Nasional Seluruh Indonesia; All Indonesia National Economic Congress (business association)

KMT. Kuomintang (Pinyin: Guomindang)

KNIP. Komité Nasional Indonesia Pusat ; Central Indonesian National Committee

Konstituante. Constituent Assembly

Kopkamtib. Komando Operasi Pemulihan Keamanan dan Ketertiban; Operational Command for the Restoration of Security and Order (army-based, political security apparatus)

Kostrad. Komando Cadangan Strategis Angkatan Darat; Army Strategic Reserve

kraton. Sultan's palace

KUHP. Kitab Undang-Undang Hukum Pidana; criminal code

KUHAP. Kitab Undang-undang Hukum Acara Pidana; Code of Criminal Procedure (1981)

kweekscholen. Normal schools

Landraden. Courts for Indonesians (colonial period)

LawAsia. Regional organization for law professionals

LBH. Lembaga Bantuan Hukum; Legal Aid Institution

LPHAM. Lembaga Pembela Hak-Hak Azasi Manusia; Institute for the Defense of Human Rights

LPKB. Lembaga Pembinaan Kesatuan Bangsa; Institute for the Promotion of National Unity

Mahkamah Agung. Supreme Court

Mahmillub. Mahkamah Militer Luar Biasa; Extraordinary Military Tribunal

Malari. *Malapetaka Limabelas Januari*; the January 15 Disaster (1974)

Manipol/USDEK. Political Manifesto/ Constitution of 1945 (Undang-undang Dasar 1945); Indonesian Socialism (Sosialisme Indonesia); Guided Democracy (Demokrasi Terpimpim); Guided Economy (Ekonomi Terpimpin); and Indonesian Identity (Kepribadian Indonesia)

Masyumi. Majelis Syuro Muslimin Indonesia; Consultative Council of Indonesian Muslims

Meester in de rechten (Mr.). Master of law, degree and title

MPR(S). Majelis Permusyawaratan Rakyat (Sementara); (Provisional) People's Deliberative Assembly (upper house of the legislature)

MULO. Meer Uitgebreed Lagere Onderwijs; Extended Primary Education (middle school)

musyawarah mufakat. Consultation leading to consensus

Nasakom. Nationalism/Religion/Communism

negara hukum. Law state, rule of law

NU. Nahdatul Ulama; Revival of Religious Scholars (Islamic political party)

onderdanen. Dutch subjects

Opstib. Anti-corruption team

Opsus. Operasi Khusus; Special Operations (New Order period)

Orba. Orde Baru; New Order (March 1966–98)

pachten. Monopolies

PAHI. Persatuan Ahli Hukum Indonesia; Union of Indonesian Lawyers

Pak. Mister, father

pamong praja. Bureaucracy

Pancasila. The five principles of state ideology

pao an tui. Self-defense corps

Parkindo. Partai Keristen Indonesia ; Indonesian Christian Party (Protestant)

Parmusi. Partai Muslimin Indonesia ; Indonesian Muslim Party

Partij van de Arbeid. Labor Party

PDI. Partai Demokrat Indonesia; Indonesian Democratic Party

PDTI. Partai Demokrat Tionghoa Indonesia; Chinese Democratic Party of Indonesia

pegawai negeri. Civil servant

pemuda. Youth

Pengabdi Hukum. Servants of the Law

pengadilan negeri. First-instance court

pengadilan tinggi. Appellate court

Peradin. Persatuan Advokat Indonesia; Indonesian Advocates' Bond (formerly PAI) *peranakan.* An acculturated Chinese who usually uses an Indonesian language; of mixed ethnic origin

Perki. Perkumpulan Keristen Indonesian; Indonesian Christian Association

Persahi. Persatuan Ahli Hukum Indonesia; Indonesian Lawyers' Association (includes advocates, judges, prosecutors, nongraduate practitioners)

Persaja (Persadja). Persatuan Jaksa; Prosecutors' Association

New PTI. Persatuan Tenaga Indonesia; Union of Indonesian Forces

PKI. Partai Komunis Indonesia; Indonesian Communist Party

pleidooi, pledoi. Defense plea, summation

PMKRI. Persatuan Mahasiswa Katolik Republik Indonesia; Union of Catholic Students Republic of Indonesia

PNI. Partai Nasional Indonesia; Indonesian National Party

po an tui. Self-defense corps

pokrol bamboo. Bush lawyer

PPP. Partai Persatuan Pembangunan; United Development Party

PP10. Presidential Regulation #10; ban on alien traders in rural areas

PRC. People's Republic of China

pribumi. Native

priyayi. Member of the Javanese aristocratic classes

proces-verbaal. A statement or affidavit

PRRI/Permesta. Rebellion in parts of Sumatra, Sulawesi, 1958–61

PSI. Partai Sosialis Indonesia; Indonesian Socialist Party

PT. Persatuan Tionghoa; Chinese Union

PTI. Partai Tionghwa Indonesi; Indonesian Chinese Party

Raad van Justitie. Appellate bench for Europeans

Rechtshogeschool. Law college

Rechtsschool. Law school (abbreviated law course)

rechtsstaat. Law state, rule of law

Reformasi. Reformation (1998 transformation from Suharto regime)

rekwisitoor, requisitoir. Prosecution's summation of charges and request for sentence

RPKAD. Resimen Para Komando Angkatan Darat; Army commando regiment (shock troops)

RTM. Military Detention Center

singkeh (pinyin: *xinke*). Chinese immigrants; literally, "new guest"

SMH. Sin Ming Hui; New Light Association (*peranakan* service organization)

Staatswacht. Town guard

STKI. Surat Tanda Kewarganegaraan Indonesia; Indonesian Citizenship Identification Card

STOVIA. School tot Opleiding van Inlandsche Artsen; School for the Training of Native Physicians

Supersemar. Surat Persetujuan Sebelas Maret; Document of Agreement of 11 March (1966)

tapol. *Tahanan politik* (political detainee)

Tiong Hoa Kie Tok Kauw Hwee. Chinese Protestant Church

totok. Newly arrived, or Chinese-speaking ethnic Chinese

tokoh. Prominent person

trias politika. Separation of powers

UI. Universitas Indonesia; University of Indonesia

UKI. Universitas Keristen Indonesia, Christian University of Indonesia

Ureca. Universitas Res Publica ; Res Publica University (later Trisakti University)

Volksraad. People's Council

Volksuniversiteit. People's University

wayang (kulit). Shadow puppet theater

WCC. World Council of Churches

Weeskamer. Dutch civil law institution in charge of the estates of widows and orphans

wijk. District, ward

wijkmeester. Ward superintendent

wilde school. Private school (nonauthorized)

WNI. *Warganegara Indonesia;* Indonesian citizen (usually connotes Chinese descent)

zendingshuis. Mission House

NOTES

ONE *Aceh*

1 For a new, voluminous, and detailed description and interpretation of ethnic Chinese as they were enveloped into Indonesian history, see Benny G. Setiono, *Tionghoa dalam Pusaran Politik* [Chinese in the vortex of politics] (Jakarta: Elkasa, 2003). A much shorter but useful introduction to ethnic Chinese in Indonesia is G. William Skinner's "The Chinese Minority," in *Indonesia,* ed. Ruth T. McVey (New Haven: Yale Southeast Asian Studies and HRAF, 1963), 97–117.

2 On the *officieren,* see Lea E. Williams, *Overseas Chinese Nationalism: The Genesis of the Pan-Chinese Movement in Indonesia, 1900–1916* (Glencoe: The Free Press, 1960), 124 and passim.

3 Ibid., 125.

4 In exchange for the monopolies (first granted before the onset of the nineteenth century during the East-Indies Company or VOC period), revenue farmers paid licensing fees to the Dutch administration. By the time the monopolies—opium above all—came under challenge in the late nineteenth and early twentieth centuries, the colonial administration was well enough organized to regulate the private economy without resorting to private monopolies. On Chinese revenue farming, see Williams, *Overseas Chinese Nationalism,* 24.

5 Thereafter the colonial administration tried to revive the *officieren* with various incentives, some of them shallow and silly, but the institution declined steadily. There was too little popular Chinese support to shore up the *officieren,* who were, after all, the servants of an administration not obviously sympathetic to the Chinese and whose services were no longer all that useful to many and were irritating to others.

6 Williams, *Overseas Chinese Nationalism,* 126–28. Once the monopolies were removed, the administration considered paying salaries to the *officieren,* but decided against it on the grounds that the wrong sort might be attracted in that case. In 1908 the *officier* families were relieved of the onerous and despised restrictions on Chinese residence and travel, which, however, remained for all other Chinese. It did not make the *officieren* more popular. The government also went so far as to design official uniforms for *officieren,* which did not help. Henri

Borel, *De Chineezen in Nederlandsch-Indie* (Amsterdam: L. J. Veen, 1900), 33–41. The pieces in [Borel's book] were originally published in Indies newspapers.

7 Skinner, "The Chinese Minority," 100, Table 2.

8 On the nineteenth-century Chinese migration to outer Indonesia, see Victor Purcell, *The Chinese in Southeast Asia*, 2d ed. (London: Oxford University Press, 1965), 419–34; W. J. Cator, *The Economic Position of the Chinese in the Netherlands Indies* (Chicago: University of Chicago Press, 1936), 127.

9 J. Langhout, *The Economic Conquest of Acheen by the Dutch* (The Hague, 1924). I am grateful to Anthony Reid for calling my attention to this source and for making other information from his files available to me.

10 Communication from Anthony Reid, 2 November 1986, whose sources were from English and Dutch archives. On political conditions at the time, see Reid's *The Contest for North Sumatra: Atjeh, the Netherlands and Britain 1858–1898* (London: Oxford University Press and University of Malaya Press, 1969). I have no information on the early Chinese *officieren* in Aceh, though it may be available in colonial archives. The first or at least an early *kapitein* may have been Hsieh Yung-kuang (1848–1916), a Hakka born in Pontianak. Hsieh traded successfully in Aceh and would have been there at about the time the Dutch were trying to encourage immigration. He lost interest in Aceh, however, and moved his commercial interests to Penang—not an unusual story. See Yen Ching Hwang, *The Overseas Chinese and the 1911 Revolution* (London: Oxford University Press, 1976), 272–73.

11 *Encyclopaedie van Nederlandsch-Indie*, vol. 2 (The Hague and Leiden: Martinus Nijhoff and E. J. Brill, n.d.), 302.

12 Although the men in the family tended to go back to Bangka for their wives, perhaps through intermediaries, two of his brothers arranged marriages with Hokkien women from Penang. (Joen Khoy had three brothers and two sisters.) That Joen Khoy also had a Hokkien name, Yap Hok Hay, may mean that he had significant commercial or other connections with Hokkien communities.

13 Williams, *Overseas Chinese Nationalism*, 24 and 126–28.

14 Yap used the term "bankrupt," but it is not clear that what happened involved a legal action. It may be that all the family's property was simply sold off to pay the accumulated debts. In either case, the effect was much the same, not least shame and a serious decline in social status.

15 Thiam Lian remained behind in Kutaraja for years after Hien and Bong departed to Java, long enough to ask as a grown woman sensitive questions about the family and to listen to stories told by her relatives. Thiam Hien and Thiam Bong did not know how their *omah* had reached Aceh. By the turn of the century, there were many Japanese resident in the colony as elsewhere in Southeast Asia. Only a small number ended up in Aceh.

16 When exactly Nakashima went to Japan the first and second time is not clear, because the children were too young to remember. Lian believes she may have taken her adopted son back to Nagasaki just before war broke out, was caught there when hostilities began, and stayed for the duration. It is even pos-

sible, according to Lian, that Nakashima was in Japan when Joen Khoy died, but returned anyway because of her affection for the Yap children. By then Nakashima was fully at home in the family and belonged there as much as anywhere else. But it is also true that nowhere else offered her quite so much by way of home and family and support as did Kutaraja.

17 Yap Thiam Bong, Arnhem, 6 August 1987.

18 See Setiono, *Tionghoa dalam Pusaran Politik*, 472.

19 Many more ethnic Chinese applied for a different, voluntary process of limited legal adaptation *(vrijwillige onderwerping aan het Europeesch privaatrecht),* promulgated in a statute of 1917. See A. C.Tobi, *De Vrijwillige Onderwerping aan het Europeesch Privaatrecht* (Ind. Stbl. 1917, no. 12) (Leiden: van Doesburgh, 1927). These applications probably were made in connection with business interests and transactions; voluntary submission did not redefine one's personal status.

TWO *Java*

1 See Benny G. Setiono, *Tionghoa dalam Pasaran Politik* (Jakarta: Elkasa, 2003), chaps. 20–29, for an Indonesian-language history of this period.

2 Go Gien Tjwan, "Introduction," to Bob Hering, *Siauw Giok Tjhan Remembers* (Townsville, Aus.: James Cook University, 1982), viii.

3 For a start, see S. L. van der Wal, ed., *Het Onderwijsbeleid in Nederlands-Indie, 1900–1940* (Groningen: Wolters, 1963).

4 J. S. Furnivall, *Netherlands India: A Study of Plural Economy* (Cambridge: Cambridge University Press, 1944), 370–71. "Thus in education, as in so many aspects of social life, the attempt to make Netherlands India a home for Europeans has made it a better home for Orientals."

5 Ibid., 370.

6 See, for example, Ruth Gay, *The Jews of Germany: A Historical Portrait* (New Haven, Conn.: Yale University Press, 1992).

7 See the discussion of conversion to Islam by Indo-Europeans and Chinese by C. Snouck Hurgronje, in a memorandum to the governor-general of 19 April 1904, "concerning amendment of the constitutional Regeringsreglement," in E. Gobée and C. Adriaanse, *Ambtelijke Adviezen van C. Snouck Hurgronje 1889–1936* (The Hague: Nijhoff, 1957), 681, 688–89.

8 See Hendrik Kraemer, *From Missionfield to Independent Church* (The Hague: Boekencentrum, 1958), 149–58, especially 152, for a discussion of *hao* and its effect on the missionary effort.

9 Ibid., 153–54.

10 When the Japanese invaded, Landsberg committed suicide.

11 Of the total number of 22, 856 students (1,089 of whom were indigenous Indonesians and 243 European) in the for-Chinese schools, 12,806 were in government schools and 10,050 in private schools. Government elementary schools for Chinese students thus averaged 206.5 pupils over seven grades, while the private schools averaged 228.4.

12 For the sake of comparison, in the same year there were 286 HIS grade schools, of which 190 were public and 96 private, serving a total of only 62,040 pupils (including 1,468 "Foreign Orientals" and 477 Europeans). The average number of students in government HIS was 215.4, roughly comparable to the HCS, but in the private schools the average was 646.2. The data are from van der Wal, *Het Onderwijsbeleid*, 695–96. I calculated the averages.

In Indonesia as in Malaysia, and perhaps elsewhere in the region, there were always some ethnic Chinese students who attended schools for ethnic Indonesians and ethnic Indonesians who went to ethnic Chinese schools, and very few European-status children (mostly Indo-European, no doubt) in both. Over the years before 1942, a few thousand indigenous Indonesians attended schools for Chinese, and a much smaller number of "Foreign Orientals," many undoubtedly of Arab origin, were in HIS. I have been able to find no useful information about who exactly these students were, why their parents chose the schools, and what effect the experience had, but it would be interesting to know.

Indonesians and ethnic Indonesians who went to ethnic Chinese schools, and very few European-status children (mostly Indo-European, no doubt) in both. Over the years before 1942, a few thousand indigenous Indonesians attended schools for Chinese, and a much smaller number of "Foreign Orientals," many undoubtedly of Arab origin, were in HIS. I have been able to find no useful information about who exactly these students were, why their parents chose the schools, and what effect the experience had, but it would be interesting to know.

THREE *Batavia*

1 Of the 203 professional advocates working nationwide at that time, 139 were Dutch, 32 were ethnic Indonesian, and 32 were ethnic Chinese. The high number of local advocates undoubtedly fulfilled the worst fears of Dutch advocates who had opposed opening the profession to Indonesians. These data were compiled from the *Regeeringsalmanak*, vol. 2, 154–57.

2 On the history of the Indonesian private legal profession, see Daniel S. Lev, "Origins of the Indonesian Advocacy, " *Indonesia* 21 (April 1976): 135–69.

3 See Siauw Giok Tjhan's description of the reactions to the war in Manchuria among Surabaya *totok*, including his own maternal grandfather, in Bob Hering, *Siauw Giok Tjhan Remembers* (Townsville. Aus.: James Cook University, 1982), 5–6 and 28–29.

4 I have not been able to locate these articles, about which Yap's memory is vague. The journal was the *Ta Hsioh Tsa Chih*, which, despite its name, was published in Dutch.

5 On *peranakan* politics during the period of the 1920s through the 1930s, see Benny G. Setiono, *Tionghoa dalam Pasaran Politik* (Jakarta: Elkasa, 2003), chapters 21–27. Also, particularly for the 1930s, Ong Eng Die, *Chineezen in Nederlandsch-Indie: Sociografie van een Indonesische Bevolkingsgroep* (Assen: Van Gorcum, 1943), 258–63.

6 See note 31, in Hering, *Siauw Giok Tjhan Remembers.*

7 See Siauw's comments in ibid., 35.

8 Thiam Bong, already in the world of work, resented university students essentially in class terms as well-heeled "haves," socially established and intellectually pretentious, to whom he refused to feel inferior.

9 Ong Eng Die, *Chineezen*, 192–94, relying on the *Indisch Verslag*, part 2, 130. In mid-1938, there were 38,109 Catholics in Java and Madura, 409,164 in the rest of the country. The number of ethnic Chinese among them is not known. In the 1980 census, there were 8,505,696 Protestants and 4,355,575 Catholics, approximately 5.8 and 3 percent, respectively, of the total population. *Sebuah Rangkuman Tentang: Monografi Kelembagaan Islam di Indonesia* [Summary of a monograph on Islamic institutions in Indonesia] (Jakarta: Ministry of Religion, 1984), 157.

10 See, for example, Dr. Hendrik Kraemer, *From Missionfield to Independent Church* (The Hague: Boekencentrum, 1958), and Dr. J. A. Verdoorn, *De Zending en het Indonesisch Nationalisme* [The mission and Indonesian nationalism] (Amsterdam: Vrij Nederland, 1945), with an introduction by Kraemer.

11 Confidential interview with a lawyer in Kuala Lumpur on 25 July 1986. I have edited my notes from the conversation back into first person.

12 Kraemer, *From Missionfield to Independent Church*, 32–35. From his report on the church in the Minahasa.

13 Ibid., 118, on Sundanese Christians.

14 Ibid., 146–47.

15 Interview of 10 July 1986.

FOUR *From Sukabumi to Leiden*

1 Interview with Yap Thiam Bong, 6 August 1987, in Arnhem, Holland.

2 On the Japanese period, see George McT. Kahin, *Nationalism and Revolution in Indonesia* (Ithaca, N.Y.: Cornell University Press, 1952), 101ff; Leo Suryadinata, *Pribumi Indonesians, the Chinese Minority and China* (Singapore: Heinemann, 1978), 5–60; Bob Hering, *Siauw Giok Tjhan Remembers* (Townsville, Aus.: James Cook University, 1982), 39–46.

3 The material in this paragraph is recorded on tape from Yap and his sister, Non, whom I interviewed in Holland.

4 On the Keibotai and its parent organization, the Kakyo Shokai, see Mary Somers, "Peranakan Chinese Politics in Indonesia" (PhD diss., Cornell University, 1965), 109. The head of the Keibotai in East Java was Siauw Giok Tjhan, who fought off the intention of some Kakyo leaders to use the Keibotai as a defense against expected attacks on Chinese by the Keibodan. Consistent with his pre-war views in the PTI, Siauw successfully argued that the Keibotai must work with the Keibodan and support the nationalist movement. *Siauw Giok Tjhan Remembers*, 43–46.

5 Interview with Yap Thiam Bong, 6 August 1987, in Arnhem, Holland.

6 Unfortunately, *Sin Po* for the year 1946 was not available to me, and I have had to rely on Yap's memory of the more important topics he took up in his articles.

7 I am grateful to the University of Leiden for releasing Yap's transcript and to the late Professor J. F. Holleman for obtaining and explaining it in full.

8 See Dr. J. Reitsma, *Geschiedenis van de Hervorming en de Hervormde Kerk der Nederlanden* (The Hague: Martinus Nijhoff, 1949), 548. One Dutch missionary friend, Jan Klop, constantly dropped in to cadge cigarettes and leave books for Hien to read. Later he went to Indonesia but could not adapt and returned in failure.

9 It would take more hubris than I can muster to try to unravel the slightly alarming complications of Dutch religious history. Apart from Reitsma, cited in note 8, and other works on Dutch Protestantism, I have also relied in part on James Whitney's *The History of the Reformation* (New York: Macmillan, 1907, 1940) and H. E. Dosker, *The Dutch Anabaptists* (Philadelphia: Judson Press, 1921).

10 Early in the revolution, following anti-Chinese violence and with the help of returning Dutch, young Chinese toughs were recruited into local paramilitary self-defense groups, the *pao an tui*. More like gangs, these groups did not make good political sense and lacked effective political direction. In the Surabaya area, where *peranakan* leadership was highly sophisticated, the *pao an tui* was consciously rejected and never got off the ground. For more about the *pao an tui*, see chapter 6.

11 Interview with Yap Thiam Hien, May 1985 (tape 2/85, side two). Transcripts of some of my interview tapes are available in Special Collections at the University of Washington Libraries, Seattle.

12 *New York Times*, 23 July 1947, 4. The ten-day conference was sponsored by the World Alliance of the Young Men's Christian Association. Fifteen hundred participants, church leaders and young people, from about seventy countries, attended. According to the *Times* report, the Dutch and Indonesian delegations considered a joint statement, but if so, given the stance of the Indonesian delegation, the discussions must have been tense.

13 There may well be an historical relationship between the Dutch *verzuiling* (pillar) and Indonesian *aliran* (current) conception of political structure. For the fullest and most enlightening discussion, see Ruth T. McVey's introduction to the translation of Soekarno, *Nationalism, Islam and Marxism* (Ithaca, N.Y.: Cornell Modern Indonesia Project, 1969). Political party systems in both countries have changed considerably, but originally they were organized around primary ideological cleavages: in Holland, Catholics, Protestants, and secularists; in Indonesia (to simplify), Islam, aristocratically led religious syncretism, and Marxism.

14 The revolution originally opposed by the party was that of 1789.

15 The Tiong Hoa Kie Kauw Hwee (Chinese Protestant Church) in 1957 changed to Kie Kauw Hwee and later still, in a reorganization in which Yap played a part, to the Gereja Kristen Indonesia (Protestant Church of Indonesia).

16 Kenneth Scott Latourette, *Christianity in a Revolutionary Age*. Vol. 4: *The Twentieth Century in Europe* (New York: Harper Brothers, 1961), 449–50.

FIVE *Jakarta*

1 In this chapter, readers will notice, the use of "Thiam Hien" and "Hien" gradually gives way to "Yap." This is merely a means of adapting to his growing age, career, and stature, and it reflects his growing public presence.

2 The marriage was validated in the civil registry (Burgerlijke Stand) for Europeans because of Yap's European legal status.

3 Hildred Geertz, "Indonesian Cultures and Communities," in *Indonesia*, ed. Ruth T. McVey (New Haven: HRAF, 1963), 24–97, 33–41.

4 *Uittreksel uit het Register der Besluiten van de Secretaris van Staat, Hoofd van het Departement van Justitie ddo.* 11 Juli 1949 Nr. J.P. 8/4/14.

5 Daniel S. Lev, "The Origins of the Indonesian Advocacy," *Indonesia* 21 (April 1976): 135–69.

6 Ibid., 161.

7 Daniel S. Lev, "Colonial Law and the Genesis of the Indonesian State," *Indonesia* 40 (October 1985): 57–74.

8 Ibid., passim.

9 *Regeeringsalmanak* 2 (1942): 164–67. The numbers are mine, arrived at by classifying the ethnic origins of the names of registered advocates.

10 Daniel S. Lev, *Bush-Lawyers in Indonesia: Stratification, Representation, and Brokerage.* Working Paper no. 1, Law and Society Program, University of California, Berkeley (1973).

11 Daniel S. Lev, *Islamic Courts in Indonesia* (Berkeley: University of California Press, 1972).

12 Daniel S. Lev, "The Politics of Judicial Development in Indonesia," *Comparative Studies in Society and History* 7, no. 2 (1965):173–99, 202.

13 ISHI (Ikatan Sarjana Hukum Indonesia, Indonesian Law Graduates Bond) was restricted to members with law degrees, while PAHI (Persatuan Ahli Hukum Indonesia, Union of Indonesian Lawyers) accepted members without law degrees, for example, the *Rechtskundigen*, graduates of the Rechtsschool, a truncated law course that preceded the Rechtshogeschool. All of the original cohort of Javanese students sent to Leiden to study in the late 1910s came out of the Rechtshogeschool. Some, like Chief Public Prosecutor Soeprapto, never went to Leiden or to the Rechtshogeschool. Many early judges and prosecutors, moreover, had only limited legal training or experience in the regional bureaucracy, the *pamong praja*, or elsewhere. ISHI and PAHI eventually gave way to the unified national law association Persahi (Persatuan Ahli Hukum Indonesia).

14 Mochtar, Komar, and Karuin, established in the 1960s. The Mochtar is Mochtar Kusumaatmadja, Indonesia's foreign minister from the mid-1970s until 1988.

15 *Proses Yap Thiam Hien S.H.* [The Yap Thiam Hien trial] (Jakarta: Peradin, 1969), 70–71. 16. Leo Suryadinata, *Eminent Indonesian Chinese: Biographical Sketches*, rev. ed. (Singapore: Gunung Agung, 1981), 134–35, and Mary Somers, "Peranakan Chinese Politics in Indonesia" (PhD diss., Cornell University, 1965), 121–22.

17 Suryadinata, *Eminent Indonesian Chinese*, 94–95. I have also relied on unpublished manuscripts by Oei and personal interviews with him. Oei's memoir, *Memoar Oei Tjoe Tat: Pembantu Presiden Soekarno* [The memoirs of Oei Tjoe Tat: Assistant to President Soekarno] (Jakarta: Hasta Mitra, 1995), made a splash when it first came out but was soon banned (though only after it had sold several thousand copies), a rare thing at the time. Oei died a few years after his book was published.

18 All of the material in this and the next paragraph comes directly from Yap, but much of it is confirmed, though in bits and pieces, by unrecorded informal conversations with others who knew him or were involved with his projects during the 1950s or thereafter. Such documentary sources as I have found will be cited on these and related matters in later chapters.

SIX *Hazardous Waters*

1 This was the Badan Penyelidik Usaha Persiapan Kemerdekaan Indonesia (BPUPKI, Investigatory Body for Preparatory Work for Indonesian Independence), which was replaced in August 1945 by the Panitia Persiapan Kemerdekaan Indonesia (PPKI, Committee for the Preparation of Indonesian Independence). The PPKI accepted most of the earlier body's recommendations for the 1945 Constitution.

2 Moh. Yamin, *Naskah-Persiapan Undang-Undang Dasar 1945* [Documents on the drafting of the 1945 Constitution] (Jakarta: Yayasan Prapantja, 1959), 402. See also the discussion of this problem by Siauw Giok Tjhan, *Lima Jaman: Perwujudan integrasi wajar* (Jakarta/Amsterdam: [Yayasan Teratai], 1981), 286, who claimed that the *asli* provision was meant to prevent a Japanese from becoming president, a point for which I can find no corroborating evidence. Supomo and the drafting committee he headed were willing to eliminate the term *asli* from Article 6, but did not prevail.

3 See Yamin, *Naskah*, 218, for the speech of Liem Koen Hian, who along with Siauw Giok Tjan, sought citizenship for all Chinese with a right of repudiation; 242–43, for those of Oei Tjang Tjoei and Oei Tjong Houw, who suggested that Chinese preferred Chinese citizenship; and 471, for Soekarno's statement. Liem Koen Hian, a Surabaya newspaper editor, founded the PTI, which supported the Indonesian nationalists. Siauw Giok Tjan was also a Surabaya journalist and a member of the PTI. Oei Tjong Houw was a son and heir of the Semarang magnate Oei Tiong Ham. He was a founding member of the CHH and represented the CHH conservative business-oriented point of view. Oei Tjang Tjoei, a Jakarta newspaperman, was a member of the HCTH, the Japanese-sponsored Association of Chinese groups. See also Leo Suryadinata, *Eminent Indonesian Chinese* (Singapore: Gunung Agung, 1981). Naturally, *peranakan* hesitation on the citizenship issue did not sit well with ethnic Indonesian nationalists, for many of whom it merely confirmed their suspicions of Chinese loyalties.

4 See Benny G. Setiono, *Tionghoa dalam Pasaran Politik* (Jakarta: Elkasa, 2003), 577ff, on the *pao an tui*, generally chapters 30–35 on the revolutionary period. The *pao an tui* was never well organized (local units evidently operated on their own) or well armed and was short lived, formally disbanding in April 1949.

5 See the 1950 speech by Liem Koen Hian, in Leo Suryadinata, ed., *Political Thinking of the Indonesian Chinese, 1900–1977: A Sourcebook* (Singapore: Singapore University Press, 1979), 134–37, at 136.

6 Donald Willmott, *The National Status of the Chinese in Indonesia* (Ithaca, N.Y.: Cornell Modern Indonesia Project, 1956), 10–22.

7 Herbert Feith, *The Decline of Constitutional Democracy in Indonesia* (Ithaca, N.Y.: Cornell University Press, 1962), 481–87.

8 Tan Ling Djie served as PKI secretary general from 1949 until 1953, when he was ousted by Aidit and his allies.

9 Leo Suryadinata, "Indonesian Chinese Education: Past and Present," *Indonesia* 14 (October 1972): 49–71. Leo Suryadinata, *Pribumi Indonesians, the Chinese Minority and China* (Singapore: Heinemann Asia, 1978, 1986), 147.

10 Preeminent sources on post-1945 ethnic Chinese politics include Willmott, *National Status*; Mary F. Somers, *Peranakan Chinese Politics in Indonesia*, Interim Reports Series (Ithaca, N.Y.: Cornell Modern Indonesia Project, 1964), and "Peranakan Chinese Politics in Indonesia" (PhD diss., Cornell University, 1965); Leo Suryadinata's *Pribumi Indonesians*, his *Eminent Indonesian Chinese* (Singapore: Gunung Agung, 1981), and his *Political Thinking of the Indonesian Chinese, 1900–1977* (Singapore: Singapore University Press, 1979); J. A. C. Mackie, ed., *The Chinese in Indonesia* (Honolulu: University of Hawai'i Press, 1976); Charles A. Coppel, *Indonesian Chinese in Crisis* (Melbourne: Oxford University Press, 1983).

11 Somers, *Peranakan Chinese Politics*, 12. In the parliamentary elections of 1955, Baperki, the *peranakan* organization formed the previous year, won over 81 percent of its votes in Java, with the remaining 18 percent scattered around the rest of the country. In national politics, too, three of the four major parties—the PNI (Nationalists), NU (Nadhlatul Ulama, the conservative Islamic party), and the PKI (Communists)—drew most of their support from Java, essentially the ethnic Javanese provinces of Central and East Java. Only the "modernist" Islamic party, Masyumi, attracted support more or less evenly from around the archipelago. On the elections of 1955, see Herbert Feith, *The Indonesian Elections of 1955* (Ithaca, N.Y.: Cornell Modern Indonesia Project, 1957).

12 A few Chinese in West Java had acquired "private lands"—*particuliere landerijen*, estates auctioned off to private buyers early in the nineteenth century—with rights to corvée labor and taxes, thus gaining extensive control over local inhabitants, both indigenous and Chinese. Also some had acquired large tea plantations, giving them a stake in the colonial economy quite like that of Dutch planter interests. Bob Hering, *Siauw Giok Tjhan Remembers* (Townsville, Aus.: James Cook University, 1982), 22. Siauw points out that one of the first *peranakan*

in the Volksraad was Kan Hok Hoei of CHH, who owned a large estate in West Java.

13 James R. Rush, "Social Control and Influence in Nineteenth-Century Indonesia: Opium Farms and the Chinese of Java," *Indonesia* 35 (April 1985): 53–64.

14 Not only *totok*. On different grounds, in the 1930s the Chung Hua Hui charged the PTI of wanting to become native. Hering, *Siauw Giok Tjhan Remembers*, 23.

15 Compared with Malaysia, where intermarriage between Malays and ethnic Chinese was and remains rare, in Indonesia it was not and is not unusual, though without statistical data being available, one has to go on impressions. The eldest brother of Khing, Yap's wife, as has been mentioned, married the niece of the famous nationalist leader Dr. Tjipto Mangoenkoesoemo, and her father, the head of the Tan family, owned a ceremonial gamelan.

16 Feith, *The Decline of Constitutional Democracy*, 5–6. "Most nationalists regarded the body with distrust, and the more radical organizations forbade their members to participate in it." Chinese, as "Foreign Orientals," were allotted seats.

17 On twentieth-century Surabaya through the early revolution, see William H. Frederick, *Visions and Heat: The Making of the Indonesian Revolution* (Athens: Ohio University Press, 1989). Unfortunately, the study does not deal with the *peranakan* community in the city.

18 Similarly, a wartime organization of Islamic groups, Masyumi, gave rise to the post-1945 party Masyumi.

19 For a useful discussion of the CHTH relationship with republican efforts, see Yap Tjwan Bing, *Meretas Jalan Kemerdekaan* [On the road to independence: Autobiography of an independence fighter] (Jakarta: Gramedia, 1988), 66–75. Yap had been chair of the organization in Bandung during the occupation and was a vice-chair of the one re-established in Yogyakarta.

20 Somers, "Peranakan Chinese," 130, and Charles Coppel, "Patterns of Chinese Political Activity in Indonesia," in J. A. C. Mackie, ed., *The Chinese in Indonesia*, 40 (Honolulu: University of Hawai'i Press, 1976).

21 Somers, "Peranakan Chinese," 130–31. As Somers points out, however, while formal contacts between older generation *peranakan* and *totok* faded, many young *peranakan* still attended Chinese-language schools sponsored by the CHTH.

22 In an interview with me, Oei Tjoe Tat said that Thio had reluctantly agreed to work with Van Mook at the request of other Chinese leaders who felt that a major figure had to represent Chinese interests to the Dutch administration. Nevertheless, it did not help the standing of the PT, with politically sophisticated peranakan leaders who had sided with the Republic, not to mention ethnic Indonesian leaders at all attentive to Chinese activities.

23 See Somers, "Peranakan Chinese," 131, and Suryadinata, *Pribumi Indonesians*, 60–63, for a more elaborate discussion of PT views.

24 This was a way of referring to Eurasians, most of whom did not have Dutch nationality before independence.

25 See Liem Koen Hian's statement announcing his new party, in Suryadinata, *Political Thinking of the Indonesian Chinese*, 134–37. Liem died in 1952.

26 Ibid., and Suryadinata, *Pribumi Indonesians*, 63–64.

27 Suryadinata, Pribumi Indonesians, 64–65.

28 Coppel, "Patterns of Chinese Political Activity." In 1939, the left-wing party Gerindo decided to allow *peranakan* to become members.

29 Ong Eng Die eventually went back to Holland, while Yap Tjwan Bing ended up in California. Yap wrote an autobiography, *Meretas Jalan Kemerdekaan* (see above, note 20). He served on the party council of the PNI for several years, he says, before his son's illness forced the family to seek medical help in the United States.

30 Feith, *Decline of Constitutional Democracy* , 481–82. Assaat was a respected nonparty leader and businessman who was close to Vice President Hatta and had served as minister of the interior in the cabinet of Mohammad Natsir (1950–1951).

31 Leo Suryadinata, "Indonesian Chinese Education," 64. In 1950, of 300,000 school-age Chinese children, 50,000 were in Indonesian schools, with the rest in Chinese medium schools. Of the latter, 150,000 were the children of citizens, overwhelmingly *peranakan*.

32 As discussed earlier, when his father assimilated to European status, Yap and his siblings were automatically given that status. Yap never considered exercising his option, under the Round Table Conference Agreements, to move to Holland with Dutch citizenship. When he had to formally reject Chinese citizenship in order to confirm his Indonesian citizenship, it pained him and he never referred to it in our conversations. After his death, I found the document by chance among his papers.

33 On the citizenship issue, see Willmott, *National Status*; Somers, *Peranakan Chinese*; and among many Indonesian sources, *Undang-undang Kewarganegaraan Indonesia* [Indonesian law of citizenship] (Jakarta: Pustaka Rakjat, 1958); Gouw Giok Siong and Ch. Huang, *Tanja-Djawab tentang Kewarganegaraan* [Questions and answers about citizenship] (Jakarta: Keng Po, 1961); Soejono Hadidjojo's thesis, "Kewarganegaraan Indonesia" [Indonesian citizenship] (Yogyakarta: Yayasan "Gadjah-Mada," 1954); Drs. Heroe Soetjiptomo, *Peranan Pendapat Umum dalam Masalah Undang-Undang no. 2/1958 tentang Dwikewarganegaraan Warganegara Tjina di Indonesia* [The role of public opinion in the problem of Law no. 2/1958 concerning dual-nationality of Chinese citizens in Indonesia] (Medan: Toko Buku DELI, 1970); and Imam Bardjo, *Masaalah Kewargaan Negara Republik Indonesia* [The problem of citizenship in the Republic of Indonesia] (Semarang: Baperki, 1958).

34 Willmott, *National Status*, 34.

35 Ibid., 34–35. The same rules applied mutatis mutandis to Chinese who wished to opt for Chinese citizenship.

36 Ibid., 36–37. Over the next several years, particularly during the Guided Democracy and New Order periods, periodical re-registration requirements imposed on ethnic Chinese proved a financial boon for first instance courts and administrative offices around the country and a serious irritant and reminder of their unfortunate status for ethnic Chinese.

37 Ibid., 39. The editorial appeared on 26 April 1955.

38 Ibid., citing *Keng Po*, 9 May 1955.

39 In various forms, however, this provision was in fact violated again and again during the New Order period.

40 Willmott, *National Status*, 42–43, citing *Keng Po*, 16 June 1955 and *Sin Min*, 27 May 1955.

41 Ibid., 81, citing *Keng Po*, 16 June 1955.

42 See Somers, *Peranakan Chinese Politics*, 14–16. Somers suggests that the PKI and Baperki representatives who had been uncomfortable with the treaty would eventually vote to ratify because they shared the widespread assumption that Chinese who voted in the 1955 elections would be exempt from the treaty obligation to declare themselves Indonesian citizens: they would be considered as such since they were voters. Afterwards, however, the government refused to exempt voters from registration.

43 Willmott estimated, with admitted uncertainty, that about 17 to 25 percent of *peranakan* Chinese throughout Indonesia opted for Chinese citizenship in the years 1949–51. Further, he suggested, 40 to 45 percent of ethnic Chinese then (1955) living in Indonesia were Chinese subjects. Willmott, *National Status*, 49–50.

44 *Star Weekly*, 10, 17, and 24 November 1951. Yap's piece was in the 17 November issue. See *Star Weekly*, 3 July 1954, for the reprint of his article and a recapitulation of the argument.

SEVEN *At Sea in* Peranakan *Politics*

1 Leo Suryadinata, *Pribumi Indonesians, the Chinese Minority and China* (Singapore: Heinemann Asia, 1978, 1986), 65; and minutes of the founding meeting of Baperki, "Laporan Rapat Pembentukan Badan Permusjawaratan Kewarganegaraan Indonesia, BAPERKI," stencil ([Jakarta? 1954?]); hereafter cited as "Laporan Rapat."

2 *Star Weekly*, 27 February 1954. While the 1950 Constitution guaranteed nine seats to the Chinese minority, the objective of an ethnic Chinese electoral association was itself to command as many seats as possible committed to defending minority interests. Otherwise *peranakan* seats would be filled by and be bound to the major parties. Not long after the parliamentary elections of 1955, a battle arose over precisely this issue in which Baperki succeeded in gaining control over several additional seats.

3 Ibid.

4 "Laporan Rapat," 9; and Mary Somers "Peranakan Chinese Politics in Indonesia" (PhD diss., Cornell University, 1965), 145, note 18.

5 See Siauw's own discussion of the session in his autobiography, *Lima Jaman: Perwujudan integrasi wajar* (Jakarta/Amsterdam: [Yayasan Teratai], 1981), 235ff.

6 In Siauw's autobiography, Yap is not mentioned, for Siauw saw the PDTI Semarang group as the major force behind retaining a Chinese stamp in the new

organization's name. He calls attention to the irony that of the two Semarang figures—Kwee Hway Gwan and Tan Tjin Lin—who took the "Chinese" line, one later became an "assimilator" in favor of giving up Chinese personal names in favor of "Indonesian" names, while the other fled Indonesia under suspicion of abetting illegal Kuomintang activities. Ibid., 235–36.

7 "Laporan Rapat," 4. Years later, in 1977, Yap joined a few other leaders of the advocates' association, Peradin, in proclaiming it an *organisasi perjuangan*, or "struggle organization."

8 Others there may have helped to convince Yap. The politically experienced Tan Po Goan, hardly an ally of Siauw, argued persuasively that it was important to avoid antithetical juxtapositions of ethnic Chinese and ethnic Indonesians; and the term "Chinese descent" obviously represented that antithesis. Thio Thiam Tjong, whom Yap admired, also said that the name of the organization was not important. Soon afterwards, apparently, Yap supported a suggestion by Kwee Hwat Djien that to Siauw's proposed Badan Permusjawaratan Kewarganegaraan be added "Indonesia" in order to make clear that the citizenship at issue was Indonesian. So it became BPKI, to which Siauw agreed, and the meeting, according to the minutes, then decided on the acronym Baperki. "Laporan Rapat," 5–6.

9 In the "Laporan Rapat," the vote count for Yap is corrected but unclear as either 33 or 13. If 33, he was eighth, followed by Go Gien Tjwan with 31. If 13, he was ninth, following Go. The relationship between the two men was tense, mainly from Yap's side.

10 There was some resentment and worry about Siauw's choice of Go Gien Tjwan, but it was Khoe Woen Sioe who proposed that the chairman should be able to choose his own secretary. Because Go was often abroad on Antara news agency business, he gave way later to Buyung Saleh, also Siauw's personal choice, who remained secretary until Baperki was banned. Both Go and Buyung Saleh were communists; the former did not, I think, belong to the Communist Party, while the latter did.

11 One other ethnic Chinese was elected to Parliament on the Communist Party list. Seven more positions thus had to be filled. In the Constituent Assembly, the number of seats reserved for each minority group was double that in the Parliament.

12 See Somers "Peranakan Chinese," 151–53, for a discussion of Baperki's handling of the reserved seats in Parliament and the Constituent Assembly. In Parliament, the government parties sought control over the reserved seats, but Siauw skillfully maneuvered to give Baperki prior claim. Somers points out that in the election campaign, Baperki denied that it represented any ethnic group, a matter of ideological importance to Siauw's conception of the organization, yet in the debates over the reserved seats, it claimed the sole right to represent *peranakan* Chinese. Baperki was able to place another of its candidates in Parliament and three or four more in the Constituent Assembly. It was a major victory, one that persuaded many *peranakan* observers that Baperki deserved support.

13 The discussion here and elsewhere in this chapter is based on a paper I wrote for a conference on *peranakan* Chinese in Indonesia held at Cornell University in July 1990. "Becoming an *Orang Indonesia Sejati*: The Political Journey of Yap Thiam Hien" was published in *Indonesia Special Issue: The Role of Indonesian Chinese in Shaping Modern Indonesian Life* (1991): 97–112.

14 Siauw, *Lima Jaman*, 241.

15 Siauw was very well connected with national leaders, who trusted his advice. He was personally close to Sartono, the PNI speaker of Parliament, and knew Soekarno reasonably well. Both in Parliament and in the Constituent Assembly, Siauw's political knowledge and skills were much in demand. My point, however, is that Baperki necessarily confined him to a set of interests and responsibilities from which he could not easily break loose. He had to speak publicly only as a *peranakan* leader.

16 Siauw evidently had been attracted to communism since the 1930s, when Tan Ling Djie, later chairman of the PKI until 1953, influenced his ideological and political education. During the 1950s, Tan, removed from the party leadership by D. N. Aidit, lived in Siauw's home. Siauw edited the Jakarta newspaper *Suara Rakjat* (People's Voice), sold to the PKI in 1951, and continued to edit its successor, *Harian Rakjat* (People's Daily), until 1953. Many believed Siauw to be a secret member of the PKI, but he may in fact have resented the Aidit leadership for having ousted Tan Ling Djie (who remained in an advisory capacity to the party), particularly if he thought that this move was inspired by anti-Chinese animus. See *Lima Jaman*, 296–97, where he hints at this. Siauw never hid his communist, or at least Marxist, views, either in Parliament or in his autobiography.

17 *Keng Po*, 8 September 1955, and *Star Weekly*, 10 September 1955. The press reported that Auwjong resigned because of disagreements over policy on experimental integrated grade schools following a Baperki conference in May concerning education. However, Auwjong was also dissatisfied with his position in the national organization and, moreover, had become increasingly alarmed by Siauw's support for PKI initiatives in Parliament. See *Star Weekly*, 27 August 1955 and 17 September 1955, for two letters reacting to the 27 August comment on Siauw in Parliament. The first, from Ko Kwat Oen, first vice chair of Baperki's Bandung branch, defended Siauw on the grounds that he had differed with the PKI, and wrote that if Siauw deviated from Baperki's program, he would be thrown out. According to Leo Suryadinata, the same Ko Kwat Oen, a Protestant Parkindo MP, later left Baperki (Suryadinata, *Mencari Identitas Nasional: Dari Tjoe Bou San Sampai Yap Thiam Hien* [In search of national identity: from Tjoe Bou San to Yap Thiam Hien] [Jakarta: LP3ES, n.d.]), 194. The other letter, indicating that its writer was distancing himself from Baperki as a result, adduced evidence to show that Siauw was close to the PKI; i.e., Siauw wanted a vote distribution agreement with the PKI; he attacked the United States and praised Communist China; and his secretary-general, Go Gien Tjwan, was known in Holland as a communist or at least a sympathizer. In an editorial note, *Star Weekly*

pointed out that Go had been appointed to his position and was a candidate for Parliament on the approval of the Baperki congress.

18 For a more detailed history of this period, see my *Transition to Guided Democracy: Indonesian Politics, 1957–1959* (Ithaca, N.Y.: Cornell Modern Indonesia Project, 1966).

19 Buyung Saleh was a nom de guerre. His original name was Puradisastra. Educated in letters, he was regarded as an expert in cultural and literary matters. Close to Siauw, he was the lone ethnic Indonesian on Baperki's executive committee.

20 Baperki documents from 1954 and 1955, during the election campaign, provide the evidence for this. Both Siauw and Yap addressed human rights issues in their presentations, but for the rest their perspectives diverged. Yap's copies of speeches by Siauw and Go are well marked in his hand with marginal notes on their Marxist implications but also on their failure to address other issues he thought important. Yet Yap later admitted to having learned a great deal from Siauw about the economics of racial discrimination.

21 See Mary Somers, *Peranakan Politics in Indonesia* (Ithaca, N.Y.: Cornell Modern Indonesia Project, 1964), 19–23, on the Chinese schools issue and Baperki's response.

22 Interview with Yap, 25 November 1987.

23 Siauw Giok Tjan, *Membina Bangsa jang Bulat Bersatu* [To develop a united nation]. Report to the fourth Baperki congress, 21–23 December 1956, in Surabaya (BAPERKI, 1957), 47–48. The purpose of establishing the university, said Siauw, was among other things to prove the minority's willingness to help reduce the shortage of university places and the reasons for racial discrimination; to educate social cadres who rejected the idea that race determines ability and who would help eliminate racial discrimination in violation of human rights; and to get rid of the mistaken conception that people of Chinese descent were interested only in money, for the new university would produce academically trained personnel to develop various sciences in Indonesia.

24 Present at this meeting were Go Gien Tjwan, Tjan Tjoe Som, Sie Boen Liep, J. B. Avé, Oei Hien Tjiang and his wife, and Buyung Saleh. This information is from the typescript record of the Baperki executive committee (*pengurus pusat harian*) meeting of 10 January 1958; hereafter "Rapat Pengurus." According to Go, in an interview in Amsterdam on 4 August 1987, after Yap's committee decided to involve the Sin Ming Hui, a question arose in Go's mind as to whether they would actually be able to pull it off. Sometime earlier an ethnic Chinese student who had placed first in the Jakarta high school examinations was initially denied admission to the University of Indonesia medical faculty (though he or she was later admitted). Evidently in reaction to this, Go's wife, Tilly, angrily accused Go and the others of being cowards. The Sin Ming Hui, she argued, would not be able to develop the university; Go and his cohorts should do it themselves. Go was convinced, he said, and persuaded Siauw, who agreed that Baperki itself should undertake the effort.

25 Actually, according to the minutes of the meeting, it was Oei Tjoe Tat who first raised the objection that it might not be wise to append the name Baperki to the new Educational Foundation. "Rapat Pengurus," 1. But it was Yap who carried the ball thereafter. The Persatuan Guru Warganegara Indonesia, or Union of Indonesian Citizen Teachers, was the Indonesianized name of the former Onderwijzersbond. Use of the term "warganegara," citizen, was usually a clear indication that an organization was ethnic Chinese.

26 On 24 January 1958, Yap wrote a letter to the executive committee in which he laid out his arguments more clearly. The essential point remained that, as Baperki had moved left, it had lost the sympathy of many of its supporters. Consequently, a foundation bearing Baperki's name would be regarded suspiciously and it would be difficult to gather the financial and moral support needed to build a university. In this Yap proved quite wrong. He was also wrong in supposing that various factions of Baperki would fight over the university. Yap also repeated the argument that an educational foundation violated the limits imposed by Baperki's charter. After the 10 January meeting, Yap and Siauw met together to talk about the issue, but Yap remained convinced that the executive committee was wrong. The copy of the letter is from the Yap papers, Lev collection.

27 See his report as general chairman to the sixth congress of Baperki, 28–30 August 1959, in Jakarta; stencil, 12, Lev collection.

28 On Baperki's vote in 1957, see Somers, *Peranakan Chinese Politics*, 18–19. Particularly in East Java, where Siauw's brother, Siauw Giok Bie, chaired the provincial organization, Baperki's showing had increased substantially.

29 From 1958 on, complaints about Baperki finances, lackadaisical dues remissions, inactive branches, and the like were constant. See the reports of the annual congresses and executive committee meetings, mimeo, 1958–62.

30 "Berita Atjara Kongres Nasional V BAPERKI Seluruh Indonesia paga tanggal 25–26–27–28 Djuni 1958 di Solo [Minutes of the fifth national congress of Baperki, 25–28 June 1958, in Solo]", 12–13, mimeo.

31 "Berita," 12. Yap's point about defending one's enemies was important to him. As a young boy his favorite stories, whether Sato Nakashima's samurai tales or Karl May's novels of the American West, were those in which the hero showed character by treating his foes fairly and humanely. Yap seems to have carried this notion with him through life, often making genuine gestures toward honorable opponents, including Siauw.

32 Ibid., 15. Yap may well have suspected, however, that Siauw was unwilling to have Baperki react to the *Keng Po* closure because of the paper's PSI sympathies. Siauw admitted that the freedom of the press problem had become difficult, and cited a UNESCO report to the effect that freedom of the press was possible only when national security was assured—a reference on his part, most likely, to the regional rebellions. In his own report, Siauw had condemned the rebellions as self-serving, to which Yap replied that while all rebellions violated the law, it was wrong to insist that all rebels were self-concerned, for every rebel also had ideals. Ibid., 12.

33 Yap pointed out that, if Baperki could not run in the election, what was at issue was not a surplus vote agreement (*stembus accord*), as Siauw and others had referred to it, but rather a voters' alliance, an electoral bloc: he wanted this made clear, he said, so that the congress would understand and be prepared to accept the consequences of approving such an agreement, an alliance with a political party, an acceptance of its goals and policy choices. Ibid., 22.

34 Ibid., 23.

35 From appendices to the minutes mailed to members of the executive committee on 9 July 1958, Lev collection. The solution to the problem, though made irrelevant by the absence of elections thereafter, was simply that, once the law made clear its status, Baperki's executive committee would consult with the four major parties along with the PSII (Partai Sarekat Islam Indonesia), Parkindo, and Partai Katolik about representation of the minority, and then decide upon its strategy. All that Siauw had wanted, but had not made quite clear, was authority to act quickly to come up with a response to whatever situation was imposed upon Baperki by the new law. Yap like others misunderstood and jumped to the conclusion that Siauw wanted a blank check to cement an alliance with the PKI.

36 Siauw was elected by a vote of 268. The vice chairs other than Yap were Go Gien Tjwan, Mrs. Lauw In Nio, Tan Eng Tie, and Thio. Of these only Go received more than 200 votes. Buyung Saleh was re-elected secretary by a vote of 257. The executive committee consisted, for the rest, of another secretary, two treasurers, and seven commissioners of various matters—law, information, cadre education, social affairs/youth/sports, women, and election coordination. Buyung Saleh doubled as commissioner for cadre education. Ibid., 30.

37 "Laporan Ketua Umum BAPERKI Kepada Konperensi Pleno BAPERKI pada tgl. 12–14 Desember 1958 di Djakarta" [Report of the chairman of Baperki to the plenary conference of Baperki (executive committee) 12–14 December 1958 in Jakarta], 1, mimeo.

38 "Notulen Konperensi Pleno Pusat Pada Tanggal 12–14 Desember 1958 di Djakarta" [Minutes of the plenary conference, 12–14 December 1958, in Jakarta] (mimeo), 3. In this first of three rounds of questions, Yap also challenged Siauw on other scores, including the chair's condemnation of the regional rebellions and the Darul Islam. Yap said that as a legalist he agreed, but should not the communist rebellion at Madiun in 1948 also be faulted? Siauw later replied that Madiun was over and no longer relevant.

39 "Notulen," 3.

40 Ibid., 3–4.

41 There was no reason for mutual suspicion, Tan said, though in fact there was. On the one hand, he agreed with Yap that Baperki would die if its leaders pushed it in only one political direction. On the other, in Baperki's struggle against racial discrimination, necessarily it had to deal with problems beyond citizenship, and the rise of Guided Democracy required it to take a position. Yet, he agreed with Yap that such important matters had to be discussed first. "Notulen," 9.

42 Ibid., 12.

43 On the second day of the Baperki executive committee meeting, 13 December 1958, the Baperki newspaper, *Republik*, reported that a Baperki–East Java conference in Jember had unanimously thrown its support behind the consolidation of the Republic of Indonesia of 17 August 1945—i.e., behind Soekarno and Guided Democracy.

44 My copies of the minutes do not show this vote, but it is mentioned in a letter from Buyung Saleh to Yap, 4 March 1959.

45 Yap's letter of 6 February 1959 to the executive committee challenged the statement of Ang Tjiang Liat, another committee member, that all members agreed to Guided Democracy, and Buyung Saleh's reply of 19 February 1959, in which he simply sent the minutes of the February 1957 executive committee meeting. (Both letters are in the Yap papers, Lev collection.) At that time Yap and two others, Thio Thiam Tjong and Gouw Soey Tjiang, had accepted the Konsepsi with significant reservations, and later Gouw and Yap had criticized a report in the Baperki daily *Republik*, which implied that Baperki accepted the entire Konsepsi per se. See minutes of executive committee meeting of 22 February 1957, and *Republik*, 25 February 1957, in which the article in question is headlined "BAPERKI supports the 'Konsepsi Pres.'" Yap wrote back on 21 February 1959, angrily pointing out that the executive committee had not answered his question about when a decision was made to support Guided Democracy. Buyung Saleh replied on 26 February that Guided Democracy was simply an extension of the Konsepsi. Both letters are in the Yap papers, Lev collection.

46 Yap letter, 27 February 1959, Yap papers, Lev collection.

47 See Lev, *Transition to Guided Democracy*, 241.

48 The 1950 Constitution also included the ethnic condition for the Presidency. The 1945 Constitution is translated in the appendix of my Transition to Guided Democracy, at 290ff. See chapter 6 above, for 1945 debates on these articles. There were other problems as well that must have given Siauw and others pause, among them that the 1945 Constitution, unlike that of 1950, included no human rights provisions.

49 *Republik*, 28 February 1959. As I mentioned in chapter 6, this argument about the origins of Article 6 became standard in the defense of the 1945 Constitution by Siauw and others. See also *Republik*, 5 March 1959, for a similar statement by Siauw personally.

50 Yap letter of 3 March 1959. Was he actually invited or not? The management committee, in its reply on 4 March, addressed to Yap and all branches, over the names of Buyung Saleh and So Sik Hoe, second secretary, claimed that he was invited, but in any case he hardly needed an invitation to a routine session. Reminders were sent out routinely to management committee members every month. In Yap's files there is a reminder for the meeting of 27 February, dated 24 February. Did he receive it in time, or was it intentionally delayed, or did he ignore it because he had already decided not to attend these meetings? The invitation is pasted on a sheet of paper with a list of those who did attend and a note that Oei Tjoe Tat, who evidently reported this to him at their law office, told the

management committee that if it issued the 27 February statement, Yap might resign from Baperki.

51 The letter, signed by Buyung Saleh and So Sik Hoe, was in the name of the secretariat. Along with insisting that Yap had been invited to the meeting of the management committee, it also claimed that the 27 February session was valid and had a quorum—which Yap later denied and may have been right. The letter objected to Yap's language about forcing views and the like, pointing out that in the December meeting of the plenary committee two out of four days had been devoted to discussing issues he raised, and he was the only one consistently in opposition. Wasn't he being undemocratic, asked the letter, for wanting to force his views on everyone else? It missed Yap's point about political subterfuge, but some points raised by the letter were not altogether off base.

52 Yap letter of 3 April 1959.

53 Letter signed by Buyung Saleh to Yap, 8 April 1959. The letter concluded by suggesting that he attend a committee meeting in order to explain his earlier letters questioning the honesty of committee members and making harsh accusations in the press, which, wrote Buyung Saleh, should be retracted. On 20 April Yap replied that he was willing to attend a committee meeting to settle important issues of principle, but he wanted assurances that the discussion would not be one-sided, about his views and behavior alone, and that there would be a full exchange on such fundamental questions as Baperki's approval of Guided Democracy, the 1945 Constitution, and the principles and objectives of Baperki. On 25 April Siauw and So Sik Hoe replied that the committee had no intention of making a fellow member of the committee a "defendant" (*terdakwa*). But no such meeting ever took place. The softer tone of this last letter, and the fact that Buyung Saleh did not sign it, suggests—only that—the possibility that Buyung Saleh himself may have had something to do with the friction between Yap and the committee. But the issues of principle were determining. All the letters are in the Yap papers, Lev collection.

EIGHT *The Baperki Wars*

1 After *Sin Po* reported on Siauw's speech in the Constituent Assembly in which he said that Baperki approved the 1945 Constitution, Yap wrote him a letter in which he pointed out sardonically that Siauw's statement obviously needed correction, given what he had said at Oei's house. Siauw never replied. Letter to Siauw of 14 May 1959. Copy of the original letter is in Yap papers, Lev collection.

2 *Inti Sari pidato-pidato anggauta Konstituante berkenaan dengan amanat Presiden tanggal 22 April 1959, Res Publica! Sekali Lagi Res Publica!* [Precis of speeches of Constituent Assembly members in connection with the presidential address of 22 April 1959, Res Publica! Once again, Res Publica!] (Jakarta: Ministry of Information, 1959?), 107–11. Also *Republik*, 12 May 1959, whose headline over the report of Siauw's speech reads: "The 1945 Constitution Intends a Mutual Help (*gotong-royong*) State That Is Anti-Racial Discrimination; You Cannot Determine

the Soul of the Constitution from Only One Article, but Rather Must Read the Constitution in Its Totality."

3 The chairman of the Bandung branch of Baperki, Tjio Peng Liong, sent a circular to the Konstituante and Baperki executive committees, Prime Minister Djuanda, all Baperki branches, and Yap, stating that because of Yap's speech and rejection of the 1945 Constitution, the Bandung group no longer recognized him as a representative of the minority and itself fully supported the return to the 1945 Constitution (1 June 1959, Yap papers, Lev collection). Yap sent Tjio a sarcastic reply on 9 June (Yap papers, Lev collection). Among other things, he wrote: "I wish to express my thanks for your goodness in confirming my impression of your character, as I had known you only incidentally in other circles. Having just become chairman of a Baperki branch, you already display such extraordinary attitude, spirit, and action. I am sure that your behavior will certainly be greeted with warm respect and applause by a certain group in Baperki."

4 Yap here associates himself with the views of Sjafiudin of the Fraksi Penjaluran, Kouthoofd of the European minority, and Simorangkir of Parkindo, who proposed revising the discriminatory articles. I worked from the typewritten manuscript of the speech, at p. 3 (Yap papers, Lev collection.)

5 The text of Yap's speech can be found in the Constituent Assembly record, *Risalah Konstituante, 1959, Sidang ke-I, Rapat ke-12, 12 May 1959*, 612–19. I have used typewritten copies available in his papers. Yap quotes Peter's letter only in part. The Revised Standard Version of the full letter reads: "(3) His divine power has granted to us all things that pertain to life and godliness, through the knowledge of him who called us to his own glory and excellence, (4) by which he has granted to us his precious and very great promises, that through these you may escape from the corruption that is in the world because of passion, and become partakers of the divine nature." Revised Standard Version (New York: Nelson, 1953), 960. Yap's extract reads: "Berusahalah supaja kamu didapati dengan sedjahtera, dengan tiada bertjatjad dan dengan tiada bertjela pada pemandangan Tuhan."

6 Daniel S. Lev, *The Transition to Guided Democracy: Indonesian Politics, 1957–1959* (Ithaca, N.Y.: Cornell Modern Indonesia Project, 1966), 267.

7 The decline of legal process during this period is treated in Lev, "Judicial Institutions and Legal Culture in Indonesia," in *Culture and Politics in Indonesia*, ed. Claire Holt et al. (Ithaca, N.Y.: Cornell University Press, 1972), 246–318.

8 Yap letter to the Baperki Executive Committee, of 3 August 1959 (carbon of original letter in the Yap papers, Lev collection).

9 So Sik Hoe to Yap, 13 August 1959 (Yap papers, Lev collection). Yap's interpretation of the regulation was, I think, correct, but Baperki was not held to it. Other Baperki members, who like Siauw had been appointed to government positions, also ignored it.

10 "Laporan Ketua Umum pada Kongres Nasional Baperki ke VI tanggal 28, 29, 30 Agustus 1959, di Djakarta" (Chairman's Report to the Sixth Baperki National Congress), mimeo, 12. Delivered, I think, on 28 August, 1959

11 *Notulen Kongres*, 4. Oei Tjoe Tat did not mention Yap by name in noting, as everyone knew, that one Baperki delegate had voted against restoring the 1945 Constitution. But the editor of the minutes typed "Mr. Yap Thiam Hien" at the bottom of the page as a footnote to the report. For all that Yap was suspicious of Oei's political style and ethics, Oei's political views were in fact closer to Yap's than to Siauw's, and he admired Yap's courage and forthrightness. As office colleagues they argued incessantly over political issues, but Oei often tried to ease Yap's way, to no great avail.

12 "Konperensi Pleno Pusat Baperki tanggal 27 Agustus 1959 di Djakarta" [Plenary conference of Baperki Central], mimeo (n.d), 1–3.

13 See J. A. C. Mackie, "Anti-Chinese Outbreaks in Indonesia, 1959–1968," in *The Chinese in Indonesia*, ed. J. A. C. Mackie (Honolulu: Hawai'i University Press, 1976), 82–97.

14 One of the most sensitive issues between Siauw and Yap was the former's embrace of China, which Yap believed would reinforce the myth. Later, when many middle-class Chinese felt comfortable again going to China as tourists, Yap, despite his own curiosity, consistently refused to do so.

15 "Konferensi Pleno Pusat Baperki di Batu (Malang) tanggal 15–16–17 April '60," session of 16 April, mimeo, 8.

16 On the assimilation movement, see Charles Coppel, "Patterns of Chinese Political Activity in Indonesia," in Mackie, *The Chinese in Indonesia*, 50–51; *Lahirnya Konsepsi Asimilasi* [The birth of the assimilation concept], 5th ed. (Jakarta: Yayasan Tunas Bangsa, 1977); and *Assimilasi dalam rangka Pembinaan Kesatuan Bangsa* [Assimilation in the framework of developing national unity]. 3d ed. (Jakarta: Yayasan Pembinaan Kesatuan Bangsa, 1965.)

17 The other signatories included Tjung Tin Jan, Tjia Dji Siong, Lo Siang Hien, Tan Bian Seng, Lauwchuantho, Tantekhian, and Kwee Hwat Djien.

18 *Star Weekly*, 26 March 1960.

19 In his memoirs, *Lima Jaman*, Siauw reiterates the charge often made that Catholics were behind the assimilation movement. No doubt he saw Auwjong Peng Koen as the mastermind. In fact, however, not all the signatories of the assimilation statement were Catholic.

20 See Siauw's *Lima Jaman*, passim, for his irate commentary on name changing and name changers.

21 Yap Thiam Hien, "Two Therapies (Part I) to Cure the Sickness of Racial Discrimination," *Star Weekly*, 16 April 1960.

22 Yap, "Two Therapies (Part II)," *Star Weekly*, 20 April 1960.

23 See *Lahirnya Konsepsi Asimilasi*, passim.

24 The quoted insight is from Louis Wirth, "The Problem of Minority Groups," in *The Science of Man in a World of Crisis*, ed. Ralph Linton, 4th ed. (New York: Columbia University Press, 1945). That Yap did not overlook this is a significant clue to the subtlety of his thinking about the minority issue.

25 "Ali-Baba" denotes a system, in which business firms were run by a Chinese ("Baba"), with an Indonesian ("Ali") as their nominal head, often to provide political protection.

26 See *Lahirnya Konsepsi Asimilasi*, 112–40, for letters in the debate.

27 Arnold M. Rose, *The Roots of Prejudice* (Paris: UNESCO, 1952).

28 Lauwchuantho (Junus Jahja) was, like Yap, a Protestant. His father, like Yap's grandfather, was a *wijkmeester*, chief of a Chinese residential district, in Jakarta. Born in 1927, fourteen years younger than Yap, he studied economics in Rotterdam, returning to Jakarta in 1960 to leap into the assimilation debate. He was among the most deeply committed and consistent of the assimilationists and the one who engaged Yap most fiercely. In 1962 he helped to establish the first assimilationist organization, the Urusan Pembinaan Kesatuan Bangsa (National Unity Development Affairs), under army sponsorship. In 1979 he converted to Islam. See Suryadinata, *Eminent Indonesian Chinese*, 35–36.

29 Yap, "Two Therapies." From the typescript version, p. 7, and *Lahirnya Konsepsi Asimilasi*, 110–11, and supra. Yap goes on: "That assimilation of individuals has occurred in the past, and now too, and will in the future, despite everything, cannot be denied. But these . . . exceptions prove the rule."

30 *Star Weekly*, 30 May 1960, and *Lahirnya Konsepsi Asimilasi*, 128, from his concluding paragraph entitled, in English, "For whom the bell tolls."

31 *Lahirnya Konsepsi Asimilasi*, 111–12.

32 Most correspondents ignored Yap's therapy, probably shrugging it off as utterly irrelevant. One who touched on it tangentially was Tjung Tin Jan, one of the ten *tokoh*, a Catholic and a civil servant, a prosecutor, who later changed his name to Jani Arsadjaja (Suryadinata, *Eminent Indonesian Chinese*, 3–4). But he raised the same question as did Lauwchuantho and other assimilationists: "Yap's therapy (heartcleansing, change in the view of man, elimination of prejudice, egoism, and so on) is directed at the majority. Yap hopes that the majority will rid itself of prejudice and discrimination. This is fine. But what does Yap propose to the minority? What does he intend the minority also do in order to eliminate prejudice?" *Star Weekly*, 16 June 1960, and *Lahirnya Konsepsi Asimilasi*, 139.

33 See *Lahirnya Konsepsi Asimilasi*, 149, for the history of the assimilation movement.

34 The invitation to the congress is dated 17 November 1960 (Yap papers, Lev collection). At the bottom of Yap's copy he noted that it was not accompanied by the agenda and materials for discussion, as the Baperki rules of order required—the agenda, dated 7 November, came later on Yap's request—nor did it indicate who determined the place and date of the congress. Yap read the charter and rules of order of the organization carefully, constantly referring to them to challenge Siauw and others. It was a lawyerly habit of which he made much use, to the irritation of other Baperki leaders. Yap wrote to the executive committee on 18 November, protesting the congress date. The angry correspondence among Buyung Saleh, Yap, and Siauw is dated 22 November (Buyung Saleh), 29

November (Yap), 3 December (Yap, two letters), 9 December (Buyung Saleh), 13 December (Siauw), 17 December (Yap), 1960, all in the Lev collection.

35 Letter of 17 December 1960, sent by courier (carbon of typed letter, Lev collection).

36 The documentation I have for the speech includes a poorly stenciled copy, dated 24 December 1960, the day when he finished writing it, as well as his handwritten draft. The two are different in places, but the essentials are the same.

37 Just before the congress, Yap had written to the executive committee to protest that its conference at Batu, 15–17 April 1960, had taken illegal decisions because it had no quorum. In violation of the rules of order (both the original article 34 and its revision), a quorum was attained by the simple expedient of improperly appointing four members who happened to attend the meeting. Carbon of typed letter of 20 December 1960, Lev collection. Baperki was not the only organization to take a lax, opportunistic view of legal rules during the Guided Democracy years, but Yap was genuinely incensed, perceiving it as more substantial evidence of the corruption of Baperki's promises.

38 Manipol/USDEK became a catchword after 1959. The Political Manifesto (Manipol) was Soekarno's independence day address of 1959 on which an exegesis of sorts had been worked out, while USDEK was an acronym that combined several other loaded political principles: the Constitution of 1945 (Undang-undang Dasar 1945), Indonesian Socialism (Sosialisme Indonesia), Guided Democracy (Demokrasi Terpimpim), Guided Economy (Ekonomi Terpimpin), and Indonesian Identity (Kepribadian Indonesia).

39 Yap here was sarcastically calling attention to the point that despite Siauw's Marxist commitments he could accept the Pancasila, whose first principle is belief in the One God.

40 Interview, 11 December 1987, at Oei Tjoe Tat's home.

NINE *Out of the Ethnic Cage*

1 "Djikaloe pranakan Tionghoa dengan mendengar soeara hatinja maoe lengketken nasibnja bersama-sama orang Indonesier pada tana Indonesia ini, ia poen moesti dianggap Indonesier sedjati." *Mata Hari*, 8 September 1934, in an article entitled "Can the Baba Become an Indonesian?" reprinted in *Baba Bisa Menjadi Indonesier* [The Baba can become an Indonesian], ed. Ridwan Saidi (Jakarta: Lembaga Pengkajian Maslah Pembauran. 1987?), 15.

2 Suryadinata, "Yap Thiam Hien: Pembela Hak Asasi Manusia yang Gigih" [Yap Thiam Hien: Persistent defender of human rights], in *Mencari Identitas Nasional*, ed. Suryadinata (Jakarta: LP3ES, 1990), 203.

3 See Lev, "Judicial Authority and Legal Culture," in *Politics and Culture in Indonesia*, ed. Claire Holt et al. (Ithaca, N.Y.: Cornell University Press, 1972), passim.

4 Persahi was another result of the unifying, consolidating impulses of Guided Democracy. Earlier there were two organizations. ISHI (Ikatan Sarjana Hukum Indonesia, Indonesian Law Graduates Bond) restricted membership to those with

law degrees. PAHI (Persatuan Ahli Hukum Indonesia, Union of Indonesian Lawyers) was for all lawyers, graduated or not. In the latter, for example, were judges, prosecutors, and others with a year or two of legal education and legal experience but no degrees. A few graduated lawyers belonged to both organizations, but the relationship between them was edged with status tensions. Largely on the initiative of Chief Justice Wirjono Prodjodikoro, in 1959 ISHI and PAHI merged into Persahi, with Wirjono as its first chairman. Persahi remains the umbrella organization for all Indonesian lawyers.

5 Among them were Muchni Djoyodisuryo from Surabaya; Hasyim Mahdan, Harsubeno, Suprapto, Padmosumasto, Yap, A. Zainal Abidin, and Lukman Wiriadinata from Jakarta; Tjio Liang Hoat and Mrs. Amartiwi Saleh from Bandung; Mohd. Dalyono and Sumarno P. Wirjanto from Solo; A. S. Soripada from Pontianak,;and Mrs. Ani Abas Manopo from Medan. For a concise history of the organization, see *Album Kongres V* (Yogyakarta: PERADIN, 1977).

6 A few words about Yap's soul mates, for they are a prominent part of his life story. Lukman Wiriadinata, a tall, dignified man, a deliberate and cautious thinker, had a sense of principled propriety as rigid as Yap's, but a calmer demeanor. Born into an aristocratic Sundanese family, he had intended to follow tradition by joining the regional administrative bureaucracy. But Sutan Sjahrir drew him into the PSI, which made him minister of justice twice, and he became an advocate for want of any other possibility thereafter. His two office partners, Hasjim Mahdan and A. Z. Abidin, were also PSI members. Jamaluddin Datuk Singomangkuto, who had gone to school with Thiam Bong in Kutaraja and knew Yap in the Konstituante, had been active in Masyumi. Suardi Tasrif, like Yap and unlike most others, knew no regional language—only Indonesian, Dutch, English, and perhaps French—because his parents were mixed Javanese and Sundanese and used Indonesian or Dutch at home in Jakarta. A journalist and an avid reader and writer, Tasrif was invaluable to Peradin as one of its most creative and imaginative leaders. Soemarno P. Wirjanto had been a *pengadilan negeri* judge in Magelang until 1954, when he left the bench to practice law, a rare step then. From his office in Solo came a constant flow of legal commentary, criticism, and interesting litigation. Ani Abas Manopo, from Medan, one of several women in the advocacy, was also one of its toughest and most outspoken practitioners, who would have been much better known in Java.

7 *Album Kongres* V, 114.

8 In 1963 the PAI had seven branches and 150 members. Ibid., 113. Only a few more joined Peradin thereafter, largely, I think, because there were no more. Not until the late 1960s, with economic growth, did the advocacy also begin to grow.

9 Apart from Yap, my sources on the Liem Koe Nio case are A. Z. Abidin, who was co-defense with Yap, the Surabaya daily *Trompet Masjarakat*, and Andrew Gunawan, who then worked for this newspaper, owned by his father, Gooi Po An.

10 Penetapan Presiden 11/1963, *Lembaran Negara* [Collected statutes], no. 101, 1963, with elucidation in *Tambahan Lembaran Negara* [Addenda to collected statutes], no. 2595.

11 See *Trompet Masjarakat*, 29 December 1964, for the report of the arrest and particulars.

12 Ibid. Susanto was from the appellate level prosecution (*kejaksaan tinggi*) rather than first instance. Why he got the job is not quite clear, unless the *kejaksaan tinggi* offices thought the case so important that it warranted a more senior prosecutor or, a touch of cynicism suggests, the senior prosecutor wanted it for obvious reasons.

13 See especially, for starters, *Trompet Masjarakat* (hereafter *TM*) 5, 7, 22, 24 January 1965. The exact nature of *Trompet Masjarakat*'s animus I do not know. The editor, Gooi Po An, a socially conscious man, was on the left but quite independent. According to his son, Andrew Gunawan, Gooi never joined Baperki, which he criticized for failing to give enough help to ethnic Chinese who went to China in 1959 in the aftermath of the alien traders' restrictions. Gooi was evidently close to the PKI, however, which financed *Trompet Masjarakat* until sometime in mid-1965. The PKI probably attacked Liem as much or more for his Kuomintang connections as anything else. Presumably the same is true of *Trompet Masjarakat*, whose reports on the Liem case were blatantly one sided. Gooi Po An was killed in the aftermath of the 1965 coup.

14 *TM*, 25 February 1965. Wirjono was speaking to a meeting of the Central Javanese Judges' Association (Ikatan Hakim) in Solo. Among other things, he insisted, following the standard argument then taking shape, that human rights in the Declaration were founded in liberal individualist thought, while the purpose of the Indonesian revolution was to produce an Indonesian form of socialism in which individual interests must be subordinated.

By coincidence, from August 1964 on, *TM* ran a series of articles on the comments of Soekarno, the PNI leader Ali Sastroamidjojo, Wirjono, and Minister of Justice Astrawinata to various meetings of judges, all of them urging the judiciary to take appropriate revolutionary lines and adapt themselves to the true wishes of the people. *TM*, 22 August; 2, 26, 29 September and 2 November 1964. Often these statements were threatening; Ali Sastroamidjojo (*TM*, 22 August) warned that judges, too, could be "retooled," the euphemism then for throwing out those who opposed official lines. As was mentioned earlier, judges were among those least edified by the decline of legal process under Guided Democracy, and some of them put up a quiet but dogged struggle to maintain some semblance of legality and legal decorum in their courtrooms. A few were courageously critical. It was in response to such recalcitrance among judges that Soekarno, Wirjono, and the others issued their warnings. In 1965, moreover, a new law on judicial organization explicitly subordinated the judiciary to political will in matters of "national interest."

15 *TM*, 17 March 1965.

16 Ibid.

17 Interview with Abidin, 23 August 1989.

18 *TM*, 6–7 April 1965.

19 Ibid., 21 April and 13 May 1965.

20 *TM* serialized the entire *rekwisitoor* in its editions from 15 June through 21 July 1965, but ignored the defense statement except for a single, rather garbled report on 5 July. In criminal procedure, the prosecutorial *rekwisitoor* (from the French and Dutch *requisitoir*) is followed by the defense plea (*pleidooi*), a prosecutorial reply (*repliek*), and a defense reply (*dupliek*).

21 Without a copy of the defense plea, I have had to rely on *TM*'s report of 5 July 1965, which unfortunately is brief.

22 Actually, Liem himself was willing to do without this defense. Yap had told Liem that while he was indictable for his acts of hoarding and the like after October 1963, when Penpres 11/1963 went into effect, the same activities earlier were legal and he should demand the return of his seized goods. Liem, much too confident according to Yap, waved the point aside as minor, for he could always amass wealth again. It is not clear just how assiduously Yap pressed the argument in his plea.

23 *TM*, 2 August 1965.

TEN *Into New Order Indonesia*

1 No less than the revolution of 1945, and many other revolutions, the coup of 1965 scattered unanswered questions everywhere. Yet relatively little has been written about it. Still the most seminal account was written quite soon after the event, in late 1965 and early 1966, though it was published only after several years; see Benedict R. Anderson and Ruth T. McVey, *A Preliminary Analysis of the October 1, 1965, Coup in Indonesia* (Ithaca, N.Y.: Cornell Modern Indonesia Project, 1971). See also Harold Crouch, *The Army and Politics in Indonesia*, rev. ed. (Ithaca: Cornell University Press, 1988), 97, and the sources cited there.

2 See Crouch, *Army and Politics in Indonesia*, especially chapters 2 and 3.

3 Soekarno had offered the position to Siauw, who declined, suggesting Oei Tjoe Tat instead. He was the only *peranakan* to serve in a Guided Democracy cabinet and the last to serve in any cabinet for the next three decades.

4 See Crouch, *Army and Politics in Indonesia*, 86.

5 For details of these events, see ibid., 97.

6 On the post-coup violence, see especially *The Indonesian Killings, 1965–1966: Studies from Java and Bali*, ed. Robert Cribb (Clayton, Victoria: Monash Papers on Southeast Asia, no. 21, 1990).

7 Interview with Harry Tjan, 30 August 1989. The PMKRI, in which many *peranakan* students were active, was better organized, ideologically prepared, and more experienced in anti-communist efforts than most other student associations. This may have been due in part to the guidance of a Dutch Jesuit, Father Beek, who apparently played a significant role in their political education. A member also of the Partai Katolik, Harry Tjan became co-chairman (along with the young NU leader Subchan Z.E.) of the KAP-Gestapu (Action Front to Crush the Gestapu—an acronym for the September 30 Movement [Gerakan September Tiga Puluh]) established on 2 October with military help. After the burning of

Ureca, Harry Tjan and others involved in the action agreed to rebuild the university, renaming it Trisakti University, of whose board Tjan became chairman.

8 Moreover, the Protestant newspaper, *Sinar Harapan*, was filled with praise for Soekarno. Yap's sense of fairness was disgusted by how quickly the paper turned on Soekarno once he fell from power. He regarded it as blatant hypocrisy. He may have carried a grudge, however, for, as mentioned earlier, Sinar had once refused to publish his criticism of Soekarno for appointing Supreme Court chairman Wirjono to the cabinet.

9 Yap and I discussed his religious views during the late 1980s, but his behavior from the 1960s on indicates that these views were already quite well formed then. An example of Yap's critical thinking on the Old-New Testament problem, and the implication of his answers for his behavior, is drawn from a discussion we had on the subject (14 July 1986): "Of course there are examples in the Old Testament of such love and sacrifice [like the example of God's sacrifice of Jesus for love of humanity in the New Testament]—as is the case of Abraham, who would give up his son. . . . Yet, how could a God ask this of a father? I cannot accept the idea . . . that God would do such a thing as ask a father to give up his son. The God of the New Testament is willing to sacrifice his own son."

10 *Simposium Kebangkitan Semangat '66: Mendjeladjah Tracee Baru*, 6–9 May 1966 (Jakarta: Yayasan Badan Penerbit Fak. Ekonomi UI, 1966).

11 "Surat Terbuka kepada Djaksa Soesanto Bangoennagoro S.H., Kepala Reserse Kriminil Kedjaksaan Surabaja" [Open letter to Prosecutor Soesanto Bangoennagoro LLB, Chief of Criminal Investigations, Surabaya Prosecution], *Kompas*, 17 May 1966. The letter is dated 13 May.

12 *Sinar Harapan*, 18 March 1966.

13 Both Go and Yap recounted the conversation to me. Go, who took up a teaching position in Holland, told me that he felt released from the promise by Yap's own activity in criticizing the New Order regime. He and Yap did not meet again until the late 1980s, when Yap decided to visit Go during a trip to the Netherlands. By then Yap had loosened up a bit and wanted to explore a few historical problems. According to Go, after they greeted one another, Yap promptly told Go that he distrusted and blamed him even more than Siauw and started an argument about the Baperki university issue. It was typical of Yap.

14 *Kompas*, 27 December 1966. Not all those sentenced to death were executed. Several, including Subandrio and Omar Dhani, the former air force commander, had their death sentences commuted to life.

15 Brig. Gen. Sutjipto S.H. (*sarjana hukum*, graduate lawyer), minister of agriculture in the new cabinet, publicly announced that he had offered to resign his portfolio if Suharto appointed him judge in the Subandrio trial. *Kompas*, 10 September 1966.

16 *Kompas*, 27 September 1966, reported that Subandrio's own nominees for defense counsel all refused, but the court documents indicate that he suggested no one, agreeing to accept whomever the court appointed.

17 There was some question whether Air Marshal Omar Dhani or Subandrio should be tried first, in part perhaps because the case against Subandrio was harder to develop. *Kompas,* 15 September 1966. But the decision was made to try Omar Dhani in December, while Subandrio's trial would begin at midnight on 30 September. *Kompas,* 21 September 1966. It actually began a day later.

18 *Kompas,* 27 September 1966.

19 *Sinar Harapan,* 30 September 1966. He also said: "At the same time the court will give an indication of how far we intend to keep to the 1945 Constitution."

20 Ibid.

21 The procedure to be followed was that in the H.I.R. (Revised Indonesian Regulation), the procedural code inherited from the colony. In inquisitorial criminal procedure, the judge is fully in charge, and defense is formally required to address all questions to witnesses via the judge. Often, however, judges allow defense counsel to question directly, which Ali Said promised.

22 *Sinar Harapan,* 29 September 1966.

23 Sources on the trial, apart from press reports and my interviews with Yap, include Ali Said and Durmawel Ahmad, *Sangkur Adil: Pengupas Fitnah Chianat* (Jakarta: Ethika, 1967), which covers all the formal submissions of the trial and the full transcript, about 1,500 pages.

24 Ali Said and Durmawel Ahmad, *Sangkur Adil,* 12; for the indictment, 13–14. The relevant provisions were criminal code (KUHP) Articles 110, para. 2, sub-para. 2, facilitating rebellion by lending opportunity or information; Article 107 and/or 108, re punishment by imprisonment for rebellion against the government; and Presidential Decree 5/1959, Article 2. The last item dealt with the authority of the chief public prosecutor and chief military prosecutor over economic crimes and increased penalties for such crimes. The reason for including Article 2 of the Presidential Decree 5/1959 must have been that, unlike the KUHP articles, which provided prison sentences, it allowed for the death penalty. To justify it the auditor had to argue that by abetting the coup, the accused, Subandrio, must have known that his actions would obstruct the government policies meant to provide basic goods to the people, see to the security of state and population, and carry out the struggle against imperialism, as stated in Article 2 of the decree. See the indictment, ibid., 16.

25 The weight given in the indictment, and in the examination of witnesses, to the Generals' Council and the Gilchrist letter, as well as to Subandrio's speeches about bureaucratic capitalists—a PKI slogan directed against army officers, among others—reveals the special grudges of army leaders and, significantly, the extent to which the Mahmillub trials were a partisan affair. At the time, I think, Yap and many others were not fully aware of this point.

26 Ali Said and Durmawel Ahmad, *Sangkur Adil,* 16.

27 The primary provision underlying the second group of charges was Presidential Decree 11/1963 (especially Article 1, para. 1, sub-para. 1 b and 1 c, and Article 13, para. 1) on the Suppression of Subversion, the same act that Yap had confronted in the Liem Koe Nio case. Article 1 b and c deal with rebelling against

or undermining state authority or the government or government apparatus, and causing enmity, conflict, and public tension among the people or between Indonesia and friendly foreign states. Presidential Decree 11/1963, which became a law during the New Order, can be found in *Lembaran Negara,* no. 101, 1963, vol. 1963, at 593. As was mentioned in connection with the Liem Koe Nio trial, the Anti-Subversion Act makes the prosecutor's work much easier than does the H.I.R. procedural code. The other acts to which the indictment calls attention are Presidential Decision 226/1963 and Presidential Decree 16/1963, which established the military tribunals extraordinary; Presidential Decree 370/1965, which gave the Mahmillub jurisdiction over those accused of supporting the 30 September Movement and gave authority to General Suharto to determine who should be tried and to appoint the Mahmillub personnel; Decision no. KEP-071/KOPKAM/9/1966, 23 September 1966, of the Minister/Army Commander as Commandant of Operations to Restore Security and Order [Gen. Suharto], which ordered the investigation of Subandrio, and idem. no KEP-073, transmitting the case to the Mahmillub.

28 Subagio spoke first, questioning the jurisdiction of the court and arguing inter alia that Subandrio's actions were political and therefore not culpable. Original transcript, at 148. I will not devote much space to Subagio's demurrers and defense, which were generally creditable but not well developed.

29 Law 6/1950 (on criminal procedure in military courts), which provides that the Supreme Court and Military Appellate Court serve in the second instance. But the Mahmillub was a single instance court without appeal. Moreover, Laws 29/1954 and 19/1964 provide, respectively, that military courts and judicial organization generally are established by statute.

30 Durmawel's response begins at page 014 of the verbatim transcript. Rather than deal with it in the text, I will refer to Ali Said's interlocutory decision, which incorporated most of Durmawel's reasoning.

31 Original transcript, 165–70.

32 There was nothing at all that the Mahmillub judges could do about this problem short of calling off the trial then. Durmawel objected that Subandrio was not a real officer, that he had not fought in the revolution, that, in any case, he had been dismissed as deputy prime minister and his rank must have fallen with his position. But it was a weak argument, to which Yap replied that, even if his rank had been rescinded, the military code provided that any trial within a year of demotion still required judges of higher rank. There was no way out. The military auditor's office, worried about the issue for the sake of appearances, finally got in touch with Yap himself after the trial to ask his advice. Yap gave them the obvious solution, which was to raise the rank of the judges, at least their titular rank. After the Subandrio trial, all military judges had higher ranks than the accused.

33 Transcript, part II, 308.

34 Transcript, part II, 312.

35 Transcript, part II, 206–7.

36 Ali Said and Durmawel Ahmad, *Sangkur Adil*, 253. Actually Yap referred here to a *negara hukum* based on Pancasila democracy. I suspect he used the term Pancasila for reasons of ideological currency.

37 Ibid., 274–75.

38 Ibid., 275–76. As mentioned earlier, in 1964 the Indonesian emblem of justice was changed from the goddess with scales to a banyan tree inscribed underneath with the term *Pengayoman* (succor), implying the government's patrimonial responsibility for the people.

39 Following the *pleidooi* of Subagio and Yap, the auditor responded (*repliek*) and defense counsel replied (*dupliek*) to the response before the court retired to consider its decision. The *repliek* and *dupliek* can be found in the transcript, part I, and in *Sangkur Adil*,

40 See the Mahmillub decision in *Sangkur Adil*, 332–462, at 434–35. Ali Said's comment is followed by imprecations in Arabic, meant presumably to imply an Islamic riposte to Yap's Christian thrust.

41 In this light, Ali Said continued, the court interprets the uses of the death sentence and the function of the judiciary, where human beings might find the executors of God's will. By the same reasoning, "legal doctrine in our State should be oriented to educating, ministering to, curing the mentality of the Indonesian nation. It should contain social-educational purposes, although the effort to treat does not exclude the possibility of an amputation, precisely to prevent the spread of infection to parts of society still healthy." *Sangkur Adil*, 436–37.

42 Verse 178 of Baqarah (the Cow) allows retaliation for bloodshed: "the free man for the free, and the slave for the slave, and the woman for the woman; but he to whom his brother shall make any remission, is to be dealt with equitably; and to him should he pay a fine with liberality." *The Koran*, trans. Rodwell (London: J. M. Dent, 1909), 356.

43 *Kompas*, 25 October 1966.

ELEVEN *Early New Order Battlefields*

1 The fullest discussion is in Charles Coppel, *Indonesian Chinese in Crisis* (Kuala Lumpur: Oxford University Press, 1983).

2 See ibid., 56–57.

3 Ibid., 59.

4 Ibid., 89–90. Neither of the two ethnic Chinese who delivered papers at the meeting, Lie Tek Cheng and Sindhunata, had mentioned anything of this sort publicly. In his paper Sindhunata had proposed compulsory military service for ethnic Chinese, of which nothing came. In private, however, he supported the idea of using the term *Cina*. This he admitted publicly in July 1990 at a conference on ethnic Chinese in Indonesia held at Cornell University. He defended the decision, as other "assimilationists" have since, on grounds that earlier in this century Cina was in common use, and still is among friends, and that no one actually found it insulting. It is a weak defense, however, for *peranakan* do find

the term painful, fully aware of its derogatory overtone. Who actually proposed using Cina is not clear, though Sindhunata, at the Cornell conference, implied that he did. If so, his motives are a bit obscure.

5 Coppel, *Indonesian Chinese*, 97.

6 See, among other sources, the two-part article by Pek Hien Liang, "Nama dan Identitas," in *Sinar Harapan*, 16 and 18 July 1966.

7 Coppel, *Indonesian Chinese*, 82–85.

8 Ibid., 97.

9 Actually, Siauw Giok Tjhan had the last word in his memoirs, where he angrily came back to the issue again and again. He held the Catholics mainly to blame, but in fact many others were involved.

10 Yap Thiam Hien, "Masalah Tjina & Sikap Sementara Pemimpin2 Kristen Keturunan Tjina" [The Chinese problem and the attitude of some Protestant leaders of Chinese descent], *Sinar Harapan*, 25, 26, and 27 January 1967.

11 Of Pek Hien Liang's argument that Chinese identity obstructed the process of national unification, Yap wrote: "Pek does not examine either the logic or the ethical basis of his proposition, but instead takes the view and proposes that as a positive step toward participating in developing national unity the Chinese minority should be willing and happy to eliminate that obstruction—i.e., their Chinese identity—by throwing away all their Chineseness, beginning with changing their Chinese names into unChinese names." Yap particularly resented the comments of Jahja Wuller (Oey Tjin San), a Bandung psychologist and member of the GKI, about the "'poison' of Baperki PKI, racialism and fascism as obstructions to the assimilation-integration of the Chinese minority." It would be better for Wuller, wrote Yap, "to provide a social-psychological analysis of the Chinese problem along with the influences of communism, fascism, and racialism . . . than to deliver kicks at defeated enemies, who quite possibly, when they were riding high, he never himself opposed." Yap did not go easy on hypocrisy of any kind.

12 *Sinar Harapan*, 27 January 1967.

13 *Kompas*, 26 January 1967. Yap's letter is dated 25 January. The editors of *Kompas*, taking Yap's letter at face value as an offer of advice, added a note indicating that leaders of church organizations in Jakarta—presumably both Catholic and Protestant—had approached the newspaper to report their willingness to give help, and not only to church members. A day earlier, *Kompas* had run a column by Mrs. Liem Tjing Hien, a lawyer, explaining the relevant cabinet decision.

14 Coppel, *Indonesian Chinese*, 111. Coppel reports that ethnic Chinese lecturers at the University of Indonesia medical faculty met on 29 January to deal with the name-changing issue following the appearance of Yap's articles.

15 Ibid., and *Kompas*, 30 January 1967.

16 *Sinar Harapan*, 3 February 1967.

17 Ibid., 2 February 1967. In his article, apart from defending the name-changing policy, Sufwandi did something from which Yap might usefully have learned. Citing several apposite passages from the Qur'an, he pointed out that Islam

too was fundamentally opposed to racial discrimination. At the time Yap knew relatively little about Islam and probably shared the common Christian doubts and suspicions about the majority religion. Only later did he become much more sympathetic to Islamic ideas and purposes.

18 Yap did not reply to the many attacks on his essay, but fired one parting shot in an article published on 9 February 1967 in the *Indonesian Observer*, a Jakarta daily. He was especially proud of it, perhaps because it was in English, well written, subtle, and nuanced. For the same reasons, it attracted little attention. The title of the article he took from Romeo and Juliet: "My Name, Dear Saint, Is Hateful to Myself Because It Is an Enemy to Thee." In it he attacked both sides of the assimilation movement, the one for wishing to eliminate a cultural heritage on principle, the other for agreeing to do so for essentially selfish, unprincipled reasons. He ended the piece with a revival of the abacus metaphor: "How many care for principles when instincts of self-preservation and self-assertion prevail? Do not look for those 'overweights' amongst us who were born with an abacus."

19 *Kompas*, 12 August 1967.

20 See Robert Cribb, ed., *Indonesian Killings, 1965–1966*, 2d printing (Clayton, Vic: Monash Centre of Southeast Asian Studies, 1991), 195–213.

21 So corrupt had the prosecution become during the years of Guided Democracy that Soekarno's last chief public prosecutor, Soetardio, from the Military Police, was given the Herculean task of trying to clean it up. He failed miserably. In 1966 Suharto's chief public prosecutor, General Sugih Arto, promised change and fired a few prosecutors, mainly for political reasons, but got little further than Soetardio.

22 The secretary of Pengabdi Hukum was Lt. Colonel Abdul Kadir Besar, assistant to MPRS chair General Nasution, who provided a bit of political clout. The four vice chairs were Marjono from the prosecution, the police official Soebagio, Yap, and the journalist Wiratmo Soekito, who later married Widojati. Pengabdi Hukum founding document of 15 October 1967 (typescript).

23 Ibid.

24 *Kompas*, 20 December 1967.

25 See Kenneth E. Ward, "Upholding the Rule of Law—The Yap Affair," *Review of Indonesian and Malayan Affairs* 2, no. 1 (January–March, 1968): 1–7, at 2.

26 It was an easy case, as all pleaded guilty, but Taufic put up a good show in court, justifying Yap's view of him as a man of integrity, albeit a criminal. When Taufic and his men were arrested, they had a table full of jewelry, money, and other valuables. Little was left, however, when the evidence was brought to court. Taufic protested that the police themselves were bandits, official bandits, much worse than himself, who at least admitted that he was a bandit. Moreover, he asked the court to sentence him alone, not the others, for he was responsible and they were merely his followers. For reports on the Taufic case and that of one of his followers tried later, see *Kompas*, 7 June 1968 and 4 February 1969. The judge was not impressed by Taufic's toughness and honesty. They were all sentenced, but Taufic most severely, to six years in prison. Yap, joined by another attorney,

Ping A, took the opportunity of the defense to protest prison conditions and detention procedures. Years later, during the early 1980s, at a time when Yap's German shepherd was poisoned and someone fired a bullet through his front window, possibly in connection with a case he was then handling against the state oil company Pertamina (see Postscript, "New Order Landmark Cases"), Taufic, long since released, read about the incident in the newspapers and came to see Yap, offering protection and revenge. Yap declined, but was grateful, I think, for Taufic's devotion.

27 Interview of 16 July 1968. The extracts are from my field notes.

28 But when it came to the Yap affair, Sujud was not about to stand on legal principle. He claimed to have no opinion on the matter, but said, "[There] is no proof at all that Mardjaman was involved in extortion. He was actually called in as an intermediary between Lies Gunarsih and the PT Quick owner; that was his only function. . . . Yap's arrest had nothing to do with the present case. He was arrested because of info from a good informant that he was a member of Baperki. It just happened that he was arrested right after the PT Quick case."

29 *Sinar Harapan*, 6 January 1968.

30 This information comes from an interview with Sri Widojati Notoprojo, then already on the Supreme Court, 10 July 1968.

31 A.B. Nasution, "Yap Thiam Hien: Advokat dan Penggugat demi Aspirasi Negara Hukum dan Demokrasi di Indonesia" [Yap Thiam Hien: Advocate and plaintiff for the aspirations of democracy and the rule of law in Indonesia], in *Yap Thiam Hien: Pejuang Hak Asasi Manusia* [Yap Thiam Hien: Fighter for human rights], ed. T. Mulya Lubis and Aristides Katoppo (Jakarta: Pustaka Sinar Harapan, 1990), 48–64.

32 From the beginning, prosecutors and police were reluctant to join Pengabdi Hukum because there were so many public complaints about them. In addition, public lawyer representatives on Pengabdi Hukum could not bind either their own professional organizations—Persadja (prosecutors), Ikahi (judges), and the police guild—or their home institutions to Pengabdi Hukum's decisions.

33 *Kompas*, 5 January 1968.

34 *Sinar Harapan*, 6 January 1968. *Mahasiswa Indonesia*, a student weekly from Bandung, weeks I and II of January 1968. Also Ward, "Upholding the Rule of Law," and the press reports cited there.

35 *Kompas*, 5 January 1968, published also in *Sinar Harapan*, 6 January 1968, and *Kompas*, 11 January 1968, which placed the Yap affair in the broader context of corruption and abuse of power and the demand of students and others for reform.

36 See *Sinar Harapan*, 6 January 1968, for Durmawel's statement.

37 Adam Malik gave this information about the cabinet session to Yap, on the day of his release.

38 *Sinar Harapan*, 6 January 1968.

39 Padmo Sumasto, as flexible and well connected in some ways as Adam Malik himself, had been a student leader after the revolution with ties to both eth-

nic Indonesian and ethnic Chinese circles. After taking his law degree at the University of Indonesia in the mid-1950s, he was asked to head the Sin Ming Hui, which saw advantages in an ethnic Indonesian leader and, in turn, offered him advantages of his own. In 1962, when Baperki tried to take over the Sin Ming Hui—largely in order to gain control of the building it owned, where Baperki had been allowed some space for a time—it tried to oust Padmo from his position. Yap and others successfully defended him. Proud of his own role in getting Yap released, Padmo told me that he had first raised the issue with Adam Malik, and so went to pick up Yap at the jail. While several organizations and individuals have claimed a key role in freeing Yap, it seems clear that the Jakarta press was the primary instrument.

40 *Kompas*, 6 January 1968. See also Lev, "Judicial Institutions and Legal Culture in Indonesia," in *Culture and Politics in Indonesia*, ed. Claire Holt et al. (Ithaca, N.Y.: Cornell University Press, 1972), 276–78.

41 Simatupang's article—"Apa Arti Peristiwa Yap Bagi Kita?" [What does the Yap affair mean for us?]—appeared in *Sinar Harapan*, 12 January 1968; Arief Budiman's article appeared in the same journal, 11 January 1968.

42 The criminal case was based on a *klachtdelict*, in Dutch-Indonesian law, a personal allegation, that engenders a public prosecution. As the civil and criminal actions were linked, and the outcome of the former depended on that of the latter, the criminal prosecution had to take place first.

43 No doubt, public recognition, even adulation, and a kind of celebrity status made a good deal of difference, too, as Yap became increasingly aware that he was a public personage whose ethnicity did not matter to many. But the respect and support of his colleagues counted a great deal.

44 *Kompas*, 5 July 1968.

45 The importance of the Yap case for the professional advocacy is evident in Peradin's decision to publish the trial in full, using press reports along with all the official documentation. *Proses Yap Thiam Hien S.H.: Test Case bagi Rule of Law di Indonesia* (Jakarta: PERADIN, 1969), including a separate short volume devoted to the appeal, *Proses Yap Thiam Hien S.H.: Memori Banding.* Almost twenty years later, in the first issue of the journal of Ikadin, the Indonesian advocates association, a new government-inspired organization, the decisions in the Yap case were taken up once more, for the issues had not yet been resolved in practice. See "Imunitas Profesi Advokat (Kasus Mr. Yap Thiam Hien)," *Era Hukum* 1, no. 1 (November 1987): 35.

46 *Berita Yudha*, 5 January 1968, cited in Ward, "Upholding the Rule of Law," 5.

47 *Kompas*, 2 July 1968.

48 The reportage of *Kompas*, on which Peradin based its book on the case, is also available in a booklet of clippings published by the newspaper itself, *Sidang Perkara Yap Thiam Hien S.H.* (Jakarta: Kompas, 1968).

49 *Kompas*, 30 June 1968. LawAsia is a professional association of law societies, bar associations, law firms, and lawyers in the Asia-Pacific region.

50 Ibid., 1 July 1968.

51 Ibid., 2 July 1968.

52 Even when judges had no financial interests in a case, many respectfully favored the prosecution, whose political influence, control of resources, and status had risen above that of judges since the Guided Democracy years. Judges resented the change, but the antagonism between them and prosecutors was submerged by their collegial alliance against private lawyers, outsiders. On tensions in the judicial system, see Lev, "The Politics of Judicial Development in Indonesia," *Comparative Studies in Society and History* 7, no.2 (January 1965).

53 A contrast with Yap was another famous *peranakan* advocate, the late Tjiam Djoe Khiam, no less tough than Yap but whose accommodating style in court was more likely to win judicial favor. Tjiam, for example, was likely to offer young judges—some of whom referred to him familiarly as *oom* (uncle)—advice and instruction, often in chambers, even during cases in which he was defense counsel. It was out of the question for Yap to do anything of the sort, just as he would never serve as an intermediary for a payoff to judge or prosecutor or opposing litigant. Consequently, more realistic clients avoided him. Tjiam and Yap knew one another but did not get along, unsurprisingly.

54 *Proses Yap*, 66.

55 Ibid., 70.

56 Ibid., 27.

57 Pilgrims climbed the mountain in Shandong Province, China, to pray and receive oracular, often enigmatic, messages.

58 *Proses Yap*, 27–28.

59 Ibid., 30.

60 Ibid., 72, 109–10, for examples. Dali was not alone in calling attention to Yap's Chinese origins. At one point Mardjaman, by then feeling beset by the trial and upset at Yap's examination of a witness, was overheard by a reporter talking to himself. According to the news account, Mardjaman muttered angrily "Vulgar Chinese. Good thing the PKI lost; if the PKI won he'd be the *jaksa agung*, we'd all be done for." Ibid., 57.

61 Ibid., 53.

62 Ibid., 130.

63 Ibid., 179.

64 Ibid., 194–95. In the text there is, I think, a misprint on page 194, "rukum," which should be either "rukun," peace or harmony, or "hukum," law. I have chosen the former "seekers after peace," but "seekers after law" may have been meant.

65 Ibid., 166–67. Waxing eloquent, Yap concluded his defense with the hope that he would be granted the ability to serve, with his fellows, the nation and state, as a light to all within the house. He drew on Matthew 5:15, "Nor do men light a lamp and put it under a bushel, but on a stand, and it gives light to all in the house."

66 Ibid., 308–9.

67 Ibid., 323.

68 This was a very quick and short decision. See "Immunitas," *Era Hukum* 1, no.1 (November 1987): 43–45.

69 The Mahkamah Agung decision is in ibid., 36. The other judges on the panel with Subekti were Sri Widojati and Indroharto.

70 During the trial, Simandjuntak, Yap heard, felt troubled enough to consult a *dukun*, a specialist in magical and spiritual matters. He died several years later. Mardjaman suffered a stroke sometime after the trial and was incapacitated.

TWELVE *Reform Frontiers*

1 Soe Hok Gie, *Catatan Seorang Demonstran* [Notes of a demonstrator] (Jakarta: LP3ES, 1983), entry for 15 June 1969, 332.

2 Letter from Yap to Miriam Brickman, Carmel's sister, 6 November 1968, replying to her request for information. All he could do then was to confirm Carmel's detention and report that officials had told him that there was strong evidence of the Budiardjos' relationships with communist leaders. I am grateful to Carmel Budiardjo for information on her release in a letter of 16 August 1991 and for sending me Yap's letter.

3 Yap's solution may have been used in conjunction with another worked out by the English solicitor, Sarah Leigh, who was informed by the Ministry of Justice in Jakarta that Carmel acquired Indonesian nationality in 1959 under the new Indonesian citizenship law of 1958. Leigh then argued that Carmel's 1954 renunciation of British citizenship, and its acceptance by the British government, was invalid as it had occurred before she had acquired Indonesian citizenship. Once this point was accepted by the British government, Carmel had both English and Indonesian nationalities. Yap's argument eliminated her Indonesian citizenship, however. I have relied on Carmel Budiardjo's letter of 16 August 1991 for the information not at Yap's disposal.

4 As letters to the WCC and ICJ did not produce much helpful material about Yap's service, I have had to rely considerably on our conversations about his experience.

5 In early 1975, before the fall of Saigon, Yap, as vice chairman of a WCC commission sub-committee on Vietnam, traveled to Vientiane, Hanoi, Haiphong, and Saigon, along with a Swede, a Dutchman, and some American Methodists. Part of the mission concerned a North Vietnamese request for assistance in developing a tennis shoe factory.

6 For a short account of the invasion, see Harold Crouch, *The Army and Politics in Indonesia*, rev. ed. (Ithaca: Cornell University Press, 1998), 340–41. See also Jill Joliffe, *East Timor: Nationalism and Colonialism* (St. Lucia: University of Queensland Press, 1978).

7 See the collection of Tasrif's articles from the period 1966–70 in *Menegakkan Rule of Law Dibawah Orde Baru* [Supporting the rule of law under the New Order] (Jakarta: PERADIN, 1971).

8 In 1969 Princen was arrested, yet again, for his revelations of the earlier killings and terrifying conditions in the Purwodadi camps in Central Java. See Robert Cribb, ed., *The Indonesian Killings, 1965–1966: Studies from Java and Bali* (Clay-

ton, Victoria: Monash Papers on Southeast Asia, no. 21, 1990),195–213. Princen was, absurdly, accused of being a communist, but was defended by, among others, army intelligence officers who knew his background, and was soon released.

9 "Masalah Tahanan" [The detention problem], *Kompas*, 13 Dec. 1968.

10 Ibid.

11 "Angan-angan Mengenai Suatu Undang-undang Hukum Atjara Pidana Baru" [Contemplations on a new code of criminal procedure], dated 26 July 1969, mimeo. It is identical to the undated typescript copy in my possession except for the last page, added, I think, for the purposes of its presentation to the Peradin congress.

12 The tendency among Indonesian private lawyers then, as now, to be drawn to the Common Law model had much to do with what they saw as the influence and centrality of the legal professions in England, America, Australia, India, and Malaysia, but also with their own view that Indonesian legal faults were fundamentally linked to the Continental legal tradition as much as to the political base on which law and legal process inevitably rest.

13 "Kuasa Menangkap dan Menahan," [The power to arrest and detain], *Kompas*, 10 March 1966, in which he argued for full judicial control over arrest and detention. Two months later, on 17 May, *Kompas* published Yap's open letter to prosecutor Soesanto Bangoennagoro from the Liem Koe Njo case, in which he called on Soesanto to answer for his violations of the law (to which the prosecutor never replied) and at the same time used the case to instruct the public on criminal procedure. During the late 1960s and early 1970s, other critics also began to focus on individual rights against the state. See, for example, Eddy Damian, ed., *The Rule of Law dan Praktek2 Penahanan di Indonesia* [The rule of law and detention practices in Indonesia], (Bandung: Alumni, 1968), the report of a seminar on human rights held in Bandung. Yap began his *Kompas* essay with an implicit reply to those—including, perhaps, himself at times—who either doubted the appropriateness of legal solutions or wondered whether they were adequate to Indonesia's problems: "Some people take this view: that good people are better than good laws. It is true. But as good people are far fewer than people who are not good, and as it is easier to make good laws than to improve bad people, therefore the opportunity to improve laws and regulations must be used to the best possible advantage."

14 "Saran Bagi Perobahan 'Hukum Atjara Pidana" [Proposals for change in the law of criminal procedure], *Kompas*, 17 and 18 June 1968.

15 "Peradilan Tjepat, Sebagai Realisasi Hak2 Azasi" [Speedy justice, as a realization of human rights], *Kompas*, 20 June 1968.

16 Yap was not the only advocate to deal with the huge intellectual and technical problems of revising the procedural code. A Jakarta advocate, Nani Razak, produced an even more considered discussion, not far conceptually from Yap's emphases on human rights and institutional controls. Her discussion was published in two articles cited below.

17 Yap, "Angan-angan Mengenai Suatu Undang-undang Hukum Atjara Pidana Baru" [Contemplations on a new code of criminal procedure], dated 26 July 1969, mimeo. In the introduction to his draft, Yap condemned the subordination of people to interests considered more worthy—e.g., the interests of a judicial investigation or the interests of development or the interests of state and nation. Leaning in the opposite direction, he wrote: "The starting assumption of this paper is that each individual is the creation of God . . . and in the eyes of God transcends all social interests." The draft was rough at this point, and I am not at all sure that Yap, given time to consider the statement, would have stuck to it. Yet he may have, for his purpose was to emphasize individual rights, so cavalierly ignored by official instances eager to appeal to "larger interest."

18 Ibid. In the 1980s the police was in fact given full responsibility for arrest, detention, and preliminary investigation, to the chagrin of the prosecutors and the delight of the police, but it did little to improve life for accused persons. Tasrif and Yap, along with many others, argued the case for giving the Mahkamah Agung review powers on the U.S. model. See Tasrif, *Menegakkan Rule of Law*, 195 and 21703.

19 Yap,"Angan-angan Mengenai Suatu Undang-undang Hukum Atjara Pidana Baru," Of the major features of common law criminal procedure, only the jury system was left out of Yap's consideration. He and other advocates were interested in it, but seldom seriously.

20 *Sinar Harapan*, 4 February 1969.

21 As so often, religious conflict helped to scotch an instrument that promised all minorities—including the Islamic majority understood as a political minority—a measure of protective leverage. Islamic objections on the conversion issue promptly aroused Christians, particularly Catholics. Well connected with the Suharto camp, the Catholic group led by Harry Tjan played a significant role in defeating the human rights charter. The army leadership had its own interest in preventing passage of a human rights charter, which might have proved the kind of minor obstruction that the regime saw no need to countenance.

22 *Lembaran Negara*, no. 36, 1969, 5 July 1969, elucidation in *Tambahan Lembaran Negara* no. 2900.

23 See *Lembaran Negara*, vol. 1969, 502ff. Rescinded acts are in LN 37, 1969, 521. Among the regulations retained, for example, was Presidential Decree 2/1962, which banned organizations that were out of line with Indonesian identity, or obstructed the completion of the revolution, or opposed the ideas of Indonesian socialism; 3/1962 on the authority to detain or expel; 4/1963 on the confiscation of printed material disturbing to public order; 2/1964 on methods of carrying out the death penalty; 7/1959 on the "simplification"—i.e., reduction—of political parties; 5/1963 on the prevention of strikes in essential industries.

24 Soebekti, "Laporan Situasi Hukum di Indonesia," 1968. Another was made available the next year, 11 June 1969, mimeo.

25 Yap Thiam Hien, "Keterbukaan-Openbaarheid: Salah Satu Mekanisme Demokrasi" [Openness: A mechanism of democracy] *Kompas*, 23 January 1969.

He returned to the same issue of the need for openness in political and institutional life—anticipating Gorbachev's *glasnost* by fifteen years—in a two-part article in 1971. "Keterbukaan (Openbaarheid) Pengadilan Sjarat Demokrasi" [Openness in the courts is a condition of democracy], *Kompas*, 31 August and 1 September 1971.

26 Yap Thiam Hien, "Penegakan & Pelaksanaan Hukum Berkembang Positif" [Maintenance and implementation of the law develops positively], *Kompas*, 8 October 1969.

27 For details about the politics of Law 14/1970 see my "Judicial Authority and the Struggle for an Indonesian Rechtsstaat," *Law and Society Review* 13, no.1 (Fall/Winter 1978).

28 See *Seminar Hukum Nasional ke-II Tahun 1968* [Second national law seminar 1968] (Jakarta: Gita Karya, 1969) at p. 108, summarizing the discussions in Committee II, on "Maintaining an independent judiciary." Yap, who may have been abroad then, did not attend, but other advocates, including Jamaluddin, were there. As chair of Persaja (Persatuan Jaksa, Prosecutors' Association) in the 1950s, Seno Adji had won equality of rank and status for prosecutors with judges. An experienced warrior in such bureaucratic conflicts, he now fought off the judges on behalf of the government. Many senior judges, who remembered their earlier battles with him, resented Seno Adji deeply. The struggle over judicial review, however, can be traced back to the constitutional discussions of June 1945, before the revolution.

29 The courts were finally extracted from the Ministry of Justice and placed under the managerial authority of the Supreme Court—the so-called "one roof" concept—in mid-2004.

30 For an elaboration of this discussion, see Lev, "Judicial Authority."

31 "Laporan Kegiatan DPP PERADIN periode 1967–1969" [Report of Peradin board activities during the period 1967–1969], mimeo, p. 1.

32 The rest of the board consisted of Lukman's office mates, Zainal Abidin and Hasjim Mahdan, along with Moh. Dalyono and Malikus Suparto.

33 Tasrif argued thereafter that the government had in effect recognized Peradin as the sole legitimate association of advocates when it asked it to provide counsel in the Mahmillub trials. The issue became critical in the 1980s when the government set out to eliminate Peradin's influence by absorbing it into an officially established advocates' association, Ikadin.

34 "Keputusan2 Kongress ke-III 'eradin" [Decisions of the third Peradin congress], mimeo. On this board only three members were not from Jakarta: Amartiwi Saleh from Bandung, Ani Abas Manopo from Medan, and Moh. Dalyono from Solo. The presence of three women on the board is an indication of the relative openness of the profession, of the considerable influence of these three advocates, and the relatively liberal attitudes of the profession. Four members of the five-member honorary council were from outside of Jakarta, but all were from Java. Among them was the elderly Ko Tjay Sing from Semarang, one of the first

Indonesian advocates and the only ethnic Chinese advocate other than Yap in a prominent organizational position.

35 Yap's draft, which he had no time to develop fully, was not published, but Nani Razak's interesting and useful consideration, which shared many ideas with Yap, was published in two parts in two issues of the first volume of Peradin's *Hukum dan Keadilan*: Nani Razak-Muthalib, "Pembaharuan Hukum Atjara Pidana Indonesia" [Renovation of the Indonesian law of criminal procedure, in *Hukum dan Keadilan* 1, no.1 (November/December 1969): 13–18, which she read to the 1969 Peradin congress; and "Suatu Usul Mengenai Pembaharuan Hukum Atjara Pidana Indonesia" [A proposal on the renovation of the Indonesian law of criminal procedure], in *Hukum dan Keadilan* 1, no. 4 (May/June 1970): 24–37.

36 See Buyung's proposal, as it went to Peradin, in the first issue of Peradin's new journal, edited by Suardi Tasrif: Adnan Buyung Nasution, "Biro Bantuan Hukum [Legal aid]," *Hukum dan Keadilan* 1, no.1 (November/December 1969): 19–23.

37 On the development of the LBH, see Daniel S. Lev, *Legal Aid in Indonesia* (Clayton, Victoria: Monash University Centre of Southeast Asian Studies, working paper 44, 1987), and A. B. Nasution, *Bantuan Hukum di Indonesia* [Legal aid in Indonesia] (Jakarta: LP3ES, 1981).

38 Soe Hok Gie, *Catatan*, 340–41, entry for 21 June 1969. He had dropped in on Yap and found him "looking old"; he thought Yap might have been sleeping. Soe Hok Gie died at the end of that year at the age of only twenty-seven.

THIRTEEN *Law as Politics*

1 The best study still of the politics of this period is Harold Crouch, *The Army and Politics in Indonesia* (Ithaca, N.Y.: Cornell University Press, 1978; rev. ed. 1988).

2 ABRI- Angkatan Bersenjata Republic Indonesia, Armed Forces of the Republic of Indonesia, includes the police as well as the land, air, and sea forces.

3 For a full discussion of the government's dealings with the parties through the 1971 elections and thereafter, see Crouch, *Army and Politics in Indonesia*, 245–72.

4 See Harold Crouch, "The Army, the Parties and the Elections," *Indonesia* 11 (April 1971): 177–92; Ken Ward, *The 1971 Elections in Indonesia: An East Java Case Study* (Clayton, Victoria: Monash University Centre of Southeast Asia Studies, 1974).

5 The PNI, NU, the newly formed Parmusi, Parkindo (Protestants), Partai Katolik, Murba, and IPKI. On the New Order fate of the parties, see Crouch, *Army and Politics in Indonesia*, 245.

6 *Kompas*, 24 and 25 July, 24 October, and 11 December 1968

7 For a subtle commentary on the social consequences of New Order corruption, see the late Umar Kayam's novel, *Jalan Menikung* [A bend in the road] (Jakarta: Grafiti, 1999), a sequel to his *Para Priyayi* [The Javanese aristocracy] published in 1992.

8 On the origins and evolution of the LBH, see Daniel S. Lev, *Legal Aid in Indonesia* (Clayton, Victoria: Monash University SEA Working Paper 44, 1987).

9 Buyung had joined Golkar for a short time but withdrew before the 1971 elections, moving instead to a "White Group" (Golongan Putih, Golput) line that favored a refusal to vote at all on grounds of electoral abuse and the political meaninglessness of the elections.

10 I happened to be present and was standing beside Yap.

11 For an interesting and provocative analysis of the Mini park, as it came to be, see John Pemberton, *On the Subject of "Java"* (Ithaca, N.Y.: Cornell University Press, 1995.)

12 Whose thugs? Some thought they might be the sons of the Military Police living in a nearby housing complex, others that they were mobilized by Ali Moertopo either to help Suharto or to weaken him. Much of the material in this discussion is drawn from my interviews in Jakarta during those months.

13 See *Sinar Harapan*, 17 December 1971. I had arrived at Yap's office in the middle of the interview. Yap pointedly reminded the reporter that in 1963, when Minister of Justice Sahardjo had insisted that the civil code should no longer be considered law and Supreme Court Chair Wirjono had supported this view, Yap wrote a criticism of that and other violations of constitutionality that *Sinar* refused to publish. (See chapter 9.)

14 Interview with Harun al'Rashid, 29 December 1971.

15 SuperSemar—Surat Persetujuan Sebelas Maret (Document of Agreement of 11 March). Semar is one of the clowns of traditional Javanese *wayang* (shadow puppet theater). He is perhaps the most popular of the *wayang* characters; though foolish and ugly, he is also immensely wise and powerful, representing, according to some, the strength of the common people.

16 See *Tempo*, 5 February and 29 January 1972.

17 Interview with Umar Kayam, 14 January 1972.

18 See Crouch, *Army and Politics in Indonesia*, 306–18.

19 From a discussion with Khing, 26 September 1995.

20 In the midst of the furor an odd thing happened at Yap's home that reflects the tension and uncertainty of the time. Before Yap himself was arrested, he had a visit from a Dr. Tan, one of whose patients was President Suharto. As Yap told Khing afterwards—he had asked her not to join the talk—the doctor said to Yap that an unspecified "they" (who? ethnic Chinese?) would follow his lead. Khing, who told me about this, was not happy with it and rather put out. Why, she asked sarcastically, didn't Tan and the others take the lead themselves? Khing, 26 September 1995.

21 Having obtained a power of attorney from Princen, he had told him to let him know immediately if he were arrested. Princen did so, but by the time Yap got the message he too had been detained.

22 The point of keeping a copy of the warrant (*surat penangkapan*) was to prove that one had indeed been arrested and was in custody. The point of denying the arrestee copies of the warrant was just the opposite—deniability if the detainee disappeared. Khing remembered the necessity from Yap's first arrest in 1966.

23 General Kanter had a long career as an army administrative officer. A Menadonese Protestant, during the revolution he had belonged to the Sulawesi group KRIS and moved into the army by that route. With a law degree from the Military Law Academy, he eventually joined the military auditor's office, which in time he headed. After the coup, as the army extended its influence over civilian organizations, Kanter, following a fierce struggle, became chair of the umbrella organization of lawyers, Persahi (Persatuan Ahli Hukum Indonesia). He and his wife were very helpful to Khing while Yap was detained.

24 The interview was on 20 July 1986. Kanter and his wife had been invited to dinner with the understanding that he and I would talk privately for a time. I had asked him why he helped Yap after his arrest, but Kanter evidently thought I had asked why Yap was arrested. It may have been the question he expected. I have rearranged my notes for the sake of a sensible chronology.

25 Haryono was a senior member and later chair of Peradin; Albert Hasibuan was also from Peradin, I think, and had been associated with the LBH.

26 The point of using the term "subversion" was to invoke the Anti-Subversion law, originally a Presidential Decree of 1963 promulgated as a statute in 1969. The Anti-Subversion law allowed detention for a year. As Kanter pointed out, there was no intention of bringing Yap or most others to trial, but simply to put them away for a time.

27 After Yap and Buyung had been arrested, said Kanter, several advocates came to see him. He refused to mention their names, but many were friends of Buyung and of the LBH. They came to suggest to Kanter that Buyung should be removed from the LBH immediately. Kanter said that he simply dismissed them, telling them frankly that it was wrong to take advantage of Buyung's detention to push him out of the LBH. That was an LBH affair. Kanter understandably took a cynical view of these advocates who had their own interests to press. But when I suggested that he was offering protection of a sort to the LBH, he denied it, insisting that he was simply acting out of fairness to both Buyung and the LBH. Like many officers, Kanter felt that the LBH was a useful organization, though it went too far and moreover was basically an opposition group.

28 This information came from Marsillam Simandjuntak, whom Yap came to know and admire at the RTM.

29 This Kartono, according to Yap, later was detailed to some position on the prison island of Buru. He and Yap apparently argued throughout much of his interrogation, but Kartono redeemed himself in Yap's eyes by showing him the letter that Princen had written after his arrest. Princen was not detained at the RTM but in Jatinegara, east Jakarta. When Yap saw the letter, he got word to Khing to give Rp. 50,000 to Princen, which, as Yap found out later, Kartono actually had delivered.

30 May 1985, Lev interview, tape 7, side one.

31 Hariman and Marsillam were medical students. Dorodjatun had begun his studies in political science at Berkeley, where he completed his dissertation after his release and transformed himself into an economist. Sjahrir studied economics,

went to Harvard after his release, and in time became one of Indonesia's most prominent private economists.

32 They were. See Pramoedya Ananta Toer's account of the exile island of Buru, *Nyanyi Sunyi Seorang Bisu* [The lonely song of a mute] (Jakarta: Lentera, 1995). Not all army officers exploited the camps, but some did and evidently were not called to account.

33 Lev interview, May 1987, tape 9, side 2.

34 A few prosecutors would have been overjoyed to detain him forever, to extract the maximum revenge. Indeed, early in his detention one prosecutor, whom Yap had upset in a traffic accident case in Bogor, had tried to get him moved out of the RTM to a prosecution holding center, but failed, possibly because of Kanter's efforts. I got this information from Yap, who got it from an unnamed source.

35 *"Jij heb't geloofd,"* he said to Soedomo, as Kanter reported it to Khing. The conversations among Khing, Kanter, Soedomo, not to mention Hasjim and Lukman, were almost always in Dutch. One has to wonder how much influence that intimacy of a shared language among a generation of educated seniors counted in getting things done.

Epilogue

1 For a full discussion of Yap's role in the Konstituante debates, see chapter 8.

2 Daniel S. Lev, "In Memoriam: Yap Thiam Hein (1913–1989)," *Indonesia* 48 (October 1989): 107–10, at 110.

3 Daniel S. Lev, "Between State and Society: Professional Lawyers and Reform in Indonesia," in *Indonesia: Law and Society*, ed. Tim Lindsey (Sydney, Aus: Federation Press, 2008), 48–67, at 60.

4 See chapter 12, note 18.

5 Lev, "Between State and Society," 60; and note 21 at 60.

6 Daniel S. Lev, "A Tale of Two Legal Professions: Lawyers and State in Malaysia and Indonesia," in *Raising the Bar: The Emerging Legal Profession in East Asia*, ed. William P. Alford (Cambridge, MA: Harvard University Press, 2007), 383–414. For the relationship between the government and the advocates during the 1980's, see 404–6.

7 Lev, "In Memoriam," 107. INGI is the International NGO Forum on Indonesia.

8 I am grateful to Bivitri Susanti for allowing me to see parts of the draft manuscript of her PhD dissertation, and for the many conversations which helped me understand the legal changes of the post-1998 period.

9 In 1993, in response to international criticism, Suharto established by presidential decree the National Commission on Human Rights. It was reestablished, this time by parliamentary law, in 1999. For a discussion of the post-New Order legal changes to protect human rights and punish violations see Jeff Herbert, "The Legal Framework of Human Rights in Indonesia," in *Indonesia: Law and Society*, ed. Tim Lindsey (Sydney, Aus: Federation Press, 2008), 456–82.

10 See chapters 12 and 13, this volume.

Postscript: New Order Landmark Cases

1 Dan Lev interview notes, 9 July 1986, tape 13, side 2, page 12. In all such references, unless otherwise indicated, these are Lev's typed transcriptions of taped interviews.

2 Interview notes, 9 July 1986, tape 13, side 2, page 12.

3 Interview notes, 6 February 1987, tape 26, side 2, page 22.

4 Lev commented that Yap Thiam Hien was disciplined in his work and the files reflect more the realities of criminal litigation than his work style. "Yap is very detailed in his work. Careful. Analytical. Constantly took notes on his reading, filling books with ideas, thoughts, quotes, and all quite serious. [illegible] His agenda, books, conference papers, scrap papers, invitations are scribbled on with notes, questions, comments, exclamation points etc. and always remarkably thorough. Very observant. . . . Always took careful notes in the courtroom and built his replies on them." Lev's handwritten notes, 20 August 1989.

5 Interview notes, 9 July 1986, tape 13, side 1, page 5.

6 Lev interview with Yap Thiam Hien, 3 November 1971: "Usually, [Yap] gives the court only a written summary of major points, then speaks at length. This time he used a tape recorder, which he brought himself, in case a full record was needed."

7 The original collection has been deposited with the University of Washington Libraries, Seattle, Washington. Lev arranged for copies to be given to the Pusat Studi dan Dokumentasi Hukum in Jakarta, where they are located in the D. S. Lev Library.

8 A random selection includes the following: Laughing it off [15 May 1985, interview]; angry [17 December 1971, interview]; enthusiastic [16 October 1978, interview]; emphatic [May 1985, tape 8]; I was amazed [May 1985, tape 8]; laugh [May 1985, tape 8]; Yap laughs. Yes . . . [May 1985, tape 8]; joking [May 1985, tape 8]; Wah, dia tidak senang. Much laughter [Ach, he was unhappy] [7 July 1986, tape 11, side 1]; Something funny for we both laugh [7 July 1986, tape 11, side 1]; enthusiastic [9 July 1986, tape 13, side 2]; nods negatively [9 July 1986, tape 13, side 2]; Lev: did they *minta maaf*, John? Both laugh [Did they apologize, John? (Dan called Yap by his nickname, John)] [9 July 1986, tape 13, side 2]; He said this almost angrily and very much from the heart [14 July 1986, tape 16, side 2]; Yap feels very angry [25 January 1987, tape 21, side 1].

9 Typed notes of Lev interview with Yap Thiam Hien, 16 October 1978. Lev commented: "Yap said this is one of his own failings too (though clearly he does not think it a failing, and neither do I)." In the Sawito case, Yap was reprimanded by the judge for being so emotional. But Yap replied: "How can I not be emotional when my client has not been provided with food for three months. And it is you as a judge who in the end is responsible for this." The highly charged attacks by Yap ensured that the judge ordered food to be given to Sawito. When, shortly after this exchange, a witness was called, who also had been detained, to the gen-

eral surprise of the court and the audience he first thanked the judge for ordering food for Sawito, since he was then fed as well.

10 In this case, Yap's client was instrumental in the sole successful sting operation against judges during the New Order. Subsequent to the operation, the client retained Yap for the principal dispute which was still ongoing when Dan Lev conducted his interviews. However, that principal dispute must be seen as separate from the corruption sting, which is what we will discuss here. Interview notes, 5 February 1987, tape 23, side 1, page 5.

11 Dan Lev, handwritten notes, 20 August 1989, cf note 4.

12 Yap was assisted in this case by Abdurrahman Saleh, who later became Attorney General in the Susilo Bambang Yudhoyono administration.

13 The summation was widely reported in Indonesia and abroad and published in translation in some foreign newspapers. Cf. documents section of *Power Struggle in Southeast* Asia, IDC (Zug, Sw.) 1976. A translation was published in full in the Dutch daily *Trouw*, 13 September 1975.

14 Yap Thiam Hien. Document in his case file "Asep Suryaman case."

15 In later years, employing Yap might harm the client. "Abbas noted (reflecting the views of others, I think) that it is dangerous to use Yap as an advocate. Referring to the Sanusi case, in which the District Court Decisions had just been announced condemning Sanusi to nineteen years, a rather shocking sentence, Abbas suggested that judges may sometimes punish the client for the behavior of the advocate. Implied that Yap so angers judges that they increase the sentence of the accused in order to punish Yap himself. There may of course be something to this." Lev interview with Yap Thiam Hien, 15 May 1985, appendix.

16 Oei Tjoe Tat, *Memoar Oei Tjoe Tat, Pembantu Presiden Soekarno* (Jakarta: Hasta Mitra 1995), 278.

17 Oei Tjoe Tat was appointed a minister without portfolio (*menteri negara*) in 1963 and served until 12 March1966, when Soekarno transferred administrative power to Suharto. Oei was arrested the next day. One of Oei's tasks in the Soekarno cabinet had been "dealing with Konfrontasi," the military conflict with Malaysia. He therefore had to meet with the military quite a bit and knew the senior officers. So in the immediate aftermath of the coup, he was delegated by Soekarno to figure out what the military was up to, using Konfrontasi as a pretext. According to Oei, Soekarno told him: "I need you to go and find out who among the military officers are still supporting me. Talk to Suharto et al. and report back to me. And so, using the Konfrontasi excuse, I went to see Suharto."

Oei met with Suharto several times and became one of the principal conduits between Soekarno and the coming man. By that time the military was already pursuing its own policies in direct opposition to Soekarno, actually capturing the Sarawak rebels who had been supporting annexation to Indonesia. Suharto tried to use Oei for his own purposes, asking him to talk to Soekarno and have him back down on Konfrontasi. Oei refused. How could he agree? Oei said: "I have been working on Konfrontasi all this time and if I had any objections, I should have raised them earlier." If Suharto wanted Indonesia to change policy on Konfrontasi, he would have to talk with Soekarno himself, said Oei. He recalled how angry Suharto was at this, "his eyes burned with dislike and anger." Suharto refused categorically to talk to Soekarno and accused Oei of being "Soekarno's lackey." Oei knew he was on Suharto's blacklist from then on as following meetings became increasingly grim. Oei believed that his case and the way it evolved could only be explained by what went on in these meetings. For all quotes, see Lev interview with Oei Tjoe Tat, 21 February 1981 (hereafter cited as OTT interview).

18 See also Oei Tjoe Tat, *Memoar*, 265.

19 Oei Tjoe Tat had become such a fixture that the state administration for a moment actually lost him. There is official correspondence in Yap's case file in which the Supreme Court asks the Minister of Justice (Mochtar Kusumaatmadja) and his director general for prisons (DGP) for the whereabouts of Oei Tjoe Tat. Mochtar washes his hands by saying: "Sorry, am out of town quite a bit, did not read your letters, and we do not have Oei in our custody anyway" (Statement, 22 August 1977). The DGP issued a note to say that Mr. Oei was not under its jurisdiction. So where was he? After a flurry of letters, DGP came back and said, "Ah well, sorry, it turns out he is with us after all." Much of this back-and-forth was prompted by Mrs. Oei Tjoe Tat, who bombarded government officials right up to the president with letters and notes, thus ensuring that the Oei file would not be forgotten. She played a key role in securing his unexpected sentence remission after the trial, as Oei recounted in his memoirs.

20 OTT interview. A *proces-verbaal* is a statement or affidavit.

21 Ibid.

22 *Review*, magazine of the International Commission of Jurists, no.13 (December 1974), 18.

23 OTT interview.

24 Oei Tjoe Tat retained his concerns even after he had engaged Yap Thiam Hien, and indeed after he had been freed. After Oei had asked Yap to be his lawyer, Oei's wife approached General Kanter (who was head of the anti-corruption team Opstib at the time and knew Yap well) to express their concern that Yap might put up too strong a defense. Kanter in fact conveyed the message to Yap and said that it might be best not to put up too strong a defense, presumably so as not to upset the court and perhaps have Kanter arrange for a release, or so Yap thought. For Yap, this was an impossible request. (Lev interview with Yap Thiam Hien, 17 July 1986, tape 18, side 1, page 32.) After his release many years later, Oei Tjoe Tat came back to the issue and asked Kanter whether he thought Yap had put up too impolitic a defense. Yap Thiam Hien heard of this and was upset. He understood this, correctly, to mean that Oei thought he had put up too strong a defense and, by implication, questioned his professional standards. Lev interview with Khing, 16 December 1987.

25 OTT interview.

26 There was a document ordering house arrest, though it had been issued not by a judge but by Suharto himself on March 12, 1966.

27 The secretary general of Partindo, Adi Sumarto, gave testimony in court which confirmed that the original October statement had been put together by himself, not by Oei, and that Oei disagreed with it forcefully and insisted on an amendment. Adi Sumarto was subsequently sentenced to twelve years imprisonment for issuing the statement.

28 In November 1965, Soekarno named Oei Tjoe Tat to the Commission of Three Ministers assigned the sensitive task of purging government departments of persons involved in the coup. Additionally, in December 1965, Oei was appointed to a fact-finding commission to investigate the coup.

29 On the Suharto link cf. OTT interview.

30 There is a little note in the Yap file of a meeting between Judge Abdullah and Oei Tjoe Tat's wife, in which the judge said: "I am but a little cog in these cases. I can be thrown out, replaced by someone else or they can beach the case. 13 years was the maximum our team of judges could get out of this." Oei's wife commented that she appreciated ("most sympathetic") that the judge had taken the initiative to come and see her and how forthcoming he had been.

31 Lev interview with Yap's wife, Khing, 16 December 1987.

32 The International Commission of Jurists wrote to President Suharto on June 29.

33 Oei Tjoe Tat in his memoirs recounted how his wife wrote letters and badgered President Suharto; the commander of the Command for the Restoration of Security and Order (Pangkopkamtib), Soedomo; the chairman of the People's Consultative Assembly, Adam Malik; Minister of Justice Mochtar Kusumaatmadja; Chief Justice Seno Adjie; the head of the Legal Department of the Armed Forces, Major General E. Y. Kanter; and others. Adam Malik and Kanter were notably sympathetic and made efforts to secure a remission. When the remission order was issued, Kanter turned up at the prison in person to see that it was properly carried out. Oei Tjoe Tat, *Memoar*, 282.

34 A. Latief died in April 2005.

35 Yap Thiam Hien to Dan Lev, 1985, tape 6, side 2. In fact, Latief was shot in one leg, while the tendons in the other leg were severed by a bayonet. A. Latief, *Pledoi Kol. A. Latief. Soeharto terlibat G30S* (Jakarta: Institut Studi Arus Informasi n.d. [2000]), 43. Latief told the story of the maggots on pages 47–48. Apparently he wrapped some of the maggots in a piece of paper and had them submitted to the prison authorities. The authorities sent down a lieutenant to check him out, and Latief later recounted in court that the officer was so revolted by what he found there that he threw up. Yap recounted the story of the brutal arrest twice in the same interview, and Lev noted that he must have admired Latief for his fortitude. The account recurred, with minor differences, in two more interviews, cf. Yap Thiam Hien to Dan Lev 5, February 1987, tape 23, side 2, and Yap Thiam Hien to Dan Lev, 25 September 1987, tape 21, side 1.

36 Yap Thiam Hien to Dan Lev, 25 September 1987, tape 21, side 1. In his book Latief reported that he did in fact receive medical treatment on a number of occasions (*Pledoi*, 44–46).

37 One of the first things Latief did when he was released from prison in 1999 was to publish a book accusing Suharto of involvement in the Gerakan 30 September. *Pledoi Kol* consists primarily of his court plea (*pledoi* or *pleidooi),* at least some of which presumably was written by Yap Thiam Hien, although there is no reference to Yap in the book.

38 There are many questions about the role of Suharto in the G30S. Reading Latief's book, published after his release in 1999, one perhaps gets the impression that Latief was something of a mystery man, and, as with most mystery men, it is possible that his knowledge and role have been exaggerated. But this is hindsight, and throughout the New Order Latief had an aura of having critical inside knowledge which compromised Suharto. Yap Thiam Hien seems to have shared this view.

39 Yap Thiam Hien to Dan Lev, 1985, tape 6, side 2.

40 Ibid. Even before Latief's trial, information had come out which suggested that there might be another angle to the story. In 1968 Suharto gave an interview in which he recounted that he had been at a hospital in the days leading up to 30 September to look after his son who had been scalded by soup in a kitchen accident. Suharto recounted that Colonel Latief had come to see him to commiserate. Suharto said that he only understood after the event that Latief was there to warn him that something was afoot, but because he (Suharto) was wholly focused on his child he could not take it in. Two years later, in a 1970 interview with the German weekly *Der Spiegel,* Suharto repeated the story of the hospital, but now said that Latief had come to kill him but stepped back when he found the entire family there. In an interview in a book by Arnold Brackman, Suharto confirmed that Latief had come to see him in the hospital (*The Communist Collapse in Indonesia* [W.W. Norton: New York, 1969], 100).

41 Yap Thiam Hien to Dan Lev, 25 September 1987, tape 21, side 1.

42 Dan Lev, 25 September 1987, tape 21, side 1.

43 Yap pointed out twice in interviews that the Latief defense team trickled away after he joined. Abdurrachman Saleh was pulled off to another case and Narimba simply failed to turn up for the final court session.

44 Latief, *Pledoi,* 5–8.

45 Asep Suryaman converted in prison; Latief included pictures of himself at Muslim prayers. Inside prison!

46 Latief, *Pledoi,* 16–19.

47 Ibid., 20–22.

48 Cf. note 9 above.

49 Conversation in English, Dutch, and Indonesian, 1985, tape 6, side 2, translated with edits by Sebastiaan Pompe (SP).

50 5 February 1987, tape 23, side 2, with edits.

51 Yap suggested that the prosecutor never appealed: "In the end, his office never lodged the appeal, and the decision stood." Yap Thiam Hien to Dan Lev, 25 September 1987, tape 21 side 1. But it is clear from Latief's book that he did: cf. Latief, *Pledoi,* xxv. Yap's recollection of the Latief case was not always solid, as

Lev pointed out. The five-year time lapse between the first instance and appeal decisions suggests that Yap was not involved in the appeal case, and lost track in the interim. It also explains the confusion on whether or not Latief ever received a copy of the decisions, which affected his right to ask for early release or an amnesty, as explained in note 52.

52 Yap recounted that he had explained to Latief that to qualify for amnesty, he needed a decision. The notes suggest that the decision never came down. Even by the shabby New Order legal standards this seems rather extraordinary. It comes close to the practices of Guantanamo Bay, and falls squarely within habeas corpus. However, in his book Latief referred to the respective reference numbers of the High Military Court and Supreme Court decisions (Latief, *Pledoi*, xxv).

53 Yap Thiam Hien to Dan Lev, 25 September 1987, tape 23, side 2: "Kawatir nanti dia bongkar lagi [Suharto is worried Latief will spill the beans—SP]."

54 Yap Thiam Hien to Dan Lev, 25 September 1987, tape 21, side 1. The text does not make a clear connection between the "cynicism and corruption" at the time of the interview (1987) and the Latief trial, which happened ten years previously. Lev, however, seems to have made that connection in his notes; one follows seamlessly on the other in the same paragraph. The connection occurred in the context of a discussion about the issue of whether there may have been more people like Latief who knew what really happened in 1965. Some of those who sided with Suharto soon found themselves in senior government positions, and their inside knowledge gave them some sort of immunity vis-à-vis Suharto, opening the door to abuse of power and corruption rackets, as Lev suggested in his notes.

55 R. Robison and V. Hadiz, *Reorganizing Power in Indonesia* (London and New York: Routledge Curzon, 2004), 120.

56 Interview notes, 28 May 1985.

57 Interview with Yap Thiam Hien in *Eksekutif* (November 1985). An English translation was published in that journal. In the same interview Yap mentioned that he defended Sanusi pro bono.

58 Daniel S. Lev, "In Memoriam Yap Thiam Hien (1913–1989)," *Indonesia* 48 (October 1989): 107.

59 "*Mu*" means "one who"; "*balligh*" means "told to deliver." *Muballigh* means preacher, one who propagates and preaches Islam.

60 All the defendants in the "Islamic cases" were not so ideological. Thus, Basuki Rahmat signed the power of attorney appointing Yap without prompting, and in the Sanusi case Yap was pulled in by Sanusi's wife. Lev interview with Yap Thiam Hien, May 1985, tape 8, side 2.

61 Ibid. Also Lev interview with Mulya Lubis, 22 May 1985.

62 Yap Thiam Hien: Yeah, Sanusi in his [defense speech] . . . said that people such as Yap are pribumi [indigenous Indonesian]. And Rahmat and . . . before they made their [defense speech] *minta maaf pada saya* (because they would say things about the Chinese (added by Dan Lev)). . . . Several times he asked my forgiveness. *Sampai even di sidang* [even during the court session] he minta maaf. And

others too, *kawan2* Rahmat [friends of Rahmat] and others. Lev interview with Yap Thiam Hien, May 1985, tape 8, side 2.

63 Ibid.

64 Written by Ibrahim Assegaf.

65 David Bourchier, *Dynamics of Dissent in Indonesia: Sawito and the Phantom Coup* (Ithaca, N.Y.: Cornell Modern Indonesia Project, 1984), 1. This study provides the best and most detailed treatment of the background, course, and outcome of the Sawito affair.

66 Ibid., 22–23.

67 Ibid., 31–32.

68 Ibid., 87, citing Rodney Lewis, "The Trial of Sawito Kartowibowo in Indonesia," *Justice* (Journal of the International Commission of Jurists, Australian Section) 8 (1981): 35–56, at 53.

69 Bourchier, *Dynamics of Dissent,* 87–88, citing Sumi Narto, *Sawito, Ratu Adil, Guruji, Tertuduh* (Solo: Sasongko, 1978), 184–85.

70 Dokumen I, dated 27 October 1977, signed by Yap.

71 A letter signed by Yap and the other lawyers, dated 17 April 1978.

72 Bourchier, *Dynamics of Dissent,* 74.

73 Ibid., 62–63, 73, 86.

74 Ibid., 76.

75 Interview notes, 12 November 1992. A notable example is Gouw Giok Siong (Sudargo Gautama), with whom relations never recovered after their court fight in the 1950s. Other lawyers had recalled Yap's conduct in civil cases with some bitterness. One prominent lawyer recalled how she faced Yap in a case in the 1970s and asked for a deferment to accompany her husband to Europe for medical treatment. Yap said, "Aha, so that's your tactic, excuses, excuses, just to further your case." This troubled her. The treatment didn't take, and her husband died shortly thereafter. Returning home she confronted Yap, but he just walked away without a word. Their rapport never recovered. There were, of course, exceptions to his way of treating lawyers in civil cases, one being Adnan Buyung Nasution (whom he faced in the Tancho case).

76 Interview notes, 1986. The case Yap refers to is the Istiqlal marble case (1986), one of the last cases he handled. It arose out of a contract between the Indonesian government and an Italian to provide Italian marble for the new Istiqlal Mosque. President Suharto had approved the deal. But some time later, he reversed his approval, saying that it would be better to use Indonesian marble from Tulung Agung. By that time, the Italian marble had been ordered and cut and was in shipment. The Italian agent ran around town trying to sort things out but found all doors closed in his face. In desperation he turned to Yap. Yap was incensed by the outrageous violation of contract in the case: here was a straightforward agreement broken unilaterally and without cause by the Indonesian government, which even refused to cover the Italian's costs and damages. The subtext, which did little to calm Yap, was that the general who chaired the Istiqlal procurement

team had allegedly asked the Italian for kickbacks. The deal collapsed when he and the Italian failed to reach agreement.

77 Such as the press restrictions in the Oei Tjoe Tat case and the pressure and reprimands in the Latief case.

78 In his interview notes, Lev pointed out that Yap Thiam Hien was in a way used by the military authorities and the regime, notably in the 1965 cases. For example, during the Subandrio trial, the military actually asked Yap for advice on how to improve the process, which Yap was willing to give. He put it to them that at least as regards Subandrio they were closing the door after the horse had bolted. "Yap: 'How can you reconcile yourselves to the fact Subandrio was sentenced to death by a court that you now yourself acknowledge to be illegally constituted?' So they were embarrassed. They could not answer. Perhaps one of the reasons the military authorities rather liked me is that I am a straight shooter. No twists and turns with me . . . So they [i.e., the Mahmillub judges and the military auditor general] could see my proposals and produced a new law." (Dan Lev commented: Yap is here oddly formalistic, legalistic, and doesn't see that perhaps he should not have helped them.) Yap went on to describe that he told the military that this was one of the first human rights cases in the country and that therefore it should be dealt with properly. He also said that as a result of his comments and input, the law and procedure were amended. Lev commented: Yap here is a bit odd in his views. He takes a kind of joy in the legal learning and propriety itself. Does not really see the political side of these issues. In a sense he allowed himself to be used.

79 Never one to hold back, Yap used the corruption case to support his appeal in the Sawito case: "It is common knowledge that there is rampant corruption in the Central Jakarta District Court under the chair of Chief Justice Moh. Soemadijono, as well as fraud and abuse of power"; Yap then pointed out that these judges had been proven to be corrupt in the Heru Gunawan case, and therefore their role in the Sawito case was questionable. *Memori Kasasi*, 3.

80 Two years after the Heru Gunawan case the issue still had not been sorted out. In fact, the diamonds were seized in evidence by the prosecution, but when they were presented in court in 1983, Yap asserted that they had been (in whole or in part) replaced with fakes. *Tempo*, 21 May 1983. Yap said that the original owner, who was seeking redress against Ms. Maria, had bribed the prosecution and replaced the original diamonds with fakes. In the 1981 case, Maria also said that the prosecutor had tried to extort money from her, but he was not caught on tape. Interview notes, 5 February 1987, tape 23, side 1, page 6.

81 Ibid., page 1.

82 Dan Lev's phrase. Ibid., page 4.

83 Ibid. Yap noted that Heru Gunawan was the only Chinese judge.

84 Lev interview with Yap Thiam Hien, 3 November 1971, in which Yap repeatedly indicates his contempt for and distrust of Soemadijono.

85 Interview notes, 5 February 1987, tape 23, side 1, pages 7–8.

86 Interview notes, 5 February 1987, tape 23, side 2, page 10.

87 Ibid., page 11.

88 Ibid., page 12.

89 There were a number of similar cases, one involving the widow of a senior oil company official who was living in a garden house (*pavilyun)* and whom Pertamina wanted to kick out. Yap referred to his secret weapon, a Pertamina document that turned out to be quite useful in a number of comparable cases.

90 Lev interview with Yap Thiam Hien, 21 August 1971.

91 "We had met before, years ago, in the *pengadilan negeri* [district court], I think, though he remembers it better than I." Lev interview with Yap Thiam Hien, 21 August 1971. There are no notes from that earlier brief meeting.

92 *Indonesia* 48 (October 1989): 110.

93 Lev interview with Yap Thiam Hien, 3 November 1971.

94 Earlier interview notes date from 29 October 1971, in which Lev briefly described Yap's office in terms that suggest he had not been there before, and from 26 November 1971, which was the first time Lev asked about Yap's background.

ACKNOWLEDGMENTS

Had he written these acknowledgments, I know that Dan would have, first and foremost, thanked those friends and colleagues in Indonesia with whom he spent countless hours recollecting, analyzing, arguing, and laughing. Together, they caught shifting and sometimes elusive personal memories and firmed them into a history of the Republic of Indonesia's first quarter-century.

As for myself, I could not have prepared Dan's incomplete manuscript for publication without the help and encouragement of my friends and coeditors, Audrey Kahin and Ben Anderson. The old saw "without whom this book would never have seen the light" has never been less an exaggeration. The manuscript benefited not only from Anderson's meticulous editing but from his tactful willingness to share with me his encyclopedic knowledge of Indonesian history and politics. Sebastiaan Pompe overcame his lawyerly need for complete documentation and, with Ibrahim Assegaf, contributed an essay so compelling that missing documents became irrelevant.

Many, many friends supported this project professionally and personally and I can thank only a few in these pages, although I owe so much to all. Arief Surowidjojo, founder of the Center for Law and Policy Studies and the Daniel S. Lev Law Library, both in Jakarta; Indrasatuti Hadiputranto; Maria Hartiningsih; Abigail Rosenthal Martin; Goenawan Mohamad; Marsillam Simandjuntak; Timothy Manring; Lee Scheingold; Laurie Sears of the Southeast Asia Center and Veronica Taylor of the Asian Law Center, both at the University of Washington; and Judith Henchy of the University of Washington Libraries' Southeast Asia Collection—all played crucial roles in this project, extending to me loving encouragement and help in navigating.

Bivitri Susanti advised me in matters of legal terminogy and in the ways the legal issues of the Guided Democracy and early New Order periods live on or have been resolved. Bivitri and Aryani Manring gathered the illustrations and Jean Sherrard edited them, jobs requiring tact and technical prowess.

I want especially to thank two families: the family of Yap Thiam Hein—Yap Hong Gie and Yap Hong Ay—and my own—Claire Lev Murata, Louis B. G. Lev, and Howard G. Lev— who understood the importance of this project and were patient and supportive in ways large and small.

Arlene O. Lev

APRIL 2011

SELECTED BIBLIOGRAPHY

Album Kongres V. Yogyakarta: Peradin, 1977.
Ali Said and Durmawel Ahmad. *Sangkur Adil: Pengupas Fitnah Chianat* [The bayonet of justice: Exposing treasonous slanders]. Jakarta: Ethika, 1967.
Anderson, Benedict R., and Ruth T. McVey. *A Preliminary Analysis of the October 1, 1965, Coup in Indonesia.* Ithaca, N.Y.: Cornell Modern Indonesia Project, 1971.
Assimilasi dalam rangka Pembinaan Kesatuan Bangsa [Assimilation in the framework of developing national unity]. 3d ed. Jakarta: Yayasan Pembinaan Kesatuan Bangsa, 1965.
"Berita Atjara Kongres Nasional V BAPERKI Seluruh Indonesia pada tanggal 25–28 Djuni 1958 di Solo [Minutes of the fifth national congress of Baperki, 25–28 June 1958, in Solo]. Stencil, Yap papers, Lev collection.
Borel, Henri. *De Chineezen in Nederlandsch-Indie.* Amsterdam: L. J. Veen, 1900.
Butwell, Richard. *U Nu of Burma.* Stanford: Stanford University Press, 1963.
Cator, W. J. *The Economic Position of the Chinese in the Netherlands Indies.* Chicago: University of Chicago Press, 1936.
Coppel, Charles A. "Patterns of Chinese Political Activity in Indonesia." In *The Chinese in Indonesia,* edited by J. A. C. Mackie, 19–76. Honolulu: University of Hawai'i Press, 1976.
———. *Indonesian Chinese in Crisis.* Kuala Lumpur/Melbourne: Oxford University Press, 1983.
Cribb, Robert, ed. *The Indonesian Killings, 1965–1966: Studies from Java and Bali.* Monash Papers on Southeast Asia, no. 21. Clayton, Victoria: Monash Centre of Southeast Asian Studies, 1990.
Crouch, Harold. "The Army, the Parties and the Elections." *Indonesia* 11 (April 1971): 177–92.
———. *The Army and Politics in Indonesia.* Rev. ed. Ithaca, N.Y.: Cornell University Press, 1988.
Damian, Eddy, ed. *The Rule of Law dan Praktek2 Penahanan di Indonesia* [The rule of law and detention practices in Indonesia]. Bandung: Alumni, 1968.
Dosker, H. E. *The Dutch Anabaptists.* Philadelphia: Judson Press, 1921.
Elson, Robert. *Suharto: A Political Biography.* Cambridge: Cambridge University Press, 2001.
Encyclopaedie van Nederlandsch-Indie. Vol. 2. The Hague and Leiden: Martinus Nijhoff and E. J. Brill, n.d.

Feith, Herbert. *The Indonesian Elections of 1955*. Ithaca, N.Y.: Cornell Modern Indonesia Project, 1957.

———. *The Decline of Constitutional Democracy in Indonesia*. Ithaca, N.Y.: Cornell University Press, 1962.

Frederick, William H. *Visions and Heat: The Making of the Indonesian Revolution*. Athens: Ohio University Press, 1989.

Furnivall, J. S. *Netherlands India: A Study of Plural Economy*. Cambridge: Cambridge University Press, 1944.

Gay, Ruth. *The Jews of Germany: A Historical Portrait*. New Haven: Yale University Press, 1992.

Geertz, Hildred. "Indonesian Cultures and Communities." In *Indonesia*, edited by Ruth T. McVey. New Haven: HRAF, 1963.

Gobée, E., and C. Adriaanse. *Ambtelijke Adviezen van C. Snouck Hurgronje, 1889–1936*. The Hague: Nijhoff, 1957.

Go Gien Tjwan. "Introduction." In Bob Hering, *Siauw Giok Tjhan Remembers*.

Gouw Giok Siong and Ch. Huang. *Tanja-Djawab tentang Kewarganegaraan* [Questions and answers about citizenship]. Jakarta: Keng Po, 1961.

Hering, Bob. *Siauw Giok Tjhan Remembers*. Townsville, Aus.: James Cook University, 1982.

Heroe Soetjiptomo. *Peranan Pendapat Umum dalam Masalah Undang-Undang no. 2/1958 tentang Dwikewarganegaraan Warganegara Tjina di Indonesia* [The role of public opinion in the problem of Law no. 2/1958 concerning dual-nationality of Chinese citizens in Indonesia]. Medan: Toko Buku DELI, 1970.

"Imunitas Profesi Advokat (Kasus Mr. Yap Thiam Hien) [Immunity of the professional advocates: The case of Mr. Yap Thiam Hien]." *Era Hukum* 1, no.1 (November 1987): 35ff.

Imam Bardjo. *Masaalah Kewargaan Negara Republik Indonesia* [The problem of citizenship in the Republic of Indonesia]. Semarang: Baperki, 1958.

Inti Sari pidato-pidato anggauta Konstituante berkenaan dengan amanat Presiden tanggal 22 April 1959, Res Publica! Sekali Lagi Res Publica! [Precis of speeches of Constituent Assembly members in connection with the presidential address of 22 April 1959, Res Publica! Once again, Res Publica!]. Jakarta: Ministry of Information [1959?].

Joliffe, Jill. *East Timor: Nationalism and Colonialism*. St. Lucia: University of Queensland Press, 1978.

Kahin, George McT. *Nationalism and Revolution in Indonesia*. Ithaca, N.Y.: Cornell University Press, 1952.

Kayam, Umar. *Jalan Menikung* [A bend in the road]. Jakarta: Grafiti, 1999.

"Konferensi Pleno Pusat Baperki di Batu (Malang) tanggal 15–17 April '60" [Plenary conference of Baperki Central in Batu (Malang) 15–17 April 1960]. Mimeograph. Yap papers, Lev collection.

Konperensi Pleno Pusat Baperki tanggal 27 Agustus 1959 di Djakarta" [Plenary conference of Baperki Central]. N.p., n.d., mimeo. Yap papers, Lev collection.

Kraemer, Hendrik. "Introduction." In Dr. J. A. Verdoorn, *De Zending en het Indone-*

sisch Nationalisme [The mission and Indonesian nationalism]. Amsterdam: Vrij Nederland, 1945.

———. *From Missionfield to Independent Church.* The Hague: Boekencentrum, 1958.

Lahirnya Konsepsi Asimilasi [The birth of the assimilation concept]. 5th ed. Jakarta: Yayasan Tunas Bangsa, 1977.

Langhout, J. *The Economic Conquest of Acheen by the Dutch.* The Hague: n.p., 1924.

"Laporan Ketua Umum pada Kongres Nasional Baperki ke VI tanggal 28, 29, 30 Agustus 1959, di Djakarta" [Chairman's Report to the Sixth Baperki National Congress]. Mimeo, 12. Yap papers, Lev collection.

"Laporan Kegiatan DPP PERADIN periode 1967–1969" [Report of Peradin board activities during the period 1967–1969]. Mimeo. n.p.,n.d. Yap papers, Lev collection.

"Laporan Rapat Pembentukan Badan Permusjawaratan Kewarganegaraan Indonesia, Baperki [Minutes of the founding meeting of Baperki]." Jakarta. Stencil. All minutes of Baperki meetings are in the Yap papers, Lev collection.

Latourette, Kenneth Scott. *Christianity in a Revolutionary Age.* Vol. 4: *The Twentieth Century in Europe.* New York: Harper Brothers, 1961.

Lev, Daniel S. "The Politics of Judicial Development in Indonesia." *Comparative Studies in Society and History* 7, no. 2 (Jan. 1965) 173–99, 202.

———. *The Transition to Guided Democracy: Indonesian Politics 1957–1959.* Ithaca, N.Y.: Cornell Modern Indonesia Project, 1966.

———. *Islamic Courts in Indonesia.* Berkeley: University of California Press, 1972a.

———. "Judicial Institutions and Legal Culture in Indonesia." In *Culture and Politics in Indonesia*, edited by Claire Holt et al., 246–318. Ithaca, N.Y.: Cornell University Press, 1972b.

———. *Bush-Lawyers in Indonesia: Stratification, Representation, and Brokerage.* Working Paper 1, Law and Society Program, Berkeley, Calif., 1973.

———. "Origins of the Indonesian Advocacy." *Indonesia* 21 (April 1976): 135–69.

———. "Judicial Authority and the Struggle for an Indonesian Rechtsstaat." *Law and Society Review* 13, no.1 (Fall/Winter 1978): 37–71.

———. "Colonial Law and the Genesis of the Indonesian State." *Indonesia* 40 (October 1985): 57–74.

———. *Legal Aid in Indonesia.* Monash Papers on Southeast Asia, no. 44. Clayton, Victoria: Monash Centre of Southeast Asian Studies, 1987.

———. "Becoming an Orang Indonesia Sejati: The Political Journey of Yap Thiam Hien." In *Indonesia, Special Issue: The Role of Indonesian Chinese in Shaping Modern Indonesian Life* (1991): 97–112.

———. "A Tale of Two Legal Professions: Lawyers and State in Malaysia and Indonesia." In *Raising the Bar: The Emerging Legal Profession in East Asia*, edited by William P. Alford, 383–414. Cambridge, Mass.: Harvard University Press, 2007.

———. "Between State and Society: Professional Lawyers and Reform in Indonesia." In *Indonesia: Law and Society*, edited by Tim Lindsey, 48–67. Sydney, Aus: The Federation Press, 2008.

Liem Koen Hian. "Apa Baba Bisa Menjadi Indonesier?" [Can the baba become an Indonesian?]. Reprinted in *Baba Bisa Menjadi Indonesier* [The Baba can become an

Indonesian], edited by Ridwan Saidi, 13–16. Jakarta: Lembaga Pengkajian Maslah Pembauran, n.d.
Mackie, J. A. C., ed. *The Chinese in Indonesia.* Honolulu: University of Hawai'i Press, 1976.
———. "Anti-Chinese Outbreaks in Indonesia, 1959–1968." In Mackie, *The Chinese in Indonesia*, 77–138.
McVey, Ruth T., ed. and trans. "Introduction." In Soekarno, *Nationalism, Islam and Marxism.* Ithaca, N.Y.: Cornell Modern Indonesia Project, 1969.
Mrázek, Rudolf. *Sjahrir: Politics and Exile in Indonesia, 1906–1966.* Studies on Southeast Asia, no. 14. Ithaca, N.Y.: Cornell Southeast Asian Program, 1994.
Nani Razak. "Pembaharuan Hukum Atjara Pidana Indonesia" [Renovation of the Indonesian law of criminal procedure]. *Hukum dan Keadilan: Madjallah Persatuan Advocat Indonesia*, no. 1 (November/December 1969): 13–18.
———. "Suatu Usul Mengenai Pembaharuan Hukum Atjara Pidana Indonesia" [A proposal on the renovation of the Indonesian law of criminal procedure]. *Hukum dan Keadilan:Madjallah Persatuan Advocat Indonesia*, no. 4 (May/June 1970): 24–37.
Nasution, Adnan Buyung. "Biro Bantuan Hukum [Legal aid]." 1 *Hukum dan Keadilan* 1 (November/December, 1969): 19–23.
———. *Bantuan Hukum di Indonesia* [Legal aid in Indonesia]. Jakarta: LP3ES, 1981.
———. "Yap Thiam Hien: Advokat dan Penggugat demi Aspirasi Negara Hukum dan Demokrasi di Indonesia" [Yap Thiam Hien: Advocate and plaintiff for the aspirations of democracy and the rule of law in Indonesia]. In *Yap Thiam Hien: Pejuang Hak Asasi Manusia* [Yap Thiam Hien: Fighter for human rights], edited by T. Mulya Lubis and Aristides Katoppo, 48–64. Jakarta: Pustaka Sinar Harapan, 1990.
"Notulen Konperensi Pleno Pusat Pada Tanggal 12–14 Desember 1958 di Djakarta [Minutes of the plenary conference, 12–14 December 1958, in Jakarta]." N.p.: [Baperki], n.d. Stencil. Yap papers, Lev collection.
Oei Tjoe Tat. *Memoar Oei Tjoe Tat: Pembantu Presiden Soekarno* [The memoirs of Oei Tjoe Tat: Assistant to President Soekarno]. Jakarta: Hasta Mitra, 1995.
Ong Eng Die. *Chineezen in Nederlandsch-Indie: Sociografie van een Indonesische Bevolkingsgroep.* Assen: Van Gorcum, 1943.
Pramoedya Ananta Toer. *Nyanyi Sunyi Seorang Bisu* [The lonely song of a mute]. Jakarta: Lentera, 1995.
Pemberton, John. *On the Subject of "Java."* Ithaca, N.Y.: Cornell University Press, 1995.
Poeze, Harry A. *Tan Malaka Strijder voor Indonesie's vrijheid: Levensloop van 1897 tot 1945* (Tan Malaka, a fighter for Indonesian freedom: Life from 1897 to 1945). The Hague: Martinus Nijhoff, 1976.
Proses Yap Thiam Hien S.H.: Test Case bagi Rule of Law di Indonesia [The Yap Thiam Hien trial: Test case for the rule of law]. Jakarta: Peradin, 1969.
Purcell, Victor. *The Chinese in Southeast Asia.* 2d ed. London: Oxford University Press, 1965.
Regeeringsalmanak. Vol. 2 (1939): 154–57.
Reid, Anthony. *The Contest for North Sumatra: Atjeh, the Netherlands and Britain, 1858–1898.* London and Kuala Lumpur: Oxford University Press and University of Malaya Press, 1969.

Reitsma, J. *Geschiedenis van de Hervorming en de Hervormde Kerk der Nederlanden.* The Hague: Martinus Nijhoff, 1949.

Ridwan Saidi, ed. *Baba Bisa Menjadi Indonesier* [The Baba can become an Indonesian]. Jakarta: Lembaga Pengkajian Maslah Pembauran, 1987[?].

Risalah Konstituante 1959, Sidang ke-I, Rapat ke-12, 12 May 1959 [Constituent Assembly Record, 1959]. N.p.

Rose, Arnold M. *The Roots of Prejudice.* Paris: UNESCO, 1952.

Rush, James R. "Social Control and Influence in Nineteenth Century Indonesia: Opium Farms and the Chinese of Java." *Indonesia* 35 (April 1985): 53–64.

Sebuah Rangkuman Tentang: Monografi Kelembagaan Islam di Indonesia [Summary of a monograph on Islamic institutions in Indonesia]. Jakarta: Ministry of Religion, 1984.

Setiono, Benny G. *Tionghoa dalam Pusaran Politik* [Chinese in the vortex of politics]. Jakarta: Elkasa, 2003.

Siauw Giok Tjhan. *Membina Bangsa jang Bulat Bersatu* [To develop a united nation]. Report to the fourth Baperki congress, 21–23 December 1956, in Surabaya . N.p.: BAPERKI, 1957.

———. "Berita Atjara Kongres Nasional V BAPERKI Seluruh Indonesia pada tanggal 25–28 Djuni 1958 di Solo" [Minutes of the fifth national congress of Baperki, 25–28 June 1958, in Solo]. Stencil.

———. Report of the General Chairman to the Sixth Congress of Baperki, 28–30 August 1959, in Jakarta. Stencil. Yap papers, Lev collection.

———. *Lima Jaman: Perwujudan integrasi wajar* [Five epochs: Achieving a fitting integration]. Jakarta/Amsterdam: [Yayasan Teratai], 1981.

Sidang Perkara Yap Thiam Hien S.H. [The trial of Mr. Yap Thiam Hien]. Jakarta: Kompas, 1968.

Simposium Kebangkitan Semangat '66: Mendjeladjah Tracée Baru, 6–9 May 1966 [Symposium on the awakening of the spirit of '66: Exploring a new trajectory]. Jakarta: Yayasan Badan Penerbit Fak. Ekonomi UI, 1966.

Skinner, G. William. "The Chinese Minority." In *Indonesia*, edited by Ruth T. McVey. New Haven, Conn.: Yale Southeast Asian Studies and HRAF, 1963.

Soeharto, G. Dwipayana, and Ramadhan K.H. *Soeharto: Pikiran, Ucapan dan Tindakan Saya, Otobiografi* [Soeharto: My thoughts, statements and actions, an autobiography]. [Jakarta]: Citra Lamtoro Gung Persada, 1988.

Soe Hok Gie. *Catatan Seorang Demonstran* [Notes of a demonstrator]. Jakarta: LP3ES, 1983.

Soejono Hadidjojo. *Kewarganegaraan Indonesia* [Indonesian citizenship]. Yogyakarta: Yayasan "Gadjah-Mada," 1954.

Somers, Mary. *Peranakan Chinese Politics in Indonesia.* Interim Reports Series. Ithaca, N.Y.: Cornell Modern Indonesia Project, 1964.

———. "Peranakan Chinese Politics in Indonesia." PhD diss., Cornell University, 1965.

Suryadinata, Leo. "Indonesian Chinese Education: Past and Present." *Indonesia* 14 (October 1972): 49–71.

———. *Pribumi Indonesians, the Chinese Minority and China.* Singapore: Heinemann, 1978.

——, ed. *Political Thinking of the Indonesian Chinese, 1900–1977: A Sourcebook.* Singapore: Singapore University Press, 1979.

——. *Eminent Indonesian Chinese: Biographical Sketches.* Rev. ed. Singapore: Gunung Agung, 1981.

——. "Yap Thiam Hien: Pembela Hak Asasi Manusia yang Gigih," [Yap Thiam Hien: Persistent defender of human rights]. In *Mencari Identitas Nasional,* edited by Suryadinata, 186–209. Jakarta: LP3ES, 1990.

——. *Mencari Identitas Nasional: Dari Tjoe Bou San Sampai Yap Thiam Hien* [In search of national identity: From Tjoe Bou San to Yap Thiam Hien]. Jakarta: LP3ES, n.d.

Tan Malaka. *Dari Pendjara ke Pendjara.* Djogjakarta: Murba, 1947[?]. Published in translation by Helen Jarvis, *From Jail to Jail.* Athens, Ohio: Ohio University Center for International Studies, 1991.

Tasrif, Suardi. *Menegakkan Rule of Law Dibawah Orde Baru* [Maintaining the rule of law under the New Order]. Jakarta: Peradin, 1971.

Tobi, A. C. *De Vrijwillige Onderwerping aan het Europeesch Privaatrecht.* Ind. Stbl. 1917, no. 12. Leiden: van Doesburgh, 1927.

Uittreksel uit het Register der Besluiten van de Secretaris van Staat, Hoofd van het Departement van Justitie ddo [Extract from the Register of Deliberations . . .], 11 Juli 1949, Nr. J.P. 8/4/14.

Undang-undang Kewarganegaraan Indonesia [Indonesian law of citizenship]. Jakarta: Pustaka Rakjat, 1958.

U Nu. *Saturday's Son.* Translated by U LawYone; edited by U Kyaw Win. New Haven, Conn.: Yale University Press, 1975.

van der Wal, S. L., ed. *Het Onderwijsbeleid in Nederlands-Indie 1900–1940* [Education policy in the Netherlands-Indies]. Groningen: Wolters, 1963.

Ward, Kenneth E. "Upholding the Rule of Law: The Yap Affair." *Review of Indonesian and Malayan Affairs* 2, no. 1 (January–March, 1968): 1–7.

——. *The 1971 Elections in Indonesia: An East Java Case Study.* Clayton, Victoria: Monash University Centre of Southeast Asia Studies, 1974.

Williams, Lea E. *Overseas Chinese Nationalism: The Genesis of the Pan-Chinese Movement in Indonesia, 1900–1916.* Glencoe, Ill.: The Free Press, 1960.

Willmott, Donald. *The National Status of the Chinese in Indonesia.* Ithaca, N.Y.: Cornell Modern Indonesia Project, 1956.

Wirth, Louis. "The Problem of Minority Groups." In *The Science of Man in a World of Crisis,* edited by Ralph Linton. 4th ed. New York: Columbia University Press, 1945.

Whitney, James. *The History of the Reformation.* New York: Macmillan, 1907 and 1940.

Yamin, Moh. *Naskah-Persiapan Undang-Undang Dasar 1945* [Documents on the drafting of the 1945 Constitution]. Jakarta: Yayasan Prapantja, 1959.

Yap Tjwan Bing. *Meretas Jalan Kemerdekaan* [On the road to independence: Autobiography of an independence fighter]. Jakarta: Gramedia, 1988.

Yen Ching Hwang. *The Overseas Chinese and the 1911 Revolution.* London: Oxford University Press, 1976.

INDEX